Database
Management
and Design

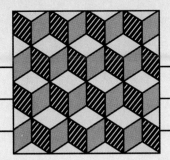

DATABASE MANAGEMENT AND DESIGN

Gary W. Hansen

Brigham Young University

James V. Hansen

Brigham Young University

PRENTICE HALL
Englewood Cliffs, New Jersey   07632

Library of Congress Cataloging-in-Publication Data

Hansen, Gary W. (Gary William)
    Database management and design / Gary W. Hansen, James V. Hansen.
       p.   cm.
    Includes bibliographical references and index.
    ISBN 0-13-200759-2
    1. Data base management.   2. Data base design.   I. Hansen, James
V. II. Title.
QA76.9.D3H348 1991
005.74—dc20   91-14063
                                                  CIP

Acquisitions Editor: Valerie Ashton
Development Editors: Linda Muterspaugh/Steve Deitmer
Production Editor: Joanne Palmer
Copy Editor: Linda Pawelchak
Interior and Cover Designer: Maureen Eide
Prepress Buyer: Trudy Pisciotti
Manufacturing Buyer: Robert Anderson
Supplements Editor: David Scholder
Editorial Assistant: Renee Pelletier

© 1992 by Prentice-Hall, Inc.
A Simon & Schuster Company.
Englewood Cliffs, New Jersey 07632

Printed in the United States of America

ISBN 0-13-200759-2

10 9 8 7 6 5 4 3 2 1

Prentice-Hall International (UK) Limited, London
Prentice-Hall of Australia PTY. Limited, Sydney
Prentice-Hall Canada Inc., Toronto
Prentice-Hall Hispanoamericana, S.A., Mexico
Prentice-Hall of India Private Limited, New Delhi
Prentice-Hall of Japan, Inc., Tokyo
Simon & Schuster Asia Pte. Ltd., Singapore
Editora Prentice-Hall do Brasil, Ltda., Rio de Janeiro

iv

To Susan and Lynne

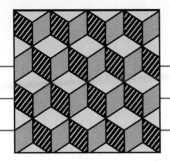

BRIEF CONTENTS

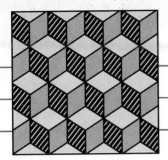

CONTENTS

part three

IMPLEMENTATION DESIGN

---

*optional

ten   THE HIERARCHICAL DATA MODEL   273

eleven   PHYSICAL DATABASE
ORGANIZATION AND ACCESS   299

part four
DATABASE SYSTEM IMPLEMENTATION

twelve DBMS SELECTION
AND IMPLEMENTATION   337

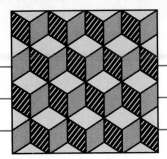

PREFACE

Information is the lifeblood of the modern organization. Effectively managing information is often the difference between success and failure. For this reason, more and more organizations have come to depend on database systems to pool and to protect this valuable commodity. At the same time, hardware and software advances have made it easy for even microcomputer users to create large and useful databases. This ease is a blessing, but it is also a curse: It tempts professionals and nonprofessionals alike to skip crucial design tasks. Thus we wrote this book to introduce students to the essential principles that guide the design, implementation, and management of effective database systems.

Our Mission We believe that a sound conceptual design is crucial to developing an effective database system—one that will meet the needs of current users and grow with them into the future. We also think that students need to understand the context of database design and see how it fits into the system development life cycle. Thus we have organized the book around this cycle, to show students how conceptual—or logical— design becomes the basis for other database development tasks.

Object-Oriented Modeling:
Our Foundation We believe that object-oriented modeling is the fastest, simplest, most powerful way to teach students to decompose user information needs into the data that will be stored in the database. After examining the context of databases in Part One, we discuss in Part Two logical design, which is based on the object-oriented model shown there. The numerous diagrams

and examples show students how to capture and to analyze the often abstract information needs of users. Chapter 4 covers the basics of modeling objects, relationships, and attributes. Chapter 5 presents two object-oriented languages, showing students how they can answer queries by navigating the object-oriented diagrams. Again, this helps readers grasp some of the more abstract aspects of data definition and manipulation. Chapter 6 then presents such advanced object-oriented topics as the use of aggregation to model more complex situations.

The object-oriented approach is then carried through our discussion of design implementation, in which we show how to convert object-oriented models to hierarchical, network, and relational models that can be implemented using state-of-the-art database management systems. (In fact, object-oriented models produce relational models that are already in Fourth Normal Form, minimizing the need for tedious normalization procedures.)

A Concern For Practical Matters

Our focus on logical design does not mean we neglect the practical aspects of database design and administration. We cover the languages used with the hierarchical, network, and relational models, including relational algebra and calculus in Chapter 8, SQL in Chapter 13, and Query-By-Example in Chapter 14. This thorough coverage of relational languages lays the groundwork for Chapter 15, which treats such leading relational microcomputer database management systems as PARADOX, RBASE, and ORACLE. We feel the microcomputer coverage is especially important because most students will get their first hands-on experience with such packages. All these topics, plus coverage of the emerging field of knowledge-base systems, are treated in the context of such strategic and tactical management issues as database planning, DBMS selection, database administration, and the need to maintain security and integrity in both centralized and distributed database systems.

Teaching and Learning Aids in the Text

As experienced teachers, we realize the importance of helping students and have provided a number of features for that purpose.

☐ Four business cases occur throughout the book and provide examples of the database concerns facing a distribution company, a manufacturer, a construction company, and a consulting firm. In addition, we provide a number of other examples to illustrate specific problems that face the database designer.

☐ Each chapter begins with a scenario that represents real-world database issues, followed by a list of learning objectives that show how the chapter content will teach the skills needed to address these issues.

☐ A generous number of two-color figures and diagrams clarify database modeling, query solutions, and other topics.

☐ A margin glossary defines key terms immediately, aiding comprehension and simplifying review. This on-page reference is supplemented by a comprehensive glossary at the end of the book.

☐ To help students test and apply their newfound knowledge, every chapter ends with a summary of key points and a generous number of review questions, problems, and exercises. In addition, the Projects and Professional Issues section gives students an opportunity to do additional research about important industry issues.

Taken together, these aids build on student knowledge and prepare students to develop database systems either as part of this course or as part of their professional lives.

A Note on Notation[1]   Throughout the book we deal with compound data names; for example, such as PRODUCT-ID. An alert reader will notice that we sometimes use hyphens to join the parts of these compound names; at other times we use an underscore. This reflects convention and the prevailing industry usage. For example, the data names in the hierarchical model use hyphens, as required by the CODASYL standard, but SQL and QBE use underscores. Although this inconsistency can be confusing, most people quickly learn the conventions of specific models, leaving them free to focus on the more important matters of database design and administration.

Flexibility in Sequencing   Different instructors use different approaches. To provide instructors with maximum flexibility in sequence of coverage, each chapter is self-contained. Also, more advanced topics are indicated with an asterisk (*). They may be emphasized or omitted. You may want to present the subject from a management viewpoint or a technical viewpoint. You may want to emphasize database design or data manipulation languages. You may want to follow a traditional approach, or you may want to embark on more advanced topics emphasizing current research. We group chapters under these broad headings in the following list. (Several chapters belong to more than one category, and so they appear more than once.)

Management Chapters   *Technical Chapters*
1, 2, 3, 12, 17, 18   4, 5, 6, 7, 8, 9, 10, 11, 13, 14, 15, 16

Database Design Chapters   *Language Chapters*
4, 6, 7, 9, 10, 11, 17, 18   5, 8, 9, 10, 13, 14, 15

Advanced Chapters
5, 6, 16

At Brigham Young University, we use the book in a two-semester sequence. The first semester focuses on database design and management, covering chapters 1-12, 17, and 18. The second semester focuses on database languages and decision support, covering chapters 8, 9, 10, and 13-16, inclusive.

☐ SUPPLEMENTS

In order to aid professors using Database Design and Management, an *Instructor's Manual* has been prepared by the text authors. The Instructor's

Manual provides the instructor with teaching suggestions, suggested answers to all problems and exercises in the textbook, test questions, and overhead transparency masters for selected figures from the textbook.

We are also providing a *Case Supplement with Data Diskette,* written by Jim Hansen. This supplement offers the student the opportunity to work through a mini-case using a microcomputer database management system. We find this kind of exercise to be particularly useful in helping the student to understand the relevance of the course material.

In addition, Prentice Hall and Borland International have joined forces to bring you Paradox. Ideal for both advanced and first-time users, the award-winning relational database management software combines powerful features with an easy-to-use interface. *Paradox®: A Student Tutorial with Cases,* by Eric L. Denna, Michael P. Briggs, and Jeff G. Gibbs; *Paradox®: A Complete Course,* by Elizabeth Swoope Johnston; and *Paradox®: A Complete Course,* also by Elizabeth Swoope Johnston, are all available for use with this text. Student software is also available. Contact your local Prentice Hall representative for further details.

□ ACKNOWLEDGMENTS

The authors would like to express appreciation to a number of people for their help and guidance in preparing this text.

Our students in the Information Management Program of the Marriott School of Management (MSM) at Brigham Young University used preliminary versions of the text. Their comments helped us improve the book.

A number of reviews provided useful insights and suggestions that helped in preparing the final version of the book. The reviewers are

Bay Arinze, Drexel University

John Eatman, University of North Carolina at Greensboro

Hermant Jain, University of Wisconsin–Milwaukee

Constance Knapp, Pace University

William L. Harrison, Oregon State University

Dennis McLeod, University of Southern California

John Boggess, Purdue University

Herman Hoplin, Syracuse University

Gerald Karush, New Hampshire College.

We are grateful for their time and effort.

Nina Whitehead and the MSM wordprocessing center staff provided many hours of service in typing and correcting the manuscript. We owe them more than a lunch.

We are also indebted to Steve Deitmer, Ray Mullaney, and Joanne Palmer of Prentice Hall. Joanne, who was our production editor, was unfailingly cheerful and cooperative and got things done.

We give special acknowledgment to the acquisitions editor, Valerie Ashton, and to the development editor, Linda Muterspaugh. Their efforts substantially improved the form and substance of the book.

part one

THE CONTEXT OF DATABASE

In Part I, you will be introduced to databases and database systems. As we outline the historical and organizational context of databases, our discussion will focus on answers to the following questions:

What is a database and what is a database system?

How did database systems originate?

How do organizations use and control databases?

How are database systems developed?

Chapter 1 deals with the first two of these questions. In this chapter, we review the historical development of database systems. We see how business needs have shaped the development of technology and how the information implicit in data has come to be regarded as a valuable corporate resource. Our discussion will conclude with a description of the four principal components of a database system: hardware, software, data, and people.

Chapter 2 addresses the next question. Here we examine database systems in their organizational context. We discuss the need for sharing data at all levels of an organization, describe the process of strategic data planning, and outline the role database administration personnel play in controlling and protecting the database.

Chapter 3 answers the last question by discussing the database development life cycle. We show that database design, although performed concurrently with system design, should be placed in a larger framework than the design of any one system. A well-conceived database will then become the foundation for many application systems.

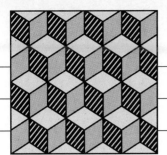

chapter one

DATABASE SYSTEMS AND THE EVOLUTION OF DATABASE TECHNOLOGY

Susan Broadbent, CEO, and Sanford Mallon, CIO (Chief Information Officer), of International Product Distribution are verbally sparring over systems technology. Susan, seeing an opportunity for some fun, needles him: "You want us to convert to a relational database, Sandy? Is this another one of your harebrained schemes?"

"Harebrained? When have I ever made a proposal that wasn't conceived with brilliance and executed with intricate precision?"

"Well, let's see. When you came here, you took us from our manual system to two file-oriented systems—first, a sequential file system and then a random access file system. Then came the database systems—hierarchical followed by network. Now you want to go to a relational database. If those schemes were brilliantly conceived, why did they have to be changed every few years?"

Sanford laughed. He could tell by the smile on Susan's face that she was well aware of the reasons for each change and of the significant benefits the company reaped each time. He replied, "It's been a long haul, hasn't it, keeping up with technology?"

"Yes. But you've been exceptional at staying abreast of developments and moving us to them when they would help our business the most. And to think that it all began so simply. . . ."

Susan Broadbent and Sanford Mallon are reflecting with satisfaction on several decades of business growth supported by data access technology. In this chapter, we review (1) the development of this technology as it affected and was affected by business needs and (2) the four major components of a modern database system—hardware, software, data, and people. After reading this chapter, you should be able to:

- ☐ Discuss the strengths and weaknesses of the early sequential and random access file systems.
- ☐ Explain how information has come to be regarded as a valuable resource in modern organizations.
- ☐ Describe the historical evolution of the hierarchical, network, and relational database systems and the business needs that led to their development.
- ☐ Explain how four components—hardware, software, data, and people—work together to form today's database systems.

☐ THE EVOLUTION OF DATABASE TECHNOLOGY

The sophistication of modern database technology is the result of a decades-long evolution in data processing and information management. Tugged on one side by the needs and demands of management, and restrained on the other side by the limits of technology, data access technology has developed from the primitive methods of the fifties to the powerful, integrated systems of today.

Management's expectations have grown along with and parallel to the evolution of technology. The early data processing systems performed clerical tasks that reduced the paper handling in businesses. More recent systems have expanded to the production and management of information, which has come to be viewed as a vital company resource. Today, the most important function of database systems is to provide the basis for corporate management information systems.

The implementation of technological change, then, has been guided by genuine business needs. Management will only authorize a new computer system when they can see a clear benefit that offsets the system's cost. And, despite pitfalls and risks, the benefits have been realized in many cases. Moreover, the end is not yet in sight and is unlikely to be for some time to come. New technology, such as object-oriented or semantic databases, addresses new problems and will result in the development of more powerful systems to be installed in the future.

The close relationship between database technology and business needs may be easier to understand if we take a closer look at the experience of International Product Distribution.

Case: International Product Distribution

Susan Broadbent is founder, owner, and President of International Product Distribution (IPD), which sells over 3500 products from more than 300 manufacturers in countries all over the world. IPD has headquarters in Chicago, with international offices in Brussels, Buenos Aires, Lagos, New Delhi, Tokyo, and Sydney. More than 2700 sales representatives work locally in over 100 countries, each of them reporting to a regional office. The company has annual revenue of about $500 million and profit of about $50 million.

After selling children's clothing for a single manufacturer to department stores in the Chicago area for a number of years, Susan decided she could increase her income significantly if she represented several manufacturers. Consequently, she founded International Product Distribution. Her concept was simple: She would identify manufacturers in various countries whose products consistently exhibited a strong standard of quality. She would also identify retail outlets that emphasized the sale of such products. She would then establish strong business relationships with both the manufacturers and the retailers by providing the retailers with appropriate products from the manufacturers.

Initially, she had a small staff and dealt only with retailers in the Chicago area and manufacturers in the Midwest. Shortly, however, she was supplying products to merchants in Milwaukee, Minneapolis, St. Louis, Detroit, Cleveland, and Indianapolis. Her first international sales were made to stores in Toronto. After three years, IPD had representatives in Europe, and two years later they opened an office in Tokyo. Offices in Buenos Aires, Sydney, Lagos, and New Delhi followed. Employees supervised by each of these offices included sales representatives and buyers. Purchased products were sold in the country of manufacture or could be exported for sale in another country. Figure 1.1 illustrates the relationship between IPD and its suppliers and retailer customers. As you can see, products flow from the manufacturer to an IPD warehouse and on to the retailer.

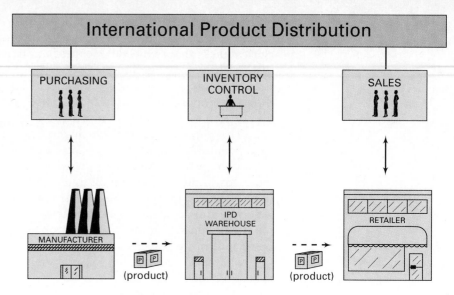

FIGURE 1.1   Product Flow for IPD

When the company was young, records of sales, product purchases, and inventory were kept by hand. By the end of the second year, though, business had grown to the extent that it was necessary to purchase a mini-computer to track this information and produce reports, billing statements, and payments, as shown in Figure 1.2. Sanford Mallon was hired to implement this file-oriented system and manage a staff of programmers, data entry operators and operations personnel.

FIGURE 1.2   Data Processing Flow for IPD

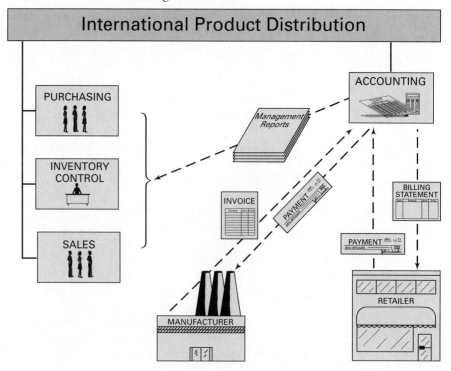

Early business computer systems were used primarily for accounting functions: accounts receivable, accounts payable, payroll, balance sheet, profit and loss statements, and so on. These were functions that had to be carried out in order for a business to operate. Consequently, computer systems that could perform these functions were easy to cost justify. The manual effort required for payroll or accounts receivable, for example, was so great that an automated system that could replace the manual system would pay for itself in a short time.

Since these systems performed accounting functions, they tended to be developed and operated under the direction of the accounting department. The large systems consulting groups one finds in today's major accounting firms can be traced to the early importance of computer systems in automating accounting.

Because these systems performed functions that would otherwise have to be carried out by hand, they were thought of as (and called) **data processing systems.** That is, they processed the data that was part of the normal record keeping of the company. Not surprisingly, the programmers and analysts who designed these systems followed their natural inclination to mimic the existing manual procedures in their programming. Thus, the computer files corresponded to paper files, and the records in the computer files contained information that an individual file folder in a manual system might contain.

data processing system An automated system for processing the data for the records of an organization.

Figure 1.3 shows some files and sample data from the original file-oriented system of International Product Distribution. Each table represents a file in the system. That is, we have a CUSTOMER file, a SALES-REP file, a PRODUCT file, and so on. Each row represents a record in the file. Thus, the PRODUCT file contains three records. Each of these records contains data about a different product. The individual data items or fields in the PRODUCT file are PROD-ID, PROD-DESC, MANUFACTR-ID, COST, and PRICE.

Assume for the moment that all of these files are sequentially accessed. That is, each record can only be read and processed after all the records preceding it in the file have been read. This was the case at IPD in the sixties, when disk storage was still relatively expensive. Most files were stored on tape, and records were accessed and processed in sequence. Usually, these files were processed in a batch mode, meaning that all the records in a file were processed at the same set time, usually each night after the close of business.

These files were used for a number of different applications. For example, the accounts receivable program was an application that generated billing statements for customers. It used the CUSTOMER and the SALE files. These files were both sorted in order by CUST-ID and were merged to create a printed statement as shown in Figure 1.4. The BE-GINNING-BALANCE field in the CUSTOMER file would be updated to reflect the new charges. Payments previously received and processed by another program against the CUSTOMER file were recorded in the MONTH-TO-DATE-PAYMENTS field in the CUSTOMER file and were shown on the billing statement.

| CUSTOMER | | | | | MONTH-TO- |
CUST-ID	CUST-NAME	ADDRESS	COUNTRY	BEGINNING-BALANCE	DATE-PAYMENTS
100	Watabe Bros	Box 241, Tokyo	Japan	45,551	40,113
101	Maltzl	Salzburg	Austria	75,314	65,200
105	Jefferson	B 918, Chicago	USA	49,333	49,811
110	Gomez	Santiago	Chile	27,400	28,414

| SALES-REPRESENTATIVE | | | | |
SALREP-ID	SALREP-NAME	MANAGER-ID	OFFICE	COMM-%
10	Rodney Jones	27	Chicago	10
14	Masaji Matsu	44	Tokyo	11
23	Francois Moire	35	Brussels	9
37	Elena Hermana	12	B.A.	13
39	Goro Azuma	44	Tokyo	10

| PRODUCT | | MANUFACTR- | | |
PROD-ID	PROD-DESC	ID	COST	PRICE
1035	Sweater	210	11.25	22.00
2241	Table Lamp	317	22.25	33.25
2518	Brass Sculpture	253	13.60	21.20

| SALE | | SALREP- | | | TOTAL- |
DATE	CUST-ID	ID	PROD-ID	QTY	PRICE
02/08	100	14	2241	200	6650.00
02/12	101	23	2518	300	6360.00
02/12	101	23	1035	150	3300.00
02/19	100	39	2518	200	4240.00
02/22	101	23	1035	200	4400.00
02/25	105	10	2241	100	3325.00
02/25	110	37	2518	150	3180.00

| MANUFACTURER | | | |
MANUFACTR-ID	MANUFACTR-NAME	ADDRESS	COUNTRY
210	Kiwi Klothes	Aukland	New Zealand
253	Brass Works	Lagos	Nigeria
317	Llana Llamps	Lima	Peru

FIGURE 1.3   Sample Data From the File-Oriented System at IPD

FIGURE 1.4   Creating the Customer Billing Statement

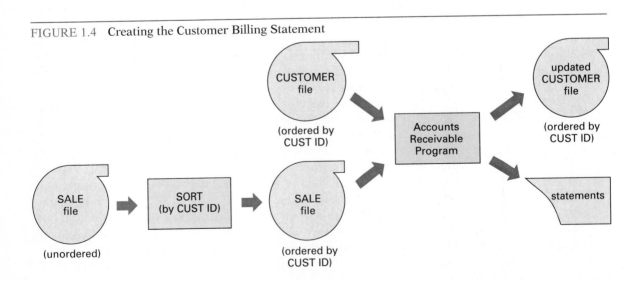

A program like this which accomplishes a specific task of practical value in a business situation is an **application program** or an example of *application software*. A set of such programs that work together to accomplish a set of related tasks is an *application system*.

Meeting the Need for Random Access Processing

The limitations of purely sequential file-oriented systems did not prevent them from being effective tools for producing payments, statements, and other reports once or twice a month. To perform many routine business tasks, however, we need **random access processing**—the ability to directly access and process a given record without first sorting the file or reading the records in a file in sequence. To understand some of the problems that occurred when random access processing was not available, let's look at two encounters from the past of IPD.

"Sandy, I don't understand why our data entry operators have to enter both the quantity and the total price whenever they enter a sales transaction. We have the price of the product in the PRODUCT file. Why can't our people merely enter the quantity and the product ID, which they're already entering anyway, and then have the system calculate the total price?"

We are in the early days of data processing at IPD, and Susan Broadbent is concerned about the amount of unnecessary work the clerks are doing. The more data the clerks have to enter, the longer it takes, and the higher IPD's labor costs. Since IPD has already invested a considerable sum of money to purchase a computer, develop application software, and pay the salary of the staff that runs it, her question is a natural one.

"Susan, we have a sequential file system. That means all records within a file must be accessed in order. When we're running the accounts receivable program, we're working with the CUSTOMER and SALE files, but we can't get at the right product record."

"I'm afraid I don't understand what you're saying."

"All right, here's some sample data from the files. [See Figure 1.3.] Notice how the CUSTOMER file is in order by Customer ID. Before we run the accounts receivable program, we sort the SALE file so that it is in order by Customer ID also. Then, when we run the accounts receivable program, we read both files. When the Customer IDs from the two files match, we update the beginning balance in the CUSTOMER file and print out a bill. On the bill, we list month-to-date payments and itemize all the charges for that customer that are shown in the SALE file. We do that by holding on to the CUSTOMER record while we in turn read each of the SALE records that apply to that customer. Notice how the SALE file in this example shows two charges for customer 100, three charges for customer 101, and one charge each for customers 105 and 110. As a result, we've minimized the amount of time spent reading data from tape, which is the slowest part of running the program.

"Now look what happens if the program has to calculate total price. The first sale on the file has a Product ID of 2241. Notice that that's in the middle of the PRODUCT file. So in order to get the price for that product, we would have to read to the middle of the PRODUCT file. The next sale record applies to product 2518, which is the next record on the PRODUCT file. But then the next SALE record applies to the product that is at the very beginning of the PRODUCT file. To get the price for that product, we would have to go clear back to the beginning of the PRODUCT file. Do you see how we would have to be continually jumping around in the PRODUCT file, reading forward a large number of records, then rewinding, and so on?"

"Yes, I see that it would be very time consuming on the computer," Susan replied.

"That's right. It costs us money to have the clerical people enter total price data, but in the long run it's much cheaper than the alternative."

"I'm not so sure it's cheaper, Sandy. The data entry operators have to rely on the accuracy of the sales order submitted by the sales representatives. The order contains both the Product ID and the total price. The sales representatives usually get the Product ID right, but they often miscalculate the price. That results in incorrect billing amounts, unhappy customers, and lower profits. We can't live with this problem. We need a solution."

Let's step back from this example for a moment and take a closer look at the problems with sequential file systems. In order for sales to be processed against the CUSTOMER file in the accounts receivable program, the sales must be in order by Customer ID. Since the sales will very likely be entered in helter-skelter order, the SALE file must be sorted before it can be used as input to this program. This is shown in Figure 1.4. If the SALE file is in order by Customer ID though, it will probably be completely out of order with respect to Product ID. Hence, the total price of a sale cannot in practicality be calculated from the price in the PRODUCT file. This leads to clerks entering redundant data, requiring additional manual effort and introducing increased probability of error.

The requirement that all files be processed sequentially leads to additional work in other ways as well. For example, another of IPD's applications calculates sales commissions and generates a commission statement. To calculate the sales representative's commission, we must sort the SALE file again, this time to put it in order by SALREP-ID. Now we can process the SALE file against the SALES-REP file to create commission statements for the sales representatives (Figure 1.5).

FIGURE 1.5   Creating the Commission Statement

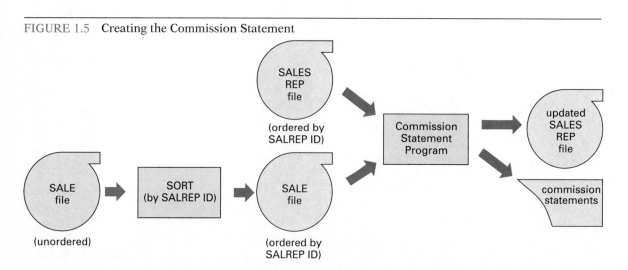

Two days later, sales manager Dick Greenberg approaches Sanford Mallon. He needs some information immediately. "What's Watabe Bros.' current balance?"

"I don't know," replies Sanford. "Have you checked the last accounts receivable run?"

"The accounts receivable program is only run once a month. I want to know what their balance is right now, not what it was three weeks ago."

"I'm sorry, but there's no way we can give it to you. The information is buried in the SALE and CUSTOMER files, and we would have to run the entire accounts receivable program to get you an answer."

"Okay then, forget it. Maybe we can figure it out by going over the paper sales receipts. Let me ask you another question. Why are the Product IDs on the customer statements wrong so much of the time? Many of those Product IDs we see on statements don't even exist. Can't your system check the Product IDs the clerks enter to see if they're valid?"

"Unfortunately, the Product IDs are on a different file, and it's impossible to get at them."

"To tell you the truth, I don't understand why we can't get at the data if it's in the system. It seems to me that if the data is there, you ought to be able to get to it and use it."

"Dick, I agree, and I know Susan's concerned about some of the system's other limitations. I'm already working on a proposal to upgrade our system to include random access files. Although it would cost some money, the upgrade would not be terribly difficult, and it would solve some of the problems we've been having."

"How?"

"We'll change the CUSTOMER, PRODUCT, SALES-REP, and MANUFACTURER files to random access [indexed sequential] files. For example, we'll use the Customer ID as the key to the customer file. Then we can write a simple program that will access any record on that file any time we want to. All we need to know is the Customer ID of the record we want. Then you can find out the Watabe Bros. up-to-date balance whenever you need it. We can also use those files to validate Product IDs, Manufacturer IDs, Salesrep IDs, and so on. That will help us clean up the errors on customer statements you were complaining about."

"That sounds great. How soon can I get it?"

These two encounters illustrate some of the most serious limitations of purely sequential file systems:

1. It is usually impractical to get at all of the data needed for an application if the data is contained on more than two files. This results in the entry of redundant data.

2. The limited access to data usually makes it impossible to validate data values (such as Product ID) that are located in inaccessible files.

3. *Ad hoc* queries to the system are impossible. The information desired must be contained on a report somewhere and will probably not be up-to-date.

These problems were partially solved by the introduction of random access files, and particularly indexed sequential (ISAM) files, which became widely available in the sixties. Random access files allow the retrieval of records on a random, as opposed to a sequential, basis. A desired record in a random access file may be retrieved directly. ISAM files are the most popular type of random access files for business processing. These files allow one or more data fields—together called a **key**—to be used as the means of identifying precisely which record is to be retrieved. ISAM files provided a practical and powerful means of adding significant flexibility to business applications systems. (We will discuss physical aspects of database systems in more detail in Chapter 11.)

However, random access files provided only a partial solution to these problems. To get a more complete resolution of these problems, it was necessary to introduce database management systems.

Information as a Resource

key A value that uniquely identifies a record in a file.

Problem 3 above has special significance. When Dick Greenberg wanted to know the current balance of the Watabe Bros. account, he was reaching beyond the data processing capability of the system and asking an **information system** question. Questions like this illustrate the important transition that took place in the late sixties and early seventies as business computer systems progressed from *data processing* to *information processing*. This change reflected a growing awareness that information was more than simple business records. Gradually, businesses began to realize the value of information and the enormous potential business computer systems have for organizing and managing this newly recognized resource. This led in the late sixties to a very strong demand for **management information systems**. These systems would use the data already available in the computer to provide answers to a broad spectrum of management questions.

information system An automated system which organizes data to produce information.

management information system A system that provides information to management.

In this context, we make a distinction between *data* and *information*. **Data** is usually thought of as isolated facts. For example,

data Isolated facts.

"Watabe Bros. is a company located in Japan"

is a fact. This fact is contained in a single record in the CUSTOMER file. The files of a system contain thousands of such facts. The files, therefore, contain "data." **Information**, on the other hand, is "processed data." We mean, in this sense of the word, that information is organized or summarized data. For example, we might want to know the total current balance of Watabe Bros., or perhaps we might ask for the average current balance of all customers in Europe. We would call the answers to such questions as these "information."

information Organized or summarized data.

Of course, every fact or data item can be called "information." But we are primarily concerned with information that would be valuable at a management or an executive level in a company—particularly for decision making. This information is normally higher-level information, summarized from a much larger set of facts. Consequently, information is different from data.

In recent years, the significant impact information has had on planning and decision making in organizations has led to an ever increasing recognition that information is a resource that has value and therefore needs to be organized and managed. Although businesses are accustomed to dealing with tangible assets such as money, facilities, and personnel, whose value can be appraised with some precision, they have found it more difficult to measure the value of information precisely. Nonetheless, it is clear that the better information managers have, the more likely they are to make sound, timely decisions that will have a positive impact on their business. Conversely, the poorer information managers have, the more uncertainty they must deal with and the less likely they are to make good decisions. The emergence of database systems is an exciting development in the effort to provide accurate and timely information to managers.

A **database** is a collection of interrelated data items that can be processed by one or more application systems. A **database system** is comprised of a database, general-purpose software—called the **database management system (DBMS)**—that manipulates the database, and appropriate hardware and personnel. A DBMS is usually purchased from a software vendor and is the means by which an application program or an end user views and manipulates data in the database. We will discuss the components of a database system in more detail at the end of this chapter.

A properly designed database system integrates data common to several functional units of a company and facilitates the manipulation of data. In addition to simplifying the everyday insertion, deletion, and updating of records, database systems facilitate the identifying and quantifying of derived relationships between data items, compiling statistical summary information concerning data, drawing inferences about business trends, and so on. Through such facilities, the database system can be used to transform raw data into information.

database A collection of interrelated data items that can be processed by one or more application systems.

database system A database, a database management system, and appropriate hardware and personnel.

database management system (DBMS) Systems software that facilitates the management of a database.

Other Limitations of Traditional File Systems

Despite the introduction of random access files, it soon became obvious that file systems of any kind contained a number of shortcomings: (1) data redundancy; (2) poor data control; (3) inadequate data manipulation capabilities; and (4) excessive programming effort.

Data Redundancy. ☐ A major difficulty was that many applications used their own special files of data. Thus, many data items were found to be common to several applications. In a bank, for example, the same customer name might appear in a checking account file, a savings account file, and an installment loan file (Figure 1.6). Moreover, even though the customer name was the same, the related field often had a different name in the various account files. Thus, CNAME in the checking account file became SNAME in the savings account file and INAME in the installment loan file. The same field might also have a different field length in the various files. For example, CNAME could be up to 20 characters, but SNAME and INAME might be limited to 15 characters. This redundancy increased the overhead costs of maintenance and storage. Data redundancy also increased the risk of inconsistency among the various versions of common data.

Suppose a customer's name was changed from Carol T. Jones to Carol T. Smith. The name field might be immediately updated in the checking account file, updated next week in the savings account file, and updated incorrectly in the installment loan file (Carole T. Smith) (Figure 1.7). Over time, such discrepancies can cause serious degradation in the

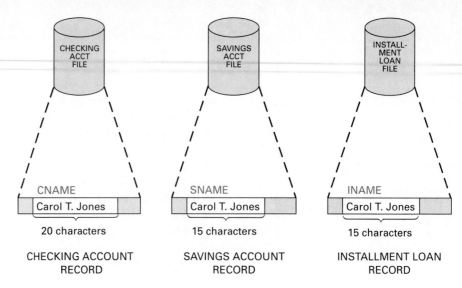

FIGURE 1.6   Customer Name Shown in Different Files

FIGURE 1.7   Inconsistent Update of Customer Name

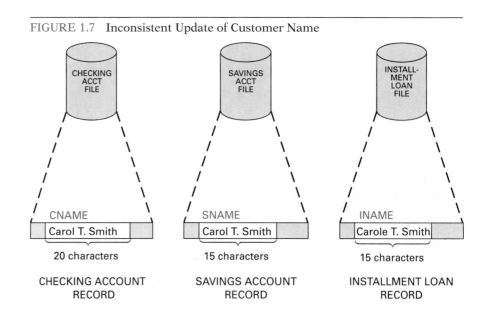

quality of information contained in the data files. These types of data inconsistency can also affect the accuracy of reports. Suppose we wished to produce a management report showing all customers who have either a checking or savings account and an installment loan. Carol T. Smith would erroneously be omitted from the report because her name appears as Carole T. Smith in the installment loan file. As we will show, database systems can eliminate data redundancy, since all applications share a common pool of data. Essential information, such as customer name or address, will appear just once in the database. Thus, we can enter a name change or change of address once and know that applications will be accessing consistent data.

Poor Data Control. ☐ In file systems, as we noted above, there was no centralized control at the data element level. It was very common for the same data element to have multiple names, depending on the file it was in.

At a more fundamental level, there is always the chance that the various departments of a company will be inconsistent in their terminology. A bank, for example, may use the term *account* to mean one thing when applied to savings and something quite different when applied to loans. A term that has different meanings in different contexts is called a **homonym.** Conversely, different words may mean the same thing. An insurance company may refer to a *policy* and a *case* and mean the same thing with both words. Two terms that mean the same thing are called **synonyms.** A database system supports centralized data control and helps eliminate the confusion caused by homonyms and synonyms.

homonym A term that has different meanings in different contexts.

synonyms Terms that mean the same thing.

Inadequate Data Manipulation Capabilities. ☐ Indexed sequential files allowed applications to access a particular record by a key, such as a Product ID. For example, if we knew the Product ID for table lamps, we could directly access the product's record within the PRODUCT file. This was adequate so long as we only wanted a single record.

However, suppose we wanted a set of related records. We might be interested, for example, in identifying all sales to IPD's customer Maltzl. Perhaps we need to know the total number of sales, or the average price, or which products are being purchased and from which manufacturers. Such information would be difficult, if not impossible, to obtain from a file system, because file systems are unable to provide strong connections between data in different files. Database systems were specifically developed to make the interrelating of data in different files much easier.

Excessive Programming Effort. ☐ A new application program often required an entirely new set of file definitions. Even though an existing file may contain some of the data needed, the application often required a number of other data items. As a result, the programmer had to recode definitions of all the needed data items from the existing file as well as the definitions of all the new data items. Thus, in file-oriented systems, there was a heavy interdependence between programs and data.

Even more importantly, data manipulation in file-oriented languages such as COBOL was difficult for complex applications. This meant that both the initial and the maintenance programming efforts for management information applications was significant.

Databases provide a separation between program and data, so that programs can be somewhat independent of the details of data definition. By providing access to a pool of shared data and by supporting powerful data manipulation languages, database systems eliminate a large amount of initial and maintenance programming.

☐ DATABASE SYSTEMS

Database systems attempt, with varying degrees of success, to overcome the limitations of file-oriented systems. By supporting an integrated, centralized data structure, database systems eliminate problems with data redundancy and data control. A centralized database is available throughout the company, and if, for example, a customer's name must be changed, the change is available to all users. Data is controlled via a Data Dictionary/Directory (DD/D) system which is itself controlled by a group of company employees known as Database Administrators (DBAs). New data access methods greatly simplify the process of relating data elements, which in turn enhances data manipulation. All of these features of database systems simplify the programming effort and reduce program maintenance.

At present we are in the midst of a decades-long effort to develop increasingly powerful database management systems. This process has seen the evolutionary development of systems based on three principal **data models,** or conceptual methods of structuring data. These three data models are the hierarchical, the network, and the relational. In the next two sections, we outline the historical development of database systems based on these three models.

data model A conceptual method of structuring data.

Hierarchical and Network Model Systems

Indexed sequential files solved the problem of directly accessing a single record within a file. For example, take another look at Figure 1.3. If we had the first sale record shown in the SALE file but wanted to know the name and address of the customer involved in the sale, we could simply use the Customer ID (100) to look up the customer's record in the CUSTOMER file. This tells us that the customer who made the order was Watabe Bros.

Now suppose that we want to reverse the process. Instead of wanting to know the customer involved in a sale, we want to know all the sales to a given customer. We start with the Watabe Bros. customer record, and now we want all their sale records. We cannot do this directly in a file system. It was for such applications that database systems were originally developed.

The first database systems, introduced in the mid-sixties, were based on the **hierarchical model,** which assumes all data relationships can be structured as hierarchies. To illustrate this we modify our database of Figure 1.3 slightly. Now, instead of sales which contain only a single product, we have invoices which in turn have invoice lines. Each customer has multiple invoices, and each invoice has multiple lines. Each line records the sale of a single product. Figure 1.8 gives some examples. The INVOICE and INVOICE LINE files replace the SALE file from Figure 1.3.

Figure 1.9 illustrates how we can make a hierarchy showing the relationships between customers, invoices, and invoice lines. A customer is thought to "own" invoices, which in turn "own" invoice lines. In a hierarchical database system, these three files would be tied together by physical pointers, or data fields added to the individual records. A **pointer** is a physical address which identifies where a record can be found on disk. Each customer record would contain a pointer to the first invoice record for that customer record. The invoice records would in turn contain pointers to other invoice records and to invoice line records. Thus, the system would easily be able to retrieve all the invoices and invoice lines that apply to a given customer.

hierarchical model A data model that assumes all data relationships can be structured as hierarchies.

pointer A physical address that identifies where a record can be found on disk.

CUSTOMER

CUST-ID	CUST-NAME	ADDRESS	COUNTRY	BEGINNING-BALANCE	MONTH-TO-DATE-PAYMENTS
100	Watabe Bros	Box 241, Tokyo	Japan	45,551	40,113
101	Maltzl	Salzburg	Austria	75,314	65,200
105	Jefferson	B 918, Chicago	USA	49,333	49,811
110	Gomez	Santiago	Chile	27,400	28,414

INVOICE

INVOICE-#	DATE	CUST-ID	SALREP-ID
1012	02/10	100	39
1015	02/14	110	37
1020	02/20	100	14

INVOICE LINE

INVOICE-#	LINE-#	PROD-ID	QTY	TOTAL-PRICE
1012	01	1035	100	2200.00
1012	02	2241	200	6650.00
1012	03	2518	300	6360.00
1015	01	1035	150	3300.00
1015	02	2518	200	4240.00
1020	01	2241	100	3325.00
1020	02	2518	150	3180.00

FIGURE 1.8   IPD Files Having a Hierarchical Relationship

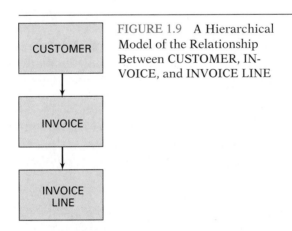

FIGURE 1.9   A Hierarchical Model of the Relationship Between CUSTOMER, IN-VOICE, and INVOICE LINE

Suppose we are interested in adding information about customers to our hierarchical database. For example, since our customers are department store companies, we may want to keep a list of stores for each customer. In that case, we would expand the diagram of Figure 1.9 to look like that of Figure 1.10. CUSTOMER is still related to INVOICE which is related to INVOICE LINE. CUSTOMER is also related, however, to STORE and STORE is related to CONTACT. By CONTACT, we mean a buyer to whom we would sell merchandise for a particular store. We see from this diagram that CUSTOMER is at the top of a hierarchy from which a large amount of information can be derived.

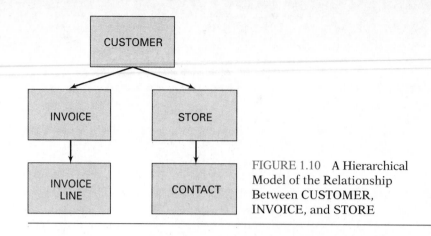

FIGURE 1.10 A Hierarchical Model of the Relationship Between CUSTOMER, INVOICE, and STORE

These figures show the kind of interfile relationships that are easily implemented in the hierarchical model. It became apparent very quickly, however, that this model had some significant limitations, since not all relationships could be expressed easily in a hierarchical framework. For example, to take the present case a step further, it is obvious that we are not only interested in the relationship between customers and invoices; we are also interested in the relationship between sales representatives and invoices. That is, we want to know all the invoices that a particular sales representative has produced so that we can issue commission statements. This new relationship is shown in Figure 1.11.

This diagram is not a hierarchy, however. In a hierarchy, a **child** can have only one **parent.** In Figure 1.10, INVOICE is a child and CUSTOMER is its parent. In Figure 1.11, though, INVOICE has two parents—SALESREP and CUSTOMER. We call diagrams like these **networks.** Because of the obvious need to handle relationships like those shown in Figure 1.11, in the late sixties *network* database systems were developed. Like hierarchical database systems, network database systems used physical pointers to tie records in different files together.

The dominant hierarchical DBMS is IBM's IMS, developed in the mid-sixties. In the late sixties and early seventies, a number of network DBMSs were developed and successfully marketed, and this data model

child An "owned" record in a hierarchical relationship.

parent An "owner" record in a hierarchical relationship.

network A data relationship in which a record can be owned by records from more than one file.

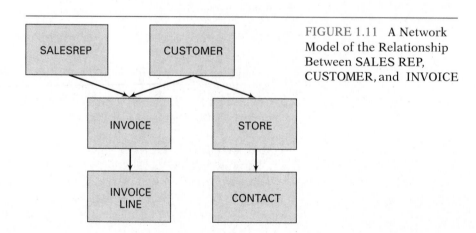

FIGURE 1.11 A Network Model of the Relationship Between SALES REP, CUSTOMER, and INVOICE

was eventually standardized as the CODASYL model. We will discuss both of these data models and their data definition and manipulation capabilities at length in Chapters 9 and 10.

Relational Database Systems

The use of physical pointers was at once a strength and a weakness of the hierarchical and the network database systems. The pointers were a strength because they allowed the quick retrieval of data having predetermined relationships. The weakness was that these relationships had to be determined *before* the system was put into operation. Data based on other relationships were difficult, if not impossible, to retrieve. As users became more familiar with database systems and their power to manipulate data, they quickly found these limitations unacceptable, as this encounter at IPD shows.

"Cordelia, we are getting quite frustrated with the number of management questions our database system *cannot* answer easily. When you and Sandy convinced us that we should convert to a network database system, you claimed that we would be able to answer most questions that we would be likely to ask."

Susan Broadbent, IPD CEO, and Dick Greenberg, IPD Sales Manager, are talking to IPD's Database Administrator (DBA), Cordelia Molini, about the shortcomings of their current network database management system. This is not a new complaint. With each new system, IPD management finds as they begin to ask "What if . . ." questions that the system does less than they would like. Although the network system has served them well for several years, they are now reaching the point where more and more of the information they need is difficult to obtain. Cordelia is well aware of these frustrations.

"Well, perhaps we should have said *many* questions you would be likely to ask. With experience, we have found that there is a very broad variety of questions users want to ask." Cordelia continues: "The problem we face is that the network system depends on *physical* pointers to tie data in different files together. If you ask a question that does not naturally follow those pointers, we can't answer the question without a significant amount of programming. Now tell me, can you give me a better idea of the types of questions you need answers to?"

Dick replies immediately. "We want to answer all kinds of questions, Cordelia. We really can't characterize them by type, because that would be too limiting. Ideally, we would like to be able to ask any question we want, and if the answer is in the data, we should be able to get the answer from the system."

Cordelia looks from Dick to Susan. "From what you say, it sounds like we need to seriously consider moving to a relational database system. In a relational system, we don't have physical pointers. Data can be connected if a *logical* connection exists, so we don't have to worry about defining which relationships are the most likely to be used by the system."

Susan asks, "Does that mean, for example, that Dick can ask whether products made in Ghana are selling well in Korea? Or how well a sales representative in Rio is doing selling electronic equipment from Amsterdam?"

"Yes. Both those questions would be easy to answer in a relational system. Besides that, you will find that you will not have to work through a programmer nearly as often. Managers who are willing to learn a relatively simple data manipulation language can answer more of their own questions by accessing the system directly. What do you think, Susan?"

"It sounds like something that deserves further investigation. If the technology is sound, we should think seriously about moving to it. Why don't you look into it and put together a proposal?"

In 1970, E.F. Codd published a revolutionary paper that strongly challenged the conventional wisdom of the database "establishment" (Codd, 1970). Codd argued that data should be related through the natural, logical relationships that were inherent in the data, rather than through physical pointers. Thus, people could combine data from different sources, if the logical information needed to make the combination was present in the data. This opened up an entirely new vista for management information systems, since database queries need no longer be limited by the relationships indicated by physical pointers.

To illustrate the shortcomings of database systems that rely on physical pointers, consider Figure 1.12. Here we have shown that CUSTOMER, INVOICE, and INVOICE LINE are connected by physical pointers. MANUFACTURER and PRODUCT are also connected. The broken line between INVOICE LINE and PRODUCT indicates that these two are *logically* related, since every invoice line refers to a specific product. Suppose, however, that PRODUCT has *not* been connected to INVOICE LINE by a physical pointer. How can the following management report be obtained?

For each customer, identify the manufacturers whose products the customer has ordered.

This requires navigating from CUSTOMER through INVOICE and INVOICE LINE, over to PRODUCT, and then up to MANUFACTURER. But since the physical connection between INVOICE LINE and PRODUCT does not exist in the database, this navigation cannot be done through the normal database facilities. Instead, old-fashioned and cum-

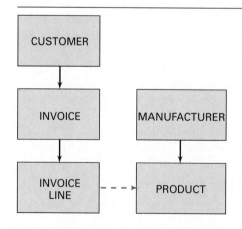

FIGURE 1.12   A Logical Relationship Not Supported by Physical Pointers

bersome file processing techniques must be used to obtain the requested information. This would necessitate a considerable amount of complex programming. In contrast to this, database systems that support the retrieval of data based on *logical* relationships would easily solve problems like these.

In the same paper, Codd proposed a simple data model in which all data would be represented in tables made up of rows and columns. These tables were given the mathematical name *relations,* and from this the model was named the relational model. Codd also proposed two languages for manipulating data in tables: relational algebra and relational calculus (to be discussed in Chapter 8). Both these languages support data manipulation on the basis of logical characteristics rather than the physical pointers used in the hierarchical and network models.

By handling data on a conceptual rather than a physical basis, Codd introduced another revolutionary innovation. In relational database systems, entire files of data can be processed with single statements. By contrast, traditional systems require data to be processed one record at a time. Codd's approach significantly improves the conceptual efficiency of database programming.

The logical manipulation of data also makes feasible the creation of query languages more accessible to the nontechnical user. Although it is quite difficult to create a language which can be used by *all* people, regardless of their previous computer experience, relational query languages make the accessing of databases realistic for a much larger group of users than was previously possible.

The publication of Codd's papers in the early seventies set off a flurry of activity in both the research and commercial system development communities as they worked to bring out a relational database management system. The result was the release of relational database management systems during the last half of the seventies supporting such query languages as Structured Query Language (SQL), Query Language (Quel), and Query-by-Example (QBE). As the personal computer became popular during the eighties, relational database management systems that ran on microcomputers also became available. All of these developments have greatly advanced the state-of-the-art in database management systems and increased the availability of information contained in corporate databases. The relational approach has proven to be quite fruitful. We should note, however, that additional research promises to provide increasingly powerful capabilities as we acquire a more complete understanding of user needs with respect to database systems.

☐ CURRENT DIRECTIONS

Today, relational systems are considered the standard in up-to-date commercial data processing operations. Of course, file-oriented systems, as well as hierarchical and network database systems, are still plentiful and, for a number of applications, the most cost effective solution. However, the clear trend for some time has been for companies to convert to relational systems whenever feasible.

It would be wrong to assume that the relational database systems now available represent the last word in DBMS development, though. The

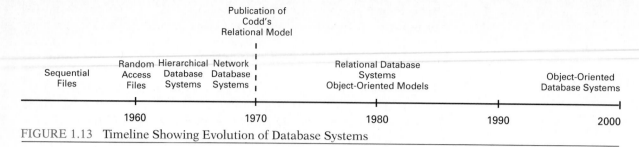

FIGURE 1.13   Timeline Showing Evolution of Database Systems

relational systems of today are still evolving and in significant respects changing their underlying nature to allow users to address more complex problems. From our point of view, the most significant of these changes are occurring in the area of object-oriented databases. We will discuss the object-oriented model in detail starting in Chapter 4.

Figure 1.13 shows a timeline describing the historical development of the data access methods we have discussed. The timeline projects into the nineties, when it is anticipated that object-oriented database systems, based on the methodology discussed in Chapters 4, 5, and 6, will become more common. Table 1.1 provides a feature comparison of the various data access methods.

□ DATABASE SYSTEMS: HARDWARE, SOFTWARE, DATA, PEOPLE

So far, we have discussed database systems and their capabilities in general terms. Now it is time to take a closer look at the components that make up such a system. A database system is more than just data or data in combination with database management software. A *complete* database

TABLE 1.1   Feature Comparison of Data Access Methods

Data Access Method	Features
Sequential Files	All records in a file must be processed in sequence
Random Access Files	Supports direct access to a specific record
	Difficult to access multiple records related to a single record
Hierarchical Database	Supports access to multiple records related to a single record
	Restricted to hierarchical data relationships
	Dependent on predefined, physical pointers
Network Database	Supports hierarchical and nonhierarchical network data relationships
	Dependent on predefined, physical pointers
Relational Database	Supports all logical data relationships
	Logical data access, independent of physical implementation techniques

system in an organization consists of four components: hardware, software, data, and people.

Hardware The *hardware* is the set of physical devices on which a database resides. It consists of one or more computers, disk drives, CRT terminals, printers, tape drives, and other auxiliary and connecting hardware.

The computers, used for processing the data in the database, may be mainframe, mini-, or microcomputers. In the example given above, IPD initially began processing with a minicomputer and then later upgraded to a mainframe computer. Mainframe and minicomputers are normally used to support multiple users accessing a common database. Microcomputers are often used with stand-alone databases controlled and accessed by a single user. However, they can also be connected in a network, providing multiple users access to a common database stored on disk drives which are also part of the network. Figure 1.14 illustrates a variety of hardware configurations.

FIGURE 1.14   Three Possible Hardware Configurations for Database Systems

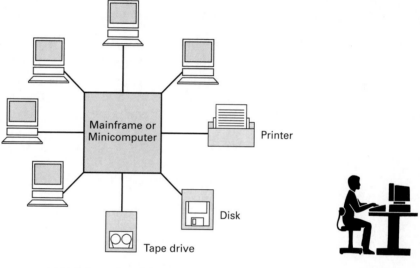

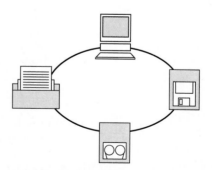

(a) Mainframe or minicomputer supporting access through multiple terminals

(b) Microcomputer used with a stand-alone database

(c) Microcomputers connected in a network, all accessing a database stored on one of the microcomputers

Disk drives are the main storage mechanism for databases and are essential since they allow random access, without which database processing would be impossible. CRT terminals and printers are used for entering and retrieving information from the database. Tape drives are used to provide rapid and inexpensive backup of data residing on the disk drives.

The success of database systems has been heavily dependent on advances in hardware technology. A very large amount of main memory and disk storage is required to maintain and control the huge quantity of data stored in a database. In addition, high-speed computers and peripherals are necessary to execute the large number of data accesses required to retrieve information in an acceptable amount of time in an environment with a large number of users. Fortunately, computer hardware has become increasingly powerful and significantly less expensive during the years of database technology development. This has made possible the widespread use of database systems.

Software   A database system includes two types of software:

- General-purpose database management software, usually called the Database Management System (DBMS)
- Application software that uses DBMS facilities to manipulate the database to achieve a specific business function, such as issuing statements or analyzing sales trends

Application software is generally written by company employees to solve a specific company problem. It may be written in a standard programming language, such as COBOL, or it may be written in a language (commonly called a Fourth Generation Language) supplied with the database management system. Application software uses the facilities of the DBMS to access and manipulate data in the database, providing reports or documents needed for the information and processing needs of the company.

The *database management system* (DBMS) is systems software, similar to an operating system or a compiler, that provides a number of services to end users, programmers, and others (Figure 1.15). As its name implies, the DBMS exists to facilitate the management of a database. To this end a DBMS typically provides most of the following services:

- A centralized data definition and data control facility known as a Data Dictionary/Directory (DD/D)
- Data security and integrity mechanisms
- Concurrent data access for multiple users
- User-oriented data query, manipulation, and reporting capabilities
- Programmer-oriented application system development capabilities

Data Dictionary/Directory (DD/D).   A Data Dictionary/Directory subsystem keeps track of the definitions of all the data items in the database. This includes elementary level data items (fields), group and

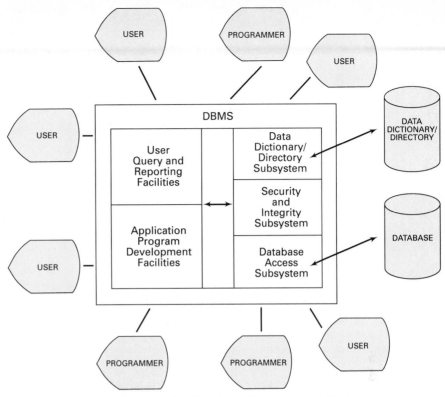

FIGURE 1.15   Components of a Database Management System

record level data structures, and files or relational tables. Not only does the DD/D maintain this information, but it keeps track of relationships that exist between various data structures. Additionally, it maintains the indexes that are used to access data quickly. It also keeps track of screen and report format definitions that may be used by various application programs.

The data dictionary can be viewed as being a part of the database itself. Thus, the database is *self-describing,* since it contains information describing its own structure. The information in the data dictionary is called **metadata,** or "data about data." The metadata is available for query and manipulation, just as other data in the database.

metadata Data in the data dictionary that describes the database.

Data Security and Integrity Mechanisms. □   The database is an important resource and needs to be protected. The DBMS provides database security by controlling access to the database by authorized personnel. Users who are allowed access to the database will generally be restricted as to the particular data they can access and whether they can update it. Such access is often controlled by passwords and by **data views,** which are definitions of restricted portions of the database, as illustrated in Figure 1.16. The integrity and consistency of the database are protected via constraints on values that various data items can have and by backup and recovery capabilities that are provided within the DBMS. Data constraint definitions are maintained in the data dictionary. Backup and recovery

data view A definition of a restricted portion of the database; also called a view.

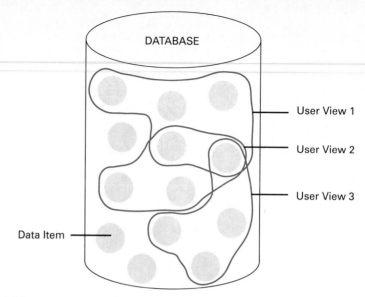

FIGURE 1.16   User Views of a Database

are supported by software that automatically logs changes to the database and provides for a means of recovering the current state of the database in case of a system failure.

Concurrent Data Access for Multiple Users. ☐   One of the chief functions of the DBMS is to support the access, retrieval, and update of data in the database. The DBMS provides the physical mechanisms allowing multiple users to access a variety of related data quickly and efficiently. This support extends to users in remote locations who must access the database through a telecommunications system. The DBMS facilities provide interface with telecommunications systems so that requests for data and the resulting responses will be properly routed.

The centralization of data in a database increases the probability that two or more users will want to access the same data concurrently. If the DBMS allowed this, the two users would certainly affect each other's work and could damage it. Thus, it is important that the DBMS protect the data being accessed by one user from simultaneous update by another user. To do this, the DBMS uses sophisticated locking mechanisms to protect the data currently being updated by a user, while at the same time providing concurrent database access and acceptable system response time to other users.

User-Oriented Data Query and Reporting. ☐   One of the most valuable aspects of a DBMS is its provision of user-oriented data manipulation tools. These easy-to-use query languages allow users to formulate queries and request one-time reports directly from the database. This relieves the company's programming staff of the burden of formulating these queries or writing special purpose application software.

Associated with query languages are report generators. Often the query language will contain facilities to format the results of queries as reports. The formulated query itself can be saved for use later and its result can be produced as a regular report. When this is the case, the query language can be viewed as a report generator. In addition, report generators may also be provided which have more powerful reporting facilities than those available in the query language.

Application Development Facilities. ☐ Besides making it easier for the user to access the database for information, the DBMS commonly provides significant assistance to the application programmer as well. Such tools as screen, menu, and report generators; application generators; compilers; and data and view definition facilities are standard. More importantly, modern database systems provide language components that are much more powerful than those of traditional languages, making the programming process itself considerably more efficient.

Data Clearly, no database system can exist without data, the basic facts upon which a company's processing and information needs are founded. The important factor to consider here, however, is that the data of which a database is constituted must be carefully and logically structured. Business functions must be analyzed, data elements and relationships must be identified and precisely defined, and these definitions must be accurately recorded in the data dictionary. Data can then be collected and entered into the database according to the defined structure. A database built in harmony with these procedures can be a powerful resource for providing the organization with timely information.

People The IPD case identified two different *types* of people concerned with the database. Susan Broadbent and Dick Greenberg are **users,** people who need information from the database to carry out their primary business responsibility, which is in some other functional area. Sanford Mallon and Cordelia Molini, by contrast, are **practitioners,** people whose primary business responsibility is to design and maintain the database system and its associated application software for the benefit of the users. Examples of people in each of these categories may be as follows:

users People who need information from the database to carry out their primary business responsibility.

practitioners People responsible for the database system and its associated application software.

> Users: Executives, managers, staff, clerical personnel
>
> Practitioners: Database Administrators, analysts, programmers, database and system designers, information systems managers

procedure Written instructions describing the steps needed to accomplish a given task in a system.

The **procedures** people use to accomplish their goals in the system constitute an important aspect of this component. Virtually no system completely automates a user task. Manual procedures must be developed to provide a smooth interface between the users of the system and the system itself. An example of such a procedure would be the audit control by which the users determine that the total amount deposited in the bank on a given day agrees with the total amount of cash received for that day as shown in the system. There are normally many such procedures in a system, and the success of the system often depends as much on the skill with which such procedures are developed to mesh with the system functions as it does on the structure of the system itself.

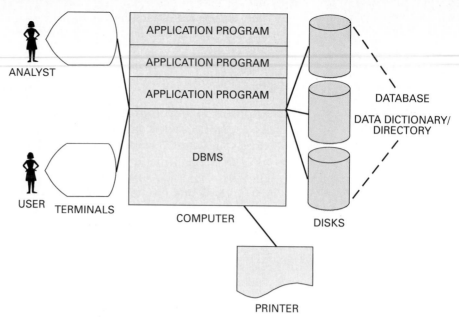

FIGURE 1.17   The Four Components of a Database System: People, Hardware, Software, and Data

Relationship of the Four System Components

Figure 1.17 summarizes the relationship among the four components of a database system. *Practitioners* (analysts and database designers) in consultation with *users* identify *data* needs and design database structures to accommodate these needs. The database structures are then specified to the *DBMS* through the data dictionary. *Users* enter *data* into the system by following specified *procedures*. The entered data is maintained on *hardware* media such as disks and tapes. *Application programs* that access the *database* are written by practitioners and users to be run on *computers*. These programs utilize the command language of the DBMS and make use of the information contained in the data dictionary. These programs generate information, which can be used by executives and managers to make business decisions. Application programs may also generate billing statements and other documents used by the customers of the business. Thus, it can be seen that in a properly designed and functioning system all four components—hardware, software, data, and people—fit together in a single system to accomplish the goals of the organization.

■ SUMMARY

In this chapter, we have reviewed the development of database technology, starting with the early file access methods and proceeding through the principal approaches to database processing. We have also identified and discussed the four main components of a database system: hardware, software, data, and people.

In the early years of data processing, during the fifties and early sixties, sequential file processing was the rule. All data resided on sequential files, which required the processing of complete files by application programs. During the sixties, as direct access disk storage became widely available, random access file processing became feasible and popular. This file access method allowed the direct access of specific data from a file.

As computer data processing systems became ever more important, businesses began to recognize that information was a corporate resource of considerable value. More and more they perceived that the data to answer numerous business questions was available in their data processing files. As a consequence they began to push for management information systems that would use the power of the computer to produce information from corporate data. This initiated the demand for database systems which would more effectively manage data access and manipulation.

In the mid-sixties, the first database systems, based on a hierarchical structuring of data, were introduced. These systems provided for the retrieval of multiple records associated with a single record of another file. Shortly after, network database systems were developed which supported significantly more complex relationships between records of different files. Both the hierarchical and network database models required the use of predefined physical pointers for linking related records.

In 1970, Codd's paper on the relational data model revolutionized the thinking of the database industry. Codd's approach called for the access and manipulation of data solely in terms of its logical characteristics. During the seventies and eighties, a number of relational database systems were developed, and at present they dominate the commercial market place.

Today, a database system in a large organization consists of hardware, software, data, and people. The hardware configuration is comprised of one or more computers, disk drives, terminals, printers, tape drives, and other physical devices. The software includes a database management system (DBMS) and application programs which use the DBMS to access and manipulate the database. The data, representing the recorded facts important to the organization, resides physically on disk but is logically structured in a way to make its access easy and efficient. People, both database system users and practitioners, work together to define the characteristics and structure of the database system and to create the application programs which will provide the information essential to the company's success.

■ REVIEW QUESTIONS

1. Define each of the following terms in your own words:
   a. data processing system
   b. random access processing
   c. management information system
   d. database
   e. database system
   f. data model
   g. hierarchical model
   h. pointer
   i. network
   j. database management system

    k. data view
    l. procedure
    m. metadata

2. What are the important characteristics of sequential and random access file systems? What weaknesses of sequential file access do random access methods remedy?

3. Discuss the importance of information as an organizational resource. How have database systems helped to increase the value of information to organizations?

4. Compare and contrast the features of hierarchical, network, and relational database systems. What business needs led to the development of each of them?

5. List and briefly describe each of the four main components of a modern database system.

6. Describe each of these components of a database management system (DBMS):
    a. Data Dictionary/Directory (DD/D)
    b. Data security and integrity
    c. Concurrent data access for multiple users
    d. Data query, manipulation, and reporting
    e. Application system development facilities

7. List three examples of each of the following:
    a. Users
    b. Practitioners

8. Define each of the following:
    a. ISAM
    b. IMS
    c. DBA
    d. SQL
    e. Quel
    f. QBE

■ PROBLEMS AND EXERCISES

1. Match the following terms with their definitions:

__data	a. Computer program that performs a task of practical value
__key	b. Organized or summarized data
__information system	c. Isolated facts
__synonyms	d. People who need information from the database
__parent	e. People responsible for the database system
__users	f. Automated system that organizes data to produce information
__application program	g. Terms that mean the same thing
__homonym	h. "Owned" record in a hierarchical relationship

__child	i. "Owner" record in a hierarchical relationship
__information	j. Has different meanings in different contexts
__practitioners	k. Data fields that uniquely identify a record

2. Define a key for each of the files in Figure 1.3.

3. Which of the following can be regarded as "data" and which as "information"?

    a. Marshall Dobry received more commission than any other sales representative this year.

    b. Marshall Dobry was born December 12, 1960.

    c. The Western region produced over $500,000 in sales during each month of the last quarter.

    d. Product A235 is profitable.

    e. Product A235 is manufactured in Des Moines.

4. Organize the following files into a hierarchy for a bank's database: PAYMENT, SAVINGS ACCOUNT, DEPOSIT, CUSTOMER, LOAN ACCOUNT, WITHDRAWAL.

5. Organize the following files into a network for a shipping company's database: SHIPMENT, TRUCK, SENDER, PACKAGE, RECEIVER.

6. For problems 4 and 5, identify fields that may be found in each file. Identify key fields for each file.

7. Explain how uncontrolled concurrent processing in a database system could lead to damaged data in the following situations:

    a. Making flight reservations in an airline reservation system

    b. Updating quantities of a product in an inventory control system

    c. Updating a checking account balance in a bank

■ PROJECTS AND PROFESSIONAL ISSUES

1. Visit a data center in your area and speak with the managers, analysts, and programmers. Ask about their experience with traditional file systems and database systems. If they are using a database system now, does it use any of the three models discussed in this chapter? What advantages and disadvantages do they perceive in the various approaches to accessing data? What hardware configuration do they have? Have they needed hardware upgrades in the past, and do they anticipate any in the near future? What are the principal management information needs being served by the system?

2. Sketch the logic of (a) a program using sequential file systems and (b) a program using ISAM files to solve the following query:
For each customer identify the manufacturers whose products the customer has ordered. (Assume the file structure given in Figure 1.3.)

3. Read Codd's 1970 paper proposing the relational data model. Investigate subsequent papers which argued the relative merits of the CODASYL network model over those of the relational model. Write a paper that analyzes the merits of both approaches to database systems.

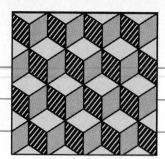

chapter two

DATABASE SYSTEMS AND THEIR ORGANIZATIONAL ENVIRONMENT

"As you can see, Susan, this strategic database plan outlines the path IPD information systems will take for the next five years. In two years, we will complete database system installations in two of our overseas offices, and in five years, we will have systems in all our offices."

Cordelia Molini, Database Administrator at International Product Distribution (IPD), is presenting a five-year database planning report to Susan Broadbent, IPD's CEO. IPD has just completed a strategic database planning project, for which Cordelia was the project leader.

Susan queries: "Did you address the problem of keeping our data secure in an international environment?"

"Yes, and we analyzed the associated costs and risks. We also considered the information needs of IPD's functional areas and different levels of management. As you review the report's details, you will see that we have indicated proposed schedules for several development projects as well as their estimated costs."

"This is excellent work. You and your team are to be congratulated for providing us with a database system framework that fits our business plan so well."

database A collection of interrelated, shared, and controlled data.

In this chapter, we focus on the organizational environment in which databases exist and how databases and their environment interrelate. To facilitate our discussion, we add to our simple definition of a database: A **database** in an organization is a collection of interrelated, shared, and controlled data. After reading this chapter, you should be able to:

☐ Discuss data sharing in an organization—between different functional areas, management levels, and geographical locations.
☐ Explain why and how strategic database planning is done in an organization.
☐ Understand the control function of Database Administration.
☐ List and explain the risks and costs of database systems.

☐ DATA SHARING AND DATABASES

IPD's database system went through several stages of evolution before it reached its current level of sophistication. To better understand why IPD decided to change from a file-oriented system to a database system, we look back several years to a conversation between Susan Broadbent and Sanford Mallon, IPD's Chief Information Officer.

"Sandy, I'm concerned that our company is becoming too compartmentalized. As the various functional groups get larger, they seem to become more and more isolated from each other. I don't think many groups care what the other groups are doing."

"I'm sorry to hear that, Susan, but what does that have to do with me?"

"Thanks a lot, pal! I can see that the isolationist attitude has reached the information systems group, too. All right, let me explain. Our groups are producing management reports that are helpful to them, but they are not sharing their information with the other groups. For example, Dick's Marketing group gets all kinds of information about customer satisfaction and dissatisfaction with products. But our Product Evaluation group never sees it. Why can't we get our people to share information more effectively?"

"Actually," Sandy replied, "Product Evaluation has seen those Marketing reports, but they tell me they cannot understand the format. I'm willing to write some programs to get Evaluation the information they need, but Marketing doesn't want to let other groups have control over their data. They're afraid it will get trashed or misused."

"You've talked before about converting to a database system. Would that help us solve this problem?"

"Yes, it certainly would. We would be able to share data in a controlled way. This means Evaluation could get the information they need without adversely affecting Marketing. Of course, we would have to assure Marketing—and all the other functional areas—that if they give up some control, the database system will protect their data. In addition, I think I can show them that a good database system will offer them many advantages."

"Sandy, that sounds good to me. If you present these ideas to the functional areas, I'm sure they will agree."

Perhaps the most significant difference between a file-based system and a database system is that data is shared. This requires a major change in the thinking of users, who are accustomed to feeling they "own" the data resulting from their daily work activities. Data sharing also requires a major change in the way data is handled and managed within the organization. Part of this comes from the sheer amount of data that needs to be organized and integrated. To help you understand the challenge of using a database to share data, let's take a closer look at the nature of organizational data that needs to be shared. We will consider three types of data sharing: (1) between functional units; (2) between management levels; and (3) between geographically dispersed locations.

Sharing Data Between Functional Units

The term *data sharing* suggests that people in different functional areas use a common pool of data, each for their own applications. Without data sharing, the Marketing group may have their data files, the Purchasing group theirs, the Accounting group theirs, and so on (Figure 2.1(a)). Each group benefits only from its own data. Thus, IPD's Product Evaluation group could not use data from Marketing.

In contrast, the effect of combining data into a database that users share is synergistic—that is, the value of the combined data is greater than the sum of the data in separate files. Not only does each group continue to have access to their own data, but, within reasonable limits of control, they have access to other data as well (Figure 2.1(b)). In this environment, the Marketing department, for example, is better off because they have access to data from Purchasing, especially product evaluations, which provides valuable input for marketing campaigns. In return, Product Evaluation gains access to Marketing's feedback about customer satisfaction. Both Marketing and Purchasing benefit by having access to accounting data, which can help Marketing identify valuable customers and

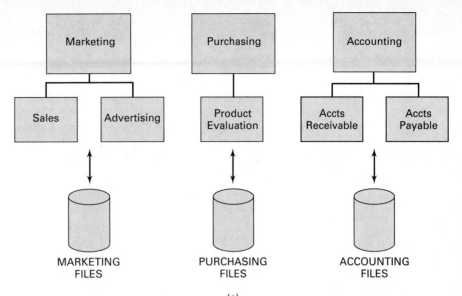

(a)
Separation of Data Without Data Sharing

FIGURE 2.1   Sharing Data Among Functional Units

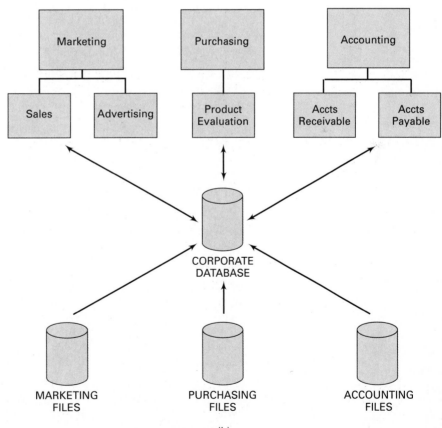

(b)
Sharing Data in a Database Environment

Purchasing identify valuable vendors. We refer to this concept of combining data for common use as **data integration.**

Sharing Data Between Different Levels of Users

Different levels of users also need to share data. Three different levels of database users are normally distinguished: operations, middle management, and executive. These levels correspond to the three different types of automated business systems that have evolved during the past three decades: **Electronic Data Processing** (EDP), **Management Information Systems** (MIS), and **Decision Support Systems** (DSS). Sprague (Sprague and Watson, 1989) gives a description of a commonly held view of these three types of systems:

EDP was first applied to the lower operational levels of the organization to automate the paperwork. Its basic characteristics include:

- a focus on data, storage, processing, and flows at the operational level;
- efficient transaction processing;
- scheduled and optimized computer runs;
- integrated files for related jobs; and
- summary reports for management. . . .

The MIS approach elevated the focus on information systems activities, with additional emphasis on integration and planning of the information systems function. In *practice*, the characteristics of MIS include:

- an information focus, aimed at the middle managers;
- structured information flow;
- an integration of EDP jobs by business function, such as production MIS, marketing MIS, personnel MIS, etc.; and
- inquiry and report generation, ususally with a database. . . .

[A] DSS is focused still higher in the organization with an emphasis on the following characteristics:

- decision focused, aimed at top managers and executive decision makers;
- emphasis on flexibility, adaptability, and quick response;
- user initiated and controlled; and
- support for the personal decision-making styles of individual managers. (pg. 11–12)

The relationships of these systems to different management levels is illustrated in Figure 2.2. These three levels of users and systems naturally require three different types of data. The EDP user at the operational level needs data for transaction processing. This might include data for new accounts or changes to existing accounts, records of purchases, payments, and so on. This is detailed data which can then be used in a summarized form for the information needs at the other two, higher levels. The MIS level would utilize summaries that might indicate, for example, which sales representatives were most productive and which were least productive. Executives at the highest level use Decision Support Systems and are interested in long-term trends as they apply to their own corporation as well as to the economic, social, and political environment in

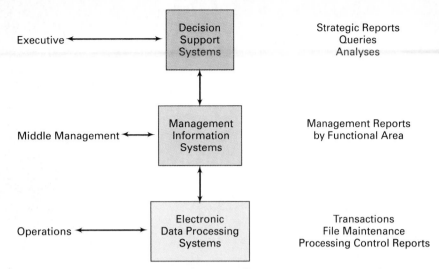

FIGURE 2.2   Systems Corresponding to Different Management Levels

which they operate. They use the DSS to help them make decisions such as building a new factory, starting or dropping a product line, opening or closing a market, and so on. Thus, a DSS must use summary data from within the company as well as market, demographic, and other data coming from outside sources.

Sharing Data Between Different Locations

A company with multiple locations will have important data distributed over a wide geographical area. Sharing this data is a significant problem. As IPD's branch offices became large, the interchange of data between the home office and the branches became increasingly inadequate, as illustrated in the following conversation.

"Now let me see if I understand what you mean, Dick. You say that with offices spread out all over the globe, it's becoming more and more difficult to get timely reports."

"That's right. By the time they send their data to Chicago and our people here enter it into the system, it's already too late for us to make a good business decision. Moreover, the people in the foreign offices want to be able to use the data right there and yet not have to make extra copies of it."

"I think it's about time for us to consider a distributed database system. It's possible that with today's telecommunications capabilities we can keep the data at the office where it originates, but we can access it from anywhere in the world via data lines. We can do queries in Sydney that use data in Brussels and Buenos Aires. It will be sophisticated, but I think we can do it in a cost effective manner."

centralized database Database physically confined to a single location.

A **centralized database** is physically confined to a single location, under the control of a single computer (Figure 2.3). Most of the functions for which databases are created are accomplished more easily if the database is centralized. For example, it is easier to update, backup, query,

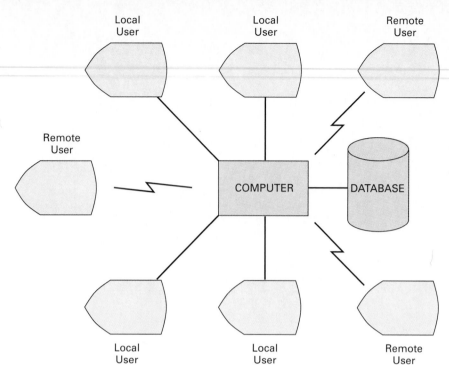

FIGURE 2.3   Centralized Database Structure

and control access to a database if we know exactly where it resides and what software is being used to control it.

The size of the database and the computer on which it resides need not have any bearing on whether the database is centrally located. A small company whose processing is entirely managed by a microcomputer has a centralized database just as does a large company with many computers, but whose database is entirely controlled by a mainframe.

As companies grow, however, they tend to open branch offices, far-flung factories, and regional distribution centers, each with their own data needs. International Product Distribution is a good example. Once IPD opened sales offices around the world, managers began to complain that they could not get timely reports from the central database system in the Chicago home office. In addition, regional managers wanted to keep relevant data in their own database systems instead of in a database system thousands of miles away. Once communications technologies improved, IPD began a serious study of a distributed database system.

distributed database system
A database system made of several systems at local sites, connected by communication lines.

A **distributed database system** is made up of several database systems running at local sites, which are connected by communication lines (Figure 2.4). A database query or update transaction is then no longer a single process controlled by one software module, but a set of cooperating processes running at several sites and controlled by independent software modules. Clearly, for distributed database systems to function effectively, adequate data communications technology must be available,

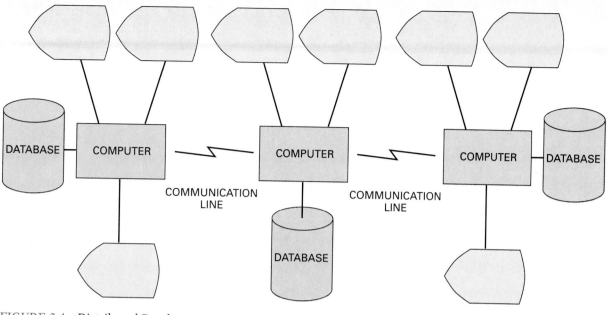

FIGURE 2.4   Distributed Database Structure

and the DBMSs in the system must be able to communicate with each other while interfacing with the data communications facilities.

Distributed database systems are attractive because they make possible the localization of data: Data resides at those sites where it is produced, updated, and referenced most frequently. With the availability of powerful database software even on microcomputers, it is reasonable to create distributed systems that allow local users to manipulate local data, while at the same time providing means for off-site users and centrally located management to access this same data as their needs require. This approach improves cost effectiveness and local autonomy. The cost, in addition to that caused by the need for data communication, is more complexity in the total database system—a problem which must be solved by system designers. Other advantages and drawbacks of distributed database systems are discussed in Chapter 18, which deals with this subject in detail.

The Role of the Database   As the discussion of centralized and distributed databases indicates, achieving the goal of sharing data is complex. With this in mind, let's take a second look at the definition of an effective database. We said above that a database can be defined as a collection of interrelated, shared, and controlled data. Both sharing and controlling data are facilitated through data *integration*. Thus, this definition contains three criteria for an effective database.

First, data must be shared. As we have seen, data can be shared between functional units, between levels of management, and between different geographic units.

Second, a database is made available to users in a controlled fashion. This control is provided by a database managment system (DBMS) whose facilities are managed by personnel from the information systems area known as Database Administration. We outlined the facilities of the DBMS in Chapter 1 and will deal more extensively with them in Chapter 12. The functions of Database Administration will be discussed later in this chapter and again in Chapter 17.

Third, the organization's data is integrated into a database in a logically sound fashion so that redundancies are eliminated, ambiguities of definition are resolved, and internal consistency between data elements is maintained. The logical structure of data integration makes data sharing and control practical on a large scale. Without integration, it would be extremely difficult to manage and maintain consistency between the large number of different files of various user groups and locations. Techniques for achieving data integration through logical structuring of data are presented at length in Chapter 3 and in Part II.

☐ STRATEGIC DATABASE PLANNING

database planning Strategic effort to determine information needs for an extended period.

Moving from a state in which data is private and fragmented to one of data sharing is easier said than done. To be successful, data must be viewed as a corporate resource, and other, significant corporate resources must be devoted to the development, implementation, maintenance, control, and use of one or more databases. An essential initial element in this process is database planning. **Database planning** is a strategic corporate effort to determine the information needs of the entire organization for an extended period into the future. A successful database planning project will be followed by operational projects to design and implement new or enhanced databases to satisfy the organization's information needs.

The Need for Database Planning

Database planning is directed by the information needs of the organization which in turn are determined by the company's business plan, as illustrated in Figure 2.5. For example, the corporation formulates its strategic business plan for the next five years. Accomplishing the objectives of this plan depends on the availability of certain identifiable types of information. The information can be obtained only if the data resources, as identified in database planning, are in place. This dictates the need for database development projects which create new databases, or enhance or integrate existing databases.

FIGURE 2.5 Operational Databases Ultimately Result From Business Plans

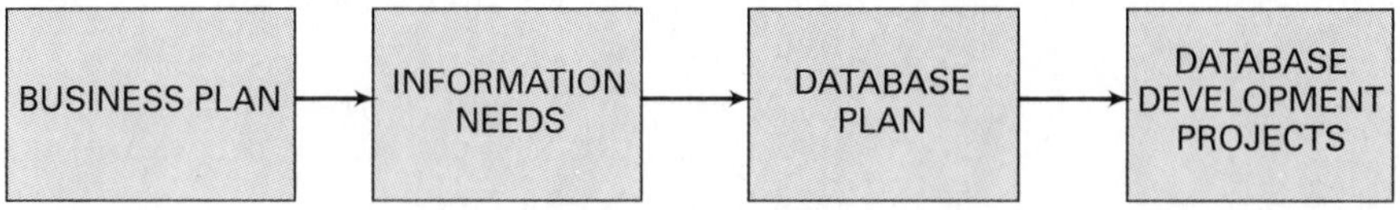

BUSINESS PLAN → INFORMATION NEEDS → DATABASE PLAN → DATABASE DEVELOPMENT PROJECTS

Database planning has significant advantages which are sometimes not recognized. James notes (in Umbaugh, 1985) that the value of a formal planning process is in forcing managers "to articulate their objectives, priorities, and action plans." He cites several advantages of a formal, documented information resource plan, including:

☐ It expresses management's current understanding of the information resource . . .

☐ It identifies and justifies resource requirements . . ., helping ensure that the resources will be available. . . .

☐ It identifies opportunities for effective resource management, including collaboration among departments or divisions within the organization. . . .

☐ It specifies action plans for achieving objectives. . . .

☐ It can . . . provide a powerful stimulus and sense of direction to employees at all levels, focusing their efforts, increasing their productivity, and making them feel that they are a genuine part of the enterprise. (pg. 6)

The Database Planning Project

Strategic database planning is initiated by the organization's senior management. They allocate the resources and identify the personnel to participate in the project, both as full-time and as part-time team members. Since they have received their commission from management, the team members have both the resources and the authority necessary to carry out a successful planning project.

The project team should have extensive experience in information systems and in the other functional areas of the company. Martin (1983) recommends a group of four full-time team members, two from information systems and two who are acquainted with most of the other functional areas of the company. All team members should be highly skilled and respected employees, since their work will have a major impact on the organization for many years. If they are not skilled in a methodology for carrying out the study, an outside consultant should be employed as an advisor to train the team in a suitable methodology. The project team leader, however, should not be a consultant, but a permanent company employee and very possibly the head of Database Administration. In the case opening the chapter, Cordelia Molini, the chief Database Administrator for IPD, was shown as the project leader for IPD's strategic database planning project.

During the course of the project, the team interacts with senior managers from all the primary user areas, as shown in Figure 2.6. The senior end users identify the principal processes, activities, and entities that are used in the information processing of the organization, whether manual or automated. The project team synthesizes this data into a corporate information model to be included as an important part of the comprehensive database plan.

Martin notes that for the project to achieve its goals within the organization, it should last no more than six months. At this time, a report

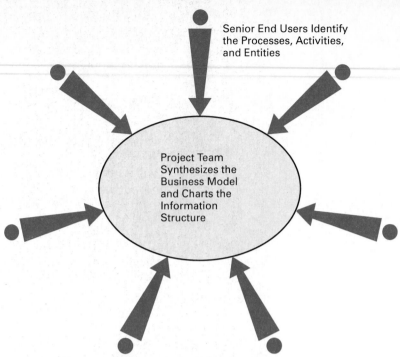

FIGURE 2.6   Interaction of Database Planning Team and Senior End Users
James Martin, MANAGING THE DATABASE ENVIRONMENT, ©1983, p. 658. Adapted by permission of Prentic Hall, Englewood Cliffs, NJ.

covering at least the next five years should be delivered to senior management. This report will include analyses of the following:

☐ Information needs of the organization's various functional areas.

☐ Information needs of different management levels.

☐ Information needs of different geographical locations.

☐ A model of these information needs.

☐ Anticipated volumes of data to be processed by geographical location and projected for the period under study.

☐ A preliminary estimate of costs associated with system upgrades. These include acquisition and maintenance costs of hardware and software, telecommunications costs for transmitting data to and from remote sites, data conversion, and training costs for converting from existing systems.

☐ Recommendations for detailed development of new or enhanced databases. Schedules for these development projects should also be estimated.

Since this is a high-level strategic plan, the project team should not strive for a detailed information model. Detailed models will be developed during subsequent database design projects. Instead, as James notes, the project team should identify the stable elements in the organization's information structure—those elements that are not likely to be altered with organizational changes or changes in the product mix. Martin states that at the end of six months, the information model is often thought to be "90% complete." This implies that most of the main elements have been identified. If the information model is made usable at that time, even though some of the details remain unresolved, the model will have value for strategic planning.

The Database Development Life Cycle (DDLC)

The strategic database planning team may conclude that the organization should have *several* databases rather than a single all-encompassing corporate database. Many companies have come to this conclusion because their operations are extremely diverse. They decided that the task of designing and implementing a single database for all their information needs would be so expensive and filled with risk that the database development project itself might never succeed. For them, comprehensive databases in several different well-defined areas were a better option. Of course, communication between these databases would now be difficult, but they viewed this as the lesser evil.

The strategic database plan will recommend the number and kind of databases that should be developed, as illustrated in Figure 2.7. It will

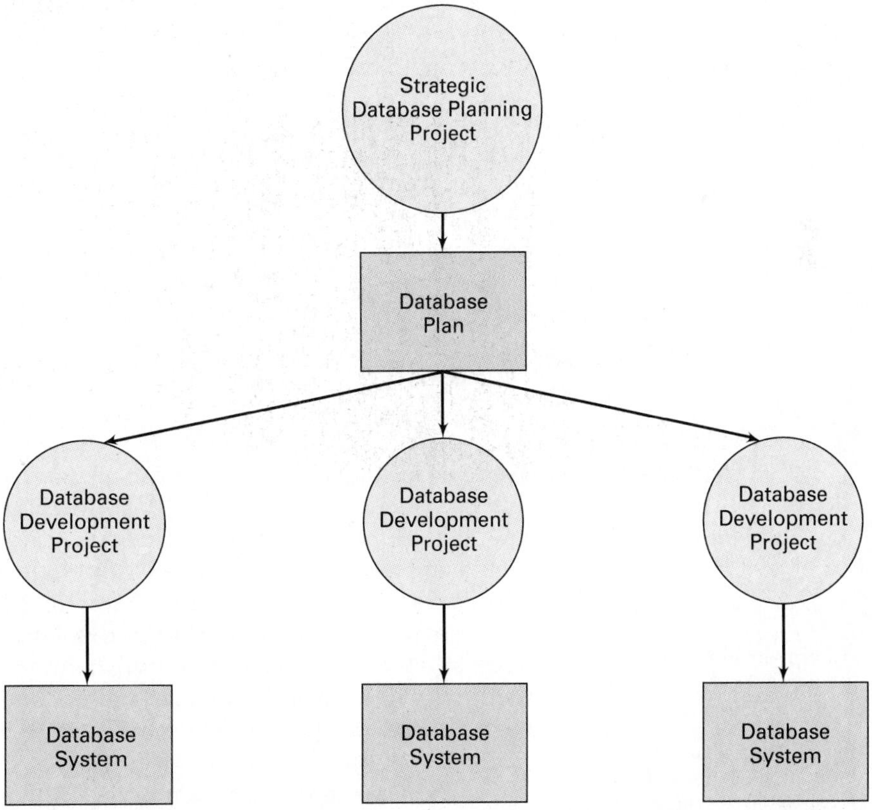

FIGURE 2.7   A Database Plan May Recommend Development of Several Databases

also indicate a schedule for these development projects. After the plan receives final approval from senior management, these plans for designing and implementing the specific databases will be carried out. The methodology for doing this is the Database Development Life Cycle.

The **database development life cycle (DDLC)** includes the gathering of information to determine user data needs; the design of a database schema, or logical structure, to satisfy those needs; the selection of a DBMS to support the implementation and use of the database; the development of computer programs to maintain and utilize the database; and the review of user information needs in the context of the developed database.

Since this life cycle constitutes the major area of interest for this book, we will be studying it in detail in Chapter 3. Nearly all of the remainder of the book is concerned with developing the necessary skills for carrying out the crucial design and implementation steps of the life cycle.

DATABASES AND MANAGEMENT CONTROL

As a company resource of significant value, the database requires control and protection. This responsibility is usually assigned to the Database Administrator (DBA). The DBA is responsible for coordinating the design of the database, training users to access and update the database, guiding the development and implementation of data security procedures, protecting the integrity of data values, and making sure that system performance is satisfactory.

In a small organization, one person may be able to carry out all the responsibilities of the DBA. Often, however, these functions are assigned to a group of people known as the **Database Administration.** This is especially likely in a large organization where the responsibilities of Database Administration are divided among several people, managed by a chief administrator.

The functions of the DBA include:

- Database Design
- User Training
- Database Security and Integrity
- Database System Performance

Database Design

Logical database design consists primarily of identifying and defining the data elements to be included in the database, the relationships that exist between them, and the value constraints that apply to the data elements and their relationships. A **value constraint** is a rule defining the permissible values for a specific data item. **Physical database design** determines the physical structure of the database and includes such decisions as which physical devices will contain the data values, what access methods will be used to retrieve and update data, and what indexes will be built and maintained to improve the performance of the database system.

To carry out the function of logical database design, the Database Administration staff must include personnel who are expert at understanding design concepts as well as skilled at working with the user groups who provide the essential application information needed for a proper design. The DBA designers work with users in various areas and design *portions* of the entire database. The portion of the database design which a given user group has defined is a **view** of the database—a view that will be utilized by the originating user group. These views must then be integrated into a complete database **schema** which defines the logical structure of the entire database. This process is illustrated in Figure 2.8.

The process of logical design requires the resolution of conflicts between different user groups. For example, different groups may use the same term in contradictory ways. Moreover, groups are likely to be jealous of their data and resist the possibility of allowing others to access it, as illustrated by the conflict between IPD's Marketing and Product Evaluation groups, discussed earlier in the chapter. Reasonable controls must be established that define which groups can access which data, and whether their access will include the capability of updating data values. DBA staff members must be able to negotiate resolutions to conflicts like these.

More technically oriented DBA staff members carry out the physical design of the database. They must know precisely how the DBMS handles data access and which access methods will be most efficient in the DBMS environment. Their goal is to use company resources most effectively, so that the total combination of hardware, software, and human resource costs is optimized. Ideally, they seek to minimize system response time within the practical constraints of the cost of hardware and software.

view A definition of a restricted portion of the database; also called a data view.

schema A definition of the logical structure of the entire database.

FIGURE 2.8   Creating User Views and Integrating Them Into a Schema

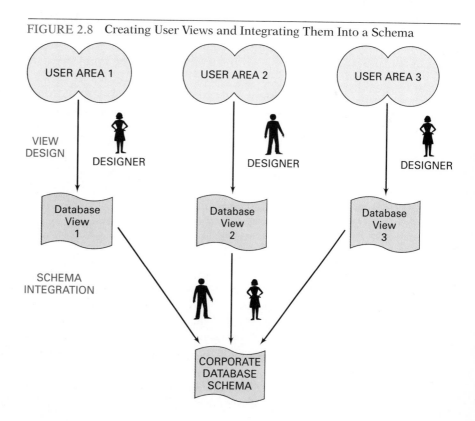

Initial database design and implementation must be followed by a continuous maintenance of the logical and physical structure of the database. Changes in business requirements, hardware and software capabilities, and processing volumes lead to the need for modifications to both the logical and physical design of the database. This ongoing maintenance of the logical and physical design of the database is also the responsibility of the DBA.

The DBA occupies a strategically advantageous position with respect to the definition and enforcement of company data standards. Since database design is centrally controlled, the DBA can define standards for data naming; data formats; and screen, report, and file formats. This simplifies documentation and training requirements and provides for a more thorough systems integration within the company.

Database design decisions are documented in the data dictionary. The DBA controls the contents of the data dictionary and records there as metadata the names of data elements, files, screens, report forms, and the like. As we noted in Chapter 1, the metadata in the data dictionary can be queried and manipulated. However, its manipulation is very carefully controlled by the DBA, since the data in the data dictionary is vital to the proper functioning of the database system as a whole.

User Training

Many of the advantages resulting from data sharing can only be realized in practice if users understand how to use the facilities of the DBMS to access the database. It is the responsibility of Database Administration to educate users in the structure of the database and in the means of database access provided by the DBMS. This can be done through formal training sessions, through interacting with users to create database views, through users manuals and periodic memos, and through company information centers.

information center An area where users have facilities to do their own computing.

An **information center** is an area within an organization where users are provided with facilities to do their own computing. Auxiliary software packages for data manipulation may be provided, as well as training and simple programming services. Such centers provide users with a ready outlet for answering questions and solving information processing problems, while relieving the organization's information systems staff from the numerous "simple" requests that are a natural part of every organization's information needs. Database Administration provides staff for the information center who assist users in developing solutions to their information needs.

Database Security and Integrity

The concept of combining an organization's data into one common pool accessible to all has both advantages and disadvantages. An obvious advantage is that different functional areas can benefit from using data that they themselves do not create or maintain. A corresponding disadvantage, however, is that data can be misused or damaged by users who do not have original responsibility and authority over it. The DBA provides procedures and controls to prevent the abuse of data.

The DBA also assigns ownership of the data in a database view to the originating group. The owning group may then grant access to the data in the view to other groups or persons within the organization. This

access may be restricted to portions of the data, to **retrieve only access,**
or to access with update allowed. The information regarding access rights
and ownership of data is maintained under the direction of the DBA in
the data dictionary.

Access to the database is ultimately controlled by a password mechanism. Any user attempting access must give a password, which is vali-
dated by the system. After successful validation, the system allows the
user only the privileges and access rights recorded in the data dictionary.
The DBMS can then control access as well as keep statistical information
about the data accessed and entered by the user. Database Administration is responsible for assigning passwords and controlling access privileges. By this means, the DBA can greatly reduce the risk of one group doing damage to another group's data.

Data integrity refers to the problem of maintaining the accuracy
and consistency of the data values in the database. Security mechanisms,
such as passwords and data views, allow the DBA to protect data integrity. In addition, value constraints can be maintained in the data dictionary. Unfortunately, value constraint definition and enforcement is a major area of weakness for current database management systems. We can
identify many more constraints than we can easily define to the DBMS.
Thus, it may be necessary for programs to be coded which will carry out
constraint verification for new data being entered. Such programming
may be reasonably assigned to the DBA staff.

The backup and recovery mechanisms supported by the DBMS are
tools for preserving data in the event of system failure. The DBA, however, must define the procedures to be followed to recover lost data. It is important that users know what they should do following a system crash so
that they will re-enter all needed data but not enter more data than is
needed.

Database System Performance

A database system that is being simultaneously accessed by a large number of users may respond very slowly at times. The physical problems associated with many users contending to use the same resources are not
trivial. For this reason, it is important that the DBA staff include technically skilled personnel who are able to diagnose and solve system problems relating to response time. The solutions to these problems may involve the acquisition of additional hardware, the physical re-arrangement
of data on one or more disks, the construction of indexes for the rapid access of certain high-volume data, or the writing of special software to improve access time. At times, the DBA may even decide to maintain several, redundant copies of data for the sake of improving system
performance. Such redundancy must be controlled by the DBA, however, so that the problems of data inconsistency that often occur with redundant data will be avoided.

☐ RISKS AND COSTS OF DATABASES

It is natural in a book about database systems to emphasize the positive
characteristics of such systems. The synergistic effect of databases, the
standardization of data design and data handling procedures, the securi-

ty benefits, the power of data design and data manipulation methods and languages, the breadth of system functions provided by the database foundation are all positive benefits of database systems.

Database systems also have drawbacks, however. The main ones include organizational conflicts, development project failure, system failure, increased overhead costs, and the need for sophisticated personnel.

Organizational Conflicts

Pooling data in a common database may not be politically feasible in some organizations. Certain user groups may not be willing to relinquish control over their data to the extent needed to integrate that data into a database. Moreover, the risk involved in data sharing—for example, that one group may damage another group's data—and the potential system problems that may limit a group's access to their own data may be viewed as more troublesome than beneficial. Such "people problems" could prevent the effectual implementation of a database system.

Development Project Failure

The project to develop a database system may fail. This can occur for a variety of reasons. Sometimes management was not fully convinced of the value of the database system in the first place. If the database project seems to be taking too long, they may withdraw support, terminating the project.

Sometimes the database project is too large in scope and becomes almost impossible to complete in a reasonable amount of time. Again, management and users become disenchanted, and the project fails. In this case, a more successful approach may have been to divide the database project into several projects to develop several databases or a single database in several stages.

During the course of a database project, key personnel may unexpectedly leave the company. If replacement personnel cannot be found, then the project might not be successfully completed.

System Failure

When the computer system goes down, all users directly involved in accessing the database must wait until the system is functional again. This may require a long wait. Moreover, if the system or application *software* fails, there may be permanent damage to the database. It is very important, therefore, to carefully evaluate all software that will have a direct effect on the database to be certain that it is as free of errors as possible. If the organization does not use a database, it is not exposed to this risk, since the data and its software are distributed.

A distributed database system also reduces the risk associated with hardware failure in a centralized database system, since the distributed system runs on several computers. If any single computer in the system fails, the system can continue running on the other computers. Of course, the data associated with the computer that is down cannot be accessed, but otherwise the system continues running intact.

Overhead Costs The database approach may require an investment in both hardware and software. The hardware to run a large DBMS must be efficient and will generally require more main memory and disk storage than simpler file-based systems. Tape drives for rapidly backing up the database are also required. In addition, the DBMS itself may be quite expensive. The DBMS usually includes many facilities, some of which may not be needed by a particular organization. Nevertheless, these features cost money and use disk and memory in the system. These are overhead costs that may not always bring corresponding benefits. Thus, in order to obtain some of the benefits of a DBMS, a company may need to spend money on software and hardware to obtain features they do not plan to use.

The DBMS may also increase operating costs, since it requires more hardware power and execution time. For example, an application system using a DBMS will usually execute more slowly than a system not using a DBMS. The DBMS itself requires a certain amount of extra time for execution because of its generalized structure. That is, a DBMS is built to be a general purpose system handling all kinds of diverse applications. As a result, it cannot be as efficient as a system built to handle a specific application. A system requiring extremely efficient real-time execution may not be able to use a general-purpose DBMS effectively.

As with any system using online updating, explicit backup is needed to protect data from system failure. However, a database system with a large amount of data sharing and online update requires more powerful backup and recovery procedures. The continual logging of transactions, together with the recording of "before" and "after" copies of database records, is part of the system overhead that consumes system time and hardware resources.

Need for Sophisticated Personnel The Database Administration function requires skilled and experienced personnel who are capable of coordinating the various needs of different user groups, designing database views, integrating those designs into a single database schema, establishing data recovery procedures, and fine tuning the physical structure of the database to meet acceptable performance criteria. This combination of skills constitutes a personnel overhead in the adoption and use of a database system. That is, once the Database Administration function has been established in an organization, then the cost of the DBA group is an ongoing expense.

In addition, there is risk involved in the identification of personnel for Database Administration, since if no person having the requisite skills can be found, the Database Administration function may not be properly performed. This could result in significant problems for the organization and may even result in the failure of a database implementation. Because of the critical value of the database system, care must be taken to hire or promote only qualified people in Database Administration.

■ SUMMARY

In this chapter, we have outlined the organizational context in which database systems function. We saw that the concept of data sharing can be viewed from three perspectives—between different functional areas, between different levels of management, and between different geographical locations. We discussed the concept of strategic database planning and indicated how it lays the foundation for all database systems to be used in the organization. We then examined the Database Administration function, outlining this group's responsibility for controlling and protecting the database. Finally, we discussed some of the risks and costs of the database approach to an organization.

Data sharing between different functional areas is based on the concept that one area can benefit from the controlled use of another area's data. Sharing data at this level benefits the organization as long as the interests of all functional areas are safeguarded.

Data sharing is also valuable at different management levels. The operational level generates transactions and updates master files. The data generated in these activities can be used by middle management to control and improve the performance of their departments in the organization. Senior management can combine the basic data used by the two lower levels with data coming from outside the organization to make information-based strategic decisions.

Data sharing in the geographical sense means combining data from different locations so that the entire organization benefits while at the same time allowing far-flung locations first access to the data they have generated. If communications costs are not prohibitive and the benefit from connecting geographically distributed systems is significant, then companies are likely to develop a distributed database system connecting remote parts of their organization.

Strategic database planning is initiated by senior management to provide a foundation for future information needs. A project team will work with experienced users in defining information and data needs. Their report will recommend and schedule the development of databases as needed to support the organization's information processing.

Database Administration has responsibility for the logical and physical design of the database; for training users in the structure of the database and in the procedures required for acessing and updating it; for protecting the database from misuse, inappropriate access, and inadvertent damage; and for assuring that the system as a whole performs at an acceptable level.

The risks and costs of database systems include organizational conflicts over data sharing, potential failure of a database development project, database system failure and consequent database damage, increased overhead costs, and the need for sophisticated personnel for database development and operation.

■ REVIEW QUESTIONS

1. Define each of the following terms in your own words:
   a. database
   b. electronic data processing
   c. management information system
   d. centralized database
   e. database development life cycle
   f. Database Administration

g. physical database design
   h. value constraint

2. Discuss the advantages and disadvantages of data sharing for each of the following:
   a. Different functional areas
   b. Different geographical locations

3. How can transaction level data be used to support information needs at management and executive levels? What other kinds of information may be needed for strategic decision making?

4. Discuss the following aspects of the strategic database planning project:
   a. Support of senior management
   b. Project team composition
   c. Length of project
   d. Scope of project
   e. Output of project
   f. Relationship of project with Database Development Life Cycle

5. What is the responsibility of Database Administration with respect to:
   a. Logical database design
   b. The information center
   c. Data integrity
   d. Database system performance

6. List all the potential drawbacks you can think of associated with implementing and using a database system. Classify them according to whether they are risks or costs. Explain why you classify them in that way.

■ PROBLEMS AND EXERCISES

1. Match the following terms with their definitions:

__decision support system	a. where users can find computing facilities
__retrieve only access	b. restricted portion of the database
__database planning	c. multiple database systems connected by communication lines
__logical database design	d. no update allowed
__data integrity	e. strategic effort to determine long-term information needs
__view	f. combining data for common use
__data integration	g. identifies elements, relationships, and constraints
__distributed database system	h. accuracy and consistency of values
__schema	i. provides strategic information
__information center	j. defines logical structure of entire database

2. IPD's functional areas include Inventory, Marketing, Sales, Purchasing, Accounting, Order Processing, and Product Evaluation. Identify the functional areas that (1) need data or (2) could use data contained in each of the following documents. Explain in each case why they need it or how they could use it.

a. An order from a department store in Canada for 100 glass crystal vases.

b. A report showing sales and returns of products for each sales representative in the Latin American region.

c. A report showing changes in quantity on hand for each product over a three-month period.

d. A report showing current quantity on hand for each product, together with average product cost and current price.

3. Classify the following types of information as to whether they are most significant at the operational, middle management, or executive level:

a. The population of Clark County is 500,000 and has doubled in each of the last two decades.

b. The Smiths are two months past due on their account.

c. Becky Daines got married and now her last name is Martinez.

d. Galen has led the Eastern region in sales for seven months in a row.

e. Wilson's check bounced again!

f. The repair costs for that old equipment in the Charlesville factory have gone through the roof, new employees are impossible to find there, and transportation costs in and out of Charlesville are becoming exorbitant.

4. In a geographically distributed organization, which types of information would be needed centrally and which types locally:

a. A country's payroll tax laws.

b. A factory's total monthly payroll.

c. A sales office's monthly sales figures by product line.

d. A sales office's weekly sales figures by sales representative.

5. Discuss the following strategic database planning projects:

a. The project team spent a full year interviewing at least one clerk from every processing unit in the company.

b. The project team carefully investigated the information needs of the home office but spent no time in the branch offices because they were only interested in high-level information.

6. Categorize each of the following into the Database Administration tasks of design, training, security/integrity, and performance:

a. Showing Helen Hessenthaler how to construct a query to identify the average percentage of returns for each product.

b. Reducing order entry response time to two seconds.

c. Reissuing passwords for every system user.

d. Directly relating every sale to the sales representative who made the sale.

7. Identify the potential difficulties in the following situations:

a. A functional area is reluctant to allow other areas to access its data.

b. Senior management initiates a database project without being fully convinced of its value.

c. The computer controlling a centralized database goes down.

d. An on-line system needs more rapid response time than the DBMS can provide.

e. The only Database Administrator for a company in a small town suddenly leaves to work for a company in another state.

1. Interview an executive in a large organization that recently conducted a strategic database planning study. Determine answers to the following questions:

a. What was the composition of the project team? How many members did it have and what were their professional backgrounds? Was a consultant engaged as a team advisor?

b. What was the nature of senior management's commitment to the project? Did they believe in its potential success or were they skeptical? What influence did their commitment have on the attitude of other employees?

c. What was the result of the project? Was a DBMS purchased? Was a new database designed and installed? How many functional areas and levels of management do the database and its application programs serve? Were distributed databases considered? What are the organization's database plans for the future?

2. Write a research paper on the difference between *a data administrator* and *a database administrator*. Determine whether most organizations make a distinction between the two in practice.

3. Write a research paper on a database implementation that failed. Try to determine why the project failed. What circumstances existed in this case that may not exist in other cases? What lessons can be drawn from the experience of the people in the project?

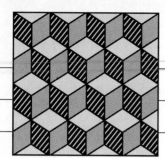

chapter three

THE DATABASE DEVELOPMENT LIFE CYCLE

"Rita, could you give me a report on the status of the database implementation? When will we start using the system to process our daily transactions and give us management information?"

Bill Blue, President of Zeus, Inc., a manufacturer of running shoes, is speaking with Rita Minkowski, the Director of Information Systems for Zeus. Zeus is nearing the end of a year-long database system development project.

"The system will be ready to use next week, Bill. We are in the final stages of training the users in the procedures for processing transactions. Overall, the project has run very smoothly. I'm certainly glad we hired a consultant to map out the steps for us, because otherwise the project's complexity may have caused a disaster. Instead, we have a comprehensive database we can use as the foundation for a number of application systems."

The strategic database plan discussed in Chapter 2 provides a high-level corporate information model and schedules one or more database development projects to create detail level database systems. In this chapter, we will examine the process of developing a specific database system. After reading this chapter, you should be able to:

☐ Diagram and explain the standard foundation for database structure, the ANSI/SPARC three-level architecture.

☐ Compare and contrast the weaknesses of function-oriented system development and the corresponding strengths of data-oriented system development.

☐ Describe the steps in the database development life cycle and their interrelationships.

☐ SEPARATING LOGICAL AND PHYSICAL DATA REPRESENTATION

As we have seen, data access has progressed during the past several decades from the awkward, physically oriented methods of early file processing through various forms of database processing. The current status of this development is found in the relational database systems of today. One of the most significant aspects of the relational database "revolution" was the concept of separating the logical structure and manipulation of data as understood by the end user from the physical representation required by the computer hardware. This important concept has been much discussed and is now universally accepted. It is an integral part of the philosophy of database structure embodied in the ANSI/SPARC model we discuss next.

Three-Level Database Architecture

The distinction between the logical and physical representation of data was officially recognized in 1978 when the ANSI/SPARC committee proposed a generalized framework for database systems (Tsichritzis and

three-level architecture Standard database structure consisting of conceptual, external, and internal levels.

conceptual level Database structural level defining logical schema of database.

Klug, 1978). This framework provided a **three-level architecture,** three levels of abstraction at which a database could be viewed. The three levels are the conceptual, the external, and the internal levels.

The **conceptual level** is the level at which logical database design is done. *Logical database design* involves the analysis of users' information needs and the identification and definition of the data items needed to meet those needs. The result of logical design is the *logical schema* or *conceptual schema,* a single logical description of all the data elements and their relationships.

external level Database structural level defining user views.

The **external level** is the level at which users view the database. It consists of the individual portions and/or derivations of the logical schema that apply to particular groups of users. Each definable user group will have its own *view* of the database. Each of these views is, in a sense, "conceptual," in that each view gives a user-oriented description of the data elements and relationships of which the user view is composed. The external level consists of the set of all such user views.

internal level Database structural level defining physical view of database.

The **internal level** provides the "physical" view of the database—the disk drives, physical addresses, indexes, pointers, and so on. This level is the responsibility of physical database designers, who decide which physical devices will contain the data, what access methods will be used to retrieve and update data, and what measures will be taken to maintain or improve database performance. No user, as a user, would be concerned with this view.

As Elmasri and Navathe (1989) note, the implementation of these three levels requires the DBMS to "map" or translate from one level to another (Figure 3.1). To understand this, recall that the database exists in reality only at the internal level. To represent data to the user at the conceptual and external levels, the system must be able to translate physical addresses and pointers into their corresponding logical names and relationships. Such translation must also take place in the other direction—from the logical to the physical. The price of this translation process is higher system overhead. The benefit is the independence of the logical and physical representation of data.

Use of the Three-Level Architecture in This Book

In this book, we will be concerned to some extent with all three ANSI/SPARC levels. In this chapter and in Parts II and III (Chapters 4 through 10), we will study the conceptual and external levels, and how they can be developed as the schemas for database systems that meet user needs. As we review the database development life cycle in this chapter, we will see how the user views of the external level are developed and then integrated into a single conceptual level schema for the entire database.

As we study the conceptual and external levels in Part II, we will examine object-oriented design methodologies and show how designs created from these methods can be implemented with commercial database management systems (Figure 3.2). These commercial systems (based on the relational, hierarchical, and network models) are themselves part way between a "purely" physical level and a "purely" logical level. They represent the current state of the art with respect to DBMS implementations.

In Chapter 11, we will discuss the internal level. Our examination of this level will include the description of the physical structures required

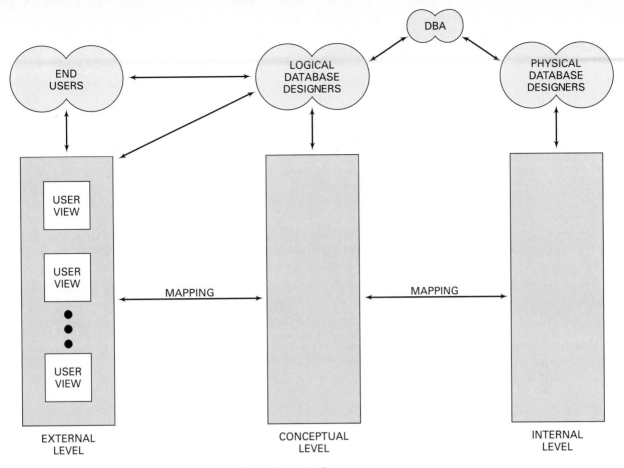

FIGURE 3.1   The ANSI-SPARC Three/Level Database Architecture

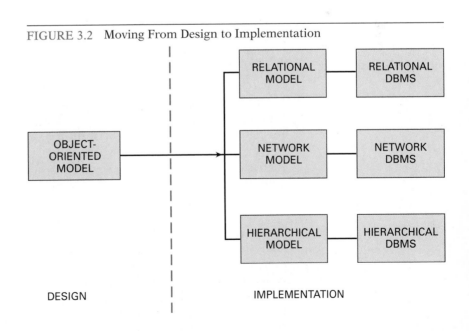

FIGURE 3.2   Moving From Design to Implementation

to manipulate data in an efficient manner. We will also see how these physical structures can map to the logical schemas defined in the conceptual and external levels.

☐ DATABASE DESIGN AND THE TRADITIONAL SYSTEM

system development life cycle (SDLC) A process for system development.

Books on systems analysis and design usually outline and investigate a system development procedure called the **system development life cycle (SDLC).** The following is an enhanced version of an SDLC given by Whitten, Bentley, and Ho (1986):

1. Survey the situation. Briefly overview the business environment and needs to determine whether a new system is feasible.
2. Study the current system. Perform a more detailed analysis of the situation to determine the specific problems and opportunities that exist.
3. Define user requirements. Identify and document the information, processing, and data needs of the users.
4. Evaluate alternative solutions. Conduct a high-level evaluation to answer such questions as which parts of the system should be automated, whether software should be purchased or developed, whether new computer hardware is needed, and so on.
5. Select new computer equipment and software (if necessary).
6. Design the new system. At the detail level, design outputs, inputs, database, and programs.
7. Program and test the new system.
8. Install the new system. Convert data from the old system, develop manual procedures, create user documentation, train users.
9. Evaluate and maintain the new system. Analyze whether the system satisfies user needs and make needed changes as determined from this analysis and from changing business needs.

The traditional SDLC places heavy emphasis on identifying specific business functions and developing application systems to perform those functions. A natural question arises: How does database design fit into this outline? The answer to this question depends upon the point of view one takes in system development. Meyer (1988) argues that to increase their effectiveness, system developers need to take a close look at the assumptions underlying the traditional system development life cycle.

Drawbacks of Function-Oriented System Development

function-oriented approach Views a system from the perspective of the functions it should perform.

One of the assumptions underlying the SDLC is that structured systems analysis and design create the most effective systems. Meyer notes, however, that these structured methods are **function-oriented.** That is, they view systems from the standpoint of the functions they perform rather than of the data they perform these functions on. Thus, structured analysis emphasizes dataflow diagrams, which track the progress of data through a sequence of transformations. The structured analysis process consists of refining these transformations through a series of levels, until they are described at a primitive level that could conceivably be implemented on a computer. The same is true of structured design, which assumes that any system consists of a single function that can be successively decomposed into subfunctions at various levels, finally arriving at a level sufficiently low for direct computer implementation to be feasible.

By concentrating on the functions to be performed, these methods tend to neglect the data, and more especially the *structure* of the data, which the functions manipulate. The result, says Meyer, is that systems are developed that have short-term value at the expense of the long-term needs of the users these systems should be serving. This happens because within a relatively short time, the functions a system is originally developed to carry out become only a small subset of the functions that the users would like the system to perform. Almost immediately, the users, a remarkably perceptive and creative lot, see a large variety of additional services they would like to get from the system. This is particularly true of managers and executives who can identify many information needs the system could fulfill. These needs and requests cause problems for systems designed around functions, since the design of these systems might require major revision in order to accommodate the additional functions desired.

Another drawback is that database design commonly tends to have a "stepchild" status in the function-oriented paradigm. Database design normally consists of little more than data field identification and logical file definition. This narrow focus tends to minimize the complexity of constructing an overall conceptual schema. As we will see in Part II, however, the proper structuring of a database schema requires careful and sophisticated analysis of classes of data items and their interrelationships. Once a logically sound database schema is built, any number of functional systems may be designed to take advantage of the data defined in the schema. If such a schema does not exist, though, or if its design is shoddy and unrepresentative of genuine real-world relationships, the database may be useful for a single application system but be difficult for other applications to use. Thus, the function-oriented approach is good for a short-term system development effort, but of considerably less real value over the longer term.

The Advantages of Data-Oriented System Development

Now that we have a clearer idea of the drawbacks of the function-oriented approach, we can repeat our earlier question: How does database design fit into the SDLC process? The answer, as stated before, depends on one's point of view. From a function-oriented viewpoint, database design does not fit very well, since this approach focuses on functions and their immediate data needs. If we interpret the SDLC from a data-oriented perspective, though, we can eliminate these problems.

The **data-oriented approach** focuses on the analysis of data used by the functions. The data elements are a considerably more stable part of a system than are the functions. This can be seen from a simple example.

Suppose we consider the problem of managing policies for an automobile insurance company. The standard factors used to calculate premium are age, sex, and marital status. Let's start with a simple file con-

data-oriented approach Focuses on the analysis of data used by the functions.

taining just one of these factors and ask some basic questions about it. The automobile insurance file of Figure 3.3(a) has only three data fields: Policy #, Name, Age. Nevertheless, we can ask a variety of questions about this data file. Thus, if we focus on age, we can ask:

How many policy holders are over age 27?

If we add a field, as in Figure 3.3(b), we can ask *twice* as many *additional* questions. For example:

How many female policy holders are there?

and

How many female policy holders are over age 27?

That is, we can ask questions regarding the gender of policy holders only, and we can ask questions regarding the gender and the age of policy holders. If we add yet another field, the number of additional questions doubles again. In Figure 3.3(c), we have added marital status. Now we can ask additional questions that involve marital status alone; marital status and gender; marital status and age; and marital status, gender, and age.

Each time we add a field, we not only can ask questions regarding the new field, but we can ask questions involving that field in combination with every other previously existing set of fields. This is why the number of query types doubles with each additional field. The result of all this is that while the number of fields is increasing arithmetically, the number of possible types of queries is increasing exponentially. In simple terms, this means that if we had, say, thirty fields, we would have one billion possible types of queries!

In an information system, a query type may be viewed as corresponding to a function giving information about some combination of

---

FIGURE 3.3   Automobile Insurance Files

(a)

POLICY #	NAME	AGE
18733	J. Canseco	25
22432	W. Boggs	28
83002	O. Winfrey	33

(b)

POLICY #	NAME	AGE	SEX
18733	J. Canseco	25	F
22432	W. Boggs	28	F
83002	O. Winfrey	33	M

(c)

POLICY #	NAME	AGE	SEX	MARITAL STATUS
18733	J. Canseco	25	F	Single
22432	W. Boggs	28	F	Married
83002	O. Winfrey	33	M	Single

data fields. It can be seen, therefore, that the number of possible functions will virtually always be enormously larger than the number of data fields. From this, it is clear that the data is likely to represent the more stable part of an information system. The data may be metaphorically viewed as the foundation on which a large variety of different buildings (functional systems) can be solidly established. Figure 3.4 expands the database plan shown in Chapter 2 and indicates how the database plan leads to one or more database systems which in turn lead to multiple functional systems.

Indeed, Whitten, Bentley, and Ho (1986) indicate that the SDLC *should* be viewed as building a foundation for present and future applications. Consider, for example, their step 3:

Define User Requirements

During the course of this step, the analysts must identify the functions or processing needed by users *and* the data needed to perform those functions. The data so identified may now be analyzed further. By exploring the uses of data and their interpretations in a multitude of possible ap-

FIGURE 3.4   Functional Systems Based on Database Systems

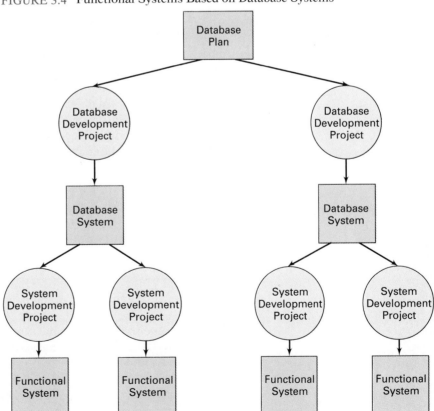

plications, analysts can determine the significance of data elements and their relationships. Applying the principles of database design, an intelligent conceptual database schema may then be built, which can be used in the analysis of additional user requirements. This further analysis will uncover other data elements, which can be integrated into the previously defined schema as the process is repeated. After a sufficient number of iterations of this analysis process, the logical schema will begin to stabilize and the analysts can turn their attention more fully to the functions desired for the current system.

Notice how the concepts of function analysis and data analysis work together. By analyzing functions, we identify data elements. As we analyze these data elements, we identify additional functions that can operate on this data. Analysis of these new functions leads to the identification of new data elements. Thus, the function analysis process which lies at the heart of the SDLC plays an essential role in database design as well.

The SDLC step of defining user requirements, then, can be expanded into a complete process for defining a database. We call this process the **database development life cycle (DDLC).** The DDLC has a form very similar to that of the SDLC. During the remainder of this chapter, we will show you how the traditional SDLC can be adapted to create the database development life cycle.

database development life cycle (DDLC) A process for designing, implementing, and maintaining a database system.

□ DATABASE DEVELOPMENT

Much has been said in the literature about the need for an overall corporate plan. We will not repeat it here. Similarly, the MIS literature is filled with discussions about the need for a corporate MIS plan that supports corporate policy and objectives. The area we emphasize is that part of the MIS plan that focuses on database development. For a specific database, this includes the development of the logical database schema, the identification of the data to be included in the database, and the development of programs to update and process the data. Thus, we are interested in the development of a complete database system.

Figure 3.5 shows a database development life cycle (DDLC), which consists of six stages:

1. Preliminary planning
2. Feasibility study
3. Requirements definition
4. Logical design
5. Implementation
6. Database evaluation and maintenance

As can be seen, this life cycle is similar to the SDLC. The difference is in its emphasis: The DDLC is concerned with the development of a comprehensive *database* and the initial programs needed to maintain and process it. In the rest of this section, we will describe the main tasks associated with each stage, using the experience of Zeus, Inc., as an illustration.

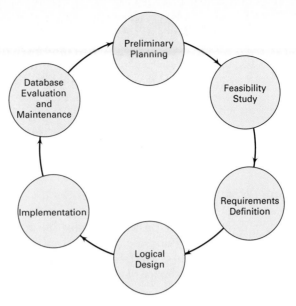

FIGURE 3.5   A Database Development Life Cycle

The Zeus Corporation was created as the result of a project completed while the Blue brothers were finishing their MBAs at a well-known Midwestern business school. The project focused on the creation of a company to manufacture and market running shoes. Both Bill and Steve Blue had been high school cross country runners and had continued to run after high school for the enjoyment and to keep in good physical condition. Occasionally, they would participate in a local road race, or even a marathon.

As part of a business strategy course, they collaborated on a plan to manufacture and distribute running shoes. Initially, they simply wanted to satisfy course requirements. As they thought through some of the details, though, their interest grew. At this time, very few companies marketed genuine running shoes, and they felt the market would be receptive. When their instructor encouraged them, they decided to test their idea by actually creating the Zeus Corporation.

Using a loan from their father, the brothers rented an old garage and purchased some basic equipment and an initial stock of materials. Most importantly, they persuaded their former high school coach to help them in return for an interest in the business. All three felt that their greatest chance for success would be to develop a very lightweight shoe that still provided good stability and support.

This strategy turned out to be a good one. Their biggest initial challenge—getting running-shoe stores to accept a new and untried brand—was largely overcome by providing free shoes to a number of elite runners, who provided free media exposure and testimonials. After two meager years, the quality of their product began to pay off, and revenues doubled over the following two years and continued to grow in subsequent years until annual revenues reached a level of about $50 million.

These sales represented a product line that had grown to include many types of athletic wear and clothing.

Zeus's information systems had basically evolved as the company grew, with new applications being developed as needs were identified. Two years ago, a consultant had helped the company establish a long-range business plan and a corresponding plan for Management Information Systems (MIS), along with the establishment of an MIS steering committee to implement the MIS plan. A central part of the MIS plan was the development of a corporate database system.

Preliminary Planning

preliminary planning Planning for a database that occurs during the strategic database planning process.

Preliminary planning for a specific database system takes place during the strategic database planning project. After the database implementation project begins, the general information model produced during database planning is reviewed and enhanced if needed. During this process, the firm collects sufficient information to answer at least the following questions:

1. How many application programs are in use, and what functions do they perform?
2. What files are associated with each of these applications?
3. What new applications and files are under development?

This information can be used to establish the interrelationships between current applications and to identify the uses of application information. It can also help in identifying future system requirements and in assessing the potential economic benefits of installing a database system. It is documented in a generalized object-oriented model, produced during database planning.

Feasibility Study

feasibility study Portion of the DDLC that determines technological, operational, and economic feasibility of database.

A **feasibility study** involves preparing a report on each of the following issues:

1. Technological feasibility. Is suitable technology available to support the database development?
2. Operational feasibility. Does the company have the personnel, budget, and internal expertise to make a database system successful?
3. Economic feasibility. Can the benefits be identified? Is the desired system expected to be cost-beneficial. Can the costs and benefits be measured?

At Zeus, the feasibility study was carried out by an interdisciplinary development team. This team was comprised of a systems analyst, an engineer, a marketing specialist, a production supervisor, a financial analyst, and a database specialist. Their activities were guided by a corporate MIS Steering Committee comprised of high-level managers from each of the firm's functional areas. Approval was obtained from the Steering Committee for each phase of the feasibility study before proceeding with the next phase. The focus of each phase was as follows:

technological feasibility Determination of hardware and software availability for database system.

1. The first phase was a **technological feasibility** study, which determined whether the hardware and software were available to service corporate information needs. This study included an analysis of whether the capabilities and resources were already present in the company or whether they would have to be purchased, and whether training was needed. It turned out that all of the required hardware was already present at Zeus, although the DBMS itself would have to be acquired.

operational feasibility Determination of availability of expertise and personnel needed for database system.

2. A study of **operational feasibility** was completed. This included an analysis of the skill and labor requirements needed to implement the database system. A preliminary assessment suggested that, although Zeus had competent, experienced programmers and analysts, a good deal of training would be required. The training needs encompassed users primarily, but also included some systems personnel. The Database Administrator had previously been identified and trained from the ranks of systems personnel.

economic feasibility Cost-benefit study of proposed database system.

3. The **economic feasibility** study turned out to be a challenging one. The expected benefits of installing a database system were very difficult to quantify. This is a fairly typical experience. The project team addressed this challenge by seeking answers to the following questions:

   a. How soon can benefits be expected?
   b. Is the sharing of data by user departments politically feasible?
   c. What risks are involved if a database system is implemented?
   d. What risks are associated with database implementation?
   e. What applications will be implemented, and what are the benefits that are sought from those applications?
   f. What is the competition doing?
   g. How will the database system aid in accomplishing corporate long-range plans?

On the cost side, the simplest factors to measure were out-of-pocket costs such as the cost of software, hardware, and programming. While these costs are not entirely subject to management control, it was felt that the firm could enjoy cost savings by ensuring that standards were established before database software was installed, and by not installing a query language before there were sufficient data to warrant its effective use.

The project team also mentioned hidden costs that could be associated with database system implementation. These costs typically result from unforeseen changes in the way systems function. For example, it is easy to underestimate the time required to integrate previously independent application systems. In addition, software changes may require unanticipated hardware upgrades to ensure adequate performance. Such changes can quickly add to development costs.

The results of each feasibility examination were favorable, and the Steering Committee gave its approval to move ahead with the next task: requirements definition.

requirements definition Determination of management and functional area information requirements.

Requirements definition involves defining the scope of the database, identifying management information requirements, determining information requirements by functional area, and establishing hardware and software requirements. The information requirements are determined from responses to questionnaires, by conducting interviews with managers and clerical users, and by gathering reports and preprinted forms that are currently being used. The general information model created during database planning is expanded to general information models for each functional area. These will be the basis for the detailed design of the database, which will be carried out during the next step. The results of this stage are described in the four tasks below.

Although not every firm will follow identical steps, there are some basic notions that are identified with successful requirements definition. At Zeus, the following tasks were completed:

1. The scope of the database system was defined. This was accomplished through analyzing the information requirements of the firm's managers. The team also considered whether the database should be distributed or centralized and what teleprocessing facilities might be required. A brief three-page narrative was produced describing the scope of the database system. It was decided that a centralized database encompassing most of the company's major functional areas would be developed.

2. User requirements at both the management and operational levels were documented with a generalized information model for each functional area, along with definitions of the application systems necessary to satisfy those requirements. The information models for each functional area were object-oriented data models, explained in Chapters 4 and 6. User requirements were also documented with narratives developed from user interviews, with reports and preprinted forms, and with the answers to a questionnaire. An example of a preprinted form used by Zeus is shown in Figure 3.6. The questionnaire appears in Figure 3.7.

3. The general hardware and software requirements of the system were established along with the facilities required and the levels of performance to be supported. Considerations in this area included the number of users who would normally be accessing the system, the number of transactions entering the system each day, and the amount of printing that would be required. This information was used to determine the size and type of computer and DBMS needed as well as the amount of disk space and printing support. A narrative report with figures showing the hardware and software configuration was produced.

4. For steps 1 to 3, a plan was drafted for a time-phased development of the entire database system. This plan included an identification of the initial applications to be implemented. The guiding principles here were that: (1) The applications should be relatively small and not critical to the firm, to limit the impact of any problems associated with introducing a database; or (2) they should be for those users who are very supportive of the database system development.

Zeus Corporation

Boswick, TN

Purchase Order

Order No. 1848

Date 2/21/9X

Date Needed	Vendor		Department	Purchasing Agent
3/15/9X	Code	Name	Parts Inventory	T. Achilles
	215	Shoe Pieces, Inc.		

Part No.	Description	Quantity	Unit Price	Extended Price
4831	Laces	5000	.17	850.00
4922	Insoles	1000	2.30	2300.00
			Total	3150.00

FIGURE 3.6   A Preprinted Purchase Order Form

FIGURE 3.7   A Questionnaire to be Used During Requirements Definition.

```
YOUR FUNCTION
Describe your area of responsibility. _____
What are your principal duties that require information from
computer applications? _____

USE OF INFORMATION
1. From what applications do you receive information? _____
2. How often is the information received? _____
3. What do you do with this information? _____
4. What security precautions must you take with respect to
   the information? _____
5. For what applications do you submit data? _____
6. Are there contemplated changes to any of your current activities
   involving any of the above information? Please describe
   briefly. _____
```

Logical Design

logical design Creation of conceptual level schema for database.

The **logical design** stage creates the logical or conceptual schema for the entire database. Specifications are developed to the point where implementation can begin. During this stage, detailed object-oriented models of individual user views are created and integrated into an object-oriented data model recording all the corporate data elements to be maintained in the database.

At Zeus, logical design focused on the development of an object-oriented model of the firm's reality. The development of the object-oriented model was guided by information contained in company policy and procedure manuals, as well as the guidelines and generalized object-oriented models for the functional areas that resulted from requirements definition. Through in-depth interviews with users and careful examination of company forms, these models were enhanced. They were then integrated as part of logical design and became the basis for implementation.

The object-oriented modeling task of the logical design step was a key component in the consultant's recommendation of the DDLC. At first, Steve Blue, Zeus's Executive Vice-President was skeptical of this technique. He queried their consultant, Linda Kelly, very carefully:

"Linda, what's wrong with the way we do things now?"

"Your current methods are tied too closely to a file-oriented way of thinking, Steve. You've inherited this approach from the early days when technology left no choice but to design databases as files. But the fact is, problems are simply not structured that way. You need an approach that is much more natural, more like the way problems are actually structured. In other words, you need to move from an approach that is physically oriented to one that is logically oriented. The object-oriented approach will do that."

"Now wait a minute. As I understand it, a relational database system will move us from the physical orientation to the logical orientation."

"A relational database will help you primarily with logical data manipulation, not with data structure. The relational model itself is still essentially file-oriented, since relational tables are really just like files. The relational model is fine as long as you are working with relatively simple problems. But to perform rigorous data analysis of complex business problems, you need a more powerful methodology. That is why I am recommending object-oriented design."

"What do you mean by 'object-oriented'?"

Linda explained, "The object-oriented design methodology is also called *semantic modeling*. *Semantic* means *meaning*. That is, we capture the *meaning* of data and relationships in our modeling. In this design methodology, we think in terms of 'objects' instead of files. 'Objects' are things like sales representatives, products, managers, sales, and so forth. Even more importantly, we think in terms of named relationships between objects. For example, a manager 'manages' a sales representative. Managers and sales representatives are objects. 'Manages' is a relationship between them. As problems become more complex, object-oriented design helps us to think more clearly and to keep a large number of complex relationships straight in our minds. Without this methodology, our systems could easily become hopelessly tangled and confused."

"Well, I agree that we need to be able to handle more complex problems. Does this mean that we shouldn't plan on getting a relational database management system?"

"No it doesn't. Think of object-oriented modeling as a tool that creates clear designs that can readily be converted to high quality relational models. You will have better systems, but they can still run on existing relational DBMS software."

"It sounds like you've got all the bases covered. Let's follow through with it."

Thus, as Zeus executed the DDLC, the logical design step consisted of, first, creating detailed object-oriented models representing user views in different functional areas. These models together constituted the external level in the three-level architecture. Second, these user views were integrated into a single object-oriented model giving the entire database schema. This was the schema at the conceptual level. When this was completed, they were ready for the database implementation.

Implementation

database implementation
The steps required to change a logical design to a functioning database.

During the **database implementation** stage, a DBMS is selected and acquired. Then the detailed object-oriented model is converted to the appropriate implementation model, the data dictionary is built, the database is populated, application programs are developed, and users are trained (Figure 3.8).

At Zeus, implementation began with the selection and acquisition of a DBMS. For a variety of reasons, they chose a relational DBMS. The next

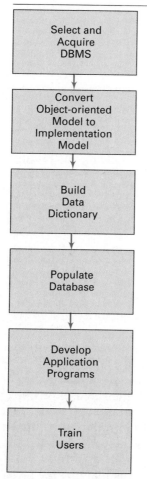

FIGURE 3.8   The Database Implementation Step

step was the mapping of the firm's object-oriented model to a relational implementation model using the procedures outlined in Chapter 7. The resulting table structures were then defined to the DBMS. This was done by using a data definition language (DDL) supplied with the DBMS to develop the data dictionary.

Building the data dictionary is a crucial step in implementation, because the DD is a central repository for definitions and descriptions of all the data structures in the database. Because it contains information about access authority, security rules, and related controls, the DD acts as a control center for the system. This allows the data dictionary to enforce data standards and eliminate many of the problems involved with coordinating the sharing of data among applications.

At this point, the database contained only the data dictionary. The next step was to populate the database by loading actual data from Zeus's files into the database. This was done through a data conversion program that used the data manipulation language (DML) supplied with the DBMS.

The development team then surveyed the user views and the applications that would be using the database. For some users, it was decided that a special application program would provide the simplest and most efficient access to the database with the least security problems. This was most often true of data access performed by clerks and other employees involved in recording the firm's daily transactions. The programming staff then wrote these application programs. For other users, the team decided that it was best to train them to use the data manipulation language to directly access the database.

The final step was to develop a set of procedures for using the database and setting up training sessions to explain these procedures and the other facilities of the database system.

Evaluating and Enhancing the Database Schema

Evaluation involves interviewing and polling users to determine whether any data needs are unmet. Changes are made to the database as needed. Over time the database system is "maintained" via the introduction of enhancements and the addition of new programs and data elements, as business needs change and expand.

☐ DEVELOPING SKILLS IN DATABASE DEVELOPMENT

As Table 3.1 shows, the majority of this book is devoted to helping you develop the skills needed to execute the database development life cycle. Thus, Part II covers the general topic of "Conceptual Database Design." These chapters (4, 5, and 6) describe the process of object-oriented data modeling, which is essential to the successful construction of a logically sound database. Part III then focuses on implementation database design, or converting an object-oriented model to an implementation model. Chapters 7, 8, 9, and 10 introduce the implementation models—the relational, hierarchical, and network data models—and show how an object-oriented model can be converted to any of these three models. Chapter 11 concludes the part by explaining the physical model.

TABLE 3.1 Coverage of the DDLC

DDLC Step	Chapter
Preliminary Planning	2
Feasibility Study	3
Requirements Definition	3, 4, 5, 6, 15
Logical Design	3, 4, 5, 6, 15
Implementation	
DBMS Selection	12
Conversion to Implementation Model	7, 8, 9, 10
Physical Model	11
Data Dictionary Development	17
Application Program Development	13, 14, 15, 16
Management Control	17, 18

Part IV expands the topic of database implementation by discussing DBMS selection (Chapter 12), commercial relational database implementations (Chapters 13 and 14), microcomputer database management systems (Chapter 15), and the more advanced concepts of knowledge-base systems and natural language processors (Chapter 16).

The final part, Part V, deals with management topics such as database administration, security and integrity, and distributed databases that were introduced in Chapter 2.

As you study this material, you will develop skills in database design and data manipulation that will be essential for your success in a business database environment. You will also understand the management issues that significantly affect many of the decisions made about database systems. The background material provided throughout the book will help you to understand the context in which database systems exist in today's business world. By acquiring these skills, understanding the key management issues, and being familiar with the context of databases, you will be well-equipped to function in the advanced environment of management information systems.

■ SUMMARY

In this chapter, we discussed the concept of database development. We explained the ANSI/SPARC three-level database architecture, indicating that database development is primarily concerned with the logical definition of a database. Then, we contrasted the function-oriented approach of the traditional system development life cycle (SDLC) with the data-oriented approach of the database development life cycle (DDLC). In the last part of the chapter, we outlined the steps of the DDLC and described the activities included in each step. We also described the written documents resulting from each step.

Three-level architecture describes a database as consisting of the conceptual, external, and internal levels. The conceptual level is the logical schema which defines the entire database from the perspective of the organization. The external level consists of the various views by which the users throughout the organization understand, access, and update the database. The internal level is the physical definition of the database by which the DBMS controls and updates the database.

The traditional SDLC views systems from the standpoint of the functions they are to perform. Since data elements tend to be more stable than functions, we saw that the database structure should be developed prior to the development of functional systems. A properly developed database system will be the foundation on which many functional systems can be built.

The DDLC consists of six steps: preliminary planning, feasibility study, requirements definition, logical design, implementation, and database evaluation and maintenance. Preliminary planning takes place primarily during strategic database planning. Information from the database plan is reviewed and brought up-to-date as part of the DDLC. The feasibility study is carried out to determine technological, operational, and economic feasibility. Requirements definition determines the information requirements of management as well as those of the functional areas to be served by the database. Logical design results in a comprehensive object-oriented data model which gives a detailed logical schema for the entire database. During implementation, the DBMS is acquired, the logical design is converted to an implementation design, the data dictionary is built, the database is populated, application programs are developed, and the users are trained. After implementation, the database itself is evaluated to determine whether it is in fact meeting users' needs. Needed enhancements to improve database useability and to address changing business needs are carried out.

■ REVIEW QUESTIONS

1. Define each of the following terms in your own words:
   a. three-level architecture
   b. internal level
   c. database development life cycle
   d. preliminary planning
   e. technological feasibility
   f. requirements definition
   g. database implementation

2. Explain the difference between the conceptual and external levels in the ANSI/SPARC three-level architecture.

3. Explain the meaning of the statement: "The database exists in reality only at the [ANSI/SPARC] internal level."

4. Discuss the differences between function-oriented system development and data-oriented system development. Why is data-oriented system development more likely to allow a broader range of functions?

5. List and briefly describe each of the six steps in the database development life cycle.

■ PROBLEMS AND EXERCISES

1. Match the following terms with their definitions:

__Operational feasibility   a. Focuses on the analysis of data used by the functions

__External level   b. Creation of a conceptual level schema

__Logical design   c. Cost-benefit study

__Data-oriented approach   d. A process for system development

__Conceptual level   e. Determines availability of expertise and personnel

__Feasibility study   f. Views a system from the perspective of the functions it should perform

__System development life cycle   g. Structural level defining the logical schema

__Function-oriented approach   h. Structural level defining user views

__Economic feasibility   i. Determines technological, operational, and economic feasibility

2. Identify the ANSI/SPARC levels for each of the following:

   a. An index giving the disk address of each record in a PERSONNEL file.

   b. A partial version of the PERSONNEL file containing only the name and address of each employee.

   c. A combination of sales transaction data and customer data which shows the product number of the product sold and the customer's number, name, and address but does not show the sales representative number.

   d. A file giving the disk address of an employee record together with the disk addresses of the records of all the employee's dependents.

   e. Data giving the names of all files and fields in the database together with definitions of interrelationships between fields in different files.

3. Identify information system functions that the following sets of data elements can be used to perform:

   a. For a department store: product number, regular price, sale price, cost, quantity sold, department, sales representative, commission rate, supervisor. (Example: Using regular price, sale price, and cost, profit at the regular price and profit at the sale price can be calculated.)

   b. For a consulting firm: consultant, consultant rank, hourly rate by rank, client, client type, hours a consultant worked for a particular client, date to which the hours billed apply, project type, project leader. (Example: Using consultant, rank, rate, hours worked, and dates, the total amount billed for a consultant's work for a client in a month can be calculated.)

4. In which step(s) in the DDLC would each of the following be performed:

   a. Obtaining a reasonable estimate of the operating cost of a database system.

b. Determining the files used by the quarterly sales report.

c. Determining whether the organization has people who are technically qualified to design and manage a database.

d. Determining the major functions performed by the Accounts Payable system.

e. Entering data into the database.

f. Identifying the information needed by the manager of Purchasing relative to the quality of service provided by vendors.

g. Determining changes needed to make the database more effective.

h. Specifying the complete logical structure of the database.

i. Writing and testing database application programs.

j. Determining which functions the database system will perform in each area.

k. Determining whether communications technology is powerful enough to make a world-wide distributed system practical.

5. Explain how the information concerning current applications and files that is gathered during preliminary planning can be used to help determine future information requirements.

6. List the preprinted forms that might be used by each of the following:
   a. An insurance company
   b. An electric company
   c. A department store
   d. A university

■ PROJECTS AND PROFESSIONAL ISSUES

1. Write a research paper on the issues that led up to the ANSI/SPARC report on three-level architecture. Why did the committee recommend the levels they did? What was the historical context for their report? Were any issues left unresolved?

2. Examine the files and the functions of an installed application system. Discuss the system with some of its users to determine whether they would like the system to perform other functions. Identify which data items from the current system and which new data items would be required by the new functions.

3. Research the concept of the database development life cycle in current textbooks and trade periodicals. Try to identify versions of the DDLC that are different from the one given in this chapter. What do these versions have in common? Try to synthesize the various versions into a single, generic DDLC.

part two

LOGICAL DATABASE DESIGN

In Part II, we deal with the problems of requirements definition and logical design in the database development life cycle. As you work through the material of this part, you will develop skills in requirements analysis, conceptual database design, and logical data manipulation. In demonstrating the methods used to create object-oriented data models, we indicate how information requirements can be used to determine the appropriate data models that will form the basis for the installed database.

In Chapter 4, you will be introduced to object-oriented design and will see how the concepts of objects, relationships, attributes, and generalization and specialization can be used to create information models. A number of examples will be given to clarify the concepts and to illustrate how they can be applied in a very large number of practical situations.

In Chapter 5, you will see how object-oriented data models can be used to answer management questions through the application of data manipulation languages. Two languages are discussed—a textual query language and a graphical query language. These languages are very natural and easy to use and will demonstrate the strength of the object-oriented approach.

Chapter 6 applies the principles of object-oriented design to more complex problems. Sophisticated analysis and design techniques are discussed and applied to a number of practical examples from a wide variety of business situations.

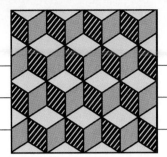

chapter four

BASIC CONCEPTS OF OBJECT-ORIENTED DESIGN

"How many checking accounts do we have? How many savings accounts? How many customers? Which customers have both savings and checking accounts? What percentage of our savings accounts have a balance under $1000? Which types of customers tend to have the highest average balance in their accounts? How many customers have loans in addition to checking or savings accounts?"

Robert Goldthumb, President of Alchemical Bank and Trust (ABT) is frustrated because he cannot get answers to these sorts of questions on a daily basis. Meanwhile, Anita Short, head of Bookkeeping, needs to be sure each customer gets the right monthly statement, and Elliott Tight, head of Consumer Loans, needs a weekly report of overdue loan payments and an application that will automatically generate reminder letters.

Clearly, each of these users' needs can be met by a database system. Just as clearly, these three users have distinct needs. Yet, it is easy to see that there is quite a bit of overlap in the types of data all three users require. Your task during requirements definition and logical design is to identify these basic data needs and create object-oriented models that accurately record needed data elements and their relationships. After reading this chapter, you should be able to:

- List and explain basic concepts in object-oriented data modeling.
- Perform logical database specification by using object-oriented models.
- Use object-oriented data modeling to capture the data and relationships inherent in simple user queries.
- Use object-oriented data modeling to capture information from existing reports and forms.

REALITY, REQUIREMENTS DEFINITION, AND OBJECT-ORIENTED DATA MODELING

The processes of requirements definition and logical design require identifying user information requirements and representing them in a well-defined model. To accomplish this, we need to look carefully at the nature of user requirements and at a precise means of logically representing them.

Reality and Models

model A representation of reality that retains only selected details.

What is a model? A **model** is a representation of reality that retains only selected details. For example, consider an accounting transaction such as a deposit to a checking account. Bookkeeping wants to keep certain details (account number, amount of deposit, time, date, teller number) and ignore others (words exchanged during the transaction, the number of people in the bank, the number of people waiting in line, the music playing over the intercom, weather conditions outside, and so on). Reality involves a myriad of details, but Bookkeeping will consider most of them irrelevant to the transaction. Thus, a model of Bookkeeping's view of the transaction will keep only those details Bookkeeping deems relevant.

Of course, some of the details regarded as irrelevant by one user may be very important to other users. Imagine, for example, that you are developing a database system for a fast-food restaurant. Outside weather conditions may be a significant aspect of the manager's reality, since a cold day may produce a far different mix of sales than a warm day. As a result, the manager may want to track these changes and order supplies accordingly. The number of people waiting in line may be another important aspect of the manager's reality, since the manager needs this information to schedule counter workers and minimize customer waiting. Thus, different users will have different models of reality.

A database incorporates a model of reality. The DBMS manages the database so that each user can record, access, and manipulate the data that constitutes his or her model of reality. By manipulating data in a large variety of ways, users can derive the information needed to run an enterprise successfully. Thus, models are powerful tools for eliminating irrelevant details and understanding the reality of individual users.

map To associate elements in one sphere with elements in another sphere.

Modeling reality is, in many ways, like solving a story problem. Both require you to sift through details to create a "correct" model of a portion of reality. This means you must associate, or **map,** elements in reality to elements in the model. If this mapping is done properly, then the model can be used to solve the problem. If not, the model cannot produce the correct solution. Many people find story problems difficult because they are not comfortable with the mapping process itself. In fact, Figure 4.1 may represent your own view of story problems. If so, we hope to help you become more comfortable with both modeling and mapping reality. We will begin with simple, basic modeling concepts and show how these can be used to build, step by step, a powerful solution to what may appear to be a complex problem. As you study the examples and work through the exercises and cases, you will develop substantial data modeling skills.

THE FAR SIDE   By GARY LARSON

Hell's library

MODELS AT DIFFERENT LEVELS

Although it may not be obvious, we are using the term *model* at three different levels in our discussion. These levels (not related to the three levels of ANSI/SPARC architecture) are illustrated in Figure 4.1S.

At the lowest level, we say that the current state of a particular database is a model of reality because it is a record of selected facts about reality that are currently true. For example, the database may record the fact: "Margaret Smith lives at 845 Puente Avenue." If Margaret's address changes, then the database state must change if it is to continue as an accurate model of reality.

At the next higher level, the schema, describing the structure of the database, is a model of a set of models (that is, it is a model of a set of database states). The schema models a huge range of database states by defining those characteristics that all of these states have in common. Thus, "Name" and "Address" are recorded in the schema as characteristics that apply to many different people and that change from time to time.

At the highest level, the database design methodology describes the constructs and rules that may be used in formulating a schema. Therefore, this level is also a model of a set of models (possible database schemas). A given design methodology, such as the object-oriented model or the relational model, is a model at this highest level and describes in general terms a potentially enormous set of schemas.

In summary then, we speak of the object-oriented model, which is a methodology for creating database schemas for particular application situations. These database schemas are themselves models that provide the logical structure to capture facts about a particular portion of reality. When these facts are captured and recorded in a computer database system, then the database itself is a model of the current state of reality. Each of the two upper levels of Figure 4.1S is a model of the level below it.

FIGURE 4.1S   Three Levels of Models

Model Level	Sample Model	Typical Construct
Design Methodology	Object-Oriented, Relational, etc.	Objects, Relationships Tables, Columns
	models a set of ↓	
Database Schema	Database Schema	Person, Name, Address, Is-Employed-By
	models a set of ↓	
Current State of Reality	Database	Margaret Smith 845 Puente Avenue

Object-Oriented Models

object-oriented model A model representing real-world entities as objects rather than records.

semantic model A model that captures the meanings of real-world entities and relationships.

The data modeling methodology we will study and use in this chapter is called **object-oriented** because it presumes a computer representation of real-world entities as "objects" having attributes and participating in relationships, rather than as records in traditional file-oriented systems. It is generally acknowledged that object-oriented representations more accurately reflect the logical essence of real-world applications than do record-based representations. Object-oriented data models are also called **semantic** because they provide a powerful means of mapping the *meanings* of things in reality to constructs in the model. Since the early seventies, a number of object-oriented models have been proposed. We will be using a generic model, which has features common to most of these proposed models.

The principal elements of object-oriented models are *objects* and *relationships*. Objects are often thought of as *nouns*, and relationships are regarded as *verbs*. Although additional constructs are provided in some object-oriented models, objects and relationships are powerful enough for the problems we will be considering.

OBJECT-ORIENTED OR SEMANTIC?

Object-oriented databases are the result of the convergence of two research disciplines: semantic data modeling and object-oriented languages. These disciplines developed independently but in recent years have begun to merge with important implications for database processing.

Semantic data modeling was originally developed for the purpose of increasing the effectiveness and accuracy of database design (Hull and King, 1987). Semantic modeling methods were found to be appropriate for many user problems and could be easily converted to "record-based" implementation models such as the hierarchical, network, and relational models. Abrial introduced the Binary Semantic Data Model in 1974, and this was followed during the next several years by Chen's Entity-Relationship model (Chen, 1976), the Semantic Data Model (SDM) of Hammer and McLeod (1981), and the Functional Data Model (Shipman, 1981). These and other data models, as well as extensions to these models, approached the problem of data modeling for purposes of database design from a variety of perspectives, yet they had in common the aim of providing a means to capture the "semantics" or the meaning of the application area being modeled.

While those involved in semantic data modeling were primarily concerned with data structure, the developers of *object-oriented programming languages* were more interested in the "behavior" of data objects. That is, they were looking for ways of manipulating data that would focus on the data *and* the manipulation (query, computation, update) capabilities of the language. Data structure was a secondary concern.

The convergence of these two areas came when researchers began to apply concepts of object-oriented languages to semantic data structures.

The result is the notion of an "object-oriented database." In this merger of disciplines, the object-oriented terminology has tended to predominate, and so we speak of "objects" rather than "entities," as we would if we were to use semantic terminology.

Because we are concerned almost exclusively with structure rather than behavior in this book, we have adopted the term *object set* rather than the normal *object class* of object-oriented languages. An *object class* is what we have called an *object set*, with the additional property, however, of having specific programs defined for it that characterize the object set's behavior. Thus, an *object class* is an *object set* with behavior. Since the question of behavior is beyond the scope of this book, we do not define object classes and have chosen the more neutral term *object set* to identify the principal building blocks in our data models.

☐ BASIC CONCEPTS

Objects

Objects represent "things" that are important to users in the portion of reality we want to model. Examples of objects are people, automobiles, trees, dishwashers, houses, hammers, and books. These are concrete objects. Conceptual objects would be companies, skills, organizations, product designs, business transactions, and job classifications.

From the preceding, it may not be clear whether an object is a particular thing (an individual person, a particular automobile, a specific bank) or a *set* of things (all people, all automobiles, all banks). To avoid ambiguity, we will use the term **object set** to refer to a set of things of the same kind and **object instance** to refer to a single member (or element) of an object set. As Figure 4.2 shows, we will use rectangles to graphically represent object sets and points to represent instances. The name of an object set, given in all capital letters, is the singular version of the object. Thus, "PERSON" is the name of the object set representing people. A "person" (lower-case) is an instance of the object set PERSON. We write "person IN PERSON" to indicate that *person* is an instance of PERSON, or that the instance "person" is in the object set "PERSON."

Object sets are either **lexical** or **abstract.** Instances in lexical object sets can be printed, while the instances in abstract object sets cannot. Thus, for example, NAME would be a lexical object set, since the instances in NAME are names, which are strings of characters that can be printed. DATE, AMOUNT, and SOCIAL-SECURITY-NUMBER are other examples of lexical object sets, since dates, amounts, and social security numbers can also be printed.

object set A set of things of the same kind.

object instance A particular member of an object set.

lexical object set An object set consisting of instances that can be printed.

abstract object set An object set consisting of instances that cannot be printed.

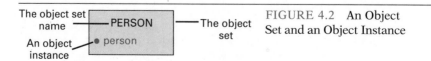

The object set name ⟶ | PERSON | ⟵ The object set
An object instance ⟶ • person

FIGURE 4.2   An Object Set and an Object Instance

PERSON on the other hand is abstract, because a person cannot be printed. While it is true that a person can be *represented* by a lexical object such as a name or social security number, we nevertheless insist that a person is *not* a name or a social security number. For example, a person's name or social security number can change, but the person continues to be the same person. Therefore, to achieve a more accurate model of reality, we distinguish between abstract object sets and lexical object sets.

In a computer implementation of an object-oriented model, a lexical object instance would be represented by a string of printable characters. An abstract object instance would be represented by an internal number which has no meaning outside the system. This internal number is sometimes called a **surrogate key,** meaning that it represents and uniquely identifies the real-world abstract object instance.

Suppose a person named Juanita Perez is in the PERSON object set. In an actual implementation of this object set, Juanita would be represented by some surrogate key, say "13948226." Her name (Juanita Perez), social security number, birthdate, height, weight, and other such information would be recorded as lexical data and would be associated in the database with the surrogate key representing her. Users would only see this lexical data. They would never see 13948226 in association with Juanita. But the system would use the surrogate in associating Juanita in all the possible numerous relationships that are part of the database.

Surrogate keys solve problems arising from traditional types of keys. For example, in many systems it is very difficult to change a key value. Social security number is often used as a key to uniquely access information about a person. What happens if the social security number is incorrect? Since this number has legal importance *outside* the database system, it *must* be corrected. But this could lead to a great many difficulties within the database, since there may be many references to that social security value. This problem is eliminated by using surrogate keys, since they are defined by the system and have no meaning outside the system. If Juanita Perez's social security number is incorrect, we merely change it. Nothing else in the database will be affected, since nothing else refers to the social security number. Instead, all references to Juanita Perez use the surrogate key.

Specialization and Generalization

Some object sets are contained within other object sets. For example, MAN (the set of men) is contained within PERSON. This means that every man (every instance of the set MAN) is also a person (an instance of the set PERSON). Similarly, WOMAN is contained within PERSON. We say that MAN is a **specialization** of (or subset of) PERSON. We can represent this by writing MAN ⊂ PERSON. PERSON, on the other hand, is a **generalization** or superset of MAN (and of WOMAN). We designate the specialization/generalization relationship graphically as shown in Figure 4.3(a). The U-shaped symbol indicates the direction of set containment. The top of the U "points" to the larger or containing set. If we placed the sets side by side, the U would be on its side, pointing in the direction of PERSON. If PERSON were the bottom box, and MAN were the top box, the U would be upside down. We could also show MAN within PERSON

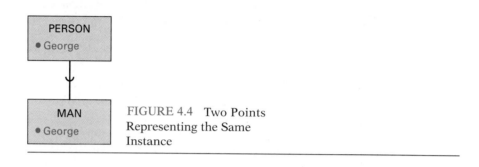

(a) The Specialization-Generalization
Relationship

(b) An Alternate Representation of
Specialization

FIGURE 4.3   Alternate Representations of Specialization and Generalization

FIGURE 4.4   Two Points
Representing the Same
Instance

(Figure 4.3(b)). Since many object sets can be contained within a single
set, however, this technique tends to cause crowded diagrams.

Suppose George is a man. Then George is also a person. This is
shown graphically in Figure 4.4. Note that two points represent the same
person. One point represents him as an instance in PERSON, and one
point represents him as an instance in MAN. There is really only one instance. It is just shown as residing in two different object sets. The importance of this will be illustrated shortly.

Relationships

relationship A linking between instances of two object
sets.

A **relationship** links two object sets. Consider the object sets MARRIED
MAN and MARRIED WOMAN. We can define the IS-MARRIED-TO relationship between these two sets by associating each married man with
his wife (or, conversely, each married woman with her husband). The IS-
MARRIED-TO relationship consists of a set of married couples, the husband coming from the MARRIED MAN object set and the wife coming
from the MARRIED WOMAN object set. Graphically, we represent a relationship between two object sets by showing a line (with an optional
embedded diamond) connecting the two sets (Figure 4.5(a)).

FIGURE 4.5   Representations of a Relationship

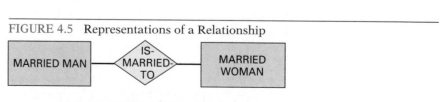

(a) The IS-MARRIED-TO Relationship

A relationship is itself an object set, consisting of pairs of instances taken from the two object sets it relates. That is, each instance of a relationship is a pair of instances from the two object sets. If

```
MARRIED MAN    = {Adam, David, John}    and
```

```
MARRIED WOMAN = {Joan, Linda, Michelle}    and
```

```
Adam       is-married-to    Joan
David      is-married-to    Linda
John       is-married-to    Michelle
```

then

```
IS-MARRIED-TO =
        {(Adam, Joan), (David, Linda), (John, Michelle)}.
```

The braces ({ }) here are used to indicate a set. Figure 4.5(b) shows this information graphically. We see then that the IS-MARRIED-TO relationship is itself an object set whose instances are married couples. An object set like IS-MARRIED-TO, which is derived from a relationship between other object sets, is called an **aggregate object set.**

aggregate object set A relationship viewed as an object set.

Aggregate object sets can be given object set names and can participate in relationships, just as normal object sets. In Figure 4.5(c), the aggregate of IS-MARRIED-TO is named MARRIED-COUPLE, and it par-

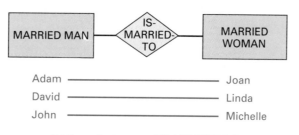

(b) Some Instances of IS-MARRIED-TO

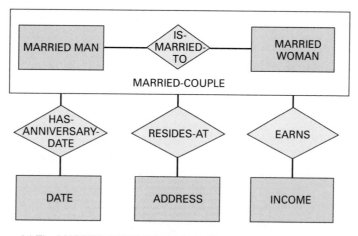

(c) The MARRIED-COUPLE Aggregate Object Set Participating in Relationships

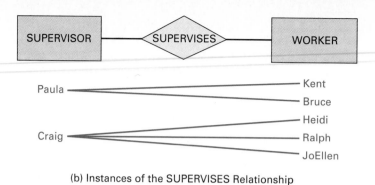

(b) Instances of the SUPERVISES Relationship

(a) The SUPERVISES Relationship

FIGURE 4.6   Representations of the SUPERVISES Relationship

ticipates in several relationships. The HAS-ANNIVERSARY-DATE relationship connects a married couple to their anniversary date; the RE-SIDES-AT relationship connects the couple to their address; and the EARNS relationship connects them to their total combined income.

As another example of a relationship, consider the two subsets of a company's employees, SUPERVISOR and WORKER. We define the instances of WORKER as employees who do not supervise other employees. The SUPERVISOR set consists of employees who supervise workers. The SUPERVISES relationship (note the verb) associates each supervisor with the workers he or she supervises (Figure 4.6(a)). Figure 4.6(b) illustrates instances that may be found in the SUPERVISES relationship.

Generalization/specialization represents a special type of relationship. In Figure 4.4, remember, two different points represented the same person—George. The point in MAN representing George is related via this subset relationship to the point in PERSON representing George. In fact, every point in MAN is related to exactly one point in PERSON. Some points in PERSON, however, are related to points in WOMAN. Thus, every point in PERSON is related to either zero or one point in MAN. We can capture this type of information about relationships by adding cardinality to our diagrams.

Cardinality

cardinality The maximum number of instances of one object set related to a single instance of the other object set.

The **cardinality** of a relationship refers to the maximum number of instances in one object set that are related to a single instance in the other object set. For example, if we assume each married person has only one spouse, the cardinality of the IS-MARRIED-TO relationship is 1 in each direction (Figure 4.7).

Although we are normally only interested in maximum cardinality, it is sometimes useful to specify minimum cardinality. Suppose, for example, that we restate the IS-MARRIED-TO relationship so that it exists between the sets MAN and WOMAN (Figure 4.8(a)). Since many men and women are not married, the minimum cardinality is 0 in both directions.

FIGURE 4.7   Cardinality of IS-MARRIED-TO

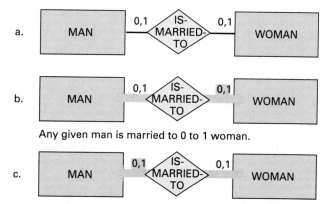

a.   Any given man is married to 0 to 1 woman.

c.   Any given woman is married to 0 to 1 man.

FIGURE 4.8   Minimum and Maximum Cardinalities
Relationship diagrams can be read from left to right or from
right-to-left.

We write "0,1" next to the WOMAN object set to indicate that any given
man is married to between 0 and 1 wives. Conversely, the 0,1 next to the
MAN object set states that each woman is married to between 0 and 1
husbands (Figures 4.8(b,c)).

   Some relationships do not have a specific value for maximum cardinality. For example, a supervisor supervises at least one and possibly
many workers. We indicate this cardinality as 1, * where "1" indicates the
minimum cardinality and "*" simply means "many." Conversely, if we assume that any given worker has one and only one supervisor, the cardinality in the other direction is 1,1 (Figure 4.9).

FIGURE 4.9   Cardinality of SUPERVISES

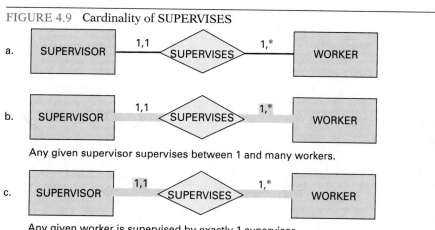

b.   Any given supervisor supervises between 1 and many workers.

c.   Any given worker is supervised by exactly 1 supervisor.

The cardinalities of the specialization or subset relationship are always the same. Every instance in the generalization set is related to zero or one instance in the specialization set, and every instance in the specialization set is related to exactly one instance in the generalization set (Figure 4.10).

Maximum cardinality is a much more important concept than minimum cardinality. To simplify our diagrams, therefore, we will only indicate minimum cardinality when it is needed. Except in the subset relationship (whose minimum cardinalities were discussed above), omitted minimum cardinalities can be assumed to be zero.

A maximum cardinality of 1 in one direction of a relationship corresponds to the mathematical concept of a function, which sets up a one-to-one or many-to-one correspondence between two sets. Therefore, a relationship with maximum cardinality 1 in one direction is called **functional** in that direction. The supervisor/worker relationship in Figure 4.9 is functional from worker to supervisor. That is, if we know who the worker is, then we can uniquely determine his or her supervisor. This relationship is *not* functional in the other direction, since a supervisor has many workers.

If the maximum cardinalities in both directions of a relationship are 1, we say the relationship is **one–one**. If the maximums are 1 in one direction and * in the other direction, we say the relationship is **one–many**. Finally, if the maximum cardinalities are * in both directions, we say the relationship is **many–many**. Table 4.1 summarizes the three basic relationship cardinalities.

functional relationship A relationship having maximum cardinality 1 in at least one direction.

one–one Relationship cardinalities of 1 in both directions.

one–many Relationship cardinalities of 1 in one direction and many in the other.

many–many Relationship cardinalities of many in both directions.

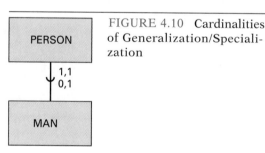

FIGURE 4.10 Cardinalities of Generalization/Specialization

TABLE 4.1 The Three Basic Relationship Cardinalities

Cardinality	Notation	Examples
One–one	1:1 or 1-1	A husband has *one* wife. A wife has *one* husband. (The marriage relationship is one–one.)
One–many	1:* or 1-*	An employee is in *one* department. A department has *many* employees. (The employement relationship is one–many)
Many–many	*:* or *-*	A student takes *many* courses. A course has *many* students. (The enrollment relationship is many–many.)

Attributes

We have represented object sets as boxes and instances as points. This is very abstract. (What could have fewer features than a point?) We normally think of object instances as having a number of attributes that serve to distinguish them. For example, a person has a name, a birthdate, a social security number, height, weight, gender, eye color, hair color, a father, mother, and possibly a spouse. How do we represent these attributes?

attribute Functional relationship from an object set to another set.

An **attribute** of an object is really just a functional relationship of that object's object set with another object set. Thus, two of the attributes listed above are shown as relationships in Figure 4.11. We will find it convenient, however, to represent some attributes more simply, as shown in Figure 4.12. Note that the relationship name and the object name are, in a sense, combined into the name of the attribute (especially BIRTHDATE). We see, then, that writing attributes in this manner is merely a shorthand notation for writing relationships. Generally, this shorthand notation may be used whenever we do not intend to use the attribute as an object in yet another relationship.

In normal usage (which we will follow), attributes are *functional* relationships from the object set to the attribute. That is, the value of the attribute is uniquely determined for each object instance. For example, each person has exactly one birthdate and (in our database) one social security number. The maximum cardinality on the attribute side of these relationships is always 1, and for this reason we will always omit attribute cardinalities from our diagrams. If a particular object instance has no value for one of its attributes, we say that that attribute has a **null value** for the object instance.

null attribute value An attribute value that does not exist for a specific object instance.

It is important to realize that attributes must be kept conceptually separate from the objects they describe. Recall from our earlier discussion that the values of attributes will frequently change while the objects associated with them remain the same. Thus, a person will change height, weight, name, and hair color but will remain the same person. This does not mean that all attributes do change values. In fact, we often try to identify attributes that do not change, because they can be used as external keys.

FIGURE 4.11 Attributes Shown as Relationships

FIGURE 4.12 **Attribute** Notation

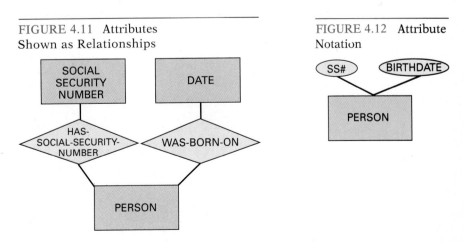

key A value that can always be used to uniquely identify an object instance.

Keys. ☐ A **key** is a value which can always be used to uniquely identify an object instance. We previously mentioned surrogate keys, which would be used within a computer system to identify instances in abstract (non-lexical) object sets. PERSON, for example, is an abstract object set. In an implementation of an object-oriented database, each person in the object set PERSON would have a surrogate key to identify that person within the database. But since the surrogate key cannot be used outside the system, database users need some other way of identifying instances of PERSON. This is accomplished through external keys.

external key A set of lexical attributes whose values always identify a single object instance.

An **external key** is a lexical attribute or set of lexical attributes whose values always identify a single object instance. A lexical attribute is an attribute formed using a lexical object set. Thus, external keys can be printed and read by users. They serve, therefore, as means by which specific object instances can be identified externally to the database system. We will usually refer to an external key as simply a "key." In Figure 4.12, for example, SS#, could be a key for PERSON if we assume each social security number corresponds to exactly one person. That is, the minimum and maximum cardinalities from SS# to PERSON are 1,1. Birthdate, on the other hand, could not be a key, since any given date is the birthdate for many different people.

Sometimes more than one attribute is needed to form a key. Suppose that PERSON in Figure 4.12 is being used in a genealogical database, which traces family trees. Because many of the people in PERSON died before social security numbers were introduced, we need something other than SS# for the key. Perhaps name, birthdate, and birth place would be sufficient. If so, then the combination of these three attributes would form the key for PERSON. If not, then something additional may be needed. If necessary, we can always make up an identification number whose uniqueness can be enforced within the system.

Not every object set needs to have a key. For example, in a database that records sales transactions, the user may be interested only in recording amount of sale and product sold. Obviously, many sales will have the same values for amount and product. It would be unreasonable to require the user to provide a unique key value for every sales transaction. Thus, the database would record only the information the user desires about each transaction, but it would still record separate instances for each transaction. Figure 4.13 shows two different sales attached to an amount of 5.95 and to product A237. The user will see two sales transactions but has no means of distinguishing between them and no interest in doing so. Thus, the absence of a key is of no consequence.

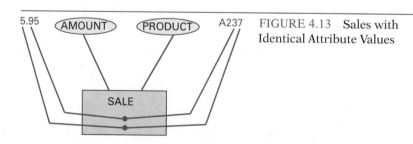

FIGURE 4.13   Sales with Identical Attribute Values

inherit The property of a specialization set that causes it to have all the attributes of its generalization set.

Specialization/Generalization and Attributes. ☐ If an object is a specialization of another object, then the specialization object **inherits** all of the attributes and relationships of the object it specializes. MARRIED PERSON, for example, is a specialization of PERSON. Thus, a married person has a name, social security number, address, and so on, just by virtue of being a person. The MARRIED PERSON object set inherits these attributes from the PERSON object set. In addition, the specialization object set can have attributes of its own. For example, SPOUSE would be an attribute of MARRIED PERSON, but not of PERSON. These concepts are illustrated in Figure 4.14.

Not only does a specialization inherit attributes, but it inherits all relationships. Figure 4.15 illustrates that PERSON is related to COMPANY via WORKS-FOR. MARRIED PERSON, being a specialization of PERSON, is also related to COMPANY via WORKS-FOR. Suppose John Doe is a married person working for XYZ Company. Then there is a point in MARRIED PERSON representing John Doe, a point in PERSON representing John Doe, and a point in COMPANY representing XYZ Company. John Doe in MARRIED PERSON is related to John Doe in PERSON which is in turn related to XYZ Company. Consequently, John Doe in MARRIED PERSON is related to XYZ Company.

Inheritance of attributes and relationships is an important concept, since it allows us to define subsets of object sets which have attributes and relationships of their own but still retain all of the attributes and relationships of the superset. This makes it possible to model reality much more precisely than we could without the inheritance concept.

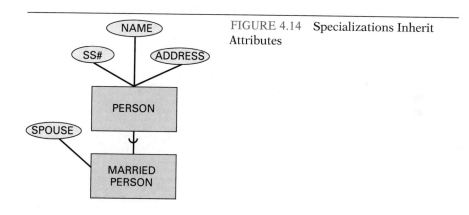

FIGURE 4.14   Specializations Inherit Attributes

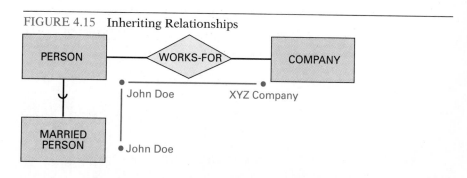

FIGURE 4.15   Inheriting Relationships

Let us try now to create object-oriented models for some real-world problems.

Example 1: The Bank Data Model

Our first example can be used to answer some of the questions posed at the beginning of the chapter. We are interested in creating an object-oriented model of the bank's business that will reflect the reality of Robert Goldthumb, President of Alchemical Bank and Trust (ABT).

The bank has checking accounts, savings accounts, and customers (Figure 4.16(a)). We establish appropriate relationships between these as shown in Figure 4.16(b). We are now in a position to answer these questions:

How many checking accounts do we have? How many savings accounts? How many customers?

The answers to these questions are obtained by merely counting the instances in each of the three object sets. With the appropriate software, Goldthumb could use his personal computer to ask these questions any time, or he could receive a periodic report.

Note how much more cleanly the database handles these questions than a traditional file-based system would. In a file-based system, without the interfile connections provided by a database, there may very well be just two files—one for the checking accounts and one for the savings accounts. In each of these files, customer information would be embedded in a number of fields (customer name, address, and so on). The third question—"How many customers"—would be difficult to answer, since

FIGURE 4.16 The Bank Data Model: Basic Objects and Relationships

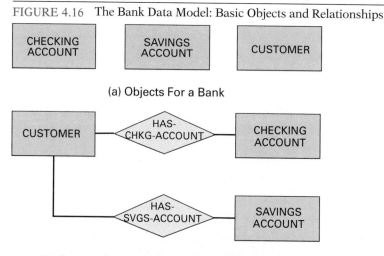

(a) Objects For a Bank

(b) Simple Relationships Between Bank Objects

we would have to extract all of the customer data from the two files, sort it, and throw out duplicates. In a database, however, this customer data can be maintained separately while still preserving the desired connections with account information.

Which customers have both savings and checking accounts?

This question can be answered only by looking at the relationships. A customer has a savings account if he or she is related via HAS-SAVINGS-ACCOUNT to an instance in SAVINGS-ACCOUNT. Similarly, a customer has a checking account if he is related via HAS-CHECKING-ACCOUNT to an instance in CHECKING-ACCOUNT. Finally, a customer has both a savings and a checking account if she's related via both these relationships to instances in SAVINGS-ACCOUNT and CHECKING-ACCOUNT. To answer the above question, we merely count all the customers who are so related.

Cardinalities. □ Figure 4.16(b) intentionally omits cardinalities from the relationships. Let's deal with them now. Suppose we indicate the cardinalities as shown in Figure 4.17. These cardinalities indicate that a customer can have no more than one checking account or savings account. For each account there is one customer.

These cardinalities may not be an accurate reflection of reality, though. Consider the cardinality next to CHECKING-ACCOUNT. Can a customer have only one checking account? ABT, like most banks, allows a customer to have more than one checking account, but the cardinalities of Figure 4.17 do not allow this.

Now look at the other cardinalities. Is it realistic to suppose that an account will be assigned to no more than one customer? This also seems unlikely, since joint accounts—between husband and wife, and between parent and child—are very common. To reflect our more precise perception of reality, we update Figure 4.17 to appear as in Figure 4.18.

The model in Figure 4.17 is incorrect because it does not reflect our perception of ABT's reality. A different perception of reality may make the model of Figure 4.17 correct. A bank, for example, may decide that any customer may have no more than one account of a given type, and that there are no joint accounts. In that case, Figure 4.17 correctly represents reality for that bank. A model is right or wrong only according to whether it correctly or incorrectly represents the reality we are interested in.

FIGURE 4.17   Cardinalities of Bank Relationships

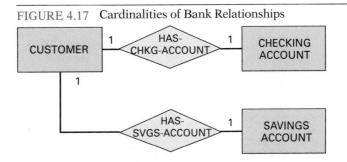

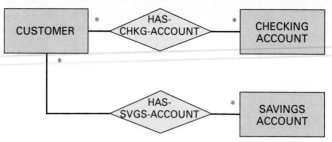

FIGURE 4.18   Revised Cardinalities for Bank Relationships

Returning to the model of Figure 4.18, we can now answer additional questions:

How many customers have multiple checking accounts? How many joint checking accounts do we have? How many customers with multiple checking accounts have a savings account?

Let's walk through the solution to the first of these questions. A customer will have multiple checking accounts if that customer is related via HAS-CHKG-ACCOUNT to at least two different instances in CHECKING-ACCOUNT. We answer the first question by examining each instance in CUSTOMER to see if it is so related and counting the instances that are. We recommend that you try to see how each of the above questions can be answered by walking through the diagram of Figure 4.18.

Specializing the Bank's Customers. ☐   Are the bank's customers always people? Perhaps some of the bank's customers are organizations: businesses, nonprofit organizations, churches, government agencies. Does Goldthumb want to distinguish between types of customers? Yes, he does, since different types of customers will have different attributes. In addition, their accounts may have different characteristics. Figure 4.19 shows two specializations of CUSTOMER. HUMAN CUSTOMER is, of course, the set of customers who are people. INSTITUTIONAL CUSTOMER contains those customers that are organizations.

One of the principal advantages of using generalization and specialization is that we can create different attributes for specializations of an object set, while at the same time retaining common attributes at the generalization level. Figure 4.20 shows that every customer has a cus-

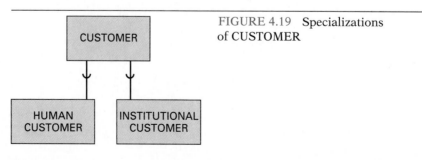

FIGURE 4.19   Specializations of CUSTOMER

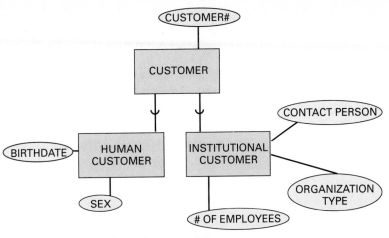

FIGURE 4.20   Attributes by Type of Customer

tomer number, which can be used as a key, but human customers have different attributes than institutional customers.

Let us now revise Figure 4.18 to reflect the specializations of CUSTOMER. Our revision is shown in Figure 4.21, which is a composite of Figures 4.18 and 4.20. (In this figure, we have omitted the optional diamonds in the relationships. We will usually do that from now on.) We have also added a BALANCE attribute to each of the account object sets. We are now prepared to answer a few more questions:

What percentage of our savings accounts have a balance under $1000? Which types of customers tend to have the highest average balance in their checking accounts?

The answer to the second question depends on what we mean by "types of customers." Our database design lets us distinguish between human

FIGURE 4.21   Accounts for Different Customer Types

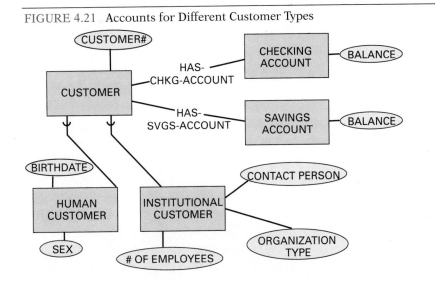

customers and institutional customers. Within INSTITUTIONAL CUS-TOMER, we can also distinguish using the ORGANIZATION TYPE attribute. For example, ORGANIZATION TYPE could possibly be Business, Nonprofit, Church, or Government Agency. To answer the second question, we start at HUMAN CUSTOMER and trace through CUSTOMER to CHECKING ACCOUNT via HAS-CHKG-ACCOUNT. We do this for each human customer and record the balance. When we're done, we compute the average balance for human customers. Then we do the same thing for INSTITUTIONAL CUSTOMER. Finally, to answer the question we compare the two averages.

Example 2: The Keepon Trucking Company

Sally Keepon's trucking company receives packages from customers with orders to ship them from one city to another. Each shipment is assigned to a truck. Each truck is assigned to one and only one driver. Keepon wants to set up a database system that will help determine that truck and drivers are being used efficiently and shipments are on time.

A data model for Keepon Trucking is shown in Figure 4.22. (We have omitted relationship names except in the case where two different relationships connect the same pair of object sets.) Note that shipment functionally determines customer, origination (SENT-FROM) city, destination (SENT-TO) city, and truck. Also, truck determines driver, and driver determines truck. (Look at the cardinalities.) Moreover, origination city and destination city are independent of customer. That is, a given customer can send packages from and to whatever city he chooses. Finally, once a shipment has been assigned to a truck, it stays on that truck until it is delivered. While these statements may not be true in the real world, they are true in the model of Figure 4.22. Now, this model can be used to answer questions about reality at the Keepon Trucking Company only if the statements it implies correspond to reality. Thus, if the above statements are false, the model must be revised to be useful as the basis for Keepon's information system.

Some of the questions this model can answer are:

How many shipments have been sent to Memphis? How many shipments has driver Foster Baire taken to Phoenix? What is their total weight? What city receives the highest number of packages from customer Jones? Which cities send out at least as many packages as they receive?

FIGURE 4.22   Data Model for Keep On Trucking Company

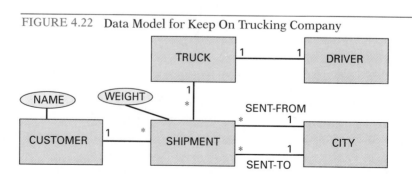

To answer the second question, we start with driver Foster Baire in DRIVER and trace via the relationships to TRUCK, SHIPMENT, and CITY, using the SENT-TO relationship for the last step.

Vern Stratton, Maple Glen fruit grower, has been in the fruit business for fifty years. Before him, his father and grandfather owned his orchards, and he anticipates that at least some of his grandchildren will inherit them. Since the nineteenth century they've kept excellent records, which could constitute the basis for a comprehensive information system.

Vern is interested in the answers to questions like these:

How many varieties of peaches do we have in the Springtown orchard? How many trees die on average in the Lee's Valley orchard each year? What is the average age of my apple trees? How many plum trees have more than one variety on them?

Figure 4.23 gives a simple data model that can be used to obtain answers to these questions. The ORCHARD object set contains an instance for each orchard. The AREA attribute describes the orchard. Thus, AREA would have values such as Springtown, Lee's Valley, and so on. Each orchard is related to those trees (instances of TREE) that are in the orchard. Therefore, the instances of TREE stand for specific, physical trees, rather than types of trees. Each tree was planted in a specific year and may or may not have died. If the tree has died, then YEAR DIED contains a value — otherwise it is null.

Trees have species and species have varieties. For example, apple is a species and Jonathan and Red Delicious are varieties. Since branches can be grafted onto trees, a given species of tree might bear more than one variety. Thus, an apple tree that was originally Red Delicious could also bear Jonathan and Roman Beauty. Each tree has only one species, but it may have multiple varieties. Of course, there are many trees of each species and variety. Finally, each variety corresponds to only one species, although a species may have many varieties.

To answer the first question, we start with the ORCHARD object set.

FIGURE 4.23 Data Model for Stratton's Orchards

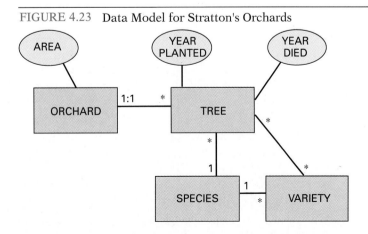

Using the AREA attribute, we identify the Springtown orchard. We then identify all the trees in that orchard by tracing to the TREE object set. From there we go to SPECIES, find "peach" and eliminate all those trees that are not peach trees. Now from TREE we trace all the Springtown peach trees to the VARIETY object set and identify all the varieties of peaches in the Springtown orchard.

Example 4: A Logic Problem Involving Mapping

You have probably seen logic problems in the games section of a newspaper or magazine. Usually such problems cannot be completely solved with the principles of this chapter, but they can be simplified by defining objects and relationships appropriately. The following comes from Wylie (1957):

> In a certain bank, the positions of cashier, manager, and teller are held by Brown, Jones, and Smith, though not necessarily respectively.
>
> The teller, who was an only child, earns the least. Smith, who married Brown's sister, earns more than the manager.
>
> What position does each man fill?

Figure 4.24 represents this problem graphically. We have four objects and corresponding relationships. Note that the minimum and maximum cardinalities for the relationship between POSITION and EMPLOYEE are 1,1 in both directions. When we make the assignments for this relationship, we will have the solution to the problem. We are trying to assign each employee to his position. We have listed the three positions and three employees next to their object sets. The clues tell us something about the employees' comparative earnings and how many brothers and sisters they have. This information is indicated on the diagram.

Figure 4.25 gives the solution to the problem. This was derived as follows: Since Smith earned the most, he could be neither the manager nor the teller. Therefore, Smith is the cashier. Brown has a sibling (his

---

FIGURE 4.24   Objects and Relationships for Bank Employees

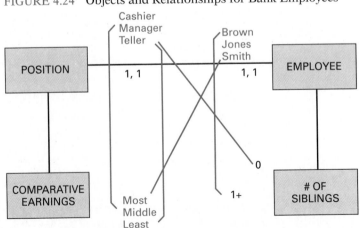

FIGURE 4.25   Solution to Bank Employees Problem

sister is married to Smith), so he's not the teller, who has no siblings. So Brown is the manager. Consequently, Jones must be the teller.

BUILDING OBJECT-ORIENTED MODELS FROM EXISTING REPORTS

The models we have been developing in this chapter are based on information implicit in the types of questions that *managers* would ask. Consequently, these models form the basis for *management information systems*. We are also interested, however, in models that could be used in the *data processing systems* which process the transactions that occur daily in most businesses. In this section, we examine two report forms that are used for transactions by many businesses and show how object-oriented models can be derived from these forms. These forms are used by Manwaring Consulting Services, a case study which we introduce now and which we will use in several future chapters to illustrate the steps in database design and implementation.

Case: Manwaring Consulting Services   Joan Manwaring, CPA, has operated Manwaring Consulting Services for the last ten years. Manwaring Consulting employs six consultants who perform consulting projects for Manwaring clients. Each project involves one or more consultants and may last several weeks or several months, depending on the scope of the project.

Estimates. □   For each engagement taken, Joan must make a proposal for services. The proposal includes a scope, objective, task structure, and fee structure, among other things. The fees Joan charges can vary greatly among the different types of engagements. Fees are based on the benefits provided to the client, and the time and effort expended in completing the engagement. All information pertaining to the engagement is kept for future reference. Any adjustments made to the estimate are shown to the client and are recorded.

Cash Receipts. □   Although many of the smaller engagements are paid for in cash, most of the customers pay on account. Payment is due upon completion of the engagement, unless credit arrangements have been made. The credit accounts are ususally paid by the clients on time, but Joan sometimes has to send second notices to the client in order to collect payment.

Cash Disbursements. □   Although many supplies are charged directly to a specific engagement, some supplies and equipment are associated with multiple engagements or overhead. All supplies are bought on account.

A Data Model for
Purchases

Manwaring's Purchase Order form, used for ordering supplies, is shown in Figure 4.26. It includes the vendor's name and address, the date, order number, and vendor number. It also gives the vendor stock number, product, and price for each product. The total, including tax, is given at the bottom.

From this form, we can derive the following object sets: VENDOR, ORDER, PRODUCT. The attributes of these three sets as well as the relationships between them are shown in Figure 4.27. Note the cardinalities of the relationships. The relationship between ORDER and VENDOR has one–many cardinality, because each order is made from only *one* vendor, but a given vendor can receive *many* orders. The INCLUDES relationship between ORDER and PRODUCT is many–many, because an order includes *many* products and a product can be found on *many* orders.

Eventually, a payment will be made for the order. To record this information, we enlarge the model to that shown in Figure 4.28. The PAYMENT object set has been added, with attributes CHECK NUMBER and DATE. The one-one cardinality indicates that each order will be paid for with one check, and each check will pay for one order.

FIGURE 4.26   A Purchase Order for Manwaring Consulting Services

MANWARING CONSULTING
SERVICES
950 MAIN
EASTON, PA 11111

PURCHASE ORDER

Date	Order Number	Vendor Number
3/19	384	23

Stock #	Product Description	Price
3821	Box of #2 Pencils	4.00
4919	Box of Legal Pads	8.90
	Tax	.77
	Total	13.67

Vendor: Consolidated Office Supplies
             414 S. Choctaw Drive
             Flagship, PA 12345

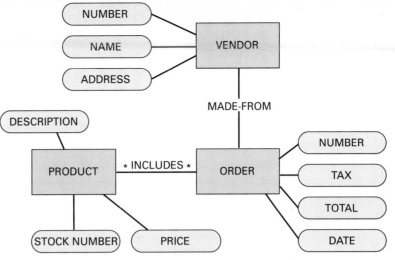

FIGURE 4.27   The Initial Purchase Order Data Model

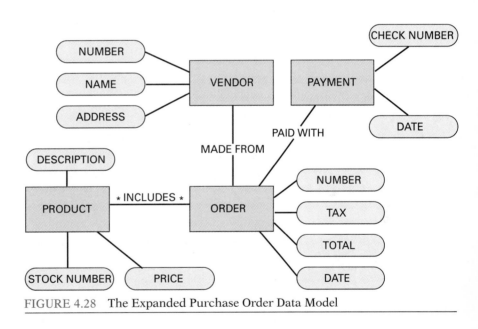

FIGURE 4.28   The Expanded Purchase Order Data Model

A Data Model for Project
Billing

When a project is complete, Manwaring often sends an invoice for services rendered and for supplies used on the project. A sample invoice is
shown in Figure 4.29. This invoice includes date, invoice number, and
project title, as well as an itemization of the services and supplies being
charged for.

From this form, we can identify CLIENT, PROJECT, and CHARGE
object sets with their attributes. These are shown with the relationships
between the object sets in Figure 4.30. Note that there are two different
types of charges: consulting service charges and supply charges. Since the
consulting service charge includes an identification of the consultant, we

MANWARING CONSULTING SERVICES
950 MAIN
EASTON, PA 11111

INVOICE

Date	Invoice Number	Project
10/27	342	Inventory Control System

Consultant	Charge Description	Amount
Rodriguez	80 hours analysis and design	4800.00
Harris	200 hours programming	8000.00
Farasapoulos	30 hours user training	900.00
	supplies (paper, photocopying, etc.)	40.00
	Total	13,740.00

Client: Storehouse Markets
318 Elm Street
Morgantown, PA 11222

FIGURE 4.29   An Invoice for Manwaring Consulting Services

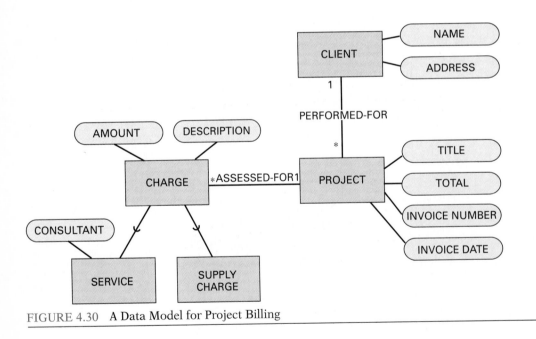

FIGURE 4.30   A Data Model for Project Billing

must divide the CHARGE object set into two subsets: SERVICE and SUP-PLY CHARGE. The CHARGE object set has two attributes, AMOUNT and DESCRIPTION, which both of these subsets inherit. In addition, the SER-VICE specialization of CHARGE has the CONSULTANT attribute.

The Purchase Order and Invoice forms illustrate the process of using existing reports to define an object-oriented model. The database analyst gathering the data needed for database design uses a wide variety of existing reports to contribute to the object-oriented data model. In addition, the analyst uses the interviewing process to determine additional information requirements by identifying the types of questions that management needs to be able to answer. The data obtained from reports and from interviews is combined in the design of a comprehensive object-oriented model. This model will eventually be implemented as a database schema and will be the basis for both data processing and management information systems.

■ SUMMARY

In this chapter, we have studied the fundamentals of object-oriented data modeling. We have defined the general concept of a data model, have described a modeling methodology called "object-oriented data modeling," and have shown how this modeling can be carried out on sets of user queries and on existing reports.

The word *model* is often used on three different levels. At the highest level, a model is really a methodology for modeling. Thus, the object-oriented model is a methodology we can use to create models on the second level. A second-level model is a database schema which defines the types of data to be captured for a particular application. A data model at this level is designed to capture only those details about business operations that the users deem relevant. Irrelevant data which would unnecessarily consume company resources is ignored. When a database schema is implemented and actual data is captured, a database is built. This implemented database is a third-level model, since it models the current state of the business for which it exists.

An object-oriented model is also called *semantic*, since it captures the meanings of things in the real world. Object-oriented models consist of object sets, relationships, attributes, specialization sets, cardinality indicators, and keys. Object sets can be lexical, containing instances which can be printed, or abstract, containing instances which cannot be printed. Instances in abstract object sets are represented by surrogate keys, which are internal identifiers with no external meaning. Relationships establish connections between instances in two object sets. Relationships can also be viewed as object sets which are called aggregate object sets. Attributes are relationships between two object sets which are functional in the direction of one of the object sets. For any given instance in one object set, the value of its attribute is uniquely determined. Specialization object sets are subsets of another object set. Specialization sets are valuable because they provide a means for defining attributes for some instances without the need for defining them for others. A relationship's cardinalities indicate how many of one set may be related under the relationship to a single element in the other set. Cardinalities for relationships are one–one, one–many, and many–many. Keys are used to uniquely identify objects. Surrogate keys are internal identifiers. External keys are sets of lexical attributes which can be used together to identify an element in an object set.

By analyzing the questions users want to answer and the reports that the organization needs, object-oriented data models can be constructed. These data models identify object sets, their attributes, specialization sets, and relationships connecting object sets, together with the cardinalities of the relationships.

■ REVIEW QUESTIONS

1. Define each of the following terms in your own words:
   a. model
   b. object-oriented model
   c. object set
   d. lexical object set
   e. surrogate key
   f. generalization
   g. aggregate object set
   h. functional relationship
   i. cardinality
   j. one-many
   k. attribute

2. Identify and describe six constructs used in object-oriented modeling.

3. Discuss how interviewing and report analysis are used with object-oriented data modeling in the process of logical database design.

4. Discuss how a series of potential user queries is analyzed to determine the following constructs in an object-oriented model:
   a. object sets
   b. attributes
   c. relationships
   d. specializations

5. Discuss how a report is analyzed to determine the following constructs in an object-oriented model:
   a. object sets
   b. attributes
   c. relationships
   d. specializations

■ PROBLEMS AND EXERCISES

Part A

1. Match each term with its definition:

   __Many–many   a. Value used to uniquely identify an object instance

   __Semantic model   b. Object set consisting of instances that cannot be printed

   __Abstract object set   c. A linking between instances of two object sets

   __Specialization   d. Particular member of an object set

   __Relationship   e. Relationship cardinalities of many in both directions

__One–one	f. Object set that is a subset of another object set
__Map	g. Having all the attributes of the generalization set it specializes
__Object instance	h. To associate elements in one sphere with elements in another sphere
__Null value	i. Relationship cardinalities of one in both directions
__Key	j. Captures the meanings of real world entities and relationships
__External key	k. Attribute value that does not exist for a specific object instance
__Inherit	l. Lexical attributes that identify a single object instance

Part B. For each of the following questions, create an object-oriented model, consisting of object sets, relationships, attributes, and so on, that can be used to answer questions similar to the questions given. Indicate cardinalities.

Assume these models are for a university environment.

2. How many faculty members are assigned to the math department? What are their names? Who is assigned to the music department?

(Note: "math" and "music" are just examples of departments. Your model should also be able to answer these questions if, say, sociology, political science, or mechanical engineering were substituted for math or music.)

3. Which students are majoring in history? In English?

4. Which faculty members are teaching courses in sociology? Which courses are they teaching?

5. How many students are taking Physics 201? Which section is Andrea Edens taking?

6. How many German majors are formally registered in the Honors Program? For those who are, who is their Honors Program advisor?

Assume these models are for a manufacturer of parts.

7. Which parts are designed and manufactured in the same facility? (Assume a part is designed in only one facility.)

8. What percentage of the parts are designed in facilities in the West? How many parts are designed, manufactured, and stored in the same region?

Assume the following models are for a bank. Derive these models by adding to the model in Figure 4.21.

9. What percentage of the bank's checking account holders are bank employees?

10. How many tellers have savings accounts with the bank? How many managers do? How many tellers do not?

11. Which managers having savings accounts with the bank manage employees having savings accounts with the bank?

Part C. Indicate which questions cannot be answered by the indicated data model and explain why.

(Figure 4.21)

12. What is the average savings account balance for manufacturers having over 500 employees?

13. How many women opened checking accounts on December 5, 1988?

(Figure 4.22)

14. Has Marion Balmforth ever delivered a package sent by Anne Shirley?

15. Which drivers have picked up 20 pound packages in Peoria?

16. To whom does Thad Burdette send packages from Detroit?

(Figure 4.23)

17. How many spaces are available for new trees in the Heber City orchard?

18. What is the average life span of Jonathan apple trees in the Pleasantville orchard? (Jonathan is a variety, apple is a species)

19. How many peach trees in the Springtown orchard bear more than two varieties?

Part D.

20. Derive an object-oriented data model by analyzing the report shown in Figure 4.1E.

MANWARING CONSULTING SERVICES

CONSULTANT PROFILE REPORT

Name	SSN	Date Hired	Skill Code	Skill Description
Farasopoulas	539-88-4242	11/22/84	A	User Training
			B	Data Entry
			D	File Conversion
Harris	560-43-1111	8/11/86	C	Programming
			D	File Conversion
			F	System Design
Rodriguez	524-33-8119	7/3/85	A	User Training
			C	Programming
			E	Systems Analysis
			F	System Design

FIGURE 4.1E   A Sample Consultant Profile Report

■ PROJECTS AND PROFESSIONAL ISSUES

1. Write a research paper on one of the following:
   a. Chen's entity-relationship data model
   b. The semantic data model of Hammer and McLeod
   c. The functional data model
   d. A comparison of these semantic data models

2. Create an object-oriented model for a portion of an organization. Your model should have at least five object sets with their attributes and relationships. Try to determine conditions when specialization sets are required.

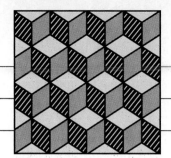

chapter five

OBJECT-ORIENTED DATA LANGUAGES

*Optional

Roberta Powell frowned as she looked over her data model of Lerner College. For the last month, she had worked with Juan Lopez, a senior systems analyst for the college, interviewing users in Administration, Records and Admissions, and individual departments about their requirements for an upgraded database system. Now she, as the intern, had been given the assignment of constructing an object-oriented data model of the user requirements. Now that the model was finished, how could she be sure that it was structured properly and contained the right data?

If you are like Roberta Powell, you may still be a little uncomfortable with data modeling. How can you become more confortable? One way is through practice and experience. Over time, you will learn to combine systems analysis skills with data modeling skills to produce accurate and effective object-oriented models. After you have developed a preliminary model, you can test its validity and completeness by using a data manipulation language (DML) to ask typical user questions of the model. If all the questions can be answered by using the DML to navigate through the model, then your model is correct.

In this chapter, you will be introduced to two data manipulation languages that can be used with object-oriented models. After reading this chapter, you should be able to:

☐ Formulate queries in TextQuery, a text-oriented data language.

☐ Explain how TextQuery solutions navigate through data models.

☐ Formulate queries in GraphQuery, a graphic-oriented data language.

☐ DATABASE DESIGN AND DATA MANIPULATION LANGUAGES

data manipulation language (DML) Computer language for querying and updating a database.

So far we have discussed **data manipulation languages (DMLs)** primarily as tools for computer professionals and end users who want to record, access, and manipulate data in an existing database system. Studying these languages can also give us further insight into the skill of data modeling, since each language reflects an underlying data model. Over time, as you gain experience with data manipulation languages, you will develop an intuitive sense of whether the data in a model is adequate for answering user queries.

In this chapter, we will be studying two prototypes of data manipulation languages—TextQuery and GraphQuery—that are based on the object-oriented data model. By showing you how these languages can be used to answer queries of a data model, we hope to help you develop your intuitive modeling skills.

The first of these languages, TextQuery, is an adaptation of Daplex, which is described in Shipman (1981). The other, GraphQuery, is modeled after the graphical language described by Campbell, Embley, and Czejdo (1987).

A portion of Roberta Powell's data model for Lerner College is shown in Figure 5.1. This model contains four object sets (FACULTY, STUDENT, COURSE, DEPARTMENT) and seven relationships. Each of the object sets has a number of attributes. To make our example more concrete, we have provided some sample data for the data model of Lerner College in Figure 5.2. This figure shows sample attribute values for instances in each of the object sets and one of the relationship sets (HAS-TAKEN). Figure 5.3 shows how instances in the object sets are related to each other via the given relationships.

Before we go on, it might be useful to review the distinction between an object instance and the values of its attributes. Thus, "John" is the name of a person, but the person we call "John" is not the same thing as his name. As an additional example, we may identify a person by a social security number, but the person is *not* a social security number. Therefore, Figure 5.1 represents object sets separately from their attributes. The advantage of this is that we can change attribute values, add attributes, and delete attributes without worrying about losing any of the underlying object instances. We can also manipulate object instances without worrying about specific attributes or attribute values.

FIGURE 5.1   A Portion of the Lerner College Data Model

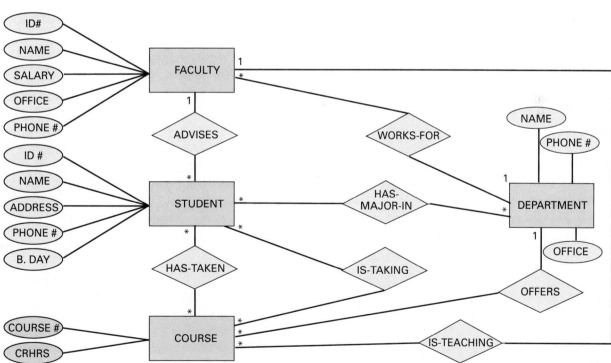

FACULTY

ID#	NAME	SALARY	OFFICE	PHONE#
821	Adams	38000	281 CB	4822
911	Clyde	27000	48 TMB	3085
237	Brown	38000	521 MCK	7324
113	Parker	33000	492 CB	6122
544	Hinman	42000	213 TMB	4188
145	Stevens	45000	312 CB	1203

DEPARTMENT

NAME	PHONE#	OFFICE#
MATH	8111	411 TMB
ENGLISH	4980	512 MCK
HISTORY	5233	313 CB

STUDENT

ID#	NAME	ADDR	PHONE#	BDAY
3825	Mary	214 HH	2112	12/3
4913	John	3A DG	3114	9/14
6255	Ann	4117 RCK	5311	3/5
4118	Kelly	311 ST	6622	4/24
3223	Roger	4214 RCK	1383	7/17

COURSE

COURSE#	CRHRS	COURSE#	CRHRS
H121	3	H250	2
E101	3	E372	3
E212	2	M336	3
M115	4	E456	3
M213	3	H312	3

HAS-TAKEN

NAME (STUDENT)	COURSE#	NAME (STUDENT)	COURSE
Mary	E101	Kelly	E456
John	H121	Roger	M115
John	E101	Roger	M213
Ann	E212	Roger	M336
Ann	H250	Roger	H312
Kelly	E372		

FIGURE 5.2   Representative Values for Lerner College Database

FIGURE 5.3   Relationship Instances

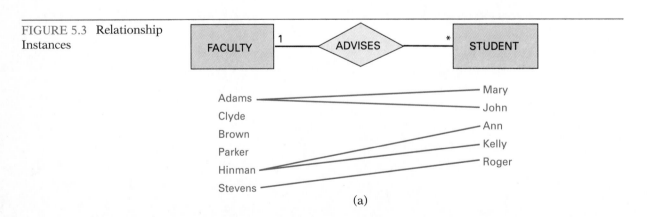

(a)

FIGURE 5-3 (a-g) (continued)

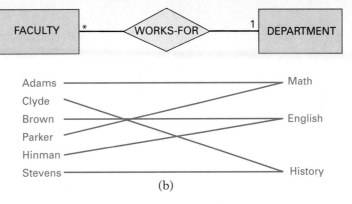

(b)

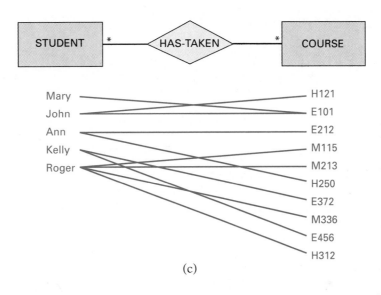

(c)

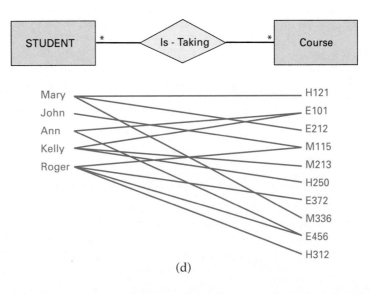

(d)

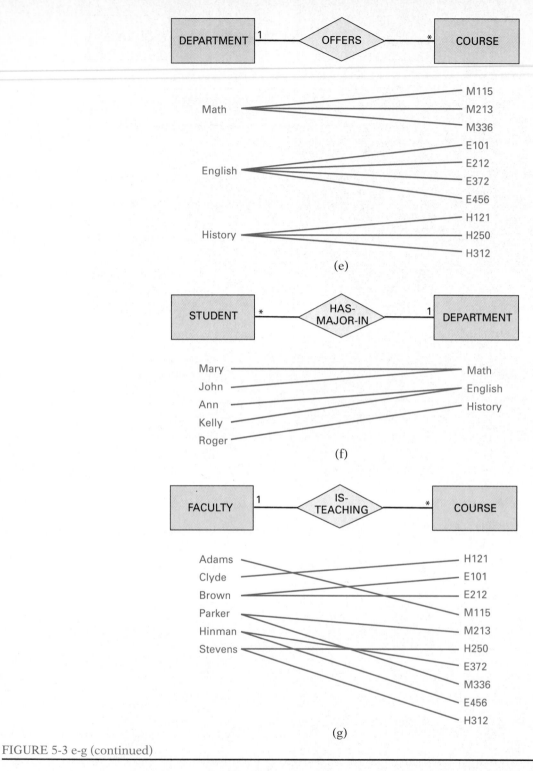

(e)

(f)

(g)

FIGURE 5-3 e-g (continued)

Figure 5.4 may help you understand the separation of object instance from attribute value. Figure 5.4(a) shows a typical representation of the STUDENT object set and the NAME attribute, while Figure 5.4(b) shows actual object instances and attribute values. In this case, the STUDENT object set contains five instances, or students, represented by the five

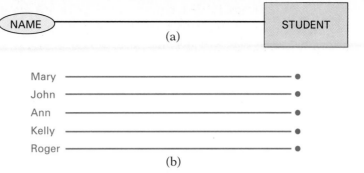

FIGURE 5.4 Distinguishing Between Attributes and Object Instances

points shown below the STUDENT box. We have a value—a specific name—for the NAME attribute for each student. This value is indicated by a line drawn from the attribute value—the name—to the point representing the student. Thus, we have a line from "Mary" to the point that represents the student named "Mary" in the STUDENT object set.

Attributes are important because they identify and help us distinguish between object instances. In fact, a *key* is an attribute or set of attributes that uniquely identifies each object instance. However, for some purposes it is not necessary to use attribute values to distinguish between object instances. Thus, treating an object instance separately from its attribute values will make it easier to do certain types of data manipulation. This will be illustrated as we carry out various queries later in this chapter.

Note that we are using attributes—NAME and COURSE #—to identify object instances in our sample database (Figure 5.3 (a–g)), rather than showing the instances as points that are connected to the attribute values. This is only done to simplify these diagrams.

☐ FORMULATING QUERIES WITH TEXTQUERY

During their interviews with personnel in Administration, Records and Admissions, and elsewhere on campus, Roberta and Juan compiled a long list of questions that these potential database users would like to have answered. The following are a representative sample:

Who are the faculty members earning over $40,000? What are their names and salaries? Which faculty members work for the English department? What are the names of faculty from whom Kelly is taking classes? Which students have taken every course offered by the math department? Which students have taken every course offered by their major department? Which students are repeating classes? Which students have taken or are taking a history course?

The answers to these questions should be contained in the object and relationship sets of our database. If we can use a computer to access that database, we can answer these questions. The key is to formulate these queries in a language, such as TextQuery, that could be translated into operations the computer can execute, allowing the computer to identify and access the appropriate data.

The Basic Format of Query Solutions in TextQuery

We begin our description of **TextQuery** with an example.

User Query: What are the names and salaries of faculty members earning over $40,000?

From Figure 5.1, we can see that the data needed to answer this query is contained in the FACULTY object set and its attributes. We formulate the TextQuery solution to this query as follows:

```
{(name, salary) : name IS-NAME-OF faculty AND
                  salary IS-SALARY-OF faculty AND
                  salary > 40000}
```

TextQuery A query language for object-oriented models with a text-based syntax.

This TextQuery solution defines a set whose definition is given within the braces. The definition should be read as: "The set of pairs of names and salaries such that the name is the name of some faculty member, the salary is the salary of the same faculty member, and the salary is greater than 40,000."

If this TextQuery solution were applied to the database, it would yield a **solution set**—a set of data values from the database, consisting of pairs of names and salaries, that satisfy the conditions that the name and salary in the pair apply to the same faculty member and that the salary is greater than 40,000. Using the data of Figure 5.2, the solution set for this query is a set consisting of two pairs:

solution set A set of data values from the database that satisfy the conditions of a query.

```
{(Hinman, 42000), (Stephens, 45000)}.
```

Let's now take the TextQuery solution apart and examine its pieces.

variable A symbolic name that represents an unspecified instance in an object set.

Terms. □   In the TextQuery solution, the words *name, salary,* and *faculty* represent instances of the object sets NAME, SALARY, and FACULTY, respectively. That is, these words are **variables** that can take on any of the values in these three sets. IS-NAME-OF and IS-SALARY-OF are relationship names corresponding to the NAME and SALARY attributes that relate the faculty member to his or her name and salary. Thus, if the variable *faculty* represents the faculty member whose name is Brown, then

```
name = 'Brown', and
salary = 38000.
```

target list A parenthesized list of variables representing the desired format of a typical member of a query's solution set.

Set Definition Parts. □   The colon (:) separates the two main parts of the set definition—the target list and the qualification expression (Codd, 1971a). The **target list,** a parenthesized list of variables, gives the desired format of a typical member of the solution set—in this case, a pair of el-

qualification expression A
true-false condition that refers
to the target list; must hold for
the elements in the solution set.

ements consisting of a name and a salary. The **qualification expression**
gives a condition that refers to the target list and must hold true for the
elements in the solution set.

The target list in our example is

```
(name, salary)
```

and the qualification expression consists of three subexpressions:

```
name IS-NAME-OF faculty
salary IS-SALARY-OF faculty
   salary > 40000
```

which are connected by logical ANDs.

By applying the TextQuery solution to the database, the solution set
is generated. This is done by allowing the target list to assume, in turn,
all possible combinations of values of name and salary. For each combination, the qualification expression is evaluated. If the expression is true,
then the name-salary pair is placed in the solution set. If not, then the
name-salary combination is discarded, and the next name-salary combination is examined.

For example, suppose

```
name = 'Adams'
salary = 42,000.
```

Then the qualification expression will be true only if some instance of
FACULTY exists whose name is Adams, whose salary is 42,000, and whose
salary is greater than 40,000. In this case, the salary is greater than 40,000,
but the qualification expression as a whole is false, because there is no
faculty member named Adams who has a salary of 42,000. (Look again at
Figure 5.2.) Therefore, the (Adams, 42000) combination is not placed in
the solution set.

Let's try this combination:

```
name = 'Adams'
salary = 38,000.
```

There *is* a faculty member named Adams having a salary of 38,000, so the
first two subexpressions of the qualification expression are true. But the
last subexpression is false, since the salary is *not* greater than 40,000.
Therefore, the qualification expression is not true for the (Adams, 38000)
combination, and this combination is not placed in the solution set, either.

It is easy to see that (Hinman, 42000) and (Stephens, 45000) are the
only two combinations that do satisfy the qualification expression. Thus,
these two pairs constitute the complete solution set for this query.

This query and its solution illustrate several rules of the TextQuery
language. Before we go on, let's look at these rules and consider some enhancements that can be used in this and other queries.

1. Variables in TextQuery that represent instances of object sets are written in lower-case. The lower-case name of an object set is considered a variable representing an instance of that object set.

2. Variables representing instances of an object set may also be defined by stating that the variable is IN the object set, as shown by the following examples:

```
f IN FACULTY
faculty2 IN FACULTY
faculty' IN FACULTY
```

These statements define *f*, *faculty2*, and *faculty'* as variables, each representing an instance in the object set **FACULTY**.

3. Attribute names of an object set can be transformed to relationship names by adding the prefix "IS-" and the suffix "-OF" to the attribute name. Thus,

```
IS-NAME-OF and IS-SALARY-OF
```

are relationship names created from the **NAME** and **SALARY** attributes, respectively.

4. A TextQuery solution is always a set definition, consisting of an expression—the target list—representing a typical element of the solution set, followed by a colon, followed by a condition—the qualification expression—that qualifies precisely the elements to be included in the solution set. The definition is enclosed in braces—{ }—to indicate that we are defining a *set*—in particular, the set of all elements whose format is the target list and that satisfy the condition stated in the qualification expression.

5. Within a set definition, a variable retains its meaning from one occurrence to the next. Thus, in our example, *salary* is defined in the target list and occurs in the qualification expression. *It means the same thing every time it occurs.* If, during the computation of the solution set for the query, *salary* assumes the value 38,000 in the target list, then it has that same value each time it appears in the qualification expression.

existentially quantified The assertion that, for a given variable, a value exists in the object set.

6. If a variable does not appear in the target list but appears in the qualification expression, we say that that variable is ***existentially quantified.*** This means that some value *exists* in the object set for that variable. For example, in the expression

```
salary IS-SALARY-OF faculty
```

faculty is existentially quantified. The expression can be interpreted as: "There exists some faculty member such that *salary* is the salary of that faculty member."

Defining Relationship Directions

Our first example was a relatively simple one that involved just one object set and its attributes. The solution to other queries, however, will involve object sets that are linked by a series of relationships. Thus, we need to take a closer look at these relationships and what they mean intuitively. As we do so, we will develop the means of solving more complex queries. In this section, we will explore this concept further. We will be more precise in the next section where we will apply these ideas to formulating queries in TextQuery.

When we defined objects and relationships in the previous chapter, we compared objects to nouns and relationships to verbs. This suggests that a text language such as TextQuery resembles a natural language to some extent. You can see this if you look at Figure 5.1. The names of each of the relationships suggests a direction for reading the relationship. Thus, we would say

```
faculty ADVISES student
```

and not, as a matter of course,

```
student ADVISES faculty.
```

The relationship name suggests the relationship is to be read from FACULTY to STUDENT. Similarly, we have

```
faculty WORKS-FOR department
faculty IS-TEACHING course
student HAS-MAJOR-IN department
student HAS-TAKEN course
student IS-TAKING course
department OFFERS course
```

and none of these would make sense if the order were reversed. Each of these is an English-language sentence in the format

```
SUBJECT VERB OBJECT
```

that is in the active voice.

Now by changing the name of the relationship and using the passive voice, we can reverse the implied direction of most of these sentences. Thus, we have

```
student IS-ADVISED-BY faculty
course IS-TAUGHT-BY faculty
course HAS-BEEN-TAKEN-BY student
course IS-BEING-TAKEN-BY student
course IS-OFFERED-BY department
```

as sentences showing the *reverse* direction for reading these relationships. We can obtain the reverse direction of the other two relationships by appropriate renaming as follows:

```
department EMPLOYS faculty
(EMPLOYS reverses WORKS-FOR)

department HAS-MAJORING-STUDENT student
(HAS-MAJORING-STUDENT reverses HAS-MAJOR-IN)
```

The last relationship name (HAS-MAJORING-STUDENT) shows that we can always find some name that will reverse the direction of a relationship, even though the new name may be awkward and inconvenient.

Thus, the name chosen for a relationship suggests an intuitive **direction** that will allow the relationship to be stated as an English sentence in SUBJECT-VERB-OBJECT format. We can also create a substitute name for each relationship that makes it possible to read that relationship in the opposite direction. We can diagram this idea by updating Figure 5.1 to show the direction of relationship names. The arrow preceding or following each relationship name in Figure 5.5 indicates its direction.

The direction of relationship names is important for solving queries requiring navigation through a series of object sets and relationships. Depending on the needs of the query, we will sometimes navigate a relationship in one direction and other times navigate the same relationship in the opposite direction. Thus, the ability to go in either direction is very important. Since nearly every query will require this kind of navigation, we are establishing here the general framework for query solution.

We need to do the same thing for attributes as we have done for relationships. Recall that we can interpret attributes as relationships. As we saw earlier, we can create verb phrase names for them by embedding the attribute name between IS and OF. We can reverse the direction of attribute relationship names by prefixing the attribute name with HAS:

```
faculty HAS-NAME name
faculty HAS-SALARY salary
faculty HAS-OFFICE office
```

direction of relationship The implied SUBJECT-VERB-OBJECT order for reading the names of a relationship and its object sets.

FIGURE 5.5   A Portion of the Lerner College Data Model Showing Relationship Directions

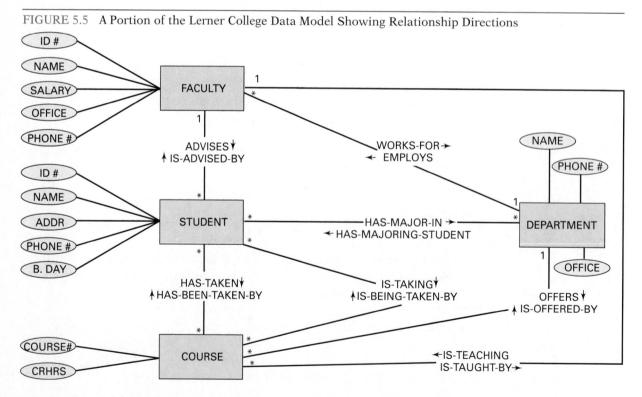

Finally, we need to derive names for specialization relationships. Suppose we have a set named MATH-COURSE that consists of all the courses offered by the math department. Then MATH-COURSE is a subset of COURSE. We name this specialization relationship IS-A, and this name holds in both directions. That is,

```
math-course IS-A course   and
course IS-A math-course
```

can both be true. The first is true for all instances of MATH-COURSE, while the second is true for only some of the instances of COURSE.

Navigating over Attributes and Relationships

In the previous section, we saw that the names we use for objects, attributes, and relationships can be tailored to more readily allow their interpretation as English-language sentences. In this section, we will show how this idea will let us solve more complex queries in the TextQuery language.

> **User Query:** What are the names of faculty members earning $38,000?

This query, just as the earlier query, requires data found only in the FACULTY object set and two of its attributes. In this case, however, salary only figures in the qualification expression, not the target list. The solution to this query illustrates the principle of navigating through relationships and object sets:

```
{name : name IS-NAME-OF faculty WHO HAS-SALARY 38000}
```

This solution may be read "the set of all names such that each name is the name of a faculty member who has a salary of 38000." It is equivalent to

```
{name : name IS-NAME-OF faculty AND
        faculty HAS-SALARY 38000}
```

Let's analyze the first solution by starting at the back and working our way forward:

```
faculty WHO HAS-SALARY 38000
```

FIGURE 5.6 Instances of FACULTY Earning $38,000

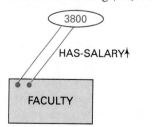

This is a statement about a faculty member that can be evaluated as true or false. It is true only for those in FACULTY who have a SALARY attribute of 38000. These faculty members constitute a subset of FACULTY (Figure 5.6). We see that there are two faculty members earning $38,000.

To explain the remainder of the query solution, we rewrite the qualification expression with parentheses:

```
name IS-NAME-OF (faculty WHO HAS-SALARY 38000)
```

This statement is true for a set of names—{Adams, Brown}. The names

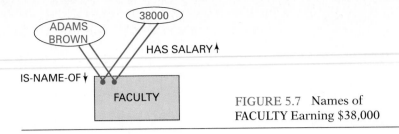

FIGURE 5.7 Names of
FACULTY Earning $38,000

in the set will be those that map under the IS-NAME-OF relationship to FACULTY instances who earn $38,000—the definition in the latter half of the query. This is shown in Figure 5.7.

Note how closely the format of the TextQuery solution matches the format of the original query, down to the position of the qualification expression, a salary of $38,000.

User Query: What are the names of faculty members earning $38,000?

TextQuery Solution: name IS-NAME-OF faculty WHO HAS-SALARY 38000

Because they follow the format of the natural language queries, such solutions are said to be in the **interrogative format.** In using a data model to visualize this solution, however, we work *backwards*. You can see this in Figure 5.8. We start at the SALARY attribute and find 38000. Then we draw back to FACULTY to find those FACULTY instances who "HAS-SALARY" of 38000. Then we draw back one more step, using IS-NAME-OF, to NAME. If we put together our TextQuery solution after this visualization, we must retrace our steps going from NAME through IS-NAME-OF to FACULTY and then through HAS-SALARY to SALARY of 38000. This backtracking suggests there may be an alternate format

FIGURE 5.8 A Visual Solution to the User Query, "What are the Names of Faculty Members Earning $38,000?"

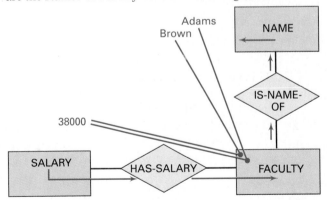

that more closely echoes the solution we visualized on the diagram. We can formulate a solution in this alternate format as follows:

```
{name : 38000 IS-SALARY-OF faculty WHO HAS-NAME name}
```

We see that the order of the qualification expression here is opposite to that of the interrogative format. Because this second format is more like a declarative sentence, it is called the **declarative format.** Either of these formats is permissible. Therefore, in developing TextQuery solutions to user queries you are encouraged to used whichever format you find more natural.

In both cases, we have simplified the target list to just a variable name, while the qualification expression we have developed traverses the object sets and their attributes via the relationships that link them. Relative pronouns such as WHO and WHICH are used in these expressions to increase their readability. They are **noise words** in the sense that they are present in the expression but have no effect on its meaning.

Let us now look at two more examples that provide further illustration of the concept of navigating over relationships.

User Query: Which faculty members work for the English department?

TextQuery Solution:
```
{faculty : faculty WORKS-FOR department
                      WHICH HAS-NAME 'English'}
```

Although this solution answers the query, it is inadequate because the set of faculty members created cannot be displayed on an output device. If we want to produce a human-readable solution, we must create a set of attribute values that is human-readable. Therefore, we revise the solution to:

```
{name : name IS-NAME-OF faculty WHO WORKS-FOR department
                      WHICH HAS-NAME 'English'}
```

In declarative format, the solution is:

```
{name : 'English' IS-NAME-OF department WHICH EMPLOYS faculty
                      WHO HAS-NAME name}
```

The solution set for this query is shown in Figure 5.9.

User Query: What are the names of faculty from whom Kelly is taking classes?

TextQuery Solution:
```
    Interrogative format
    {name : name IS-NAME-OF faculty WHO IS-TEACHING course
            WHICH IS-BEING-TAKEN-BY student
            WHO HAS-NAME 'Kelly'}
Declarative format
{name : 'Kelly' IS-NAME-OF student WHO IS-TAKING course
        WHICH IS-BEING-TAUGHT-BY faculty
        WHO HAS-NAME name}
```

declarative format A qualification expression format that takes the form of a declarative sentence.

noise words Words used in a qualification expression that increase readability but do not affect its meaning.

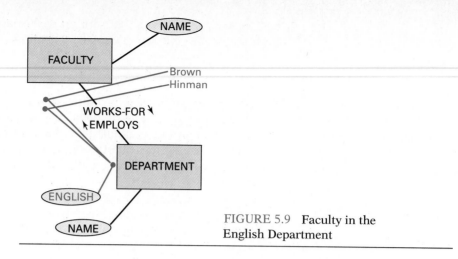

FIGURE 5.9   Faculty in the
English Department

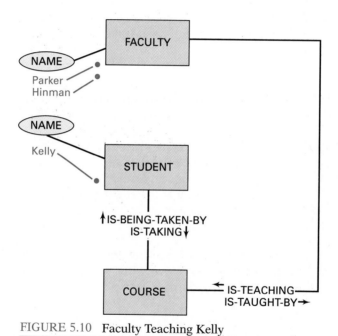

FIGURE 5.10   Faculty Teaching Kelly

The solution set is shown in Figure 5.10.

Figure 5.10 does *not* show the instances for the courses Kelly is taking, but from the previous examples it should be easy to visualize what is happening here. The name "Kelly" is connected to the student instance having that name. This student instance is in turn connected to the set of courses Kelly is taking. Each of these courses is connected to the faculty member teaching the course, and the faculty member is connected to his or her name.

Incidentally, this query provides an example of using an abstract object set (COURSE) without using any of its attributes. The solution to the query did not have to identify, for example, the precise course numbers of the courses Kelly is taking in order to identify which faculty members Kelly is taking courses from. It sufficed to use course instances in their abstract (attribute-less) form.

Assigning Names to Derived Sets

The solution sets resulting from the queries already illustrated were derived through the use of TextQuery. Often such sets are useful in their own right. We may, for example, find it convenient or faster to use these derived sets in other TextQuery queries without having to derive them again. We can do this if we simply assign a name to the derived set by which we can refer to it later. For example, if we want to identify the set of all math courses, we can assign the name MATH-COURSE to the appropriate set as follows:

```
MATH-COURSE := {course : course IS-OFFERED-BY department
                         WHICH HAS-NAME 'Math'}
```

This example illustrates that names are assigned by stating the set's name, followed by the ":=" notation, and then the TextQuery definition of the set. The ":=" notation can be read "is the name assigned to."

*Set Comparison Qualification Expressions**

set comparison expression A qualification expression that involves comparing two sets to see if one set is contained in the other.

Some queries can be solved best by using qualification expressions that involve **set comparison.** Consider the query:

```
User Query: Which students have taken every course offered by
the math department?
```

We solve this query by generating the set of courses offered by the math department and then, for each student, comparing that set with the set of courses that the student has taken. If the set of all math courses *is contained in* the set of the student's courses, then the student has taken all the math courses and the student's name is placed in the query's solution set. Our TextQuery solution is in three steps and utilizes the facility of assigning names to derived sets:

```
TextQuery Solution:
MATH-COURSE := {course : course IS-OFFERED-BY department
                         WHICH HAS-NAME 'Math'}
STUDENT-ALL-MATH :=
{student : MATH-COURSE IS-CONTAINED-IN
           SET-OF (course WHICH HAS-BEEN-TAKEN-BY student)}
NAME-STUDENT-ALL-MATH := {name : name IS-NAME-OF student
                                 AND student IN STUDENT-ALL-
                                 MATH}
```

These three steps may be explained as follows:

1. The first step defines MATH-COURSE, the set of all math courses, and

---

*This section may be omitted without loss of continuity.

is identical to the definition of MATH-COURSE given in the previous section.

2. The second step defines STUDENT-ALL-MATH, the set of students who have taken every math course, and includes some unfamiliar notation that we now explain.

Recall that for each student, we wish to compare the set of math courses—MATH-COURSE—with the set of courses taken by that student. We defined the set of math courses in step 1. How do we define the set of courses taken by each particular student? This is done with the construct:

```
SET-OF (course WHICH HAS-BEEN-TAKEN-BY student)
```

This SET-OF construct is used to generate the set of courses that have been taken by the particular student being evaluated by the query. For example, if the student is Ann, then this construct is equivalent to:

```
{course : course HAS-BEEN-TAKEN-BY 'Ann'}
```

dynamically generated set A set whose value varies depending on the particular value of a variable from the target list.

This is an example of a **dynamically generated set.** That is, a different set is generated for each value of the variable *student*. As the query is executed, the SET-OF construct will generate a set for Mary, a set for John, a set for Ann, a set for Kelly, and a set for Roger.

In step 2, the system evaluates each student in STUDENT by comparing the MATH-COURSE set with the set of courses taken by the student, using the IS-CONTAINED-IN comparison operator. If the entire set of math courses is contained in the student's set of courses, then the qualification expression using the IS-CONTAINED-IN operator evaluates to "true." In that case, the student is selected for inclusion in the set STUDENT-ALL-MATH.

3. NAME-STUDENT-ALL-MATH gives us the names of the students who have taken every math course. We could have avoided this step by expanding the qualification expression of step 2 to include this step's qualification expression, but that would have made step 2 more complicated and difficult to comprehend. We broke out step 1 as a separate step for the same reason. Thus, we see that the facility of assigning names to derived sets makes it possible to break query solutions down into a series of steps. This makes the process simpler and easier to grasp.

Applying this query to our sample database and using the information in Figures 5.3(c) and 5.3(e), we see that Roger is the only student who has taken all the math courses. Thus, the answer to the query is {Roger}.

The converse of the IS-CONTAINED-IN operator is the CONTAINS operator. If we had used it in the preceding example, step 2 of our solution would have been:

```
STUDENT-ALL-MATH :=
{student : SET-OF (course WHICH HAS-BEEN-TAKEN-BY student)
          CONTAINS MATH-COURSE}
```

Let's look at another example.

User Query: Which students have taken every course offered by their major department?

In the previous problem, we compared every student's set of courses taken with a single, fixed set (MATH-COURSE). In this problem we must compare each student's courses with a set of courses that varies with each student, since the major department varies from one student to the next.

```
TextQuery Solution:
STUDENT-ALL-COURSE :=
{student : SET-OF (course WHICH HAS-BEEN-TAKEN-BY student)
           CONTAINS SET-OF (course WHICH IS-OFFERED-BY
           department WHICH HAS-MAJORING-STUDENT student)}
```

This example shows that we can compare two dynamically generated sets. Of course, this only gives us the students, not their names. We obtain the set of names in the same way we did in the previous query.

Boolean Connectives

Boolean connective Any of the logical connectives AND, OR, NOT.

Our first TextQuery example used the **Boolean** (or logical) **connective** AND in the qualification expression. The qualification expressions for the other queries we have considered are *atomic* in the sense that they are made up of simple expressions not connected by AND, OR, or NOT. As with most computer languages, TextQuery lets us combine atomic qualification expressions by using the Boolean connectives. Further, we can use parentheses to group expressions and thus eliminate ambiguities. These features give TextQuery increased power.

```
User Query: Which students are repeating classes?
TextQuery Solution:
REPEATING-STUDENT := {student : student IS-TAKING course AND
                               student HAS-TAKEN course}
```

Recall that the variable *course* in this qualification expression has the same value throughout the expression. That is, the meaning of *course* in

```
student IS-TAKING course
```

is the same as it is in

```
student HAS-TAKEN course.
```

The Boolean connective AND, which is being used here to join two atomic expressions, means that the qualification expression as a whole is true for a given student and course only if *both*

```
student IS-TAKING course
```

and

```
student HAS-TAKEN course
```

are true.

As before, another step is needed to obtain the students' names. To keep our presentation simple, we omit this step throughout this section.

```
User Query: Which students have taken or are taking a history
course?
{student : student HAS-TAKEN course WHICH IS-OFFERED-BY
            department WHICH HAS-NAME 'History' OR
            student IS-TAKING course WHICH IS-OFFERED-BY
            department WHICH HAS-NAME 'History'}
```

A second, simpler version creates the history subset of COURSE and uses the IN operator.

```
HISTORY-COURSE := {course : course IS-OFFERED-BY department
                            WHICH HAS-NAME 'History'}
STUDENT-HAS-TAKEN-HISTORY := {student : (student HAS-TAKEN
                                         course AND
                                         course IN HISTORY-
                                           COURSE) OR
                                         (student IS-TAKING
                                         course AND
                                         course IN HISTORY-
                                           COURSE)}
```

Here the Boolean OR is interpreted to make the qualification expression true when either the first half or the second half (or both halves) of the qualification expression is true. We also used AND in each half and grouped the halves with parentheses to prevent potential ambiguities.

```
User Query: Which students majoring in math have not yet taken
a math course?
MATH-COURSE := {course : course IS-OFFERED-BY department
                         WHICH HAS-NAME 'Math'}
STUDENT-HAS-TAKEN-MATH :=
  {student : (student HAS-TAKEN course AND
             course IN MATH-COURSE) OR
             (student IS-TAKING course AND
             course IN MATH-COURSE)}
NEW-MATH-STUDENT :=
  {student : student HAS-MAJOR-IN department WHICH
             HAS-NAME 'Math'
             AND student NOT IN STUDENT-HAS-TAKEN-MATH}
```

The last line of the qualification expression could have been written:

```
AND NOT student IN STUDENT-HAS-TAKEN-MATH
```

That is, the NOT can be embedded in the atomic part of the expression to negate the effect of IN, or it can be part of the Boolean connective AND, to negate the entire atomic expression. NOT can also be applied to the other comparison operators (CONTAINS, IS-CONTAINED-IN, <, >, =).

TextQuery provides a simple, elegant, and natural means of extracting data from an object-oriented database. It is similar to many traditional programming languages in that it uses a textual representation of data, variables, and statements. It also has a nice connection with natural language, since the object sets and relationships on which it operates are themselves modeled as nouns and verbs. However, it does not have the ease of use that a more visual approach, based on the object-oriented model itself, might provide. Such an approach can be found in graphical query languages, such as GraphQuery, which we study next.

☐ FORMULATING QUERIES WITH GRAPHQUERY

GraphQuery A query language for object-oriented models that uses direct interaction with the model.

GraphQuery, our graphical query language, makes direct use of the object-oriented model in developing query solutions. The basic idea of any graphical query language is that the user can form query solutions graphically or visually. That is, by drawing appropriate diagrams, users can develop the solution to a query. *The diagram itself will be the solution.* As an example consider the simple query:

User Query: What are the names and salaries of faculty members earning over $40,000?

The information needed to solve this query is in the FACULTY object set and its NAME and SALARY attributes. The portion of Figure 5.1 containing these is shown in Figure 5.11. This diagram represents the set of all faculty members and their respective names and salaries. To illustrate more clearly what is happening, we have shown specific data values from the database of Figure 5.2. Now to solve this query, we must restrict FACULTY so that it contains only those members earning over $40,000. This is shown in Figure 5.12. The condition at the bottom of the figure

```
SALARY(faculty) > 40000
```

is part of the diagram. It states a condition that applies to each instance

FIGURE 5.11   The FACULTY Object Set and Its Name and Salary Attributes

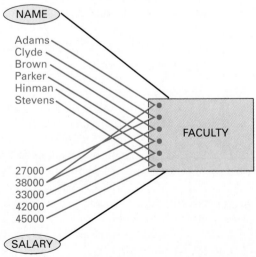

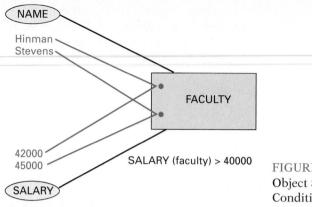

FIGURE 5.12   The FACULTY Object Set Restricted by a Condition

of FACULTY. We represent this by using the lowercase variable, *faculty,* to represent a typical member of FACULTY. The condition may be read as: "Salary of faculty is greater than 40000"—meaning that the salary of each instance of the FACULTY object set must exceed $40,000. If the salary of the faculty member does not meet this condition, then the faculty member is not part of the FACULTY object set *in this diagram.* This is shown by the fact that only those instances of FACULTY satisfying the condition are shown in Figure 5.12.

The query calls for the names and salaries to be listed. We indicate this by highlighting the desired attributes (Figure 5.13). Figure 5.13 is the GraphQuery solution to the user query. The highlighted attributes correspond to the target list used in TextQuery. Note that the GraphQuery solution does not involve the showing of instances. We included them in Figures 5.11 and 5.12 only to clarify what is happening during each step of the query. A display of the data resulting from the solution of Figure 5.13 is shown in Figure 5.14.

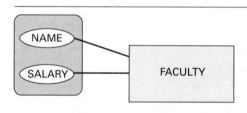

FIGURE 5.13   Solving a Query Graphically by Highlighting the Appropriate Attributes

SALARY (faculty) > 40000

NAME	SALARY
Hinman	42000
Stevens	45000

FIGURE 5.14   The Names and Salaries of Faculty Members Earning Over $40,000

In an actual computer system implementation of GraphQuery, the
user formulating the query solution would probably be given a copy of
the complete object-oriented data model from Figure 5.1 on the monitor.
Then using the keyboard and a mouse, the user would eliminate irrelevant object sets, relationships, and attributes; would add any desired conditions applying to the diagram; and would use the mouse to highlight
the lexical attributes. These **highlighted attributes** contain the data requested in the query. The process itself would be interactive. The system
would likely provide a command menu, and the user would have access
to it via the mouse, the function keys, or other keys on the keyboard. Upon
the completion of the query solution, the system would calculate the result of the query and display the answer (the solution set) on the screen.
The answer could also be formulated into a report for printing.

To develop solutions to other, more complex queries, we must resolve an ambiguity in our diagrams. To illustrate the problem, we consider the following query:

> **User Query:** Which faculty members work for the English depart-
> ment?

Figure 5.3(b) shows the relationship between faculty members and the
departments they work for. If we restrict the DEPARTMENT object set
so that any instance in DEPARTMENT must have the name "English," we
obtain Figure 5.15. Note that FACULTY still contains the same elements,
but DEPARTMENT now only contains one element. Thus, we have lost
some of the links the WORKS-FOR relationship maintains between the
two object sets. Now if we highlight NAME of FACULTY, do we obtain
the names of faculty members in the English department or the names of
all faculty members? The problem is that FACULTY is being used in two
ways:

1. As a container for elements representing all the faculty members
2. As a participant in the WORKS-FOR relationship.

We can resolve this ambiguity by adopting a new interpretation for our

FIGURE 5.15   Ambiguity in Data Model Diagrams

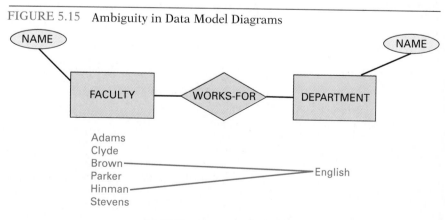

NAME(department) = 'ENGLISH'

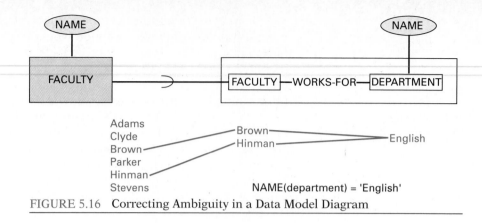

Adams
Clyde
Brown
Parker
Hinman
Stevens

Brown
Hinman

English

NAME(department) = 'English'

FIGURE 5.16   Correcting Ambiguity in a Data Model Diagram

diagrams—for use only in GraphQuery. Figure 5.16 illustrates the convention we will adopt. FACULTY within the larger box participates in the WORKS-FOR relationship and contains *only* those faculty members who actually participate in the relationship. FACULTY outside the large box contains all faculty members and consequently is a superset of FACULTY within the larger box—as indicated by the U-shaped set containment symbol shown on the line connecting the two FACULTY boxes. Our convention then is that an object box contained within a larger box—which in turn contains a relationship—denotes only those instances participating in the relationship. Figure 5.17 gives the solution to the query. Since FACULTY in the large box is a subset of FACULTY outside the box, according to the inheritance principle, both representations of FACULTY have the same attributes. Thus, we show the NAME attribute attached to FACULTY within the large box in Figure 5.17. To solve the query, we merely highlight this attribute.

> **User Query:** Which faculty members are either advising a student or teaching a course (or both)?

set-theoretic union A set made up of elements from one or the other or both of two other sets.

Figure 5.18 gives the solution. We have introduced some new notation here. The **set-theoretic union** sign ($\cup$) in the circle connecting the two FACULTY boxes to FACULTY' indicates that the box to which the arrow is pointing is the union of the other two. This means that the instances in

FIGURE 5.17   Solving a Query Graphically by Highlighting the Appropriate Attribute

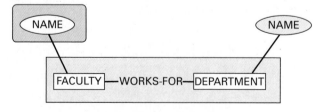

NAME(department) = 'ENGLISH'

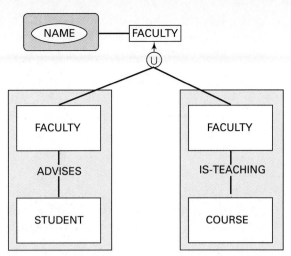

FIGURE 5.18   A Graphic Solution Using the Set-Theoretic Union Sign

FACULTY' are in one or the other (or both) of the two FACULTY boxes. It is easy to see that this is what the query requires. We use one or more primes (') after the object name to indicate that it is a subset of or another copy of the object set of the same name.

User Query: Which faculty members are neither advising a student nor teaching a course?

Figure 5.19 gives the solution to this query. In this case, we have merely added to Figure 5.18. The FACULTY box at the top of the diagram is the **disjoint union** of FACULTY' and FACULTY". This is indicated by the cir-

disjoint union A set made up of elements that are in one or the other of two other sets, but not in *both*

FIGURE 5.19   A Graphic Solution Using a Disjoint Union

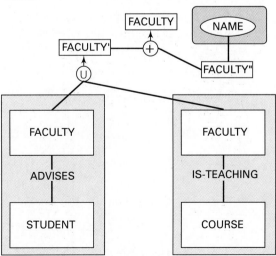

cled + sign that is connected to FACULTY' and FACULTY". This means that the elements of FACULTY are either in FACULTY´ or in FACULTY"´, but none of them is in both. Thus, FACULTY" must contain precisely those faculty members who are not in FACULTY'—that is, those who are neither advising a student nor teaching a course, as required by the query.

We complete our discussion of GraphQuery by looking at some of the other queries we used to illustrate the TextQuery language.

User Query: What are the names of faculty from whom Kelly is taking classes?

The GraphQuery solution is given in Figure 5.20. Note that we are not concerned in these diagrams about the order in which relationships are to be read. Thus, in Figure 5.20, we might read

COURSE IS-TAKING STUDENT

if we read the relationship from the top down. But we don't. This is because the language is *graphical* and not *textual*. This picture is the solution, and the relationships in the picture can be read in any order we choose. The important thing is that the relationship itself is valid in the context of the data model we are using.

Notice that COURSE is in two different relationships. This means that the instances in COURSE must participate in *both* relationships. That is, any instance in COURSE must be currently in the process of being taken by Kelly and must be being taught by a faculty member—certainly not a stringent requirement in this case.

User Query: Which students have taken every course offered by the math department?

See Figure 5.21. This solution contains two diagrams with a condition for each diagram. The first diagram, with its condition, identifies all the courses offered by the math department. These courses are those contained in the object set COURSE.

FIGURE 5.20   Names of Faculty Teaching Kelly

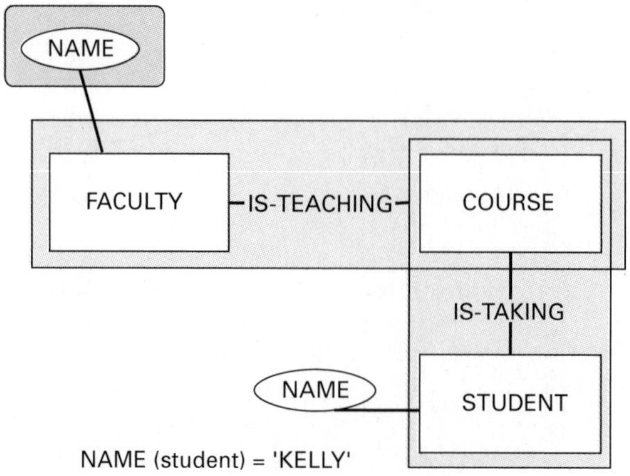

NAME (student) = 'KELLY'

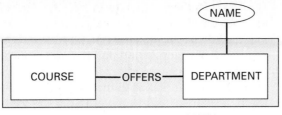

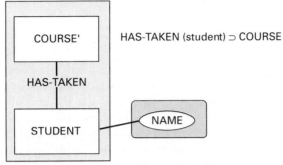

FIGURE 5.21   Students Who Have Taken Every Math Course

The second diagram shows the relationship HAS-TAKEN between STUDENT and a second copy of the original COURSE object set, identified as COURSE´. Since COURSE´ is not subject to the same condition as COURSE in the first diagram, COURSE´ contains *all* courses offered by all departments. The condition

```
HAS-TAKEN(student) ⊃ COURSE
```

requires some explanation.

The HAS-TAKEN relationship relates students to courses. Thus, both STUDENT and COURSE' participate in this relationship. Now suppose we wish to identify all the courses taken by a particular student. We fix the student and look at all those courses related to the student by the HAS-TAKEN relationship. We do this with our notation by writing HAS-TAKEN(student), meaning the set of all courses taken by the student represented by the variable *student*. We could also identify the set of all students who have taken a given course by writing HAS-TAKEN(course').

The statement

```
HAS-TAKEN(student) ⊃ COURSE
```

is a condition placed on the STUDENT object set. It states that a student is in that object set if and only if the set of courses the student has taken contains (⊃) COURSE, which in this diagram is the set of all courses offered by the math department. Since this is precisely the condition of the query, STUDENT contains the solution to the query. We highlight the attribute NAME to produce a list of students who meet this condition.

GraphQuery is a data manipulation language based on the concept of direct interaction with object-oriented models. It can therefore be classified as a "visual" language, one of a group of computer languages that have been developed and have become increasingly popular over the past twenty years. These languages have shown a great deal of potential both as user query and as system development languages and will probably be the object of substantially more development in the future. GraphQuery gives a concrete example of how the visual language concept can be applied to object-oriented databases.

■ SUMMARY

In this chapter, we have examined two query languages designed for object-oriented models—TextQuery and GraphQuery. TextQuery uses a text-based syntax, typical of the traditional approach to computer languages. GraphQuery is based on the concept of solving queries through the direct manipulation of object-oriented diagrams. Both query languages are capable of solving simple and complex queries.

TextQuery produces set definitions as query solutions. If the set definition were to be applied to a particular object-oriented database, a solution set consisting of values satisfying the query will result. Each set definition consists of (1) a target list of variables which together represent a typical element in the solution set, and (2) a qualification expression which defines a condition the solution set elements must satisfy. The variables used in the target list and qualification expression are written in lower-case and represent elements in object sets of the object-oriented model.

GraphQuery uses the object-oriented model itself for query solution formulation. The solution of any given query involves discarding irrelevant object sets, attributes, and relationships; specifiying conditions applying to the remaining object sets and relationships; and highlighting the attributes which contain the information requested. Highlighting attributes in a GraphQuery solution is equivalent to specifying the target list in TextQuery.

■ REVIEW QUESTIONS

1. Define each of the following terms in your own words:
   a. target list
   b. qualification expression
   c. existentially quantified
   d. direction of relationship
   e. dynamically generated set
   f. interrogative format
   g. set-theoretic union
   h. data manipulation language (DML)

2. Identify and describe five components of a TextQuery solution to a user query.

3. How does the interpretation of a GraphQuery solution differ from the interpretation of an object-oriented model?

4. Compare and contrast TextQuery and GraphQuery. Discuss what you feel are the advantages and drawbacks of each language. Which language do you prefer for simple queries? For more difficult queries?

■ PROBLEMS AND EXERCISES

1. Match each term with its definition:

___Solution set
    a. Qualification expression that takes the form of a declarative sentence

___Variable
    b. Query language with a text-based syntax

___Highlighted attributes
    c. A logical connective

___Disjoint union
    d. Indicate the data requested in the user query

___Declarative format
    e. Qualification expression that involves a containment comparison

___Noise words
    f. Symbolic name that represents an unspecified instance in an object set

___Set comparison expression
    g. Query language that uses direct interaction with the model

___TextQuery
    h. Made up of elements that are in one or the other of two other sets, but not in *both*

___Boolean connective
    i. Used in a qualification expression to increase readability

___GraphQuery
    j. Set of data values satisfying the conditions of a query

Using the model of Figure 5.1E, create solutions to each of the following user queries in TextQuery and in GraphQuery.

2. A list of shipment numbers for shipments weighing over 20 pounds.

3. Names of companies with more than $10 million in annual revenue.

4. The population of Atlanta.

FIGURE 5.1E Data Model for Keepon Trucking

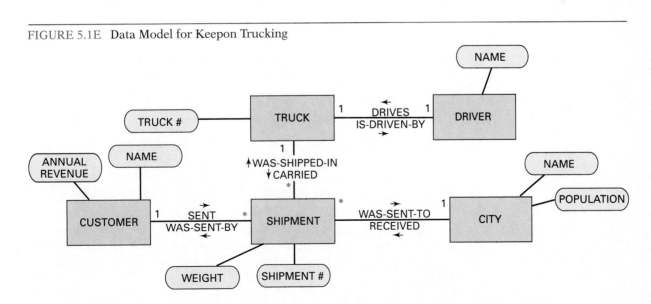

5. The driver of Truck #45.

6. The name and population of cities which have received shipments weighing over 100 pounds.

7. The name and annual revenue of customers who have sent shipments weighing over 100 pounds.

8. The truck numbers of trucks which have carried shipments weighing over 100 pounds.

9. The names of drivers who have delivered shipments weighing over 100 pounds.

10. Cities which have received shipments from customers having over $15 million in annual revenue.

11. Customers having over $5 million in annual revenue who have sent shipments weighing less than 1 pound.

12. Customers having over $5 million in annual revenue who either have sent shipments weighing less than 1 pound or have sent a shipment to San Francisco.

13. Customers who have had shipments delivered by truck driver Jensen.

14. Drivers who have delivered shipments for customers with annual revenue over $20 million to cities with population over 1 million.

15. Customers who have had shipments delivered by every driver. (Hint: For the TextQuery solutions to exercises 15–18, use the SET-OF construct with set comparison.)

16. Cities which have received shipments from every customer.

17. Drivers who have delivered shipments to every city.

18. Customers who have sent shipments to every city with population over 500,000. (Hint: First create the set of cities with population over 500,000.)

Create solutions to the following user queries in TextQuery:

19. Give a list of customers and annual revenue for those customers whose annual revenue is the maximum for the customers in the database.

20. Give a list of customers, all of whose shipments weigh over 25 pounds.

21. Give a list of customers that send all their shipments to a single city. (Note: The city may or may not be the same for each of these customers.)

■ PROJECTS AND PROFESSIONAL ISSUES

1. Write sketches of programs in a language like COBOL, BASIC, or Pascal to solve queries 2, 6, 10, 14, and 18 in the previous section. Of course, you must first represent the object-oriented model of Figure 5.1E as a set of files. Note the varying degrees of complexity of the programs. Which programs are the most complex?

2. Analyze the Stratton Fruit Orchards model of Figure 4.23 (Chapter 4) to determine the types of user queries which could be answered from this model. Develop sample TextQuery and GraphQuery solutions for each of them.

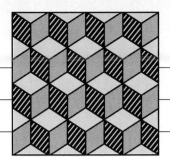

chapter six

ADVANCED OBJECT-ORIENTED MODELING: MAPPING REALITY

Joan Manwaring needs more information than her reports are giving her. She wants to make the best use of personnel, and so she needs to know how many hours each consultant spent on each billable activity during the past year. For example, how many hours had John Rodriguez spent programming and how many hours in systems analysis and design? In the current system, the number of hours is embedded in a nonnumeric field called description from which it cannot be easily extracted. In addition, she wants information relating consultants to the client accounts they worked on. Yes, she concluded, what she really needs is a way of directly relating consultants, activities, and clients and of finding how many billable hours a consultant spent in each activity for each client. Then she could get reports giving billable hours for any one of these factors, for any pair of them, or for all three together. That information would be very helpful.

The object-oriented models we developed in Chapter 4 for Manwaring Consulting Services as well as for other applications reflected the basic modeling ideas introduced in that chapter. In this chapter, we expand these relatively simple techniques to encompass the more complex situations which arise naturally in business. We will focus on aggregate object sets and conceptual object sets, two concepts which occur often in practical situations. We will also introduce the concept of view integration with a simple example. After reading this chapter, you should be able to:

☐ Show how aggregate object sets can be created from existing relationships.

☐ Explain how aggregates function as object sets, which have attributes and participate in relationships.

☐ Demonstrate how information needs that occur frequently in business can be addressed by using aggregates appropriately.

☐ Discuss the difference between conceptual object sets and physical object sets and give examples of when this distinction is important.

☐ Demonstrate a process for combining different database views into a single, unified data model.

By understanding these techniques, you will increase your skill in carrying out the requirements definition and logical design steps of the database development life cycle.

☐ AGGREGATES AND HIGHER-LEVEL RELATIONSHIPS

aggregate A relationship viewed as an object set.

higher-level relationship A relationship between three or more object sets.

The models we created with the object-oriented modeling concepts introduced in Chapter 4 were relatively simple. Yet despite their simplicity, it is easy to see their power and usefulness. However, most problems we actually encounter in business are considerably more complex and often involve the use of an **aggregate**—a relationship viewed as an object set—or a **higher-level relationship,** which involves three or more object sets.

We saw in Chapter 4 that a relationship can be used as an object set. For example, when we initially defined and discussed relationships, we noted that each man and woman who are related by the IS-MARRIED-TO relationship constitute a *married couple,* which is itself an object. As such, the married couple can have its own attributes, such as anniversary date, total earnings, and address. Moreover, it can participate in other relationships, such as OWN-AUTOMOBILE and ARE-PARENTS-OF. Thus, the IS-MARRIED-TO relationship can be viewed as an object set whose elements are married couples.

This is true of any relationship. Relationships can be viewed as objects and can have attributes and participate in other relationships. As we noted, such relationships are called aggregates. Graphically, we will represent an aggregate by drawing a box around the relationship and its participating object sets (Figure 6.1). Sometimes, for convenience, we will give the aggregate an object-like name—a noun—in addition to its relationship name. In Figure 6.1, for example, MARRIED-COUPLE is the object set name given to the IS-MARRIED-TO relationship. This is reasonable if a relationship is to be used as an object set.

binary relationship A relationship between two object sets.

n-ary relationship A relationship between n object sets.

All of the relationships we have considered to this point involve two object sets. Such relationships are called **binary.** However, relationships can also involve three or more object sets. We call such relationships *higher-level,* and we will denote them as ***n*-ary relationships,** where n stands for the number of object sets being related. A 3-ary relationship is called *ternary.* To use more understandable terminology, however, we will often refer to 3-ary or 4-ary relationships as "3-way" or "4-way" relationships.

Let's illustrate these concepts with an example. Suppose Dick Greenberg of International Product Distribution (IPD) wants to track sales of a line of products by country. To help him we create an object set PRODUCT and an object set COUNTRY and establish a relationship (IS-SOLD-IN) between them (Figure 6.2(a)). An instance in PRODUCT, say "dishwasher soap #5," is related to an instance in COUNTRY, say England, if dishwasher soap #5 is sold in England. If we treat the IS-SOLD-IN relationship as an object set, then we can give it the attribute QUANTITY to indicate how many of each product were sold in each country.

Notice that the QUANTITY attribute depends on *both* product *and* country. That is, we cannot determine the value of quantity from product alone nor from country alone—we need both of them. This is why QUANTITY is an attribute of the *relationship* between product and country, rather than an attribute of either product or country alone. For this reason, the models of Figures 6.2(b) and 6.2(c) are both incorrect. In case (b), the model does not distinguish between quantities sold in different *countries,* and in case (c), the model does not distinguish between quantities sold of different *products.*

FIGURE 6.1   A Relationship Viewed as an Object

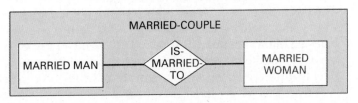

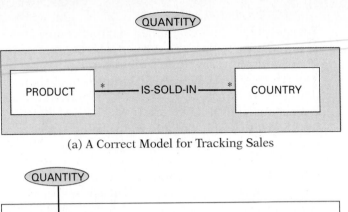

(a) A Correct Model for Tracking Sales

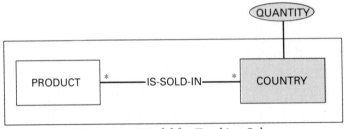

(b) Incorrect Model for Tracking Sales

(c) Incorrect Model for Tracking Sales

FIGURE 6.2

The model of Figure 6.2(a) gives Dick the ability to track sales of products by country. Suppose, however, that he wants a finer breakdown of sales than this model can give. In particular, he would like to record the quantity of each product sold in each country *on each day*. Then we relate IS-SOLD-IN to DATE and give this new relationship the attribute QUANTITY (Figure 6.3(a)). Once again, the attribute applies to the outer relationship, because instances from all three object sets—PRODUCT, COUNTRY, DATE—are needed to determine quantity.

Figure 6.3(a) gives the solution to this problem as two binary relationships, the first of which (IS-SOLD-IN) is an object set in the second relationship (SOLD-ON). We may find it more convenient to express this model as a single, 3-way relationship as in Figure 6.3(b). Again we see that QUANTITY is an attribute of the relationship among the three object sets.

Any higher-level relationship can be broken down into a series of nested binary relationships. However, some of these binary relationships may not make sense to us when we try to relate them to something in the real world. Thus, we will sometimes use higher-level relationships to ex-

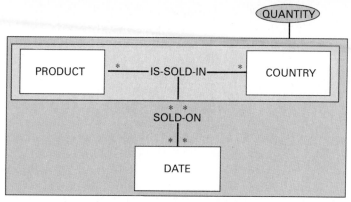

(a) Using 2 Binary Relationships

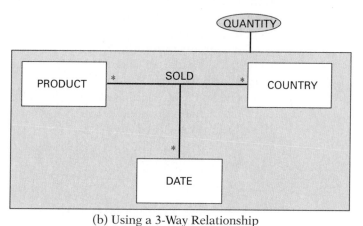

(b) Using a 3-Way Relationship

FIGURE 6.3   Different Ways to Track Sales by Country and Date

press concepts that we are trying to capture in a particular data model, since these relationships may be easier to relate to our problem.

With respect to maximum cardinalities in higher-level relationships, we will assume that all the binary relationships that make up the higher-level relationship are many-many binary relationships. This assumption will almost always hold in practice.

We will now illustrate the power of these concepts by considering a number of other examples, all of them somewhat more complex than those we have previously considered.

Example 1: Premier Construction Company   Premier Construction erects buildings at a variety of locations. Each building requires a number of different types of materials in quantities that vary by building. Different crews carry out different portions of the project. For example, there may be a crew for framing, a crew for drywall, a crew for plumbing, a crew for masonry, and so on. In scheduling the construction of a building, Premier assigns different crews to different dates. Workers are assigned to different crews, depending on their skills. Thus, Hank Brigman can do both carpentry and masonry work and so is assigned at various times to framing, drywall, and masonry crews. The size of a crew varies according to the size and requirements of the building. Consequently, crews are made up as needed for a particular building. Also, a foreman is assigned to a particular crew for a particular building. A worker can be a foreman on one crew and simply a worker on another crew. Marcus Brown, owner of Premier, wants to know which of his workers are assigned to crews for various buildings, what materials are being used on the buildings, and when work on each building is scheduled. We will now design an object-oriented model that can provide the information Brown is seeking.

Figure 6.4(a) models the relationship between buildings and materials. The BUILDING object set contains an instance for each building in the database. The MATERIAL TYPE object set represents types of material such as "2×4×10' lumber," "#10 nails," and so on. The cardinalities of the relationship between BUILDING and MATERIAL TYPE state that each building requires many types of material and each type of material is used on many buildings. Note that the ADDRESS attribute applies only to BUILDING. The ADDRESS can be used as a key to uniquely identify a particular building.

The box around the REQUIRES relationship indicates that we wish to consider that relationship as an aggregate object set. We will then give this object set the attribute QUANTITY. The instances of this aggregate object set consist of pairs: a building and a type of material. Thus, for ex-

---

FIGURE 6.4   Modeling the Relationship of Buildings and Materials

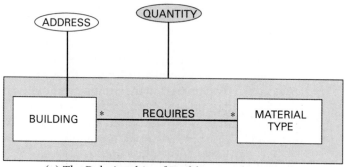

(a) The Relationship of Buildings and Materials

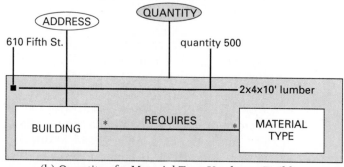

(b) Quantity of a Material Type Used on a Building

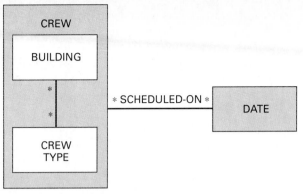

FIGURE 6.5   A Model of Construction Crews

ample, the pair made up of the building at 610 Fifth St. and 2×4×10' lumber may be an instance in the REQUIRES relationship. This pair is then assigned a quantity—say, 500 pieces—which is the quantity of 2×4×10' lumber required for this building (see Figure 6.4(b)).

It is important to note that the MATERIAL TYPE object set in this example represents a **conceptual** rather than a **physical object**. That is, each instance in MATERIAL TYPE represents a *type* of material rather than a specific, physical piece of material. This notion of conceptual as opposed to physical objects will have frequent application in our modeling and will be discussed at length later in this chapter.

We now show how to represent the formation of crews and the assignment of workers and foremen to crews. Figure 6.5 shows a relationship between CREW TYPE and BUILDING object sets. CREW TYPE is another example of a conceptual object set. That is, the instances of CREW TYPE do not represent *particular* crews; rather, they represent *types* of crews, such as masonry or drywall. The relationship of a crew type and a building represents a particular crew—the crew assigned for that building to perform the task associated with its crew type. Therefore, we can view this relationship as an object and give it the name CREW.

Each crew, as an instance in the object set CREW, is scheduled to work on a number of different dates. For example, the plumbers will require a number of days to complete the plumbing in a given building. Thus, we have a many–many relationship, SCHEDULED-ON, between CREW and DATE.

Figure 6.6 shows the assignment of workers and foremen to crews. Note that the IS-FOREMAN-OF relationship is one–many. This is because a crew will have only one foreman. However, a worker can be foreman of many different crews. Figure 6.7 gives the composite diagram showing the complete data model for Premier Construction Company.

conceptual object An object representing a type of thing.

physical object An object representing a specific, physical thing.

Example 2: International Product Distribution

Susan Broadbent's International Product Distribution (IPD) markets products all over the world. She is interested in understanding how different marketing approaches succeed in different places and which products are most successful in which areas. As a rough measure of cultural differences, she wants to identify regions and countries according to the languages spoken there.

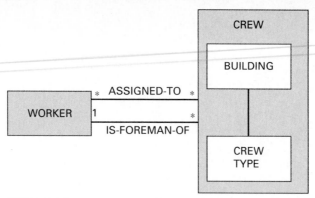

FIGURE 6.6 Assigning Workers to Crews

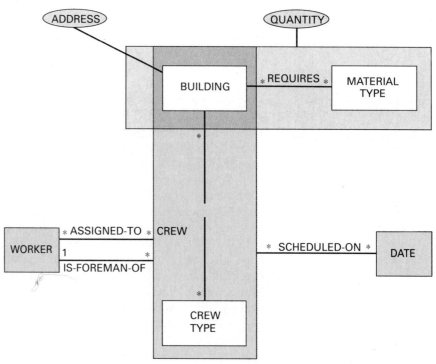

FIGURE 6.7 Data Model for Premier Construction Company

She has divided each country into a number of regions. She wants the database to track the quantity of each product sold each day in each region. She also wants to keep track of advertising. Advertisements are developed for each product, and a given advertisement can be run on several different media, including newspapers, magazines, radio, and television. Records should be maintained of when a given advertisement runs, which medium it runs on, in which language, and in which region. This information will be correlated with sales in the region targeted by the advertisement and used to judge the success of the advertisement.

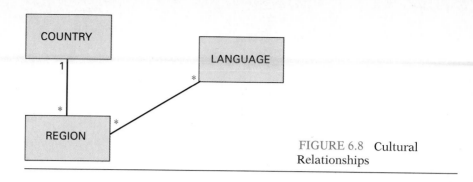

FIGURE 6.8   Cultural Relationships

Figure 6.8 shows the relationship of COUNTRY, REGION, and LAN-GUAGE. Note that the one–many cardinality between COUNTRY and RE-GION restricts a region to a single country. We are assuming that a given region is a geographical object within a country, and multiple languages could be spoken there. Therefore, we have a many–many relationship between REGION and LANGUAGE.

Figure 6.9 shows the structure for recording the quantity of each product sold in each region on each date. All of the relationships are many–many except the final one to QUANTITY, which is an attribute of the 3-way relationship among PRODUCT, DATE, REGION.

Figure 6.10 provides a model for keeping track of IPD's advertising. ADVERTISEMENT is a conceptual object. That is, we consider an advertisement for a product as conveying a particular message about that product. This message may be conveyed in different ways, depending on the medium chosen. Thus, a particular advertisement may run in the newspaper and on television. Even though the two media are different, the advertising message is considered to be basically the same. We relate ADVERTISEMENT and MEDIUM via a many–many relationship to capture the connection between advertising message and medium. This relationship is connected to the date on which it is run. Finally, this last relationship (ADVERTISEMENT, MEDIUM, DATE) is related to the REGION and LANGUAGE in which it is run on that date. All of the relationships in this figure are many–many, except that between ADVER-

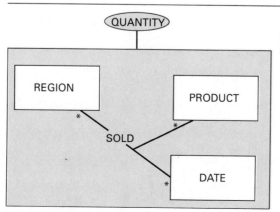

FIGURE 6.9   Tracking Quantity Sold by Region, Product, Date

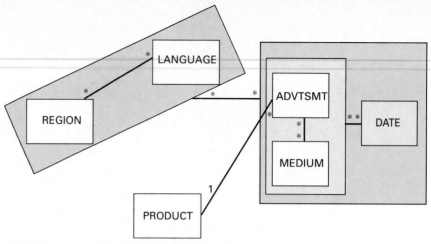

FIGURE 6.10   A Model to Track Advertising

TISEMENT and PRODUCT, since an IPD advertisement is always focused on a single product.

Figure 6.11 is a composite diagram that shows the entire data model for IPD's marketing program. Some of the questions this model can provide answers to are:

Which products were advertised in Switzerland last summer? Which medium was used the most? Does the most-used medium change if we consider only ad-

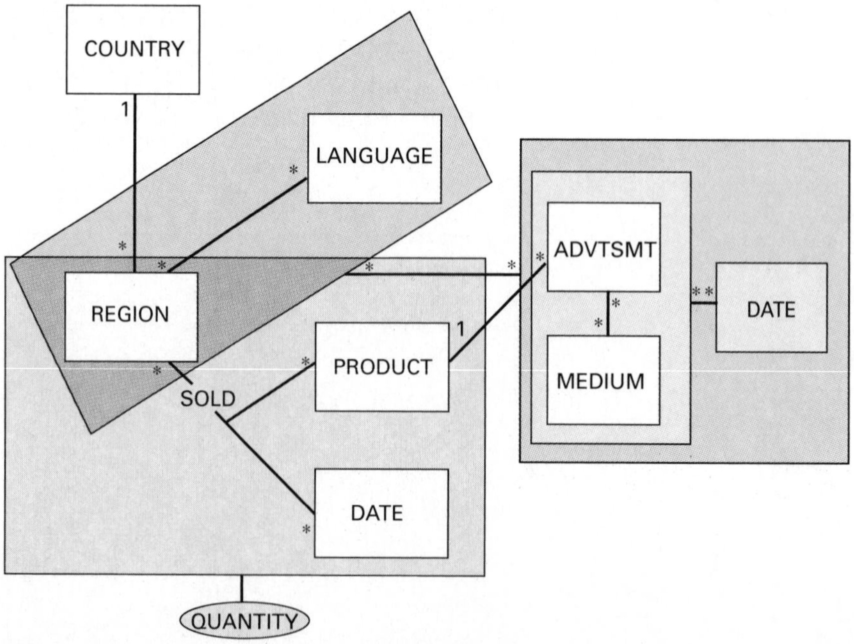

FIGURE 6.11   Composite International Product Distribution Marketing Data Model

vertisements in German? How are sales of a specific product affected in the three days immediately following a television advertisement? Do they increase, decrease, or stay the same? If they increase, at what rate?

Let's see how the third question can be answered. First, we rephrase the question to incorporate the information implied by the previous two questions:

Is the most-used medium for advertisements in Switzerland in German last summer different from the most-used medium for advertisements in all languages?

Using the model of Figure 6.11, we start with the COUNTRY object set and identify Switzerland. We then trace to REGION to find all the regions in Switzerland. Now we determine all the pairs of region and language where the region is in Switzerland. We separate those pairs having German as the language from the pairs having another language. Then we trace to the (ADVERTISEMENT, MEDIUM, DATE) object set and see how many times (region, language) are related to (advertisement, medium, date) for German and non-German. We count how many times each medium is used for German to determine the most-used medium, and we do the same for non-German. This gives us the answer we are seeking.

Example 3: Stratton's Fruit Orchards

Example 3 in Chapter 4 gave some information on Vern Stratton's fruit-growing business. We now add some information and use it to derive the corresponding data model, which is somewhat more complex than the earlier model. This model will be more powerful and will be able to provide information needed for scheduling workers, for planting new trees, and for other management decisions needed in running the business.

Trees in Vern's orchards are planted in rows and columns. Each pair of consecutive rows is 20 feet apart, and each pair of consecutive columns is 20 feet apart. When a tree dies, it is pulled out, and eventually another tree is planted in its place.

Recall that species represent broad categories of fruit—such as apple, peach, or cherry—and varieties represent subcategories, like Jonathan and Red Delicious (apples). Depending on weather conditions during the early months of the year, varieties blossom at different times. Harvest begins a set number of days from full blossom for a given variety.

In addition to handling this new information, our data model must be constructed so that questions such as the following can be answered:

How many bushels of Red Delicious apples did we get out of the Paynesville orchard last year? What was the average harvest date in all orchards for cling (variety) peaches in the last ten years? When will the Jonathans in the Lee's Valley orchard be ready for harvest this year? How many spaces are there in each orchard for new trees? How many would there be if we tore out trees whose average production the last five years is under one bushel?

Figure 6.12 gives the enhanced version of Figure 4.23. The LOCATION object set is another example of a *conceptual object*. It does not represent a specific location, but it is rather a row and column number that

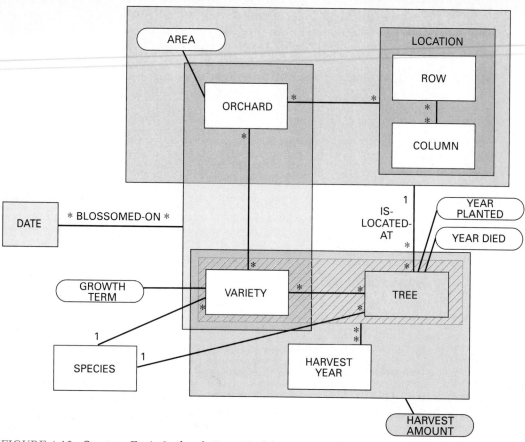

FIGURE 6.12   Stratton Fruit Orchards Data Model

could occur in any orchard. Thus, an instance in LOCATION might be (10, 17), meaning the 10th row and the 17th column of *no* specific orchard. When this instance is related to a specific orchard—say, the Springtown orchard—then the *triple* (Springtown, 10, 17) stands for row 10, column 17 in the Springtown orchard.

In Figure 4.23, we merely related the trees to their orchards. Now we can identify both the orchard and the specific location (row and column) within the orchard where the tree is planted. This lets us answer the questions about the number of empty spaces in each orchard as follows:

The relationship that ties trees to their specific locations within an orchard is named IS-LOCATED-AT. Why is this relationship one–many? Clearly, a tree can have only one location, but why can a location have many trees? If we recall that we maintain the year that a tree died, we can see that the database keeps track of all the trees that have been at a specific location over the years. Now we merely identify all the trees associated with a particular space in the orchard. If they have all died, then we may assume that the space is available for a new tree.

This information can also be used to determine where the more fertile areas within each orchard are to be found. This is because we are also keeping track of the number of bushels of fruit each tree is producing each year. Over the years, the trees in the more fertile areas will consistently produce more fruit.

To determine when harvest time is for a given variety in a given orchard, we must record when full blossom took place for the variety in that orchard. Therefore, we connect ORCHARD and VARIETY in a relationship and further connect these two to DATE in the BLOSSOMED-ON relationship. This tells us when full blossom occurred for each variety in each orchard. The GROWTH TERM attribute of VARIETY tells us the number of days from full blossom until the beginning of harvest. By using the GROWTH TERM attribute in combination with the BLOSSOMED-ON relationship, we can tell when harvest time will be for each variety in each orchard. This information is essential for scheduling workers during the harvest season.

To record the amount of each variety harvested each year from each tree, we must relate each instance of the (TREE, VARIETY) relationship to the HARVEST YEAR. This 3-way relationship will have the HARVEST AMOUNT attribute, which will tell us how many bushels were harvested of each variety from each tree each harvest year.

Example 4: Manwaring Consulting Services

In Chapter 4, we created data models for a Purchase Order and an Invoice from Manwaring Consulting Services. The forms used there were simplified to fit the basic modeling concepts available to us in that chapter. Using the more advanced concepts of this chapter, we can create data models for more sophisticated report forms. We will now examine enhanced versions of the Purchase Order and the Invoice and create data models for them.

Figure 6.13 shows an enhanced Purchase Order for Manwaring Con-

FIGURE 6.13   An Enhanced Purchase Order for Manwaring Consulting Services

MANWARING CONSULTING SERVICES
950 MAIN
EASTON, PA 11111

PURCHASE ORDER

Date	Order Number	Vendor Number
3/29	388	23

Stock #	Product Description	Quantity	Unit Price	Extended Price
3821	#2 Pencils	3	4.00	12.00
4919	Legal Pads	4	8.90	35.60
	Tax			2.86
			Total	50.46

Consolidated Office Supplies
414 S. Choctaw Drive
Flagship, PA 12345

sulting Services. As you compare this form with that of Figure 4.26, please note that the new form includes columns for *Product Description, Quantity, Unit Price,* and *Extended Price,* whereas the original had only *Product Description* and *Price.* In the original form, the quantity being ordered was embedded in *Product Description,* while in the new form it is broken out separately. *Unit Price* did not appear at all on the original form. *Price* on the original form is the same thing as *Extended Price* on the new form.

There are two advantages to the new form: (1) Since *Unit Price* is a function of the product being ordered, *Extended Price* can automatically be calculated from *Quantity* and *Unit Price.* The old form required this calculation to be done by hand. (2) Since *Quantity* is listed separately, it is possible to perform calculations with it, both on the Purchase Order form itself and in determining the total quantity of any product ordered over an extended period of time. Such calculations can be used to answer questions like:

How many pads of legal paper did we use last year?

Figure 6.14 shows the data model derived from the new Purchase Order form. Note that we have aggregated the relationship between PRODUCT and ORDER. QUANTITY and EXTENDED PRICE are attributes of the *aggregate* because they depend on both PRODUCT and ORDER. That is, the *quantity* is the number of the *product* being ordered on that particular *order.* EXTENDED PRICE is a calculated attribute that applies to both PRODUCT and ORDER in the same way as QUANTITY. Notice also that DESCRIPTION, STOCK NUMBER, and UNIT PRICE are all attributes of PRODUCT, since they depend only on PRODUCT and not on ORDER. DESCRIPTION in the new model has a different meaning than it did in the model of Figure 4.27, since in the earlier model DESCRIPTION included the quantity being ordered.

FIGURE 6.14   Data Model for Enhanced Purchase Order

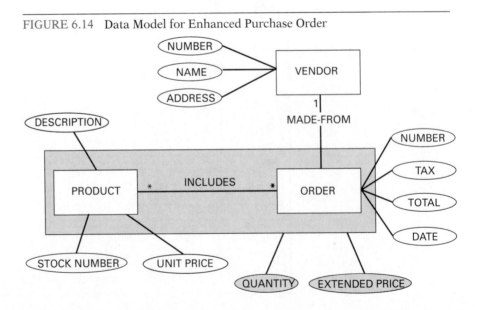

MANWARING CONSULTING
SERVICES
950 MAIN
EASTON, PA 11111

INVOICE

Date	Invoice Number	Project
12/27	349	Cost Accounting System

Consultant	Activity	Hours	Rate	Amount
Rodriguez	System Analysis	30	$60/hr.	1800.00
Rodriguez	System Design	30	$60/hr.	1800.00
Rodriguez	Programming	20	$60/hr.	1200.00
Chatman	Programming	60	$40/hr.	2400.00
			Consulting Total	7200.00

OTHER CHARGES

Description	Amount
Supplies (Paper, Photocopying, etc.)	35.00
Other Total	35.00
Invoice total	7235.00

Client: Robespierre Manufacturing
1793 Bonaparte Road
Bastille, PA 10000

FIGURE 6.15   Enhanced Invoice for Manwaring Consulting Services

Figure 6.15 shows an enhanced version of the Manwaring Invoice. In comparing this invoice with that of Figure 4.29, note that charges have been separated into *Consulting Charges* and *Other Charges*. In the enhanced invoice, we show *Activity* and *Hours* rather than *Charge Description* as in the original. *Charge Description* was a free-form field in which the user could write whatever descriptive information seemed appropriate. *Activity* and *Hours,* on the other hand, are much more precise. *Activity* includes only a specified number of predefined activities—such as systems analysis, system design, programming, and user training—which the consultants could be engaged in. *Hours,* of course, must be numeric. This approach makes it much easier for an automated system to calculate the number of hours each consultant has been involved in each type of activity for each client.

The data model for this invoice is shown in Figure 6.16. We have aggregated the relationship between CONSULTANT and ACTIVITY, as well as the relationship between this aggregate and PROJECT. The larger aggregate, then, has attributes of HOURS and AMOUNT. This is because the value of the HOURS attribute depends on the three factors of consultant, activity, and project. That is, the HOURS attribute tells us how long a given *consultant* engaged in a given *activity* on a given *project*.

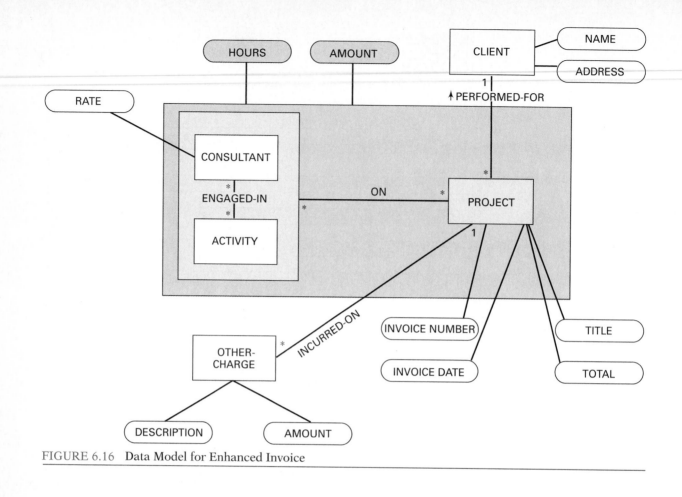

FIGURE 6.16 Data Model for Enhanced Invoice

Notice that the RATE attribute is attached directly to the CONSULTANT object set, since it depends only on the consultant. That is, Manwaring charges the same hourly rate for a given consultant regardless of the activity the consultant is engaged in. This is shown in Figure 6.15—the enhanced invoice—where we can see that the rate for Rodriguez is always $60 per hour.

AMOUNT indicates the charge for the consultant's work on an activity for a project. This is calculated by multiplying the *rate* from the consultant's RATE attribute by the *hours* from the HOURS attribute for the appropriate *consultant, activity,* and *project.*

At the beginning of the chapter, we saw that Joan Manwaring was interested in a system that would relate consultants, activities, and clients so that she could obtain information about their relationships. Figure 6.16 provides the data model needed. The data supported by this data model can be manipulated to create a large number of reports, two of which are shown in Figures 6.17(a) and 6.17(b).

The consultant activity report of Figure 6.17(a) shows how many hours each consultant spent in each activity during the past year. For example, Chatman spent 950 hours programming, 600 hours training users, and 450 hours in the office in analysis activities billed to clients. The consultant-client report of Figure 6.17(b) shows how many hours each consultant spent in billable activity for each client.

MANWARING CONSULTING
SERVICES

CONSULTANT ACTIVITY REPORT
For Year Ending December 31, 19__

CONSULTANT	ACTIVITY	HOURS
Chatman	Programming	950
	User Training	600
	Office Analysis	450
Farasopoulos	Data Entry	30
	File Conversion	1400
	User Training	350
	Office Analysis	220
Harris	File Conversion	1140
	Programming	500
	System Design	120
	Office Analysis	240
Rodriguez	Programming	150
	System Design	800
	Systems Analysis	750
	User Training	100
	Office Analysis	200

(a) A Report Relating Consultants to Activities

MANWARING CONSULTING
SERVICES

CONSULTANT-CLIENT REPORT
For Year Ending December 31, 19__

CONSULTANT	CLIENT	HOURS
Chatman	Robespierre	60
	Statten	400
	Sunderman	950
	Universal	140
Farasopoulos	Storehouse	30
	Sunderman	1100
	Watanabe	650
Harris	Goldman	950
	Martino	425
	Storehouse	200
	Universal	185
Rodriguez	Goldman	800
	Martino	840
	Robespierre	80
	Storehouse	80

(b) A Report Relating Consultant to Clients

FIGURE 6.17   Typical Reports Used at Manwaring

The data model of Figure 6.16 could be used to obtain a number of other similar reports. For example, a report could be generated showing precisely which activities each consultant performed for each client and on which project. Of course, the number of hours they spent on each activity could also be shown. Another report could be the average percent of each project's billable hours spent in each activity. For example, if the report showed that, on average, Systems Analysis took only 5% of the project time, additional training could be scheduled to teach consultants better Systems Analysis skills.

Aggregation and higher-level relationships are powerful tools that have frequent application in modeling complex business problems. Indeed, nearly every business problem has sufficient complexity to require the application of this concept. The examples given in this chapter illustrate the power of aggregation and the rich variety of situations to which it can be applied.

☐ MODELING CONCEPTUAL OBJECTS VS. PHYSICAL OBJECTS

Although aggregation and higher-level relationships are very useful tools for solving a large variety of data modeling problems, there are certain problems whose more difficult aspects can be solved with more basic tools. In this section, we look at problems that arise because of ambiguities in our daily language. As you will see, once we understand and separate the concepts involved in these ambiguities, we can solve the data modeling problems simply by defining the appropriate object sets. Aggregates and other concepts can then be used to build additional constructs into the data models, as needed.

conceptual object set An object set whose instances are conceptual objects.

In the previous section, we noted several instances of **conceptual object sets.** For example, MATERIAL TYPE and CREW TYPE in the Premier Construction Company data model were conceptual object sets, since their instances represented *types* of things rather than specific, concrete examples of those types. A material type might be "2×4×10' lumber" rather than a specific piece of lumber. A *crew type* could be "roofing" or "electrical," whereas a specific *crew* might be "roofing for the 320 Main Street building."

physical object set An object set whose instances are physical objects.

It is often necessary to distinguish between conceptual object sets and the **physical object sets** that correspond to them, because both types of object sets need to be represented in the same data model. This is illustrated in the following example.

The Library Problem   A student calls a library and asks:

STUDENT: Do you have *The Pickwick Papers* by Charles Dickens?
LIBRARIAN: (Enters query of online catalog) No, we don't.
S: How about *Bleak House?*
L: (Enters second query) No.
S: How many books *do* you have by Dickens?
L: (Enters a third query) We have twelve.
S: Really? What are they?
L: We have *A Tale of Two Cities*, Copy 1; *A Tale of Two Cities*, Copy 2; *A Tale of Two Cities*, Copy 3; and so forth, through Copy 12.

S: Those are all the same book! You don't have twelve books by Dickens, you only have one.

L: No, they aren't all the same. One is the Signet Classic Edition, one is a German translation, one a French translation, one is a condensed version, and so on.

S: But the fact remains that they are all *really* the same book. No matter what may be done to put it into a different edition, it is still *A Tale of Two Cities.* You really only have one book by Dickens.

This conversation, based on Kent (1978), would never happen since no librarian would make the kind of argument that our librarian is making. However, it serves to point up a significant problem we have with the natural language that we as humans use in normal conversation. In this example, what do we mean by "book"? Without giving it further thought, and outside the context of this conversation, we might think that "a book is a book," and there should not be any ambiguity in our use of the word. Yet the student and the librarian are using "book" in two very different senses. One sense—the student's—is that a book is something conceptual that can have many different physical versions. Thus, *A Tale of Two Cities* is "really" the same book whether it is Copy 1 or Copy 8, whether it is in English or French, or whether it is the full, unabridged version or a condensed version. The librarian, on the other hand, is using (at least initially) the other sense: A book is something physical that we can hold, leaf through, and put up on a shelf. The library needs to account for every *physical* book it has, regardless of whether it is the first or the twelfth copy of a given *conceptual* book.

Sometimes we distinguish between these two usages by insisting that physical books be referred to as "copies" or "volumes." Thus, we may say "How many volumes does the library contain?" But as analysts interviewing users, we need to recognize that people frequently don't observe such conventions. They simply say "book," and sometimes they mean "conceptual book" and sometimes "physical book." In designing a database, we need to be able to detect the differences in intended meanings. In some cases, users will be referring to a *conceptual object,* which is an abstract or generalized version of an object. In other cases, users will be referring to a *physical object,* or a specific instance of a conceptual object. If we are to meet the needs of all database users, though, our data models must capture the conceptual-physical distinction.

There may be other subtle distinctions to capture as well. In the discussion between student and librarian, the librarian eventually concedes that there is a difference between a physical and conceptual book but insists that books are conceptually different if their editions are different. That is, the Signet Classic Edition of *A Tale of Two Cities* is a different conceptual book than a condensed version. The student insists, however, that the edition is irrelevant and that, conceptually, the book remains the same through all its various editions.

Certainly both parties have a legitimate viewpoint. Since we are interested in database design, we don't have to determine which party is "right." We only need to decide what kind of questions the users want the system to answer. Once we have identified the type of information needed, we can make decisions about the data design. Ideally, we would like to satisfy all points of view, including *both* the student's and the librarian's.

Creating the Library Data Model

During the requirements definition phase of the DDLC, we as analysts are involved in interviewing users to determine their needs and expectations from a database system. During this phase, it is very important that we correctly identify the objects and relationships that make up the normal part of the users' day-to-day activity. Thus, if there are subtle distinctions in the meanings of different terms that occur naturally in business transactions, we need to be able to identify them so that we will model business relationships accurately.

As we create a model for the library problem, let us consider the following sample questions:

How many books does the library have by Charles Dickens? How many different books does the library have in the Signet Classic Edition? How many books does the library have that are in their second edition? How many copies does the library have of *Pride and Prejudice?*

From these questions we can identify three different types of "books":

A conceptual book

An edition of a conceptual book

A physical book

From the first two of these, we can construct two object sets and a relationship (Figure 6.18). Notice the minimum and maximum cardinalities for CONCEPTUAL-BOOK. These cardinalities show that the CONCEPTUAL-BOOK-EDITION object set is **dependent** on the CONCEPTUAL-BOOK object set. That is, each conceptual book edition is an edition of one and only one conceptual book.

dependent object set An object set whose instances *must* be related to at least one other instance of another object set.

FIGURE 6.18   A Preliminary Solution to the Library Problem

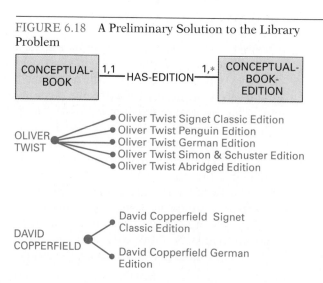

Although this solution answers some of the questions, it ultimately fails because it is unable to answer questions like:

How many different books does the library have in the Signet Classic Edition?

The problem lies with the CONCEPTUAL-BOOK-EDITION object set. Since each instance is an edition of a particular book, we cannot match identical editions of different books. An additional problem with this solution is that it requires CONCEPTUAL-BOOK-EDITION to contain considerably more object instances than are actually necessary.

Figure 6.19 gives a better solution. In this case, EDITION is an independent object set that stands on its own. Since a conceptual book can have many editions, EDITION cannot be an attribute of CONCEPTUAL-BOOK. Thus, the relationship between CONCEPTUAL-BOOK and EDITION is many–many. With this model, the questions about editions can be answered, and there is no unnecessary duplication of conceptual editions. For example, Signet Classic Edition appears only once in the EDITION object set, whereas it appeared twice, embedded in "Oliver Twist Signet Classic Edition" and "David Copperfield Signet Classic Edition," in the CONCEPTUAL-BOOK-EDITION object set of Figure 6.18. Since there could be many books in the Signet Classic Edition, our new approach eliminates a great deal of potential duplication.

Using Figure 6.19, we can add the notion of "physical books" to our model (Figure 6.20). An instance of PHYSICAL-BOOK represents an actual volume which can be marked with a call number and which can be checked out to only one library patron at a time. For this example, we assume that the call number includes *all* the information needed to uniquely identify a particular physical book. Therefore, the **external key** for each physical book is the call number, or "physical identification number," by which it can be tracked for inventory control purposes. The call number may include information such as *copy number* that distinguishes one copy of a given conceptual book from another copy of the same book.

Notice the one–many cardinality of the IS-CONTAINED-IN relationship of Figure 6.20. Such cardinality asserts that a given book-edition combination can be contained in many different physical books. This corresponds to our understanding of reality. But the cardinality also asserts that a given physical book can contain only one book-edition. Is this accurate?

external key A set of lexical attributes whose values always identify a single object instance.

FIGURE 6.19   A Better Solution to the Library Problem

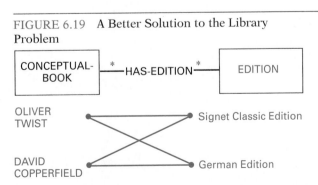

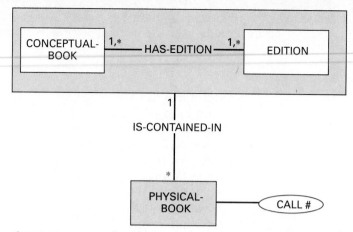

FIGURE 6.20   A Third Solution to the Library Problem

Consider a book containing the collected works of Jane Austen. Such a book contains a number of different conceptual books, although we might say they all have the same edition. All of these conceptual books are contained in the same physical book, as shown in Figure 6.21. Since this situation is not unusual, for the sake of accuracy we must amend the cardinality of Figure 6.20 from one–many to many–many (Figure 6.22). That is, a single physical book can be related to multiple conceptual books.

FIGURE 6.21   An Instance of a Collected Works Edition

```
  CONCEPTUAL-  1,*                          1,*    EDITION
  BOOK     ————————  HAS-EDITION  ————————

                        |
                IS-CONTAINED-IN
                        |

                  PHYSICAL-
                    BOOK
```

Pride and Prejudice
Sense and Sensibility
Emma
Persuasion
Northanger Abby

COLLECTED
WORKS EDITION

call # = 123.45CW1
PHYSICAL BOOK

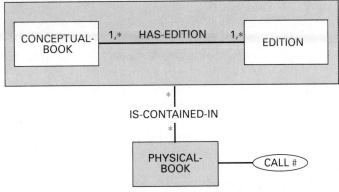

FIGURE 6.22   An Amended Solution to the Library Problem

Our data model still may not go far enough. If library users need to identify books by the language in which they are published, we will need to break out language as a separate object. Language might be an attribute of a book-edition combination (assuming that an edition of a book can be in only one language), or it might be a separate object set, which has a many–many relationship with book-edition. That is, a given edition of a book might contain portions in Italian, French, Spanish, English, and so on. Figure 6.23 shows LANGUAGE as an object set related through the IS-IN-LANGUAGE relationship to the aggregate of HAS-EDITION. A physical book then would map to an object instance consisting of conceptual book, edition, and language, which is in the aggregate of IS-IN-LANGUAGE.

The distinction between conceptual books and physical books is crucial to the solution of this problem. More importantly, this conceptual-

FIGURE 6.23   Showing Language as a Separate Object in the Solution to the Library Problem

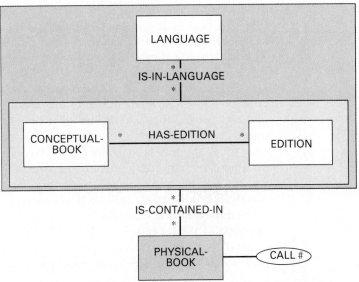

physical distinction is useful in solving many similar data modeling problems. The library model itself can be extended to capture data about non-book items, such as paintings and musical compositions, in addition to audio tapes and videotapes. For example, the library might keep prints of famous paintings that it lends to patrons. It might also have recordings of famous (and not-so-famous) pieces of music. Ravel's *Bolero* might be available on LP record, cassette, and compact disk. The library could have recordings by the New York Philharmonic, the Philadelphia Orchestra, and the Vienna Philharmonic. Thus, in our model we would have conceptual paintings (for example, the *Mona Lisa*) and physical paintings (prints of the *Mona Lisa*). We would also have conceptual musical works and physical copies of those musical works. Tracking such information, while at the same time maintaining control over physical inventory, requires a database design that distinguishes between physical and conceptual works, in music and art as well as in literature.

This problem is not unique to libraries. You will encounter it in many types of business situations. Any time a word is used ambiguously, the potential for the problem exists. As we have shown, however, the solution is quite simple. By defining separate object sets, one for each distinct meaning of the ambiguous term, and by defining appropriate relationships between these object sets, a data model can be constructed that will provide all the information the users require. Additional examples will help to clarify this.

Tracking Manufactured Parts

Let's look at another problem for which the conceptual-physical distinction is useful.

Robespierre Manufacturing ("Products on the Cutting Edge") has design facilities, manufacturing facilities, and warehouses. These facilities design, produce, and store parts. A part is designed in only one facility but may be manufactured and stored in several facilities. After interviewing the owners, Louis and Marie Blades, and several other officers and managers of Robespierre, the database analysts determined that the following questions were typical:

Which parts were designed in which facility? If a particular part fails, can we trace it back to the facility that designed it and the facility that manufactured it? What quantity of part A235 is stored in the Lexington warehouse?

It is clear that most of these questions have to do with tracking specific parts, which are designed at one facility, manufactured at another, and then stored in a warehouse. Figure 6.24 is the result of our first attempt at a data model for this problem. Note the cardinalities. We can answer the first question—"Which parts were designed in which facility?"—because each part is designed in only one facility. Moreover, if a part fails, we can use the part number to identify the part and determine where it was designed. But we cannot tell where the part was manufactured, since a given part can be manufactured in many different facilities. The third question—"What quantity of part A235 is stored in the Lexington warehouse?"—can be answered since our model captures the quantity of the part stored in the warehouse for each part/warehouse combination. Thus,

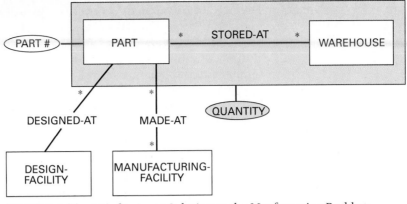

FIGURE 6.24   A Preliminary Solution to the Manfacturing Problem

the data model of Figure 6.24 provides most of the information needed to answer the questions.

A better data model, that answers all these questions, is shown in Figure 6.25. Here we have distinguished between conceptual parts and physical parts. A conceptual part represents a *type* of part and has a part number, which is assigned when the part is designed. It is precisely what was meant by PART in Figure 6.24. A physical part is a particular instance of its corresponding conceptual part. Therefore, the relationship between CONCEPTUAL PART and PHYSICAL PART is one–many: A physical part corresponds to only one conceptual part, but a conceptual part corresponds to many physical parts. A physical part has a serial number that uniquely identifies it. Moreover, it was manufactured in only one facility and, at any given time, is stored in only one warehouse.

This data model answers all the questions listed above. Note that we have omitted QUANTITY as an attribute in this data model. The quantity of parts in a warehouse can be determined by finding the desired warehouse instance in the WAREHOUSE object set and then counting the number of physical parts related to the warehouse by the IS-STORED-AT relationship. Since the computer can easily count the number of such instances, it is unnecessary for us to create a superfluous QUANTITY attribute.

FIGURE 6.25   A Better Solution to the Manfacturing Problem

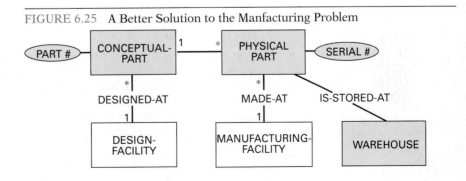

The need to distinguish between conceptual and physical objects occurs frequently in practice. We have already discussed books, paintings, pieces of music, and parts. Other examples include automobiles, trucks, airplanes, computers, and appliances. Indeed, anything that is planned, designed, and then manufactured involves the conceptual-physical distinction. For example, *the* Ford Escort is a type of automobile, but *a* Ford Escort is a specific automobile with a unique vehicle identification number.

Many words in our natural language are used in ambiguous ways. Consider the phrases:

> the annual inventory
>
> the inventory of part A235

It is clear that *inventory* in the first phrase refers to a procedure undertaken for accounting and tax purposes, while *inventory* in the second phrase means the store of a specific part available to Sales.

Another example is an airline's use of the word *flight* to refer to an airplane route that, say, begins each day in St. Louis and stops in Cincinnati before flying on to Boston. On the other hand, when passengers say *flight,* they may mean a particular instance of an airplane traveling from one airport to another on a given date: "On January 31 at 2 P.M., my flight will leave St. Louis for Cincinnati."

Conceptual Objects for Manwaring Consulting Services

Over a period of several years, Manwaring has developed a number of computer applications systems for its clients. After working with many different clients, the Manwaring staff has found that clients often have similar needs and the same basic software can be used for these needs. For example, Statten needs an Accounts Receivable system, an Accounts Payable system, and a Cost Accounting system. Sunderman needs an Accounts Payable system, a Cost Accounting system, and a Payroll system. By creating generalized systems for Accounts Receivable, Accounts Payable, Cost Accounting, Payroll, Inventory Control, and so forth, Manwaring can satisfy many clients' needs at reduced cost. From this experience came the decision to create "base" systems in each of these areas.

Figure 6.26(a) shows a data model that gives the relationship between the base systems and the client systems that use them. The base systems have *version numbers* to indicate different versions of the system. For example, the first version of the Accounts Payable system may have had version number 1.0. The second and third versions may have had numbers 1.1 and 2.0, respectively. Since each base system can have many version numbers, and since each version number can apply to many base systems, the relationship between BASE SYSTEM and VERSION NUMBER is many–many.

Each client system is related to the base system(s) from which it is constituted. However, since the client will always receive a specific *version* of the base system, the client system is related to *both* the base system and the version number. That is, the IS-INCLUDED-IN relationship is between CLIENT SYSTEM and the *aggregate* of BASE SYSTEM and VERSION NUMBER. The IS-INCLUDED-IN relationship is many–many because a given client system will include many base-system/version-number combinations, and a given base-system/version-number combination will be included in many different client systems.

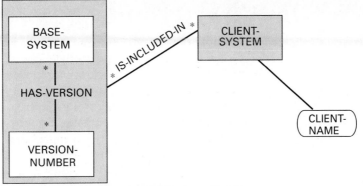

(a) Data Model for Installed Systems

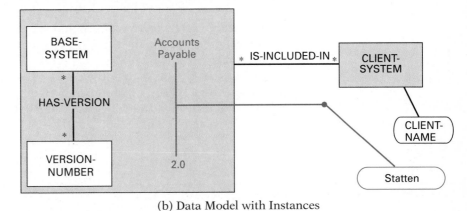

(b) Data Model with Instances

FIGURE 6.26   Data Models of Conceptual and Physical Systems

Figure 6.26(b) shows instances from this data model. The system for client Statten is shown as a dot beneath the CLIENT SYSTEM box. This system includes Accounts Payable, Version 2.0, and so in the diagram it is connected to the (Accounts Payable, 2.0) pair. If the Statten system included other base system versions, there could be other such instances illustrated.

This data model further illustrates the conceptual-physical distinction. The BASE SYSTEM object set is a conceptual object set, and the CLIENT SYSTEM object set is a physical object set. In fact, this example is very similar to the library example given earlier. If you compare Figure 6.26(a) with Figure 6.22, you can see the following correspondence:

CONCEPTUAL BOOK—BASE SYSTEM

EDITION—VERSION NUMBER

PHYSICAL BOOK—CLIENT SYSTEM

The purpose of this example, as well as those that precede it in this section, is to illustrate the ambiguities lurking in the natural language used to describe the requirements of database users. To make sure our data models are accurate and complete, we must carefully analyze the circumstances of the application and the kind of information desired by the users of the database system.

☐ VIEW INTEGRATION: AN EXAMPLE

view A definition of a restricted portion of the database.

The examples we have been using in the last three chapters tend to be unified in that we create a single model to satisfy all the requirements of the users with whom we are working. In a large organization, such a simple approach is impossible; and a database development project would require the creation of a number of different data models by analyst teams working with users in different areas. These separate data models are called **views,** since each of them represents the way a given user group looks at the database. To create a single, integrated database, it is necessary to integrate these different views into a single data model.

The data models for Manwaring Consulting Services given earlier in this chapter represent different user views. Let's take two of them and see how they can be integrated into a single data model. The approach will be to preserve each view in its original state, to the extent possible, and to connect object sets in the different views by creating new relationships between them.

Consider Figures 6.16 and 6.26(a). Figure 6.16 contains a CLIENT object set with a NAME attribute, and Figure 6.26(a) contains a CLIENT SYSTEM object set with a CLIENT NAME attribute. Since the CLIENT NAME attribute of Figure 6.26(a) and the NAME attribute of Figure 6.16

FIGURE 6.16   Data Model for Enhanced Invoice

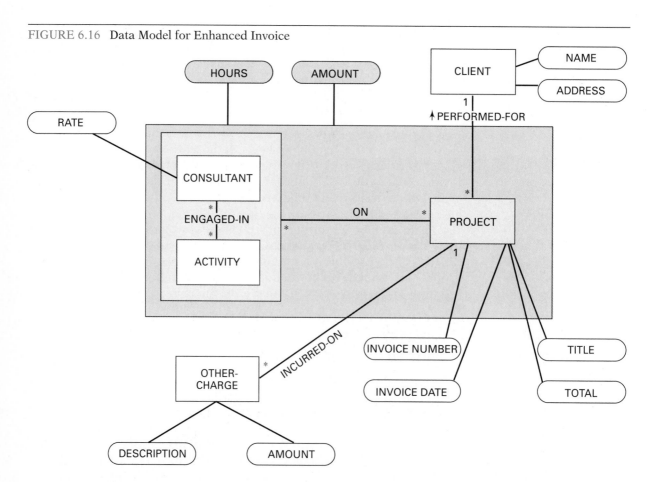

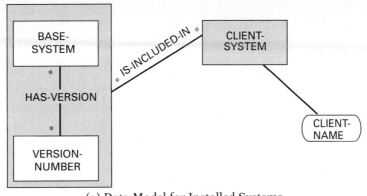

(a) Data Model for Installed Systems

FIGURE 6.26   Data Models of Conceptual and Physical Systems

represent the same attribute, an integrated model would drop one of them as redundant. A possible solution would be to relate CLIENT SYSTEM to CLIENT and drop CLIENT NAME as an attribute of CLIENT SYSTEM, as in Figure 6.27(a).

FIGURE 6.27   Examples of View Integration

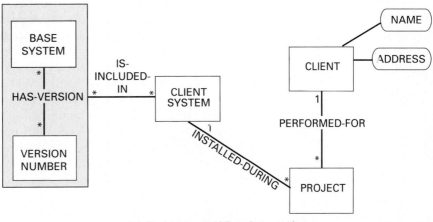

(a) A First Attempt at View Integration

(b) An Improved View Integration

However, this solution fails to consider other portions of Figure 6.16. Client systems, for example, are developed during projects. Thus, it seems more reasonable to relate the CLIENT SYSTEM object set to the PROJECT object set, as shown in Figure 6.27(b). The INSTALLED-DURING relationship indicates that a given client system was created during a series of projects, all of them for the same client. Thus, we can trace from a *client system*, through the *projects* used to install it, to the *client* for whom the projects were performed. This solution integrates the two views and gives the single, unified data model we are seeking.

View integration for a large organization's database is a complex problem requiring analysis of the object sets, attributes, and relationships of the views by the analysts and users most familiar with them. This requires communication to take place between the analysts and users responsible for the different views to be integrated. We have shown here a simple example which illustrates some of the basic concepts involved in the process. This process involved defining one or more new relationships to connect the object sets in different views. In other cases, the views involved may already have object sets in common, and the integration process will then merely consist of creating a composite of the views. This was done earlier in this chapter when we created the model of Figure 6.7 from the models of Figures 6.4, 6.5, and 6.6.

In an actual business situation, the process of view integration may work in some cases and may not in others. As indicated earlier, some organizations, because of the complexity of the database development project, have chosen *not* to have a single corporate database for all information needs. By choosing this approach, they have avoided some of the more difficult aspects of view integration. Of course, the smaller databases will still represent a variety of user views, and each of these databases will require the view integration process for their successful design.

■ SUMMARY

This chapter introduced advanced object-oriented data modeling concepts, building on the concepts introduced in Chapter 4. We developed the concept of relationship aggregation and showed how aggregates and higher-level relationships could be used to model more complex business problems. We also showed that a number of significant data modeling problems result from ambiguities in natural language. Through logical resolution of these ambiguities, data models can be developed which establish the structure for answering questions resulting from the ambiguities. In the last section of the chapter, we showed how different data models or views can be integrated into a single data model.

An aggregate is a relationship which is viewed as an object set. A higher-level relationship is a relationship among three or more object sets. By using aggregates or higher-level relationships, it is possible to address more complex modeling problems which involve more than two object sets. Aggregates can have attributes and participate in other relationships. These new relationships can also be aggregated and can be used as object sets in other relationships.

Conceptual object sets represent entities that are "types of things." For example, a book in a conceptual object set is not a specific, physical book, but rather represents a complex, conceptual entity developed by the author. The conceptual book can have many different editions, and each edition can result in the printing of many physical copies of the book. The physical copies are physical books which would be represented in a data model in their own object set, separate from the object set representing the conceptual books. Many other examples of the conceptual-physical distinction exist. Parts are designed and manufactured. The designed part is conceptual; the manufactured part is physical. By understanding how a single word, such as "book" or "part," is used in ambiguous ways, the analyst is better prepared to separate meanings and to create separate modeling structures to handle the different possible meanings.

In a large database development project, different analysts will work with different user groups to create a variety of data models. To create a single, unified database, these data models or views of the database must be integrated. The process involves leaving the views intact to the extent possible; removing only those object sets, relationships, and attributes which are redundant between views; and connecting the views by defining, as needed, new relationships between object sets in the different views. This process requires analysts and users working in different areas to communicate to understand how the views can be accurately integrated. It may not be economically feasible in some cases to carry out complete view integration. Database development projects that are particularly large may result in a decision to create a number of smaller databases rather than a single, integrated database.

■ REVIEW QUESTIONS

1. Define each of the following terms in your own words:
   a. aggregate
   b. *n*-ary relationship
   c. conceptual object set
   d. physical object set
   e. view

2. In what situations are aggregates needed in data modeling? When are higher-level relationships appropriate? Give examples from business situations.

3. Discuss the possible ambiguities in meaning of each of the following terms:
   a. book
   b. musical work
   c. part
   d. flight
   e. toy
   f. aircraft
   g. insurance policy
   h. computer software system
   i. Chevrolet

4. Suppose you are required to integrate two data views into a single data model. Describe the steps you would follow.

■ PROBLEMS AND EXERCISES

Part A.

1. Match the following terms with their definitions.

__Binary relationship
  a. Relationship between three or more object sets

__Aggregate
  b. Lexical attributes whose values identify a single instance

__Conceptual object
  c. Object representing a type of thing

__View
  d. Object set whose instances *must* be related to at least one other instance of another object set

__Physical object
  e. Relationship between two object sets

__External key
  f. Relationship viewed as an object set

__Dependent object set
  g. Object representing a specific, physical thing

__Higher-level relationship
  h. Defines a restricted portion of the database

Part B.

2. For each of the following statements, draw a data model showing a relationship between object sets, an aggregation of the relationship, and attributes of the aggregate.

  a. Students take classes and get grades in the classes.

  b. Sections of courses are offered at specified times and in specified rooms and buildings.

  c. Each school term can be represented as a season (Fall, Winter, Spring, Summer) and a year and begins and ends on specified dates.

  d. Each day, employees work some number of hours.

  e. People subscribe to magazines and their subscriptions have beginning and ending dates.

  f. Pilots have a certain number of hours of training on each type of aircraft.

For each of the following problems, create an object-oriented model, consisting of object sets, relationships, attributes, and so on, that can be used to answer questions similar to the questions given. Use aggregates and higher-level relationships as needed. Indicate cardinalities.

3. How many students are taking Physics 201? Which section is Andrea Edens taking? How many times has Jim Hardy taken Accounting 201, when, who were his instructors, and what grades did he receive?

Dustin Tomes, history professor, wants to use a database to get answers to questions about European history. Create a separate data model for each problem.

4. How many of the kings of Prussia were named Fredrick? When did they live and when did they reign? Did they rule over any other countries during their lifetimes? Were any of the countries in Europe ruled by women in the seventeenth century? Which ones?

5. Was Marie Antoinette's grandfather the ruler of any country? Which one and when? Who was her mother? Were rulers of two different countries ever married to each other? How many of Henry VIII's children became monarchs of England? Who were their mothers?

Brick Wall Communications owns a group of television stations. These stations televise syndicated programs, commercial messages, and live sporting events. Create a separate data model for each problem.

6. Which stations have broadcast "Batman" syndicated programs? Did Brick Wall rebroadcast any of the episodes from the 1988 season of "The Cosby Show" last year? Did they show the fifth episode? When and on which stations?

7. How many baseball games did Brick Wall broadcast last year? On what dates did they broadcast games between the Dodgers and the Mets? Which teams were featured the most often? What about football games? Basketball games? Tennis matches? Golf tournaments? Other types of sports? Did Steffi Graf play tennis on any Brick Wall stations? Which station and when?

8. Which commercial messages has Brick Wall shown more than three times during an hour on a single station? When did this happen? During which hour on which date and station? How much did Brick Wall charge for each of these commercial message broadcasts?

Frank Howe, managing partner of the law firm of Dewey, Kleenem, Outt, and Howe, has decided that the firm's attorneys would be helped substantially by having a database directly applicable to legal questions. For each problem, create a separate data model.

9. In what cases have opinions been offered on Section 411.3c of the federal code? Which courts were involved? When were these opinions handed down? What sections of the federal code were interpreted by the *Black* v. *Williams* case?

10. Which law firms have represented General Continental in court during the last ten years? What were the cases; which party did the verdict favor; and what was the size of the award? What were the opposing law firms? What other large companies were these law firms representing in cases at the same time?

Part C.

11. As part of a project for Acme Insurance Company, one of Manwaring's analysts created a report to measure the productivity of Acme's data entry personnel. This report gives a tally for each day of the month of the number of transactions of each type entered by each clerk. Derive an object-oriented data model which could be used as the basis for the report shown in Figure 6.1E.

Part D. Use conceptual and physical object sets in creating data models for the following problems:

```
                    ACME INSURANCE COMPANY


                MONTHLY CLERICAL PRODUCTIVITY REPORT
                       For Month Ending March 31


     Employee No.     Name      Date     Transaction      Number
                                            Type         Completed
         3855       J. Perkins   3/1     New Policy          15
                                         Payment             75
                                         Claim               22

                                3/2      New Policy          18
                                         Policy Change       53
                                         Claim               25

                                • • •

         3921       S. Stallone  3/1     Payment             45
                                         Policy Change       83
                                         Claim               10

                                3/2      New Policy           8
                                         Payment             63
                                         Policy Change       35

                                • • •
```

FIGURE 6.1E   Report Giving Daily Tally of Transaction Types Entered by Each Clerk

---

12. An airline wants to answer questions like the following about its airplanes:

> What is the seating capacity of the Boeing 727? How many engines does it have? What is the average age of the 727s we have in our fleet? Who is the chief mechanic responsible for servicing aircraft number 1388? What company manufactured that aircraft?

13. The Administrative Services Division of a large city must keep track of its computer equipment. It also wants to answer questions about the computer models it has. Create a data model for the following questions:

> What is the maximum memory the IBM PC can have? How about the PC-XT and PC-AT? What is the maximum possible memory size for the Macintosh II? Which of our employees have IBM PCs in their offices? Who has the computer with serial number 4538842? How much main memory does it have?

Part E. View Integration.

14. Create an integrated data model from the views (or data models) you created in problems 4 and 5.

15. Create an integrated data model from the views you created in problems 6, 7, and 8.

16. Create an integrated data model from the views you created in problems 9 and 10.

1. Read papers on each of the following data models and determine how these models handle aggregation. Determine whether the papers provide enough information to answer these questions: Can an aggregate have attributes in the model? Can it participate in relationships? Can these relationships also be aggregated?

    a. The Entity-Relationship Model (Chen, 1976).

    b. The Semantic Data Model (Hammer and McLeod, 1981).

    c. The Functional Data Model (Shipman, 1981).

2. Read the first chapter of Kent (1978). List as many examples as you can of instances of the conceptual-physical distinction that are given in that chapter.

3. Write a research paper on views and view integration. Identify problems with view integration that were not discussed in this chapter.

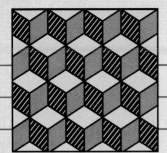

part three

IMPLEMEN-TATION DESIGN

In Part III, you will learn how logical design models can be transformed to database implementation models. The predominant models for database implementation in today's business environment are the relational, the network, and the hierarchical models. We also show how physical structures are used to implement databases at the lowest, internal level.

Chapter 7 introduces the relational model and explains its significance in the history of database processing. The process of database normalization and the process of object-oriented model conversion are also defined and illustrated.

In Chapter 8, we discuss Codd's relational algebra and relational calculus. Numerous examples are used to clarify both of these foundational data manipulation languages.

In Chapter 9, the definition of the network model is presented. Object-oriented model conversion is defined and illustrated, and the network model data manipulation language is introduced and discussed.

Chapter 10 presents the hierarchical model. As with the other models, we examine object-oriented model conversion. Additionally, the IMS data manipulation language is introduced and discussed.

Chapter 11 discusses physical implementation techniques. We examine direct access storage devices, data formats, and traditional file organizations. Moreover, we define techniques of mapping by using pointers, chains, rings, inverted lists, and B$^+$-trees and show how these may be used to map logical data structures. We also discuss secondary key structure and query optimization techniques.

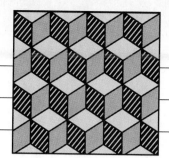

chapter seven

THE RELATIONAL DATA MODEL

Marcus Brown, owner of Premier Construction Company, is discussing database implementation with Tony Melton, Premier's Information Systems Manager. Conceptual design for the database system has been completed, and the project team is now ready to move into implementation design for a relational database management system.

"It's not clear to me, Tony, why we went through the conceptual design step to produce an object-oriented database model, if we knew from the start that we would have to convert to a relational model anyway."

"Conceptual design is essential for creating a database schema that is logically sound, Marcus, but at present there are few systems that can actually run an object-oriented database. Now that we've created a good logical model for our business, we need to implement it on a system suited to our application needs. We've chosen a relational database management system, because for our purposes it is the most advanced available."

"That's fine, but I understand it is necessary to normalize a relational database before it is ready for implementation. I'm not exactly sure what that means, but won't it require you to do additional database design?"

"The process used to convert an object-oriented data model to a relational model is one of the powerful aspects of conceptual data modeling. By following a straightforward, mechanical conversion process, we will create a relational implementation design that is completely normalized. In essence, we have the best of both worlds."

The focus of this chapter is the relational data model and its use as a database implementation design model. We will define the model constructs, discuss the normalization process, and show how any object-oriented model can be easily converted to an equivalent relational model. After reading this chapter, you should be able to:

- Explain the fundamental concepts of the relational model, including relations, attributes, domains, keys, foreign keys, entity integrity, and referential integrity.
- Demonstrate how relations can be normalized. The normalization process requires an understanding of First through Fourth Normal Forms, Functional Dependencies, and Multivalued Dependencies.
- Transform an object-oriented data model to a relational data model in Fourth Normal Form.

□ THE RELATIONAL DATA MODEL AND SYSTEM DEVELOPMENT

In 1970, the way people viewed databases was permanently changed when E.F. Codd introduced the relational data model (Codd, 1970). At that time, the existing approaches to database structure used physical pointers, or disk addresses, to relate records in different files. Suppose, for example, we need to relate record *A* to record *B* in one of these early systems. To do this, we would add to record A a field containing the disk address of record B. This added field, or physical pointer, would always point from record A to record B. Codd demonstrated that these databases signifi-cantly limited the types of data manipulation that could easily be done by the end user. Moreover, they were highly vulnerable to changes in the physical environment. Whenever new disk drives were added to the com-puter system configuration and data was moved from one physical loca-tion to another, extensive data file conversion could be required. If fields were added to a record format in a file, all the existing records in the file would have new physical locations, requiring additional data conversion. Thus, users and software were restricted by physical considerations from using data in the large variety of ways that the logical structure would have allowed.

The relational model, based on logical relationships in data, over-came these problems. It allowed the user to be totally unconcerned with, even unaware of, the physical structure of data. In addition, Codd pro-posed two logically based data manipulation languages that promised more power in accessing and processing data. These languages, relation-al algebra and relational calculus, are discussed in Chapter 8. Today, these languages provide the basis for the commercial relational database lan-guages used in many of the most popular commercial database manage-ment systems (DBMSs). We will describe these DBMSs in more detail in Part IV.

In this chapter, we will review two approaches to relational database design. The first approach is more traditional. In this approach, concep-tual design does not include object-oriented modeling but proceeds di-rectly to the creation of a relational database schema consisting of rela-tional table definitions. Design is then completed by "normalizing" these table definitions according to a well-defined process.

The second approach assumes the creation of an object-oriented data model during conceptual design. This model is then mechanically converted to a relational model. The conversion process will automati-cally guarantee normalization of the resulting relational model.

The first approach was traditionally used before object-oriented models became known and established. It is still useful today in situations requiring a relatively simple database schema. In such cases, the analyst may find it easier to create and normalize relational table definitions di-rectly from user information. The second approach, using object-orient-ed models, is valuable in the design of large, complex database schemas needed for corporate database systems.

After we introduce the concepts of the relational model, we will dis-cuss the normalization process and the process of converting an object-oriented model.

☐ THE RELATIONAL DATA MODEL: FUNDAMENTAL CONCEPTS

Relations

relational data model A data model representing data in the form of tables.

relation A two-dimensional table containing rows and columns of data.

The **relational data model** organizes and represents data in the form of tables or *relations*. **Relation** is a term that comes from mathematics and represents a simple, two-dimensional table, consisting of rows and columns of data. Examples of relations are found in the database devel-oped for Premier Construction Company, a company we encountered ear-lier.

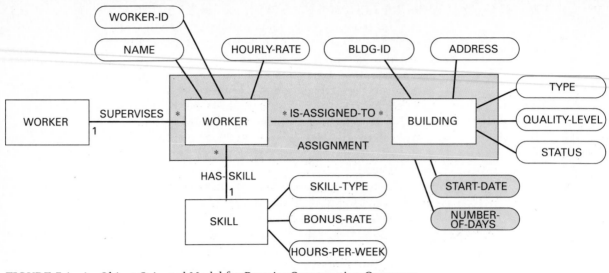

FIGURE 7.1 An Object-Oriented Model for Premier Construction Company

Figure 7.1 gives a revised object-oriented data model that provides the basis for Premier's relational database. Note that this data model contains three object sets—WORKER, BUILDING, and SKILL—and one aggregate object set—ASSIGNMENT. Although the WORKER object set appears twice in the model, it is the same object set *both* times. Thus, both copies of WORKER have the same attributes and participate in the same relationships. The ASSIGNMENT object set is the aggregation of the IS-ASSIGNED-TO relationship between WORKER and BUILDING. That is, each assignment consists of a pair—a worker and a building—and means that the worker is assigned to work on the building. Each of these assignments has two attributes—START-DATE, or the date on which the worker is assigned to start work on the building, and NUMBER-OF-DAYS, meaning the anticipated number of days required for the worker to complete work on the building. Thus, the ASSIGNMENT aggregate object set has the two attributes, START-DATE and NUMBER-OF-DAYS.

Besides the IS-ASSIGNED-TO relationship, the model contains the HAS-SKILL relationship and the SUPERVISES relationship. The HAS-SKILL relationship associates a skill, such as plumbing, roofing, or framing, with each worker. The skill has a description, a bonus rate, and the number of hours per week that a worker of that skill type can work before the bonus becomes effective. Since workers are supervised by other workers, the SUPERVISES relationship assigns to each worker a supervisor from the WORKER object set. A relationship like SUPERVISES, that relates an object set to itself, is **recursive.**

By using a process discussed later in the chapter, this data model can be converted into a relational data model. Figure 7.2 shows a relation, with sample data values, which represents the WORKER object set, its attributes, and two of its relationships. Each column in the relation is an **attribute** of the relation. The name of the column is called the *attribute name.* We use the terms *attribute* and *attribute name* rather than *column* and *column name* to be consistent with relational database conventions.

recursive relationship A relationship that relates an object set to itself.

relation attribute A column in a relation.

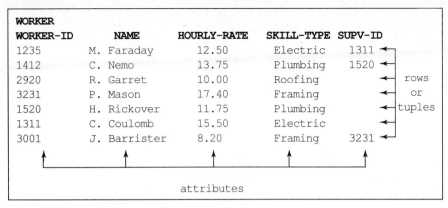

FIGURE 7.2   A Portion of the Relation WORKER

The attribute names of WORKER are WORKER-ID, NAME, HOURLY-RATE, SKILL-TYPE, and SUPV-ID. These attributes correspond to attributes and relationships in the object-oriented data model as follows:

Object-Oriented Model	Relation Attribute
WORKER-ID (Attribute)	WORKER-ID
NAME (Attribute)	NAME
HOURLY-RATE (Attribute)	HOURLY-RATE
HAS-SKILL (Relationship)	SKILL-TYPE
SUPERVISES (Relationship)	SUPV-ID

A relational database equivalent to the entire object-oriented data model for Premier is shown, together with sample values, in Figure 7.3. As noted, we will explain the process of converting such an object-oriented data model to a relational model later in the chapter.

degree of a relation The number of attributes in a relation.

The number of attributes in a relation is called the **degree of the relation.** The degree of WORKER is five. So that the user does not have to remember the order of attributes in a relation, it is assumed that the order in which the attributes are listed is immaterial. From this, it follows that no two attributes in a relation can have the same name.

tuple A row in a relation.

The rows of a relation are also called **tuples.** It is assumed that there is no prespecified order to the rows, or tuples, of a relation and that no two tuples have identical sets of values.

A common notation used to represent relations such as the one in Figure 7.2 is

```
WORKER (WORKER-ID, NAME, HOURLY-RATE, SKILL-TYPE, SUPV-ID)
```

That is, the name of the relation is followed by the names of its attributes in parentheses.

attribute domain The set from which an attribute takes its values.

The set of all possible values that an attribute may have is termed the **domain** of the attribute. Two domains are the same only if they have

```
WORKER
WORKER-ID        NAME          HOURLY-RATE   SKILL-TYPE     SUPV-ID
   1235       M. Faraday         12.50       Electric        1311
   1412       C. Nemo            13.75       Plumbing        1520
   2920       R. Garret          10.00       Roofing
   3231       P. Mason           17.40       Framing
   1520       H. Rickover        11.75       Plumbing
   1311       C. Coulomb         15.50       Electric
   3001       J. Barrister        8.20       Framing         3231


ASSIGNMENT
WORKER-ID       BLDG-ID       START-DATE    NUM-DAYS
   1235           312           10/10           5
   1412           312           10/01          10
   1235           515           10/17          22
   1412           460           12/08          18
   1412           435           10/15          15
   1412           515           11/05           8
   1311           435           10/08          12


BUILDING
BLDG-ID      BLDG-ADDRESS       TYPE        QLTY-LEVEL     STATUS
   312       123 Elm          Office            2             2
   435       456 Maple        Retail            1             1
   515       789 Oak          Residence         3             1
   210       1011 Birch       Office            3             1
   111       1213 Aspen       Office            4             1
   460       1415 Beech       Warehouse         3             3


SKILL
SKILL-TYPE       BONUS-RATE    HOURS-PER-WEEK
Plumbing           3.00             35
Electric           3.50             37
Roofing            2.00             40
Framing            5.00             35
```

FIGURE 7.3   Sample Relations in the Premier Construction Company Database

the same meaning. Thus, NAME and SKILL-TYPE reference different domains, even though each consists of strings of characters. It is not necessary for two attributes with the same domain to have the same name. SUPV-ID, for example, has the same domain as WORKER-ID. In both cases, the domain consists of worker identification numbers.

Null Values

null value The value given an attribute in a tuple if the attribute is inapplicable or its value is unknown.

Suppose an attribute is not applicable in a specific case. For example, some employees in the WORKER relation do not have supervisors. Consequently, no value exists for SUPV-ID for these employees. In addition, when we are entering data for a row in a relation, we might not know the values of one or more of the attributes for that row. In either case, we enter nothing, and that row is recorded in the database with **null values** for those attributes. A null value is not blank or zero; it is simply "unknown" or "inapplicable" and may be supplied at a later time.

Keys

It is clear that the rows of WORKER contain information about individual employees. In fact, we would expect each employee to be represented by one and only one row in WORKER. Thus, if some attribute uniquely identifies an employee, we should expect the same attribute to uniquely identify the row for that employee in WORKER. Let us assume that the WORKER-ID attribute uniquely identifies an employee. Then the value of the WORKER-ID attribute uniquely identifies a row in WORKER, and we say that WORKER-ID is a "key" in the WORKER relation.

Any set of attributes that uniquely identifies each tuple in a relation is termed a **superkey.** A **key** of a relation is a *minimal* set of such attributes. That is, a key is a "minimal superkey." By *minimal*, we mean that no subset of the set of key attributes will uniquely identify tuples in a relation. A key can also be described as a minimal set of attributes that uniquely determines, or **functionally determines,** each attribute value in a tuple.

In our discussion of the object-oriented model in Chapter 4, we referred to *surrogate keys*, which are internal object identifiers that have no meaning outside a computer system, and *external keys*, which are lexical attributes that do have meaning outside the system. *Keys* in the relational model are external keys in the sense of Chapter 4. That is, they are externally meaningful attributes and their values are assigned by users.

To illustrate the relational model concepts of keys and superkeys, let us consider the database of Figure 7.3. In the WORKER relation, the values of the attribute set

```
{WORKER-ID, NAME}
```

uniquely identify any tuple in the relation. Therefore, this set is a superkey for WORKER. However, this set of attributes is not minimal and is therefore not a key. In this example, WORKER-ID by itself is a key, since any row in the relation is uniquely identified by WORKER-ID.

In the ASSIGNMENT relation, the key consists of the WORKER-ID and the BLDG-ID attributes. Neither WORKER-ID alone nor BLDG-ID alone uniquely identifies every row, but the two attributes together do provide the unique identification required for a key. A key consisting of more than one attribute is called a **composite key.**

In any given relation, there may be more than one set of attributes that could be chosen as a key. These are called **candidate keys.** It may appear, for example, that NAME is a candidate key in the WORKER relation. This would be so if we could assume that NAME will *always* be unique. If we cannot make that assumption, then NAME is not a candidate key. When one of the candidate keys is selected as *the* relation key, it may be called the **primary key.** The candidate key that is the easiest to use in day-to-day data entry work is normally selected as the primary key. We will ordinarily use the term *key* to mean primary key.

Having introduced the concept of a key, we can augment the notation used to identify a relation by underlining the key attributes. The relations of Figure 7.3 are designated as follows:

superkey A set of attributes that uniquely identifies each row in a relation.

key A minimal set of attributes that uniquely identifies each row in a relation.

functionally determine To uniquely determine a value.

composite key A key consisting of more than one attribute.

candidate key Any set of attributes that could be chosen as a key of a relation.

primary key The candidate key designated for principal use in uniquely identifying rows in a relation.

```
WORKER (WORKER-ID, NAME, HOURLY-RATE, SKILL-TYPE, SUPV-ID)
ASSIGNMENT (WORKER-ID, BLDG-ID, START-DATE, NUM-DAYS)
BUILDING (BLDG-ID, BLDG-ADDRESS, TYPE, QLTY-LEVEL, STATUS)
SKILL (SKILL-TYPE, BONUS-RATE, HOURS-PER-WEEK)
```

Note that since ASSIGNMENT has two key attributes, both of them are underlined. This means that WORKER-ID and BLDG-ID *together* are a key for ASSIGNMENT. It does *not* mean that each of them is, by itself, a key.

Foreign Keys

The database schema given above has instances of the same attribute name being used in different relations. Examples of this are SKILL-TYPE in the WORKER and SKILL relations, and BLDG-ID in the ASSIGNMENT and BUILDING relations. Both of these attributes provide instances of the concept of a *foreign key*.

foreign key A set of attributes in one relation that constitute a key in some other (or possibly the same) relation; used to indicate logical links between relations.

A **foreign key** is a set of attributes in one relation that is a key in another (or possibly the same) relation. SKILL-TYPE in the WORKER relation and BLDG-ID in the ASSIGNMENT relation are examples of foreign keys, since SKILL-TYPE is the key of the SKILL relation, and BLDG-ID is the key of the BUILDING relation. Foreign keys are the essential links between relations. They are used to tie data in one relation to data in another relation. Thus, SKILL-TYPE links the WORKER relation to the SKILL relation, and WORKER-ID and BLDG-ID in the ASSIGNMENT relation show the link between WORKER and BUILDING.

Foreign key attributes need not have the same names as the key attributes to which they correspond. For example, WORKER-ID and SUPV-ID in the WORKER relation have different names but both take their values from the domain of worker identification numbers. Thus, SUPV-ID is a foreign key in the WORKER relation that references the key of its own relation. For any worker, the SUPV-ID attribute indicates the worker's supervisor—who is another worker. Consequently, SUPV-ID must contain a value that is a key of some other tuple in the WORKER relation. For example, in Figure 7.3, the supervisor of worker 1235 is worker 1311. In other words, M. Faraday's supervisor is C. Coulomb. SUPV-ID is an example of a **recursive foreign key**—a foreign key that references its own relation.

recursive foreign key A foreign key that references its own relation.

Because of the vital importance of foreign key information in the definition of a relational database schema, we will now revise the previously defined schema to show foreign key definitions:

```
WORKER (WORKER-ID, NAME, HOURLY-RATE, SKILL-TYPE, SUPV-ID)
Foreign Key: SKILL-TYPE REFERENCES SKILL-TYPE IN SKILL
             SUPV-ID REFERENCES WORKER-ID IN WORKER
ASSIGNMENT (WORKER-ID, BLDG-ID, START-DATE, NUM-DAYS)
Foreign Key: WORKER-ID REFERENCES WORKER-ID IN WORKER
             BLDG-ID REFERENCES BLDG-ID IN BUILDING
BUILDING (BLDG-ID, BLDG-ADDRESS, TYPE, QLTY-LEVEL, STATUS)
SKILL (SKILL-TYPE, BONUS-RATE, HOURS-PER-WEEK)
```

Note that a relation's foreign keys are defined immediately after the definition of the relation name, attribute, and keys. The statement is a foreign key definition for the WORKER relation and indicates that the SKILL-TYPE attribute in WORKER is a foreign key that references the key attribute SKILL-TYPE in the SKILL relation.

A listing such as this one, that gives relation names followed by their attribute names, with key attributes underlined, and with foreign keys designated, is called a **relational database schema.** It is the primary output of implementation design in a DDLC that implements a relational database. Moreover, it corresponds to the conceptual level of the ANSI/SPARC model.

relational database schema
A listing showing relation names, attribute names, key attributes, and foreign keys.

Integrity Constraints

constraint A rule that restricts the values in a database.

A **constraint** is a rule that restricts the values that may be present in the database. Codd's relational data model includes several constraints that are used to verify the validity of data in a database as well as to add meaningful structure to the data. We will consider the following constraints:

Entity integrity
Referential integrity
Functional dependencies

We will consider entity integrity and referential integrity now and discuss functional dependencies later in the chapter. The integrity constraints provide a logical basis for maintaining the validity of data values in the database, thus preventing errors in database updating and in information processing. Such capability has obvious value, since a principal purpose of database processing is to provide accurate information for management and executive decisions.

Entity Integrity. ☐ The rows in a relation represent instances in the database of specific real-world objects or "entities" (as we will call them here to be consistent with relational terminology). For example, a row in WORKER represents a specific employee, a row in BUILDING represents a specific building, a row in ASSIGNMENT represents a specific assignment of an employee to a building, and so on. The key of the relation uniquely identifies each row, and hence each entity instance. Thus, if users want to retrieve or manipulate the data stored in a specific row, they must know the value for the key of that row. That means we do not want any entity to be represented in the database unless we have a complete identification of the entity's key attributes. Thus, we cannot allow the key, or any part of the key, to be a null value. This is summed up in the **entity integrity rule:**

entity integrity rule No key attribute of a row may be null.

No key attribute of any row in a relation may have a null value.

Referential Integrity. ☐ In constructing relations, foreign keys are used to tie rows in one relation to rows in another. For example, SKILL-TYPE is used in the WORKER relation to tell us the principal skill of each employee so that bonus pay rates may be calculated. Therefore, it is extremely important that the value of SKILL-TYPE in any employee's row correspond to an actual SKILL-TYPE value in the SKILL relation. Otherwise, the employee's SKILL-TYPE would point nowhere. A database in which all non-null foreign keys reference actual key values in other relations observes referential integrity. Thus, we have the **referential integrity rule:**

Every foreign key must either be null, or its value must be the actual value of a key in another relation.

referential integrity rule The value of a non-null foreign key must be an actual key value in some relation.

□ THE NORMALIZATION PROCESS

Consider the relation of Figure 7.4, which partially combines the data of WORKER and ASSIGNMENT. Let us assume for this section that the relational database schema was not transformed from an object-oriented model but was designed directly from information collected from potential database users. We assume also that the original design of the database did not include the relations of Figure 7.3 but *did* include the relation of Figure 7.4. We want to see how problems can arise through careless database design, and how such problems can be avoided by following a set of well-defined principles called **normalization.**

normalization The process of converting a relation to a standard form.

data redundancy Repetition of data in a database.

data integrity Consistency of data in a database.

With a little analysis, we can see that the relation of Figure 7.4 is not well designed. For example, the four tuples for worker 1412 repeat the same name and skill type information. This **data redundancy,** or repetition, not only wastes space; it can lead to loss of **data integrity** (loss of consistency) in the database. The problem is brought about by the fact that one individual may be working on more than one building at a time. Suppose C. Nemo's skill type is in error, but only the first tuple is corrected. We would then have an *inconsistency* among the tuples containing information about C. Nemo. This is called an **update anomaly**.

update anomaly Data inconsistency resulting from data redundancy and partial update.

Alternatively, suppose that Nemo has been on sick leave for three months and all the buildings to which he was assigned are completed. If it is decided to delete all the rows containing information about completed buildings from the relation, then the information about C. Nemo's worker ID, name, and skill type will be lost. This is termed a **deletion anomaly.** Conversely, we might have hired a new employee named Spandolf, who has not yet been assigned to a building. If we assume null en-

deletion anomaly Unintended loss of data due to deletion of other data.

FIGURE 7.4   A Different Version of the Relation WORKER

WORKER				
WORKER-ID	**NAME**	**SKILL-TYPE**	**SUPV-ID**	**BLDG-ID**
1235	M. Faraday	Electric	1311	312
1235	M. Faraday	Electric	1311	515
1412	C. Nemo	Plumbing		312
1412	C. Nemo	Plumbing		460
1412	C. Nemo	Plumbing		435
1412	C. Nemo	Plumbing		515
1311	C. Coulomb	Electric		435

insertion anomaly Inability to add data to the database due to absence of other data.

tries are not allowed, then we cannot enter information regarding Spandolf until he has been assigned to a building. This is termed an **insertion anomaly.**

Update, deletion, and insertion anomalies are obviously undesirable. How can we prevent, or at least minimize, such problems? Clearly, dividing the WORKER relation of Figure 7.4 into the two relations, WORKER and ASSIGNMENT, of Figure 7.3 appears to do away with the anomalies. This is an intuitive solution. We will now show a more formal method, called decomposition, for achieving the same result. **Decomposition** is the process of splitting relations into multiple relations to eliminate anomalies and maintain data integrity. To do this, we use **normal forms,** or rules for structuring relations.

decomposition of relations Splitting a relation into multiple relations.

normal forms Rules for structuring relations that eliminate anomalies.

First Normal Form

First Normal Form (1NF) All attribute values must be atomic.

atomic value Value that is not a set of values or a repeating group.

A relation is in **First Normal Form (1NF)** if the values in the relation are **atomic** for every attribute in the relation. By this we mean, simply, that no attribute value can be a set of values or, as it is sometimes expressed, a "repeating group." Codd's definition of a relation includes the condition that the relation be in first normal form. Therefore, all the relation schemes we will encounter will be 1NF. However, to clarify the concept, let's look at an example of a table that is not a 1NF relation.

In Figure 7.5, consider the values entered for the attribute BLDG-ID. Here we have combined each worker's building assignments into a single set. The value of the attribute BLDG-ID is the set of buildings on which the person is working. Suppose we are interested in only one of the worker's buildings. This information may be difficult to extract, since the identifier for the building of interest is buried within a set within a tuple.

The relation in Figure 7.5 is not 1NF because BLDG-ID is not atomic. That is, in any given tuple, BLDG-ID can have multiple values. The relation shown in Figure 7.4 would be 1NF, though, because the value in which we are interested, that of an individual building, can be identified merely by referencing an attribute name, BLDG-ID.

Since Codd's original definition of the relational model required *all* relations to be 1NF, Figure 7.5 is not even a legitimate relation. We will follow Codd's definition and assume that all relations must be 1NF.

The next two normal forms, Second Normal Form and Third Normal Form, apply to relations that are constrained by functional dependencies. Before proceeding to these normal forms, then, we must first explain functional dependencies.

FIGURE 7.5   A Version of the Relation WORKER That Is Not in First Normal Form

WORKER				
WORKER-ID	**NAME**	**SKILL-TYPE**	**SUPV-ID**	**BLDG-ID**
1235	M. Faraday	Electric	1311	{312, 515}
1412	C. Nemo	Plumbing		{312, 460, 435,515}
1311	C. Coulomb	Electric		435

Earlier in the chapter, we discussed the entity and referential integrity constraints. Functional dependencies (FDs) provide a means for defining additional constraints on a relational schema. The essential idea is that a tuple's value in one attribute uniquely determines the tuple's value in another attribute. For example, in every tuple in Figure 7.4, WORKER-ID uniquely determines NAME, and WORKER-ID uniquely determines SKILL-TYPE. We write these two functional dependencies as:

```
FD: WORKER-ID -> NAME
FD: WORKER-ID -> SKILL-TYPE
```

functional dependency The value of an attribute in a tuple determines the value of another attribute in the tuple.

More formally, we can define a **functional dependency** as follows: if A and B are attributes in a relation R, then

```
FD: A -> B
```

means that if any two tuples in R have the same value for their A attribute, they *must* have the same value for their B attribute. This definition also applies if A and B are sets of columns, rather than just single columns.

The notation "—>" is read "functionally determines." Thus, in these examples, WORKER-ID functionally determines NAME, WORKER-ID functionally determines SKILL-TYPE, and A functionally determines B.

determinant The attribute(s) on the left side of a functional dependency; determine(s) the value of other attributes in the tuple.

The attribute on the left hand side of an FD is called a **determinant,** because its value "determines" the value of the attribute on the right hand side. A relation's key is a determinant, since its value uniquely determines the value of every attribute in a tuple.

Second Normal Form

Second Normal Form (2NF) No nonkey attribute may be functionally dependent on just a part of the key.

Second and Third Normal Forms deal with the relationship between key and nonkey attributes. A relation is in **Second Normal Form (2NF)** if no nonkey attribute is functionally dependent on just a part of the key. Thus, 2NF can be violated only when a key is a composite key, or, in other words, one that consists of more than one attribute.

Examine the relation scheme of Figure 7.6. Here the key consists of WORKER-ID and BLDG-ID together. NAME is determined by WORKER-ID and so is functionally dependent on a part of the key. That is, knowing WORKER-ID for the worker is sufficient to identify the worker's

---

FIGURE 7.6   The Relation ASSIGNMENT

```
ASSIGNMENT (WORKER-ID, BLDG-ID, START-DATE, NAME)
```

ASSIGNMENT

WORKER-ID	BLDG-ID	START-DATE	NAME
1235	312	10/10	M. Faraday
1412	312	10/01	C. Nemo
1235	515	10/17	M. Faraday
1412	460	12/08	C. Nemo
1412	435	10/15	C. Nemo

name. Thus, the relation is not 2NF. Leaving this relation in its present, non-2NF form can lead to the following problems:

1. The worker name is repeated in every row that refers to an assignment for that worker.
2. If the name of the worker changes, every row recording an assignment of that worker must be updated. This, as you may remember, is an update anomaly.
3. Because of this redundancy, the data might become inconsistent, with different rows showing different names for the same worker.
4. If at some time there are no assignments for the worker, there may be no row in which to keep the worker's name. This is an insertion anomaly.

To resolve these problems, the relation can be decomposed into the following two relation schemes, both of which are 2NF:

```
ASSIGNMENT(WORKER-ID, BLDG-ID, START-DATE)
Foreign Key: WORKER-ID REFERENCES WORKER-ID IN WORKER
WORKER(WORKER-ID, NAME)
```

Can you see that these relations are 2NF and that they eliminate the problems listed above? Thus, 2NF reduces redundancy and inconsistency. However, it may complicate certain retrieval applications. If we wanted the names of all workers assigned to a given building, we have to somehow combine the information in these two relations. We will show how to do this in later chapters which discuss relational data languages.

projection of a relation A relation consisting of selected attributes from another relation.

These two smaller relations are called **projection**s of the original relation. It is easy to see that a projection simply selects certain attributes from an existing relation and represents them as a new relation. This seems simple enough. The contents of ASSIGNMENT and WORKER are now as shown in Figure 7.7. Notice that in ASSIGNMENT we still have five rows, since the values for WORKER-ID, BLDG-ID, and START-

FIGURE 7.7   The Relations ASSIGNMENT and WORKER, Both 2NF

ASSIGNMENT

WORKER-ID	BLDG-ID	START-DATE
1235	312	10/10
1412	312	10/01
1235	515	10/17
1412	460	12/08
1412	435	10/15

WORKER

WORKER-ID	NAME
1235	M. Faraday
1412	C. Nemo

DATE, taken together, were unique. However, in the relation WORKER we now have just two rows, since there were only two unique sets of values for WORKER-ID and NAME. Thus, data redundancy and the possibility of anomalies have been eliminated.

The process of decomposing the non-2NF relation into two 2NF relations follows a few simple steps, the first two of which were illustrated in our example: (1) Create a new relation by using the attributes from the offending FD as the attributes in the new relation. The determinant of the FD becomes the key of the new relation. (2) The attribute on the right side of the FD is then eliminated from the original relation. (3) If more than one FD prevents the relation from being 2NF, repeat steps 1 and 2 for each FD. (4) If the same determinant appears in more than one FD, place all the attributes functionally dependent on this determinant as nonkey attributes in a relation having the determinant as key.

Third Normal Form

Third Normal Form (3NF)
Every determinant is a key.

A relation is in **Third Normal Form (3NF)** if *for every FD: X —> Y* , X is a key. We note in passing that it follows from the definition of Third Normal Form that if a relation is 3NF, then it is also 2NF. The converse is not true, however, as we will now see.

Consider the relation WORKER' of Figure 7.8. We see that

```
FD: WORKER-ID -> SKILL-TYPE
FD: WORKER-ID -> BONUS-RATE
```

are functional dependencies for this relation since WORKER-ID is a key. However,

```
FD: SKILL-TYPE -> BONUS-RATE
```

is also a functional dependency. It is clear that the 3NF criterion is satisfied for the first two of these FDs, but what about the last one? Obviously, SKILL-TYPE is not a key, so the 3NF criterion fails. Therefore, WORKER' is not 3NF. Note, however, that WORKER' *is* 2NF. (It must be, since its key consists of only one attribute.) Thus, it is possible for a relation to be 2NF without being 3NF.

Why should we be concerned if a relation is not 3NF? The problems are similar to those listed for violation of 2NF design.

1. The skill type's bonus rate is repeated in the row of every employee having that skill type. This data redundancy wastes storage space.

FIGURE 7.8   The Relation WORKER'

WORKER'		
WORKER-ID	SKILL-TYPE	BONUS-RATE
1235	Electric	3.50
1412	Plumbing	3.00
1311	Electric	3.50

2. If the bonus rate of the skill type changes, every such row must be updated. If a row is deleted, we may lose data giving the bonus rate for a skill type. Thus, the relation is subject to update and deletion anomalies.

3. If there are currently no permanent employees for a given skill type, there may be no row in which to keep the skill type's bonus rate. This is an insertion anomaly.

Fortunately, if we establish that a relation is 3NF we can be assured that it is 2NF. But how can we convert a relation scheme that is not in 3NF to a set of relations that satisfy 3NF? Decomposition is the easiest method. This is the method we used to convert a non-2NF relation (AS-SIGNMENT of Figure 7.6) into two relations in 2NF (Figure 7.7). We now show how to apply the decomposition process to non-3NF relations.

We begin with the relational scheme of WORKER'. Form a new relation (R1) by removing from WORKER' the attributes on the right side of any FD that fails the 3NF criterion. In our example, this is BONUS-RATE. Form a new relation consisting of those attributes on both the left and right side of the FD that fails the 3NF criterion. In our example, these are SKILL-TYPE and BONUS-RATE. The determinant of the FD, SKILL-TYPE, is the key. If we call this new relation R2, then

```
R1(WORKER-ID, SKILL-TYPE)
Foreign Key: SKILL-TYPE REFERENCES SKILL-TYPE IN R2
```

and

```
R2(SKILL-TYPE, BONUS-RATE)
```

are the schemas of the two relations that take the place of WORKER'. If either R1 or R2 are not 3NF, we continue to apply the decomposition process until all relations are 3NF. In this case, R1 and R2 are both 3NF, so we may stop.

We have decomposed WORKER' into R1 and R2, both of which are 3NF. You should convince yourself that R1 and R2 are both 3NF. Please note, also, that SKILL-TYPE is a foreign key in R1.

Because every relation is, by definition, 1NF, and because 3NF relations are always 2NF, the following chain of implications is valid:

3NF   implies   2NF   implies   1NF

For this reason, to put relations in Second and Third Normal Form, it is only necessary to use the Third Normal Form criterion. If we verify that every determinant in every relation is a key in that relation—the Third Normal Form criterion—then all relations are in First, Second, and Third Normal Forms. This greatly simplifies the normalization process, since we now need check only one criterion.

Our version of Third Normal Form is often called **Boyce-Codd Normal Form (BCNF)**. The criterion used for 3NF by many authors is logically slightly weaker than the BCNF criterion that we are using. This weaker criterion states that a relation is 3NF if it has no "transitive dependencies." A **transitive dependency** occurs when a nonkey attribute

Boyce-Codd Normal Form (BCNF) Every determinant is a key.

transitive dependency Occurs when a nonkey attribute is functionally dependent on one or more other nonkey attributes.

is functionally dependent on one or more other nonkey attributes. This criterion does not handle two cases:

1. A nonkey attribute is dependent on a key attribute in a composite key (the criterion for non-2NF relations).

2. A key attribute in a composite key is dependent on a nonkey attribute.

BCNF handles both of these. Thus, if a relation is BCNF, then it is also 3NF, in the transitive dependency sense, and it is 2NF. We see then that our definition of 3NF further simplifies the normalization process.

Fourth Normal Form

First Normal Form prohibits relations from having nonatomic or multivalued attributes. Many data modeling situations exist, however, which require multivalued attributes. For example, in a group health insurance system, the multiple dependents of an employee must be tracked. In a college setting, a faculty member is assigned to multiple committees and is responsible for multiple courses. Such examples as these could be multiplied many times. How can they be modeled in a relational database that does not allow multivalued attributes?

Figure 7.9 shows four possible approaches to solving this problem for the college faculty member's committees and courses. Each solution seems unsatisfactory in some way. They all waste space, either by using null values or by entering redundant data. Those that use null values violate entity integrity, since all attributes together constitute the relation's key. In addition, suppose Jones were placed on the Promotion committee, and an update were required. Would a new row be added or would an existing row be updated? Finally, it is not clear that the COMMITTEE and COURSE attributes are independent of each other. For example, in Figure 7.9(a), is the Admissions committee in some way related to course IM101?

The apparent relationship between independent attributes can be eliminated by requiring that every value of one attribute appear in at least one row with every value of the other attribute. This is illustrated in Figure 7.10, where both Admissions and Scholarship appear in rows with IM101, IM102, and IM103.

multivalued dependency (MVD) A constraint that guarantees the mutual independence of multivalued attributes.

A condition that enforces attribute independence by requiring this duplication of values is called a **multivalued dependency (MVD)**. MVDs are constraints on relations just as FDs are constraints. Clearly, since they require an enormous duplication of data values, an important aspect of the normalization process should be to eliminate multivalued dependencies. This is done with Fourth Normal Form.

Fourth Normal Form (4NF) A relation that is in Third Normal Form and has no multivalued dependencies.

A relation is in **Fourth Normal Form (4NF)** if it is 3NF and has no multivalued dependencies. Since the problem of multivalued dependencies arises from multivalued attributes, we can reach a solution by placing all multivalued attributes in relations by themselves, together with the key to which the attribute values apply. Figure 7.11 illustrates this. FNAME is a key value in some other relation that identifies the faculty member to whom the information applies. We list the committees Jones is assigned to by including one row for each committee. Jones's name is repeated each time. The same is true of the courses that Jones teaches.

FACULTY	FNAME	COMMITTEE	COURSE
	Jones	Admissions	IM101
	Jones	Scholarship	IM102
	Jones	Scholarship	IM103

(a) Minimal number of records with repetitions

FACULTY	FNAME	COMMITTEE	COURSE
	Jones	Admissions	IM101
	Jones	Scholarship	IM102
	Jones		IM103

(b) Minimal number of records with null values

FACULTY	FNAME	COMMITTEE	COURSE
	Jones	Admissions	
	Jones	Scholarship	
	Jones		IM101
	Jones		IM102
	Jones		IM103

(c) Rows with no repetitions

FACULTY	FNAME	COMMITTEE	COURSE
	Jones	Admissions	IM101
	Jones	Scholarship	
	Jones		IM102
	Jones	Scholarship	IM103

FIGURE 7.9   Representing Multi-valued Attributes in a Single Relation

FACULTY	FNAME	COMMITTEE	COURSE
	Jones	Admissions	IM101
	Jones	Scholarship	IM101
	Jones	Admissions	IM102
	Jones	Scholarship	IM102
	Jones	Admissions	IM103
	Jones	Scholarship	IM103

FIGURE 7.10   The Relation FACULTY with a Multivalued Dependency

FIGURE 7.11   The Relations FAC-COMM and FAC-COURSE Are Both 4NF

FAC-COMM	FNAME	COMMITTEE
	Jones	Admissions
	Jones	Scholarship

FAC-COURSE	FNAME	COURSE
	Jones	IM101
	Jones	IM102
	Jones	IM103

The relations in Figure 7.11 are in Fourth Normal Form (4NF) because all multivalued attributes (in this case, COMMITTEE and COURSE) have been placed in relations by themselves. Moreover, this approach overcomes the problems of the various approaches shown in Figure 7.9. As a final note, we point out that the keys of these 4NF relations are *both* the attributes in the relation. That is, the key of FAC-COMM is (FNAME, COMMITTEE) and the key of FAC-COURSE is (FNAME, COURSE).

Other Normal Forms

Several other normal forms have been proposed to eliminate additional anomalies. We will briefly discuss two of these: Fifth Normal Form (5NF) and Domain/Key Normal Form (DKNF).

Fifth Normal Form. □ Functional dependency and multivalued dependency constraints result in the need for Second, Third, and Fourth Normal Forms. **Fifth Normal Form (5NF)** eliminates anomalies that result from a special type of constraint called *join dependencies*. These dependencies are principally of theoretical interest and are of highly dubious practical value. Consequently, Fifth Normal Form has virtually no practical application.

Fifth Normal Form (5NF) A normal form that eliminates join dependencies.

Domain/Key Normal Form. □ Fagin (1981) proposed a normal form based on the definitions of keys and attribute domains. He showed that a relation is in **Domain/Key Normal Form (DKNF)** if and only if every constraint on the relation is a consequence of the definitions of domains and keys. This is an important result. However, he did not provide a general method for converting a non-DKNF relation into a DKNF relation.

Domain/Key Normal Form (DKNF) Requires every constraint to result from definitions of domains and keys.

□ TRANSFORMING AN OBJECT-ORIENTED MODEL TO A RELATIONAL MODEL

It is generally agreed that object-oriented models provide a more accurate representation of the complexities of an application problem than do the relational and other early data models. Thus, in Chapters 4, 5, and 6, we discussed object-oriented modeling and demonstrated how a large variety of applications problems could be solved with object-oriented models. However, few systems exist at present on which object-oriented models are implemented. Thus, we need some method for translating object-oriented models to models that can be implemented. Since we are studying the relational model in this chapter, we will focus on methods of transforming any object-oriented model into a relational model.

An object-oriented data model consists of objects, relationships, attributes, specializations, aggregates, and so forth. We will now show methods of transforming each of these constructs to relations. An important characteristic of the process we will describe is that it results in the creation of relations normalized to Fourth Normal Form. Consequently, following conversion of an object-oriented model to a relational model, further normalization is unnecessary.

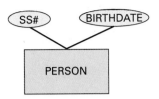

FIGURE 7.12   An Object-Oriented Model of Person

Consider the simple object-oriented model of Figure 7.12. We see an object set with two attributes. PERSON is an abstract (that is, nonlexical) object set, but SS# and BIRTHDATE are lexical attributes. Since attributes in the relational model must be lexical, SS# and BIRTHDATE can both be attributes in a relation. Therefore, we can transform this diagram into a relation with attributes as follows:

```
PERSON (SS#, BIRTHDATE)
```

What is the key? Since we can (and will) assume that SS# uniquely identifies a person, we conclude that SS# is the key. We have, therefore

```
PERSON (SS#, BIRTHDATE)
```

as the transformation of the object-oriented model of Figure 7.12 to a relational model.

Now consider Figure 7.13. We may attempt to transform this model in the same way, resulting in:

```
SALE (AMOUNT, PRODUCT-#)
```

But in this case there is no key, since there may be many sales having the same values for AMOUNT and PRODUCT-#. Therefore, we must add a key attribute, SALE-#:

```
SALE (SALE-#, AMOUNT, PRODUCT-#)
```

We may summarize this process as follows. An object set with attributes can be transformed into a relation by using the object set name as the relation's name, and the object set's attributes as the relation's attributes. If any set of these attributes can be used as a key for the relation, then they become the relation's key. Otherwise, we add an attribute to the relation with the understanding that its values uniquely identify object instances in the original object set, and it can thus serve as a key for the relation. In the example above, we added SALE-# as an attribute to the relation—meaning that SALE-# uniquely identifies an instance in the SALE object set.

We have shown a simple and fast method for generating a key for a relation that does not otherwise have one. In actual practice, the database

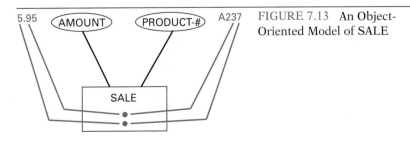

FIGURE 7.13   An Object-Oriented Model of SALE

designer must consult with the user in selecting a key for the relation. Often there will be an invoice number or some other value that is recorded that can serve as the relation's key. This would be the logical choice for the key attribute. Another possibility is that the user would recommend the addition of some combination of attributes that together would constitute a key. The analyst has the responsibility of working with the users to determine which attribute(s) will make up the key.

Transforming Specialization and Generalization Object Sets

Now consider Figure 7.14. The PERSON object set is easily transformed:

```
PERSON (SS#, NAME, ADDRESS)
```

But what do we do with **MARRIED PERSON**? Since it is a subset of PERSON, it inherits all of PERSON's attributes. Additionally, it has attributes of its own. Consequently, we derive the following relation:

```
MARRIED-PERSON (SS#, NAME, ADDRESS, SPOUSE)
Foreign Key: SS# REFERENCES SS# IN PERSON
```

Thus, a specialization of an object set will have all of the attributes of the object set it specializes, plus all of its own attributes as well. The two relations will have the same key. It is important to note that the key (SS#) of the specialization relation (**MARRIED-PERSON** in our example) is also a foreign key which points to the generalization relation (**PERSON** in the example). This is because every instance in a specialization must also be in the generalization. Consequently, NAME and ADDRESS in MARRIED-PERSON constitute duplicated information. To eliminate this data redundancy, we simply remove from the specialization relation all the non-key attributes that are duplicated. Finally then our **MARRIED-PERSON** relation is:

```
MARRIED-PERSON(SS#, SPOUSE)
Foreign Key: SS# REFERENCES SS# IN PERSON
```

Transforming Relationships

Relationships are transformed in three different ways, depending on the relationship's cardinality. We handle one–one, one–many, and many–many relationships separately.

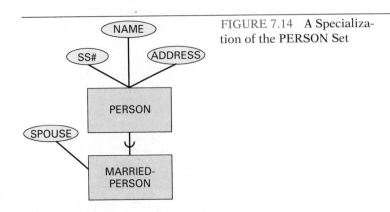

FIGURE 7.14   A Specialization of the PERSON Set

One–One Relationships. □ Let's take another look at an example from Alchemical Bank. The relationship HAS-CHKG-ACCOUNT, shown in Figure 7.15, is one–one. That is, a customer has at most one checking account, and a checking account is assigned to at most one customer. If we assume the key attributes CUSTOMER-# for CUSTOMER and CH-ACCOUNT-# for CHECKING-ACCOUNT, then we have the two one-column relations:

```
CUSTOMER(CUSTOMER-#)
CHECKING-ACCOUNT(CH-ACCOUNT-#)
```

To show the connection between the two relations, we may add CH-ACCOUNT-# to CUSTOMER and CUSTOMER-# to CHECKING-ACCOUNT. Note that each of these columns is a foreign key that points to the other relation:

```
CUSTOMER(CUSTOMER-#, CH-ACCOUNT-#)
Foreign Key: CH-ACCOUNT-# REFERENCES CH-ACCOUNT-# IN
             CHECKING-ACCOUNT
CHECKING-ACCOUNT(CH-ACCOUNT-#, CUSTOMER-#)
Foreign Key: CUSTOMER-# REFERENCES CUSTOMER-# IN CUSTOMER
```

Obviously, this solution duplicates data, since only one CUSTOMER-#, CH-ACCOUNT-# combination is needed. Which one should we eliminate? If a customer does not have a checking account, then in the CUSTOMER relation CH-ACCOUNT-# is null for that customer. However, in the CHECKING-ACCOUNT relation, there will always be a CUSTOMER-# for each CH-ACCOUNT-#. This is shown by the minimum cardinalities of the relationship as shown in Figure 7.15. That is, the minimum cardinality on the CHECKING ACCOUNT side is zero, whereas the minimum cardinality on the CUSTOMER side is one. Therefore, in this case *the best choice* would be to eliminate CH-ACCOUNT-# from the CUSTOMER relation. This yields:

```
CUSTOMER(CUSTOMER-#)
CHECKING-ACCOUNT(CH-ACCOUNT-#, CUSTOMER-#)
Foreign Key:CUSTOMER-# REFERENCES CUSTOMER-# IN CUSTOMER
```

Of course, in a complete database schema for a real application, both of these relations will have many more attributes. Here we show only the attributes needed to transform the simple object-oriented model of Figure 7.15. If the object sets in Figure 7.15 had additional attributes, these would be placed in the relations corresponding to them. For example, CUSTOMER could have NAME, ADDRESS, and PHONE-# as attributes, and CHECKING-ACCOUNT could have BALANCE and DATE-OPENED.

FIGURE 7.15 Cardinalities of Alchemical Bank Relationships

These additional attributes would cause our database schema to look like this:

```
CUSTOMER(CUSTOMER-#, NAME, ADDRESS, PHONE-#)
CHECKING-ACCOUNT(CH-ACCOUNT-#, CUSTOMER-#, BALANCE, DATE-
OPENED)
     Foreign Key:CUSTOMER-# REFERENCES CUSTOMER-# IN CUSTOMER
```

In summary, one–one relationships are transformed by showing one of the object sets as an attribute of the other's relation. The relation chosen is determined by the needs of the application itself. In many cases, either relation may be chosen.

One–Many Relationships. □ Suppose the HAS-CHKG-ACCOUNT relationship had "many" cardinality on the side of the CHECKING ACCOUNT object set. That is, a customer may have many checking accounts, but any one checking account is still assigned to only one customer. In this case, the one–many cardinality *by itself* determines that the relation structure must be as follows:

```
CHECKING-ACCOUNT (CH-ACCOUNT-#, CUSTOMER-#)
Foreign Key: CUSTOMER-# REFERENCES CUSTOMER-# IN CUSTOMER
CUSTOMER(CUSTOMER-#)
```

Thus, in any one–many relationship, the relation describing the object on the "many" side of the relationship receives the foreign key column that points to the other object. In our example, CHECKING-ACCOUNT is the relation corresponding to the object set on the "many" side of the relationship, and CHECKING-ACCOUNT therefore receives the CUSTOMER-# foreign key column.

Many–Many Relationships. □ Figure 7.16 shows HAS-CHKG-ACCOUNT as a many–many relationship. In this context, we assume that a customer may have multiple checking accounts and that a checking account may be assigned to multiple customers. To transform many–many relationships, we create an *intersection relation*. In this case, we need three relations—one relation for each object set and one for the HAS-CHKG-ACCOUNT relationship:

```
CUSTOMER(CUSTOMER-#)
CHECKING-ACCOUNT(CH-ACCOUNT-#)
HAS-CHKG-ACCOUNT(CUSTOMER-#, CH-ACCOUNT-#)
Foreign Keys: CUSTOMER-# REFERENCES CUSTOMER-# IN CUSTOMER
              CH-ACCOUNT-# REFERENCES CH-ACCOUNT-# IN
                   CHECKING-ACCOUNT
```

FIGURE 7.16   A Many–Many Alchemical Bank Relationship

Since CUSTOMER-# doesn't determine CH-ACCOUNT-#, and CH-AC-COUNT-# doesn't determine CUSTOMER-#, the key of the relation HAS-CHKG-ACCOUNT is both of these columns. HAS-CHKG-ACCOUNT contains the data that identifies which customers are associated with which checking accounts. Figure 7.17 shows some sample data for these three relations. Note that customers 2222 and 1111 are each associated with two different checking accounts, and accounts CA777 and CA888 are each associated with two different customers. These relationships are indicated in the HAS-CHKG-ACCOUNT relation.

Note also that only the key columns from CUSTOMER and CHECK-ING-ACCOUNT are used in HAS-CHKG-ACCOUNT. That is, even if CUS-TOMER and CHECKING-ACCOUNT had other columns, HAS-CHKG-ACCOUNT would only use the key columns from these two relations. The following schema illustrates this:

```
CUSTOMER(CUSTOMER-#, NAME, ADDRESS, PHONE-#)
CHECKING-ACCOUNT(CH-ACCOUNT-#, BALANCE, DATE-OPENED)
HAS-CHKG-ACCOUNT(CUSTOMER-#, CH-ACCOUNT-#)
Foreign Keys: CUSTOMER-# REFERENCES CUSTOMER-# IN CUSTOMER
              CH-ACCOUNT-# REFERENCES CH-ACCOUNT-# IN
                 CHECKING-ACCOUNT
```

intersection relation A relation representing instances where two other relations meet in a many–many relationship.

The foreign key descriptions indicate that both of the key attributes of HAS-CHKG-ACCOUNT are also foreign keys. This is why we call HAS-CHKG-ACCOUNT an **intersection relation**—because it represents the instances where CUSTOMER and CHECKING-ACCOUNT meet, or "intersect." As we will see in the next section, it is possible for an intersec-

FIGURE 7.17   An Intersection Relation for a Many–Many Relationship

CUSTOMER	
CUSTOMER-#	
1111	
2222	
3333	

CHECKING-ACCOUNT	
CH-ACCOUNT-#	
CA888	
CA777	
CA999	

HAS-CHKG-ACCOUNT	
CUSTOMER-#	**CH-ACCOUNT-#**
2222	CA999
2222	CA888
3333	CA777
1111	CA777
1111	CA888

tion relation, such as HAS-CHKG-ACCOUNT, to have additional nonkey attributes that apply only to it.

Consider Figure 7.18, which shows an object-oriented model for tracking sales of International Product Distribution. IS-SOLD-IN, a relationship aggregated to be considered an object set, has a QUANTITY attribute. We transform this model in accordance with the rules given above. Since the relationship is many-many, we create three relations:

```
PRODUCT (PRODUCT-#)
COUNTRY (COUNTRY-NAME)
IS-SOLD-IN (PRODUCT-#, COUNTRY-NAME, QUANTITY)
Foreign Keys: PRODUCT-# REFERENCES PRODUCT-# IN PRODUCT
              COUNTRY-NAME REFERENCES COUNTRY-NAME IN
              COUNTRY
```

We have created key attributes of PRODUCT-# and COUNTRY-NAME to distinguish them from the names of their respective relations. We have also placed QUANTITY in the IS-SOLD-IN relation, because it is an attribute that applies to that relation. If IS-SOLD-IN had other attributes that applied to it, they would be added to the relation in a similar manner. The PRODUCT and COUNTRY relations are shown with only one attribute, but of course they could have other attributes as well. If no other attributes are needed for these relations in the database, then they can be eliminated from the schema; and the schema will consist of the IS-SOLD-IN relation only.

Figure 7.19 shows IS-SOLD-IN related to DATE. In this case, the QUANTITY attribute applies to those products sold in a particular country on a particular date. We can transform this model to a relational model as:

```
IS-SOLD-IN (PRODUCT-#, COUNTRY-NAME)
SOLD-ON (PRODUCT-#, COUNTRY-NAME, DATE, QUANTITY)
```

(We have omitted the one-column relations that define the object sets.) Notice, however, that all of the information contained in IS-SOLD-IN is also contained in SOLD-ON. Thus, we can eliminate IS-SOLD-IN from the schema. If IS-SOLD-IN had nonkey attributes, then it could not be eliminated. By eliminating IS-SOLD-IN from the schema, we are saying

FIGURE 7.18   An Aggregate Object Set

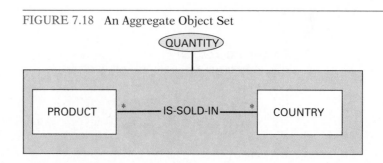

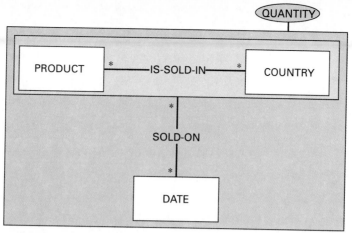

FIGURE 7.19   Nested Aggregates

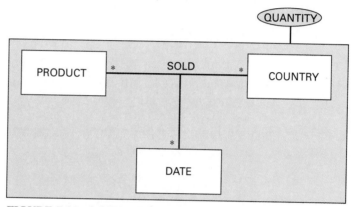

FIGURE 7.20   A 3-Way Relationship

that the model of Figure 7.19 is essentially a 3-way relationship with an attribute. Thus, it is equivalent to Figure 7.20. The relational model for Figure 7.20 would be

```
SOLD (PRODUCT-#, COUNTRY-NAME, DATE, QUANTITY)
```

which is the same as **SOLD-ON** above, except for the name of the relation.

Transforming Recursive Relationships   Figure 7.21 shows a portion of the model of Figure 7.1. It is important to realize that the WORKER object set, which appears twice in the diagram, is the *same object set* both times. Both copies of WORKER have the same attributes, even though they are only shown attached to the copy on the right. The model uses two copies of WORKER for convenience in showing the SUPERVISES relationship which exists between WORKER and WORKER. This relationship is called *recursive*, because it exists between

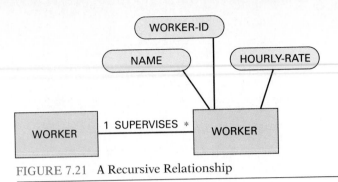

FIGURE 7.21　A Recursive Relationship

an object set and itself. In this case, the relationship with its one–many cardinality means that one worker supervises many workers.

How do we transform the **WORKER** object set, together with its attributes and the **SUPERVISES** relationship, into a relation? Using the approaches we have already studied, we would arrive at the following:

```
WORKER (WORKER-ID, NAME, HOURLY-RATE, WORKER-ID)
```

This solution is incorrect, because the **WORKER** relation has two attributes named **WORKER-ID**, and no two attributes within a relation are allowed to have the same name. The solution is to change the name of the second **WORKER-ID** attribute to a name that reflects the **SUPERVISES** relationship it represents. Thus, we change it to **SUPV-ID**:

```
WORKER (WORKER-ID, NAME, HOURLY-RATE, SUPV-ID)
Foreign Key: SUPV-ID REFERENCES WORKER-ID IN WORKER
```

Notice that SUPV-ID is a recursive foreign key, since it references WORK-ER-ID, which is the key of the relation SUPV-ID is in. That is, recursive foreign keys will result from the transformation of recursive relationships. Sample data for the **WORKER** relation is shown in Figure 7.22.

In summary, we have shown ways of translating object-oriented model constructs—objects, attributes, relationships, specializations, and aggregates—to relations. After all translation of specific constructs is

FIGURE 7.22　A Relation With a Recursive Foreign Key (SUPV-ID)

WORKER			
WORKER-ID	NAME	HOURLY-RATE	SUPV-ID
1235	M. Faraday	12.50	1311
1412	C. Nemo	13.75	1520
2920	R. Garret	10.00	
3231	P. Mason	17.40	
1520	H. Rickover	11.75	
1311	C. Coulomb	15.50	
3001	J. Barrister	8.20	3231

complete, then the resulting schema should be reviewed for redundancy. Any redundant relations—that is, relations whose information is entirely contained in other relations in the schema—should be eliminated from the schema.

In addition, note that all of the relations are normalized to Fourth Normal Form. The reason for this is as follows: Functional dependencies, as defined for the relational model, are attributes, one–one relationships, or one–many relationships. The process we described for converting each of these to attributes in a relation guaranteed that they would only be dependent on key attributes. Thus, each relation will be 3NF. The multivalued attributes of the relational model occur only in many–many relationships. Since these are converted to relations whose composite keys consist of the keys of the individual object sets, they are guaranteed to be 4NF.

Transformation Examples: Manwaring Consulting Services

In Chapter 4, we created an object-oriented model for Manwaring Consulting Service's project billing. This model is shown in Figure 7.23. Applying the principles of this chapter, we will now convert this model to a relational schema.

The relations for the PROJECT and CLIENT object sets are as follows:

```
CLIENT (CLIENT-NAME, CLIENT-ADDRESS)
PROJECT (PROJECT-#, CLIENT-NAME, PROJECT-TITLE,
         TOTAL-CHARGE, INVOICE-#, INVOICE-DATE)
Foreign Key: CLIENT-NAME REFERENCES CLIENT-NAME IN CLIENT
```

PROJECT-# was added as an attribute, because we needed an external key for PROJECT. PROJECT-TITLE does not uniquely identify a project. INVOICE-# is unique but is not an appropriate key for a relation describing projects. For the sake of clarity, we have also changed some of

FIGURE 7.23   A Data Model for Project Billing

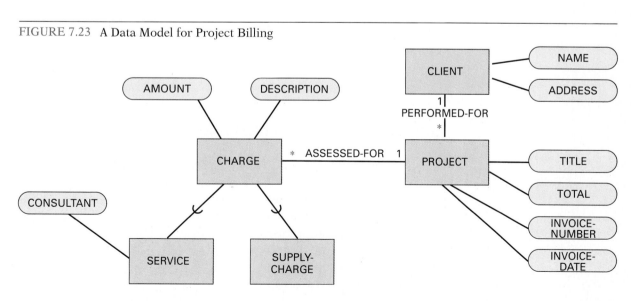

the attribute names—for example, CLIENT-NAME and PROJECT-TI-TLE. The change to CLIENT-NAME was essential, since it is used as a foreign key in PROJECT.

In addition to these two relations, we need relations for CHARGE and SERVICE:

```
CHARGE (CHARGE-#, PROJECT-#, AMOUNT, DESCRIPTION)
Foreign Key: PROJECT-# REFERENCES PROJECT-# IN PROJECT
SERVICE (CHARGE-#, PROJECT-#, CONSULTANT)
Foreign Key: CHARGE-#, PROJECT-# REFERENCE
                     CHARGE-#,PROJECT-# IN CHARGE
```

In converting the CHARGE object set to a relation, we had to make a decision about its key. In this case, we decided that the project to which a specific charge applies partially identifies the charge. Therefore, we used PROJECT-# as a part of the key. We then added CHARGE-# as the remaining part of the key. This means that different charges can have the same CHARGE-# if they are not related to the same project.

The SERVICE object set is a specialization of the CHARGE object set. For this reason, the SERVICE relation must have the same key as the CHARGE relation. Of course, this means that this two-column key is a foreign key that references CHARGE. In addition, the SERVICE relation has the CONSULTANT attribute, which indicates the consultant who performed the service. Even though SUPPLY CHARGE is also a specialization of CHARGE, it does not merit its own relation, because it has no attributes of its own. All the information needed about supply charges can be found in the CHARGE relation.

Figure 7.24 shows the data model we developed for Manwaring's project billing in Chapter 6. We will now convert it to a relational model. The CLIENT and PROJECT object sets are converted as before:

```
CLIENT (CLIENT-NAME, CLIENT-ADDRESS)
PROJECT (PROJECT-#, CLIENT-NAME, PROJECT-TITLE,
         TOTAL-CHARGE, INVOICE-#, INVOICE-DATE)
Foreign Key: CLIENT-NAME REFERENCES CLIENT-NAME IN CLIENT
```

The object set OTHER-CHARGE in this model corresponds to CHARGE in the previous model:

```
OTHER-CHARGE (CHARGE-#, PROJECT-#, AMOUNT, DESCRIPTION)
Foreign Key: PROJECT-# REFERENCES PROJECT-# IN PROJECT
```

We also need a relation for CONSULTANT:

```
CONSULTANT (CONSULTANT-NAME, RATE)
```

Finally, we need to represent the relationships in the large box. Since the ENGAGED-IN relationship has no attributes of its own, we can embed it in the relation representing the ON relationship. This relation is equivalent to a 3-way relationship, so its key will consist of three attributes. It also has two nonkey attributes, HOURS and AMOUNT.

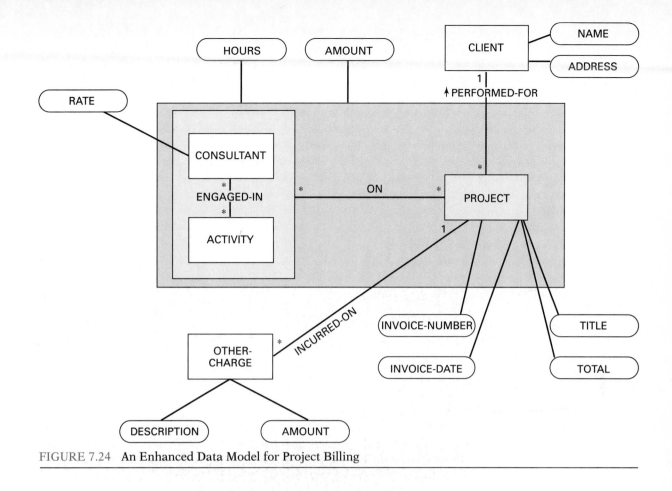

FIGURE 7.24 An Enhanced Data Model for Project Billing

```
ENGAGED-IN-ACTIVITY-ON (CONSULTANT-NAME, ACTIVITY, PROJECT-#,
                        HOURS, AMOUNT)
Foreign Keys: CONSULTANT-NAME REFERENCES CONSULTANT-NAME IN
              CONSULTANT
              PROJECT-# REFERENCES PROJECT-# IN PROJECT
```

Since "ON" does not give a very good description of the meaning of the relation, we have given it a new name that we feel is more descriptive.

While the process of converting an object-oriented model to a relational model is mechanical and straightforward, it does require some human intelligence. We have illustrated this in the previous two examples, where we selected keys in various ways and changed the names of attributes and relations as needed. Nevertheless, the process is comparatively simple, and all resulting relations are in Fourth Normal Form.

■ SUMMARY

This chapter introduced Codd's relational data model, the normal forms associated with it, and a process for converting an object-oriented model to a relational model. We showed ways of designing a relational database directly from user information or by transforming an object-oriented model.

The relational data model was introduced in 1970 by E.F. Codd, who showed that a logical approach to data definition and manipulation is superior to the physical approaches that prevailed at the time. The relational model is based on the mathematical notion of a relation, consisting of rows and columns of data. The columns are called attributes, and the rows are called tuples. Each relation has a set of attributes, known as a key, that uniquely identifies each row. Inter-relation references are handled through foreign keys, which are logical pointers from a row in one relation to a row in another. To ensure the validity of data in a relational database, Codd formulated the entity integrity and referential integrity rules. These rules state that a key value cannot be null and that a foreign key value must correspond to an actual value of a key in another relation.

Relations that are designed as a part of a database's conceptual design may have update anomalies. These usually occur because of functional dependencies, or functional relationships, between attributes, neither of which is a key attribute in the relation. By making functional dependencies a natural consequence of the relation`s key definitions, many common anomalies are eliminated. Relations that correspond to this rule are in Third Normal Form. In addition, the existence of multivalued attributes and rules designed to guarantee independence between attributes results in the need for a higher normal form. Fourth Normal Form is used to guarantee that relations in Third Normal Form will properly handle multivalued attributes. Fifth Normal Form and Domain/Key Normal Form are additional normal forms that have been discussed in the literature and are briefly described in this chapter.

The process of transforming an object-oriented model to a relational model involves creating a relation for each object set in the model. The attributes of the object set are attributes of the relation. If an external key attribute exists, it can be used as the relation's key. Otherwise, a key attribute may be created by the analyst. However, it is best if such an attribute arises naturally in the application being modeled. One–one and one–many relationships are converted to the relational model by making them attributes of the appropriate relation. Many–many relationships correspond to multivalued attributes and are converted to Fourth Normal Form by creating a relation whose two-column key is taken from the keys of the two object sets participating in the relationship. Specialization sets are converted by creating separate relations, which take their key from the relation corresponding to the generalization set. Recursive relationships may also be modeled by creating a new attribute name, which is descriptive of the relationship.

■ REVIEW QUESTIONS

1. Define each of the following terms in your own words:
    a. relational data model
    b. recursive relationship
    c. degree of a relation
    d. attribute domain

e. superkey
f. functionally determine
g. candidate key
h. foreign key
i. relational database schema
j. entity integrity rule
k. normalization
l. data redundancy
m. update anomaly
n. insertion anomaly
o. normal forms
p. atomic value
q. determinant
r. projection of a relation
s. Boyce-Codd Normal Form
t. multivalued dependency
u. Fifth Normal Form
v. intersection relation

2. Compare and contrast:
a. Keys and superkeys
b. Foreign keys and keys
c. Foreign keys and recursive foreign keys
d. Attributes and domains
e. Attributes and columns
f. Tuples and rows
g. Entity integrity and referential integrity
h. Candidate keys and primary keys

3. React to the following statement, paraphrased from Kent (1983): A relation is in Third Normal Form if every nonkey attribute is dependent on the key, the whole key, and nothing but the key. Which part of the statement applies to Second Normal Form, and which applies to Third Normal Form?

4. Explain why it is undesirable to have relations that are not in Second or Third Normal Form.

5. Describe the process of transforming an object-oriented model to a relational model for each of the following:
a. Object set and attributes with and without an external key
b. One–one relationship
c. One–many relationship
d. Many–many relationship
e. Specialization relationship
f. Aggregate
g. Recursive relationship

■ PROBLEMS AND EXERCISES

1. Match each term with its definition:

| __Domain/Key Normal Form | a. A nonkey attribute is functionally dependent on one or more other nonkey attributes |

__Second Normal Form	b. Every determinant is a key
__Relation attribute	c. Value of an attribute if the attribute is inapplicable or its value is unknown
__Referential integrity	d. Consistency of data in a database
__Tuple	e. Two-dimensional table containing rows and columns of data
__Null value	f. Minimal set of attributes that uniquely identifies each row
__Third Normal Form	g. In Third Normal Form with no multi-valued dependencies
__Primary key	h. Foreign key that references its own relation
__Relation	i. A column in a relation
__Recursive foreign key	j. The value of a non-null foreign key must be an actual key value in some relation
__Constraint	k. Key consisting of more than one attribute
__Data integrity	l. Splitting a relation into multiple relations
__Composite key	m. Row in a relation
__Decomposition of relations	n. No nonkey attribute may be functionally dependent on just a part of the key
__First Normal Form	o. All attribute values must be atomic
__Functional dependency	p. Unintended loss of data due to deletion of other data
__Deletion anomaly	q. Rule that restricts the values in a database
__Fourth Normal Form	r. Requires every constraint to result from definitions of domains and keys
__Key	s. Candidate key designated for principal use in identifying rows
__Transitive dependency	t. The value of an attribute in a tuple determines the value of another attribute in the tuple

2. Consider the following relation (capitalized letters are attribute names, lower-case letters and numbers are values):

X

A	B	C	D	E
a1	b2	c1	d3	e2
a3	b2	c3	d2	e4
a1	b3	c1	d1	e2
a2	b4	c1	d4	e2

Circle the functional dependencies that do *not* apply to X.

a. A —> C   b. D —> E   c. C —> A   d. E —> B
e. E —> A   f. C —> B   g. B —> D   h. B —> A

Identify a key for X.

3. Consider the following relation (capitalized letters are attribute names, lower-case letters and numbers are values):

Y

A	B	C	D	E
a1	b2	c1	d3	e2
a2	b2	c3	d3	e4
a1	b3	c2	d1	e2
a2	b4	c5	d1	e5

Circle the functional dependencies that do *not* apply to Y.

a. A —> C   b. D —> E   c. C —> A   d. E —> B
e. E —> A   f. C —> B   g. B —> D   h. B —> A

Identify a key for Y.

4. Consider the following relation (capitalized letters are attribute names, lower-case letters and numbers are values):

Z

A	B	C	D	E
a1	b2	c2	d3	e2
a1	b2	c2	d1	e4
a2	b3	c2	d1	e5
a2	b4	c5	d1	e5

Circle the functional dependencies that do *not* apply to Z.

a. E —> D   b. D —> E   c. C —> A   d. E —> B
e. E —> A   f. B —> C   g. B —> D   h. B —> A

Identify a key for Z.

5. For each of the following relations, indicate which normal forms the relations conform to (if any) and show how the relation can be decomposed into multiple relations each of which conforms to the highest normal form.

a. EMPLOYEE(SS#, NAME, ADDRESS, PHONE, FATHER, SKILLS)
FD: NAME —> ADDRESS

b. WORKER(W-ID, W-NAME, SPOUSE-SS#, SPOUSE-NAME)
FD: SPOUSE —>SPOUSE-NAME

c. SALE(DATE, CUSTOMER, PRODUCT, VENDOR, VENDOR-CITY, SALESREP)
FD: CUSTOMER —> SALESREP

d. EMPLOYEE(SS#, NAME, ADDRESS, PHONE, FATHER, FATHERS-ADDRESS)
FD: FATHER —> FATHERS-ADDRESS

e. WORKER(W-ID, W-NAME, SPOUSE, CHILDREN)

f. SALE(DATE, CUSTOMER, PRODUCT, VENDOR, VENDOR-CITY, SALESREP)
FD: VENDOR —> VENDOR-CITY, FD: PRODUCT —> VENDOR

g. STUDENT (<u>STUDENT-#</u>, NAME, BLDG, FLOOR, SENIOR-RESI-DENT)
FD: FLOOR —> SENIOR-RESIDENT

h. ENROLLMENT (<u>COURSE-#</u>, <u>STUDENT-#</u>, GRADE, INSTRUCTOR, ROOM-#)
FD: COURSE-# —> INSTRUCTOR, FD: COURSE-# —> ROOM-#

i. ACTIVITY (<u>STUDENT-#</u>, <u>DESCRIPTION</u>, DATE, BLDG, ROOM, COST)
FD: DESCRIPTION —> BLDG, FD: DESCRIPTION —> ROOM,
FD: BLDG —> COST

6. Create a relational schema, with all relations 4NF, for the following information about a life insurance company:

> The company has a large number of policies. For each policy, we want to know the policyholder's social security number, name, address, and birthdate. We also need to know the policy number, annual premium, and death benefit amount. Moreover, we want to know the agent number, name, and state of residence of the agent who wrote the policy. A policyholder can have many policies, and an agent will write many policies.

7. Convert the following object-oriented models to relational schemas that show relation names, attributes, keys, and foreign keys.

a. Figure 7.1E

b. Figure 7.2E

FIGURE 7.1E   Purchase Order Data Model for Manwaring Consulting Services

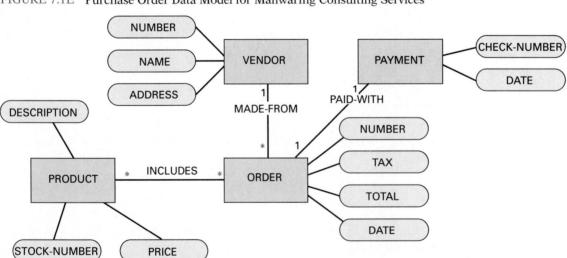

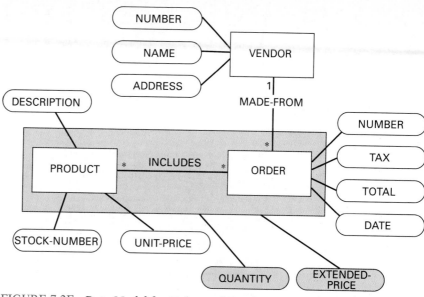

FIGURE 7.2E   Data Model for Enhanced Purchase Order

▪ PROJECTS AND PROFESSIONAL ISSUES

1. Without using an object-oriented model for conceptual design, create a relational database schema for some organization that you have contact or experience with. Create at least eight relations that are normalized to Fourth Normal Form.

2. Carry out project 1 again, this time by first designing an object-oriented model and converting it to a relational model using the methods of this chapter. Compare your experience in the two projects.

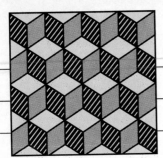

chapter eight

RELATIONAL ALGEBRA AND CALCULUS

Cordelia Molini and Reggie Townsend, information systems practitioners at International Product Distribution (IPD), are discussing the differences in relational database languages. Reggie has recently been introduced to relational databases and is striving to comprehend their conceptual basis. However, he does not understand the significant structural differences between some of the commercial languages. Cordelia explains:

"When Codd originally proposed the relational data model, he recommended a procedural language, relational algebra, and a nonprocedural language, relational calculus."

"I'm afraid I don't understand those terms, Cordelia. What do you mean by procedural and nonprocedural?"

"In a nonprocedural language, we tell the computer what has to be done, not how to do it. In a procedural language, we tell the computer how each step is to be executed. Traditional computer languages are procedural. The relational model has made the development of nonprocedural languages more practical."

"It would appear, then, that nonprocedural languages are superior to procedural languages. So why aren't all relational languages modeled after relational calculus?"

"The more popular ones, such as SQL, QBE, and QUEL, tend to be. Relational algebra does have definite advantages, however, and some languages, such as those in the R:base systems, are modeled after it. To fully understand the relational model and the languages used to manipulate it, it's important to completely grasp both approaches."

This chapter provides a comprehensive introduction to relational algebra and relational calculus, which form the basis for the commercial languages used with relational databases. After becoming acquainted with these two languages, you will be prepared to learn and use any of the many database languages that are based on them. After reading this chapter, you should be able to:

- List the operations of relational algebra and show how they can be used to create new relations from existing relations.
- Demonstrate the structure of query solutions in relational calculus, most especially the conditional statements that must be formed to define a query solution.
- Formulate solutions to specific types of queries in both languages.

□ A REVOLUTIONARY ADVANCE IN DATA MANIPULATION

In 1970–1971, E.F. Codd published two papers introducing the relational data model and the relational data manipulation languages, relational algebra and relational calculus. Although the relational data model itself was important, the relational languages were more significant in touching off the relational database revolution. After all, the relational model, in which data is represented in tables, is very similar to the file-oriented models that already existed. Admittedly, the changes in terminology— from "file" to "relation," from "field" to "attribute," and so on—were important, since they emphasized the logical meaning of data, rather than its physical structure. But, in retrospect, it appears that the most important aspect of the new model was its concrete data languages, which allow the manipulation of data solely on the basis of its logical characteristics. In this chapter, we will study the two languages Codd proposed, relational algebra and relational calculus.

In his original paper, Codd introduced the relational data model and relational algebra (Codd, 1970). **Relational algebra** is a **procedural** language for manipulating relations. That is, relational algebra uses a step by step approach to create a relation containing the data that answers the query. In subsequent papers, Codd introduced relational calculus (Codd, 1971a, 1971b). **Relational calculus** is **nonprocedural**. In relational calculus, a query is solved by defining a solution relation in a single step.

Codd showed that relational algebra and relational calculus are logically equivalent—a fact of considerable importance. It meant that any query that could be formulated in relational calculus could be formulated in relational algebra, and vice versa. This provided a means of measuring the logical power of a query language. If a language was at least as powerful as relational algebra, it was called **relationally complete**. This means that any query that can be formulated in relational algebra must be formulable in the "relationally complete" language. Thus, as commercial relational languages are developed, their logical power can be tested by comparing them with relational algebra or relational calculus. If a language is less powerful than either of these, then there will be certain queries which cannot be formulated in the commercial language.

Relational algebra is also important because it contributes much of the vocabulary and many of the basic relational data manipulation concepts that are commonly found in commercial database languages. Such terms as *select*, *project*, *join*, and *union compatible* all originate in relational algebra. In addition, some commercial database languages are based on relational algebra.

Relational calculus is important for two reasons: (1) It is based on the predicate calculus of formal logic, which is a powerful method of determining the truth of a statement from the truth of its components. Consequently, relational calculus has as firm a logical foundation as any programming language in existence. (2) Several commercial relational languages are conceptually close to it. We will be studying some of these languages in later chapters.

Both relational algebra and calculus, as formulated by Codd and as discussed in this chapter, are theoretical languages. That is, here we are interested only in the conceptual aspects of algebra and calculus, not in specific implementations of them. Therefore, we will be rather free and informal in our definition and use of syntax. If these were actual, commercial languages—such as those we will study later in the book—we would need to be more precise. Throughout this chapter, we will use the database of Figure 8.1 to illustrate our examples. This database is taken from the International Product Distribution case introduced in Chapter 1.

relational algebra A procedural language for manipulating relations.

procedural Language that provides a step by step method for solving problems.

relational calculus A nonprocedural language for defining query solutions.

nonprocedural Language that provides a means for stating *what* is desired rather than *how* to get it.

relationally complete Having the same logical power as relational algebra or calculus.

CUSTOMER

CUST_ID	CUST_NAME	ADDRESS	COUNTRY	BEGINNING BALANCE	CURRENT BALANCE
100	Watabe Bros	Box 241, Tokyo	Japan	45,551	52,113
101	Maltzl	Salzburg	Austria	75,314	77,200
105	Jefferson	B 918, Chicago	USA	49,333	57,811
110	Gomez	Santiago	Chile	27,400	35,414

SALESPERSON

SALPERS_ID	SALPERS_NAME	MANAGER_ID	OFFICE	COMM %
10	Rodney Jones	27	Chicago	10
14	Masaji Matsu	44	Tokyo	11
23	Francois Moire	35	Brussels	9
37	Elena Hermana	12	B.A.	13
39	Goro Azuma	44	Tokyo	10
27	Terry Cardon		Chicago	15
44	Albert Ige	27	Tokyo	12
35	Brigit Bovary	27	Brussels	11
12	Buster Sanchez	27	B.A.	10

PRODUCT

PROD_ID	PROD_DESC	MANUFACTR_ID	COST	PRICE
1035	Sweater	210	11.25	22.00
2241	Table Lamp	317	22.25	33.25
2249	Table Lamp	317	13.55	24.80
2518	Brass Sculpture	253	13.60	21.20

SALE

DATE	CUST_ID	SALPERS_ID	PROD_ID	QTY
02/28	100	10	2241	200
02/12	101	23	2518	300
02/15	101	23	1035	150
02/19	100	39	2518	200
02/02	101	23	1035	200
02/05	105	10	2241	100
02/22	110	37	2518	150
02/14	105	10	2249	50
02/01	101	23	2249	75
02/04	101	23	2241	250

MANUFACTURER

MANUFACTR_ID	MANUFACTR_NAME	ADDRESS	COUNTRY
210	Kiwi Klothes	Auckland	New Zealand
253	Brass Works	Lagos	Nigeria
317	Llama Llamps	Lima	Peru

FIGURE 8.1   Sample Data From the IPD Database

☐ A REVOLUTIONARY ADVANCE IN DATA MANIPULATION

Relational algebra operations manipulate relations. That is, these operations use one or two existing relations to create a new relation. This new relation may then be used as input to a new operation. This powerful concept—the creation of new relations from old ones—makes possible an infinite variety of data manipulations. It also makes the solution of queries considerably easier, since we can experiment with partial solutions until we find an approach that will work.

Relational algebra consists of the following nine operations: union, intersection, difference, product, select, project, join, divide, and assignment. The first four of these operations are taken from mathematical set theory and are largely the same as the operations found there. This is reasonable, since relations are themselves sets, so set operations can be applied to them. The next four are new operations that apply specifically to the relational data model. The last operation—assignment—is the standard computer language operation of giving a name to a value. In this case, assignment is used to give a name to a new relation that is created from existing relations. We will use the ":=" ("is the name assigned to") sign to indicate assignment of names to relations. We will discuss these operations in the order they are listed above.

Union

union Relational algebra operation that creates the set union of two union compatible relations.

The **union** operation ($\cup$) allows us to combine the data from two relations. For example, suppose the SALESPERSON relation of Figure 8.1 did not exist in our database. Instead, we have two relations as in Figure 8.2. These two relations represent all salespeople who are subordinate to some other salesperson (SP_SUBORD) and all salespeople who manage some other salesperson (SP_MGR). Obviously, we have created redundant data here. This could have happened through the execution of a series of relational algebra commands prior to the command we are about to illustrate. If we wish to obtain a relation containing *all* salespeople, we must take the *union* of SP_SUBORD and SP_MGR.

```
SALESPERSON := SP_SUBORD  ∪  SP_MGR
```

SALESPERSON (Figure 8.3) is the name assigned to the resulting rela-

---

FIGURE 8.2   An Alternate Relational Representation of **SALESPERSON**

SP_SUBORD

SALPERS ID	SALPERS NAME	MANAGER ID	OFFICE	COMM %
10	Rodney Jones	27	Chicago	10
14	Masaji Matsu	44	Tokyo	11
23	Francois Moire	35	Brussels	9
37	Elena Hermana	12	B.A.	13
39	Goro Azuma	44	Tokyo	10
44	Albert Ige	27	Tokyo	12
35	Brigit Bovary	27	Brussels	11
12	Buster Sanchez	27	B.A.	10

SP_MGR

SALPERS ID	SALPERS NAME	MANAGER ID	OFFICE	COMM %
27	Terry Cardon		Chicago	15
44	Albert Ige	27	Tokyo	12
35	Brigit Bovary	27	Brussels	11
12	Buster Sanchez	27	B.A.	10

SALESPERSON SALPERS ID	SALPERS NAME	MANAGER ID	OFFICE	COMM %
10	Rodney Jones	27	Chicago	10
14	Masaji Matsu	44	Tokyo	11
23	Francois Moire	35	Brussels	9
37	Elena Hermana	12	B.A.	13
39	Goro Azuma	44	Tokyo	10
27	Terry Cardon		Chicago	15
44	Albert Ige	27	Tokyo	12
35	Brigit Bovary	27	Brussels	11
12	Buster Sanchez	27	B.A.	10

FIGURE 8.3   The Union of SP_SUBORD and SP_MGR

tion and consists of rows that are either in SP_SUBORD or SP_MGR or both.

It is important to note that any row that exists in both relations appears only once in the union relation. This follows from the definition of a relation as a set, since a given element is found only one time in a set. This is illustrated in Figures 8.2 and 8.3. Three rows, identified by SALPERS_ID 44, 35, and 12, are found in both of the relations of Figure 8.2, but each of these rows appears only once in the relation of Figure 8.3.

We must point out a special requirement of the union operation that makes it slightly different from the normal set union of mathematics. In mathematics, any two sets can be combined through a union operation. But in relational algebra, before the union can be applied to two relations, the relations must have exactly the same columns, both as to number of columns and domains of columns. If this is the case, we say that the two relations are **union compatible**. Obviously, SP_SUBORD and SP_MGR are union compatible.

union compatible Two or more relations that have equivalent columns as to number and domains.

Union compatibility is required so that the result of the union operation is a relation. If we took the union of, say, CUSTOMER and PRODUCT, we would obtain a set but not a relation. The rows in the resulting set would not have common columns so they could not be grouped into a relational table. Union compatibility is clearly essential for the union operation. For the same reason, it is essential for the intersection and difference operations.

Intersection

intersection Relational algebra operation that creates the set intersection of two union compatible relations.

The **intersection** operation ($\cap$) allows us to identify the rows that are common to two relations. If we want to identify the salespeople who are subordinate to some manager *and* who are managers themselves, for example, we take the *intersection* of SP_SUBORD and SP_MGR, calling the result SP_SUBORD_MGR:

SP_SUBORD_MGR := SP_SUBORD $\cap$ SP_MGR

This yields the following relation:

SP_SUBORD_MGR SALPERS ID	SALPERS NAME	MANAGER ID	OFFICE	COMM %
44	Albert Ige	27	Tokyo	12
35	Brigit Bovary	27	Brussels	11
12	Buster Sanchez	27	B.A.	10

The result of an intersection operation is the relation consisting of all rows that are in both of the relations. That is, if C is the intersection of A and B,

```
C := A ∩ B,
```

then C consists of those rows that are in A and in B. As before, A and B must be union compatible.

Difference

difference Relational algebra operation that creates the set difference of two union compatible relations.

The **difference** operation (indicated by a minus sign) allows us to identify rows that are in one relation and not in another. Suppose we are interested in identifying the managers who are *not* subordinate to any other manager. Then we take the *difference* between SP_MGR and SP_SUBORD, in that order.

```
SP_MGR_MGR := SP_MGR - SP_SUBORD
```

This yields the following relation:

SP_MGR_MGR

SALPERS_ID	SALPERS_NAME	MANAGER_ID	OFFICE	COMM_%
27	Terry Cardon		Chicago	15

The difference between two relations is defined as the relation consisting of all rows that are in the first relation and *not* in the second relation. Thus, if

```
C := A - B
```

then a row is in C if and only if it is in A and not in B.

Note that

```
A - B
```

is not the same thing as

```
B - A.
```

If we were to reverse the order of the relations used in the example above,

```
SP_SUBORD - SP_MGR
```

the resulting relation would consist of all those salespeople who do not manage anybody, which is just the opposite of the salespeople who are not managed by anybody. Thus, the order of the relations in a difference operation is very important. Once again, both relations must be union compatible.

subtraction The relational algebra difference operation.

The difference operation may also be called the **subtraction** operation. This particular operation is very valuable in solving some difficult problems that otherwise would be unsolvable. We will give an example at the end of our discussion of relational algebra.

Product

product Relational algebra operation that creates the Cartesian product of two relations.

The **product** operation, indicated by the * symbol, is valuable as a building block for the join, which is probably the most important operation in relational algebra. It is identical to the operation in mathematics which creates the Cartesian product of two sets. We now explain what this means by illustrating the product operation with a simple, abstract example.

Consider the relations of Figure 8.4(a). A and B are two two-column relations, having attributes X, Y and W, Z, respectively. The product of A and B is C, shown in Figure 8.4(b).

```
C := A * B
```

Note that the product is created by:

1. Concatenating, or adjoining, the attributes of the two relations;
2. Attaching to each row in A, each of the rows in B.

That is, C's attributes are all the attributes of A and B together. Since A and B have two attributes each, C has four attributes. The rows of C are created by stringing the rows of A and B together. Each row of A is matched with each row of B. Thus, since there are three rows in B, each row of A is matched three times with a row in B, and so appears in three different rows of C. It is easy to see that the number of rows in C will always be the number of rows in A *times* the number of rows in B.

To give another example using the database of Figure 8.1, if we were to take the product of PRODUCT (no pun intended) and SALE

```
P_S := PRODUCT * SALE
```

FIGURE 8.4   An Example of the Product Operation

(a) The relations A and B

A

X	Y
10	22
11	25

B

W	Z
33	54
37	98
42	100

(b) The product of A and B

C   (:= A * B)

X	Y	W	Z
10	22	33	54
10	22	37	98
10	22	42	100
11	25	33	54
11	25	37	98
11	25	42	100

P_S would have 10 columns and 40 rows. There is a small problem in this case, since a column in PRODUCT and a column in SALE (PROD_ID) have the same name. This is overcome by modifying the column name in each case by adding the name of the originating relation. Thus, in P_S, we have columns named

```
PRODUCT.PROD_ID  and  SALE.PROD_ID.
```

There seems to be no obvious application for the product operation. That is, it is not clear what kind of query would be answered by taking the product of two relations. No matter. As we will see, the product is used as a building block operation for the join. It is conceptually important, therefore, and will have ample application later in the chapter. It is also used in the SQL query language, which is the most important commercial relational language.

Select

select Relational algebra operation that uses a condition to select rows from a relation.

The **select** operation is used to create a relation from another relation, by selecting only those rows from the original relation that satisfy a specified condition. For example, consider the following query:

Query: Give all information for salespeople in the Tokyo office.

This can be solved by selecting rows from the SALESPERSON relation of Figure 8.1, subject to the condition that a row is selected only if the OFFICE attribute is equal to 'Tokyo.' We do this in relational algebra as follows:

```
SP_TOKYO := SELECT(SALESPERSON: OFFICE = 'Tokyo')
```

The name "SP_TOKYO" is one that we just made up to identify the relation. The keyword "SELECT" is used to indicate that a select operation is being performed. Following "SELECT," we place in parentheses the name of the relation from which rows are to be selected, followed by a colon (:), followed by a selection condition. Those rows that satisfy the selection condition will be selected and placed in the resulting relation. The result of this select operation is the following relation:

SP TOKYO

SALPERS_ID	SALPERS_NAME	MANAGER_ID	OFFICE	COMM_%
14	Masaji Matsu	44	Tokyo	11
39	Goro Azuma	44	Tokyo	10
44	Albert Ige	27	Tokyo	12

Selection conditions are essentially the same as the conditions used in IF statements in traditional programming languages. However, the column names used in any given selection condition must be found in the relation named in the select operation. Some examples of selection conditions that could be used with the SALESPERSON relation are:

```
SALPERS_ID = 23
SALPERS_NAME = `Brigit Bovary'
MANAGER_ID >= 20
OFFICE not = 'B.A.'
COMM_% < 11
```

Notice that we can use comparison operators such as "<" and ">". There are five such comparison operators: =, <, >, <=, >=. For each of these, there is a corresponding operator that uses the Boolean operator "not." Thus, we have "=" and "not =" as well as "<" and "not <", and so forth. We can also use the Boolean connectives "and" and "or." The "not" can also be used in a general way to negate an entire condition. These concepts are illustrated in the following queries.

Query: Which salesperson has ID 23?
   Solution: SELECT(SALESPERSON: SALPERS_ID = 23)
Result:

SALPERS_ID	SALPERS_NAME	MANAGER_ID	OFFICE	COMM_%
23	Francois Moire	35	Brussels	9

Query: Give all information about salesperson Brigit Bovary.
   Solution: SELECT(SALESPERSON: SALPERS_NAME = 'Brigit Bovary')
Result:

SALPERS_ID	SALPERS_NAME	MANAGER_ID	OFFICE	COMM_%
35	Brigit Bovary	27	Brussels	11

Query: Who are the salespeople working for managers having an ID greater than or equal to 20?
   Solution: SELECT (SALELSPERSON: MANAGER_ID >= 20)
Result:

SALPERS_ID	SALPERS_NAME	MANAGER_ID	OFFICE	COMM_%
10	Rodney Jones	27	Chicago	10
14	Masaji Matsu	44	Tokyo	11
23	Francois Moire	35	Brussels	9
39	Goro Azuma	44	Tokyo	10
44	Albert Ige	27	Tokyo	12
35	Brigit Bovary	27	Brussels	11
12	Buster Sanchez	27	B.A.	10

Query: Give information on all salespeople *except* those in the Buenos Aires office.
   Solution: SELECT(SALESPERSON: OFFICE not = 'B.A.')
Result:

SALPERS_ID	SALPERS_NAME	MANAGER_ID	OFFICE	COMM_%
10	Rodney Jones	27	Chicago	10
14	Masaji Matsu	44	Tokyo	11
23	Francois Moire	35	Brussels	9
39	Goro Azuma	44	Tokyo	10
27	Terry Cardon		Chicago	15
44	Albert Ige	27	Tokyo	12
35	Brigit Bovary	27	Brussels	11

Query: Which salespeople are getting less than 11% commission?
   Solution: SELECT(SALESPERSON: COMM_% < 11)

Result:

SALPERS_ID	SALPERS_NAME	MANAGER_ID	OFFICE	COMM_%
10	Rodney Jones	27	Chicago	10
23	Francois Moire	35	Brussels	9
39	Goro Azuma	44	Tokyo	10

Query: Who are the salespeople in Tokyo getting more than 10% commission/
   Solution: SELECT 9SALESPERSON; OFFICE = 'Tokyo'
and COMM % > 10)
Result:

SALPERS_ID	SALPERS_NAME	MANAGER_ID	OFFICE	COMM_%
14	Masaji Matsu	44	Tokyo	11
44	Albert Ige	27	Tokyo	12

Query: Who is reporting to manager 27 or getting over 10% commission?
   Solution: SELECT(SALESPERSON: MANAGER_ID = 27 or COMM_% > 10)
Result:

SALPERS_ID	SALPERS_NAME	MANAGER_ID	OFFICE	COMM_%
10	Rodney Jones	27	Chicago	10
14	Masaji Matsu	44	Tokyo	11
37	Elena Hermana	12	B. A.	13
27	Terry Cardon		Chicago	15
44	Albert Ige	27	Tokyo	12
35	Brigit Bovary	27	Brussels	11

Project

project Relational algebra operation that creates a relation by deleting columns from an existing relation.

projection Relation resulting from a project operation.

Several of the queries used to illustrate the select operation asked "Who . . .," which suggests that users wanted just the names of the salespeople satisfying the query condition. Yet the answer to each query included entire rows of data taken from the SALESPERSON relation, since the select operation always selects entire rows. Clearly we need some way to eliminate unwanted columns. If the select operation may be thought of as eliminating unwanted rows, the **project** operation can be thought of as eliminating unwanted columns. The relation resulting from a project operation is called a **projection** of the original relation.

Unlike the other relational algebra operations, the project operation does not require any special keyword or symbol. Rather, to create a projection—a relation consisting of only certain identified columns of another relation—we merely list the original relation followed by brackets enclosing the columns that we want to keep. For example, if we wish to identify the salespeople in the Tokyo office, we could project the name column from the SP_TOKYO relation shown on p. 000.

```
SP_TOKYO [SALPERS_NAME]
```

This gives the following relation:

SALPERS_NAME
Masaji Matsu
Goro Azuma
Albert Ige

We could have chosen more than one column. Thus, if we want the ID, the Name, and the Manager of these salespeople we enter:

```
SP_TOKYO [SALPERS_ID, SALPERS_NAME, MANAGER_ID]
```

The result would be:

SALPERS_ID	SALPERS_NAME	MANAGER_ID
14	Masaji Matsu	44
39	Goro Azuma	44
44	Albert Ige	27

Suppose we are interested in knowing all the different commission percentages being paid to salespeople. We can obtain these by merely projecting on the COMM_% column of the SALESPERSON relation:

```
SALESPERSON [COMM_%]
```

This gives the following result:

COMM_%
10
11
9
13
15
12

Notice that each commission rate appears only one time, even though several different salespeople have the same commission rate. Because a relation is a set, a given rate appears only once. This is an important feature of the project operation. It automatically eliminates duplicate rows from the resulting relation. This also happens when the resulting relation consists of more than one column. If any two entire rows in a relation are identical column for column, the row appears only once in the relation.

The project operation presents a convenient opportunity for showing the nesting of operations in relational algebra. By *nesting,* we mean the execution of more than one operation without explicitly assigning a name to the intermediate result relations. For example, let's add a project operation to one of the queries used to illustrate the select operation:

Query: Which salespeople are getting less than 11% commission?
Solution: SELECT(SALESPERSON: COMM_% < 11) [SALPERS_NAME]
Result:

SALPERS_NAME
Rodney Jones
Francois Moire
Goro Azuma
Buster Sanchez

In this example, the select operation is performed first, followed by the projection of the resulting relation on the SALPERS_NAME column. It is permissible to nest relational algebra operations as desired, using parentheses where needed to show the order of operations.

Join

join Relational algebra operation that connects relations.

The **join** operation is used to connect data across relations—perhaps the most important function in any database language. There are several versions: the natural join, the "theta" join, and the outer join. Of these, the natural join is by far the most important.

Natural Join. □ Consider the SALE relation of Figure 8.1. This relation records the customer, salesperson, and product involved in any particular sales transaction by including the respective IDs of these three data items. This information allows us to make logical connections between the CUSTOMER, SALESPERSON, and PRODUCT relations. For example, suppose we want to know the names of the customers who have made purchases from salesperson 10. First, we select those sales applying only to salesperson 10 and place them in a relation we name SALE_10. This yields the following relation:

SALE_10

DATE	CUST_ID	SALPERS_ID	PROD_ID	QTY
02/28	100	10	2241	200
02/05	105	10	2241	100
02/14	105	10	2249	50

Then we can obtain the desired information by *joining* the SALE_10 and CUSTOMER relations. This operation proceeds as follows:

1. The product of SALE_10 and CUSTOMER is created. This results in a relation with 11 columns (5 from SALE_10, 6 from CUSTOMER) and 12 rows (3 in SALE_10 * 4 in CUSTOMER).

2. All of the rows of this product relation are eliminated except those in which CUST_ID from SALE_10 is equal to CUST_ID from CUSTOMER. This results in the relation shown in Figure 8.5. Note that there are two CUST_ID columns in the relation and that in each row the values in these two columns are identical.

FIGURE 8.5   Result of Step 2 in Natural Join

DATE	CUST_ID	SALPERS_ID	PROD_ID	QTY
02/28	100	10	2241	200
02/05	105	10	2241	100
02/14	105	10	2249	50

CUST_ID	CUST_NAME	ADDRESS	COUNTRY	BEGINNING BALANCE	CURRENT BALANCE
100	Watabe Bros	Box 241, Tokyo	Japan	45,551	52,113
105	Jefferson	B 918, Chicago	USA	49,333	57,811
105	Jefferson	B 918, Chicago	USA	49,333	57,811

3. Since the two CUST_ID columns contain identical information, one of them can be eliminated. This results in the natural join of SALE_10 and CUSTOMER, shown in Figure 8.6.

Of course, we have obtained much more information than just the customers' names. If we wanted only the names we would have to project the CUST_NAME column of the relation of Figure 8.6.

Perhaps an easier way to see what's happening in a join is to simply view the process as a table lookup. For each row in the SALE_10 relation, we look up the rows in the CUSTOMER relation that have the same value for CUST_ID. Since CUST_ID is the key of CUSTOMER, and since our database observes referential integrity, there will always be exactly one such row. Thus, since there are originally 3 rows in the SALE_10 relation, joining the CUSTOMER relation to SALE_10 creates a relation that also has 3 rows. We have merely expanded each SALE_10 row by adding all the available information about the customer involved in the sale.

The natural join operation in this example is written as follows:

```
JOIN(SALE_10, CUSTOMER)
```

natural join Join operation that connects relations when common columns have equal values.

The general definition of the **natural join** is as follows: Assume we want to take the natural join of two relations, A and B, which have columns $C_1, \ldots, C_n$ in common. Then JOIN(A, B) is obtained through these three steps:

1. Take the product of A and B. The resulting relation will have two columns for each of $C_1, \ldots, C_n$.

2. Eliminate all rows from the product except those on which the values of the columns $C_1, \ldots, C_n$ in A are equal, respectively, to the values of those columns in B.

3. Project out one copy of the columns $C_1, \ldots, C_n$.

For most of our examples, the two relations being joined will have only one column in common. However, as the general definition shows, if two relations have more than one column in common, then the join depends on equality of values in *all* common columns. We point out that if A has k columns and B has m columns, then the natural join of A and B will

FIGURE 8.6   Natural Join of SALE_10 and CUSTOMER

DATE	SALPERS_ID	PROD_ID	QTY
02/28	10	2241	200
02/05	10	2241	100
02/14	10	2249	50

CUST_ID	CUST_NAME	ADDRESS	COUNTRY	BEGINNING BALANCE	CURRENT BALANCE
100	Watabe Bros	Box 241, Tokyo	Japan	45,551	52,113
105	Jefferson	B 918, Chicago	USA	49,333	57,811
105	Jefferson	B 918, Chicago	USA	49,333	57,811

SALPERS_ID	SALPERS_NAME	MANAGER_ID	OFFICE	COMM_%
10	Rodney Jones	27	Chicago	10
10	Rodney Jones	27	Chicago	10
10	Rodney Jones	27	Chicago	10
23	Francois Moire	35	Brussels	9
23	Francois Moire	35	Brussels	9
23	Francois Moire	35	Brussels	9
23	Francois Moire	35	Brussels	9
23	Francois Moire	35	Brussels	9
37	Elena Hermana	12	B.A.	13
39	Goro Azuma	44	Tokyo	10

DATE	CUST_ID	PROD_ID	QTY
02/28	100	2241	200
02/05	105	2241	100
02/14	105	2249	50
02/12	101	2518	300
02/15	101	1035	150
02/02	101	1035	200
02/01	101	2249	75
02/04	101	2241	250
02/22	110	2518	150
02/19	100	2518	200

FIGURE 8.7   The Natural Join of SALESPERSON and SALE

have (k + m - n) columns, where n is the number of columns A and B have in common.

We will now illustrate the use and power of the join with a number of sample queries.

> **Query:** Attach sales information to the information about salespeople.
> **Solution:** JOIN(SALESPERSON, SALE)
> **Result:** See Figure 8.7.

This is essentially the same query as in the previous example, except in this case we have used the SALESPERSON relation instead of the CUS-TOMER relation. We give this example to illustrate another way of looking at the join. In this case, the query as stated starts by looking at the SALESPERSON relation and asks that sale information be attached to the rows of this relation. Since the various salespeople may have more or less than one sale, we find that the rows for some salespeople are repeated several times, while the rows for others don't appear at all. Many people feel that something is lost in a case like this where the salespeople who have no sales in the database do not appear in the result of the natural join. The *outer join*, which is discussed below, has been defined to address this problem.

> **Query:** What is the name of the customer involved in each sale?
> **Solution:** A := CUSTOMER[CUST_ID, CUST_NAME]
> B := JOIN(SALE, A)

Result:

B

DATE	SALPERS_ID	PROD_ID	QTY	CUST_ID	CUST_NAME
02/28	10	2241	200	100	Watabe Bros
02/12	23	2518	300	101	Maltzl
02/15	23	1035	150	101	Maltzl
02/19	39	2518	200	100	Watabe Bros
02/02	23	1035	200	101	Maltzl
02/05	10	2241	100	105	Jefferson
02/22	37	2518	150	110	Gomez
02/14	10	2249	50	105	Jefferson
02/01	23	2249	75	101	Maltzl
02/04	23	2241	250	101	Maltzl

In this example, we projected out the undesired information from CUS-TOMER before making the join. The answer to the query is found in the relation we have named B.

> **Query:** Give the names of customers who have purchased product 2518.
>
> **Solution:** A := SELECT(SALE: PROD_ID = 2518)
> B := JOIN(A, CUSTOMER)[CUST_NAME]
>
> **Result:** B
> CUST_NAME
> Maltzl
> Watabe Bros
> Gomez

Our solution in this example first creates a reduced SALE relation by placing in relation A only those sales that involve product 2518. This relation is then joined to the CUSTOMER relation, and CUST_NAME is projected out, leaving the desired result in relation B.

The select operation could have been specified second instead of first. In that case, the solution would have been:

```
A := JOIN(SALE, CUSTOMER)
B := SELECT(A: PROD_ID = 2518)[CUST_NAME]
```

This solution is *logically* equivalent to the first solution. That is, both solutions yield the same result. However, the first solution is normally preferable, because it would execute much more quickly. This follows from the fact that the A relation in the first solution is much smaller than the SALE relation. Thus, far fewer comparisons would be required to complete the join. As a rule, it is most efficient to perform operations such as joins, which require numerous comparisons, *after* operations that reduce the number of rows to be compared, such as select. Of course, this is only possible if there is more than one logically valid solution.

> **Query:** Who has bought table lamps?
>
> **Solution:** A := SELECT(PRODUCT: PROD_DESC = 'Table Lamp')
> B := JOIN(A, SALE)
> C := JOIN(B, CUSTOMER)[CUST_NAME]

```
Result:  C
         CUST_NAME
         Watabe Bros
         Jefferson
         Maltzl
```

In this example, we must follow a logical path from 'Table Lamps' in the PRODUCT relation to CUST_NAME in the CUSTOMER relation. To do this, we identify all table lamp products and then follow the path from PRODUCT to SALE to CUSTOMER. This requires the joining of three relations. We have done this by executing the join operation twice. Since we are only interested in obtaining the customer name, we project out all other columns in the final step.

```
Query:  Which salespeople have sold products manufactured in
Peru?
   Solution:  A := SELECT(MANUFACTURER: COUNTRY = 'Peru')
              B := JOIN(A, PRODUCT)
              C := JOIN(B, SALE)
              D := JOIN(C, SALESPERSON) [SALPERS_NAME]
Result:  D
         SALPERS_NAME
         Rodney Jones
         Francois Moire
```

This query is essentially the same as the previous query, only the path from country of manufacture to salesperson is one relation longer. Thus, we must execute three joins to connect four relations. One of the intermediate relations will have 16 columns, but since the only attributes that concern us are country and salesperson name, we can ignore the other attributes. The final relation, D, however, will have only a single column, as shown above.

Theta Join. □   Consider the following query.

```
Query:  Identify salespeople whose manager gets a commission
rate exceeding 11%.
```

All the data needed to solve this query is contained in the SALESPERSON relation, since it contains data about *all* salespeople—both those who are managers and those who are not. This query cannot be solved by a simple select operation, however, because the commission rate in the salesperson's record applies to the salesperson, not to the salesperson's manager. To obtain the commission rate of a salesperson's manager, we must join the manager's record, in the SALESPERSON relation, to the salesperson's record. That is, we must join the SALESPERSON relation to *itself*. Then we will have the manager's commission rate in the same row as the salesperson's name and can easily complete the solution to the query.

For example, the first row of SALESPERSON contains information for Rodney Jones. As you can see, the ID of his manager is 27. This is the SALPERS_ID for Terry Cardon, so she is Rodney's manager. Since her-commission rate is 15%, Rodney Jones's manager receives more than 11% commission, and Rodney Jones is part of the solution to the query. By joining **SALESPERSON** to itself, we can attach the manager record to every salesperson record, and we can use a select statement on the joined relation to solve the query.

But how do we join a relation to itself? We cannot use the natural join, because that is based on equality of *all* common columns in the two relations being joined. If both relations in the join operation are the same relation, then *all* columns will be common to the two relations, and the join will be meaningless.

We solve this problem by defining a new version of the join. This version will allow us to specify a condition for joining rows. The following solution illustrates this new version of join, after first creating two copies of **SALESPERSON**:

```
SP1 := SALESPERSON
SP2 := SALESPERSON
  A := JOIN(SP1, SP2: SP1.MANAGER_ID = SP2.SALPERS_ID)
```

The last statement shows the new version of join. The condition following the colon states that two rows should be joined if the **MANAGER_ID** from the first is equal to the **SALPERS_ID** from the second. In other words, we are attaching to each salesperson's row the row containing information about that salesperson's manager. This is shown in Figure 8.8. Notice that there is no row showing Terry Cardon with her manager. This is because Terry Cardon, having no manager, has a null value in the MANAGER_ID column. However, her row does appear as a *manager* with many other salespeople.

FIGURE 8.8   The Theta Join of SP1 and SP2

A

SP1.SALPERS_ID	SP1.SALPERS_NAME	SP1.MANAGER_ID	SP1.OFFICE	SP1.COMM_%
10	Rodney Jones	27	Chicago	10
14	Masaji Matsu	44	Tokyo	11
23	Francois Moire	35	Brussels	9
37	Elena Hermana	12	B.A.	13
39	Goro Azuma	44	Tokyo	10
44	Albert Ige	27	Tokyo	12
35	Brigit Bovary	27	Brussels	11
12	Buster Sanchez	27	B.A.	10

SP2.SALPERS_ID	SP2.SALPERS_NAME	SP2.MANAGER_ID	SP2.OFFICE	SP2.COMM_%
27	Terry Cardon		Chicago	15
44	Albert Ige	27	Tokyo	12
35	Brigit Bovary	27	Brussels	11
12	Buster Sanchez	27	B.A.	10
44	Albert Ige	27	Tokyo	12
27	Terry Cardon		Chicago	15
27	Terry Cardon		Chicago	15
27	Terry Cardon		Chicago	15

We are not yet finished with this query. We must still identify those salespeople whose manager gets a commission rate exceeding 11%. We can finish the query by simply using the select operation on the relation A:

```
B := SELECT(A: SP2.COMM_% > 11) [SP1.SALSPERS_NAME]
```

This yields the following relation: B

```
SP1.SALPERS_NAME

Rodney Jones
Masaji Matsu
Goro Azuma
Albert Ige
Brigit Bovary
Buster Sanchez
```

Note that we *had* to specify **SP2.COMM_%**, and *not* **SP1.COMM_%**. The former contains the manager's commission rate, while the latter contains the salesperson's commission rate.

The **theta join** is a join with a specified condition involving a column from each relation. This condition specifies that the two columns should be compared in some way. The comparison operator can be any of the six:

```
=
not =
<
>
<=
>=
```

The general way of saying this is that the theta join takes the form

```
JOIN(A, B: X [θ] Y)
```

where A and B are the relations to be joined, X and Y are columns from the two relations, and the Greek letter [θ] is one of the six comparison operators listed above.

Our example illustrates the theta join where the comparison operator is "=". This join is also called the **equijoin**. Joins using the other operators are also needed for some problems. We illustrate one of these later in the chapter.

As a final note, we point out that the theta join, unlike the natural join, does *not* include the elimination of one or more columns as its final step. In other words, if A has k columns and B has m columns, then the theta join of A and B will have k + m columns.

Outer Join. ☐ Let's look again at a query discussed earlier:

Query: Attach sales information to the information about salespeople.
    JOIN(SALESPERSON, SALE)

The result of this was shown in Figure 8.7.

This result is unsatisfactory, however, because the intent of this query is to show *all* salespeople together with their sales. If we use the natural join, though, no rows are shown for salespeople who do not have sales. Therefore, we cannot use the natural join if we wish to list the salespeople who have had no sales along with those who have. The outer join remedies this problem.

outer join Expansion of the natural join that includes *all* rows from both relations.

The **outer join** expands the natural join by making sure that every record from both relations is listed in the join relation at least once. The outer join consists of two steps. First, a natural join is executed. Then, if any record in one relation does not match a record from the other relation in the natural join, that unmatched record is added to the join relation, and the additional columns are filled with nulls. This is illustrated for the present problem in Figure 8.9. This relation is the result of the following operation:

```
OUTERJOIN(SALESPERSON, SALE)
```

Some versions of SQL, such as Oracle, provide an outer join. Although the need for it is minor, we see that there are some occasions when it is desirable.

Divide*

Suppose we have a query like the following:

Query: List salespeople who have sold every product.

Our sample database contains four different products with ID numbers: 1035, 2241, 2249, and 2518. A salesperson will satisfy the query if he or she has sold each of those products at least once. In other words,

*This section may be omitted without loss of continuity.

FIGURE 8.9   The Outer Join of SALESPERSON and SALE

SALPERS_ID	SALPERS_NAME	MANAGER_ID	OFFICE	COMM_%	DATE	CUST_ID	PROD_ID	QTY
10	Rodney Jones	27	Chicago	10	02/28	100	2241	200
10	Rodney Jones	27	Chicago	10	02/05	105	2241	100
10	Rodney Jones	27	Chicago	10	02/14	105	2249	50
14	Masaji Matsu	44	Tokyo	11				
23	Francois Moire	35	Brussels	9	02/12	101	2518	300
23	Francois Moire	35	Brussels	9	02/15	101	1035	150
23	Francois Moire	35	Brussels	9	02/02	101	1035	200
23	Francois Moire	35	Brussels	9	02/01	101	2249	75
23	Francois Moire	35	Brussels	9	02/04	101	2241	250
37	Elena Hermana	12	B.A.	13	02/22	110	2518	150
39	Goro Azuma	44	Tokyo	10	02/19	100	2518	200
27	Terry Cardon		Chicago	15				
44	Albert Ige	27	Tokyo	12				
35	Bridget Bovary	27	Brussels	11				
12	Buster Sanchez	27	B.A.	10				

for each of those products there must be at least one row in **SALE** containing the **SALPERS_ID** of that salesperson. A query like this can be solved using the relational algebra **divide** operation.

The pivotal word in this query is "every," since it requires that for each salesperson we examine **SALE** rows until we have found whether that salesperson has sold *every* product. The requirement here is different from those described earlier, since in those cases we could work with one or two rows at a time in performing the operation. The divide (or *division*) operation requires that we look at an entire relation at once.

How do we solve this query? We will follow a procedure close to one we would use intuitively and show how the divide operation corresponds to this procedure.

Obviously, if we want to know whether a salesperson has sold every product, we must first obtain a relation listing every product. The **PRODUCT** relation is such a relation. However, in other relations, a product is identified only by the *key* column, not by an entire row from **PRODUCT**. Thus, the key passes for the product itself. Our first step, then, is to obtain a relation consisting of the key attribute for all the products in the database. We do this by projecting **PRODUCT** on **PROD_ID**:

```
PI := PRODUCT [PROD_ID]
```

PI is a relation containing all the values of **PROD_ID**.

Next, we must obtain a relation containing all instances where a salesperson and a product are together in a single sale. This is clearly done by projecting the **SALE** relation on **PROD_ID** and **SALPERS_ID**:

```
PI_SI := SALE [PROD_ID, SALPERS_ID]
```

An instance in **PI_SI** consists of a **PROD_ID** and a **SALPERS_ID** and means that the product represented by **PROD_ID** was sold by the salesperson represented by **SALPERS_ID**. Therefore, **PI_SI** consists of all product/salesperson combinations where the salesperson has sold the product.

The result of these two projections is as follows:

```
PI

PROD_ID
 1035
 2241
 2249
 2518
```

```
PI_SI
SALPERS_ID      PROD_ID
    10            2241
    23            2518
    23            1035
    39            2518
    37            2518
    10            2249
    23            2249
    23            2241
```

Now we merely need to determine which salespersons represented in PI_SI are associated with every product ID in PI. This is done automatically by the divide operation:

```
A := PI_SI / PI
```

with the result: A

SALPERS ID
23

This probably looks like magic. It is not, however, since it simply corresponds with the definition of division in relational algebra. We give a general description of the operation as follows. Assume that A, B, and C are relations, and we desire to divide B by C, giving A as the result.

1. The columns of C must be a subset of the columns of B. The columns of A are all *and only* those columns of B that are *not* columns of C. Note that this corresponds to our example above. The columns of PI_SI are PROD_ID and SALPERS_ID, while the column of PI is PROD_ID and the column of A is SALPERS_ID.

2. A row is placed in A if and only if it is associated in B with *every* row of C. This also corresponds to our example, since A's only row (having SALPERS_ID = 23) is associated in PI_SI with all the rows of PI, and it is the *only* SALPERS_ID so associated.

The divide operation is the reverse of the product operation. It is easy to verify that if a relation is the product of two relations B and C, then we can obtain B, say, by dividing the product by C. That is:

```
(B * C) / C  =  B
```

This explains, by analogy with ordinary arithmetic, why the divide operation is so called. Codd included it in relational algebra to provide the capability needed for the universal quantifier of relational calculus. This will be discussed below. In practical terms, the divide operation was provided so that we could solve queries involving "every" or "all" as part of the condition. In the example we have been discussing, the query was:

```
List salespeople who have sold every product.
```

As we have seen, the divide operation was essential for solving this query.

Assignment

We have been using the **assignment** operation throughout the chapter to give names to relations. For example, in the statement

```
A := SELECT(SALESPERSON: COMM_% > 11)
```

the name A is being assigned to the result of the select operation. The symbol ":=" means "is the name assigned to."

assignment Relational algebra operation that gives a name to a relation.

Relational algebra is remarkably powerful in its flexibility and ability to solve a large range of problems. In this section, we give an example of a problem that can be solved using relational algebra, even though it may not seem easy to solve at first glance. The solution involves using relational algebra operations in creative ways.

> **Query:** What is the maximum commission rate?

The immediate difficulty with this problem is that it appears we have no way of comparing all the values in the commission rate column to determine which is largest. The comparison needed is between rows, so the select operation will not work, since it applies to only one row at a time. However, the theta join does allow at least a two row comparison. We will use it in joining a relation to itself:

```
A := SALESPERSON[COMM_%]
B := A
C := JOIN(A, B: A.COMM_% > B.COMM_%)
```

The result of this join follows:

C

A.COMM_%	B.COMM_%
10	9
11	10
11	9
13	10
13	11
13	9
13	12
15	10
15	11
15	9
15	12
15	13
12	10
12	11
12	9

How can we use this relation to solve the problem? If we examine the columns separately, we discover an important fact. The left column, **A.COMM_%**, contains all the commission rates *except* the lowest one, and the right column, **B.COMM_%**, contains all the commission rates *except* the highest. This leads us to the solution to the problem. By *subtracting* the set of commission rates in the right column from the set of *all* commission rates, we are left with the highest commission rate, as requested by the query.

```
D := C [B.COMM_%]
E := A - D
```

D is the right column of C and so contains all the commission rates except the highest, and A contains all the commission rates. Their difference, E, contains only the highest commission rate and is therefore the solution to the query.

It should be clear that to obtain the *minimum* commission rate, it is only necessary to substitute the A.COMM_% column for the B.COMM_% column in the definition of D. The rest of the solution remains the same.

The solution to this query involves two "tricks": (1) joining a relation to itself, using the theta join, and (2) subtracting a relation containing everything *except* what the query asks for from the set of all possible values. This second point is important and often necessary for solving the more difficult queries in relational algebra.

☐ RELATIONAL CALCULUS

Relational calculus uses an entirely different approach than relational algebra. Nevertheless, the two languages are logically equivalent. This means that any query that can be solved in one language can be solved in the other. We will be more brief in our coverage of relational calculus, since the language itself has fewer constructs.

Query: Who are the salespeople in the Tokyo office?

This query is solved in relational calculus as follows:

```
{r.SALPERS_NAME : r IN SALESPERSON and r.OFFICE = 'Tokyo'}
```

The braces ({ }) enclosing the statement indicate that the solution to the query is a set of data values. Precisely what is in this set is described by the statement. The solution given here illustrates most of the features of relational calculus. We list the parts of the solution and explain their meanings:

1. r
2. r.SALPERS_NAME
3. The colon (:)
4. r IN SALESPERSON
5. r.OFFICE = 'Tokyo'

1. *r* is a variable that stands for an arbitrary row. The relation from which *r* comes is defined by "r IN SALESPERSON," which means that *r* is a row in SALESPERSON. We will use lower-case letters near *r* in the alphabet, such as *s*, *t*, *p*, and *q*, as row variables.

2. r.SALPERS_NAME is the value of the SALPERS_NAME attribute in row *r*.

3. The colon (:) separates the target list from the qualifying statement. The target list in this case is

```
r.SALPERS_NAME
```

and the qualifying statement is

```
r IN SALESPERSON and r.OFFICE = 'Tokyo'
```

We will explain the meanings of these shortly. The colon can be read as "such that."

4. "r IN SALESPERSON" was explained in point 1.

5. "r.OFFICE = 'Tokyo'" means that the value of the OFFICE attribute in row *r* is 'Tokyo'.

Target List and Qualifying Statement

target list A parenthesized list of variables representing the desired components of a typical member of a query's solution set.

qualifying statement A condition in a relational calculus statement that restricts membership in a solution relation.

The solution to every query in relational calculus is a relation which is defined by a target list and a qualifying statement. The **target list** defines the attributes of the solution relation. The **qualifying statement** is a condition used to determine which values from the database actually go into the solution relation. We now explain how this works.

In the example above, the target list was r.SALPERS_NAME. In other words, the solution relation has only one attribute, the name of the salesperson. The actual values that go into the solution relation are those taken from the rows that satisfy the qualifying statement. In this example, a salesperson's name is taken from a row *r* and placed in the solution relation if the row *r* satisfies the condition

```
r IN SALESPERSON and r.OFFICE = 'Tokyo'
```

The system examines the rows of SALESPERSON, as shown in Figure 8.1, one by one. The first row is temporarily given the name *r*, and the qualifying statement is tested for truth or falsity. In this case, since r.OFFICE = 'Chicago', the qualifying statement is false, so r.SALPERS_NAME (Rodney Jones) is *not* placed in the solution relation. The system then moves on to the second row, gives it the name *r*, and tests the qualifying statement again. This time the statement is true, so Masaji Matsu is placed in the solution relation. This process is repeated for every row in SALESPERSON. The result is shown as follows:

```
SALPERS_NAME
Masaji Matsu
Goro Azuma
Albert Ige
```

For most queries, the target list will consist of a single attribute. However, the target list can consist of multiple attributes. For example, consider the query:

Query: Give all attributes for salespeople in the Tokyo office.
Solution: {r : r IN SALESPERSON and r.OFFICE = 'Tokyo'}

Here we have indicated that all attributes are to be included by merely listing *r*. This means that the entire row should be included. We also could have listed all of the attributes separated by commas:

```
{(r.SALPERS_ID, r.SALPERS_NAME, r.MANAGER_ID, r.OFFICE,
r.COMM_%)
   : r IN SALESPERSON and r.OFFICE = 'Tokyo'}
```

In addition, we may choose to list any subset of these attributes we desire.

From our explanation so far, it should be easy to see how the select and project operations of relational algebra are supported in relational calculus. Union, intersection, difference, and product operations can also be readily derived from the constructs of relational calculus we have discussed to this point. Since calculus does not use the step by step procedure of algebra, the assignment statement is not needed. Thus, the only relational algebra operations for which we have not yet shown relational calculus equivalents are join and divide. These require the *quantifiers*: existential for join and universal for divide.

The Existential Quantifier

existential quantifier Relational calculus expression affirming the existence of at least one row to which a condition applies.

A quantifier *quantifies*, or indicates the quantity of something. The **existential quantifier** states that at least one instance of a particular type of thing exists. In relational calculus, the existential quantifier is used to state that a particular type of row in a relation exists.

Let's consider an example to clarify this concept:

Query: List names of customers who have purchased product 2518.

Obviously, the solution to this query is a relation containing the names of certain customers. This is a single column relation so the target list is clearly

```
r.CUST_NAME
```

where *r* is a row in CUSTOMER.

So we have the target list, but what is the qualifying statement? To be in the solution, the customer must meet the condition of having purchased product 2518. In other words, if a given customer's ID is found in a row of SALE with PROD_ID = 2518, then that customer is in the solution. Thus the condition must be that there exists at least one row in SALE that contains the customer's ID and a PROD_ID of 2518. We state this as follows:

```
there exists s IN SALE
(s.CUST_ID = r.CUST_ID and s.PROD_ID = 2518)
```

This is read as: "There exists a row *s* in SALE, such that s.CUST_ID = r.CUST_ID, and s.PROD_ID = 2518." (The words "there exists" constitute the existential quantifier.)

Notice that this is a statement about the row *r*. If it is true that for a given *r* such a row *s* exists, then r.CUST_NAME is placed in the solution relation. If the statement is false — that is, if no such *s* exists for this *r* — then r.CUST_NAME is not placed in the solution relation.

The complete relational calculus solution for this query is:

```
{r.CUST_NAME : r IN CUSTOMER and there exists s IN SALE
             (s.CUST_ID = r.CUST_ID
             and s.PROD_ID = 2518)}
```

This solution describes a relation consisting of a single column and containing customer names taken from the rows of the relation CUSTOMER. A given name is placed in the solution relation if its row (*r*) satisfies the condition following the colon. Let's look at a few of the rows in CUSTOMER to see how the condition would be applied.

Consider Figure 8.10. The first row of CUSTOMER (which we have marked *r*) has CUST_ID = 100. The CUST_NAME (Watabe Bros) will be placed in the solution relation if a row exists in SALE having CUST_ID = 100 and PROD_ID = 2518. Such a row does in fact exist, and we have marked it *s*. Thus, *r* satisfies the qualifying statement, and *r*.CUST_NAME is placed in the solution. We repeat this process for each row of CUSTOMER. When the second row is designated *r*, we must find a corresponding *s* in SALE. In this case, the corresponding *s* is the second row of SALE. So Maltzl is placed in the solution. As we proceed further, we see that customer 105 (Jefferson) is *not* placed in the solution, but customer 110 (Gomez) is. The solution set would be:

```
CUST_NAME
Watabe Bros
Maltzl
Gomez
```

In relational algebra, the solution to this query would involve the join. Thus, we have shown how the existential quantifier is used in relational calculus to accomplish the function of the join. As a final example, we look at a more complex query that requires two joins.

Query: Who has bought table lamps?

FIGURE 8.10   The Existential Quantifier Applied to the CUSTOMER and SALE Relations

CUSTOMER

CUST_ID	CUST_NAME	ADDRESS	COUNTRY	BEGINNING BALANCE	CURRENT BALANCE	
100	Watabe Bros	Box 241, Tokyo	Japan	45,551	52,113	r
101	Maltzl	Salzburg	Austria	75,314	77,200	
105	Jefferson	B 918, Chicago	USA	49,333	57,811	
110	Gomez	Santiago	Chile	27,400	35,414	

SALE

DATE	CUST_ID	SALPERS_ID	PROD_ID	QTY	
02/28	100	10	2241	200	
02/12	101	23	2518	300	
02/15	101	23	1035	150	
02/19	100	39	2518	200	s
02/02	101	23	1035	200	
02/05	105	10	2241	100	
02/22	110	37	2518	150	
02/14	105	10	2249	50	
02/01	101	23	2249	75	
02/04	101	23	2241	250	

```
CUSTOMER
                                                     BEGINNING    CURRENT
CUST_ID    CUST_NAME        ADDRESS        COUNTRY    BALANCE      BALANCE
  100     Watabe Bros  Box 241, Tokyo      Japan      45,551       52,113
  101     Maltzl       Salzburg            Austria    75,314       77,200
  105     Jefferson    B 918, Chicago      USA        49,333       57,811   r
  110     Gomez        Santiago            Chile      27,400       35,414


SALE
 DATE    CUST_ID   SALPERS_ID    PROD_ID   QTY
02/28      100         10          2241    200
02/12      101         23          2518    300
02/15      101         23          1035    150
02/19      100         39          2518    200
02/02      101         23          1035    200
02/05      105         10          2241    100   s
02/22      110         37          2518    150
02/14      105         10          2249    50
02/01      101         23          2249    75
02/04      101         23          2241    250


PRODUCT
PROD_ID           PROD_DESC          MANUFACTR_ID     COST     PRICE
 1035          Sweater                   210         11.25    22.00
 2241          Table Lamp                317         22.25    33.25    t
 2249          Table Lamp                317         13.55    24.80
 2518          Brass Sculpture           253         13.60    21.20
```

FIGURE 8.11   The Existential Quantifier Applied to CUSTOMER and SALE

This query was used to illustrate the join in our discussion of relational algebra. The solution relation is given on page 000. The solution in relational calculus is:

```
{r.CUST_NAME : r IN CUSTOMER and there exists s IN SALE and
               there exists t IN PRODUCT
               (r.CUST_ID   = s.CUST_ID and
                s.PROD_ID   = t.PROD_ID and
                t.PROD_DESC = 'Table Lamp')}
```

Note that just as the relational algebra solution required two joins, the relational calculus solution requires two existentially quantified row variables, s and t. A sample set of values for r, s, and t is shown in Figure 8.11. This sample set shows that Jefferson is included in the solution relation because there exist rows in SALE and in PRODUCT that prove that Jefferson has bought table lamps.

The Universal Quantifier*

universal quantifier Relational calculus expression stating that some condition applies to *every* row of some type.

The **universal quantifier** states that some condition applies to *all* or to *every* row of some type. It is used to provide the same capability as relational algebra's divide operation. We illustrate it using the same query we used for the divide.

---

*This section may be omitted without loss of continuity.

Query: `List salespeople who have sold every product.`

Note that the condition for selecting a salesperson includes the word "every." Only salespeople who have sold *every* product are included in the solution relation. If you skip ahead to the result below, you can easily see that only one salesperson satisfies the condition of the query.

The calculus solution to this query follows:

```
{r.SALPERS_NAME : r IN SALESPERSON and for every p IN PRODUCT
                  there exists s IN SALE
                  (r.SALPERS_ID = s.SALPERS_ID and
                  s.PROD_ID = p.PROD_ID)}
```

The result is:

SALPERS_NAME
Francois Moire

A salesperson's name from a row *r* in SALESPERSON is placed in the solution relation if the qualifying statement is true about that row *r*. Figure 8.12 shows how the qualifying statement is true when *r* is the row con-

FIGURE 8.12 The Universal Quantifier applied to SALESPERSON, PRODUCT, and SALE

SALESPERSON

SALPERS_ID	SALPERS_NAME	MANAGER_ID	OFFICE	COMM_%	
10	Rodney Jones	27	Chicago	10	
14	Masaji Matsu	44	Tokyo	11	
23	Francois Moire	35	Brussels	9	r
37	Elena Hermana	12	B.A.	13	
39	Goro Azuma	44	Tokyo	10	
27	Terry Cardon		Chicago	15	
44	Albert Ige	27	Tokyo	12	
35	Brigit Bovary	27	Brussels	11	
12	Buster Sanchez	27	B.A.	10	

PRODUCT

PROD_ID	PROD_DESC	MANUFACTR_ID	COST	PRICE	
1035	Sweater	210	11.25	22.00	p(1)
2241	Table Lamp	317	22.25	33.25	p(2)
2249	Table Lamp	317	13.55	24.80	p(3)
2158	Brass Sculpture	253	13.60	21.20	p(4)

SALE

DATE	CUST_ID	SALPERS_ID	PROD_ID	QTY	
02/28	100	10	2241	200	
02/12	101	23	2518	300	s(4)
02/15	101	23	1035	150	s(1)
02/19	100	39	2518	200	
02/02	101	23	1035	200	
02/05	105	10	2241	100	
02/22	110	37	2518	150	
02/14	105	10	2249	50	
02/01	101	23	2249	75	s(3)
02/04	101	23	2241	250	s(2)

taining data about Francois Moire. For each row p in **PRODUCT**, there must be a row s in **SALE** satisfying the condition. The figure shows the correspondence between rows of **PRODUCT** and rows of **SALE** in satisfying the condition. That is,

s(1)	corresponds to	p(1)
s(2)	corresponds to	p(2)
s(3)	corresponds to	p(3)
s(4)	corresponds to	p(4)

In each of these rows of **SALE**, the SALPERS_ID is François Moire's (23), and each of the four sale rows corresponds to one of the four possible products. Therefore, Moire has sold *every* product.

RELATIVE DIFFICULTY OF RELATIONAL ALGEBRA AND RELATIONAL CALCULUS

The conventional wisdom in database languages holds that nonprocedural languages should be easier to use than procedural languages. This has not been borne out by experiment, however. The results of a number of experiments (Welty and Stemple, 1981; Hansen and Hansen, 1987, 1988) indicate that people generally perform better in solving problems with a procedural language than they do with a nonprocedural language. This is particularly true when the problems are logically more complex. In the specific case of relational algebra vs. relational calculus, users tend to find the universal quantifier of calculus difficult to comprehend. Consequently, they are often unable to solve queries requiring this quantifier. Although the corresponding operation in relational algebra — division — is difficult to grasp, the percentage of people who do so successfully is far larger than the percentage of people who learn to use the universal quantifier successfully.

Our own view on this subject is that no good alternative has yet been developed for solving the more difficult queries that involve "every" in the condition. As will be discussed in Chapter 13, the approach used by SQL, the NOT EXISTS predicate, seems no better than the alternatives provided by algebra and calculus. Hopefully, additional research will strengthen database languages in this area.

■ SUMMARY

In this chapter, we have presented Codd's relational algebra and relational calculus. Both of these theoretical languages manipulate relations in a relational database on the basis of their logical characteristics and without regard to the physical structures used for implementation. Relational algebra is a procedural language that uses step by step solutions to query problems. Relational calculus, however, is nonprocedural, meaning that the solution to a query is formulated as a definition of the desired result, rather than as a process that will produce the desired result. Codd showed that relational algebra and calculus are logically equivalent, or, in other words, that any query that can be solved in one language can also be solved in the other.

Relational algebra consists of nine operations: union, intersection, subtraction, product, select, project, join, divide, and assignment. Union, intersection, subtraction, and product are very similar to the set operations of the same names. Select is used to apply a condition to a relation and produce a new relation consisting of those rows satisfying the condition. Project creates a new relation by removing columns from an existing relation. Join connects relations on columns containing comparable information. Divide identifies the rows in a relation that match every row in another relation. Assignment gives a name to a relation.

Relational calculus defines the solution to a query as a relational set. The relation definition consists of a target list, defining the attributes in the solution relation, and a qualifying statement, which is a condition that the elements in the target list must satisfy. Relational calculus takes its name from predicate calculus in symbolic logic and uses the Boolean connectives (and, or, not) to link conditions which may be true or false. It also uses the existential and universal quantifiers which state, respectively, that an instance of some type *exists*, or that a condition is true for *every* instance of a specified type.

Although conventional wisdom holds that a nonprocedural language is easier for people to use than is a procedural language, research suggests that, in the case of relational languages, this may not always be true. For some difficult queries, the step by step approach of a procedural language like relational algebra provides the flexibility people need for formulating query solutions. Further research in this area will perhaps result in the development of languages that users can easily apply to the solution of queries having a wide range of complexity.

■ REVIEW QUESTIONS

1. Define each of the following terms in your own words:
   a. relational algebra
   b. nonprocedural
   c. relationally complete
   d. union compatible
   e. intersection
   f. subtraction
   g. project
   h. natural join
   i. theta join
   j. qualifying statement
   *k. divide
   *l. universal quantifier

2. Describe the circumstances when you would use each of the following relational algebra operations:
   a. Select
   b. Project

---

*This question pertains to the chapter's optional material.

c. Join

d. Assignment

e. Subtraction

f. Intersection

*g. Divide

3. Explain the function of each of the following in a relational calculus query solution:

a. Target list

b. Qualifying statement

c. Boolean connective (and, or, not)

d. Existential quantifier

*e. Universal quantifier

4. Why doesn't relational calculus need something similar to the assignment statement of relational algebra?

5. Consider the following statement: "Nonprocedural languages are easier for naive users to use." Using your experience, discuss this statement.

6. Discuss the significance of saying that relational algebra and relational calculus are relationally complete and what that means for evaluating commercial DBMSs.

PROBLEMS AND EXERCISES

1. Match each term to its definition.

__Difference

__Union

__Procedural

__Existential quantifier

__Select

__Join

__Product

__Equijoin

__Outer join

__Relational calculus

__Assignment

__Projection

__Target list

a. Gives a name to a relation

b. Theta join based on equality of specified columns

c. List that defines the attributes of the solution relation

d. Language that provides a step by step method for solving problems

e. Operation that connects relations

f. Relation resulting from a project operation

g. Expansion of the natural join that includes *all* rows from both relations

h. Creates the Cartesian product of two relations

i. Creates the set difference of two union compatible relations

j. Affirms the existence of at least one row to which a condition applies

k. Creates the set union of two union compatible relations

l. Relational algebra operation that uses a condition to choose rows from a relation

m. A nonprocedural language for defining query solutions

2. Using the following relational schema, indicate which relational algebra operation(s) might be used to answer the given query:

CUSTOMER (CUST_ID, CUST_NAME, ANNUAL_REVENUE)
SHIPMENT (SHIPMENT_#, CUST_ID, WEIGHT, TRUCK_#, DESTINATION)

    a. Which customers have annual revenue exceeding $5 million?
    b. What is the name of customer 433?
    c. What is the destination city of shipment #3244?
    d. Which trucks have carried packages weighing over 100 pounds?
    e. What are the names of customers who have sent packages to Sioux City, Iowa?
    f. To what destinations have companies with revenue less than $1 million sent packages?

Use this relational schema for the following set of queries:

```
CUSTOMER (CUST_ID, CUST_NAME, ANNUAL_REVENUE)

SHIPMENT (SHIPMENT_#, CUST_ID, WEIGHT, TRUCK_#, DESTINATION)

Foreign Key: DESTINATION REFERENCES CITY_NAME IN CITY

TRUCK (TRUCK_#, DRIVER_NAME)

CITY (CITY_NAME, POPULATION)
```

3. Give relational algebra solutions to the following queries:
    a. A list of shipment numbers for shipments weighing over 20 pounds.
    b. Names of customers with more than $10 million in annual revenue.
    c. The driver of Truck #45.
    d. The names of cities which have received shipments weighing over 100 pounds.
    e. The name and annual revenue of customers who have sent shipments weighing over 100 pounds.
    f. The truck numbers of trucks which have carried shipments weighing over 100 pounds.
    g. The names of drivers who have delivered shipments weighing over 100 pounds.
    h. Cities which have received shipments from customers having over $15 million in annual revenue.
    i. Customers having over $5 million in annual revenue who have sent shipments weighing less than 1 pound.
    j. Customers having over $5 million in annual revenue who have sent shipments weighing less than 1 pound or have sent a shipment to San Francisco.
    k. Customers whose shipments have been delivered by truck driver Jensen.
    l. Drivers who have delivered shipments for customers with annual revenue over $20 million to cities with population over 1 million.

*m. Customers who have had shipments delivered by every driver.

*n. Cities which have received shipments from every customer.

*o. Drivers who have delivered shipments to every city.

*p. Customers who have sent shipments to every city with population over 500,000. (Hint: First create the set of cities with population over 500,000.)

q. Give a list of customers and annual revenue for those customers whose annual revenue is the maximum for the customers in the database.

r. Give a list of customers, all of whose shipments weigh over 25 pounds. (Hint: First find customers who have at least one shipment less than 25 pounds.)

s. Give a list of customers that send all their shipments to a single city. (Note: The city may or may not be the same for each of these customers.) (Hint: First find customers that send shipments to more than one city.)

4. Give relational calculus solutions for the queries of problem 3.

■ PROJECTS AND PROFESSIONAL ISSUES

1. Compare your solutions to the queries in problems 3 and 4 above. Which queries seemed easier to solve in relational algebra and which in relational calculus? In each case why do you suppose the one language was easier to use than the other? Which of the two languages do you prefer? Why?

2. Read Codd's papers on relational algebra and calculus (Codd 1970, 1971a, 1971b). Write an essay comparing the two languages and discuss how Codd showed their logical equivalence.

3. Write sketches of programs in a language like COBOL or Pascal to solve the queries 3 a, e, m, and r. Compare the complexity of these programs with that of the query solutions in relational algebra and calculus.

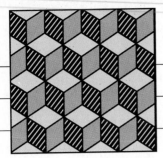

chapter nine

THE NETWORK
DATA MODEL

Rita Minkowski, the Director of Information Systems for Zeus, Inc., was attending the monthly meeting of the local chapter of the Association for Computing Machinery (ACM). That evening's topic was "Relational Database Systems versus Network and Hierarchical Database Systems."

John Stiller, regional sales manager for a popular network DBMS, began. "Relational systems can be expected to work well in satisfying user needs for ad hoc queries, but they can never achieve the performance needed for production systems. However, most database systems are going to be running a mixture of production transactions—such as updating inventory and sending out invoices—and ad hoc queries, with an emphasis on production systems. Unfortunately, highly efficient production systems and ad hoc queries are mutually disruptive activities. That is why we continue to support the network model. It supports the needs of most users with the greatest speed and efficiency."

The next speaker was Andrea Villa, an MIS professor at a local university. "Network and hierarchical systems are typically devoted almost entirely to production activities because that is what they do best. However," she continued, "they do not provide the flexibility needed to fully support ad hoc queries. With a network DBMS, you can churn out information on sales by region, but it may be more time-consuming to retrieve the type of summary data a marketing manager needs. Yet, we have a whole generation of managers who want—and expect—this kind of capability. That is why so many professionals have supported the relational model, which offers the flexibility needed to answer the sort of ad hoc queries managers have for summarized information."

In rebuttal, Stiller cited his own research, which showed that relational systems tend to be slower than network and hierarchical database systems, which have proven performance records. To get the same performance with a relational model, he indicated that users might have to undertake an expensive upgrade of their equipment and a redesign of their system.

Villa nodded her head. "Indeed, some of the newer relational systems may not yield the same performance statistics as some of the long-established network and hierarchical systems. And, in situations where the data structures and transaction patterns are very well understood in advance of design and implementation, the network and hierarchical systems can be customized to produce more impressive performance than some of the relational DBMSs. "But what happens," she asked, "if the data structures change? Or the marketing manager wants summary data that was not a part of the original data structure or transaction patterns? To get the information, you may have to write a new application program or even redesign part of the database system. Either of these options are time-consuming and expensive. In a relational model, however, we can easily extract this information. This means that we can give managers the information they need to make sound strategic decisions. In the long run, this capability makes relational systems more efficient for more users."

The meeting was then opened up to questions and answers. What ensued was a lively debate that suggested that network and hierarchical databases are alive and well today, but perhaps not the models of the future.

In this chapter, we present the fundamentals of the network data model. After reading this chapter, you should be able to:

☐ Describe the basic data structure from which the network data model is constructed.

☐ Explain the terminology used in describing the network data model.

☐ Use the fundamental methods of mapping from an object-oriented model to the network data model.

☐ Explain how the Data Description Language is used to implement the network data structures.

☐ Describe how the DBTG Data Manipulation Language operates to retrieve and update data.

☐ Evaluate the CODASYL DBTG model.

☐ HISTORICAL BACKGROUND

directed graph A mathematical structure in which points or "nodes" are connected by arrows or "edges."

node Part of a network structure represented by a point.

edge Part of a network structure represented by an arrow.

network data model Represents data in network structures of record types connected in one–one or one–many relationships.

Conference on Data Systems Languages (CODASYL) An organization composed of representatives from hardware vendors, software vendors, and users—known principally for development of the COBOL language.

Database Task Group (DBTG) A subgroup of CODASYL given responsibility for developing standards for database management systems.

Integrated Data Store (IDS) One of the earliest database management systems; its architecture greatly influenced the DBTG recommendations for a network database model.

Networks are a natural way of representing relationships among objects. They are widely used in mathematics, operations research, chemistry, physics, sociology, and other fields of inquiry. Since objects and their relationships are useful ways of modeling many of the business phenomena that concern us, it is not surprising that the network architecture applies to the organization of databases as well.

Networks can generally be represented by a mathematical structure called a **directed graph.** Directed graphs have a simple structure. They are constructed from points or **nodes** connected by arrows or **edges**. In the context of data models, the nodes can be thought of as data record types, and the edges can be thought of as representing one–one or one–many relationships. Thus, the **network data model** represents data in network structures of record types connected in one–one or one–many relationships. The graph structure enables simple representation of hierarchical relationships (such as genealogical data), membership relationships (such as department to which an employee is assigned), and many others. Moreover, once a relationship has been established between two objects, retrieval and manipulation of the related data can be efficiently executed.

As will be explained shortly, a hierarchy is a special case of a network. Correspondingly, the hierarchical data model, to be discussed in the next chapter, is a special case of the network data model. Even though the hierarchical data model historically precedes the network data model, it seems useful to discuss the more general graph structure of the network model first. Thus, we cover the network data model in this chapter and the hierarchical model in the next chapter.

The **Conference on Data Systems Languages (CODASYL)**—an organization comprised of representatives from major hardware vendors, software vendors, and users—initially developed and standardized the COBOL language in the early 1960s. In the late 1960s, it appointed a subgroup named the **Database Task Group (DBTG)** to develop standards for database management systems. The DBTG was heavily influenced by the architecture used on the earliest DBMSs, the **Integrated Data Store**

(IDS), developed earlier at General Electric. That influence led to recommendations for a network model in a preliminary report published in 1969.

This first report generated a number of suggestions for improvement, and a revised official report was published in 1971 and submitted to the American National Standards Institute (ANSI) for possible adoption as a national standard for DBMSs. ANSI took no action, and the 1971 report was followed by modified reports in 1978, 1981, and 1984.

Nonetheless, the 1971 document remains the fundamental statement of the network model, which came to be referred to as the CODASYL DBTG model. It has served as the basis for the development of network database management systems by several vendors. IDS (Honeywell) and IDMS (Computer Associates) are two of the better-known commercial implementations.

Although the network data model may in the future increasingly yield to the relational data model as the DBMS of choice, it is currently serving effectively in a number of database systems.

☐ BASIC CONCEPTS AND DEFINITIONS

Three-Level Structure

The DBTG network model conforms to the ANSI/SPARC three-level database architecture (Chapter 3) as follows:

schema A definition of the logical structure of the entire database.

The conceptual level (the logical view of all data and relationships in the database) is called the **schema**.

The external level (the users' views of the data needed for various applications) is called the **subschema**.

subschema Subsets of the schema which are defined by the user's view of the database.

The internal level (the physical details of storage) is implicit in the implementation.

Records and Sets

There are just two fundamental data structures in the network model, record types and sets. **Record types** are defined in the usual way, as collections of logically related data items. For example, a customer record type might include the following data items: CustomerID, Name, Address, AmountOwed, and Date-of-Last-Payment. Note that we identified this collection as a *customer* record type, thus specifying by name the record type. All record types are given names such as CUSTOMER, INVOICE, SALESPERSON, and so forth.

record type A collection of logically related data items.

A **set** in the DBTG model expresses a one–many (or one–one) relationship between two record types. (Note that this is not the usual mathematical definition of a set, which is just a collection of elements.) For example, one set might express the one–many relationship between customers and their outstanding invoice records. In every network set, one record type is the **owner**, and the other record type is the **member.** In the example just given, the customer record type is the owner and the invoice record type is the member. The one–many relationship incorporates the possibility that zero, one, or many invoice records may be related to a given customer record. That is, at a given time, a customer may have, say, 10, one, or zero outstanding invoices. The "many" really expresses capability, rather than constraint.

set In the DBTG model, a one–many relationship between two record types.

owner record type The record type on the "one" side of the one–many relationship of a DBTG set.

member record type The record type on the "many" side of the one–many relationship of a DBTG set.

Of course, there are situations where a relationship is strictly one–one, such as with truck and driver, but this is handled in the same way. Once the owner record type and the member record type are defined, all definitions apply as given.

These conventions are illustrated by the example shown in Figure 9.1. Figure 9.1(a) shows the general form of the data structure. This type of figure is called a "Bachman diagram" in honor of Charles Bachman, who was instrumental in the development of the IDS system at General Electric. Figure 9.1(b) shows actual values, termed **instances** or **occurrences**, which could occur in the structure of the Bachman diagram.

In Figure 9.1(a), we note certain conventions represented in the diagrams. First, sets are denoted by the arrow between record types, with the arrow pointing to the member record type (the "many" in the one–many relationship). Second, each set type is constructed of an owner record type, a member record type, and a name for the set type. The set name is the label given to the arrow. This corresponds to a graph in which the nodes are the record types and the edges are represented by the arrow-tipped lines connecting the record types. Third, the data structure is constructed from these simple set relationships. Figure 9.1(a) shows

FIGURE 9.1   Example of Network Data Structure

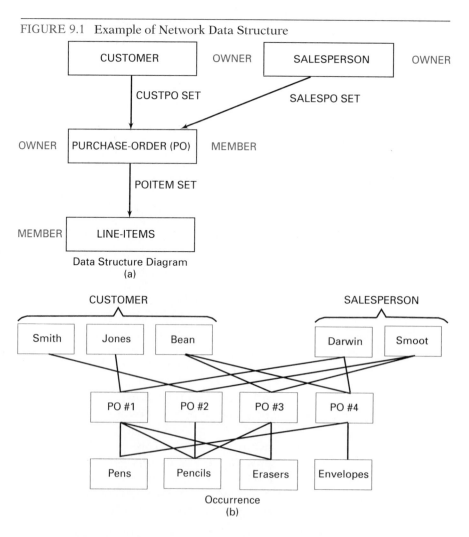

Data Structure Diagram
(a)

Occurrence
(b)

three sets: the CUSTPO set with owner CUSTOMER and member PUR-CHASE-ORDER; the SALESPO set with owner SALESPERSON and member PURCHASE-ORDER; and the POITEM set with owner PUR-CHASE-ORDER and member LINE-ITEMS.

Figure 9.1(a) provides an example of the difference between the network data model and the hierarchical data model. Notice that PUR-CHASE-ORDER is a member record type of two sets: CUSTPO and SALE-SPO. In the hierarchical data model, no record type can be a member of two different sets. However, this *is* allowed in the network data model. Thus, additional representational power is provided in the network data structure. This distinction is important because it is one of the principal differences between the network data model and the hierarchical data model to be discussed in the next chapter.

Since the network model allows only one–many relationships between record types, one might wonder how a many–many relationship is modeled. Figure 9.2 is a classic example of a relationship that is many-many. One student may be enrolled in many classes, and a given class can have many students. The DBTG model allows only **simple networks** in which all relationships are one–one or one–many. A **complex network**, which includes one or more many–many relationships, cannot be directly implemented in the DBTG model. There is, however, a method for transforming a complex network, such as the one in Figure 9.2, into the simple network form required for DBTG implementation.

The method is similar to the method by which object-oriented diagrams are mapped to relational tables. Recall that when the cardinality between two object sets is many–many, a relational table is created that contains the key attributes from the two related object sets. A similar method applies here. When two record types, such as STUDENT and CLASS, are connected in a many–many relationship, we create an **intersection**, or link, **record type** consisting of at least the keys from the STUDENT and CLASS records. Other attributes may be added at the discretion of the designer.

In Figure 9.3, this procedure is illustrated. An intersection record type named SC has been created, consisting of the fields STUDENT-ID and CLASS-ID. As shown in Figure 9.3(a), the SC record type partitions the many–many relationship into *two* one–many relationships. The SC record type accordingly becomes a member of two sets, the TAKING-CLASS SET and the ENROLLED SET. Figure 9.3(b) illustrates how an SC record instance is created for every student/class pair. For example, Rex Lupus owns three SC records, one for each class in which he is enrolled. Botany 500, in like manner, owns two SC records, one for each stu-

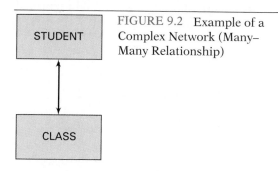

FIGURE 9.2 Example of a Complex Network (Many–Many Relationship)

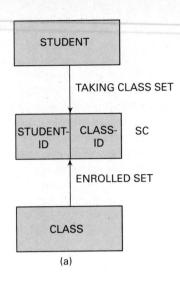

(a)

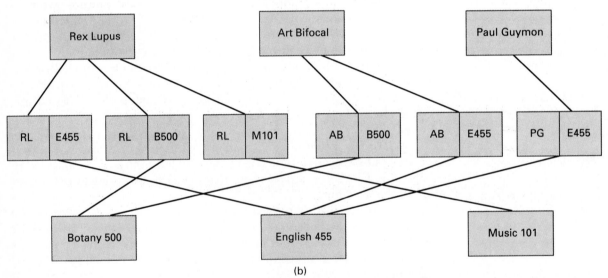

(b)

FIGURE 9.3   Example of Use of Intersection Records to Convert a Complex Network to a Simple Network

dent enrolled. Additional storage and processing requirements are inherent in the creation of the artificial records, but the data model is now in simple network form and satisfies the DBTG requirements.

☐ THE NETWORK MODEL'S RELATIONSHIP TO OBJECT-ORIENTED SEMANTICS

As we have taken an object-oriented semantic approach to studying database systems, it is appropriate to examine the relationship between the network data model and the object-oriented model. In this section, we show how an object-oriented model can be transformed to a network model.

Transforming Object Sets and One–Many Relationships

logical record A record type as seen from the user's perspective.

physical link A means of connecting records by using the records' disk addresses.

The network model can be thought of as an object-oriented model with all the relationships limited to binary (two-object) sets and one–many or one-one relationships. This allows an uncomplicated graphical representation of data structures. Instead of the object sets of the object-oriented model, we have **logical records,** which are connected with other logical records through **physical links** consisting of the records' addresses on disk. Each link represents a relationship between exactly two records. The relationship between two record types connected by the binary link is referred to as a set.

To clarify this, let's take another look at an example from International Product Distribution (IPD). We assume the same case facts as before and add that IPD is organized into the usual functional departments such as accounting, marketing, and so forth. Figure 9.4(a) is a fragment of an object-oriented model for IPD illustrating the relationship between customers and IPD accounts. Figure 9.4(b) shows how the model fragment is mapped to a network data structure.

The correspondence is quite direct. The names of the objects become the names of the records. The attributes of the objects become the fields of the records. The relationship between objects becomes the relationship between records. If the reality is that a customer may have many accounts, and that an account may belong to only one customer—as indicated in Figure 9.4(a), then an arrow would be added at the ACCOUNT end of the HAS-ACCOUNT link (Figures 9.4(b) and 9.5(a)). If a customer could only have one account, but that account could belong to several customers, then the arrow would be added at the customer end of the HAS-ACCOUNT link, as shown in Figure 9.5(b).

From the foregoing examples, we are led to the expression of these mapping rules:

Rule 1: For each object set *O* in an object-oriented diagram, create

FIGURE 9.4   Mapping of Data Model to Network Structure

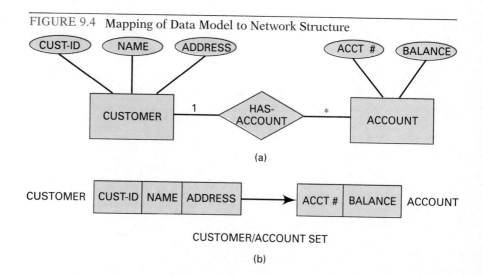

(a)

CUSTOMER/ACCOUNT SET

(b)

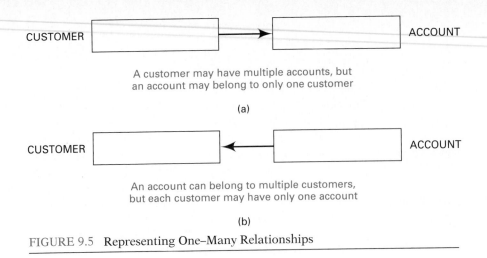

A customer may have multiple accounts, but
an account may belong to only one customer

(a)

An account can belong to multiple customers,
but each customer may have only one account

(b)

FIGURE 9.5   Representing One–Many Relationships

a record type R in the network data structure. All attributes of O are represented as fields of R.

Rule 2: For one–many relationships, the record type on the "one" side of the relationship becomes the owner, and the record type on the "many" side of the relationship becomes the member record type. If a relationship cardinality is strictly one–one, then the owner and member record types may be arbitrarily chosen.

Transforming n-ary
Relationships

IPD also has some three-way relationships as shown in Figure 9.6(a), which do not satisfy the binary-relationship requirement. There is, however, an easy way of satisfying that requirement, as illustrated in Figure

FIGURE 9.6   Converting a Three-Way Relationship to Binary Network Representation

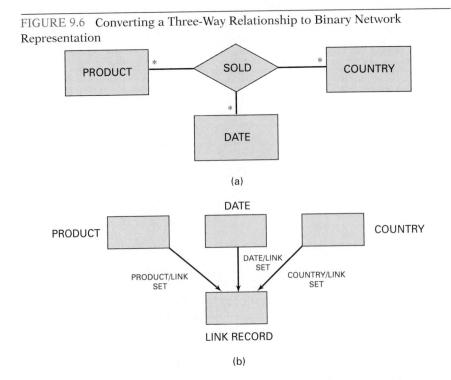

(a)

(b)

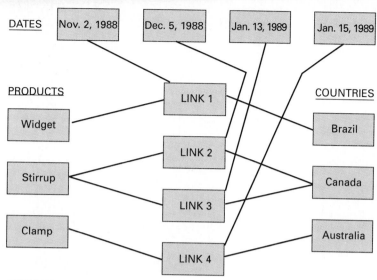

FIGURE 9.7 Sample Database for the Diagram of Figure 9.6

9.6(b). A link record is created, which must be composed of at least the key from each object set. The creation of this link record allows representation of the object-oriented structure in network form. All three relationships are now binary.

Note that the relationship between the existing records and the link record is one–many, with the link record always being the member record in the set. Occurrences are shown in Figure 9.7. The strategy of creating linking record types can be extended without modification to mapping n-ary relationships to the required form. We express our third mapping rule as

> *Rule 3:* For each n-ary relationship, $n > 2$, create a linking record L, and make it the member record type in n set types. Designate the owner of each set type as the record type on the "one" side of the resulting one–many relationships.

Transforming Many–Many Relationships

As we saw with the earlier STUDENT-CLASS example, a similar situation could arise when many–many relationships are involved. As another example, consider a situation that exists at IPD. A manufacturer may produce many products, and any one of these products can be made by several manufacturers. A diagram of this situation is shown in Figure 9.8(a). Implementation requires that an intersection record be created—which we name IREC. This is shown in Figure 9.8(b). The relationship between PRODUCT and IREC is one–many, as is the relationship between MANUFACTURER and IREC. The requirements of the DBTG network model are satisfied.

An instance of this data model is given in Figure 9.9. Manufacturer Smith supplies products 115 and 116. Product 115 is supplied by Shirdlu, Inc., as well. Can you see what would happen if Joe Bean Mfg. also supplied product 116, or if Shirdlu began manufacturing product 120, or a new product—135?

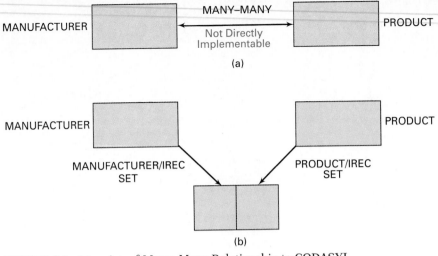

(a)

(b)

FIGURE 9.8   Mapping of Many–Many Relationship to CODASYL

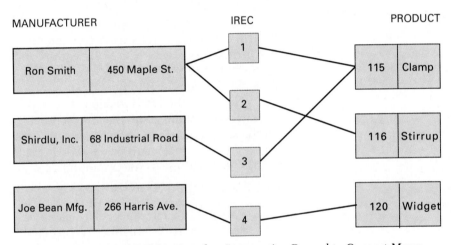

FIGURE 9.9   Example of the Use of an Intersection Record to Convert Many–Many Relationships to One–One Relationships

Our final rule deals with this many–many situation.

Rule 4: For each many–many relationship between object sets O_1 and O_2 create an intersection record type I and make it the member record type in two set types, of which the set type owners are the record types corresponding to O_1 and O_2.

☐ THE DBTG DATA DEFINITION LANGUAGE (DDL)

Data Definition Language (DDL) The language used to specify a database schema.

We now turn to the languages by which the network data model is implemented. These languages are the means by which the data structure or schema is specified and by which the data are stored and manipulated. The language used to specify the schema is called **Data Definition**

Data Manipulation Language (DML) The language used to store and manipulate data.

Language (DDL), and the language used to store and manipulate data is called **Data Manipulation Language (DML)**. We cover the DBTG DDL in this section and DML in the next.

From Data Model to Schema

As noted earlier, the overall definition of a network database—its records and sets—is called a schema. In particular, the schema describes the relationships between record types, identifies the data items that make up each record type, and defines the owner-member record types that define the set types. A procedure for using the DDL in defining a schema is as follows:

> Create the object-oriented data model.
>
> Map the object-oriented data model to network data-structure diagrams.
>
>> Check to see whether there are one–many relationships between record types. These can be implemented directly as DBTG sets.
>>
>> If there are many–many relationships, transform them into two sets having one–many relationships by constructing the necessary intersection records.
>>
>> If there are *n*-ary relationships, convert them to binary relationships by the method illustrated earlier.
>
> Use the DDL to implement the schema.

A schema is made up of the following components:

schema section The section of the DBTG schema that names the schema.

record section The section of the DBTG schema that defines each record, its data items, and its location.

set section The section of the DBTG schema that defines sets and includes owner record types and member record types.

> A **schema section**, which names the schema
>
> **Record sections**, which provide specifications of each record structure, its data items, and its location
>
> **Set sections**, which specify all sets, including the owner and member record types.

Consider the object-oriented model in Figure 9.10. IPD wishes to implement the related schema. The mapping to the network data structure

---

FIGURE 9.10   Object-Oriented Diagram (Fragment) for IPD

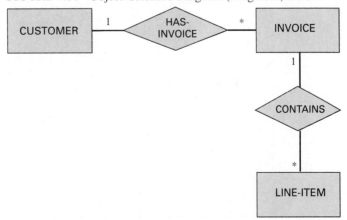

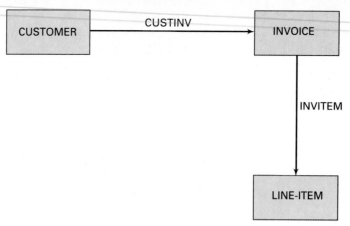

FIGURE 9.11   Mapping of Figure 9.10 to a Network Data Structure

is shown in Figure 9.11. The use of the DDL to implement the schema is shown in Figure 9.12. The lines of code are numbered for reference in our discussion.

The schema section is represented on Line 1. This line identifies what follows as a schema description for a database named AC-COUNTSREC. This name is supplied by the user.

FIGURE 9.12   Schema Example

```
1. SCHEMA NAME IS ACCOUNTSREC
2. RECORD NAME IS CUSTOMER
3. CUST-ID         TYPE IS  NUMERIC INTEGER
4. NAME            TYPE IS  CHARACTER 15
5. ADDRESS         TYPE IS  CHARACTER 20
6. ACCOUNT-BALANCE TYPE IS  NUMERIC (5,2)


7. RECORD NAME IS INVOICE
8. INVNO   TYPE IS  NUMERIC INTEGER
9. DATE    TYPE IS  CHARACTER 9
10.AMOUNT  TYPE IS  NUMERIC(5,2)
11.STATUS  TYPE IS  CHARACTER 2


12.RECORD NAME IS LINE-ITEM
13.STOCKNO      TYPE IS  NUMERIC INTEGER
14.DESCRIPTION  TYPE IS  CHARACTER 20
15.PRICE        TYPE IS  NUMERIC (4,2)


16.CUSTINV
17.OWNER IS CUSTOMER
18.MEMBER IS INVOICE


19.INVITEM
20.OWNER IS INVOICE
21.MEMBER IS LINE-ITEM
```

Lines 2 through 15 are devoted to the record section. Each record type is identified by name: CUSTOMER, INVOICE, and LINE-ITEM. For each record type, the component data items are defined. For CUSTOMER these are CUST-ID, NAME, ADDRESS, and ACCOUNT-BALANCE. Each data item is given a data type and a length specification. For example, AC-COUNT-BALANCE is assigned the NUMERIC data type and given a length of 5 characters, with 2 characters to the right of the decimal point. Those identified as INTEGER have an implied length.

When all records have been defined, sets can be specified. Lines 16 through 21 in Figure 9.12 show examples for the ACCOUNTSREC schema. Definition of a set requires at least the three lines shown. The first line is to name the set type, the second line is to name the owner record type, and the third line is to name the member record type. In Figure 9.12, one set is named CUSTINV, and has CUSTOMER as its owner record type and INVOICE as its member record type.

From Schema to Subschema

Whereas the schema defines the overall logical structure of the database, the subschema describes the external view of a user or application program. Subschemas are basically subsets of the schema. However, data independence (to allow for the variety of users' terminology) is provided by allowing some elements of the schema to differ. Data items can be grouped that were not grouped in the schema; data items, records, and sets can be renamed; and the order of the descriptions may be changed.

There is no accepted DBTG standard for the subschema; however, the following divisions are commonly used:

A **title division** that enables naming of the subschema and its associated schema

A **mapping division** that provides for changes in names from the schema to the subschema, if desired

A **structure division** that specifies the records, data items, and sets from the schema that are present in the subschema. This division is composed of record and set sections. The **subschema record section** defines the records and the data items from those records that are to be included, along with their data types. The **subschema set section** identifies the sets that are to be included.

We use as an example an application from IPD that computes the number of outstanding invoices by customer, as well as the amounts owed on those invoices. From the ACCOUNTSREC schema, the application requires only the CUSTOMER and INVOICE record types, and the CUSTINV set. The subschema is shown in Figure 9.13.

The name of the subschema (SS) is INVSTATUS. The mapping division shows that the CUSTOMER record of the schema has been renamed OWEDBY in the INVSTATUS subschema, and the CUST-INV set has been renamed OWEDBY-INV. This is done in the ALIAS section, where AD denotes "alias description." The CUSTOMER record from the schema has been renamed with the alias OWEDBY for the subschema, and just three of the four data items comprising CUSTOMER in the schema have been included. The INVOICE ALL statement indicates all

---

title division That portion of the DBTG subschema that provides for naming the subschema and its associated schema.

mapping division The portion of the DBTG subschema that provides for changing the names used in the schema to names chosen for the subschema.

structure division The division of the DBTG subschema where records, data items, and sets from the schema are defined.

subschema record section The section of the structure division that specifies subschema records, data items, and data types.

subschema set section The section of the structure division that defines the sets to be included.

```
SS INVSTATUS WITHIN ACCOUNTSREC.
MAPPING DIVISION.
ALIAS SECTION.
AD RECORD CUSTOMER IS OWEDBY.
AD SET CUST-INV IS OWEDBY-INV.
STRUCTURE SECTION.
RECORD SECTION.
01     OWEDBY.
       05     CUST-ID.
       05     NAME.
       05     ACCOUNT-BALANCE.
01     INVOICE ALL.
SET SECTION.
SD     OWEDBY-INV.
```

FIGURE 9.13   Subschema Example

data items from the record INVOICE in the schema have been included, so there is no need to specify them again.

As you can see, the subschema allows the user to use a predefined schema to tailor the schema to the requirements of a particular application.

☐ THE DBTG DATA MANIPULATION LANGUAGE (DML)

navigational commands DBTG DML commands used to find database records.

retrieval commands DBTG DML commands used to retrieve database records.

update commands for records DBTG DML commands used to change the values of records.

update commands for sets DBTG DML commands used to create, change, or delete set instances.

The DBTG data manipulation language (DML) provides powerful commands for manipulating a network database system. It is the means by which the data contained in the database can be used to support organizational information requirements. Once the database is designed and created using the DDL, the DML allows users to execute operations on the database for purposes of providing information and reports, as well as updating and modifying record content.

As opposed to the DMLs of relational database systems, whose operators process entire relations at one time, the DBTG DML operators process records one at a time. Moreover, the DML must be embedded in a host language, such as COBOL. The basic commands used by the DML can be classified as **navigational commands**, **retrieval commands**, **update commands for records**, and **update commands for sets**. Commands from each of these groups are listed in Figure 9.14.

FIGURE 9.14   Basic DBTG DML Commands

Type	Command
Navigation	FIND
Retrieval	GET
Record Update	ERASE
	STORE
	MODIFY
Set Update	CONNECT
	DISCONNECT
	RECONNECT

Before we illustrate the DBTG DML with examples, we need to define terms that will be necessary for our discussion.

The first concept is that of the **user working area (UWA)**. Every
user or application program has a UWA. The records in the subschema
are stored in the UWA, along with **currency indicators** and **status flags**.
The way in which the record is formatted in the UWA is called the **record
template**.

Consider Figure 9.15. Here we show a possible working area related to the subschema defined in Figure 9.13. The OWEDBY currency
pointer marks the location of the last processed record of that record type.
The INVOICE currency pointer marks the location of the last processed
record of that record type. The OWEDBY-INV currency pointer marks the
location of the associated owner or member record of that set which was
last accessed. The RUN-UNIT currency pointer marks the location of the
last accessed record of any type.

We see that currency indicators function as placemarkers. When the
user issues a FIND command (to be discussed), the record is found, and
its place is marked in the currency indicator. When a second command
is issued, the DBMS refers to the currency indicator to determine which
record is to be acted upon. Briefly, the type and function of the currency
pointers are the following:

Current of Run-Unit: Run-unit refers to the user's program. Current
of the run unit contains the address of the record, or set instance,

FIGURE 9.15   Relationship of User Working Area to Database Instances

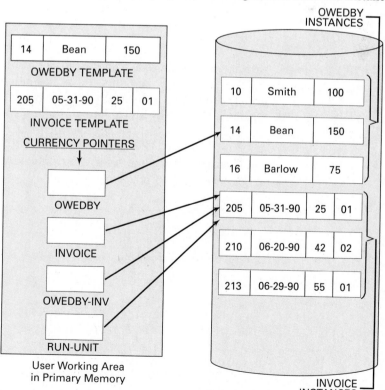

most recently accessed by the application program. In Figure 9.15, this is invoice 205.

Current of Record Type: There is one currency indicator for each record type in the subschema. For each record type, the UWA contains the address of the record of that type most recently accessed by the program. In Figure 9.15, we have currency indicators for the OWEDBY and INVOICE record types, and they are pointing to the records for Bean and invoice 205, respectively.

Current of Set Type: A currency pointer contains the address of the most recently accessed record of a given set type. A separate currency pointer is maintained for each set type. The pointer may point to a record of either the owner or member type depending on which was most recently accessed. Figure 9.15 shows the currency indicator for the only set type in this subschema, OWEDBY-INV, and it is pointing to the member record, invoice 205.

The above pointers are updated automatically as accesses take place in the database system. It is instructive to think of currency indicators as variables in a table. Figure 9.15 illustrates possible currency indicators for the INVSTATUS subschema.

Status flags are a set of variables used to communicate the outcome of the last operation applied in the application program. The flag used most frequently is *db-status*. Its value is set to "0" if the most recent operation succeeded; otherwise, it is set to an error code. The most common use of this flag is to signal the end of data. Other status flags include *db-set-name*, *db-record-name*, and *db-data-name*. These flags are set, as a means of identifying the source of a problem, when the last operation fails. We shall see examples of their use in the queries that follow.

DBTG Retrieval and Update Facilities

FIND commands select and locate a desired record or instance of a set. That is why they are called navigational commands. A GET command must then be used to actually retrieve the data. The FIND command could also be followed by an update command such as ERASE or MODIFY.

Syntactically, there are two forms of the FIND command as shown below. The optional parts of the commands are denoted by brackets ([. . .]) and names to be supplied by the user are indicated by the angle brackets (<. . .>).

```
FIND ANY <record name> [USING <field list>]
FIND DUPLICATE <record name> [USING <field list>]
```

We give several examples.

Example 1: A Simple Record Retrieval

Suppose that IPD wants the Customer information for Customer 105. The following commands apply:

```
MOVE 105 TO CUST-ID IN CUSTOMER
FIND ANY CUSTOMER USING CUST-ID
GET CUSTOMER
```

The FIND command sets the current of run-unit, current of CUSTOMER, and current of CUSTINV to point to the record of Customer 105. The GET command then brings the record into the CUSTOMER template in the UWA.

Example 2: Retrieval of All Records Having a Particular Characteristic

Suppose next that IPD wants all the records of customers having account balances of zero.

```
MOVE 0 TO ACCOUNT-BALANCE IN CUSTOMER
FIND ANY CUSTOMER USING ACCOUNT-BALANCE
DOWHILE DB-STATUS = 0
     GET CUSTOMER
     (process customer record)
     FIND DUPLICATE CUSTOMER USING ACCOUNT-BALANCE
END-DO
```

In this example, we have a loop that is controlled by DB-STATUS. That is, DB-STATUS will be set to a non-zero code when there are no more CUSTOMER accounts with zero balances. The first FIND locates the first CUSTOMER record having a zero balance. The next FIND looks for a DUPLICATE, meaning another record that has the same value of ACCOUNT-BALANCE that the current of CUSTOMER has.

Example 3: Deleting Records Using the ERASE Command

IPD now wants to delete CUSTOMER accounts that have a zero AC-COUNT-BALANCE.

```
MOVE 0 TO ACCOUNT-BALANCE IN CUSTOMER
FIND FOR UPDATE ANY CUSTOMER USING ACCOUNT-BALANCE
DOWHILE DB-STATUS = 0
     ERASE CUSTOMER
     FIND FOR UPDATE DUPLICATE CUSTOMER USING ACCOUNT-BALANCE
END-DO
```

Comparing this query to that of Example 2, it may be seen that the ERASE command is used in place of GET. Additionally, the words FOR UPDATE are added to the FIND command, which communicates to the DBMS that an update is to occur and that the record must then be locked for the run-unit. Record locking prevents other users from updating this record while our run-unit is processing it. FOR UPDATE is required when seeking records for operations other than GET.

We now turn to an example of modifying the content of stored records.

Example 4: Modifying the Contents of a Record

As previously indicated, a special form of the FIND command—FIND FOR UPDATE—is used to modify record contents. FIND FOR UPDATE is used to locate the record; GET is used to move it to the UWA, where the changes are made. The MODIFY command is then used to replace it in the database.

Suppose that IPD Customer 502 has just moved its offices and needs to have the address field of its record changed. The DML could be used in the following way:

```
MOVE 502 TO CUST-ID IN CUSTOMER
FIND FOR UPDATE ANY CUSTOMER USING CUST-ID
GET CUSTOMER
IF DB-STATUS = 0
    THEN MOVE '455 Cherry Lane, San Marino, CA' tO
    ADDRESS IN CUSTOMER
        MODIFY ADDRESS
    ELSE (perform error routine)
END-IF
```

In this example, the MODIFY statement is used to identify the record field that is to be changed. If no record field identifier is supplied, the DBMS assumes that the entire record is to be changed.

Example 5: *Adding a New Record to the Database*

The STORE command is used to insert new records into the database. The record is constructed in the UWA and then placed in the database by STORE.

IPD has a new customer record to add. The new customer's name is Harry Z. Smith, located at 201 S. Main, San Marino, California. Smith's company has just purchased $500.00 worth of goods. IPD has assigned a customer identification number of 503.

```
MOVE 503 TO CUST-ID IN CUSTOMER
MOVE 'Harry Z Smith' TO NAME IN CUSTOMER
MOVE '201 S. Main, San Marino, Ca' to ADDRESS IN CUSTOMER
MOVE 500.00 TO ACCOUNT-BALANCE IN CUSTOMER
STORE CUSTOMER
```

DBTG Set-Processing Facility

Sets are used to process records by relationship. The DBTG DML provides facilities for inserting records into set instances, removing records from set instances, and moving records around within set instances. Options are available to specify constraints on set membership, as well. We explain this facility next.

Set Operations

The DBTG language provides three commands for processing sets. CONNECT adds a record to a set. DISCONNECT removes a record from a set. RECONNECT allows set membership to be changed. In order to add a new record to a particular set instance, the record must first be added to the database. Then, the currency pointers of the record type and the set type must be set to point to the appropriate record and set instance. We give the following example.

Example 6: *Placing a Record in a Set*

Suppose that IPD Customer 431 has just made a $100.00 purchase on account, and the associated invoice (#231) has been prepared. Customer 431 is now the owner of a new invoice instance. The INVOICE record occurrence must be created, then connected to the CUSTINV set. This is done in the following way:

```
MOVE 231 to INVNO IN INVOICE
MOVE '7/7/90' TO DATE IN INVOICE
MOVE 100.00 TO INVOICE-AMOUNT IN INVOICE
STORE INVOICE
MOVE 431 TO CUST-ID IN CUSTOMER
FIND ANY CUSTOMER USING CUST-ID
CONNECT INVOICE TO CUSTOMER
```

The first four statements create the new invoice record and insert it into the database as in Example 5. At this point in processing, the new INVOICE record is the current of run-unit, the current of INVOICE, and the current of CUSTINV. The CONNECT command connects the current of the INVOICE record to the existing instance of the set. In this example, the new INVOICE record is connected to the CUSTINV occurrence owned by Customer 431.

Thus, after the STORE command, 431 is moved to the data item CUST-ID, and Customer 431's record becomes the current of CUSTINV. The CONNECT command then puts the new INVOICE record into this instance of the CUSTINV set.

A DISCONNECT command removes the run-unit's current record from one or more sets. This operation does not delete a record from the database, *it only removes a record from a set*. If deletion is desired, it is completed using the ERASE command as illustrated previously. We demonstrate the use of the DISCONNECT command in Example 7.

Example 7: Removing a Record from a Set

When an IPD invoice is paid, it is deleted from the set of outstanding invoices for that customer. Suppose, for example, that IPD Invoice 254 has just been paid in full.

```
MOVE 254 TO INVNO OF INVOICE
FIND ANY INVOICE USING INVNO
DISCONNECT INVOICE FROM CUSTINV
```

The first two statements locate the desired invoice. The final statement disconnects it from the set of which it is currently a member record. The record still remains in the database for audit and record-keeping purposes.

The RECONNECT command allows a record to have its set membership changed. For example, suppose that Invoice 510 is mistakenly assigned to the set owned by Customer 425, when it should have been connected to the set owned by Customer 431. The change to correct this situation would proceed as shown in the next example.

Example 8: Changing Set Membership

```
MOVE 510 TO INVNO OF INVOICE
FIND ANY INVOICE USING INVNO
MOVE 431 TO CUST-ID IN CUSTOMER
FIND ANY CUSTOMER USING CUST-ID
RECONNECT INVOICE IN CUSTINV
```

The first two statements locate the desired INVOICE record. The third and fourth statements locate the desired CUSTOMER record. The last statement connects Invoice 510 to the set owned by Customer 431. This also affects removal of Invoice 510 from the set owned by Customer 425.

Set Membership Classification

Two classes of set membership are **set insertion class** and **set retention class**. Set insertion is associated with the way in which a member gets placed in a set occurrence. Once a member record is assigned to a set, the set retention class determines how and when a member record can be removed from that set.

Set insertion modes are defined by the statement

```
INSERTION IS <insert mode>,
```

where the insert mode options are manual or automatic.

set insertion class In DBTG, the way in which a member record gets placed in a set occurrence; can be manual or automatic.

set retention class In DBTG, determines how and when a member record can be removed from a set; can be fixed, mandatory, or optional.

manual insertion mode In DBTG, requires that the member record be placed in a set by using a CONNECT command to link it to the desired set occurrence.

The **manual insertion mode** requires that the member record must be placed in a set by using a CONNECT command to link it to the desired set occurrence. Manual insertion is accomplished by the statement

```
CONNECT  <record type> TO <set type>
```

Assume that we have the following subschema fragment:

```
SET NAME IS CUSTINV.
OWNER IS CUSTOMER
MEMBER IS INVOICE
     INSERTION IS MANUAL
     RETENTION IS OPTIONAL.
```

An example of its use was seen in Example 6.

automatic insertion mode In DBTG, when a new member record is created, the DBMS will automatically connect it to the correct set occurrence.

Automatic insertion mode means that when a new member record is created, the DBMS will automatically connect it to the correct set occurrence. This connection will occur whenever statements of the following type are executed:

```
STORE <record type>
```

Suppose in the subschema fragment above that MANUAL is replaced by AUTOMATIC. Example 6 would change in the following way:

```
MOVE 431 TO CUST-ID IN CUSTOMER
FIND ANY CUSTOMER USING CUST-ID
MOVE 231 to INVNO IN INVOICE
MOVE '7/7/90' TO DATE IN INVOICE
MOVE 100.00 TO INVOICE-AMOUNT IN INVOICE
STORE INVOICE
```

The first two lines make customer 431 the current of the CUSTINV set. The next three statements create the new INVOICE record. The

STORE command will insert the record into the desired CUSTINV set, since connection to this set is defined as AUTOMATIC.

Set retention options are

fixed retention In DBTG, once a member record has been assigned to a set occurrence, it cannot be removed from that set occurrence unless the record is deleted from the database.

mandatory retention In DBTG, once a member record has been placed in a set occurrence, it must always be in some occurrence of that set.

optional retention In DBTG, there are no restrictions imposed on connections or reconnections to set types.

Fixed, meaning that once a member record has been assigned to a set occurrence, it cannot be removed from that set occurrence unless the record is deleted from the database

Mandatory, meaning that once a member record has been placed in a set occurrence, it must always be in some occurrence of that set. It cannot be disconnected, or reconnected, to a set of another type.

Optional, meaning that there are no restrictions imposed on connections or reconnections to set types. A record so designated need not be connected to any set whatsoever.

The set retention mode also governs what is allowed when a record that is a set owner is erased. If the retention mode is FIXED, the entire set will be erased. If the retention mode is MANDATORY, then the deletion operation is illegal since member records must belong to a set occurrence. If the retention mode is OPTIONAL, then the record will be deleted and the member records of the set it owns will be disconnected and remain in the database without set membership.

Example 9: Set Insertion and Retention Status

Consider the schema of Figure 9.12. We illustrate the use of set insertion and retention status specification by extending the definition of CUSTINV and INVITEM. Assume that we want to specify MANUAL insertion and OPTIONAL retention. The modified schema is shown in Figure 9.16.

☐ IDMS/R—A DBTG DBMS

IDMS/R stands for Integrated Database Management System/Relational. It is based on the DBTG network model and is perhaps the most successful of the DBTG-based products. The R was added to indicate the addition of certain relational features to IDMS. The relational interface is primarily

---

FIGURE 9.16   An Example of the Use of Set Insertion and Set Retention Status

```
CUSTINV
OWNER IS CUSTOMER
MEMBER IS INVOICE
    INSERTION IS MANUAL
    RETENTION IS OPTIONAL


INVITEM
OWNER IS INVOICE
MEMBER IS LINE-ITEM
    INSERTION IS MANUAL
    RETENTION IS OPTIONAL
```

of interest to the user. The basic structure of IDMS remains closely aligned to DBTG network specifications.

IDMS applies the structural concepts of record and set as defined by DBTG. The IDMS schema is comprised of a SCHEMA DESCRIPTION section, RECORD DESCRIPTION sections, and SET DESCRIPTION sections according to DBTG design. In addition, it includes a FILE DESCRIPTION section, which defines all internal files and assigns them to external files. IDMS also includes an AREA DESCRIPTION section, which assigns file partitions to specified areas. An **area** is a location in storage that contains one or more record types.

The IDMS subschema contains no MAPPING division, because aliases are not generally allowed for records, sets, or data items. When an entire record from the schema is used in the subschema, it is expressed by

```
ELEMENTS ARE ALL
```

If some subset of the record data items are required, it is denoted by

```
ELEMENTS ARE <data item 1> <data item 2> . . .
    <data item n>,
```

where data items can be permuted according to the needs of the application.

Sets are defined in a manner similar to that prescribed by DBTG, with some important differences. FIXED set retention is not available. Only MANDATORY and OPTIONAL retention capabilities are provided. There are also certain restrictions on which records are to be included in the subschema. IDMS/R mandates that sets that might be deleted by erasing an owner record be included in *any* subschema containing that record. This is to avoid propagating an ERASE to records that are not included in the set defined in this subschema. This could happen if the owner record were erased, causing the erasure of member records, which were, in turn, owners of another set not included in this schema.

Overall, IDMS structures are faithful to the recommendations of the DBTG report.

> **area** In IDMS/R, location in storage that contains one or more record types.

□ CODASYL DBTG EVALUATION

In this section, we compare the CODASYL DBTG model with the relational model to assess its comparative strengths and weaknesses.

Data Representation A significant difference between the relational model and the network model is in the way in which relationships are represented. In the relational model, links between two relations are established by including in those two relations an attribute with the same domain of values—often with the same attribute name. Rows in each relation that are logically related will have the same values for that attribute. In the DBTG network model, one–many cardinalities between two record types are established by explicit definition of set type. The DBMS then connects records in each set type by physical pointers.

This means that records are physically connected when they participate in the same set occurrence. This explicit representation of set types has been asserted to be an advantage for the network model. A counter argument is that the network model uses two modeling concepts, the record type and the set type, whereas the relational model only uses one simple concept, the relation.

Data Manipulation Language

The DBTG DML navigational and retrieval operations are carried out on single records, in contrast to the relational model's operations which are carried out on entire relations. These DBTG operations must be embedded in a host programming language such as COBOL. Since the record-oriented manipulation operations are based on traditional file-processing operations, the programmer needs to be intimately familiar with the currency indicators and their meanings to avoid error.

It would appear that the relational model may have the advantage when it comes to the DML. This is partially confirmed by the addition of relational user interfaces to IDMS, making it IDMS/R. The relational language systems provide high-level capabilities for operating on sets of tuples. Commercial implementations of these systems have incorporated complementary capability for grouping, sorting, and arithmetic. Additionally, the relational DMLs can be used directly or can be embedded in a host language.

Integrity Constraints

The DBTG network model provides a useful set of integrity constraints. It is particularly strong in its capability for protecting the integrity of sets. The set retention features allow the designer to determine how owner records may behave with respect to member records, and vice versa. MANDATORY and FIXED retention requires that every record must have an owner, for example, whereas OPTIONAL does not.

Semantic constraint capability, such as limiting the hours worked as recorded in an employee record to 60 or less, can only be implemented in the application program that operates on those records.

Implementation

The DBTG network model is especially well suited for database systems that are characterized by

> large size
> well-defined repetitive queries
> well-defined transactions
> well-defined applications.

If these factors are all present, then the users and designers of the database system can focus efforts on ensuring that applications are programmed in the most efficient manner. The negative side is that unanticipated future applications may not work well—and may even require difficult database system reorganization.

■ SUMMARY

In this chapter, we have presented the fundamentals of the DBTG network data model. This model has a rich history and is the basis for several successful DBMSs. We observed that a network forms a graph structure, which is a natural way of representing the relationships among data. We outlined the history of the DBTG recommendations for network standards, and we used those recommendations as a basis for the remainder of the chapter.

We found that the network data model utilizes two basic constructs: the record type and the set type. Records are defined as collections of logically related data items. Sets are defined by owner and member records that have a logical linkage. A data structure diagram for the network data model consists of boxes, which represent record types, and arrows, which establish relationships between record types. These named relationships form set types.

The way in which object-oriented models are mapped to network data structures was demonstrated, and rules were provided to guide that process. Methods of mapping one–one, one–many, and many–many relationships were demonstrated. It was also shown how to convert n-ary relationships to an equivalent set of binary relationships by creating a link record.

The DBTG languages were then presented. The DBTG DDL provides a means of creating and defining the database. Concepts used to define the data base included the schema, which defines the logical structure of the network in terms of its record types and set types.

Once the schema is defined, external views of that structure needed by database users and applications are defined using a subschema for each such view. The subschema allows selection of only that data needed from the schema. Data items can be renamed or reordered to suit the needs of the application.

The DBTG DML was then discussed, and a number of examples were given. We saw that the DBTG DML is single-record oriented and provides a number of features to ensure maintenance of database integrity. DML commands can be classified as navigational commands, retrieval commands, and update commands. Update commands are used for updating records, as well as for updating set occurrences.

The most widely used commercial implementation of the DBTG network data model, IDMS/R was briefly outlined. While the "R" indicates that some relational user interface features have been added, IDMS/R basically follows the design recomendations of DBTG.

This was followed by a summary evaluation of the DBTG model. It is generally accepted that for predetermined transactions on the database, programs can be devised that make the network model very efficient. Its disadvantages seem to center on weak facilities for adapting to changed requirements and *ad hoc* queries.

■ REVIEW QUESTIONS

1. Define each of the following terms in your own words:
   - a. CODASYL
   - b. DBTG
   - c. IDS
   - d. network data model
   - e. DML
   - f. logical record
   - g. physical link
   - h. DDL
   - i. title division
   - j. mapping division
   - k. structure division
   - l. record occurrence/instance
   - m. subschema record section
   - n. set occurrence
   - o. owner record type
   - p. member record type
   - q. subschema set section
   - r. user working area
   - s. currency indicator
   - t. status flag
   - u. retrieval commands
   - v. navigational commands
   - w. directed graph
   - x. node
   - y. edge
   - z. record section
   - aa. set section
   - bb. update commands for records
   - cc. update commands for sets
   - dd. record templates
   - ee. set insertion class
   - ff. set retention class
   - gg. manual insertion mode
   - hh. automatic insertion mode
   - ii. fixed retention
   - jj. mandatory retention
   - kk. optional retention
   - ll. area

2. Briefly define what funtion is performed by each of the following DBTG DML commands:
   - a. FIND
   - b. GET
   - c. STORE
   - d. ERASE

3. Briefly discuss the three-level architecture of the DBTG network model. Focus on the functions of each of the three levels and how they relate to one another.

4. How is the DBTG definition different from the mathematical definition of a set as a collection of objects?

5. Using an example, show how the use of an intersection record allows a complex network to be transformed into a simple network.

6. What would happen if an n-ary relationship ($n > 2$) were not transformed into equivalent binary relationships in the network data structure?

7. Compare the ways in which the relational data model and the DBTG model represent relationships.

8. How do relational data manipulation languages differ from the DBTG DML?

9. Suppose your boss asked you to explain the relative advantages and disadvantages of relational database systems versus the DBTG network model. What would you say?

1. Match the following terms with their definitions:

__Schema   a. A name given to the relationship between an owner record type and a member record type

__Subschema   b. The user's view of the logical data structure of a database

__Record type   c. In DBTG, determines when a member record can be removed from a set

__Set   d. The logical structure of all data and relationships in the database

__Set retention class   e. The name given to records of the same type

__Complex network   f. Occurs when there is at least one many–many relationship

__Simple network   g. A dummy record created in order to allow implementation on a DBTG system

__Intersection record type   h. A data structure in which all binary relationships are one-many

2. State any rules from the chapter that would be used in transforming the object-oriented diagram of Figure 9.1E to a DBTG data structure. Show the resulting data structure.

3. Complete the requirements of Problem 2 using the object-oriented diagram of Figure 9.2E.

4. Map the object-oriented diagram of Figure 9.3E to a DBTG data structure. From that structure create a DBTG schema. State any necessary assumptions.

5. For the schema of Problem 4, create a subschema for an application that views only the VENDOR and ORDER record types.

6. For the DBTG data structure created in Problem 4, write DML statements to do the following:

     a. Retrieve the record for Vendor 13.

     b. Retrieve all orders in the amount of $100.00.

     c. Delete order #256.

     d. Change the address for Vendor 13 to '912 Adams Street, Gainesville, FL'.

     e. Add Vendor 15 to the database. Vendor 15's name is 'Mike Otteson', and the address is 'Buster Building, Suite 95, Toronto, Canada'.

FIGURE 9.1E   Object-Oriented Diagram for Problem 2

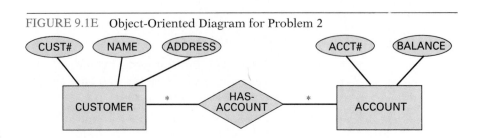

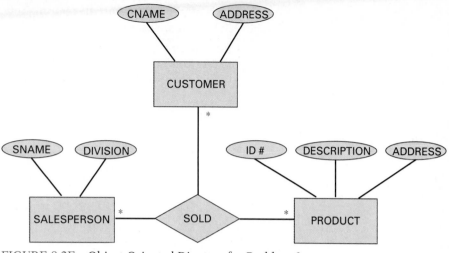

FIGURE 9.2E   Object-Oriented Diagram for Problem 3

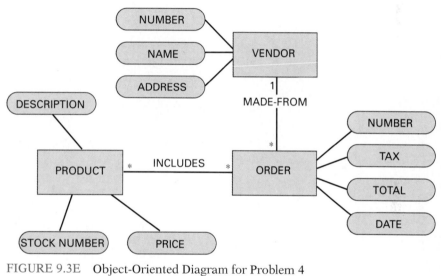

FIGURE 9.3E   Object-Oriented Diagram for Problem 4

    f. Add Invoice #285 to the database; connect it to Vendor 15.

    g. Delete Invoice #842 from the database.

■ PROJECTS AND PROFESSIONAL ISSUES

1. Research the database literature to find discussions of the various database models. Based upon your findings, develop a report to help Rita Minkowski resolve the debate she heard at the ACM meeting.

2. Find more detailed descriptions of IDMS/R. What relational features have been added? Can you conclude that these features overcome any advantages that may have been claimed for relational database systems? Explain.

3. If you were charged with developing recommendations for improving the DBTG network model, what suggestions would you make? Be specific.

4. Can you develop any improvements in the method of transforming an object-oriented model to a DBTG data structure? What are they, and how do they improve the transformation method?

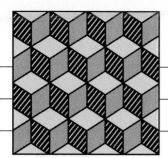

chapter ten

THE HIERARCHICAL DATA MODEL

273

William (Bill) Orange, the chairperson of the local chapter of the Association for Computing Machinery (ACM), was on the phone with Rita Minkowski. "Rita, our discussion of database systems at the last meeting was so well received that we've decided to devote the next three meetings to surveys of the hierarchical, network, and relational models. Do you think you could cover the hierarchical model in the next meeting?"

"Certainly, Bill. What would you like me to discuss?"

"The philosophy of the model and some of the more general aspects of database implementation. Perhaps you could indicate some of the reasons it might be chosen over the competing models. I believe you have had quite a bit of experience with IBM's IMS database system, and that alone should qualify you to describe the hierarchical model."

"Well, I have spent a lot of time with IMS, and I would be glad to represent that point of view at the next meeting. Thanks for the invitation."

In this chapter, we present the fundamentals of the hierarchical data model. After reading this chapter, you should be able to:

- ☐ Describe the basic data structure from which the hierarchical data model is constructed.

- ☐ Explain the terminology used in describing the hierarchical data model.

- ☐ Use the fundamental methods of mapping from an object-oriented model to the hierarchical data model.

- ☐ Describe the terminology and structure of the IMS implementation.

- ☐ Explain how the IMS Data Description Language is used to implement hierarchical data structures.

- ☐ Discuss how the IMS Data Manipulation Language operates to retrieve and update data.

- ☐ Discuss the practical advantages and disadvantages of the hierarchical model.

☐ INTRODUCTION

IMS IBM's Information Management System; leading DBMS based on the hierarchical data model.

TDMS System Development Corporation's Time-Shared Data Management System; DBMS based on the hierarchical data model.

Unlike the relational data model, which is firmly grounded in mathematics, and the network data model, which evolved from an effort to establish detailed standards, the hierarchical data model has developed from practice. There is no original document that delineates the hierarchical model, as there is with the other two models. Since the hierarchical data model has no standard, its study requires an examination of DBMSs used in practice. Fortunately for the student, the hierarchical database implementations are dominated by one system, **IMS** (IBM's Information Management System). In fact, IMS is currently the most widely used of all DBMSs. Expositions on the hierarchical model invariably incorporate the vocabulary and conventions of IMS. We will do the same.

Other hierarchical systems are in use, however, including **TDMS** (System Development Corporation's Time-Shared Data Management System), **MARK IV** (Control Data Corporation's Multi-Access Retrieval System), and **System-2000** (SAS Institute).

Both hierarchical and network DBMSs were developed in the early 1960s. IMS was developed in a joint effort between IBM and North American Aviation (later to become Rockwell) to develop a DBMS to support the Apollo moon project—one of the largest engineering projects undertaken to that time. A key factor in the development of IMS was the need to manage the millions of parts that were related to one another in a hierarchical manner. That is, smaller parts were used to construct larger subassemblies, which became the components of larger modules, and so forth.

Although the relational system, DB2, is rapidly gaining on IMS in terms of number of installations, for large planned-transaction systems requiring rapid response, IMS remains a competitive system. A complementary reason for the durability of IMS is that many data structures are inherently hierarchical. For example, a company may contain departments (one level), departments have employees (a second level), and employees have skills (a third level). While this data structure could be implemented in the network model, that model's more robust representational capability may provide more system complexity (overhead) than needed. In fact, one reason that developers of IMS did not adopt the IDS approach used at General Electric (see Chapter 9) was that the IDS approach would require more disk storage than IMS.

☐ BASIC CONCEPTS AND DEFINITIONS

The hierarchical data model is, on the conceptual level, simply a special case of the network data model. As described in the previous chapter, a network is a directed graph constructed of points connected by arrows. Applying this concept to data models, the points are data record types, and the arrows represent one–one or one–many relationships. An arrow in a network has a point at each end. The point at the tail of the arrow is called the **parent** in hierarchical model terminology, and the point at the head of the arrow is called the **child.** The principal difference between the network and hierarchical models is that the network model allows a child record type to have more than one parent record type, whereas the hierarchical model does not. The kind of network structure permitted by the hierarchical model is called a **tree.** Relationships in the **hierarchical data model** are organized as collections of trees, rather than as arbitrary graphs.

While the vocabulary of the hierarchical model varies somewhat from that of the network data model, there are many natural architectural similarities. As with the network model, there are two basic concepts associated with the hierarchical data structure: **segment types**, or simply **segments**, and **parent-child relationship types (PCR types)**. Segment is used analogously to the network record type. A PCR type is similar to the network set type, except that a segment type can only participate as a child in one PCR type.

As an example, consider Figure 10.1. Figure 10.1(a) shows an object-oriented model defining one–many relationships between DEPARTMENT and EMPLOYEE and between RETIREMENT PLAN and EM-

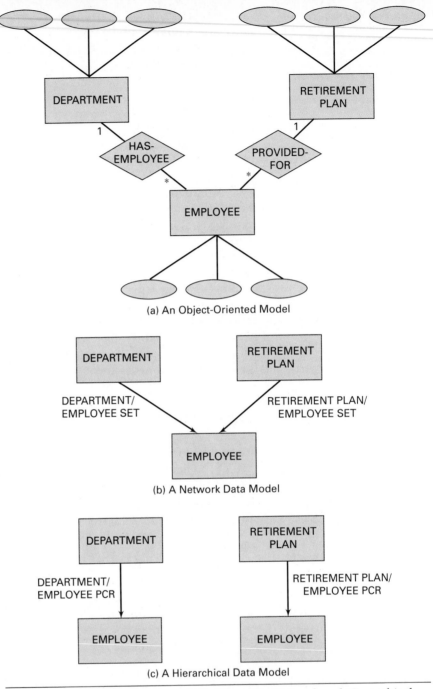

(a) An Object-Oriented Model

(b) A Network Data Model

(c) A Hierarchical Data Model

FIGURE 10.1   An Object-Oriented Model and Its Network and Hierarchical Representations

PLOYEE. The DEPARTMENT, EMPLOYEE, and RETIREMENT PLAN object sets each have their own attributes, although for the present example, the attribute names are omitted. In addition, the relationships' cardinalities indicate that each department occurrence has many employees, while each employee is assigned to only one department. Also, each employee has only one retirement plan, but a given retirement plan is provided for many employees. The representation of these object sets and relationships in the network and hierarchical models is shown in Figures 10.1(b) and 10.1(c).

Figure 10.1(b) illustrates a data structure where (in network terminology) the EMPLOYEE record type is a member of the DEPARTMENT/EMPLOYEE set, as well as a member of the RETIREMENT PLAN/EMPLOYEE set. While this data structure is directly implementable in the network model, it cannot be directly implemented in the hierarchical model. In order to be implemented in the hierarchical model, it must be modified as shown in Figure 10.1(c). Note that in Figure 10.1(c) the DEPARTMENT/EMPLOYEE and the RETIREMENT PLAN/EMPLOYEE sets of Figure 10.1(b) have been transformed to their hierarchical analogs: the DEPARTMENT/EMPLOYEE and the RETIREMENT PLAN/EMPLOYEE PCR types. Also, the EMPLOYEE segment has been shown twice, since in the hierarchical model no segment can participate as a child in more than one PCR type. The EMPLOYEE segment can actually only participate in *one* of these PCRs. EMPLOYEE in the other PCR will consist of pointers to the original EMPLOYEE segment, as we will explain later.

The reason for the transformation of Figure 10.1(c) is that the hierarchical model uses the tree as its fundamental structure. A tree data structure is comprised of a hierarchy of segments conforming to the following conventions:

1. There is a single segment, called the root, at the highest level. The **root segment** does not participate as the child segment in any PCR type.

2. With the exception of the root segment, every segment participates as a child segment in exactly one PCR type.

3. A segment can participate as a parent segment in more than one PCR type (for example, EMPLOYEE in Figure 10.2).

FIGURE 10.2   Hierarchical Arrangement of Segment Type for the DEPARTMENT Database

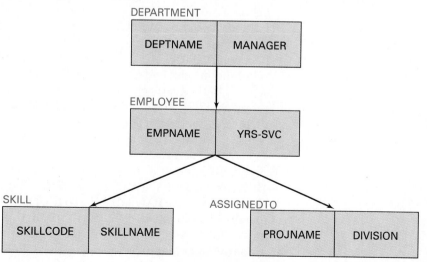

leaf segment In a tree, any segment type that has no child segment types.

ancestor In a hierarchy, a segment type that is found on the same path, but at a higher level in the tree.

dependent segment type All record types other than the root segment type.

database tree A tree that has a root.

database record An occurrence of a root and all its dependent segment types.

4. A parent segment occurrence may have any number of child segment occurrences (children), but each child segment may have only a single parent segment. This establishes a one–many constraint on the relationship between parent and child segments in a tree.

5. A segment that has no children is termed a **leaf segment.**

6. For any segment type *A*, there is a single path in the tree from the root to *A*. The records along this path are called the **ancestors** of *A*. *A* is a **dependent segment** of all segments on that path, including the root.

7. A segment *A* may itself be the root of a subtree.

Figure 10.2 is an example of a three-level tree, in this case representing DEPARTMENT, EMPLOYEE, SKILL, and ASSIGNEDTO segment types and their relationships. A hierarchical database schema is a collection of rooted trees of this type. Each such tree is referred to as a **database tree.** The tree of Figure 10.2 has DEPARTMENT as its root segment and has two subtree types, rooted in the EMPLOYEE segment. One of these subtree types goes from EMPLOYEE to SKILL and the other from EMPLOYEE to ASSIGNEDTO. EMPLOYEE, in turn, has two subtree types, rooted in the SKILL and ASSIGNEDTO segment types. These last two subtree types are, in a sense, trivial, since they consist merely of SKILL alone and ASSIGNEDTO alone. An occurrence of a root and all its dependent segments is termed a **database record**. One database record for the model of Figure 10.2 would consist of an occurrence of a DEPARTMENT segment, together with all its associated EMPLOYEE segments, together with all their associated SKILL and ASSIGNEDTO segments.

Note that DEPARTMENT is the parent segment type of the DEPARTMENT-EMPLOYEE PCR type. All remaining segment types (that is, EMPLOYEE, SKILL, and ASSIGNEDTO) are *dependent* segment types. EMPLOYEE is the child segment type of the DEPARTMENT-EMPLOYEE PCR type. EMPLOYEE also functions as a parent segment type of the EMPLOYEE-SKILL PCR type, as well as a parent segment of the EMPLOYEE-ASSIGNEDTO PCR type. As with the network model, the arrowheads indicate the "many" side of the one–many relationships.

Figure 10.2 also gives us an opportunity to compare the hierarchical data model with the relational data model. Relationships that in a relational model would be represented by foreign keys are represented in the hierarchical data model by parent-child links. For instance, the link between DEPARTMENT and EMPLOYEE might be accomplished in the relational model by placing a DEPTNAME attribute in the EMPLOYEE record. In the hierarchical data model of Figure 10.2, this relationship is represented by the DEPARTMENT-EMPLOYEE link, which is implemented in hierarchical databases by placing a physical disk address (or "pointer") in the DEPARTMENT segment.

We next turn to a consideration of occurrences of database trees. Figure 10.3 shows a sample segment occurrence for the model of Figure 10.2. For each database tree occurrence, there is by definition exactly one occurrence of DEPARTMENT. That is, each department will be the root of a distinct database tree occurrence. In this example, the Marketing Department is in a root segment that has three employee segments. Each employee segment owns one or more SKILL segments, and one or more

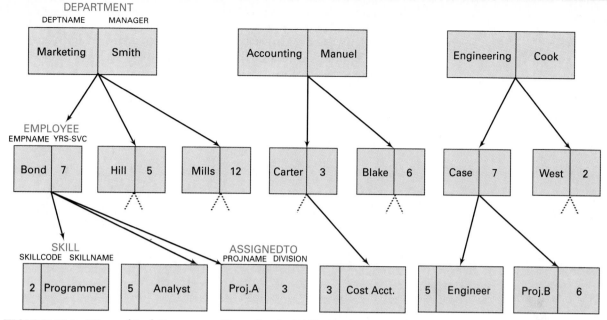

FIGURE 10.3   Hierarchical Occurrence Trees for the DEPARTMENT Database

ASSIGNEDTO segments. This database tree occurrence, then, includes the DEPARTMENT segment for Marketing as well as all its associated EMPLOYEE, SKILL, and ASSIGNEDTO segments.

We use Figure 10.3 to add a new definition to our vocabulary. Occurrences of the same segment type having the same parent are termed **twin segments.** For the Marketing Department segment, employees Bond, Hill, and Mills are twin segment occurrences (Twin segments are not limited to just two.) The tree shown in Figure 10.3 is also called a **hierarchical occurrence tree.**

Hierarchical occurrence trees can be represented in storage by using the **preorder traversal** method of creating a file. We demonstrate the method on the slightly more complex tree of Figure 10.4. The procedure is as follows:

twin segments Segment type occurrences that have the same parent segment type occurrence (more than two segment occurrences may qualify as twins, so the biological analogy is incomplete).

hierarchical occurrence tree Representation of segment occurrences in a tree structure that reflects all PCR types.

preorder traversal A method of converting a tree structure to a flat file that retains the necessary information about the hierarchical relationships.

1. Begin at the root of the tree and record the root segment in the file (segment A in Figure 10.4).

FIGURE 10.4   Example Tree for Illustrating Preorder Traversal

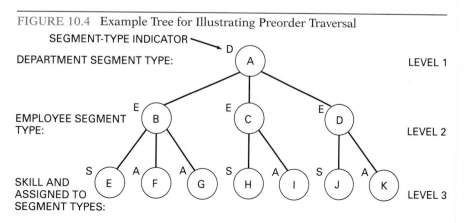

2. At any point, after recording a segment, record the left-most child segment of the segment just recorded. If the segment has no child segment, move back up the tree one level and record the left-most un-recorded child segment of the segment at that level. Continue until all segments are accounted for.

This procedure would generate the following file:

Iteration	Segment	Segment-Type Indicator
1	A	D
2	B	E
3	E	S
4	F	A
5	G	A
6	C	E
7	H	S
8	I	A
9	D	E
10	J	S
11	K	A

The segment-type indicator (D for DEPARTMENT, E for EMPLOY-EE, and so on) is necessary for implementation because of the variable number of child segments possible in each PCR. Since the file is being written sequentially, the system needs to know when a group of segments of one type ends and a group of a new type begins.

Figure 10.4 happens to be a "balanced tree," in that every path from the root segment to a leaf segment has the same length (2). This is coincidental with our example and is not a requirement. Figure 10.5 is an example of an unbalanced tree. The path to segment G is of length 2, but the path to segment L is of length 3.

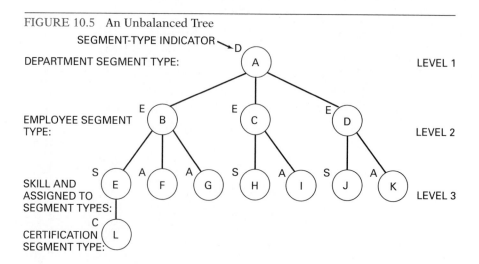

FIGURE 10.5 An Unbalanced Tree

☐ THE HIERARCHICAL MODEL'S RELATIONSHIP
TO OBJECT-ORIENTED SEMANTICS

Transforming an object-oriented model to a hierarchical data structure is very similar to mapping to the network model but with some important variations due to the tree-structure requirement of the hierarchical model. We examine various object-oriented structures and show how they can be transformed into structures of the hierarchical model.

Transforming One–Many Relationships

Examine the object-oriented model of Figure 10.6(a). The mapping of this model to a corresponding hierarchical data structure is shown in Figure 10.6(b). The example suggests that the mapping is identical to that applied to the network model. Each object set with its attributes becomes a logical segment. Each relationship becomes a binary link, and relationships are restricted to being one–many.

We remind the reader that in the network model, however, the employee record type could belong to more than one owner record as suggested by the object-oriented model of Figure 10.7(a). In a network model version of this model, the EMPLOYEE record type would be owned by two record types: DEPARTMENT and RETIREMENT-PLAN. In the hierarchical model, this is not allowed. The corresponding data structure would require two trees, as suggested in Figure 10.7(b). Note that this introduces redundancy into the model since each EMPLOYEE segment occurrence is recorded twice.

This redundancy can be limited, however. The first occurrence of a segment (in this case, EMPLOYEE) would be stored in the usual way.

FIGURE 10.6 Mapping a Simple Object-Oriented Model to a Hierarchical Data Structure

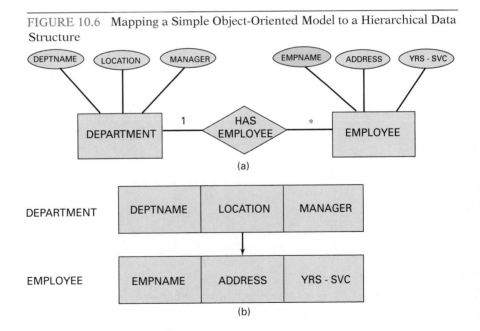

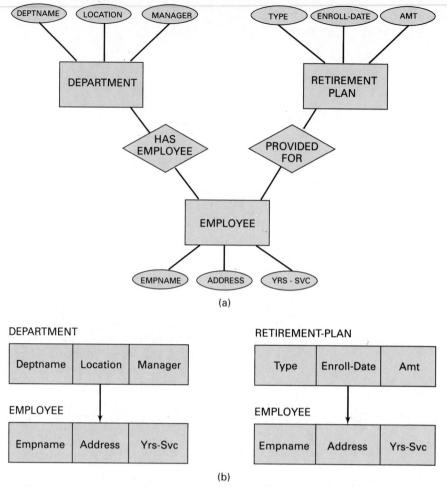

FIGURE 10.7   Mapping an Object-Oriented Diagram with Two PCRs

Subsequent occurrences would not store the actual segment but would store a pointer in the form of a physical disk address giving the location of the stored segment. Thus, there is no data redundancy, but there is additional storage space required for the pointer.

Our first rules for mapping follow.

Rule 1. □   For each object set O in an object-oriented diagram, create a segment type S in the hierarchical model. All attributes of O are represented as fields of S.

Rule 2. □   For one–many relationships between two object sets, create corresponding tree structure diagrams, making each object set a segment and making the one–many relationship a parent-child relationship. The segment on the "many" side of the relationship becomes the child segment, and the segment on the "one" side of the relationship becomes the parent.

Rules 1 and 2 cover a large number of mapping requirements. We may, however, generate object-oriented models requiring the mapping of many–many binary relationships. Recall that we had similar situations in mapping from the object-oriented model to the network model.

Figure 10.8(a) illustrates an object-oriented model fragment of a manufacturer-product relationship. This relationship is many–many, since a given product may be supplied by many manufacturers, and a given manufacturer supplies a number of products. The object-oriented fragment is mapped to the hierarchical data structure as shown in Figure 10.8(b). We have created two trees, one having PRODUCT as the root, and the other having MANUFACTURER as its root. This provides the desired one–many relationships in each tree. The rule we have followed is this:

Rule 3. □ For object sets, O_1 and O_2, that have a many–many binary relationship, and from which segments S_1 and S_2 have been defined, construct two different one–many PCRs: S_1 to S_2, and S_2 to S_1. In one of the PCRs, the actual data segments for both segment types will be replaced by pointers.

FIGURE 10.8 Mapping of Many–Many Relationships to Hierarchical Data Model

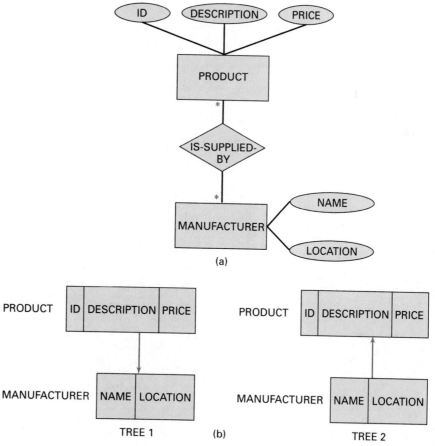

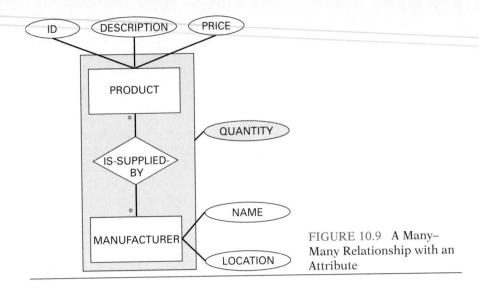

FIGURE 10.9   A Many–Many Relationship with an Attribute

A somewhat more complex situation arises when the object-oriented relationship carries an attribute as shown in Figure 10.9. The attribute QUANTITY has been added to the aggregate of the IS-SUPPLIED-BY relationship to indicate the maximum quantity of a product that can be supplied in one shipment from a manufacturer. In cases like this, an additional segment type is created in mapping to the hierarchical data structure.

This is shown in Figure 10.10. Both of the object sets involved in the binary many–many relationship will function as the parent segment type in separate trees. A new segment type QUANTITY is inserted between the PRODUCT and MANUFACTURER segments to indicate the maximum quantity a particular manufacturer will ship of a particular product. In one tree, one–many links are established from PRODUCT to QUANTITY and from QUANTITY to MANUFACTURER. The process is reversed in

FIGURE 10.10   Mapping a Many–Many Relationship to Hierarchical Data Model, Where the Relationship Carries an Attribute

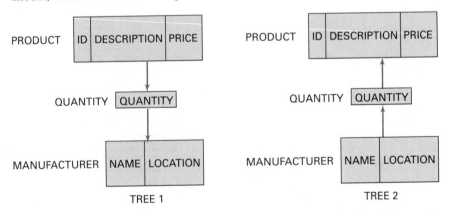

the other tree. We have two parent-child relationships in each three-level tree structure. This procedure is captured in the following rule:

Rule 4. ☐ If a binary many–many relationship has attribute data, create a new intersection segment *I*, which contains that data. Each of the segment types created from the object sets will function as the root of a distinct tree. Insert the new segment between the two object set segment types and establish the corresponding one–many relationships between parent-child segments. If any of those parent-child relationships are exactly one–one, the attribute data might be combined into the segments created from the object sets.

☐ THE IMS ARCHITECTURE

Since the hierarchical data model has no standard, we continue to use its most widely used implementation, IMS, as a basis for exposition. In this way, IMS is presented as a baseline hierarchical model, if not a true standard.

IMS records must be hierarchically ordered as suggested by Figure 10.1(c). Here we see a pair of two-level trees. In Figure 10.2, we see a three-level tree. IMS allows at most 15 levels in a tree, although it is rare for an implementation to contain more than four levels in a tree. IMS also limits the number of segment types to 225.

DL/1 Data Language 1, the IMS data manipulation language.

database description (DBD) The way in which data is physically stored in IMS (internal database structure).

external database The user view of the data in IMS.

program specification block (PSB) Specifies the names of each segment an application program will access; corresponds to a user view or subschema.

program communication block (PCB) A component of the PSB.

(DL/1) (Data Language 1) is the component of IMS that provides for database storage and retrieval. A rough counterpart to the schema used in the network data model is the **database description (DBD)**. This provides the framework for the internal database structure. It establishes the way in which data is stored for use by IMS. The DBD defines the format, length, and location of each data item to be accessed by DL/I. It also defines the position of each segment in the tree structure.

The **external database**, or user view, which was expressed by the subschema in the network model, is described in IMS by the **program specification block (PSB)**. The PSB specifies the names of each segment that a program will access. The PSB, in turn, is subdivided into **program communication blocks (PCBs)** that define the view of the database required for each user application. The PCB contains the name of the DBD of which it is a subset.

Examples of the DBD and the PCB will illustrate the fundamental IMS architecture.

Defining the Physical Database—the DBD

As observed above, the DBD is similar to the network schema, and the PSB is similar to the network subschema. We first clarify the DBD functions with an example. Figure 10.2 depicts four segment types: DEPARTMENT, EMPLOYEE, SKILL, and ASSIGNEDTO. The DBD for this tree is presented in Figure 10.11. The statements have been numbered for purposes of explanation.

Statement 1 is the DBD statement. This statement identifies the name of the database, in this case NAME = DEPTPERS. The statement also specifies the method of database access to be used, in this case

HISAM, which denotes the hierarchical index sequential access method. (IMS access methods will be discussed in a later section of this chapter.)

SEGM An IMS statement that defines the fields to be included in a segment to be used by a program.

The DBD statement is followed by a series of segment **(SEGM)** statements. The SEGM statement defines the group of data items (fields in IMS) comprising that segment and how they are ordered. The first segment in Figure 10.11 is identified in statement 2. The segment is named DEPARTMENT. The assignment PARENT = 0 means that DEPARTMENT is a root segment, "0" meaning that it has no parent segment. BYTES = 20 establishes the length of the segment. In statement 3, DEPTNAME is the first field in the DEPARTMENT segment. It is identified as a sequence field for the DEPARTMENT segment by the NAME = (DEPTNAME,SEQ,U) assignment. That is, as new occurrences of segments are stored, they will be arranged in sequence according to the value of this field in the segment. The "U" means that DEPTNAME must be unique—no two segments can have the same DEPTNAME. As can be seen, the remaining specifications establish the starting location of the field in the segment, the length of the field, and the data type. The common data types are P (packed decimal) and C (character).

We need to describe at least one more segment in order to see how the parent-child relationships are established. Statement 5 begins the definition of the EMPLOYEE segment. After it is given a name, it is assigned a PARENT = DEPARTMENT parameter. This establishes the parent-child relationship between the DEPARTMENT and EMPLOYEE segments. Segment occurrences will be added in sequence by employee name [NAME = (EMPNAME,SEQ)], but those names need not be unique as with DEPTNAME in the prior segment.

With these two descriptions, the remainder of Figure 10.11 is easily interpreted.

FIGURE 10.11 DBD for Model of Figure 10.2

```
 1 DBD     NAME  = DEPTPERS, ACCESS = HISAM

 2 SEGM    NAME  = DEPARTMENT, PARENT = 0, BYTES = 20
 3 FIELD   NAME  = (DEPTNAME,SEQ,U), BYTES = 10, START = 1, TYPE = C
 4 FIELD   NAME  = MANAGER, BYTES = 10, START = 11, TYPE = C

 5 SEGM    NAME  = EMPLOYEE, PARENT = DEPARTMENT, BYTES = 22
 6 FIELD   NAME  = (EMPNAME,SEQ), BYTES = 20, START = 1, TYPE = C
 7 FIELD   NAME  = YRS-SVC, BYTES = 2, START = 21, TYPE = P

 8 SEGM    NAME  = SKILL, PARENT = EMPLOYEE, BYTES = 17
 9 FIELD   NAME  = (SKILLCODE,SEQ), BYTES = 2, START = 1, TYPE = P
10 FIELD   NAME  = SKILLNAME, BYTES = 15, START = 3, TYPE = C

11 SEGM    NAME  = ASSIGNEDTO, PARENT = EMPLOYEE, BYTES = 4
12 FIELD   NAME  = (PROJNO,SEQ), BYTES = 2, START = 1, TYPE = P
13 FIELD   NAME  = DIVISION, BYTES = 2, START = 5, TYPE = C

14 DBGEN
```

sensitive segment A segment that is accessible to a program; abbreviated SENSEG.

Recall that the PSB is something like the network subschema, in that it specifies the view of the data to be used by an application program. The PSB contains one or more program communication blocks (PCBs). The PCB specifies the segments that an application program is allowed to access. Programs cannot access segments not defined in a PCB. Accordingly, the PCB identifies the relevant database and specifies any **sensitive segments (SENSEG)** to be included.

Consider the example shown in Figure 10.12. Suppose that Zeus, Inc., has an application that requires just the DEPARTMENT names and EMPLOYEE names from those two segments. Beginning with line 1, TYPE = DB is required for each PCB to be defined. The database from which this PCB is drawn is called DEPTPERS (DBDNAME = DEPTPERS). PROCOPT is used to denote processing options, meaning the operations that the application program may execute on the PCB. These options include

G = GET

I = INSERT

R = REPLACE

D = DELETE

A = ALL

GET specifies read-only access to segments in the PCB. INSERT allows the addition of new segments to the PCB. REPLACE permits segments to be retrieved and modified. DELETE allows segments to be retrieved and deleted. PROCOPT = A, as shown in Figure 10.12 means that all these processing options are allowed for this application. When a segment is used by the program, IMS identifies its location in the database by recording a **fully concatenated key**. The KEYLEN = 18 establishes the longest concatenated key that the program can access. Roughly, this refers to the longest key that would be obtained by adjoining the key fields along any path through the hierarchy.

The SENSEG and SENFLD statements (lines 2–5) identify those segments and fields that are accessible to the application. In Figure 10.12, there are two sensitive (accessible to the program) segments: DEPARTMENT and EMPLOYEE. The sensitive fields for the respective segments are denoted by the SENFLD statements, with the same meaning (accessibility) applying. Note that dependent segments must explicitly identify their parent segments. For example, the parent of EMPLOYEE is DEPARTMENT, as indicated by the PARENT = DEPARTMENT clause on line 4. START = 1 means that the field starts in the first byte of the segment.

fully concatenated key Means of identifying the location of a segment in the database.

FIGURE 10.12   PCB Example

```
1 PCB      TYPE  = DB, DBDNAME = DEPTPERS, PROCOPT = A, KEYLEN = 18
2 SENSEG  NAME  = DEPARTMENT, PARENT = 0
3 SENFLD  NAME  = DEPTNAME, START = 1
4 SENSEG  NAME  = EMPLOYEE, PARENT = DEPARTMENT
5 SENFLD  NAME  = EMPNAME, START = 1
```

IMS provides for four access methods: HSAM, HISAM, HDAM, and HIDAM. Recall that this choice is reflected in the DBD by the entry "ACCESS = <choice of access method>". The following subsections summarize the four methods.

HSAM

HSAM IMS access method; very fast for sequential retrieval of segments.

HSAM denotes the Hierarchic Sequential Access Method of database access. Segments are physically adjacent on the storage media, so HSAM could be implemented on either tape or disk. Segments are ordered according to the preorder traversal scheme that allows the hierarchical data structure to be maintained.

HSAM is practical only for reading the data. That is to say, this structure is not flexible enough to support effective updating of the database. Updating segments requires that a new version of the database be created and stored.

HISAM

HISAM IMS access method; provides capability for both sequential and direct segment retrieval.

HISAM, Hierarchic Indexed Sequential Access Method, stores segments in hierarchic sequence, as in HSAM, but provides the ability to gain direct access to specific root segments according to an index. Thereafter, dependent segments of the accessed root segment are accessed sequentially, as with HSAM.

HDAM

HDAM IMS access method; provides rapid direct access of segments, but no capability for sequential processing.

HDAM stands for Hierarchic Direct Access Method. This method does not relate segments by an index or by physical proximity, but through pointers (fields containing physical disk addresses). Access to roots is gained through use of a hashing algorithm (see Chapter 11). Examine the tree occurrence of Figure 10.13. The pointers that link segments of an oc-

FIGURE 10.13   Tree Occurrence Example

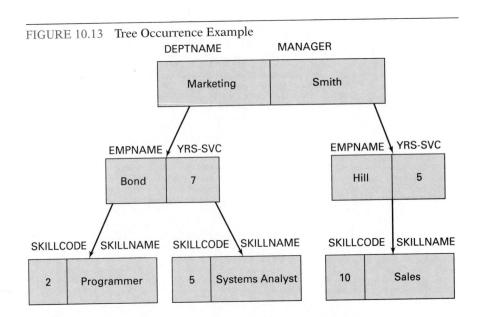

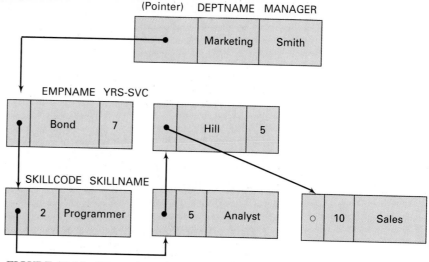

FIGURE 10.14 Hierarchical Pointers in Preorder Traversal Sequence

currence can be *hierarchical* as shown in Figure 10.14, or *child-and-twin* as shown in Figure 10.15.

When hierarchical pointers are used, each segment points to its successor in preorder traversal sequence ("0" indicates no segment follows). For example, to access the record for employee Hill in Figure 10.14, we would start at the Marketing department record, use its pointer to get the record for employee Bond, then follow that record's pointer to the Pro-

FIGURE 10.15 Child and Twin Pointers

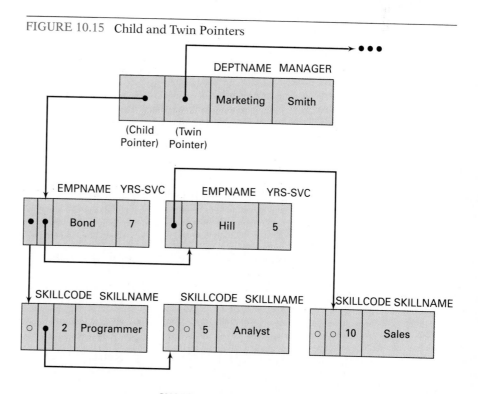

grammer skill record, thence to the Analyst skill record, and finally to Hill's record.

When child-and-twin pointers are used, each segment contains a pointer to the next segment on the same level (twin) and a pointer to the next child segment. In Figure 10.15, the left-most pointer in each segment is the child pointer, and the pointer to its right is the twin pointer. Twin pointers are simpler to implement since every segment contains exactly two pointers. To access Hill's record in Figure 10.15, we start once more at the Marketing department record, follow the child pointer to the first employee record (Bond), and follow that record's *twin* pointer to Hill's record. To access Hill's Sales skill record, we merely follow the child pointer in Hill's record directly to the desired record.

HIDAM

HIDAM IMS access method; provides for direct access of root segments, as well as sequential retrieval.

HIDAM, Hierarchic Indexed Direct Access Method, is basically the same as HDAM, but permits indexed access to roots, as well as pointer access to dependent segments.

☐ THE IMS DATA MANIPULATION LANGUAGE

In this section, we define and illustrate the features of the IMS data manipulation language, DL/1. The programmer accessing and manipulating an IMS database needs to understand these features to properly interact with them.

Program Work Area

segment template Program work area format for a segment.

currency pointer Contains the address of the segment in the tree that was accessed last.

status flag Field whose value indicates the result of the last database operation (e.g., successful or not successful).

In order for DL/1 (or any application program) to execute operations on an IMS database, the system maintains a program work area that contains the following variables:

Segment templates giving the segment layout for each segment type in the database.

Currency pointers for each database tree. These contain the address of the segment in the tree that has been most recently accessed.

Status flags that indicate the outcome of the last database operation. For example, a "0" might be assigned if the last operation was successful and another symbol if it was not. Following an operation, the program can refer to the status flag to determine what to do next.

DL/1: An Overview

The data manipulation language for IMS is termed DL/1, for Data Language 1. Below, we give examples of the most commonly used commands of DL/1:

Command	Meaning
GET UNIQUE (GU)	Retrieve the first segment that satisfies a given condition
GET NEXT (GN)	Retrieve the next segment

GET NEXT WITHIN PARENT (GNP)	Retrieves the next segment, but only within the current parent segment
<hold options>	
GHU, GHN, GHNP	Lock the database for GU, GN, GNP
INSERT (ISRT)	Add a new segment to the database
REPLACE (REPL)	Modify the value of a segment field
DELETE (DLET)	Delete a segment.

The common syntax for DL/1 is

```
Command <segment name> <WHERE qualification>.
```

Let's now look at some examples of the use of these commands.

GET UNIQUE (GU)

The GET command is used to select a segment occurrence. **GET UNIQUE** selects a segment having a particular value into the working area. The segment desired is defined in parentheses by a qualifying condition called a segment search argument (SSA).

Example 1: A Simple Segment Retrieval

```
GU DEPARTMENT (DEPTNAME = 'Marketing')
```

In this example, the SSA is DEPTNAME = 'Marketing'. The GU command will retrieve the first segment that satisfies the SSA. In the next example, note the difference when we wish to retrieve the segment for employee Steve Smith who is assigned to the Marketing Department.

Example 2: Retrieval of a Dependent Segment

```
GU DEPARTMENT (DEPTNAME = 'Marketing')
   EMPLOYEE (EMPNAME = 'Steve Smith')
```

Since the EMPLOYEE segment is dependent, a hierarchical path is specified. The GU operator will retrieve only the segment at the bottom of the path. That is, no Marketing segment will be retrieved.

Now, suppose that we didn't know the department to which Steve Smith is assigned. The query could be handled as shown in the next example.

Example 3: Retrieval of Dependent Segment When Parent Occurrence Is Not Known

```
GU DEPARTMENT
   EMPLOYEE (EMPNAME = 'Steve Smith')
```

This query will result in a sequential scan of DEPARTMENT segments until the dependent segment for Steve Smith is found.

GET NEXT (GN)

If instead of merely retrieving the first occurrence of a segment having a specified value, we wish to retrieve all segments having that value, we may use GU in concert with the GET NEXT (GN) command. For example, suppose that we want to retrieve all the EMPLOYEE segments for the Marketing Department. This would be done in the following way.

<table>
<tr><td>Example 4: Retrieval of a
Set of Segments</td><td>

```
GU DEPARTMENT (DEPTNAME = 'Marketing')
    EMPLOYEE
GN EMPLOYEE
```
</td></tr>
</table>

The GU operator will effect the retrieval of the first EMPLOYEE segment for the Marketing Department. The GN operator will then direct the retrieval of the next employee segment for the Marketing Department. As long as there is a second employee occurrence for the Marketing Department, this query does what we want. However, if there were no remaining employee segments when the GN command was executed, the system would go on to find the next EMPLOYEE segment, irrespective of the department to which she was assigned. This possibility can be prevented by using the GNP command, as we will demonstrate in Example 6. But, first we show a simple modification to the query of Example 4 that allows retrieval of all employee segments in the database.

<table>
<tr><td>Example 5: Retrieving All
Segments of a Particular
Type</td><td>

```
GU DEPARTMENT
    EMPLOYEE
MORE GN EMPLOYEE
    GOTO MORE
```
</td></tr>
</table>

As long as there is another occurrence of an EMPLOYEE segment, the loop identified by the statement label MORE will be executed.

GET NEXT WITHIN

GNP differs from GN in that IMS only retrieves the segments that are dependent on a single parent occurrence. Turning again to Example 4, that query could be modified to use GNP as in Example 6.

<table>
<tr><td>Example 6: Retrieving
Segments for Just One
Parent</td><td>

```
GU DEPARTMENT (DEPTNAME = 'Marketing')
    EMPLOYEE
GNP EMPLOYEE
```
</td></tr>
</table>

In this instance, if there was not another EMPLOYEE segment in the Marketing Department, execution would stop, and the user would have the desired restriction to employees in the Marketing Department.

As another example, suppose that we seek all the SKILLS segments for employee Steve Smith who works in the Marketing Department. The following commands would apply.

<table>
<tr><td>Example 7: Retrieving
Segments for Just One
Parent</td><td>

```
GU DEPARTMENT (DEPTNAME = 'Marketing')
    EMPLOYEE (EMPNAME = 'Steve Smith')
    SKILLS
NEXT GNP SKILLS
    GOTO NEXT
```
</td></tr>
</table>

The GU command retrieves the first SKILL segment for Steve Smith. The GNP command then sequentially retrieves the remaining SKILL segments for Steve Smith.

GET HOLD

The GET HOLD command may occur in one of three forms: GET HOLD UNIQUE (GHU), GET HOLD NEXT (GHN), and GET HOLD NEXT WITHIN PARENT (GHNP). The programmer uses these commands in the same way as GU, GN, and GNP, except that the GET HOLD commands must be used to inform the DBMS that a change or deletion is to be performed on the retrieved segment. That is, GHU, GHN, and GHNP are used in conjunction with REPLACE or DELETE commands.

REPLACE (REPL)

To modify an existing segment, it must be transferred into the work area, where the desired changes to the segment fields are made. Using DL/1, the target segment must first be retrieved using one of the GET HOLD commands. The segment is then modified, and the REPL command writes the updated segment. The following example illustrates how we would proceed if we desired to change the salary of Irving Schatz, who is an employee in the Marketing Department, from $20,000 to $25,000.

Example 8: Modifying Segment Field Values

```
GHU DEPARTMENT (DEPTNAME = 'Marketing')
    EMPLOYEE (EMPNAME = 'Irving Schatz')
MOVE 25000 TO SALARY
REPL
```

DELETE (DLET)

A segment is deleted by first targeting the segment using a GET HOLD and then using the DLET statement. Suppose that Irving Schatz leaves the firm. Example 9 would apply.

Example 9: Deleting a Segment

The commands

```
GHU DEPARTMENT (DEPTNAME = 'Marketing')
    EMPLOYEE (EMPNAME = 'Irving Schatz')
DLET
```

will delete the EMPLOYEE segment for Irving Schatz from the database. When a segment is deleted, any dependent segments are also deleted, so Schatz's SKILL and ASSIGNEDTO segments would also be deleted.

INSERT (INSRT)

New segments are added to the database using the INSRT command. The associated field values must first be moved into a work area. These are then linked to the relevant parent-segment names. Thus, if the segment to be inserted is a dependent segment, the parent segment must already exist.

Bob Lee has just completed the Engineering Drafting curriculum at a local junior college. We wish to add a new SKILL segment for Bob Lee to the database.

```
MOVE 598 TO SKILLCODE
MOVE 'ENGINEERING DRAFTSMAN' TO SKILLNAME
MOVE 0 TO YRS-EXPERIENCE
INSRT DEPARTMENT (DEPTNAME = 'Engineering')
       EMPLOYEE (EMPNAME = 'Bob Lee')
       SKILL
```

This segment will be inserted as the last skill segment under Bob Lee's name.

☐ HIERARCHICAL DATA MODEL EVALUATION

In this section, we examine the strengths and weaknesses of the hierarchical data model. We look at data representation and data manipulation.

Data Representation   There are three features that define the hierarchical data structure: trees, segments, and fields of segments. While any object-oriented model can be transformed to a hierarchical data structure, the requirement that all database records be trees may result in segment duplication. Any situation whose natural mapping results in a segment being a child segment of two distinct parent segments requires that those parent segments occur in separate trees.

While such duplication eliminates certain implementation difficulties, it has these negative results:

1. Storage space is used inefficiently since the segment is repeated.
2. The possibility of inconsistent data is created. If the data is changed in one segment copy, but not the other, the database is inconsistent.

This problem has been dealt with by the use of "virtual segments" and pointers. A virtual segment contains no data but has a pointer to a physical data segment where data is stored. When a segment is required to be replicated in two or more database trees, the actual data is stored in just one of the trees. All other instances of that data segment will contain a pointer to the location where the actual data is stored. Refer to Figure 10.16. Notice that the pointer shown by the broken line addresses the root of the tree containing the actual data in a dependent segment.

A major limitation of the hierarchical model is that there are many applications for which a tree is not the natural data structure. We have seen this, for example, in the manipulations required to convert a situation where a child segment naturally belongs to two parents into two tree structures. These types of occurrences can generate many trees and an associated inefficiency in the use of storage space.

For applications that are inherently hierarchical in nature and for which the query transactions are stable, the hierarchical model may be quite satisfactory. The fact that there are about 7000 IMS installations tends to support this conclusion—although some are switching to relational database systems.

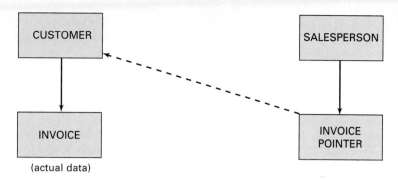

(actual data)

FIGURE 10.16   Tree Data Structure Using Pointers to Reduce Data Redundancy

Data Manipulation Language

The language interface provided for the hierarchical model generally differs with the vendor. This means that programmers need to be aware of which relationships must be predefined to the system and which do not. This programmer reliance is not entirely satisfactory, since the programmer may not be knowledgeable about all of the integrated requirements that have been built into the system. Additionally, if the hierarchical database is reorganized, it may have a negative effect on the performance of existing production programs, since the structure that supports application A may not be the best structure to support application B.

On the positive side, since IMS dominates the hierarchical implementations, a programmer who has worked with IMS may be quite familiar with the internal workings of the DL/1 Language. Moreover, for stable database use, the concern about reorganization may be minor.

■ SUMMARY

The nomenclature of the hierarchical model can be summarized in the following way:

1. A hierarchical data structure is constructed from a group of segments.

2. Each hierarchical data structure must take the form of a tree. A tree is characterized by one or more parent-child relationships, where each such relationship is one–many. Every tree will have one segment that functions only as a parent segment. This segment is called the root.

3. All parent-child relationships in a tree extend from the root downward.

4. Any segment in a tree, excepting the root segment, is a child segment of some parent segment. If a path of parent-child relationships is traced from a higher-level segment, *H*, to a lower-level segment, *S*, all segments on that path, including *S*, are dependent (also descendant) segments of *H*.

5. No segment may appear on more than one path from the root seg-

ment. If the natural model results in more than one path, a separate tree must be created for each additional path.

The hierarchical data model continues to play an important role in practical database implementations. It is especially prevalent in large data-processing centers that are supported by IBM mainframe computers.

A hierarchical database is constructed of collections of segments that are connected to one another by pointers. Each segment is a collection of fields, each of which contains only one data value. A pointer establishes the necessary logical links between two segments. In this sense, the hierarchical model is very similar to the network model where data and relationships are represented by record types and pointers.

The hierarchical model differs in that the segments are organized as collections of trees (only one parent segment allowed), rather than arbitrary graphs (where more than one parent record type is allowed).

Some limitations of the hierarchical data model are

1. The logical and physical characteristics of the model are not clearly separated.

2. Manipulations are required in order to represent nonhierarchical data relationships.

3. *Ad hoc* query requirements may require reorganizing the database.

From the standpoint of efficiently processing a database, the hierarchical data model is competitive. However, as business leaders look increasingly at using information as a strategic tool, the hierarchical data model is likely to fall short of providing the necessary capability.

■ REVIEW QUESTIONS

1. Define each of the following terms in your own words:
   a. IMS
   b. TDMS
   c. MARK IV
   d. System-2000
   e. parent
   f. child
   g. tree
   h. hierarchical data model
   i. ancestor
   j. dependent segment type
   k. database tree
   l. database record
   m. twin segments
   n. hierarchical occurrence tree
   o. preorder traversal
   p. DL/1
   q. external database
   r. SEGM
   s. HSAM
   t. HISAM
   u. HDAM
   v. HIDAM
   w. segment template
   x. currency pointer
   y. status flag

2. Define the function that is performed by each of the following DL/1 commands

GU	GHU	ISRT
GN	GHN	REPL
GNP	GHNP	DLET

3. Briefly discuss the DBD, its structure and function.

4. Describe the composition and function of the PSB.

5. What is the purpose of creating an intersection record in mapping object-oriented models to hierarchical networks?

6. In IMS, how many subtrees can there be in a tree?

* 7. Compare the data representation methods of the relational data model, the network model, and the hierarchical data model.

* 8. Do you think DL/1 is simpler than the DBTG DML? Support your answer.

9. What advantages does IMS offer, as compared to the DBTG model and the relational model?

■ PROBLEMS AND EXERCISES

1. Match the following terms with their definitions:

__Segment type   a. The way in which data is physically stored in IMS

__Parent-child relationship   b. A component of the PSB

__DBD   c. A collection of PCBs

__PSB   d. A segment that can be accessed by an application program

__PCB   e. A segment type that does not participate as a child segment in any PCR

__Sensitive segment   f. A segment type that has no child segment types

__Root segment   g. Corresponds to an object in the object-oriented model

__Leaf segment   h. Logical relationship between a parent segment type and a child segment type

2. State any rules from the chapter that would be used in transforming the object-oriented diagram of Figure 10.1E to a hierarchical data structure. Show the resulting transformation.

3. Map the object-oriented diagram of Figure 10.2E to a hierarchical data structure.

4. Write a DBD to match the data structure of problem 3.

5. Write a PSB to allow the DBD to be accessed by an application that uses only the VENDOR and ORDER segments (see problem 4).

FIGURE 10.1E   Object-Oriented Diagram for Problem 2

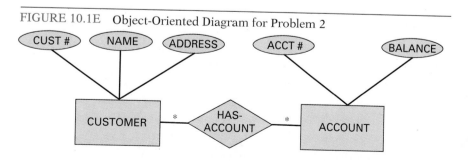

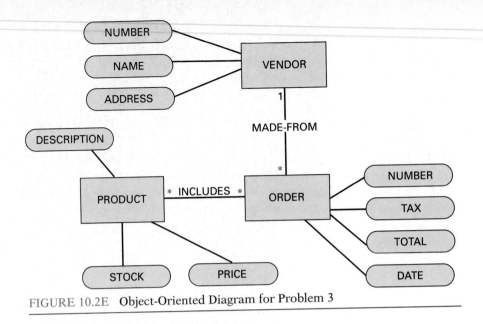

FIGURE 10.2E   Object-Oriented Diagram for Problem 3

6. For the hierarchical data structure of problem 3, write DL/1 commands to do the following:
   a. Retrieve the record for Vendor 13.
   b. Retrieve all orders in the amount of $100.00.
   c. Delete order #256.
   d. Change the address for Vendor 13 to '912 Adams Street, Gainesville, FL'.
   e. Add Vendor 15 to the database. Vendor 15's name is 'Mike Otteson', and the address is, 'Buster Building, Suite 95, Toronto, Canada'.
   f. Add Invoice #285 to the database.
   g. Delete Invoice #842.

■ PROJECTS AND PROFESSIONAL ISSUES

1. Write a short report comparing the advantages and disadvantages of the hierarchical data model. Compare and contrast it to the relational and network models.

2. Find a commercial firm that uses IMS. Are the users satisfied with its capabilities? How is it used? Is the firm planning to change?

3. If you were charged with developing recommendations for improving the hierarchical model, what suggestions would you include?

4. Can you refine and improve any of the suggested rules for transforming object-oriented models to hierarchical data structures? What are they? When do they apply? Give examples.

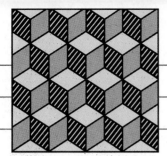

chapter eleven

PHYSICAL DATABASE ORGANIZATION AND ACCESS

Billie Tollefson, currently the Manager of Computing Services at the Zeus Corporation, is finding the attitude of one of her fellow workers unsettling. Archie Krepsbach, who is in charge of materials requirements planning (MRP) in the manufacturing division, had complained to the vice-president of manufacturing about the questionable performance of Computing Services in satisfying MRP's information needs. "Here we have this new database system, which is touted as moving us into the forefront of information management, but I can't always get the information I need when I need it. I am frustrated with the response times I am getting from our DBMS."

Upon hearing this from her boss, Billie responded: "I can appreciate Archie's frustration with our response time, but what he apparently doesn't understand is that the types of reports he needs are particularly difficult to produce in a timely fashion. If he had a better understanding of the complexities of physical database organization, he might find it easier to be patient with our turnaround time. He would also see the need to identify reports that require rapid turnaround and those that can wait a little longer. Then we could fine tune the database to provide better response on the high-priority information." After contemplating the matter for a day or two, Billie decided to recommend to her boss that in-house training seminars be offered to acquaint users with the fundamentals of physical database design and operation.

This chapter deals with the physical structures that are used to implement databases. After reading this chapter, you should be able to:

- ☐ Describe the structures for physically accessing the database.
- ☐ Explain the fundamentals of disk storage, retrieval, and performance.
- ☐ Understand the three basic types of file organization and how they function.
- ☐ Describe the use of pointers to create linked lists, inverted lists, and B^+-trees.
- ☐ Understand how logical data models are mapped to physical data structures.
- ☐ Define and understand secondary keys.
- ☐ Understand basic principles of query optimization.

☐ INTRODUCTION

Physical database organization is a vast topic, and its detail is primarily of interest to technical specialists involved with hardware and systems software design. Yet the overall performance of a database system is determined in large part by the physical data structures used and the efficiency with which the system operates on those structures. Although users should not have to master physical database design details, these details do affect performance, a major consideration in a user's satisfaction with a database system. Can the user get the information desired, in the appropriate format, and in timely fashion? This last factor, "timely fashion," can be generally expressed as acceptable response time. The "information desired" and the "appropriate format" are not greatly affected by the physical database organization—but response time *is*. Response time is the elapsed time between the initiation of a database operation and the availability of the result. Slow response time is the most fequently expressed complaint by users of database systems, possibly because it is the most easily observed.

A good physical database design will store data in such a way that it can be retrieved, updated, and manipulated in as short a time as possible. In this chapter, we are concerned with those aspects of physical database organization that foster efficient database system operation. Although you, as a business system analyst, will very likely not be involved directly in the details of physical design and implementation, it is important for you to understand physical implementation problems and their typical solutions, since they will affect your systems at the user level.

□ PHYSICAL ACCESS OF THE DATABASE

strategy selector Software that translates a user request into an effective form for execution.

buffer manager Software that controls the movement of data between main memory and disk storage.

file manager Software that manages the allocation of storage locations and data structures.

The system for physically accessing the database is shown in Figure 11.1. We see the *user* interacting with the database system by initiating a request. The **strategy selector** translates the user's command into its most efficient form for execution. The translated request then activates the **buffer manager** that controls the movement of data between main memory and disk storage. The **file manager** supports the buffer manager by managing the allocation of storage locations on disk and the associated

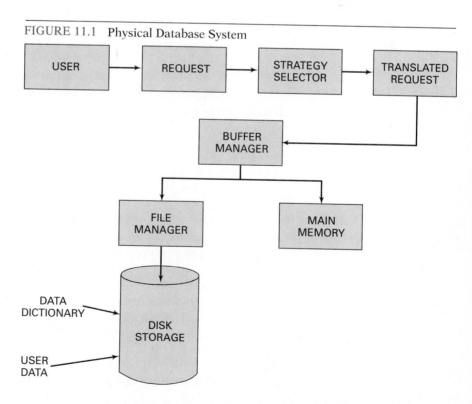

FIGURE 11.1   Physical Database System

data dictionary That part of the DBMS that defines the structure of user data and how it is to be used.

data structures. In addition to the user data, the disk contains the **data dictionary,** which defines the structure of the user data and how it may be used.

The user data is stored as a physical database or collection of records. For example, one row in a relation may be stored as a physical record, with each attribute value of the row being stored in its own data field. Similarly, a logical record of a network or hierarchical model may be stored as a physical record, with the logical data items becoming physical data items of the stored physical record.

☐ PHYSICAL STORAGE MEDIA

main memory Storage located in the central processing unit; used for data made available for user operations.

Main memory is the storage medium used for data that is available for user operations. This is where the executing program resides. As data is required for the program to execute its functions, those data are transmitted from secondary storage to main memory. Although main memory may be able to store several megabytes of data, it is usually too small to store the entire database, and secondary storage is required.

Secondary Storage

Secondary storage for database systems is usually composed of disk storage and magnetic tape storage. Typically, the entire database is stored on disk, and portions are transferred from disk to primary memory as needed. Disk storage is the principal form of database storage, since individual records can be accessed directly or sequentially. Although magnetic tape storage is less expensive than disk storage, records can only be accessed sequentially (and more slowly than with disk). Its role in database systems is basically limited to archiving data.

disk drive Physical unit that contains the disk storage unit.

The physical unit in which the disk recording medium is contained is called a **disk drive.** Each disk drive contains one disk pack or volume. Figures 11.2 and 11.3 show the principal components of the disk pack and the read/write mechanism required for data transmission. The disk pack is made up of a set of recording surfaces (disks) mounted on a shaft. In operation, the shaft and the disks rotate at a high rate of speed. Data is recorded on tracks which are circular recording positions found on each surface (Figure 11.2). There may be several hundred tracks on a single surface. A common metaphor for the disk pack is a stack of phonograph records on a spindle, except that here the tracks are concentric and therefore do not spiral inward to the center.

As shown in Figure 11.3, a set of read/write heads, roughly like the teeth of a comb, moves as a group so that the read/write heads at the end of an arm can be positioned over all those tracks having the same radius. The set of such tracks is termed a **cylinder.** That is, a set of tracks of the same diameter rotating at high speed forms a conceptual cylinder. This is a useful definition since any positioning of the set of read/write heads can be described by the cylinder location (for example, cylinder 199). Thus, all tracks in a given cylinder can be written to, or read from, without further movement of the read/write heads. The address of a record on disk usually requires specification of a cylinder number, a surface number, and a block number (discussed next).

cylinder The same track extending through all surfaces of the disk storage unit.

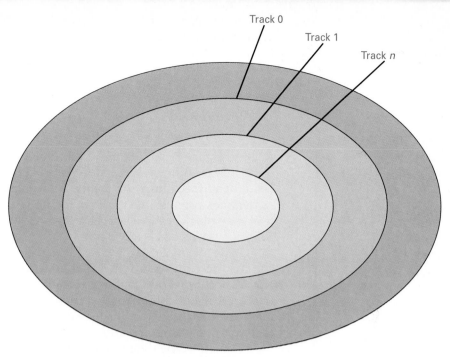

FIGURE 11.2   Structure of a Disk Surface

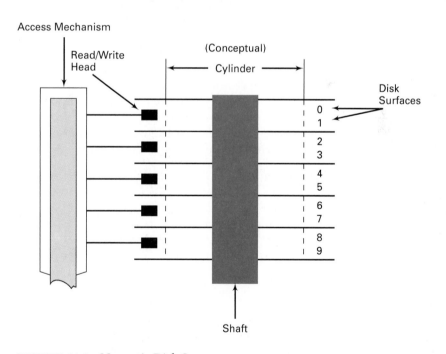

FIGURE 11.3   Magnetic Disk System

Physical Storage Blocks   The physical record, or block, is the smallest physically addressable unit of data on a disk. Each track on a surface is made up of a number of blocks. A block may contain one or more logical records. Suppose that we have a blocking factor of 3, meaning that three logical records are stored in each block. We wish to retrieve the record of John Jones, stored at the following address:

Cylinder number: 5

Surface number: 2

Block number: 1

Refer to Figure 11.4. To retrieve John Jones's record, the read/write heads move into position over cylinder 5 (track 5 on all surfaces), the read/write head for surface number 2 is then activated and block numbers are read as the track rotates under the read/write head. When block 1 is detected, the entire block of three logical records is read into main memory, where John Jones's record is selected.

In our example, we have assumed the most general disk pack nomenclature where the read/write heads are attached to a movable access arm. Not all disk units are configured this way. A few have read/write heads that are permanently fixed for each cylinder. These units are typically more expensive but are faster since there is no delay in moving the read/write heads into position over a new cylinder.

Generally, the time required to perform computations on a block is much less than the time required to transfer the data between secondary storage and primary storage. Therefore, a good design strategy is to identify, where possible, logical records that are likely to be required for the same operations and to group them in blocks. For example, suppose that a firm stocks three kinds of wire, *A*, *B*, and *C*, and that they are usually delivered in the same shipment. If blocks contain three records each, and the *A*, *B*, and *C* records are contained in separate blocks, three input/output (I/O) operations are required to update their records. However, if they are blocked together, then only one I/O operation is required. Since disk access is often a bottleneck in database operations, careful assignment of records to blocks can significantly enhance response time.

FIGURE 11.4   Block Addressing

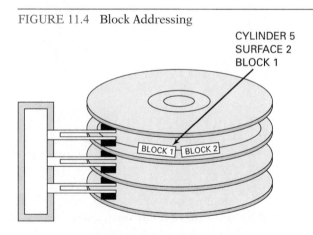

CYLINDER 5
SURFACE 2
BLOCK 1

BLOCK 1   BLOCK 2

☐ DISK PERFORMANCE FACTORS

In general, there are four factors that directly affect the speed with which data are transferred to and from disk storage: access motion time, head activation time, rotational delay, and data transfer rate.

Access Motion Time

access motion time The time required to position the read/write heads of the disk drive over the desired cylinder.

Access motion time *(A)*, sometimes termed "seek time," is the time required to move the read/write heads from their current position to a new cylinder address. Obviously, a move to an adjacent cylinder will not take the same amount of time as a move across the entire disk surface (innermost track to outermost track, or vice versa). As a compromise in calculations, the average access motion time is used—roughly the time required to move across one-half of the cylinders. The assumption is that the likelihood of access for every record is the same, giving a uniform probability distribution. The average for a uniform distribution is halfway between the extreme values. For access motion time, the extreme values would be these: stay positioned over the current cylinder and move from the innermost cylinder to the outermost (or vice versa). Given the uniform distribution assumption, the average will be the time to move across one-half of the cylinders. Twelve to twenty milliseconds are typical average access motion times, varying with the make and model of the disk drive.

Head Activation Time

head activation time The time required to activate a read/write head.

Head activation time is the time required to electronically activate the head that is over the surface where data transfer is to take place. Relative to other performance factors, this time is generally regarded as being negligible. Consequently, head activation time is seldom used in performance calculations.

Rotational Delay

rotational delay The time required for the disk to rotate the sought-for record under the read/write head.

Rotational delay, or "latency," is the third timing factor. It denotes the amount of time required for the desired block to rotate to the head, so that data transfer may commence. Rotational delay depends upon two factors: how fast the disk is rotating and the location of the block being sought in relationship to the read/write head at the time of its activation. Physically, this time could range from zero to the time required to complete one complete revolution of the disk *(R)*. As an analogy, suppose you wanted to ride on the purple horse on the merry-go-round (assuming there is just one such horse). If you bought a ticket and ran to get on the merry-go-round, the likelihood that the purple horse would be just where you stepped on would be the same as that of any of the other horses. If you were a fanatic and attempted this a large number of times, you might eventually step on at precisely the point where the purple horse was located. You might also find that on occasion you just missed it and had to wait for a complete revolution of the merry-go-round. Over time, you would find that you were waiting about one-half revolution on average to get the purple horse. The implication of this story is that performance computations usually assume an average rotational delay of $R/2$.

Data Transfer Rate

data transfer rate The rate at which data can be read from the disk to main memory, or equivalently, the rate at which data is written from main memory to disk.

Data transfer rate *(D)* refers to the amount of time required to transfer data from the disk to (or from) primary memory. It is a function of the rotational speed and the density of the recorded data. Data transfer rate is usually expressed in thousands of bytes per second.

Data Transfer Time

The expected time *(T)* to access a disk address and transfer a block of data is estimated as

$$T = A + R/2 + L/D$$

where A is the access motion time, R is the rotational delay, L is the length of the block in bytes, and D is the data transfer rate.

Example of a Randomly Accessed Record ☐ Suppose that claim records for an insurance company are stored three per block on disk (a blocking factor of 3), and that each claim record is 200 bytes long. The data transfer rate is 806,000 bytes per second. The average access motion time is 30 milliseconds. The disk unit rotates at a speed of 3600 revolutions per minute. Suppose that a policyholder calls to inquire about the status of a claim. What is the data transfer time for the requisite block of data? In order to answer this question, we assign appropriate values to the variables denoted above, as follows:

```
A = .030 seconds

Revolutions per second = 3600/60 = 60
R = 1/60 second = 0.0166 second
R/2 = 0.0166 × 1/2 (average wait is 1/2 revolution) = 0.0083

L/D = 600/806000 = 0.00074
```

Thus,

$$T = 0.030 + 0.0083 + 0.00074 = 0.03904 \text{ seconds}$$

Example of a Sequentially Accessed Record ☐ We now look at the problem of calculating average access time for a record on a sequentially accessed file. Suppose that instead of responding to a random access of a data block, as in the above example, we are now updating an insurance company's policyholder file with payments received at the beginning of the month. It makes sense that such files be organized sequentially by, say, policy number and that they are in sequential blocks by cylinder. That is, first, cylinder N is filled with sequential blocks, then cylinder $N + 1$, and so forth. In this way, we minimize head movement time. In particular, if the read/write heads are positioned at the starting cylinder, then all records on that cylinder may be transferred without further access motion time. Thus, in calculating the average access time for each record in a sequentially processed file, access motion time is of little consequence and can be ignored.

There will be an average of one-half rotational delay each time the read/write function switches from one track of the cylinder to another. This is necessary in order to locate the first record in sequence on the next track. Once the beginning record has been found, all remaining blocks from the track can be transmitted without further rotational delays. Thus, if the policyholder file occupies eight tracks on a given cylinder, the number of rotational delays will be 8. Suppose further that each track contains 1000 blocks. Then we have a total of 8000 blocks and, with a blocking factor of 3, 24,000 policy records. We assume as before that each record is 200 bytes long, so our blocks are 600 bytes long.

If we are processing the entire file sequentially, the average time to access a record can be computed as follows:

```
Total time to read all blocks =
0.0083(8) + 0.00074(8000) = 0.0664 + 5.92 = 5.9864

T = 5.9864/8000 = 0.0007483 seconds
```

T represents the average transfer time for a sequentially accessed record in the policyholder file.

DATA STORAGE FORMATS ON DISK

In this section, we examine the physical aspects of data management on disk media. We look at formats on tracks and in physical records and at input/output management.

Track Formats

Records can be stored on disk in either a **count-key format** or a **count-data format**, as shown in Figures 11.5 and 11.6. The fundamental difference is that the count-key format includes a key that is external to the data record itself. This key is used by the operating system to access a particular record. We use the term *record* here in the general sense of a **physical record**, which is another name for a block. Both the count-data and the count-key formats can be described by the definitions that follow.

Each track has an index point which is a special mark to identify the beginning of each track. Since the track is circular, it also identifies the end of the track.

The home address (HA) identifies the cylinder and the number of the read/write head that services the track, as well as the condition of the track (flag), whether it is operative or defective. If the track is defective, an alternative track to be used is indicated. A two-byte cyclic check is included as a means of error detection in input/output operations.

Gaps (G) separate the different areas on the track. The length of the gap may vary with the device, the location of the gap, and the length of the preceding area. The gap that follows the index point is different in length from the gap that follows the home address, and the length of the gap that follows a record depends on the length of that record. The reason for this is to provide adequate time for required equipment functions

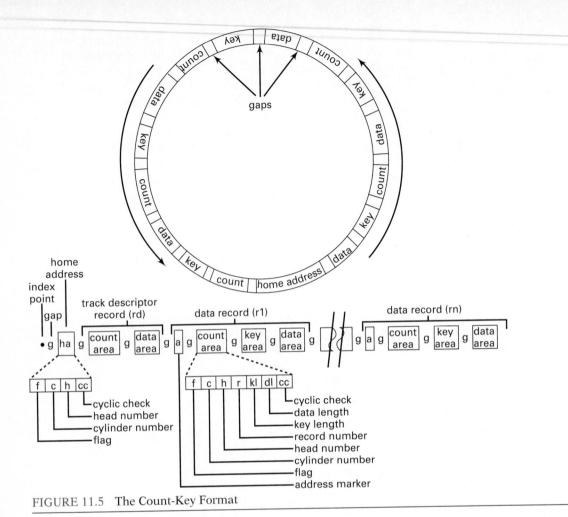

FIGURE 11.5   The Count-Key Format

FIGURE 11.6   The Count-Data Format

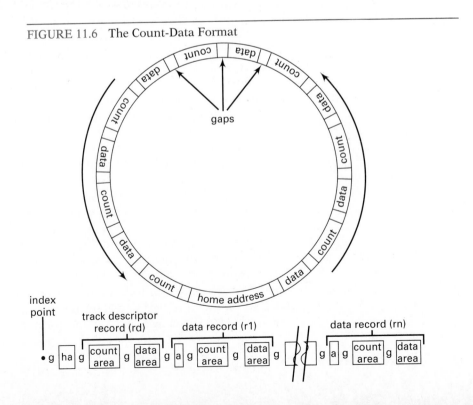

308

that are necessary as the gap rotates past the read/write head. These funcions may vary with the type of area that has just preceded the gap.

The address marker (A) is a two-byte segment supplied by the control unit (the hardware that controls the disk drive) as the record is written. It enables the control unit to locate the beginning of the record at a later time.

The count area is detailed in Figure 11.6. The flag field repeats the information about the track condition and adds information used by the control unit. The cylinder number, head number, and record number fields collectively provide a unique identification for the record. The key-length field is a one-byte field. It always contains a 0 for a record of the count-data format. The data-length field supplies two bytes, which specify the number of bytes in the data area of the record, excluding the cyclic check. The cyclic check provides two bytes for error detection.

Record Formats
Physical records, or blocks, can be stored on tracks in any of the four formats illustrated in Figure 11.7.

Fixed-length records. □ In this case, all records are of the same length. If the physical records are *unblocked*, there will be one logical record (for example, one payroll record) for each physical record (the data that is actually stored in the record area of the track). If the records are blocked, more than one logical record will comprise each physical record. For instance, if there are three payroll records comprising every physical record, we then have blocked records with a blocking factor of three. In this case, the Key Area is typically assigned the key of the *highest* record in the block. This facilitates locating records of interest. Suppose that we have two succeeding blocks containing records 10,12,14, and 15,19,24, respectively. If the operating system is seeking logical record 15, the key for the first block will read 14, so record 15 cannot be in that block. The key for the next

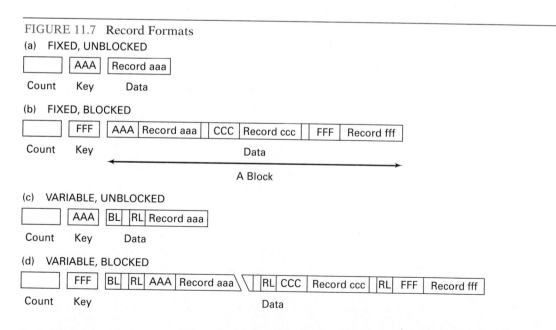

FIGURE 11.7   Record Formats

(a)   FIXED, UNBLOCKED

Count   Key   Data

(b)   FIXED, BLOCKED

Count   Key   Data

A Block

(c)   VARIABLE, UNBLOCKED

Count   Key   Data

(d)   VARIABLE, BLOCKED

Count   Key   Data

block will read 24. Since 24 is greater than 15, record 15 must be in that block. The entire block is then read into main memory where it is searched for record 15.

Variable-length records. ☐ The variable-length format, as the name implies, allows records to be of varying length. If database users need a logical customer record that stores data on outstanding invoices, this format would be appropriate, since the number of invoices will vary among customers. Because the record length is not uniform, a method of indicating where the record ends is required. This information is provided by the BL (block length) and RL (record length) areas. As with fixed-length formats, unblocked indicates that each block contains exactly one logical record. The blocked format allows several logical records to be stored in one block.

Input/Output Management   Based on the data formatting concepts of this section, we now briefly consider DBMS input/output operations. Suppose that an I/O instruction received from a user or application program is to be executed. The DBMS first checks to determine if the subschema associated with that I/O statement is defined in its data dictionary, as well as whether the user or program that is the source of that command is allowed to access that subschema. Assuming that all is well, the DBMS issues relevant I/O commands to the host operating system to access the specific physical records required. The operating system then searches the secondary storage devices and accesses the appropriate physical records. The operating system transfers those records to main memory where the DBMS extracts from the physical records those logical records requested and passes them to the user or application program for further disposition.

☐ FILE ORGANIZATION AND ADDRESSING METHODS

So far, you have learned something about the devices used to store data and the I/O operations used to transmit data to and from those devices. We now consider the methods of arranging data on those devices and addressing them in a way that facilitates storage and I/O operations.

There are three basic ways of physically organizing files on storage devices: sequential organization, indexed-sequential organization, and direct organization. This is not an entire set of all organization options available, but those that are omitted are modifications of these basic organizational types. Therefore, it is not necessary to be exhaustive in order to cover the essential concepts.

In discussing the topic at hand, the terms *organization* and *access* are often used loosely, if not interchangeably. The reason is that the way in which data are stored is closely intertwined with the method of access. We will attempt to clarify this in the discussion that follows.

Sequential File Organization

Sequential file organization means that records are stored adjacent to one another according to a key such as employee number, account number, and so forth. A conventional implementation arranges the records in ascending order of key values. This is an efficient method of organizing records when an application, such as a payroll program, will be updating a significant number of the stored records.

If a sequential file is maintained on magnetic tape, its records can only be accessed in a sequential manner. That is, if access to the tenth record in sequence is desired, generally the preceding nine records must be read. Direct access of a particular record is impossible. Consequently, magnetic tapes are not well suited for database operations and are usually relegated to producing log files and recording archival information.

Indexed-Sequential File Organization

When files are sequentially organized on a disk pack, however, direct access of records is possible. Indexed-sequential file organization provides facilities for accessing records both sequentially and directly. Records are stored in the usual physical sequence by primary key. In addition, an index of record locations is stored on the disk. This allows records to be accessed sequentially for applications requiring the updating of large numbers of records, as well as providing the ability to access records directly in response to user queries.

A simplified version of how indexed-sequential access operates is shown in Figure 11.8. The indexes and the records are both stored on disk.

FIGURE 11.8   Example of Indexed-Sequential Organization and Access

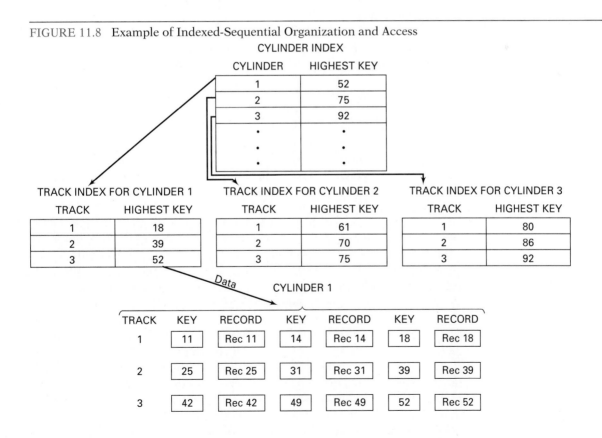

We have greatly limited the number of cylinders and tracks for purposes of our example. First notice that the records are organized sequentially on the three tracks shown for cylinder 1. Sequential processing is facilitated by simply beginning at the first record of the file, then proceeding through the file from first record to last. Direct access of records is also facilitated. Suppose that we wished to retrieve record 31. A search of the cylinder index reveals that record 31 is on cylinder 1. That is, the highest record key on cylinder 1 is 52, and since records are ordered sequentially by key, record 31 must be on cylinder 1. A search of the track index for cylinder 1 shows that record 31 is on track 2. Thus, the read/write heads are moved to cylinder 1, then the read/write head for track 2 is activated. Track 2 is then searched sequentially to locate record 31. While sequential searching has not been completely eliminated, its scope has been reduced sufficiently to justify the term *direct access*.

Our example uses unblocked records, but it can easily be extended to blocked records. Think of the data area as containing, say, three records and the key area as now denoting the highest record key in the block. The search procedure would proceed in similar fashion.

Direct File Organization

Thus far, we have discussed two forms of file organization: sequential and indexed sequential. We have concurrently outlined the two associated methods of file access: sequential access and direct access. Records in a simple sequential file organization can only be accessed sequentially. Records in an indexed-sequential file organization can be accessed directly, as well as sequentially. We now turn to a discussion of a third type of file organization called direct, or hashed. Only direct access methods are applicable to this type of file organization.

One disadvantage of index schemes is that an index must be accessed and read to locate records. The use of *hashing* is a method of record addressing that eliminates the need for maintaining and searching indexes. Elimination of the index avoids the need to make two trips to secondary storage to access a record: one to read the index, and one to access the file.

There are important applications whose predominant need is for direct access of records, whose services could be encumbered by the use of indexing methods. Examples include reservations systems for airlines, hotels, and car rentals, as well as electronic funds transfer.

The basic idea is that of trading the time and effort associated with storing, maintaining, and searching an index for the time required for the central-processing unit (CPU) to execute a hashing algorithm, which generates the record address. The hashing algorithm is a procedure for calculating a record address from some field in the record, usually the key. We turn to an example to help illustrate the method.

Suppose that 500 payroll records, each 100 bytes long, are to be stored on a magnetic disk having a 2000-byte per block capacity. Exactly 25 blocks would be required if the records were addressed in a way that assigned exactly one record to each possible location in each of the 25 blocks. Since no hashing algorithm devised to date can be guaranteed to accomplish this, additional storage space, say 20 percent, is usually added to reduce the number of instances when the algorithm calculates the same address for more than one record (a **collision**). The ratio of the space ac-

collision Occurs when the keys of two records hash to the same physical address.

tually required by the records in a file to the actual space allocated for the file is termed the **load factor.** In our example, the records require 25 blocks of storage space, but we are allocating $(25) \times (1.2) = 30$ blocks to reduce the number of collisions. The load factor is $(25/30 =)$ 83 percent.

Effective strategies for direct storage of records will result in low search times and few collisions. This can be best accomplished by selecting low load factors, using large blocking factors, and by using a hashing algorithm that distributes records uniformly over the storage area. The best method of accomplishing the latter objective is by the use of a division remainder method, which we will illustrate.

Since we have allocated 30 blocks for storing our file, a uniform distribution of records to blocks will mean that roughly four out of every five possible storage addresses will be assigned a record. Suppose the first record to be stored has a key (upon which the algorithm will operate) of 1562. We do the following (Figure 11.9):

1. Divide the key by the number of storage blocks allocated. The remainder gives the relative storage location.

```
Remainder of (1562/30) = 2
Relative storage block = 2
```

Keeping the remainder is in effect guaranteeing that an address is always computed that is in the range 0 to 29 inclusive.

2. Add the result of (1) to the beginning block address to obtain the address at which the record is to be stored.

Suppose that our series of 30 blocks begins at address 3048 and runs through address 3077. Then record 1562 will be located at block location $(2 + 3048 =)$ 3050. If there is to be just one record stored in each block,

---

FIGURE 11.9   Using a Common Hashing Algorithm to Determine a Record Storage Location

Step 1:   Divide key by allocated file size in blocks

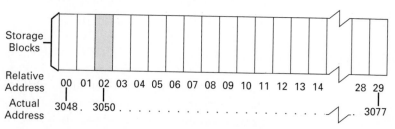

Step 2:   Add result of Step 1 to beginning address to obtain actual address of record with key value 1562

then no more records can be stored at address 3050. If several records are to be stored in each block, then records can continue to be stored at that address until the block is filled.

Let's assume that only one record is to be stored in each block, and that in the process of hashing, a second record is encountered that has key value 1592. It also computes to relative record address 2, and we have a collision. One method of dealing with collisions is to use the division hashing function with a refinement termed the *quadratic quotient method*. When no collisions occur, the resulting address is exactly the same as before, but if a collision does occur we now have a method of continuing on.

With the quadratic quotient method, when the key is divided by the table size, both the quotient, Q, and the remainder, R, are saved. Using Q and R, we can generate a sequence of relative record addresses by the formula

$$(R + Qi^2 + i) \text{ (modulo the number of blocks)}$$

where i runs through the integers beginning with 0 until no collision results.

Continuing with our example, for record 1562 we have,

$$(2 + 52 \times 0^2 + 0)_{\text{modulo 30}} = 2$$

as before. (Modulo 30 means divide by 30 and keep the remainder.) But the new record 1592 yields

$$(2 + 53 \times 0^2 + 0)_{\text{modulo 30}} = 2$$

Record 1562 is already at that relative address, so we iterate using the next value for i until we find an unoccupied address. For this example, we next compute

$$(2 + 53 \times 1^2 + 1)_{\text{modulo 30}} = 26$$

and we have an unoccupied address where this record can be stored.

When record 1592 must be found, the algorithm is computed in the usual way, first yielding a location where record 1562 is located. Since this is not the record being sought, the algorithm will be repeated until the desired record is found.

Another method of dealing with collisions is to simply store a pointer at the location computed by the algorithm. This pointer would indicate the address where the next record is located whose key also hashed to this location. If there are several such records, a pointer would be maintained at each storage location. In this way, there is a chain of pointers that can be followed until the desired record is found.

IMPLEMENTING LOGICAL RELATIONSHIPS

Next we outline the fundamentals of physical data structures, which are the underlying "molecular structures" that enable the "universe" of the database system to perform its functions. These physical data structures can be characterized in two ways: first by the way in which one database record is linked to another, and second by the way in which these linkages are used to support database operations.

Linked Lists

pointer A physical address that identifies where a record can be found on disk.

A fundamental concept in linking one physical database record with another is the use of *pointers*. A **pointer** is a field associated with one data record that is used to find a related data record. What does this mean?

Suppose that the Zeus Corporation stores personnel information in the form of the logical records shown in Figure 11.10. One field of interest is SKILL. Suppose that a new position opens for an engineer. It may be desirable to retrieve for evaluation all the records of personnel who are engineers. Notice that for each of the personnel records, the SKILL POINTER data item contains the address of the next record that contains the same value for SKILL as does the current record. A **head list,** maintained separately on the disk, points to the first record in the database that contains the value "engineer" in the Skill field. In our example, this would be Smith's record. This record points to Black, which in turn points to Steel. Such **chains** of pointers provide a means of linking records containing common values for attributes of interest. A list of records linked by such pointer chains is called a **linked list.** In our example, it facilitates rapid retrieval of the set of records for engineers. Linked lists require some type of direct access file organization in order to perform their function.

head list A list of pointers, each of which points to the first record in a file.

chain A collection of pointers that link a set of physical records—also called a linked list.

linked list A set of physical records that are linked by pointers that are maintained in the records themselves.

We could have accomplished the same goal if the personnel records were physically arranged on the disk so that all the engineers were in se-

---

FIGURE 11.10   Sample Data from the Zeus Corporation EMPLOYEE File, in Sequence by Employee ID

HEAD LIST

Accountant = 1	Seattle = 1
Draftsman = 2	Los Angeles = 2
Engineer = 3	Portland = 6

RECORD NUMBER	EMPLOYEE ID	NAME	LOCATION	SKILL	SKILL POINTER	LOCATION POINTER
1	0123	James	Seattle	Accountant	4	3
2	0211	Poirot	Los Angeles	Draftsman	6	4
3	0223	Smith	Seattle	Engineer	5	7
4	0245	Cubic	Los Angeles	Accountant	7	5
5	0301	Black	Los Angeles	Engineer	9	0
6	0401	Iwerks	Portland	Draftsman	10	8
7	0601	Ivans	Seattle	Accountant	8	9
8	0711	Nell	Portland	Accountant	0	10
9	0908	Steel	Seattle	Engineer	0	0
10	1067	Schwartz	Portland	Draftsman	0	0

quence beginning with the first record. There would be no need for pointers to retrieve all the records for engineers. The first record would be retrieved, then the second, and so on until the first record was encountered having another skill. So far, so good. If at a later time, however, there were a need to retrieve all the employees assigned to the Seattle office, this scheme would no longer work. We would have to have a copy of the file maintained elsewhere on disk that was physically ordered by location. This is obviously a storage inefficiency, and we have only considered one alternative query. Imagine the difficulty of anticipating all the query needs in advance and creating physical files to service each one.

What we have here is a conflict between physical ordering of records and logical ordering as required by the user. The use of pointers resolves this dilemma by allowing any finite number of logical lists to be represented, without requiring a reorganization of the physical sequence of the file.

In the example of Figure 11.10, note that the value contained in the Skill Pointer field for Steel's record is "0." This is our notation to indicate a null pointer, or the end of the list. It communicates to the operating system that there are no more records in the linked list for engineers. Alternatively, the last record in a linked list may contain a pointer to the first record in the list, thus completing a **ring structure.** Ring structures can be useful for network DBMS systems where entry can occur at locations other than at the top of the linked list.

ring structure A linked list whose last record contains a pointer to the first record in the list.

Inverted Lists

While linked lists are a useful way of implementing logical relationships among records, they do have limitations. If the list is extremely long, traversing the chain of records can be time consuming. List maintenance can be cumbersome, particularly if there are frequent additions or deletions. Long lists are also subject to becoming disconnected due to operating system malfunction.

inverted list A directory wherein each entry contains pointers to all physical records containing a specified value.

An alternative method of accessing records according to logical order is through the use of **inverted lists.** An inverted list is a separate file, or index, that generally contains just two data items: a value of interest, such as "engineer," and all the addresses where records are located having that value. Figure 11.11 shows two inverted lists for the data of Fig-

SKILL	ADDRESSES			
Accountant	1	4	7	8
Draftsman	2	6	10	
Engineer	3	5	9	

(a) Inverted List of Skills

LOCATION	ADDRESSES			
Los Angeles	2	4	5	
Portland	6	8	10	
Seattle	1	3	7	9

(b) Inverted List of Locations

FIGURE 11.11   Examples of Inverted Lists

ure 11.10. The use of the inverted list would eliminate the need for SKILL POINTER and LOCATION POINTER fields in the records themselves. In practice, both the inverted list and the file it references are maintained on direct access files.

Again, the linked list requires that pointers be stored with the data records, whereas the inverted list eliminates that need by storing the pointers separate from the data. Both methods are supported by most DBMS products.

Balanced-Tree Index (B$^+$-Tree)

A refinement of the inverted-list strategy is the B$^+$-tree. B$^+$-trees were developed in an effort to provide an efficient method for maintaining a hierarchy of indexes. The B$^+$-tree provides multilevel indexing that is efficient for both sequential and direct processing of data records. A B$^+$-tree consists of a hierarchy of index records together with a file of data records. The index records contain keys and pointers that are used to locate the data records. A typical index record (IR) in the B$^+$-tree is shown in Figure 11.12. In this example, we have 3 pointers and 2 keys. In general, we may have n pointers and n-1 keys, n being determined by the designer.

In order to describe the B$^+$-tree, we need to define certain terms. A **rooted tree** is a hierarchy of IRs that has a single IR at the highest level. This IR is termed the *root*. An IR is a **leaf** if it is at the lowest level in the rooted tree. The pointers in all nonleaf IRs point to other IRs. The pointers in leaf IRs, however, point to the data records. A B$^+$-tree is balanced in the sense that all the leaf IRs are the same distance from the root IR. Distance is measured by the number of IRs that must be examined to reach a leaf IR. The sequence of IRs to be examined is called a **path.** This concept of balance guarantees access to all database records with the same degree of efficiency. In the discussion that follows, we will further establish the conventions for the B$^+$-tree and clarify their use with some examples.

Formally, a B$^+$-tree is a rooted tree satisfying the following requirements:

FIGURE 11.12 B$^+$-Tree Index Record (IR) ($n = 3$)

Keys

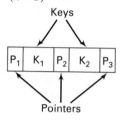

Pointers

rooted tree A hierarchy of index records that has a single index record at the highest level; that record is called the root.

leaf In a tree, any segment type that has no child segment types.

path A set of pointers leading from one index record to another.

1. All paths from the root IR to a leaf IR are of the same length.
2. Each IR that is not a root or a leaf contains at least $[n/2]$ and at most n pointers to lower-level IRs. ([./.] denotes the arithmetic operation of rounding up to the next integer value. Thus, if n is 3, then $[n/2]$ is 2. If n is 4, then $[n/2]$ is 2.)
3. A leaf IR contains at least $[(n-1)/2]$ and at most n-1 pointers to records in the data file.
4. The keys in an IR are ordered $K_1 < K_2 \ldots < K_{n-1}$.
5. All keys in the subtree to which P_1 points are strictly less than K_1.
6. For $2 \le i \le n - 1$, all the keys in the subtree to which P_i points have values greater than or equal to K_{i-1} and less than K_i.
7. All the keys in the subtree to which P_n points are greater than or equal to K_{n-1}. Therefore, for $i > 1$, K_{i-1} will always be the *lowest* key in the subtree pointed to by P_i.

Let's clarify these conventions by working through an example. Figure 11.13 shows an example of a B⁺-tree for $n = 3$ that indexes records having the following keys:

1, 3, 5, 18, 29, 31, 35

The dashed lines in some positions indicate that no key is present. We'll assume that the records were added in the order given. We will now show how this tree was built by adding records to an empty tree. Refer to Figure 11.14. The first record to be added has the key "1." It is simply inserted into an IR as shown in Figure 11.14(a). Since our tree has only one IR, it is both a leaf and the root IR. In Figure 11.14(b), we find that there is space for indexing record 3 with no additional IRs being required. To keep matters simple, we have illustrated the data file only in Figure 11.14(a).

Things change when we index record 5. Recall that a leaf IR can have at most n-1 pointers to records in the data file; in this case, only two are allowed. Consequently, we must add a new leaf IR as shown in Figure 11.14(c). Here we have added key "5" to the new IR. Since we have more than one leaf node now, we need to add a higher-level IR in the tree to index the leaf nodes, as shown. This higher-level IR is now the root IR.

Note that there are $n = 3$ pointers in each IR. In each leaf IR, the leftmost pointer (P_1) points to the storage location where the complete record is stored for key K_1. P_2 performs the same function for K_2. P_3, however, points to the next leaf node in sequence, so that the file can be processed sequentially when needed.

Note also that in the newly created nonleaf node shown in Figure 11.14(c) P_1 and P_2 are the only pointers necessary and they satisfy the necessary conventions described above. The pointer to the left of key value 5 points to a subtree whose key values are all less than 5. The pointer to the right of key value 5 points to a subtree whose smallest value is 5.

Figure 11.14(d) through Figure 11.14(f) show the result of adding records 18 through 31. Proceeding from Figure 11.14(f) to Figure 11.14(g) is a bit more complex, requiring the following steps:

1. A leaf IR must be added for record 35. This would force the top-level IR to add a fourth pointer, which is not allowed.

FIGURE 11.13   Example B⁺ -Tree with n = 3

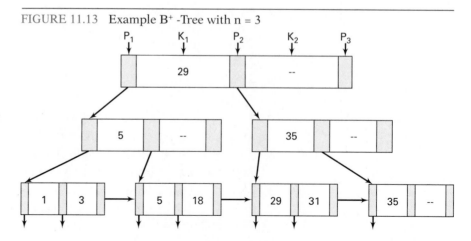

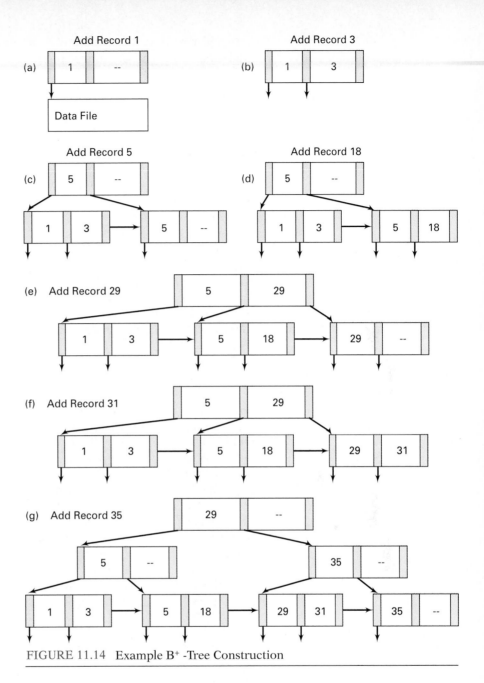

FIGURE 11.14   Example B⁺-Tree Construction

2. The solution is to split the top-level IR, which requires that we add a higher-level IR as the new root. (Recall that there is always only one IR at the root level.) Since the current top-level IR contains the key values "5" and "29," a natural way of splitting that IR is to use the larger of those values as the basis for the split. That is, we enter the value "29" in the new root IR, with two subtrees (the split) being created, one that contains values less than "29," and the other that contains values greater than or equal to 29.

3. Adjustments are then made to the contents of the subtree IRs to reflect the appropriate key values, as shown in Figure 11.14(g). Note

that every key value has a pointer to its right. The key value is always the *smallest* value in the subtree pointed to by that pointer. The leftmost pointer in an IR points to a subtree whose key values are all less than that of the key value to the right of the pointer.

We have now produced the B+-tree of Figure 11.13.

Let's now see how a query is processed using our B+-tree. Suppose we wish to access record 31. The root node is examined first. Since 31 is greater than 29, the middle pointer is followed to the IR at the next-lowest level where 35 is the first index key. Since 31 is less than 35, the left pointer is followed to the leaf IR at the third level. At this level, the second key is 31 so we can follow the pointer to the left of this key to the storage location of the record being sought.

Insertion and deletion can be more complex than a simple record access since it is sometimes necessary to split an IR that would become too large as the result of an insertion, as shown in our discussion of Figure 11.14(g), or to combine IRs if an IR would become too small as the result of a deletion.

In the simplest case, an insertion or a deletion will not require splitting or combining IRs. Refer to the B+-tree of Figure 11.14(g). Suppose record 37 is to be inserted. Using the same procedure as if we were to access record 37, we locate the leaf IR where "37" should appear. We then insert the key value "37," with a pointer to the record storage location. The result is shown in Figure 11.15.

Suppose that we later wish to delete record 37. We would simply access the leaf IR containing key "37," follow its pointer to the record location, then delete both the record and its IR value.

We have now seen two examples of insertions, one requiring a change in the index structure (Figure 11.14(g)), and one requiring no change in the index structure (Figure 11.15). Deleting the latter required no change in the index structure, either. We next supply an example of a deletion that does require modification of the index structure.

Refer to Figure 11.14(g). Suppose that we wish to delete record 35 from this tree. When 35 is deleted, its leaf node contains nothing, and so it is now deleted as well. The IR above it, containing the key value "35," would then have just one pointer, which is below the minimum required.

FIGURE 11.15   Result of Inserting Record 37

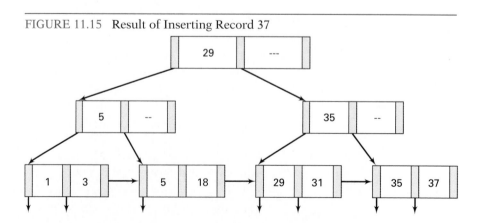

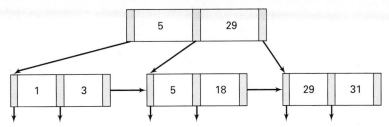

FIGURE 11.16   B+-Tree Resulting from Deletion of Record 35 from
Figure 11.14(g)

Thus, we "coalesce" the IRs at the middle level, so that our tree now looks like Figure 11.16. Note that this is identical to Figure 11.14(f).

The B+-tree is the most widely used strategy for maintaining efficiency in the face of insertions and deletions. Similar concepts exist for an indexing method called a "B-tree" (without the "+"). A B-tree only allows a key to occur once in the tree, thus reducing space requirements, but complicating IR maintenance. Consequently, it has not realized the usage level of the B+-tree.

☐ MAPPING LOGICAL DATA STRUCTURES TO PHYSICAL DATA STRUCTURES

We now look at the application of these ideas to database systems. In this section, we examine some of the physical aspects of implementing the data structures needed for relational, network, and hierarchical databases.

Mapping Relational Databases

Some database systems store each relation as a file, with one record for each tuple (row). For small databases, this is often suitable, but as the database grows in size, it may be more efficient to store several relations in one file.

Consider the relations shown in Figure 11.17 and a query requiring for each sale the customer name, the salesperson, the amount of the sale, and the product number. For every tuple of the SALES relation, tuples must be found in the CUSTOMER relation that match on the value of customer number. If CUSTOMER and SALES are stored in different files, then one file read operation must be completed for each record required by the query. A more efficient method is suggested by Figure 11.18. This file structure mixes tuples of the two relations together in order to facilitate a joining of the two relations. SALES tuples for each customer number are stored near CUSTOMER tuples having the same customer number value. When a tuple of the CUSTOMER relation is read, the entire block containing that tuple is copied to primary memory. Since the related SALES tuples are stored nearby, the block containing the SALES tuples necessary to complete the query may be in the same block—which is now in primary memory. Even if other tuples are necessary, they will be stored in blocks that are nearby on the disk.

CUSTOMER #	NAME	CREDIT LIMIT	BALANCE OWED
251	H. Barlow	$ 5,000	$1,250
095	J. Krupke	$10,000	$5,000
312	O. Reed	$ 5,000	$ 800
419	M. Little	$15,000	$7,500

SALES

INV. #	CUSTOMER #	AMT.	SALESPERSON	PROD. #
12	095	120	V. Blab	W851
13	312	592	J. Wells	O912
15	312	750	V. Blab	W851
18	261	157	J. Wells	R950

FIGURE 11.17   Sample CUSTOMER and SALES Relations

CUSTOMER

251	H. Barlow	5000	1250	
12	095	120	V. Blab	W851
13	312	592	J. Wells	0912
095	J. Krupke	10000	5000	
312	O. Reed	5000	800	
15	312	750	V. Blab	W851
18	251	157	J. Wells	R950

FIGURE 11.18   Clustering of CUSTOMER and SALES Relations

clustering Placing in the same block the records of relations that are likely to be joined frequently.

This **clustering** strategy can speed up the joining of the CUSTOMER and SALES relations, but it may slow down processing involving other relations. Determining when clustering is in order is dependent upon the frequency with which a query occurs.

Another factor also becomes important in mapping relations to physical storage. Refer to Figure 11.19. Here, the relation CUSTOMER is related to the relation CASH-RECEIPTS with a one–many cardinality. The primary key for CUSTOMER is CUST-ID, and there may be additional arbitrary attributes. CUST-ID must then appear as a foreign key in the CASH-RECEIPTS relation, as shown. If CUST-ID is used as the actual key for physical implementation, difficulties could arise if, for example, the CUST-ID is in error or later gets changed. In that case, every physical location where a CUST-ID appears would have to be changed. This not only involves time and effort, but it is an opportunity for errors to occur. To avoid this, DBMSs will often create a surrogate key, which is known only to the DBMS. In this way, if the actual primary key, CUST-ID, must be changed, the surrogate key is unaffected and there is no possibility of the physical representations being disturbed thereby.

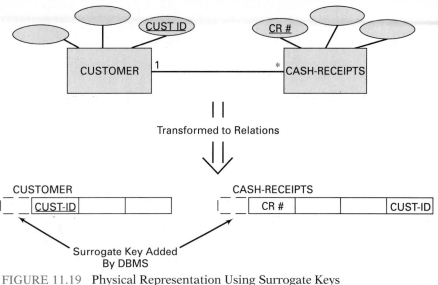

FIGURE 11.19   Physical Representation Using Surrogate Keys

Any complex network (many–many) relationship can be reformulated as a simple network by introducing intersection records. Thus, our discussion of mapping need only focus on the simple network. Consider the example shown in Figure 11.20. This is a simple network since the relationships are one–many between owner and member record types. The invoice record type is a member of two sets: CUST-INV and SALESP-INV. That is, each INVOICE record has a CUSTOMER owner record and a SALESPERSON owner record.

This simple network can be represented by linked lists by creating pointers for each set. One group of pointers is necessary to connect CUSTOMER records to their INVOICE records, and another group of pointers is needed to connect SALESPERSON records to their INVOICE records. An instance of the logical relationship is shown in Figure 11.21. As a physical implementation method, however, this is awkward because the number of pointers required is variable: If there are three invoice records owned by a customer, three pointers are required; if there are five invoice records owned by a customer, then five pointers are required. As

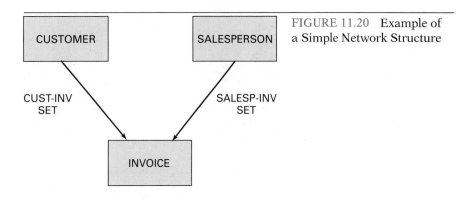

FIGURE 11.20   Example of a Simple Network Structure

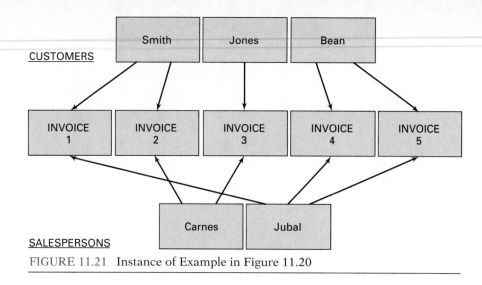

CUSTOMERS

SALESPERSONS

FIGURE 11.21   Instance of Example in Figure 11.20

a practical matter, maintaining a variable number of pointer fields in an owner record is difficult. However, the linked list provides a way of avoiding that difficulty.

The way in which this is done is illustrated in Figure 11.22. Each customer record contains a pointer to the record number of the first invoice it owns. That invoice record will contain a record number pointer to the next invoice owned by the same customer. This process continues until the last invoice for a customer is linked. For example, Customer Smith's record points to Invoice #1 (record number 6), which points to

FIGURE 11.22   Simple Network Mapped to Linked List

	RELATIVE RECORD NUMBER	DATA RECORD	CUSTOMER INVOICE POINTER	SALESPERSON INVOICE POINTER
CUSTOMER RECORDS	1	Smith	6	
	2	Jones	8	
	3	Bean	9	
SALESPERSON RECORDS	4	Carnes		7
	5	Jubal		6
INVOICE RECORDS	6	Inv #1	7	9
	7	Inv #2	0	8
	8	Inv #3	0	0
	9	Inv #4	10	10
	10	Inv #5	0	0

RELATIVE ADDRESS	DATA RECORD	CUSTOMER INVOICE POINTER	SALESPERSON INVOICE POINTER
1	Smith	6	
2	Jones	8	
3	Bean	9	
4	Carnes		7
5	Jubal		6
6	Inv #1	7	9
7	Inv #2	1	8
8	Inv #3	2	4
9	Inv #4	10	10
10	Inv #5	3	5

CUSTOMER RECORDS: rows 1–3
SALESPERSON RECORDS: rows 4–5
INVOICE RECORDS: rows 6–10

FIGURE 11.23   Simple Network Mapped to Ring Structure

Invoice #2 (record number 7), which is the last of Smith's invoices. The end of the list of invoices is indicated by a record number of 0 in the pointer field.

A more practical method of implementation is shown in Figure 11.23. Comparing Figure 11.23 to Figure 11.22, you can see that the only change is that the last record in each list contains a pointer back to the owner record. This *ring structure* facilitates the execution of the FIND OWNER, FIND FIRST, and FIND NEXT queries of common network data manipulation languages. Following the ring of pointers facilitates locating the desired record. (Network data manipulation languages were discussed in Chapter 9.)

Mapping Hierarchical Databases

As with network data structures, multiple pointers in parent records may be used to represent the relationships of a hierarchy or tree, as suggested in Figure 11.24. While the method of multiple pointers within a record provides connections between parent and child records, it is not often

FIGURE 11.24   Example of Hierarchical Relationships

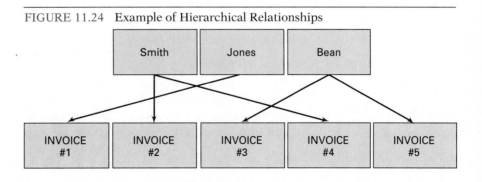

RELATIVE ADDRESS	PARENT RECORD	CHILD POINTER	TWIN POINTER
1	Smith	5	2
2	Jones	4	3
3	Bean	6	0
4	Inv #1	0	0
5	Inv #2	0	7
6	Inv #3	0	8
7	Inv #4	0	0
8	Inv #5	0	0

0 = End of Invoice List

FIGURE 11.25   Hierarchy Mapped to Linked List

FIGURE 11.26   Hierarchy Mapped to Inverted List

CUSTOMER RECORD ID	INVOICE RECORD POINTER
Smith	5
Smith	7
Jones	4
Bean	6
Bean	8

used because of the variable number of pointers that may be necessary in each parent record. Variable-length records are particularly cumbersome when additions and deletions must be made.

The use of what can be termed child-and-twin pointers reduces the complexity of maintaining multiple pointers and the restriction of child-to-parent mapping. Examine Figure 11.25. Here you see that the first pointer of each record contains the address of one child record, and the second pointer indicates the location of a twin record. In this fashion, each record contains exactly two pointer fields, which is much easier to maintain. As with any linked list, the pointers may be removed from the record itself and placed in an inverted list directory. For our example, this is shown in Figure 11.26.

□ SECONDARY-KEY ACCESS

primary key A data item value that uniquely identifies a record.

secondary key A data item value that identifies a set of records.

To this point, we have been using the word *key* rather freely to mean a data item whose value uniquely identifies a record. Technically, this definition defines a **primary key.** There are also **secondary keys** that can be unique but are not required to be. A secondary key is one that identifies a *set* of records having the same value for the secondary key. Secondary keys play an important role in supporting the information requirements of DBMS users.

We illustrate the fundamental concepts by way of an example. The Cosmos Credit Union has several types of users of its database system. The tellers need to access customer account records in order to answer customer questions and to update records as transactions take place. Some customers may have only checking accounts. Others may have, in addition, savings accounts, credit-card accounts, or long-term loans.

The teller can probably get by using a primary key such as customer identification number to access all needed records. A loan officer, however, may at times need to retrieve those records having a certain credit-card account limit (say $2000), or those loans outstanding that have balances of over $50,000. A branch manager of the credit union may be interested in knowing the total loans outstanding of a particular type: auto, home improvement, personal, and so forth. These needs can all be serviced through use of secondary-key access methods.

Secondary-key access is accomplished by establishing indexes that traverse desired paths through the physical data records. Consider the following query:

Identify names of customers having 48-month loans.

Using Figure 11.27 as a sample instance, we show how this information would be provided through the use of linked lists. The primary key is CUSTOMERNAME, and the secondary key is LOAN-PERIOD. There are three financing periods for loans: 24 months, 36 months, and 48 months. Thus, the secondary key allows the retrieval of sets of records associated with each of the three financing periods. Three pointers are thus required to identify the beginning record in each set (the head list). These pointers are stored separately from the data records themselves.

To compute the answer to the query, the list of head pointers is accessed, and the address 1 is found for the head of the list of records having financing period values of 48. The record located at address 1 contains a pointer to the next record having that value, and so on until the complete set is found.

The discerning reader will have noticed that secondary-key access was used earlier in the chapter when we introduced the idea of linked lists. You will recall that in that case we were retrieving records on the secondary keys SKILL and LOCATION.

Linked lists of secondary keys are particularly useful when physical files are very large. If in an extended version of the file used in Figure 11.27 we had 50,000 records of which only 100 had loan periods of 48

FIGURE 11.27   Use of Embedded Pointers on Secondary Key

HEAD LIST
24 = 3
36 = 2
48 = 1

RELATIVE ADDRESS	CUSTOMER NAME	LOAN-TYPE	LOAN-PERIOD	LOAN-PERIOD POINTER
1	Nixon	Auto	48	6
2	Patton	Auto	36	4
3	Fortius	Boat	24	0
4	Wood	Auto	36	5
5	Cayman	Home	36	7
6	Vance	Auto	48	8
7	Costas	Home	36	0
8	Ubu	Auto	48	0

LOAN-PERIOD

24	3			
36	2	4	5	7
48	1	6	8	

FIGURE 11.28   Use of
Inverted List on Secondary
Key

months, the use of the secondary key LOAN-PERIOD saves having to search the entire file of 50,000, a factor of (50,000/100 =) 500.

As you may have surmised, whenever we can represent lists with pointers embedded in the records, we also have the alternative of removing the pointers and maintaining them in an inverted list. Figure 11.28 shows the inverted list for the example of Figure 11.27.

□ QUERY OPTIMIZATION

Query optimization is an important consideration in a database system since the difference in execution time between a good strategy and a poor strategy may be substantial. With the network and hierarchical data structures, optimization is left to the application programmer since the data manipulation commands are embedded in a host programming language and are at the level of individual record manipulation. Relational queries, however, can be completely expressed in the relational query language, which can manipulate entire sets of records at a time. It is therefore possible and desirable to optimize queries automatically.

Our purpose in this section is to acquaint the reader with the fundamental ideas of query optimization without exploring all the details of what is a large field of study. We focus on the general question of how to efficiently compute an answer to a query in relational algebra. We will focus on the following three operators:

Select
Project
Join

And we will use the following sample database:

```
EMPLOYEE(EMP-NAME, STREET, EMP-CITY)
ASSIGNMENT(PROJ-NAME, EMP-NAME, SKILL, HOURS)
PROJECT(PROJ-NAME, BUDGET, PROJ-CITY)
```

Combining Selection and
Join Operations

Consider the following query:

Find the budgets and names of all projects that have employees living in Pasadena.

One way this query might be written and interpreted is as follows:

```
A := Join(EMPLOYEE, ASSIGNMENT, PROJECT)
B := Select(A: EMP-CITY = "Pasadena")
C := B[PROJ-NAME, BUDGET]
```

Since the Join operates on the three relations in their entirety, all tuples in all three relations must be examined. Thus, if there are n tuples in EMPLOYEE, m tuples in ASSIGNMENT, and k tuples in PROJECT, then $n \times m \times k$ inspections must be made. Contrast this with the strategy shown below.

```
A:= Select(EMPLOYEE: City = "Pasadena")
B:= Join(A,ASSIGNMENT,PROJECT)
C:= B[PROJ-NAME,BUDGET]
```

Suppose that there are t employees who live in Pasadena ($t \leq n$). Then there are $t \times m \times k$ inspections that must be made, where

$$(t \times m \times k) \leq (n \times m \times k)$$

If t is significantly smaller than n, this latter strategy will require considerably fewer inspections. Consequently, efficient execution suggests that selections be performed as early as possible.

Combining Projection, Selection, and Join Operations

In the example above, even the second query formulation carried unnecessary information with its operations. The desired relation requires only the values for two attributes: **PROJ-NAME** and **BUDGET**. All that is really needed, then, are the attributes necessary for the desired result and the attributes needed for the join. Appropriate use of the projection operator makes the query even more efficient, as follows:

```
A:= Select(EMPLOYEE: EMPCITY = 'Pasadena') [EMPNAME]
B:= ASSIGNMENT[PROJ-NAME, EMPNAME]
C:= PROJECT[PROJ-NAME, BUDGET]
D:= Join(A,B,C) [PROJ-NAME,BUDGET]
```

In each step of this solution, we have projected out all unnecessary attributes, leaving only those required for the solution. The guideline, then, is to perform selections and projections as early as possible. Joins, being very time consuming, should be performed as late as possible.

■ SUMMARY

In this chapter, basic concepts of file organization and access—which can be of value to both users and systems designers—were introduced. Both groups should be conversant with the terminology and basic concepts of physical file organization and access in order to communicate better with technical personnel, to ask relevant questions of vendors, to be aware of alternatives, and to otherwise be able to contribute to the effective implementation of database systems.

We first discussed the physical storage media that support database system operations. We examined the way in which data is stored on disk and outlined the process of accessing data on disk. We further showed how access times are computed.

We outlined three basic methods of physical file organization: sequential, indexed-sequential, and direct. Sequential organization is efficient when applications involve only the processing of significant numbers of records each time the file is accessed. Indexed-sequential organization is effective when there are significant applications that require sequential processing and there are significant applications that require direct processing. Direct organization is necessary when most critical applications require direct access to records.

We also surveyed fundamental physical data structures that enable logical data relationships to be implemented. The most basic tool is the pointer. The pointer is a data item that contains a physical address of a stored record. Pointers may be embedded in the records themselves, thus chaining together a list of related records. Alternatively, an index of values, along with pointers to records containing those values, can be maintained separate from the records themselves. This is called an inverted list. An indexing scheme that maintains its efficiency irrespective of the number of insertions and deletions is called the B^+-tree. We presented the concepts of the B^+-tree and showed how one would be constructed and used.

An outline was given of the methods by which logical data models are mapped to physical representations. In this way, we completed the journey from conceptual model to logical implementation model to physical implementation.

We then showed how pointers can be used in concert with secondary keys to facilitate retrieval of data.

Finally, we briefly discussed the topic of query optimization. While good relational DBMSs provide the necessary optimization, knowledge of the motivation and methods can provide insight to users of database systems.

■ REVIEW QUESTIONS

1. Define each of the following terms in your own words:

   a. strategy selector
   b. file manager
   c. main memory
   d. cylinder
   e. count-data format
   f. physical record
   g. data transfer rate
   h. count-key format
   i. collision
   j. head list
   k. chain
   l. inverted list
   m. rooted tree
   n. leaf
   o. rotational delay
   p. disk drive
   q. clustering
   r. primary key

2. Why is the allocation of records to blocks a factor in database system performance?

3. Compare sequential, indexed-sequential, and direct file organization.

4. What are the desired features of a good hashing algorithm?

5. What is the purpose of the gap in a record format?

6. Distinguish between the count-data format and the count-key data format.

7. What is latency?

8. Describe the principal operations involved in input/output management.

9. What efficiency is accomplished by using pointers?

10. Distinguish between a simple linked list and a ring.

11. What is a null pointer, and what does it signify?

12. What does the term B⁺-tree stand for? What is the purpose of a B⁺-tree?

13. Distinguish between a primary key and a secondary key.

■ EXERCISES AND PROBLEMS

1. Match each term with its definition

__Buffer manager   a. A data item containing a physical address

__Data dictionary   b. The time required to position the read/write heads over a given cylinder

__ring structure   c. The time required to activate the read/write heads

__Access motion time   d. Defines the structure of user data and how it is to be used

__Head activation time   e. a linked list whose last record contains a pointer to the first record on the list

__load factor   f. Software that controls the movement of data between main memory and disk storage

__Pointer   g. A sequence of pointers connecting index records

__Linked list   h. Physical records that are linked by embedded pointers

__Path   i. A data item value that identifies a set of records

__Secondary key   j. The ratio of the number of records to be stored to the number of storage locations

2. Suppose that we store records on a disk device having the following characteristics:

> average access motion time: 0.02 seconds
> disk rotation speed: 3600 revolutions per minute
> data transfer rate: 312,000 bytes per second

What is the expected data transfer time for a randomly accessed physical record that is 500 bytes in length?

3. How would your answer to (2) be changed if you were using a disk device with fixed read/write heads—that is, each track in each cylinder has its own read/write head?

4. Using the same parameters as given in (2), suppose that ten physical records are stored on a track. What would be the comparative data transfer times for (a) 30 records stored sequentially on the same cylinder, and (b) 30 records stored on three tracks not in the same cylinder?

5. If blocking facilitates efficient storage and retrieval of records, why not store entire files in one very large block?

6. Suppose that logical records are stored in blocks of four, and that two succeeding blocks contain logical records 11, 13, 14, 19, and 21, 23, 24, 26. Describe how the operating system will locate record 23.

7. Why would sequential file organization be efficient for processing the weekly payroll? Why would it not be efficient for responding to user queries?

8. Since indexed-sequential file organization provides for both sequential and direct access of records, why do we need any other methods of file organization?

9. Use the quadratic quotient hashing algorithm to compute the relative addresses at which the following records are to be stored. Assume a loading factor of 80 percent. How many blocks are needed if this is the entire file? (Assume one record per block.)

Key	Name
14	Smith
24	Bean
28	Harris
23	Scott

10. Which do you think would be easier to maintain: an inverted list or a simple linked list? If your answer is that "it depends," give an example illustrating your point.

11. Create a B⁺-tree for the following records: 20, 63, 34, 56, 43, 89, 45, 68, 52, 54, 14, 19, 7, 70, and 82. Let $n = 3$.

12. Show how the network of Figure 11.1E could be physically represented by
    a. Using child-and-twin pointers
    b. Using address pointers maintained in an index
    c. A ring structure.

13. Construct a diagram of a hierarchical data model, and show how it could be mapped to a physical representation.

FIGURE 11.1E   Network for Problem 12

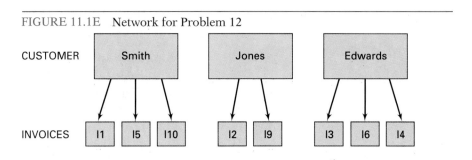

14. Construct a diagram of a simple network, and show how it could be mapped to a physical representation.

15. Construct a diagram of a complex network, and show how it could be mapped to a physical representation.

16. Construct two relations which may need to be joined to satisfy a user query. Show how clustering might be used to make that query formulation more efficient.

17. Give an example of a personnel file that is physically ordered by Employee Number and includes linked lists to provide secondary keys on Insurance Plan (there are three types: A, B, and C), Employee Type (Hourly or Salaried), and Retirement Plan (X or Y).

18. Repeat problem 17 using an inverted list.

19. Consider the following database:

CUSTOMER(*CUST#*, NAME, CUSTCITY)
ACCOUNT(*ACCT#*, TYPE, CUST#, BALANCE, OFFICE#)
LOCATION(*OFFICE#*, ASSETS, CITY)

Show how the following queries could be written to execute more efficiently:

a. Query—Find the assets and office numbers of all locations that have customers living in Midway.

A: = JOIN(CUSTOMER, ACCOUNT, LOCATION)
B: = SELECT(A:CUSTCITY = "Midway")[OFFICE#, ASSETS]

b. Query—Find the assets and office numbers of all locations that have customers living in Midway with deposit balances over $1500.

A: = JOIN(CUSTOMER, ACCOUNT, LOCATION)
B: = SELECT(A: CUSTCITY = "Midway" and BALANCE > 1500)[OFFICE#, ASSETS]

■ PROJECTS AND PROFESSIONAL ISSUES

1. For each of the following, discuss which might be the appropriate method of file organization:

a. A hospital database system to support its business operations
b. An order-entry system for a manufacturing firm
c. A car-rental agency
d. A distributor of pharmaceuticals
e. A student records system at a university
f. A hotel reservation system

2. Since physical data structures are determined by neither the systems analyst nor the user, is there any advantage to making either one literate on the topic?

3. Effective clustering of records to facilitate relational language operations may depend on the type and frequency of various types of queries. Can you think of a way of providing information that would aid in determining how to cluster records?

4. If you have access to information on commercial DBMSs, see if you can determine what types of physical data structures are supported.

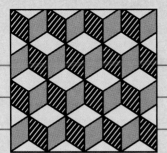

part four

DATABASE SYSTEM IMPLEMEN- TATION

In this part, you will learn about the concerns and issues involved in the implementation stage of the database development life cycle. As you work through these chapters, you will come to understand DBMS capabilities and the work that needs to be done *before* a database system is implemented. You will also learn more about the user interfaces of popular relational implementations and the emerging field of knowledge-base systems.

We begin in Chapter 12 by taking a closer look at the database management system, the software that makes the database system possible. This chapter shows you how to analyze management information needs and then use this information to evaluate various DBMS packages. You will also learn about the major issues to consider in implementing a database system.

Chapters 13 and 14 present the main features of SQL and QBE—two commercial query languages based on the relational model. Understanding this material will give you a solid foundation for using and evaluating relational DBMS language implementations.

The increasing power of microcomputers has made it easy to create microcomputer-based database systems. In fact, your first experience with a database system may involve a microcomputer. Chapter 15 discusses the role of microcomputer DBMSs, as well as the basics of using the popular relational micro DBMSs—PARADOX, RBASE, and ORACLE—to develop and query a database system.

The final chapter in this part, Chapter 16, introduces the emerging area of knowledge-base systems. These systems promise to extend the

335

data management capabilities of a traditional database system to include logic-based rules that operate on data, presenting more refined and useful information to users. In this chapter, we explain how knowledge can be represented as rules, reference the most promising languages being developed for use with knowledge-base systems, and consider the promise and obstacles of developing natural-language systems.

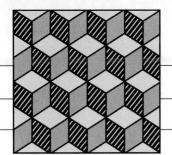

chapter twelve

DBMS SELECTION AND IMPLEMENTATION

*Optional

Steve Blue, Executive Vice-President of the Zeus Corporation, was being interviewed by Honoria Remington, a graduate student studying information systems at a nearby university. As a course project, Honoria was attempting to develop a case study on how Zeus had proceeded in selecting and implementing its DBMS: What factors had been considered important, how they were measured, and what methods of analysis were used.

In response to Honoria's inquiry, Steve said: "We thought that selecting a DBMS would be simple. We'd just have a couple of sales representatives visit us, tell us about their product, give us a price, and then we'd make the decision. Obviously, we were very naive. When the sales reps started filling the air with jargon and promotional assertions, we soon realized that we needed to back off and take a more reasoned and informed approach."

"And how did you do that?" asked Honoria.

"Well, we had a great deal of confidence in our consultant, Linda Kelly. She had done good work for us in the past, so we asked her what to do. Essentially, she outlined what the basic functions were that should be provided by a DBMS. She further showed us how to redefine those functions in terms of their underlying features. She did this in order to break the analysis down into capabilities that were objectively measurable. She then suggested ways of classifying our needs and ways of gathering information. Finally, she showed us how we could rate the capabilities of each DBMS and use a formal model for producing an overall rating for it."

"Sounds like a big job," said Honoria. "Did Linda charge you a lot?"

Steve smiled and said, "You bet, but it was worth it. We did a lot of work to satisfy her plan, but when we got the results, we knew that we had done the best job possible, and we felt confident in our final decision. We also asked her to work with our Database Administrator in developing an implementation plan."

The focus of this chapter is the **DBMS** selection and implementation process. This topic could fill a book by itself, but we will limit our discussion to an outline of its most important aspects. We first consider the relationship between management information needs and the database system. We then discuss basic **DBMS** functions, outlining some of the underlying features that are important in evaluating alternative **DBMS**s. We will then discuss a method for classifying **DBMS** features, followed by a discussion of two methods that allow an overall comparison and evaluation. Finally, we outline the key components of successful **DBMS** implementation.

After reading this chapter, you should be able to:

- ☐ Discuss the relationship between management information needs and a database system.
- ☐ Explain how an evaluation of a **DBMS** can be improved by iden-

tifying the features that enable each function to meet strategic information needs.

- ☐ Classify features according to their importance.
- ☐ Apply useful methods of combining multiple-feature evaluation into an overall decision model.
- ☐ List and discuss the tasks that should be completed in order to successfully implement a DBMS.

☐ ANALYZING MANAGEMENT INFORMATION NEEDS

management information Information to support company operations and decision makers.

We use the term **management information** in the general sense of information required to support a firm's operations and its decision makers in pursuit of company goals. The management information required by a firm providing a product that changes slowly in a stable market may be quite different from the information required by a firm that is in a volatile market, or that produces a variety of products subject to rapid obsolescence.

Consider the information needs of a manufacturing firm that uses material requirements planning (MRP) to manage its production processes. MRP requires an extensive database containing information on final product scheduling, inventories, bills of material, routing, and lead times to coordinate all phases of manufacture. If information on costs and resource needs for each manufacturing step is added, the MRP data can be used for cost accounting, shop floor control, and capacity planning and management. Such a database provides nearly all planning and control information needed for a manufacturing plant.

This information forms the nucleus of management information required by the manufacturing firm. What kind of database system might best service such information needs? The database required for MRP provides a wealth of management information, but it is very difficult to build and maintain. Every manufacturing environment is dynamic—new products are added and old ones are deleted from the product line; designs and manufacturing methods change regularly; lead times vary; inventory problems and adjustments may occur frequently. Such requirements might favor a relational DBMS.

Contrast this with the manufacturing firm that operates a just-in-time (JIT) inventory system. The intent of a JIT system is that raw materials and subassemblies will move immediately from delivery through manufacturing to the consumption center. Parts are made in small batches, which are delivered frequently to the user. The information requirements for JIT are fairly simple. For example, when products are made in small batches, the production system makes only a few bad parts before errors are discovered, and the short lead times make it easy to trace problems back to their origins.

JIT systems function best when demand is high and production requirements result in nearly continuous production. A hierarchical or network DBMS might be appropriate here.

Of course, it is inappropriate to make blanket recommendations based on these simplified scenarios. Our main point is that the management information needs of the firm should influence the choice of DBMS. Characteristics of management information needs that may affect the choice of DBMS could include the following:

1. The potential need for information that may require data from more than one application.
2. The number of applications where the relationships among data are well established and subject to little change.
3. The current and expected volume of insertions and deletions pertaining to existing and new data structures.
4. The way in which data needs to be classified for decision making. For example, a manufacturer of packaged foods may make marketing promotion decisions based upon nation-wide sales of its items. Another firm of the same type may make the same decisions based upon sales in various locations within major cities. The former company requires a simpler set of data than the latter. If the latter wants to experiment with different views of the information in order to test several strategies, a good deal of flexibility is required.

Having introduced the problem of information needs at a general level, we now proceed to an examination of specific information requirements.

Determining Application Requirements

Determining the information requirements to be supported by a database system is a complex process that is essential in guiding the selection of a DBMS. The analysis process can be simplified, however, if you realize that users typically fall into two classes: regular, repetitive users and occasional users.

The repetitive user is the one whose applications may be described as production systems. The requirements for these transaction-driven systems are planned in advance and generally support routine company operations such as recording of sales, keeping track of inventory, and so forth. Ideally, the DBMS should be able to support these applications in an efficient way.

The occasional users may require the greatest flexibility, since their requirements are often unforeseen. Such users tend to require information for analysis and decision making, as opposed to support of routine operations. This type of user needs powerful capabilities for classifying and combining data, as well as an easy-to-use query language.

Proponents of hierarchical and network data models have asserted that these models have superior capabilities for production-system applications (recall the discussion in Chapters 9 and 10). Advocates of relational DBMSs claim these systems now provide improved performance in support of production systems, in addition to more powerful capabilities for supporting *ad hoc* information needs than other models. The development of IDMS/R, which offers relational features on a network-based system, attempts to serve both needs.

Most firms are going to have a mix of needs and may go with a system that best supports their major type of need. Products such as IDMS/R are intended to minimize the sacrifice made in behalf of the less prominent need. At the same time, relational DBMSs are improving their efficiency in serving both types of information requirements.

Maintaining Data Consistency

The need to share data across multiple applications is the primary reason for implementing a database system. As discussed in Chapter 1, redundant data can result in a myriad of problems, most of which result from inconsistencies among duplicate copies of data records. Even in well-run installations, it is common for duplicate records to be updated on different time cycles. Thus, in such installations, data inconsistency is inevitable.

A good DBMS cannot guarantee that data inconsistencies will never occur, but it should provide capabilities for minimizing their occurrence. Consequently, any DBMS evaluation ought to include a consideration of the features that will ensure consistency between duplicate copies of the same data.

Response-Time Requirements

A DBMS has to perform at an expected level to be valuable to users. Unacceptable response time to user requests will lead to frustration; frustration will lead users to pursue other means of satisfying their information needs. Getting users to specify realistic response time requirements can be a challenge, yet a dialogue with users focused on identifying ideal and minimum response-time requirements can be productive. The results can then be used in evaluating DBMS performance under varying application and volume requirements.

☐ DBMS FUNCTIONS AND CAPABILITIES

To evaluate a DBMS's ability to service the firm's information requirements, we need to consider the functions provided and their underlying features.

The Data Dictionary/Directory

An effective database system will allow growth and modification in the database without compromising the integrity of its data. The data dictionary/directory (DD/D) aids the accomplishment of this objective by allowing the definitions of data to be maintained separate from the data itself. This allows changes to be made to the data definitions, with no effect on the stored data. For example, the subschema used by a particular program could be modified without in any way affecting the stored data. Other benefits provided by the DD/D include these:

Physical storage structures can be changed without affecting the programs that use the data.

Passwords and other security measures can be stored in the DD/D to facilitate control over data access.

Centralized data definition enables easy reporting on the status of the database: who is responsible for the various data items, what controls are applied to them, and what programs and users are accessing the data.

To yield these benefits, the DD/D usually includes the following features:

A language for defining entries in the DD/D.

A manipulation language for adding, deleting, and modifying entries in the DD/D.

Methods for validating entries in the DD/D.

Means for producing reports concerning the data contained in the DD/D.

An important development in relational DBMSs is the common practice of storing the directory itself as a set of relations. This enables the use of the DBMS data manipulation language for querying, updating, and maintaining the data dictionary. Figure 12.1 shows a fragment of a catalog (the name for a data dictionary used by DB2, IBM's relational DBMS). This catalog fragment contains information on the relations shown in Figure 12.2.

FIGURE 12.1 Catalog Fragment

SYSTABLES	NAME	CREATOR	COLCOUNT
	PRODUCT	JHANSEN	3
	MFR	JHANSEN	4

SYSCOLUMNS	NAME	TBNAME	COLTYPE
	PRODID	PRODUCT	INTEGER
	PRODDESC	PRODUCT	CHAR
	MFRID	PRODUCT	INTEGER
	MFRID	MFR	INTEGER
	MRFNAME	MFR	CHAR
	ADDRESS	MFR	CHAR
	COUNTRY	MFR	CHAR

```
PRODUCT
   PRODID            PRODDESC           MFRID
    1035              Sweater            210
    2241             Table Lamp          317
    2518            Brass Sculpture       253

MFR
   MFRID             MFRNAME           ADDRESS        COUNTRY
    210             Kiwi Klothes       Auckland     New Zealand
    253             Brass Works         Lagos         Nigeria
    317             Llama Llamps         Lima           Peru
```

FIGURE 12.2 Base Relations for Catalog Fragment of Figure 12.1

Data Security and Integrity

Data security and integrity are essential to effective database operations and are covered in some depth in Chapter 17. They are also important considerations in selecting a DBMS. Specifically, you should be alert to the following capabilities:

access controls Controls that limit user access to programs and data.

Access controls are an important factor because they are a means of preventing unauthorized access to data. In the data-sharing database environment, good access controls are essential.

concurrency controls Controls that maintain database integrity when two or more users simultaneously request a database record.

Concurrency controls are a means of maintaining data integrity in the multiuser environment. Suppose user *A* and user *B* both access a given record at (essentially) the same time in order to process a transaction against that record. The DBMS must somehow limit access by one of the users until the other's transaction has been completed. Without this type of facility, the accuracy and consistency of the database can rapidly erode.

view controls Those controls that restrict access to views (subsets of base relations).

View controls provide an automated means of limiting what a user is allowed to access from a given relation. This is a powerful feature that is commonly provided by relational DBMSs. The ease of creating views and the capability of the view facility can be a useful distinguishing factor among DBMSs. The DBMS purchaser may also be interested in whether views can be updated and what limitations may apply.

encryption Encoding data to make it unintelligible to unauthorized persons.

Encryption facilities may be important to institutions whose databases contain very sensitive data. Encryption can also be important for the maintenance of a secure password directory.

backup-and-recovery controls Those controls that provide for restoring the database in case of system failure.

Effective **backup-and-recovery controls** are absolutely essential to efficient operation of the database system. The ease of use of backup-and-recovery controls, their completeness, and their reliability should be major factors in the DBMS selection decision.

Query, Data Manipulation, and Reporting Capabilities

The DBMS's ability to support reporting requirements, along with users' query and data manipulation needs, is the cornerstone of today's management information systems. A sound DBMS will provide the capability to generate structured reports in a variety of formats. In addition, the

DBMS will provide a query language that is powerful, yet easy to learn and use. The language should be able to support both planned and unplanned query requirements.

Support of Specialized Programming Requirements

Developing specialized programs to interface with the DBMS requires facilities for supporting program development and program testing. A worthy DBMS will provide a host language for expressing standard procedural program structures or will provide an interface capability with one or more procedural languages. Some DBMSs may provide additional capability for quick prototyping of applications.

Physical Data Organization Options

The firm acquiring a DBMS may not wish to involve itself in the details of physical data organization. Instead, it may gauge the efficiency of a DBMS's physical organization by running sample applications.

For those who are interested, however, exploring the physical organization features may be of value. For example, it is known that the inverted list is most efficient in supporting multikey retrieval, whereas the chain list is superior for file updating, since there is no need for updating a separate file. Information on other architectural features may be elicited in the process of considering the DBMS's capability to support the types of applications common to the firm.

☐ CLASSIFYING DBMS FEATURE REQUIREMENTS

The functions and capabilities outlined in the previous section can provide a guide to determining key evaluation criteria for choosing a DBMS. Ideally, we would like to partition functions into their component parts at a level that allows objective measurement. For example, suppose that we define the necessary security and control functions as being satisfied by the following DBMS features:

☐ Access control provided for programs and users.
☐ Password-protected security tables.
☐ Ability to abort transactions in process.
☐ Automatic logging of failed attempts to access data.
☐ Utilities to create and maintain password tables.

By defining required features that can be verified, the analyst avoids the ambiguities of attempting to evaluate whether security capability is good, bad, or somewhere between—since those terms may have different meanings to different analysts. Of course, this puts the burden on the analyst to define exactly those features that constitute security capability.

CODASYL (CODASYL, 1976) recommended that such features be classified for further analysis into the following categories:

Mandatory

Important

mandatory feature A DBMS feature that must be provided.

important feature A DBMS feature that is not mandatory but makes the DBMS more attractive.

optional feature A DBMS feature that is of secondary importance; may help to distinguish among otherwise equally rated DBMSs.

unnecessary feature A DBMS feature that contributes nothing to the value of the DBMS to the firm.

undesirable feature A DBMS feature that detracts from its value to the firm.

Optional

Unnecessary

Undesirable

A **mandatory feature** is defined as one that must be provided by the DBMS. Without this feature, the candidate DBMS is dropped from further consideration. An **important feature** is one that makes the DBMS more attractive. Without this feature, the system is less responsive, and implementation may be more difficult. **Optional features** are of secondary importance and are primarily of value in discriminating between systems that are otherwise similar. An **unnecessary feature** is not relevant to the evaluation. **Undesirable features** are not often a factor. This classification refers to a feature that is not required and degrades performance.

☐ GATHERING DATA ON FEATURE AVAILABILITY AND PERFORMANCE

The process of obtaining data for DBMS evaluation involves contacting the DBMS vendor for information and benchmarking the DBMS in an environment close to that of the application.

Acquiring Data from Vendors

Information regarding DBMS features and how well they perform will typically be acquired by (1) asking other users, (2) direct testing, or (3) asking the vendor. Asking other users can be very useful because they have had actual experience and are not trying to sell the DBMS. However, in evaluating these users' opinions, the firm must exercise caution since other users may have different information needs, and, therefore, their evaluation may not accurately reflect how the DBMS might perform in other environments. Moreover, this information is usually of a general nature, not providing detailed evidence on types of applications and respective performance. At the very least, however, such information can prompt a list of questions to pose to the vendor.

Comprehensive direct testing can be very expensive and time-consuming when several DBMSs are being considered. The "mandatory requirements" analysis can help in reducing the number of DBMSs that might be tested. Direct testing produces the best results when it most closely imitates actual operating requirements and conditions.

Information supplied by vendors is, of course, subject to promotional bias. However, they often have statistics on performance and reliability, they may be willing to run demonstration tests, and they may be able to provide performance and reliability statistics that can be useful.

request for proposal (RFP) A formal document that outlines performance requirements and asks vendors to respond with a proposal for meeting those requirements.

The most common way of acquiring vendor information is to issue a **request for proposal (RFP)**. The RFP is useful in that it specifies the requirements the DBMSs must satisfy and requests information from the vendors to show how their DBMSs will satisfy those requirements. The response to the RFP can be a source of information to be compared to feedback received from users of a vendor's product. Discrepancies or inconsistencies can be referred to the vendor for clarification. This process may also suggest areas that should be directly tested. A suggestive list of requirements in four categories is shown in Figure 12.3.

Benchmark Tests

benchmarking A method of comparing DBMS performance by testing its performance on actual applications.

Benchmarking is a conventional method for generating performance information to be used in the DBMS evaluation process. The intent is to simulate the application environment in order to generate realistic performance data. Modeling the real environment can be challenging, since it is difficult to keep all parameters of the operating environment constant: the operating system, the sequence of operations, multiprogramming, and so forth. The desired invariance can usually only be accomplished by the dedicated use of a computer for the benchmark. It can also be costly to train users to a desired level of knowledge concerning each DBMS.

Although the vendors of DBMSs often supply standard benchmark tests and demonstrate them as a service to the prospective buyer, it remains the purchaser's responsibility to determine the system features that are important and to ensure that those features are sufficiently demonstrated.

One useful approach is to include a requirement for benchmark specifications in the RFP in order to eliminate in advance those vendors whose product will not meet those specifications.

When the actual benchmark testing is done, the following elements should be considered:

The test should be representative of the firm's application environment.

The nature of the benchmark test should be established prior to the actual testing: requirements to be met, relative weights to be assigned to various components of the test, and the evaluation procedures to be followed.

FIGURE 12.3   Examples of DBMS Information That Might Be Requested from Vendors

```
          FUNCTIONS                    SECURITY AND INTEGRITY
       Data Dictionary                     Authentication
  Data Manipulation Language               Authorization
      Built-in Functions                     Encryption
       Access Control                     Rollback Features
                                         Rollforward Features
                                       Transaction Processing


          PERFORMANCE                      VENDOR SUPPORT
       Benchmark Results                      Training
      Memory Requirements                   Documentation
     Optimization Features                  Responsiveness
                                              Upgrading
```

While the nature of benchmarking may vary from one firm to another, there are certain aspects of a DBMS that are necessary to every firm: main memory requirements, database storage requirements, service to multiple users that access the system concurrently, input/output requirements, and backup and recovery facilities.

□ EVALUATION MODELS

The acquisition of a DBMS reflects a major commitment by the firm. Methods of collecting and recording data may be affected. At a higher level, a commitment to providing better management information is implied. Most important, the acquisition of a DBMS represents a commitment to using information to improve the way in which the firm does business. These commitments require that the process of choosing a DBMS include consideration of important DBMS features in a rational and consistent manner. The attainment of these objectives can be aided by the use of a formal methodology. In the following discussion, we present two formal methods—a scoring model and a data envelopment model. The scoring model is easy to apply and has been widely used to aid in the DBMS selection process. The data envelopment model is more powerful, yet still easy to apply.

Scoring Model The scoring model that we present has been widely used in practice. Many firms limit the recommended classification of requirements to just two: mandatory and desirable. As nearly as possible, the verification of "must" requirements should not be subject to judgment or opinion. "Desirable" requirements may, and often do, include features that are harder to measure.

Conceptually, the scoring model is easy. Providing good input data is the hard part. We illustrate with a simple, but representative, example.

Scoring Model Example: Divide the required features into two categories, Mandatory and Desirable, as follows:

FEATURE \VENDOR	*A*	*B*	*C*
Mandatory	*Desirable*		
Views	Relational Query Language		
Password Control	User Training		
Backup Facility			

The selection of a weighting scheme is somewhat arbitrary, but it will work if it is consistent. One simple scheme is to assign a weight of 10 to each mandatory requirement and a weight of 1 to 9 to each desirable feature with the higher numbers indicating a higher degree of desirability.

When this has been determined, a value between 1 and 10 can be assigned to each feature for each vendor, depending on how well the vendor's DBMS satisfies the requirement. A completed scoring table might look like this:

FEATURE \VENDOR		A	B	C
Mandatory	*Weight*			
Views	10	5	7	9
Password Control	10	7	7	9
Backup Facility	10	9	8	7
Desirable	*Weight*			
Relational Query Language	7	10	0	10
User Training	9	6	7	4

The final scores for the vendors are determined by multiplying the feature weight times the value assigned to the vendor for that feature. The results are summed for each vendor to compute a total score, as follows:

FEATURE \VENDOR		A	B	C
Mandatory	*Weight*			
Views	10	50	70	90
Password Control	10	70	70	90
Backup Facility	10	90	80	70
Desirable	*Weight*			
Relational Query Language	7	70	0	70
User Training	9	54	63	36
TOTAL SCORES:		334	283	356

Based on the results of this example, the firm might eliminate Vendor *B* from further consideration. However, the scores of vendors *A* and *C* are sufficiently close as to warrant additional consideration. The difference could easily have come about because of uncertainty in the assignment of values to the vendor. In any case, the results of such scoring models usually have the following two functions:

1. To screen alternatives from further consideration
2. To provide information for the decision process, including the need for additional study or testing.

In the next section, we present a more sophisticated evaluation model which provides a wealth of comparative information. It is a model that is easy to use, yet mathematically powerful.

Data Envelopment Analysis (DEA) is a powerful methodology for evaluating decision alternatives such as DBMS selection, especially when there are several criteria bearing upon the selection. A basic understanding of the concepts and access to linear programming software—widely available for microcomputer use—is all that is required.

Fundamentals. ☐ We can present the basic concepts of DEA with a numerical example. Figure 12.4 contains data pertaining to the rating of the comparative performances of DBMSs *A* through *F* using just two criteria: Access Control and Backup and Recovery. The rows of the figure identify the six DBMSs to be evaluated, and the columns identify the selection criteria. Each criterion is measured on a scale from 1 to 10, where 1 is the lowest performance level, and 10 is the highest.

Figure 12.5 plots the six DBMSs and provides a graphic basis for discussing how to measure the relative performance of a DBMS. Well-performing DBMSs are away from the origin (0) in both directions. The northeast boundary defined by *A*, *C*, and *B* identifies the dominant DBMSs in the set. This outer boundary is called the **efficient frontier.**

DEA measures the relative efficiency of each DBMS by its position relative to the frontier. A point on the frontier has an efficiency of 1.0, and the origin has an efficiency of 0.0. Points inside the frontier represent values between 0 and 1, depending on how close to the frontier they are. In Figure 12.5(a) Access Control capability is plotted on the horizontal axis, and Backup and Recovery capability is plotted on the vertical.

To explain the DEA capability measure, we first introduce some additional definitions. The DBMS being evaluated is called the **reference unit**, and the path from the origin through the reference unit is called the **expansion path** for that unit. Any point on the expansion path is termed an **expansion point**, and any point on the frontier is called a **frontier point**.

Considering Figure 12.5(a) again, it may be seen that the expansion path for *D* begins at the origin (0), passes through *D* and intersects the frontier at *D'*. The significance of an expansion path is that all points thereon have the same ratio of Access Control capability to Backup and Re-

efficient frontier The outer boundary in DEA analysis.

reference unit The DBMS currently being evaluated in DEA analysis.

expansion path The path from the origin through the reference unit in DEA analysis.

expansion point Any point on the expansion path in DEA analysis.

frontier point Any point on the frontier in DEA analysis.

FIGURE 12.4   Relative DBMS Ratings

DBMS	ACCESS CONTROL	BACKUP AND RECOVERY
A	3	9
B	9	2
C	7	7
D	3	2
E	4	5
F	3	6

*This section may be omitted without loss of continuity.

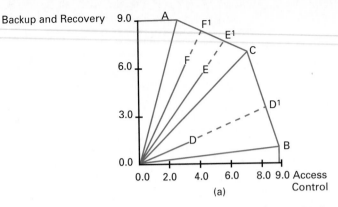

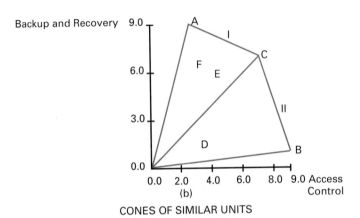

FIGURE 12.5   Graphic Illustration of DEA

covery capability and therefore can be compared directly to one another. For example, D has an Access Control rating of 3 and a Backup and Recovery rating of 2, so (3,2) is on the expansion path. The point (6,4) is also on the expansion path for (3,2), and a DBMS at (6,4) is twice as good as a DBMS at (3,2), since both the Access Control and Backup and Recovery are twice as much as (3,2).

The point D' where the expansion path intersects the frontier has an expansion factor of 2.58, meaning that Access Control and Backup and Recovery at D' are 2.58 times the corresponding values at D. The relative efficiency of a given DBMS is the inverse of the expansion factor at the frontier. Therefore, D's relative efficiency is $1/2.58 = 0.39$, meaning that D has 0.39 of the Access Control and Backup and Recovery capability of a comparable DBMS on the frontier.

Figure 12.5(b) shows that the DEA process of measuring relative capability partitions the DBMSs being evaluated into similar units. The relative capability of D is evaluated by comparing the actual DBMS to hypothetical D' that is on the frontier segment joining B and C. D, B, and C are all relatively strong in Access Control capability compared to Backup and Recovery capability. However, E and F are relatively strong in Backup and Recovery capability, and their relative capability is computed by comparing them to *A* and *C*. Thus the cone labelled I in Figure 12.5(b) contains the DBMSs that are strong in Backup and Recovery, while the cone labeled II contains those that are strong in Access Control. DBMS *C*, which is strong in both categories, is in both cones.

This graphical method of measuring relative capability is a valuable tool for illustrating DEA concepts, but it is limited to two criteria. To measure the relative capability of DBMSs characterized by more than two criteria, we must use linear programming (LP) models. The most realistic and practical formulation is based on assessing relative values of criteria.

Application. □ The heart of making a decision about the choice of a DBMS is to be able to incorporate judgments about the relative importance of the criteria. Continuing with our example, *A* is best in Backup and Recovery but is weak in Access Control. *B* is best in Access Control but weak in Backup and Recovery. Both are on the frontier and have a relative capability of 1.0 as measured by DEA. However, to compare *A* and *B* in overall performance capability, we need to make some judgments about the relative importance of Access Control capability and Backup and Recovery capability.

A criterion-based LP model allows us to focus on the relative importance of the criteria. The decision variables are weights on the attributes, which express the relative importance of the attributes. The objective in using the LP model is to choose criterion weights that maximize the relative efficiency of the reference unit. Relative capability is measured as a ratio of the overall value of the reference unit compared to the overall value of the best in the set of DBMSs.

Figure 12.6 shows how the choice of criterion weights affects relative capability. When Backup and Recovery capability is assumed to be twice as important as Access Control capability, *A* and *C* exhibit the best overall capability, each with an overall rating of 21 [= 1 × (Access Control rating) + 2 × (Backup and Recovery rating)]. The relative capability of each DBMS is measured as the ratio of the overall rating to the highest overall rating. With these weights, *B* is considered to be 61.9% (=13/21) as good in terms of capability as *A* or *C*.

FIGURE 12.6   Effect Of Attribute Weights On Relative Efficiency

DBMS	ACCESS CONTROL	BACKUP AND RECOVERY	WEIGHT (ACCESS CONTROL) 1 (BACKUP AND RECOVERY) 2		WEIGHT (ACCESS CONTROL) 3 (BACKUP AND RECOVERY) 1	
			OVERALL SCORE	RELATIVE EFFICIENCY	OVERALL SCORE	RELATIVE EFFICIENCY
A	3	9	21*	1.000	18	0.621
B	9	2	13	0.619	29*	1.000
C	7	7	21*	1.000	28	0.966
D	3	2	7	0.333	11	0.379
E	4	5	14	0.667	17	0.586
F	3	6	15	0.714	15	0.517

MAX = 21   MAX = 29

The last two columns lead to a much different result when Access Control capability is assumed to be three times as important as Backup and Recovery capability. With these weights, B has the highest overall score of 29. A now has a relative capability of 62.1% (18/29), while C has dropped to 96.6% (28/29).

D, E, and F yield lesser overall capability ratings for both sets of weights. In fact, units off the frontier will never be the best for any set of weights and will always have a relative capability less than 1.0. In contrast, for any DBMS on the frontier, there will always be at least one set of weights for which the frontier DBMS will have the best overall score and, therefore, a relative efficiency of 1.0.

This observation leads directly to the criterion-based LP model to measure relative efficiency. The decision variables are the criteria weights and the objective is to maximize the relative capability of a given reference unit. The constraints are that each DBMS has a relative capability that does not exceed 100%. The verbal model is

MAXIMIZE THE VALUE OF THE REFERENCE UNIT

SUBJECT TO THE OVERALL VALUE OF EACH UNIT BEING LESS THAN
    OR EQUAL TO 1

The full criterion-based model to measure D's relative capability is

MAX $3P + 2Q$		(D's overall rating; P = Access Control rating; Q = Backup and Recovery rating)
ST	$3P + 9Q <= 1$	(Limit on A's overall rating)
	$9P + 2Q <= 1$	(Limit on B's overall rating)
	$7P + 7Q <= 1$	(Limit on C's overall rating)
	$3P + 2Q <= 1$	(Limit on D's overall rating)
	$4P + 5Q <= 1$	(Limit on E's overall rating)
	$3P + 6Q <= 1$	(Limit on F's overall rating)
	$P,Q >= 0$	(nonnegativity)

☐ IMPLEMENTATION ISSUES

Implementation planning and administration is as important to database systems as it is to the effective implementation of any new technology. In this section, we outline some of the important considerations associated with DBMS implementation.

Database Administration   The responsibility for database administration is usually assigned to an individual given the title, Database Administrator (DBA). The DBA is charged with ensuring that the database system operates effectively and efficiently. In order to do this, the DBA's daily activities are concerned with the following tasks:

1. Servicing end-user requirements.

2. Ensuring database security and integrity.

3. Establishing backup-and-recovery procedures.

Servicing End-User Requirements ☐ The DBA is responsible for tracking the frequency of database use by end users and the response times needed by their database applications. This is done to be sure that user needs are being satisfied. The DBA is also involved with satisfying the training needs of users. This training includes providing appropriate tools to make the end users more productive. Examples might be special utilities or language capabilities.

Ensuring Database Security and Integrity ☐ By tracking the frequency of database use by users, the DBA obtains information that can help in determining needs for database controls. Unexpected user requests, for instance, may prompt an evaluation of the adequacy of access controls. For example, suppose that user U1 is not allowed to access individual records in the payroll file. Recently, U1 has been requesting aggregate data such as counts and sums of various fields in the table. U1 may be gathering data from which he or she is able to deduce individual attribute values that cannot be accessed directly. Additional access controls may be needed to prevent this.

In terms of database integrity, the DBA must make sure that there is a correct correspondence between the database and its definition as reflected in the data dictionary. The DBA must also maintain controls to restrict the updating of the database to authorized users. Maintaining the level of restriction put upon each user is the DBA's responsibility.

The DBA must further ensure that user-specified data controls are implemented and monitored. For example, users may have better knowledge than the DBA as to which data is sensitive and should be restricted and to what level. Cost data pertaining to manufacturing operations may be unrestricted from access by the cost accounting department, for example, but should not be accessed by other functional groups without prior permission.

Backup and Recovery. ☐ DBMSs provide facilities for maintaining data integrity during operations. However, they cannot otherwise guarantee database integrity. Corruption of data because of a disk failure, for example, may be outside the control of the DBMS. Such possibilities require that the DBA devise methods for restoring a complete and consistent database after a failure.

Restoration procedures typically involve utilities provided by the DBMS as part of a larger recovery plan designed by the DBA. This means that the DBA must be familiar with all DBMS functions and capabilities. The recovery plan would generally include the following actions:

1. Identify backup-and-recovery utilities that are available to handle system failures.

2. Establish procedures to be followed by all who have a role in the recovery plan.

3. Create a plan for informing users who are affected by database fail-

ure concerning the potential impact the failure will have on their operations, as well as the estimated time to restore the database.

4. Create and conduct a schedule of tests for the recovery plan, and standards by which to gauge the results. This ensures that the recovery plan will accomplish its objectives if a real disaster occurs.

Database Testing   Good testing procedures are needed to ensure that the database system fulfills user requirements and operates without major problems. In the development of new applications, testing runs second only to programming in terms of time required. Testing is normally focused on validating the operations such as these:

1. The loading of the database has been accomplished without violating the data integrity.
2. The applications interface correctly with the database.
3. The performance of the system satisfies the requirements for which the DBMS was acquired.

An objective of testing, which is sometimes overlooked, is finding out where the database system does not function as expected. Most problems arise when input values are unusual or erroneous, when combinations of conditions yield unexpected results, or when users take unanticipated actions. Consequently, test data should be generated to determine how the system handles the following types of inputs:

1. Values that have erroneous negative signs.
2. Invalid codes or keys.
3. Data that threatens referential integrity.
4. Null values.
5. An unauthorized user's attempts to change data.
6. Extreme values such as unusually large hours worked or unusually large receipts of goods.
7. Inappropriate units of measure.
8. Unauthorized attempts to change information contained in the data dictionary.

On the operational control level, the firm should be concerned with monitoring the use of computing resources. Management should be interested in:

1. Who is using the database system, what data is being used, and how long is it being used?
2. What hardware resources are being used by the database system, when are they being used, and are there bottlenecks?
3. How much time is being used for routine processing versus *ad hoc* queries, and are there trends in such usage?

To make these ideas more concrete, we note some of the performance measures incorporated in IBM's relational DBMS DB2. The DB2 Performance Monitor is used in concert with the DB2 Instrumentation Facility to generate information on system performance. The DB2 Instrumentation Facility collects database system performance data, which can then be analyzed by the DB2 Performance Monitor in order to generate information of interest to the DBA and other management personnel. Examples of such information include the processing time for SQL queries, traces of SQL query execution, statistics on input and output data, and summary information on waiting times for execution of queries and programs.

Generation of test data that will check every possible undesired condition has been shown to be an intractable problem (Garey and Johnson 1979). Consequently, sound testing of the database system requires thoughtful design of test data that are at once reasonably thorough and involve moderate resource requirements.

Decision tables have been used with some success in generating test data. More sophisticated approaches are available to automatically generate test data.

Preparing Users for Change

Since user acceptance is essential to a successful database system implementation, preparing the users for the changes that will affect them is essential. How is this best accomplished?

Conceptually, the answer is simple: Involve the users in the development of the new systems, train them thoroughly, and include user-acceptance tests as part of the implementation effort. Carrying out these activities may be a bit more complex.

Involving the users in the development of the database system is facilitated if users are convinced of the need for that system. Top management, in concert with functional analysts and systems analysts, should communicate clearly to users what the expected benefits might be, as well as any startup costs that might be borne by the user. This should be done at the earliest possible point in the development cycle.

Experience has shown that users develop feelings of support for a system when they have participated in its development and implementation. Key users may actually be selected as part of the development team; others should be consulted as the project progresses. Users need to participate and contribute. The objective here is not simply political. Often, users may contribute ideas or observe considerations that have been overlooked and that would make the database system function better. We emphasize that user involvement is most effective when users participate throughout development and implementation. A courtesy consultation at the beginning and the end of the project will rarely work.

Involving users in the development and implementation of the database system provides another benefit: It prepares them for training in the use of the system. Users may subsequently receive training in system use through (1) reading operations and procedures manuals, (2) formal training sessions conducted by the vendor and the firm, and (3) informal training by an internal coordinator charged with assisting users as questions and problems arise. If the same types of questions are repeatedly encountered, the coordinator may arrange for a formal training session addressing the problem procedures.

Among other things, users will need to know how to process documents, present input, produce reports, correct errors, generate queries, and so on. As primary users become trained they can be used as a resource to train other users in their functional area.

Loading the Database

Often the data to be stored in the database already exists on some computer-based medium such as magnetic tape. In the best cases, all the required data exists, and database loading may simply involve restructuring the existing data. That is to say, a program can be written that reads the old files and creates the structure needed for the new ones.

More often, the existing files do not contain all the data required by the new database. A commonly used approach for this case is to convert the existing files so that they contain the necessary data before the time comes to switch over to the database system. A limitation of this approach is that the old system must continue to process daily transactions while this modification is being done.

Database Maintenance

Once the DBMS is installed and in operation, maintenance activities need to be organized and performed to ensure that effective service and operations are provided. In this section, we describe some of the necessary maintenance functions.

Managing Resources. ☐ Over time, new data will be added to the database, some data may be deleted, and applications will be added or modified. Most firms will experience database growth. New requirements may change the mix of database applications, and it is important to monitor the effect of such changes. Database system resources such as storage devices, buffers, indexes, and tables need to be checked to determine their adequacy as system requirements change. This information is a help in making decisions about adding or upgrading resources, as well as forecasting future needs.

Backup and Recovery. ☐ Saving a copy of the database at selected time intervals should be a standard backup practice. In this way, if the database being used is damaged or destroyed, it can be reconstructed by loading the backup copy and rerunning all transactions that had been processed since the backup copy was made.

Database saves are usually made by using an operating system utility or a DBMS utility. The former backs up the entire disk file, including the physical data structures. Similar backup is available through use of the DBMS. However, the data structures are not actually represented in the saved data but are reconstructed during loading of the saved data. This process can be somewhat slow for large files.

Managing Changes to the Database System. □ Changes to the database system are inevitable as user needs change over time. Users may become more facile with the query language and extend the range and complexity of applications required of the system. As time passes, users often see new ways in which information from the database can be organized and retrieved to support the needs of their job. As these changes accumulate, enhancements to the database system may be needed.

Changes in user needs that amount to arranging data in more complex forms can degrade DBMS performance if they are widespread, but they may not require that the contents and structure of the database be changed. New applications, however, may require that attributes be added to tables, that new tables be created, that new views be formulated, that added indexes be constructed, and so on.

Changes such as these can be disruptive to operations and can degrade system performance. There is no pat solution to this possibility, but successful database implementations attempt to make the process of change orderly and subject to analysis and management involvement. Management may be called upon when one user's request for change degrades the availability and performance of the database system for other users.

Since decisions on change involve estimating effects, it is useful to monitor new implementations in order to assess the actual impact. Such monitoring can help to build expertise in forecasting the effects of changes requested in the future.

DBMS Monitoring Facilities □ DBMSs offer differing capabilities. In this section, we give an overview of representative monitoring facilities that might be contained in a generic DBMS we call *G*.

G provides online capability for checking on current DBMS activities. A menu allows selection of monitoring fuctions such as these:

1. Input/output usage by user.
2. Number of read and write operations executed in a set time period.
3. Number of completed transactions per set time period.
4. Provision of an audit trail for activities of interest. For example, it might be desired to check on who is modifying the data in the PAYROLL TABLE. This could be accomplished with the following command

```
AUDIT UPDATE ON PAYROLL BY SESSION;
```

The ON clause identifies the table to be audited, and the BY clause specifies how fine the level of auditing should be. BY SESSION, for example, writes an entry to the audit trail for each user *session* accessing the audited relation.

As you can see, DBMSs need to have a reasonable range of monitoring capabilities.

■ SUMMARY

In this chapter, we have addressed the tasks of DBMS selection and implementation. Our approach has been to begin with management information needs, proceeding to the types of system requirements those needs imply. We then characterized the basic DBMS functions that are available to service those system requirements and gave examples of how to subdivide them into their underlying features at a level that allows objective evaluation measurement. We then discussed a simple means of making an initial DBMS analysis by classifying features according to their importance. This was followed by a discussion of sources of information on commercial DBMSs.

Our discussion then considered two methods of overall DBMS evaluation: the multiattribute scoring model, which is simple and well known and data envelopment analysis, which is less well known but can be quite useful in that it is straightforward to use and provides powerful capabilities for handling decision-maker input and yielding valuable comparative information as its output. It is particularly effective in categorizing DBMSs whose overall capabilities are similar.

We then discussed the principal factors that should be a part of a DBMS implementation strategy. Many of these factors carry over to long-term DBMS management as well. We saw that the database administration function plays an important role in implementation and that thorough testing is essential. We also discussed the need for preparing users for change through project participation as well as training.

The need for mechanisms for accommodating changing needs for database information was summarized, along with the requirement for backup and recovery. Finally, the role of performance monitoring was outlined.

■ REVIEW QUESTIONS

1. Define each of the following terms in your own words:
   a. management information
   b. access controls
   c. encryption
   d. backup-and-recovery controls
   e. important feature
   f. optional feature
   g. unnecessary feature
   h. request for proposal (RFP)
   i. DEA
   j. efficient frontier
   k. expansion point
   l. frontier point

2. Describe each of the following DBMS functions and capabilities:
   a. Data dictionary/directory
   b. Data security and integrity

c. Query, data manipulation, and reporting capabilities
d. Support of specialized programming requirements
e. Physical data organization options

3. Identify features that would be important for each of the functions in (2).

4. How should an analytical model's output be used in selecting a DBMS?

5. Describe how the scoring model can be used to assist in DBMS selection.

6. What value is there in including classifications such as UNNECESSARY and UNDESIRABLE?

7. Discuss the major issues of implementing a DBMS.

■ PROBLEMS AND EXERCISES

1. Match the following terms with their definitions:

Concurrency controls	a. Controls that limit user access to a subset of a base table
View controls	b. Testing DBMS performance by running actual applications on it
Mandatory feature	c. In DEA analysis, the DBMS currently being evaluated
Undesirable feature	d. A DBMS feature that detracts from its value to the firm
Benchmarking	e. Controls that maintain database integrity when two or more users simultaneously request a database record
Reference unit	f. In DEA analysis, the path from the origin through the reference unit
Expansion path	g. A DBMS feature that must be provided

2. Gather information on two network DBMSs. (This can usually be found in the library.) Do these DBMSs include the functions outlined in the chapter? Is there information on the features that enable those functions? Can you create a "generic" classification of features for firms in a particular industry?

3. Gather information on two relational DBMSs, and repeat the process described in exercise 2. Then see if you can find similar information on a hierarchical model or a network model and compare it to one of the relational systems. Is it easier or more difficult to find similar information? Why?

4. Using the data from two or three of the above DBMSs, create a scoring model. Justify your selection of criteria weights and DBMS ratings.

5. Linear programs (LPs) are widely available in business schools and computer science departments, often on a microcomputer. Use an LP to analyze the data for DBMSs *A–F* in the chapter. You might begin by using the exact data given, without weights. Then try the given weights. Finally experiment with some weights of your own.

6. After completing exercise 5, try applying DEA to the analysis you developed in exercise 4.

7. Based upon the chapter material, write a short procedural guide to be used in selecting a DBMS for a hypothetical company.

8. Write a brief guide to DBMS implementation procedures.

■ PROJECTS AND PROFESSIONAL ISSUES

1. Contact one or two local institutions that use DBMSs. Find out what approach they used to select their DBMS. Are they satisfied with the result?

2. Contact a vendor to acquire data on its DBMS. What information is contained in that data that would be useful input to the DBMS selection process?

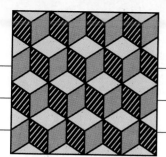

chapter thirteen

RELATIONAL IMPLEMENTATION WITH SQL

Tony Melton and Annette Chang, information systems practitioners at Premier Construction Company, are discussing their recently installed relational database management system.

"Tony, what advantages are there in having SQL as the language of our system, rather than one of the other available relational database languages?"

"Probably the chief advantage, Annette, is that SQL is both the ANSI standard relational language as well as the de facto standard for business. This means that it is widely supported and that we can feel confident of minimizing our risk if we change hardware or software vendors."

"But what about the language itself? How does SQL stack up as a relational language in its own right?"

"SQL is a powerful language. It has all the logical power of Codd's relational calculus, as well as the additional capability of handling groupings of rows and applying statistical functions to those groupings. Moreover, we can define our database schemas, identify keys and non-null columns, and embed SQL statements in programs written in other languages. In addition to all that, in our system the catalog that contains defining information for all of our databases is itself a relational database which we can query with SQL. Through SQL, we can truly take advantage of the power of the 'relational revolution.'"

In this chapter, we study the parts of relational database management systems having to do with the SQL language. After reading this chapter, you should be able to:

- Explain basic facts about the historical development of relational database management systems.
- Define a relational database schema in SQL.
- Formulate SQL queries of varying complexity.
- Insert, update, and delete data in a relational database through SQL commands.
- Discuss some aspects of embedding SQL statements in a traditional or "host" programming language.
- Define and query data views in SQL.
- Explain some basic elements in the structure of the catalog of IBM's DB2.

☐ RELATIONAL IMPLEMENTATIONS: AN OVERVIEW

The aftermath of the publication of Codd's papers introducing the relational model and relational languages (algebra and calculus) was a great deal of activity in the commercial and research communities to develop implemented versions of relational languages. The three most important languages to come out of this effort are probably SQL (Structured Query Language), QBE (Query-by-Example), and QUEL (Query Language). SQL and QBE both originated at IBM during the seventies and perform many similar functions, although SQL is a textual language while QBE is graphical. QUEL is the language of INGRES, a relational database management system developed during the seventies at the University of California, Berkeley.

SQL was the outgrowth of IBM's System R research project. This project included the development of a relational database system and the language SEQUEL (for Structured English Query Language). In the late seventies, SQL (changed from SEQUEL) became part of the public domain and was first available as a language for a commercial system from Oracle Corporation. In 1981, IBM released SQL/DS, which is a commercial database management system (DBMS) that supports SQL. In 1983, IBM released SQL as part of the DB2 DBMS. These versions of SQL run in different operating environments: SQL/DS for VM and VSE, and DB2 for MVS. In addition, IBM has released versions of SQL for the OS/2 Extended Edition environment and the OS/400 environment.

In October 1986, the ANSI standard for SQL was approved. At present, SQL is the only ANSI standard relational database language. Moreover, SQL is the de facto standard in business, since it is by far the relational language of choice in commercial systems. Many vendors have released implementations of SQL since 1980.

In addition to the mainframe versions of SQL listed above, many microcomputer versions of SQL are now available. These include XDB, SQLBase, SQLServer, and Oracle. Besides these, there are versions of R:Base and dBASE that include SQL support.

The INGRES system was originally developed as a database management system with its own data language, QUEL, which, like SQL, is modeled on relational calculus. Relational Technology, Inc., was formed in the early eighties to commercially market INGRES and QUEL. In the last few years, commercial INGRES has been expanded to support SQL as well as QUEL. This is important since SQL has been adopted as the ANSI standard.

Relational database management systems support a wide variety of features in addition to their language capability. These features include security, integrity, high performance data access and update, and data dictionary or catalog control. While some of these features are covered in this chapter, others are discussed elsewhere (see, for example, Chapters 11, 12, and 17). In this chapter, we will discuss the SQL language and the catalog features of a relational DBMS.

Although the name SQL suggests that it is a "query" language, it does include table definition, database update, view definition, and privilege granting, in addition to query facilities. In this chapter, we will study the table definition, query, update, and view definition capabilities of SQL — in that order. Our coverage of SQL will conform to the ANSI standard. We will also examine the catalog feature of IBM's DB2 system. To illustrate our examples, we will use a relational database taken from a simple version of the case of the Premier Construction Company. The sample database is shown in Figure 13.1.

WORKER

WORKER_ID	WORKER_NAME	HRLY_RATE	SKILL_TYPE	SUPV_ID
1235	M. Faraday	12.50	Electric	1311
1412	C. Nemo	13.75	Plumbing	1520
2920	R. Garret	10.00	Roofing	2920
3231	P. Mason	17.40	Framing	3231
1520	H. Rickover	11.75	Plumbing	1520
1311	C. Coulomb	15.50	Electric	1311
3001	J. Barrister	8.20	Framing	3231

ASSIGNMENT

WORKER_ID	BLDG_ID	START_DATE	NUM_DAYS
1235	312	10/10	5
1412	312	10/01	10
1235	515	10/17	22
2920	460	10/05	18
1412	460	12/08	18
2920	435	10/28	10
2920	210	11/10	15
3231	111	10/10	8
1412	435	10/15	15
1412	515	11/05	8
3231	312	10/24	20
1520	515	10/09	14
1311	435	10/08	12
1412	210	11/15	12
1412	111	12/01	4
3001	111	10/08	14
1311	460	10/23	24
1520	312	10/30	17
3001	210	10/27	14

BUILDING

BLDG_ID	BLDG_ADDRESS	TYPE	QLTY_LEVEL	STATUS
312	123 Elm	Office	2	2
435	456 Maple	Retail	1	1
515	789 Oak	Residence	3	1
210	1011 Birch	Office	3	1
111	1213 Aspen	Office	4	1
460	1415 Beech	Warehouse	3	3

FIGURE 13.1   Premier Construction Company Database

TABLE DEFINITION

Defining a database schema in SQL is straightforward. It is only necessary to identify the start of a schema definition and then define each table and view. In this section, we show how this is done for tables. Later in the chapter, we show how views are defined.

Tables are defined in three steps:

1. The name of the table is given.

2. Each column is defined.

3. Multicolumn keys and alternate keys, if any, are defined.

The following is a schema definition for the database of Figure 13.1.

```
CREATE SCHEMA
     AUTHORIZATION TONY_MELTON
CREATE TABLE WORKER
     WORKER_ID       NUMERIC (4)  NOT NULL UNIQUE
     WORKER_NAME     CHARACTER (12)
     HRLY_RATE       NUMERIC (5,2)
     SKILL_TYPE      CHARACTER (8)
     SUPV_ID         NUMERIC (4)
CREATE TABLE ASSIGNMENT
     WORKER_ID       NUMERIC (4) NOT NULL
     BLDG_ID         NUMERIC (3) NOT NULL
     START_DATE      CHARACTER (5)
     NUM_DAYS        NUMERIC (2)
     UNIQUE (WORKER_ID, BLDG_ID)
CREATE TABLE BUILDING
     BLDG_ID         NUMERIC (3)  NOT NULL UNIQUE
     BLDG_ADDRESS    CHAR (12)
     TYPE            CHAR (9)
     QLTY_LEVEL      NUMERIC (1)
     STATUS          NUMERIC (1)
```

schema owner Person who has authority and responsibility for granting access to tables, columns, and views in a database.

Each **CREATE SCHEMA** statement indicates to the DBMS that what follows is a database schema. The **AUTHORIZATION** clause indicates the name of the **owner** of the schema. This person is known to the system and can grant to other users access and update privileges for the database defined in the schema. Obviously, this structure implies that many database schemas and, therefore, many databases can exist in the same installation. These can be owned by different individuals, but, under the control of the DBMS, each database can be accessed by users other than their owner.

Following the **CREATE SCHEMA** statement are **CREATE TABLE** statements—one for each table to be defined as part of the database. The **CREATE TABLE** statement itself identifies the name of the table. The statements following **CREATE TABLE** either (1) define columns or (2) define multicolumn keys.

Column Definition. ☐ Let's look at the definitions of the first three columns of WORKER:

```
WORKER_ID       NUMERIC (4)  NOT NULL UNIQUE
WORKER_NAME     CHARACTER (12)
HRLY_RATE       NUMERIC (5,2)
```

The column is defined by giving its name, its data type, and whether specific constraints (NOT NULL and UNIQUE) apply to it. The first three columns in our example are named, respectively, WORKER_ID, WORKER_NAME, and HRLY_RATE. Their data types are numeric and character. Several other data types are available, but most of them are variations on these.

A numeric data type means that the column's data values must be numbers, possibly with a decimal point. WORKER_ID's data type, NUMERIC (4), means that it has 4 significant digits and *no* digits to the right of the decimal point. HRLY_RATE has a data type of NUMERIC (5,2), meaning that it has 5 significant digits, 2 of which are to the right of the decimal.

A character data type means that the column's data values consist of character strings, made up of alphanumeric characters, possibly in combination with special characters. The maximum length of the character string is indicated in parentheses. Thus, WORKER_NAME may have character string values no more than 12 characters in length.

WORKER_ID is also subject to two constraints: NOT NULL and UNIQUE. The NOT NULL constraint means that WORKER_ID is not allowed to have a null value. UNIQUE means that no two rows in the WORKER table may have the same value for WORKER_ID. This last constraint implies that WORKER_ID is a key for WORKER, which we intend. The NOT NULL constraint enforces the entity integrity rule, which states that no key column can be null.

We have now explained the entire schema with the exception of one statement. The CREATE TABLE ASSIGNMENT section of the schema contains the following statement:

```
UNIQUE (WORKER_ID, BLDG_ID)
```

This statement indicates that the two columns, WORKER_ID and BLDG_ID, within the ASSIGNMENT table, must together be unique. In other words, this statement defines WORKER_ID, BLDG_ID as a two-column key for ASSIGNMENT. Within the definitions of these two columns, we have indicated that they may not be null, so we have also indicated the entity integrity rule for this table.

schema definition Description of a database to the DBMS.

This **schema definition** *describes* the database to the DBMS, but it does not cause any actual data values to be entered. Data values are entered and manipulated by the SQL data manipulation language, which we describe in detail in the next section.

Besides the CREATE TABLE statement, which defines a new table, most systems provide other statements for changing the definitions of tables or for deleting tables from the schema. For example, DB2 has the ALTER TABLE statement for changing a table definition and the DROP statement for deleting a table (or other object, such as a view) from the database. In addition to these schema definition statements, other statements—such as CREATE INDEX—may provide for the creation of indexes and other physical-oriented objects which improve system performance in database access.

☐ DATA MANIPULATION

SQL contains a wide variety of data manipulation capabilities, both for querying and for updating a database. These capabilities depend only on the logical structure of the database, not on its physical structure, consistent with the requirements of the relational model. We will describe the query language first, followed by the operations for entering and changing data. The data change operations are described last, because their structure depends to some extent on the structure of the query language.

Simple Queries

simple query A query involving only one database table.

For us, a **simple query** is one involving only a single database table. Simple queries help to illustrate the basic structure of SQL.

```
Query: Who are the plumbers?
    SELECT WORKER_NAME
    FROM WORKER
    WHERE SKILL_TYPE = 'Plumbing'
Result:
    WORKER_NAME
    C. Nemo
    H. Rickover
```

This query illustrates the three most often used clauses of SQL: the SELECT clause, the FROM clause, and the WHERE clause. Although we have placed them on separate lines in this example, they could all appear on the same line. They may also be indented, and terms within clauses may be separated by an arbitrary number of blank spaces. Let's discuss the features of each clause.

SELECT clause Identifies the columns desired in the query.

SELECT □ The **SELECT clause** lists the *columns* desired in the result of the query. They are always the columns of a relational table. In our example, the resulting table has a single column (WORKER_NAME), but it could have several columns, or it could include computed values and literal values. We will show examples of each of these. If the desired result contains more than one column, the columns are all listed in the SELECT clause and separated by commas. For example, SELECT WORKER_ID, WORKER_NAME would cause both WORKER_ID and WORKER_NAME to be listed as columns in the resulting table.

FROM clause Lists the existing tables referenced by the query.

FROM □ The **FROM clause** lists one or more *tables* to be referenced by the query. All columns listed in the SELECT or WHERE clauses must be found in one of the tables of the FROM clause.

WHERE clause Gives the condition for selecting rows from identified tables.

WHERE □ The **WHERE clause** contains a *condition* for selecting rows from the table(s) listed in the FROM clause. In our example, the condition is that the SKILL_TYPE column must have the literal value 'Plumbing,' placed in single quotes, as is customary for alphanumeric literals in SQL. The WHERE clause is easily the most versatile clause of SQL and can contain a wide variety of conditions. Much of our discussion will illustrate the different constructions allowed in the WHERE clause.

The SQL query given above is processed by the system in the order FROM, WHERE, SELECT. That is, the rows of the table referenced in the FROM clause (WORKER) are set up in a work area for processing. Then, the WHERE clause is applied to each row, one by one. Any row not satisfying the WHERE clause is eliminated from consideration. Those rows that satisfy the WHERE clause are then processed by the SELECT clause. In our example, the WORKER_NAME from each of these rows is selected, and all of these selected values are displayed as the result of the query.

Query: List all data about office buildings.
```
    SELECT *
    FROM BUILDING
    WHERE TYPE = 'Office'
```
Result:

BLDG_ID	BLDG_ADDRESS	TYPE	QLTY_LEVEL	STATUS
312	123 Elm	Office	2	2
210	1011 Birch	Office	3	1
111	1213 Aspen	Office	4	1

The "*" in the SELECT clause means "the entire row." This is a convenient shorthand we will employ often.

Query: What is the weekly wage rate for each electrician?
```
    SELECT WORKER_NAME, 'Weekly Wage Rate = ', 40 * HRLY_RATE
    FROM WORKER
    WHERE SKILL_TYPE = 'Electric'
    ORDER BY WORKER_NAME
```
Result:
```
WORKER_NAME
C. Coulomb      Weekly Wage Rate = 620.00
M. Faraday      Weekly Wage Rate = 500.00
```

character string literals Literals formed from alphanumeric and "special" characters.

This query illustrates the use of both alphanumeric literals, or **character string literals,** (in this example, 'Weekly Wage Rate = '), and of computations in the SELECT clause. Computations involving numeric columns and numeric literals in combination with the standard arithmetical operations (+, -, *, /), grouped as needed with parentheses, can be defined in the SELECT clause. We have also included a new clause, the ORDER BY clause, that is used to sort the result of the query in ascending alphanumeric order of the indicated column. If descending order is desired, it must be specified by adding "DESC" to the command. Multiple columns may be specified in the ORDER BY clause, and some may be in ascending order and some in descending order. The primary sort key column is specified first.

Query: Who gets an hourly rate between $10 and $12?
```
    SELECT *
    FROM WORKER
    WHERE HRLY_RATE >= 10 AND HRLY_RATE<=12
```
Result:

WORKER_ID	WORKER_NAME	HRLY_RATE	SKILL_TYPE	SUPV_ID
2920	R. Garret	10.00	Roofing	2920
1520	H. Rickover	11.75	Plumbing	1520

comparison operators =, <>, <, >, <=, >=

Boolean connectives Any of the logical connectives AND, OR, NOT

This query illustrates some additional features of the WHERE clause: comparison operators and the Boolean connective AND. The six **comparison operators** (=, <> [not equals], , =) may be used to compare columns with other columns or with literals. The **Boolean connectives** AND, OR, and NOT may be used to create compound conditions or to negate a condition. Parentheses may also be used as they ordinarily are in programming languages to group conditions.

Query: List the plumbers, roofers, and electricians.
```
SELECT *
FROM WORKER
WHERE SKILL_TYPE IN ('Plumbing', 'Roofing', 'Electric')
```
Result:

WORKER_ID	WORKER_NAME	HRLY_RATE	SKILL_TYPE	SUPV_ID
1235	M. Faraday	12.50	Electric	1311
1412	C. Nemo	13.75	Plumbing	1520
2920	R. Garret	10.00	Roofing	2920
1520	H. Rickover	11.75	Plumbing	1520
1311	C. Coulomb	15.50	Electric	1311

This query introduces and illustrates the use of the IN comparison operator. The WHERE clause evaluates to 'true' if the skill type for the row is found *in the set* contained in parentheses—that is, if the skill type is plumbing, roofing, or electric. We will have more occasion to use the IN operator with subqueries.

Multiple-Table Queries   The ability to connect data items across table boundaries is essential in any database language. In relational algebra, this is accomplished through the *join*. Although SQL is modeled primarily after relational calculus, it connects data between tables in a manner similar to the join of relational algebra. We will now show how this is done. Consider this query:

Query: What are the skill types of workers assigned to building 435?

The data needed to solve this query is found in two relations: WORKER and ASSIGNMENT. The SQL solution requires the listing of both of these relations in the FROM clause, together with a particular type of WHERE clause condition:

```
SELECT SKILL_TYPE
FROM WORKER, ASSIGNMENT
WHERE WORKER.WORKER_ID = ASSIGNMENT.WORKER_ID AND
    BLDG_ID = 435
```

What is happening here? We must consider two steps in the system's processing of the query.

Cartesian product Result of pairing each row in one table with every row in another table.

1. As usual, the FROM clause is processed first. In this case, however, since there are two tables in the clause, the system creates the **Cartesian product** of the rows in these tables. This means that one huge table is (logically) created, consisting of all the *columns* from both tables, and pairing up every *row* in one table with every *row* in the other table in the clause. In our example, since there are 5 columns in WORKER and 4 columns in ASSIGNMENT, there will be 9 columns in the Cartesian product created by the FROM clause. The total num-

ber of rows in this Cartesian product relation is m x n, where m is the number of rows in WORKER and n is the number of rows in AS-SIGNMENT: Since WORKER has 7 rows and ASSIGNMENT has 19 rows, the Cartesian product will have 7 x 19 or 133 rows. An illustration of this is given in Chapter 8, Figures 8.4(a) and 8.4(b). If there are more than two tables in the FROM clause, the Cartesian product is created from *all* the tables in the clause.

2. After creating this giant relation, the system applies the WHERE clause as before. Each row of the relation created by the FROM clause is examined for conformity to the WHERE clause. Those not satisfying the WHERE condition are eliminated from consideration. The SELECT clause is then applied to the remaining rows. Figure 13.2 illustrates the process for the first three rows of WORKER.

The WHERE clause in this query contains two conditions:

1. WORKER.WORKER_ID = ASSIGNMENT.WORKER_ID

2. BLDG_ID = 435

The first of these is the join condition. Note that since both the WORKER and ASSIGNMENT relations contain a column named WORKER_ID, the product relation will contain two columns with this name. To distinguish between them, we prefix to the column name the name of the relation from which the column originated.

The first condition states that for any given row to be selected, the value of the WORKER_ID column that came from the WORKER relation must be equal to the value of the WORKER_ID column that came from the ASSIGNMENT relation. In effect, we are joining the two relations on WORKER_ID. All rows for which these two columns are not equal are eliminated from the product relation. This is precisely what happens in the natural join of relational algebra. (This differs from the natural join, however, in that the redundant WORKER_ID column is *not* automatically eliminated in SQL.) The complete join of these two relations, with the additional condition that BLDG_ID = 435, is shown in Figure 13.2. The application of the SELECT clause produces the final result of the query:

```
    SKILL_TYPE
    Plumbing
    Roofing
    Electric
```

FIGURE 13.2   The Join of Worker and Assignment

WORKER.WORKER_ID	WORKER_NAME	HRLY_RATE	SKILL_TYPE	SUPV_ID
1412	C. Nemo	13.75	Plumbing	1520
2920	R. Garret	10.00	Roofing	2920
1311	C. Coulomb	15.50	Electric	1311

ASSIGNMENT.WORKER_ID	BLDG_ID	START_ID	NUM_DAYS
1412	435	10/15	15
2920	435	10/28	10
1311	435	10/08	12

We now show how a relation can be joined to itself in SQL.

Query: List workers with the names of their supervisors.
```
SELECT A.WORKER_NAME, B.WORKER_NAME
FROM WORKER A, WORKER B
WHERE B.WORKER_ID = A.SUPV_ID
```

alias Alternate name given to a relation.

The FROM clause in this example defines two "copies" of the WORKER relation, given the alias names A and B. An **alias** is an alternate name given to a relation. The A and B copies of WORKER are joined in the WHERE clause by setting the WORKER_ID in B equal to the SUPV_ID in A. Thus, each row in A has attached to it the row from B containing the information about the A row's supervisor (Figure 13.3). By selecting the two worker names from each row we obtain the required list of workers paired with their supervisors:
A.WORKER_NAME represents the worker, and B.WORKER_NAME rep-

```
A. WORKER_NAME      B. WORKER_NAME
   M. Faraday          C. Coulomb
   C. Nemo             H. Rickover
   R. Garret           R. Garret
   P. Mason            P. Mason
   H. Rickover         H. Rickover
   C. Coulomb          C. Coulomb
   J. Barrister        P. Mason
```

resents the supervisor. Notice that some workers supervise themselves, as indicated by the fact that SUPV_ID = WORKER_ID for those workers.
More than two relations can be joined at once in SQL:

Query: List the names of workers assigned to office buildings.

FIGURE 13.3   Joining a Relation to Itself

A.WORKER_ID	A.WORKER_NAME	A.HRLY_RATE	A.SKILL_TYPE	A.SUPV_ID
1235	M. Faraday	12.50	Electric	1311
1412	C. Nemo	13.75	Plumbing	1520
2920	R. Garret	10.00	Roofing	2920
3231	P. Mason	17.40	Framing	3231
1520	H. Rickover	11.75	Plumbing	1520
1311	C. Coulomb	15.50	Electric	1311
3001	J. Barrister	8.20	Framing	3231

B.WORKER_ID	B.WORKER_NAME	B.HRLY_RATE	B.SKILL_TYPE	B.SUPV_ID
1311	C. Coulomb	15.50	Electric	1311
1520	H. Rickover	11.75	Plumbing	1520
2920	R. Garret	10.00	Roofing	2920
3231	P. Mason	17.40	Framing	3231
1520	H. Rickover	11.75	Plumbing	1520
1311	C. Coulomb	15.50	Electric	1311
3231	P. Mason	17.40	Framing	3231

We need to join all three relations to get the required data in one place. This is done in the following query:

```
SELECT WORKER_NAME
FROM WORKER, ASSIGNMENT, BUILDING
WHERE WORKER.WORKER_ID = ASSIGNMENT.WORKER_ID AND
      ASSIGNMENT.BLDG_ID = BUILDING.BLDG_ID AND
      TYPE = 'Office'
```
Result: WORKER_NAME
      M. Faraday
      C. Nemo
      R. Garret
      P. Mason
      H. Rickover
      J. Barrister

Notice that if a column name (for example, WORKER_ID or BLDG_ID) appears in more than one relation, we must prefix the column name by the originating relation name to eliminate ambiguity. But if the column name appears in only one relation, as does TYPE in this example, then there is no ambiguity, so the relation name need not be prefixed.

This SQL statement causes the creation of a single relation from the three relations in the database. The first two relations are joined on WORKER_ID after which the resulting relation is joined with the third relation on BLDG_ID. The condition

```
TYPE = 'Office'
```

in the WHERE clause causes all rows to be eliminated except those that apply to office buildings. This satisfies the requirement of the query.

Subqueries

subquery A query within a query.

A **subquery,** or "query within a query," can be placed within the WHERE clause of a query, resulting in the expansion of the WHERE clause's capability. Let's consider an example.

Query: What are the skill types of workers assigned to building 435?

We used this example to illustrate the join. Thus, subqueries give us at least a partial equivalent to the join.

```
SELECT SKILL_TYPE
FROM WORKER
WHERE WORKER_ID IN
     (SELECT WORKER_ID
      FROM ASSIGNMENT
      WHERE BLDG_ID = 435)
```

The subquery in this example is

```
(SELECT WORKER_ID
FROM ASSIGNMENT
WHERE BLDG_ID = 435)
```

The query that contains this subquery is called the **outer query** or the "main query." The subquery causes the following set of worker IDs to be generated:

```
WORKER_ID
  2920
  1412
  1311
```

This set of IDs then takes the place of the subquery in the outer query. At this point, the outer query is executed using the set generated by the subquery. The outer query causes each row in WORKER to be evaluated with respect to the WHERE clause. If the row's WORKER_ID is *IN* the set generated by the subquery, then the SKILL_TYPE of the row is selected and displayed as part of the result of the query:

```
SKILL_TYPE
 Plumbing
 Roofing
 Electric
```

It is very important that the SELECT clause of the subquery contain WORKER_ID and *only* WORKER_ID. Otherwise, the WHERE clause of the outer query, which states that WORKER_ID is IN a set of worker IDs, would not make sense.

Note that the subquery may logically be executed before any row is examined by the main query. In a sense, the subquery is independent of the main query. It could be executed as a query in its own right. We say that this kind of subquery is **noncorrelated** or not correlated to the main query. As we will see shortly, subqueries may also be "correlated."

Here is an example of a subquery within a subquery.

Query: List the names of workers assigned to office buildings.

Again, we are looking at a query we used to study the join.

```
SELECT WORKER_NAME
FROM WORKER
WHERE WORKER_ID IN
      (SELECT WORKER_ID
       FROM ASSIGNMENT
       WHERE BLDG_ID IN
            (SELECT BLDG_ID
             FROM BUILDING
             WHERE TYPE = 'Office'))
Result:  WORKER_NAME
         M. Faraday
         C. Nemo
         R. Garret
         P. Mason
         H. Rickover
         J. Barrister
```

Observe that we did not have to prefix any column names with relation names. This is so because each subquery deals with one and only one relation, so no ambiguity can result.

The evaluation of this query proceeds from the inside out. Thus, the innermost (or "bottom-most") subquery is evaluated first, then the subquery that contains it, followed by the outer query.

Correlated Subqueries ☐ The subqueries we have studied so far are independent of the main queries that use them. By this we mean that the subqueries could exist as queries in their own right. We are now going to look at a class of subqueries whose value upon execution depends on the row being examined by the main query. Such subqueries are called **correlated subqueries.**

correlated subquery A subquery whose result depends on the row being examined by an outer query.

> **Query:** List workers who receive a higher hourly wage than their supervisors.

The pivotal word in this query is "their." That is, the supervisor row to examine depends directly on the worker row being examined. This query can be solved by using a correlated subquery.

```
SELECT WORKER_NAME
FROM WORKER A
WHERE A.HRLY_RATE >
    (SELECT B.HRLY_RATE
    FROM WORKER B
    WHERE B.WORKER_ID = A.SUPV_ID)
```

> **Result:** WORKER_NAME
>   C. Nemo

The logical steps involved in executing this query are as follows:

1. The system makes two copies of the WORKER relation, copy A and copy B. As we have defined them, A refers to the worker, and B refers to the supervisor.
2. The system then examines each row of A. A given row is selected if it satisfies the condition in the WHERE clause. This condition states that the row will be selected if its HRLY_RATE is *greater than* the HRLY_RATE generated by the subquery.
3. The subquery selects the HRLY_RATE from the row of B whose WORKER_ID is equal to that of the SUPV_ID of the row of A currently being examined by the main query. This is the HRLY_RATE of A's supervisor.

Note that since A.HRLY_RATE can only be compared to a single value, the subquery must of necessity generate only one value. This value *changes depending on the row of A being examined.* Thus, the subquery is "correlated" to the main query. We will see other applications for correlated subqueries below when we study built-in functions.

Suppose we want to identify all the workers who are not assigned to a particular building. On the face of it, a query like this would seem easily solved by the simple negation of the affirmative version of the query. Suppose, for example, that the building of interest has the BLDG_ID 435. Then consider this "solution":

```
SELECT WORKER_ID
FROM ASSIGNMENT
WHERE BLDG_ID <>435
```

Unfortunately, this is a misformulation of the solution. This "solution" will merely give the IDs of the workers who are working on buildings other than building 435. Obviously, some of these workers may be assigned to building 435 as well.

A correct solution could utilize the NOT EXISTS operator:

```
SELECT WORKER_ID
FROM WORKER
WHERE NOT EXISTS
    (SELECT *
    FROM ASSIGNMENT
    WHERE ASSIGNMENT.WORKER_ID = WORKER.WORKER_ID AND
        BLDG_ID = 435)
```

Result: WORKER_ID
             1235
             3231
             1520
             3001

EXISTS operator Evaluates to true if resulting set is not empty.

NOT EXISTS operator Evaluates to true if resulting set is empty.

The **EXISTS** and **NOT EXISTS operators** always precede a subquery. EXISTS evaluates to "true" if the set resulting from the subquery is not empty. If the resulting set is empty, then the EXISTS operator evaluates to "false." The NOT EXISTS operator, naturally, works in precisely the opposite manner. It evaluates to "true" if the resulting set is empty and "false" otherwise.

In this example, we have used NOT EXISTS. The subquery selects all those rows in ASSIGNMENT that have the same WORKER_ID as the row currently being examined by the main query and a BLDG_ID equal to 435. If that set is empty, then the worker row being examined by the main query is selected, since that means that the worker in question does *not* work on building 435.

The solution we gave here involves a correlated subquery. If we use NOT IN instead of NOT EXISTS, we can use a noncorrelated subquery:

```
SELECT WORKER_ID
FROM WORKER
WHERE WORKER_ID NOT IN
    (SELECT WORKER_ID
    FROM ASSIGNMENT
    WHERE BLDG_ID = 435)
```

*This section may be omitted without loss of continuity.

This solution is also simpler than the solution using NOT EXISTS. It is natural to ask, therefore, why we should use EXISTS or NOT EXISTS at all. The answer is simply that NOT EXISTS provides the only means available to solve queries containing the "every" quantifier in their condition. In Chapter 8, we saw that such queries are solved with division in relational algebra and with the universal quantifier in relational calculus. The following is an example of a query containing "every" in its condition:

Query: `List workers who are assigned to every building.`

This query may be solved in SQL by using a double negative. We restate the query with such a double negative as follows:

Query: `List workers such that there is no building to which they are` *`not`* `assigned.`

We have emphasized the two negatives. It should be clear that this query is logically equivalent to the previous one.

Now we wish to formulate a solution in SQL. To make the final solution clearer we first give a solution to a preliminary problem: the problem of identifying the buildings to which a hypothetical worker, "1234," is *not* assigned.

```
(I)  SELECT BLDG_ID
     FROM BUILDING
     WHERE NOT EXISTS
         (SELECT *
         FROM ASSIGNMENT
         WHERE ASSIGNMENT.BLDG_ID = BUILDING.BLDG_ID AND
             ASSIGNMENT.WORKER_ID = 1234)
```

We have labeled this query (I) because we will refer to it below. If there are no buildings that satisfy this query, then worker 1234 must be assigned to *every* building and so would satisfy the original query. To obtain a solution to the original query then, our second step is to generalize query (I) from the specific worker 1234 to the variable WORKER_ID and to make this modified query a subquery in a larger query. The following accomplishes this:

```
(II) SELECT WORKER_ID
     FROM WORKER
     WHERE NOT EXISTS
         (SELECT BLDG_ID
         FROM BUILDING
         WHERE NOT EXISTS
             (SELECT *
             FROM ASSIGNMENT
             WHERE ASSIGNMENT.BLDG_ID = BUILDING.BLDG_ID AND
                 ASSIGNMENT.WORKER_ID = WORKER.WORKER_ID))
```

Observe that the subquery that starts on the fourth line of query (II) is identical to query (I) above, except that we have replaced "1234" with WORKER.WORKER_ID. Query (II) may be read as follows:

Select WORKER_ID from WORKER if there does not exist a building to which WORKER_ID is not assigned.

This satisfies the requirement of the original query.

We see then that NOT EXISTS can be used to formulate answers to the types of queries for which the division operation of relational algebra and the universal quantifier of relational calculus (Chapter 8) were needed. In terms of ease of use, however, the NOT EXISTS operator doesn't seem to offer any particular advantages. That is, it does not appear that SQL queries using NOT EXISTS twice are any easier to understand than solutions using division in relational algebra or universal quantifiers in relational calculus. Additional research needs to be done to develop language constructs that allow a more natural solution to these types of queries.

Built-In Functions

Consider questions like these:

What are the highest and lowest hourly wages? What is the average number of days that workers are assigned to building 435? What is the total number of days allocated for plumbing on building 312? How many different skill types are there?

built-in function Statistical function that operates on a set of rows—SUM, AVG, COUNT, MAX, MIN.

set function A built-in function.

These questions require statistical functions that examine a set of rows in a relation and produce a single value. SQL provides five such functions, called **built-in** or **set functions.** The five functions are SUM, AVG, COUNT, MAX, and MIN.

```
Query: What are the highest and lowest hourly wages?
    SELECT MAX(HRLY_RATE), MIN(HRLY_RATE)
    FROM WORKER
Result: 17.40, 8.20
```

The MAX and MIN functions operate on a single column in a relation. They select the largest or the smallest value, respectively, to be found in that column. The solution for this query does not include a WHERE clause. For most queries, this need not be the case, as our next example shows.

```
Query: What is the average number of days that workers
are assigned to building 435?
    SELECT AVG(NUM_DAYS)
    FROM ASSIGNMENT
    WHERE BLDG_ID = 435
Result: 12.33
```

To calculate the average, only rows in ASSIGNMENT for building 435 are considered. As is normally the case in SQL, the WHERE clause restricts consideration to these rows.

Query: What is the total number of days allocated for plumbing on building 312?
```
SELECT SUM(NUM_DAYS)
FROM ASSIGNMENT, WORKER
WHERE WORKER.WORKER_ID = ASSIGNMENT.WORKER_ID  AND
      SKILL_TYPE = 'Plumbing'  AND
      BLDG_ID = 312
```

Result: 27

This solution used the join of ASSIGNMENT and WORKER. This was necessary since SKILL_TYPE is in WORKER, and BLDG_ID is in ASSIGNMENT.

Query: How many different skill types are there?
```
SELECT COUNT (DISTINCT SKILL_TYPE)
FROM WORKER
```

Result: 4

DISTINCT Operator that eliminates duplicate rows.

Since the same skill type is repeated in several different rows, it is necessary to use the keyword "DISTINCT" in this query, so that the system will not count the same skill type more than once. **DISTINCT** may be used with any of the built-in functions, although, naturally, it is a redundant operator with the MAX and MIN functions.

SUM and AVG must be used with columns that are numeric. The other functions can be used either with numeric or with character string data. All the functions except COUNT may be used with computed expressions. For example:

Query: What is the average weekly wage?
```
SELECT AVG(40 * HRLY_RATE)
FROM WORKER
```

Result: 509.14

COUNT may refer to entire rows rather than just a single column:

Query: How many buildings have quality level 3?
```
SELECT COUNT(*)
FROM BUILDING
WHERE QLTY_LEVEL = 3
```

Result: 3

As all these examples show, if a built-in function appears in the SELECT clause, then nothing but built-in functions may appear in that SELECT clause. The only exception to this occurs in conjunction with the GROUP BY clause, which we now examine.

GROUP BY and HAVING

Management is often interested in knowing statistical information as it applies to each group in a set of groups. For example, consider the following query:

Query: `For each supervisor, what is the highest hourly wage paid to a worker reporting to that supervisor?`

To solve this query, we must divide the workers into groups, each reporting to a single supervisor. Then we determine the maximum wage paid in each group. We do this in SQL in this manner:

```
SELECT SUPV_ID, MAX(HRLY_RATE)
FROM WORKER
GROUP BY SUPV_ID
```

Result:

SUPV_ID	MAX(HRLY_RATE)
1311	15.50
1520	13.75
2920	10.00
3231	17.40

In processing this query, the system proceeds by first dividing the rows of WORKER into groups, using the following rule: Rows are placed in the same group if and only if they have the same SUPV_ID. Now the SELECT clause is applied to each group. Since a given group can have only one value for SUPV_ID, there is no ambiguity as to the value of SUPV_ID for that group. The SELECT clause calls for the SUPV_ID to be displayed and for the MAX(HRLY_RATE) to be calculated and displayed *for each group*. The result is as shown.

Only column names appearing in a GROUP BY clause may appear in a SELECT clause with a built-in function. Note that SUPV_ID can appear in the SELECT clause, since it appeared in the GROUP BY clause.

The **GROUP BY clause** suggests the possibility of doing some sophisticated computations. For example, we may want to know the average of all these maximum hourly rates. Computations within built-in functions are restricted, however, in that no built-in function may contain another built-in function. Thus an expression like

```
AVG(MAX(HRLY_RATE))
```

is illegal. Solving such a query would require two steps. The first step would place the maximum hourly rates in a new relation, and the second step would calculate the average of these.

It is permissible to use the WHERE clause with GROUP BY:

Query: `For each type of building, what is the average quality level for buildings of status 1?`
```
SELECT TYPE, AVG(QLTY_LEVEL)
FROM BUILDING
WHERE STATUS = 1
GROUP BY TYPE
```

> **GROUP BY clause** Indicates that rows should be grouped on a common value of specified column(s).

Result:

TYPE	AVG(QLTY_LEVEL)
Retail	1
Residence	3
Office	3.5

The WHERE clause is executed before the GROUP BY clause. Thus, no group may contain a row with a status other than 1. The rows of status 1 are grouped by TYPE and the SELECT clause is applied to each group.

HAVING clause Places conditions on groups.

We can also apply a condition to the groups formed by the GROUP BY clause. This is done with the **HAVING clause.** Suppose, for example, we wish to make one of the previous queries more specific.

> **Query:** For each supervisor *managing more than one worker,* what is the highest hourly wage paid to a worker reporting to that supervisor?

We could indicate this by the proper use of the HAVING clause:

```
SELECT SUPV_ID, MAX(HRLY_RATE)
FROM WORKER
GROUP BY SUPV_ID
HAVING COUNT(*) > 1
```

Result:

SUPV_ID	MAX(HRLY_RATE)
1311	15.50
1520	13.75
3231	17.40

The difference between the WHERE clause and the HAVING clause is that the WHERE clause is applied to *rows* while the HAVING clause is applied to *groups*.

A query may contain both a WHERE clause and a HAVING clause. In that case, the WHERE clause is applied first, since it applies before the groups are formed. For example, consider the following revision to a query given above:

> **Query:** For each type of building, what is the average quality level for buildings of status 1? Consider only those types of buildings having a maximum quality level no higher than 3.
> ```
> SELECT TYPE, AVG(QLTY_LEVEL)
> FROM BUILDING
> WHERE STATUS = 1
> GROUP BY TYPE
> HAVING MAX(QLTY_LEVEL) <=3
> ```

Result:

TYPE	
Retail	1
Residence	3

Observe that, starting with the FROM clause the clauses in SQL statements are applied in order, and then the SELECT clause is applied last.

Thus, the WHERE clause is applied to the BUILDING relation, and all rows having a STATUS other than 1 are eliminated. The rows remaining are grouped by TYPE, with all rows of the same TYPE being in the same group. This creates a number of groups—one for each value of TYPE. The HAVING clause is then applied to each of the groups, and those having a maximum quality level over 3 are elminated. Finally, the SELE CT clause is applied to the groups that remain.

Built-In Functions with Subqueries

A built-in function may appear only in a SELECT clause or a HAVING clause. However, a SELECT clause contianing a built-in funtion may be part of a subquery. In the following, we see an example of such a sub-query:

Query: Which workers receive a highger-than-average hourly wage?

```
SELECT WORKER_NAME
FROM WORKER
WHERE HRLY_RATE >
      (SELECT AVG(HRLY_RATE)
      FROM WORKER)
```

RESULT: WORKER_NAME
            C. Nemo
            P. Mason
            C. Coulomb

Note that this subquery is a noncorrelated subquery, which produces precisely one value—the average hourly wage. The main query selects a worker only if the hourly wage for that worker is above this calculated average.

Correlated subqueries may also be used with built-in functions:

Query: Which workers receive an hourly wage higher than the average of those workers reporting to the worker's supervisor?

In this case, instead of calculating a single average for all workers, we must calculate an average for each group of workers reporting to the same supervisor. Moreover, this calculation must be performed anew for each worker being examined by the main query.

```
SELECT A.WORKER_NAME
FROM WORKER A
WHERE A.HRLY_RATE >
      (SELECT AVG(B.HRLY_RATE)
       FROM WORKER B
       WHERE B.SUPV_ID = A.SUPV_ID)
```

Result: A. WORKER_NAME
            C. Nemo
            P. Mason
            C. Coulomb

The WHERE clause of the subquery contains the crucial correlation condition. This condition guarantees that the average will only be calculated for those workers having the same supervisor as the worker being examined by the main query.

Database Change Operations

SQL provides three database change operations, INSERT, UPDATE, and DELETE, to allow the addition of rows, the changing of values in rows, and the deletion of rows, respectively, to or from a specified relation in the database. We will discuss each of these separately.

INSERT Operation that causes rows to be added to a relation.

INSERT □ **INSERT** operations allow either a single row to be inserted into a relation, by the specification of values for columns in the row, or a set of rows to be inserted by the specification of a query defining the rows to be inserted.

```
INSERT INTO ASSIGNMENT (WORKER_ID, BLDG_ID, START_DATE)
VALUES (1284, 485, 05/13)
```

This statement inserts a single row into ASSIGNMENT. The names of the columns to which the respective values are to be given are shown in parentheses following the name of the table to be updated. Since we have omitted NUM_DAYS, a null value will be placed in that column of the inserted row.

Suppose we created a new relation named BUILDING_2 consisting of BLDG_ID, TYPE, and QLTY_LEVEL columns, and we wished to populate it with rows from BUILDING having status 2. Then we would use the second form of the INSERT statement.

```
INSERT INTO BUILDING_2
    SELECT BLDG_ID, TYPE, QLTY_LEVEL
    FROM BUILDING
    WHERE STATUS = 2
```

UPDATE Operation that changes column values in rows.

UPDATE □ **UPDATE** operations always apply to all the rows that satisfy the WHERE clause in the UPDATE statement. If we wanted to give everybody working for supervisor 1520 a 5% wage increase, the following statement would be needed:

```
UPDATE WORKER
SET HRLY_RATE = 1.05 * HRLY_RATE
WHERE SUPV_ID = 1520
```

If there is no WHERE clause, then the operation applies to every row in the relation. For example, if we wanted to give *every* worker a 5% increase, we would merely omit the WHERE clause from this UPDATE statement.

DELETE Operation that removes rows from a relation.

DELETE □ **DELETE** operations also apply to all rows that satisfy the WHERE clause in the DELETE statement. If there is no WHERE clause, then all rows in the relation are deleted. Suppose everybody working for supervisor 1520 has been laid off, and we wish to delete them from the database. Then this statement will do the job:

```
DELETE FROM WORKER
WHERE SUPV_ID = 1520
```

Using SQL with Data Processing Languages

The relational approach of using single statements to manipulate sets of rows in a relation is an advancement over the one-record-at-a-time data manipulation methods of traditional languages. Since SQL is intended to be used in large organizations which use traditional languages, however, a method is needed to allow the integration of SQL statements into programs of traditional languages. This is provided with embedded SQL.

embedded SQL A set of statements that allows SQL to be used with traditional programming languages.

host language Language of programs in which SQL statements can be embedded.

Embedded SQL provides a set of statements used to embed SQL statements in programs of languages like COBOL, C, and Pascal (called the **host language**). These statements include "flag" statements which notify a preprocessor that what follows should be replaced by CALLs to DBMS routines. They also include special facilities, called cursors, which allow single-record processing on the results of SQL queries.

The following is an example of embedded SQL code:

```
EXEC SQL
    DECLARE WORK_ASGNMNT CURSOR
    FOR
        SELECT *
        FROM ASSIGNMENT
        WHERE WORKER_ID = REQUESTED-WORKER-ID
END-EXEC
```

flag statements SQL statements embedded in an application program to signal the beginning or end of a set of SQL statements.

cursor Embedded SQL facility where the result of an SQL query is stored for subsequent processing.

OPEN cursor statement Embedded SQL statement that causes the DBMS to process a cursor's query and store its result in the cursor.

This code could be embedded in a program written in COBOL as the host language. The first line (EXEC SQL) and the last line (END-EXEC) are **flag statements** and indicate that the lines contained between them are SQL code. The COBOL program containing this SQL code would be processed by a "precompiler" before it is compiled. The precompiler recognizes the flag statements and replaces them with CALL statements to DBMS subprograms which at execution time will handle the SQL code. When the COBOL program is compiled, the compiler ignores the SQL CALL statements and compiles the remainder of the program.

The rest of our example contains an SQL declare cursor statement, which defines a cursor. A **cursor** is like a file, whose contents are generated at execution time. Notice that the definition of the cursor includes a SELECT statement. The WHERE clause references a column in ASSIGNMENT (WORKER_ID) and states that a row should be selected if WORKER_ID is equal to a variable in the (COBOL) program (REQUESTED-WORKER-ID). No data is selected until the cursor is *opened* by a separate statement. The **OPEN cursor statement**

```
OPEN WORK_ASGNMNT
```

will cause the DBMS to execute the SELECT statement. Individual rows placed in the cursor during execution of the OPEN can be retrieved by

FETCH statement A statement
that retrieves a single row from
an opened cursor.

the execution of a **FETCH statement,** which is analogous to a READ statement. Other statements are provided to allow the updating and deletion of data from database tables. A CLOSE statement removes the data from the cursor, so that it can be OPENed again with new data reflecting the current contents of the database.

Embedded SQL provides the interface needed for the successful use of SQL in the large scale batch and online programs of large processing organizations. With time, this need will probably decrease, as new languages emerge which are capable of making full use of the relation-at-a-time processing capability of SQL.

□ VIEW DEFINITION

base table A table that contains basic or "real" data.

Early in the chapter, we showed how tables are defined in a database schema. These tables are called **base tables,** because they contain the basic data of the database. Portions of these base tables as well as information derived from them can be defined in database views, which are also defined as part of the database schema.

view A definition of a restricted portion of the database.

A **view** is a window into a portion of the database. Views are useful for maintaining confidentiality by restricting access to selected parts of the database and for simplifying frequently used query types. For example, to preserve confidentiality, we may wish to create a view showing all information about workers except their hourly wage rate.

```
CREATE VIEW B_WORKER
AS   SELECT WORKER_ID, WORKER_NAME, SKILL_TYPE, SUPV_ID
     FROM WORKER
```

B_WORKER in this example is the name of the newly created view. The view name may be followed by the names of the columns in the view, enclosed in parentheses. In this case, we have omitted column names, so the view columns simply inherit their names from the relation they are taken from. The portion of this statement following the word "AS" is called a **query specification.** Any legal query specification may appear in a view definition.

query specification Definition of a query used in a view definition, cursor declaration, or other statement.

The system does not actually generate the data values for B_WORKER until it is accessed. At that time the query specification defining B_WORKER is executed, creating B_WORKER from the data that exists in WORKER at the time of execution. Thus, the data in views changes dynamically as the data in the underlying, base tables changes.

Suppose we are often interested in information about electricians, the buildings they are assigned to, and the starting date of the assignment. This view definition will work:

```
CREATE VIEW ELEC_ASSIGNMENT  AS
    SELECT WORKER_NAME, BLDG_ID, START_DATE
    FROM WORKER, ASSIGNMENT
    WHERE SKILL_TYPE = 'Electric'  AND
        WORKER.WORKER_ID = ASSIGNMENT.WORKER_ID
```

If ELEC_ASSIGNMENT were accessed, the system would first generate its data values. Using our database, ELEC_ASSIGNMENT would appear as follows:

```
ELEC_ASSIGNMENT
WORKER_NAME     BLDG_ID     START_DATE
  M. Faraday       312         10/10
  M. Faraday       515         10/17
  C. Coulomb       435         10/08
  C. Coulomb       460         10/23
```

Views may be queried. Suppose we are interested in the electricians assigned to building 435.

Query: Who are the electricians assigned to building 435 and when do they start work?
```
    SELECT WORKER_NAME, START_DATE
    FROM ELEC_ASSIGNMENT
    WHERE BLDG_ID = 435
```
Result: C. Coulomb 10/08

The system first created the relation shown above, and then the query was applied to that relation.

We may also use the result of a grouping operation to define a view. Let's take another look at a query given earlier that derived supervisors together with the maximum hourly rate of workers reporting to them:

```
CREATE VIEW MAX_WAGE (SUPV_ID, MAX_HRLY_RATE) AS
    SELECT SUPV_ID, MAX(HRLY_RATE)
    FROM WORKER
    GROUP BY SUPV_ID
```

Notice that in this example we have included names for the columns in the view. These immediately follow the name of the view (MAX_WAGE). It was necessary to include column names in this case, because one of the columns is a computation from a built-in function and has no name it can inherit.

Restrictions on View Queries and Updates

A view that is defined with a GROUP BY clause in the query specification is called a "grouped view." In ANSI standard SQL, there are severe limitations on queries on grouped views. These limitations are:

1. The SELECT clause of a query on a grouped view may not contain a built-in function.
2. The FROM clause may contain no other table or view names than the name of the grouped view.
3. There may be no WHERE, GROUP BY, or HAVING clauses.

Users will frequently want to update the database by referring to a view. A view can be updated only if its defining query specification:

1. Has only column names (i.e., no computations or literals) in the SELECT clause;
2. Has only one table name in the FROM clause;

3. Has no subquery in its WHERE clause;

4. Does not contain a GROUP BY or HAVING clause.

Of course, base tables can be updated without these restrictions. If a view does not allow update, then the base tables themselves must be accessed to achieve the desired update.

☐ THE SYSTEM CATALOG

metadata Descriptive information about databases.

system catalog Database containing metadata.

One of Codd's criteria for a DBMS to be "fully relational" (Codd, 1985) is that system information describing the database be maintained in relational tables, just as all other data values. This descriptive information, or **metadata,** is normally maintained in the data dictionary, a version of which is sometimes called the **system catalog**. IBM's DB2 system catalog conforms to this requirement, since it is structured as a set of tables, each row of which provides descriptive information about some database object, such as a table, a column, or an index. In this section, we give a brief description of DB2's catalog and some of its features.

The catalog tables have predefined names and functions, with each table having a primary key. The tables themselves are linked via foreign keys that point from one table to another. The following are some examples of catalog tables:

SYSDATABASE—each row contains data about a database

SYSTABLES—each row contains data about a table

SYSCOLUMNS—each row contains data about a column

SYSINDEXES—each row contains data about an index

SYSLINKS—each row contains data about a primary key/foreign key link between two tables

Not only does the catalog contain information about user database tables, but it also contains information about itself as well. For example, *for each table in each database* SYSLINKS indicates which columns in the table are a foreign key referencing another identified table in the database. SYSLINKS therefore contains linking information about the tables in the system catalog database (named SYSIBM). Thus, since SYSCOLUMNS (a table in SYSIBM) references SYSTABLES (another table in SYSIBM), some column(s) within SYSCOLUMNS must be a foreign key referencing SYSTABLES. SYSLINKS will indicate which columns these are. Consequently, the catalog is completely self-contained.

An important advantage of the relational structure of DB2's catalog is that authorized users can query the catalog using SQL. For example, suppose an auditor knows very little about the Premier Construction Company database but, for auditing purposes, needs to access it. The following query will list the names of all the tables and views in the database named "Premier":

```
SELECT NAME
FROM SYSTABLES
WHERE DBNAME = 'Premier'
```

NAME and DBNAME are columns in the SYSTABLES table identifying the table name and the database name, respectively. If only views are desired, the query can be modified as follows:

```
SELECT NAME
FROM SYSTABLES
WHERE DBNAME = 'Premier' AND TYPE = 'V'
```

The TYPE column in SYSTABLES identifies whether the table is a base table ('B') or a view ('V').

If the user needs to know descriptive information about the columns in the WORKER table, the following query can be used:

```
SELECT NAME, COLTYPE, LENGTH, NULLS
FROM SYSCOLUMNS
WHERE TBNAME = 'WORKER'
```

TBNAME is a column in SYSCOLUMNS which gives the column's table name. This query will provide the name, the data type (COLTYPE), and the length of each column in WORKER. For each column, it will also indicate whether the column can contain null values.

Other queries can determine whether an index has been created for a table, how many indexes exist for the table, what key columns are used for each index, and so forth. Also, the primary key/foreign key links among all tables can be identified. Many other types of system information, relating both to the logical definition and the physical structure of the databases controlled by DB2 can be obtained from the catalog through the formulation of SQL queries.

The advantages of the relational structure of the system catalog should be clear. An existing, and very powerful, query language can be used to ask a large variety of questions relating to the structure of the system databases. Earlier, non-relational systems do not automatically have such advantages.

■ SUMMARY

In this chapter, we studied aspects of relational database implementations with the SQL query language. We briefly reviewed the historical development of SQL systems; we showed how SQL database schemas can be defined; we studied the SQL data manipulation language in detail; we outlined view definition; and we gave a brief introduction to the system catalog of IBM's DB2, an SQL relational DBMS for large mainframes.

SQL originated at IBM during the seventies, as part of the System R project. Since that time, it has been implemented by a large variety of commercial vendors as the language of their relational DBMS. It is available in both the mainframe and microcomputer environments, and it has become the ANSI standard for relational languages.

SQL database schemas are defined through CREATE SCHEMA and CREATE TABLE commands. These define specific schemas and their owners, tables, and columns. Keys can also be defined.

SQL data manipulation includes all of the relational algebra capability defined by Codd; yet, it is based on a relational calculus structure.

In addition, SQL provides the capability of grouping rows on a common value for a specified column and of calculating statistical functions for these groups. Data manipulation also allows the insertion, update, and deletion of single rows as well as groups of rows. Finally, SQL statements can be embedded in traditional programs written in languages such as COBOL, C, or Pascal. Through cursors, SQL statements can generate query results which can be processed one row at a time by the program written in the host language.

Views are defined in the database schema by using the SQL query language. Views can be queried, and, under certain conditions, they can be updated.

The system catalog in a "truly relational" system should be structured as a relational database. We saw how DB2 satisfies this requirement. Distinct advantages are found in systems that have catalogs with this structure. In particular, the catalog can be queried using the same language as is used for normal database queries. We saw several examples of this in SQL.

■ REVIEW QUESTIONS

1. Define each of the following terms in your own words:

   a. schema owner
   b. character string literals
   c. comparison
   d. Boolean connectives
   e. outer query
   f. correlated subquery
   g. built-in function
   h. DISTINCT
   i. GROUP BY clause
   j. INSERT
   k. DELETE
   l. embedded SQL
   m. host language
   n. cursor
   o. FETCH
   p. view
   q. query specification
   r. system catalog

2. Briefly describe the early development of SQL. Which vendor was the first to offer a commercial release of SQL? Describe the variety of systems on which SQL is now available.

3. What are the SQL commands used to define a database schema? How can a single column or a multicolumn key be defined?

4. Describe the kinds of things that can be found in each of these SQL clauses:

   a. SELECT
   b. FROM
   c. WHERE
   d. GROUP BY
   e. HAVING
   f. ORDER BY

5. How are query specifications used in each data change operation?

6. Describe how a cursor works.

7. What is a database view and how can it be used?

8. Describe how SQL can be used with the system catalog to obtain information about a database.

■ PROBLEMS AND EXERCISES

1. Match each term with its definition.

__Alias   a. Contains basic or "real" data

__Subquery   b. Alternate name given to a relation

__FROM clause   c. Lists the existing tables referenced by the query

__Cartesian product   d. Evaluates to true if resulting set is *not* empty

__Noncorrelated subquery e. Gives the condition for selecting rows from identified tables

__EXISTS operator   f. A built-in function

__Schema definition   g. Query involving only one database table

__Set function   h. Operation that changes column values in rows

__HAVING clause   i. Evaluates to true if resulting set is empty

__UPDATE   j. Causes the DBMS to process a cursor's query and store its result in the cursor

__Simple query   k. Result of pairing each row in one table with every row in another table

__NOT EXISTS operator   l. Its value does not depend on any outer query

__SELECT clause   m. Description of a database to the DBMS

__Flag statement   n. Places conditions on groups

__Base table   o. Signals beginning or end of a set of SQL statements

__Metadata   p. A query within a query

__WHERE clause   q. Identifies the columns desired in the query

__OPEN cursor   r. Descriptive information about databases

2. Write the SQL commands to create a database schema for the following relational schema:

```
CUSTOMER (CUST_ID, CUST_NAME, ANNUAL_REVENUE)
SHIPMENT (SHIPMENT_#, CUST_ID, WEIGHT, TRUCK_#, DESTINATION)
Foreign Key: DESTINATION REFERENCES CITY_NAME IN CITY
TRUCK (TRUCK_#, DRIVER_NAME)
CITY (CITY_NAME, POPULATION)
```

Use the schema created in exercise 2 to express the following queries in SQL.

Simple Queries

3. a. What is the name of customer 433?

    b. What is the destination city of shipment #3244?

    c. What are the truck numbers of trucks that have carried packages (shipments) weighing over 100 pounds?

d. Give all data for shipments weighing over 20 pounds.

e. Create an alphabetical list of names of customers with more than $10 million in annual revenue.

f. What is the customer ID for Wilson Brothers?

g. Give names and average monthly revenue of customers having annual revenue exceeding $5 million but less than $10 million.

h. Give IDs for customers who have sent packages (shipments) to Chicago, St. Louis, or Baltimore.

Joins

4. a. What are the names of customers who have sent packages (shipments) to Sioux City?

b. To what destinations have companies with revenue less than $1 million sent packages?

c. What are the names and populations of cities that have received shipments weighing over 100 pounds?

d. Who are the customers having over $5 million in annual revenue who have sent shipments weighing less than 1 pound?

e. Who are the customers having over $5 million in annual revenue who have sent shipments weighing less than 1 pound or have sent a shipment to San Francisco?

f. Who are the drivers who have delivered shipments for customers with annual revenue over $20 million to cities with population over 1 million?

Subqueries

5. a. List the cities that have received shipments from customers having over $15 million in annual revenue.

b. List the names of drivers who have delivered shipments weighing over 100 pounds.

c. List the name and annual revenue of customers who have sent shipments weighing over 100 pounds.

d. List the name and annual revenue of customers whose shipments have been delivered by truck driver Jensen.

NOT EXISTS

6. a. List customers who have had shipments delivered by every driver.

b. List cities that have received shipments from every customer.

c. List drivers who have delivered shipments to every city.

Built-In Functions

7. a. What is the average weight of a shipment?

b. What is the average weight of a shipment going to Atlanta?

c. How many shipments has customer 433 sent?

d. Which cities in the database have the largest and smallest populations?

e. What is the total weight of packages (shipments) carried in truck 82?

f. Give a list of customers and annual revenue for those customers whose annual revenue is the maximum for the customers in the database. (Hint: Use a subquery.)

g. Give a list of customers, all of whose shipments weigh over 25 pounds. (Hint: Use a correlated subquery.)

h. Give a list of customers who send all their shipments to a single city. (Note: The city may or may not be the same for each of these customers.)

GROUP BY and HAVING

8. a. For each customer, what is the average weight of a package (shipment) sent by that customer?

b. For each city, what is the maximum weight of a package sent to that city?

c. For each city with population over 1 million, what is the minimum weight of a package sent to that city?

d. For each city that has received at least 10 packages, what is the average weight of a package sent to that city?

Database Change Operations

9. Write database change operations to accomplish each of the following:

a. Add truck 95 with driver Winston.

b. Delete all cities from the database with population under 5000. Don't forget to update the SHIPMENT relation.

c. Convert the weight of every shipment to kilograms by dividing the weight by 2.2.

Cursors

10. Create a cursor declaration which will identify all information about customers who have sent a shipment to a city with more than 500,000 population.

Views

11. Create views for each of the following:

a. Customers with annual revenue under $1 million.

b. Customers with annual revenue between $1 million and $5 million.

c. Customers with annual revenue over $5 million.

12. Use these views to answer the following queries:

a. Which drivers have taken shipments to Los Angeles for customers with revenue over $5 million?

b. What are the populations of cities which have received shipments from customers with revenue between $1 million and $5 million?

c. Which drivers have taken shipments to cities for customers with revenue under $1 million, and what are the populations of those cities?

1. Write a research paper on the development of SQL from its earliest stages at IBM. Discuss its first commercial releases from Oracle and IBM, its status as the ANSI standard, and recent mainframe and microcomputer releases.

2. Write a research paper that critiques the ANSI standard of SQL. Compare this standard with two or three commercial products.

3. tudy embedded SQL in detail. Determine how it interfaces with one or two host languages.

4. Study the system catalogs of two different relational database management systems. How can they be used with SQL to provide information to users?

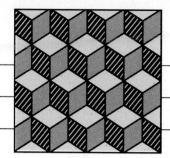

chapter fourteen

RELATIONAL IMPLEMENTATION WITH QUERY-BY-EXAMPLE

"How do you like working with the system now that we've added Query-by-Example, Irv?"

Annette Chang is interested in users' reactions to the new relational database query language that Premier Construction Company has recently installed. She's talking with Irv Bernstein, company controller.

"Annette, I can honestly say that I never thought any computer language would be so easy to use. Once I understood how the data tables were laid out, it was easy to see how to construct queries. Of course, I'm only using simple queries now, and I might not find it so easy to use as my needs grow more sophisticated."

"I think you'll find that for most of the things you want to do, the language is easy to understand. I will be glad to help you with any queries that you feel you can't solve; but I think that in any case, you'll be on your own in a very short time."

Query-by-Example is a graphical version of the SQL relational data language. It is particularly well suited to the needs of the typical user. In this chapter, you will become familiar with many of the features of this language. After reading this chapter, you should be able to:

☐ Discuss some of the background and historical facts relating to the theoretical and commercial implementation of Query-by-Example (QBE).

☐ Develop solutions to a large variety of queries in QBE.

☐ Make changes to the database in QBE.

☐ Evaluate the strengths and weaknesses of QBE as a relational language.

☐ INTRODUCTION

Query-by-Example (QBE) was developed during the seventies at IBM's Thomas J. Watson Research Center (Zloof 1975). The time of its development roughly parallels that of SQL, and the two languages are logically similar. QBE has been released as a commercial product for some time now and is commonly used as a query tool by end-users. Typically, QBE is supported when SQL is also supported, and the tables accessed by QBE are defined through the SQL table definition facility.

Both languages are supported in the Query Management Facility (QMF) offered by IBM. QMF is a shell program that provides a user interface to QBE and SQL. Users interact with QMF through online terminals using menu screens and function keys. The user selects either of the two languages and formats and executes queries in the selected language. QMF then provides means for printing the results of these queries in reports with formatting that includes headings and other standard features.

QBE is also supported by other vendors. Borland, for example, offers Paradox as a full-functioned version of QBE which includes table definition. Although the syntax is slightly different from IBM's, the language is basically the same. Lotus 1-2-3 also provides a simple database query language which uses an approach similar to that of QBE. Because QBE allows nontechnical users to formulate queries so easily, it is likely to remain an important part of commercial database systems for some time.

In this chapter, we will study the data manipulation features of QBE in some detail. We will use the IBM commercial implementation as our standard.

☐ DATA MANIPULATION

textual language A computer language whose statements consist of character string symbols.

graphical language A computer language that uses pictorial representations to solve problems.

Traditional computer languages are **textual,** providing for the formulation of problem solutions in textual character string symbols. QBE, however, is a **graphical** language that structures query solutions by means of pictorial representations of database tables. By placing symbols in the proper places in table columns, the user can specify query selection conditions, grouping, data display, and database update operations.

Although QBE is a graphical language, it has many structural similarities with SQL. Both languages support a similar array of conditional expressions, built-in functions, grouping, multiple-table queries, and the like. There are also areas of difference between the two languages. In particular, some SQL features do not appear in QBE. We will point out the most important similarities and differences as our discussion proceeds. Except as noted, we will use the same queries to illustrate QBE features as we used for SQL. The resulting data values will therefore be the same.

Since most QBE systems use databases that have been defined using SQL data definition commands, we will not discuss data definition in QBE.

Simple Queries

simple query A query involving only one database table.

example table In QBE, a skeleton table showing the table name and the column names above blank spaces used for entry of query conditions.

As with SQL, we will first investigate **simple queries** involving only one database table.

As a graphical language, QBE must provide some means for the user to interact graphically with the database. This is done through the display of skeleton tables or, in QBE terminology, **example tables.** By executing a system command, the user can cause the display of an example table for any table in the database. A sample database is shown in Figure 14.1, and Figure 14.2 shows example tables for each of the three tables in the database. In each case, the name of the table appears in the first column, followed in order by the names of each of the table's columns. A blank space is left below each of these table and column names, allowing user query input. We will now illustrate the use of example tables through sample queries.

Query: Who are the plumbers?

The QBE solution appears in Figure 14.3. We have placed "P." below the WORKER_NAME column to indicate that we want the value in that column displayed (or "printed"). This is equivalent to placing WORKER_NAME in the SELECT clause of an SQL statement. By placing the literal value "Plumbing" in the SKILL_TYPE column, we are stating the con-

```
WORKER
WORKER_ID   WORKER_NAME    HRLY_RATE    SKILL_TYPE    SUPV_ID
  1235      M. Faraday       12.50       Electric       1311
  1412      C. Nemo          13.75       Plumbing       1520
  2920      R. Garret        10.00       Roofing        2920
  3231      P. Mason         17.40       Framing        3231
  1520      H. Rickover      11.75       Plumbing       1520
  1311      C. Coulomb       15.50       Electric       1311
  3001      J. Barrister      8.20       Framing        3231


ASSIGNMENT
WORKER_ID      BLDG_ID     START_DATE    NUM_DAYS
  1235           312         10/10          5
  1412           312         10/01         10
  1235           515         10/17         22
  2920           460         10/05         18
  1412           460         12/08         18
  2920           435         10/28         10
  2920           210         11/10         15
  3231           111         10/10          8
  1412           435         10/15         15
  1412           515         11/05          8
  3231           312         10/24         20
  1520           515         10/09         14
  1311           435         10/08         12
  1412           210         11/15         12
  1412           111         12/01          4
  3001           111         10/08         14
  1311           460         10/23         24
  1520           312         10/30         17
  3001           210         10/27         14


BUILDING
BLDG_ID      BLDG_ADDRESS      TYPE       QLTY_LEVEL    STATUS
  312        123 Elm          Office          2           2
  435        456 Maple        Retail          1           1
  515        789 Oak          Residence       3           1
  210        1011 Birch       Office          3           1
  111        1213 Aspen       Office          4           1
  460        1415 Beech       Warehouse       3           3
```

FIGURE 14.1 Premier Construction Company Database

FIGURE 14.2 Example Tables

WORKER	WORKER_ID	WORKER_NAME	HRLY_RATE	SKILL_TYPE	SUPV_ID

ASSIGNMENT	WORKER_ID	BLDG_ID	START_DATE	NUM_DAYS

BUILDING	BLDG_ID	BLDG_ADDRESS	TYPE	QLTY_LEVEL	STATUS

FIGURE 14.3

WORKER	WORKER_ID	WORKER_NAME	HRLY_RATE	SKILL_TYPE	SUPV_ID
		P.		Plumbing	

dition that only those rows having SKILL_TYPE equal to "Plumbing" should be selected.

Notice that the QBE command in this example is followed by a period. Thus, "P." is the display command. The literal value "Plumbing" indicates a data selection condition. QBE commands always end with a period, and literal values appear exactly as they are normally written. The result of the query is shown in Figure 14.4. Notice that the result is a relational table, as is always the case with relational languages.

FIGURE 14.4

WORKER_NAME
C. Nemo
H. Rickover

Query: List all data about office buildings.

In the QBE solution (Figure 14.5), the "P." appears below the table name, indicating that the entire row for each office building should be displayed. "Office" appears under TYPE as the qualifying condition for selecting rows.

FIGURE 14.5

BUILDING	BLDG_ID	BLDG_ADDRESS	TYPE	QLTY_LEVEL	STATUS
P.			Office		

Result:

BLDG_ID	BLDG_ADDRESS	TYPE	QLTY_LEVEL	STATUS
312	123 Elm	Office	2	2
210	1011 Birch	Office	3	1
111	1213 Aspen	Office	4	1

Query: What is the weekly wage rate for each electrician?

target table In QBE, a table without column headings that is used to define query output.

In this QBE solution (Figure 14.6), we have introduced a second table having no column headings. Such a table is called a **target table,** because it contains information about the final result, or the "target," of the query. In this query, it is the equivalent of the SELECT clause of SQL. Note that "P." appears in the first column of the target table. This means that every column in the target table is to be displayed. The second and fourth columns contain the example elements _WN and _HR. An **example element** is a variable that represents a typical, unspecified value of a column in a table. In this case, the example elements are defined in columns three and four of the example table shown above the target table. Note that QBE variables begin with an underscore (_). Since _WN is in the WORKER_NAME column, it stands for any possible value in this column of the WORKER relation. Similarly, _HR stands for the corresponding HRLY_RATE. In this query, we have shown both a computation (column 4 of the target table) and a literal value (column 3 of the target table).

example element In QBE, a variable representing an unspecified value in a column of a table.

FIGURE 14.6

WORKER	WORKER_ID	WORKER_NAME	HRLY_RATE	SKILL_TYPE	SUPV_ID
		_WN	_HR	Electric	
P.	_WN	'Weekly Wage Rate = '	40 * _HR		

Result: WORKER_NAME
C. Coulomb   Weekly Wage Rate = 620.00
M. Faraday   Weekly Wage Rate = 500.00

Query: Who gets an hourly rate less than $10?

We have given this new query to illustrate the specification of simple comparison conditions in QBE (Fig. 14.7). Note that the condition,

   < 10

can be placed right in the example table.

FIGURE 14.7

WORKER	WORKER_ID	WORKER_NAME	HRLY_RATE	SKILL_TYPE	SUPV_ID
		P.	< 10		

Result: WORKER_NAME
J. Barrister

Query: Who are the plumbers receiving over $12 per hour?

The solution (Fig. 14.8) to this new query shows that a compound condition can be expressed in an example table. The conditions in this table are equivalent to:

   HRLY_RATE > 12 AND SKILL_TYPE = 'Plumbing'

That is, when two conditions appear on the same line in an example table,

---

FIGURE 14.8

WORKER	WORKER_ID	WORKER_NAME	HRLY_RATE	SKILL_TYPE	SUPV_ID
P.			> 12	Plumbing	

both conditions must hold for a row to be selected. In this case, we chose to display all data from the selected rows, so we placed "P." in the first column.

Result:

WORKER_ID	WORKER_NAME	HRLY_RATE	SKILL_TYPE	SUPV_ID
1412	C. Nemo	13.75	Plumbing	1520

Query: List workers who are plumbers or who are receiving over $12 per hour.

The solution (Figure 14.9) to this new query illustrates that conditions

WORKER	WORKER_ID	WORKER_NAME	HRLY_RATE	SKILL_TYPE	SUPV_ID
		P.	P. > 12	P.	
		P.	P.	P. Plumbing	

FIGURE 14.9

specified on two different lines of a QBE query are equivalent to conditions connected by a Boolean OR. Note the placement of the "P." command. It appears on both lines and in every column that is to be displayed.

Result:

WORKER_NAME	HRLY_RATE	SKILL_TYPE
M. Faraday	12.50	Electric
C. Nemo	13.75	Plumbing
P. Mason	17.40	Framing
H. Rickover	11.75	Plumbing
C. Coulomb	15.50	Electric

Query: Who gets an hourly rate between $10 and $12?

The solution appears in Figure 14.10.

FIGURE 14.10

WORKER	WORKER_ID	WORKER_NAME	HRLY_RATE	SKILL_TYPE	SUPV_ID
P.			_HR		

CONDITIONS
_HR >= 10 AND _HR <= 12

Result:

WORKER_ID	WORKER_NAME	HRLY_RATE	SKILL_TYPE	SUPV_ID
2920	R. Garret	10.00	Roofing	2920
1520	H. Rickover	11.75	Plumbing	1520

condition box In QBE, a box in which a complex query condition can be expressed.

To solve this query, we have introduced a **condition box.** This box, labeled CONDITIONS, contains any constraints on data values that the user desires. In this example, since two conditions apply simultaneously to values in the same column, it is convenient to create a single condition, using a Boolean AND, and place it in the condition box.

Multiple-Table Queries

multiple-table query A query involving more than one table.

The most important aspect of **multiple-table queries** involves connecting data *across* tables, or, in other words, joining tables. We now see how to perform a join in QBE.

Query: What are the skill types of workers assigned to building 435?

WORKER	WORKER_ID	WORKER_NAME	HRLY_RATE	SKILL_TYPE	SUPV_ID
	_WI			P.	

ASSIGNMENT	WORKER_ID	BLDG_ID	START_DATE	NUM_DAYS
	_WI	435		

FIGURE 14.11

The important thing to notice in the QBE solution (Fig. 14.11) to this query is that the same example element, _WI, appears in both example tables, WORKER and ASSIGNMENT. This is how a join condition is expressed in QBE. It means that a selected *pair* of rows from the two tables must have the *same value* for the two respective columns. We chose _WI as the example element since it is an appropriate abbreviation of the column name, WORKER_ID. We could have chosen another example element, such as _X, but that would not have been meaningful in this context. Additionally, the literal 435 is placed in the BLDG_ID column of ASSIGNMENT to indicate that only rows for building 435 should be considered. Finally, the "P." in the SKILL_TYPE column means the value in that column will be displayed.

Result: SKILL_TYPE
Plumbing
Roofing
Electric

Query: List workers with the names of their supervisors.

The solution (Fig. 14.12) to this query illustrates the ease with which a relation can be joined to itself in QBE. Observe that by using the example element _SI in both example tables, we have required that SUPV_ID in the first copy of WORKER be equal to WORKER_ID in the second copy of WORKER. The WORKER_NAME column from both tables is then displayed as shown in the target table. The second column represents the supervisor's name. It is assumed in the database that workers having no supervisors are their own supervisors.

FIGURE 14.12

WORKER	WORKER_ID	WORKER_NAME	HRLY_RATE	SKILL_TYPE	SUPV_ID
		_WN			_SI

WORKER	WORKER_ID	WORKER_NAME	HRLY_RATE	SKILL_TYPE	SUPV_ID
	_SI	_SN			

P.	_WN	_SN			

400 PART FOUR/DATABASE SYSTEM IMPLEMENTATION

Result:	WORKER_NAME	WORKER_NAME
	M. Faraday	C. Coulomb
	C. Nemo	H. Rickover
	R. Garret	R. Garret
	P. Mason	P. Mason
	H. Rickover	H. Rickover
	C. Coulomb	C. Coulomb
	J. Barrister	P. Mason

Query: List the names of workers assigned to office buildings.

The solution (Fig. 14.13) to this query illustrates the joining of three tables. It is hard to imagine such a join being more easily or clearly accomplished than it is here in QBE. The power of graphical programming should be obvious from this example.

FIGURE 14.13

WORKER	WORKER_ID	WORKER_NAME	HRLY_RATE	SKILL_TYPE	SUPV_ID
	_WI	P.			

ASSIGNMENT	WORKER_ID	BLDG_ID	START_DATE	NUM_DAYS
	_WI	_BI		

BUILDING	BLDG_ID	BLDG_ADDRESS	TYPE	QLTY_LEVEL	STATUS
	_BI		Office		

Result:	WORKER_NAME
	M. Faraday
	C. Nemo
	R. Garret
	P. Mason
	H. Rickover
	J. Barrister

Query: List workers who receive a higher hourly wage than their supervisors.

We have once again joined WORKER to itself (Fig. 14.14). This time, how-

FIGURE 14.14

WORKER	WORKER_ID	WORKER_NAME	HRLY_RATE	SKILL_TYPE	SUPV_ID
		_WN P.	_WR		_SI

WORKER	WORKER_ID	WORKER_NAME	HRLY_RATE	SKILL_TYPE	SUPV_ID
	_SI		_SR		

CONDITIONS
_WR > _SR

ever, we needed a condition box to select only those workers who receive a higher wage than their supervisors. The condition box is the only means available for comparing values in two different columns. Note that this query was solved with a correlated subquery in our SQL discussion.

Result: WORKER_NAME
C. Nemo

Built-In Functions

built-in function Statistical function that operates on a set of rows—SUM, AVG, MAX, MIN, CNT.

QBE also supports **built-in** (or statistical) **functions,** as does SQL. These are used to find the largest and smallest elements in a column, to calculate the average or total value of a column, and to count the total number of elements in a column. The built-in functions have the names MAX., MIN., AVG., SUM., and CNT. (count) in QBE. They may appear in target tables or condition boxes.

Query: What are the highest and lowest hourly wages?

The solution appears in Figure 14.15.

FIGURE 14.15

WORKER	WORKER_ID	WORKER_NAME	HRLY_RATE _HR	SKILL_TYPE	SUPV_ID
P.	MAX._HR	MIN._HR			

Result: 17.40, 8.20

This result, consisting of two values, can be thought of as a two-column table with one row. The column headings could be MAX_RATE and MIN_RATE. Thus, the result of every query is still a relational table.

Query: What is the average number of days that workers are assigned to building 435?

The solution appears in Figure 14.16.

FIGURE 14.16

ASSIGNMENT	WORKER_ID	BLDG_ID	START_DATE	NUM_DAYS
		435		_ND
P.	AVG._ND			

Result: 12.33

Query: What is the total number of days allocated for plumbing on building 312?

The solution appears in Figure 14.17.

The solution appears in Figure 14.17.

FIGURE 14.17

WORKER	WORKER_ID	WORKER_NAME	HRLY_RATE	SKILL_TYPE	SUPV_ID
	_WI			Plumbing	

ASSIGNMENT	WORKER_ID	BLDG_ID	START_DATE	NUM_DAYS
	_WI	312		_ND

P.	SUM._ND			

Result: 27

Query: How many different skill types are there?

The UNQ. operator (Fig. 14.18) guarantees that only unique occurrences of skill type will be counted. That is, duplicates will be discarded in figuring the count.

FIGURE 14.18

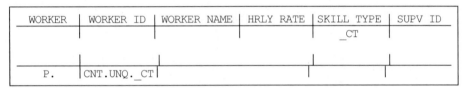

WORKER	WORKER_ID	WORKER_NAME	HRLY_RATE	SKILL_TYPE	SUPV_ID
				_CT	
P.	CNT.UNQ._CT				

Result: 4

Query: What is the average weekly wage?

The solution appears in Figure 14.19.

FIGURE 14.19

WORKER	WORKER_ID	WORKER_NAME	HRLY_RATE	SKILL_TYPE	SUPV_ID
			_HR		
P.	AVG.(40*_HR)				

Result: 509.14

Query: How many buildings have quality level 3?

The solution appears in Figure 14.20.

FIGURE 14.20

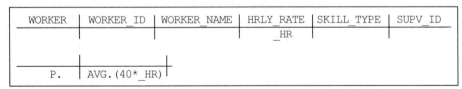

BUILDING	BLDG_ID	BLDG_ADDRESS	TYPE	QLTY_LEVEL	STATUS
	_BI			3	
P.	CNT._BI				

403

Result: 3

Group By Just as in SQL, we can group rows having a common value in one or more columns. This means that the rows of a relation are split into groups, one group for each value of a designated column. Statistical functions can then be applied to each group.

> **Query:** For each supervisor, what is the highest hourly wage paid to a worker reporting to that supervisor?

"G." indicates the grouping column (Fig. 14.21). In this case, we are grouping by SUPV_ID, since we want the maximum wage of workers by supervisor. The target table is then used to indicate the display of the grouping column together with any built-in functions that apply to the groups.

FIGURE 14.21

WORKER	WORKER ID	WORKER NAME	HRLY RATE _HR	SKILL TYPE	SUPV ID G. _SI
P.	_SI	MAX._HR			

Result:

SUPV_ID	
1311	15.50
1520	13.75
2920	10.00
3231	17.40

And of course we can combine grouping with the specification of conditions.

> **Query:** For each type of building, what is the average quality level for buildings of status 1?

The solution appears in Figure 14.22.

FIGURE 14.22

BUILDING	BLDG_ID	BLDG_ADDRESS	TYPE G. _T	QLTY_LEVEL _QL	STATUS 1
P.	_T	AVG._QL			

Result:

TYPE	
Retail	1
Residence	3
Office	3.5

Query: For each supervisor managing more than one worker, what is the highest hourly wage paid to a worker reporting to that supervisor?

In the solution (Fig. 14.23), the condition in the condition box states that each group must have more than one row. Thus, the condition box in this example is equivalent to the HAVING clause of SQL.

FIGURE 14.23

WORKER	WORKER_ID	WORKER_NAME	HRLY_RATE	SKILL_TYPE	SUPV_ID
	_WI		_HR		G. _SI

CONDITIONS
CNT._WI > 1

P.	_SI	MAX._HR			

Result:

SUPV_ID	
1311	15.50
1520	13.75
3231	17.40

Query: Which workers receive a higher than average hourly wage?

We needed two copies of the WORKER table for this query and two *different* variables to designate HRLY_RATE (Fig. 14.24). One variable (_HR1) was used to calculate the average hourly wage for all workers, while the other variable (_HR2) was used to designate the HRLY_RATE for a specific worker.

FIGURE 14.24

WORKER	WORKER_ID	WORKER_NAME	HRLY_RATE	SKILL_TYPE	SUPV_ID
			_HR1		
WORKER	WORKER_ID	WORKER_NAME	HRLY_RATE	SKILL_TYPE	SUPV_ID
		P. _WN	_HR2		

CONDITIONS
_HR2 > AVG._HR1

Result:

WORKER_NAME
C. Nemo
P. Mason
C. Coulomb

Query: Which workers receive an hourly wage higher than the average of those workers reporting to the worker's supervisor?

In this solution (Fig. 14.25), we have merely modified the previous query by adding grouping to the SUPV_ID column of the first table and by connecting the tables via SUPV_ID.

FIGURE 14.25

WORKER	WORKER_ID	WORKER_NAME	HRLY_RATE	SKILL_TYPE	SUPV_ID
			_HR1		G. _SI
WORKER	WORKER_ID	WORKER_NAME	HRLY_RATE	SKILL_TYPE	SUPV_ID
		P. _WN	_HR2		_SI

CONDITIONS
_HR2 > AVG. _HR1

Result: WORKER_NAME
C. Nemo
P. Mason
C. Coulomb

Database Change Operations

QBE supports the three database change operations: insert, update, and delete.

Insert □ As with SQL, rows can be inserted singly by specifying individual column values, or a group of rows can be inserted through the specification of a query. As an example of the first method, consider the QBE query shown in Figure 14.26. This query is an insertion statement, as the "I." in the first column indicates. It causes a row to be added to AS-SIGNMENT, having the values shown. Since the NUM_DAYS column has been left blank, that column will contain a null value in the inserted row.

The next query (Fig. 14.27) will add rows to a relation named BUILD-ING_2, which consists of BLDG_ID, TYPE, and QLTY_LEVEL columns. The rows added are those in BUILDING having status 2.

FIGURE 14.26

ASSIGNMENT	WORKER_ID	BLDG_ID	START_DATE	NUM_DAYS
I.	1284	485	05/13	

FIGURE 14.27

BUILDING	BLDG_ID	BLDG_ADDRESS	TYPE	QLTY_LEVEL	STATUS
	_BI		_T	_QL	2

BUILDING_2	BLDG_ID	TYPE	QLTY_LEVEL
I.	_BI	_T	_QL

FIGURE 14.28

WORKER	WORKER_ID	WORKER_NAME	HRLY_RATE	HRLY_RATE	SKILL_TYPE	SUPV_ID
			_H	U. _H*1.05		1520

FIGURE 14.29

WORKER	WORKER_ID	WORKER_NAME	HRLY_RATE	SKILL_TYPE	SUPV_ID
D.					1520

Observe that we have placed a condition (STATUS = 2) on the rows of BUILDING, while the insert command (I.) is in the BUILDING_2 table. Thus, we are performing a query on BUILDING, and the rows selected are inserted into BUILDING_2. A table such as BUILDING_2 could be used, for example, as a temporary table on which a large variety of queries would be carried out.

Update ☐   The QBE query shown in Figure 14.28 gives everybody working for supervisor 1520 a 5% wage increase.

We needed to show the HRLY_RATE column twice: once to define the variable _H, and once to indicate the update command (U.) and formula (_H * 1.05). Incidentally, this facility, of displaying multiple copies of the same column in an example table, may also be used in queries (e.g., if multiple conditions apply to the same column under the AND relationship).

Delete ☐   If we want to delete everybody working for supervisor 1520, then we may use the query shown in Figure 14.29, where D. indicates the delete command.

☐ CONCLUSION

QBE offers a graphical data manipulation language that seems to be quite easy to use in practice. By providing example tables, a template for solving many queries is immediately available. In addition, target tables, condition boxes, and example elements are available, and their application is straightforward.

However, there are also some disadvantages to QBE. For example, QBE cannot be used with traditional data processing languages. SQL can be embedded in COBOL and C programs, for example, but there is no facility to do that with QBE. Thus, it appears that QBE has utility primarily as a user query and update language. It is at present too limited to be used in more highly structured information processing situations.

■ SUMMARY

In this chapter, we have studied the data manipulation features of Query-by-Example (QBE). We looked briefly at the history and commercial implementations of the language, and then we studied simple, single-table queries, multiple-table queries, queries with built-in functions, queries involving grouping of rows, and database change operations. At the end of our discussion, we briefly compared QBE with SQL.

QBE was developed during the seventies by IBM as a graphical, relational database language. It was later implemented and released as a commercial package which runs together with SQL under IBM's Query Management Facility. Other vendors, such as Borland with Paradox, have released commercial products using QBE.

QBE provides the display of example tables, which are skeletons of tables in the database. Example tables show the name of the table as well as the names of all the table's columns. Users formulate queries by entering conditions into the example tables in the columns to which the conditions apply. Variables, called example elements, can also be used to state conditions—that is, example elements can be used to connect two tables and to state more complex conditions in condition boxes. Target tables can also be used to formulate definitions of complex output.

Statistical functions applying to sets of rows in tables are also available. These functions can be used to calculate the average of a set of values, the total of a set of values, the maximum and minimum, and the total number of a set of values. Rows can also be grouped, and statistical functions can be applied to each of the individual groups. In addition, queries can be formulated to add rows, change rows, and delete rows from selected tables in the database.

QBE is used primarily as an end-user query and update language. It is logically weaker than SQL, since it cannot be embedded in the programs of a traditional language. Still, it is much easier to use than a purely textual language and will probably have substantial importance for a number of years.

■ REVIEW QUESTIONS

1. Define each of the following terms in your own words:
   a. graphical language
   b. example table
   c. target table
   d. example element
   e. condition box

2. Discuss the relationship between SQL and QBE.

3. When should each of the following be used in a QBE query:
   a. Condition box
   b. Target table
   c. Example element
   d. Multiple example tables

4. Discuss the strengths and weaknesses of QBE as a relational language.

PROBLEMS AND EXERCISES

1. Match each term with its definition.

__Example element

__Built-in function

__Example table

__Graphical language

__Target table

__Simple query

__Condition box

__Multiple-table query

__Textual language

a. In QBE, a table without column headings that is used to define query output

b. A query involving more than one table

c. In QBE, a skeleton table showing the table name and the column names above blank spaces used for entry of query conditions

d. In QBE, a variable representing an unspecified value in a column of a table

e. A query involving only one database table

f. A computer language that uses pictorial representations to solve problems

g. A computer language whose statements consist of character string symbols

h. In QBE, a box in which a complex query condition can be expressed

i. Statistical function that acts on a set of rows—SUM, AVG, MAX, MIN, CNT

Formulate QBE solutions to the following queries. Use this relational schema:

```
CUSTOMER (CUST_ID, CUST_NAME, ANNUAL_REVENUE)
SHIPMENT (SHIPMENT_#, CUST_ID, WEIGHT, TRUCK_#, DESTINATION)
Foreign Key: DESTINATION REFERENCES CITY_NAME IN CITY
TRUCK (TRUCK_#, DRIVER_NAME)
CITY (CITY_NAME, POPULATION)
```

Simple Queries

2. a. What is the name of customer 433?

b. What is the destination city of shipment #3244?

c. What are the truck numbers of trucks that have carried packages (shipments) weighing over 100 pounds?

d. Give all data for shipments weighing over 20 pounds.

e. Create a list of names of customers with more than $10 million in annual revenue.

f. What is the customer ID for Wilson Brothers?

g. Give names and average monthly revenue of customers having annual revenue exceeding $5 million but less than $10 million.

Multiple-Table Queries

3. a. What are the names of customers who have sent packages (shipments) to Sioux City?

b. To what destinations have companies with revenue less than $1 million sent packages?

c. What are the names and populations of cities that have received shipments weighing over 100 pounds?

d. Who are the customers having over $5 million in annual revenue who have sent shipments weighing less than 1 pound?

e. Who are the customers having over $5 million in annual revenue who have sent shipments weighing less than 1 pound or have sent a shipment to San Francisco?

f. Who are the drivers who have delivered shipments for customers with annual revenue over $20 million to cities with population over 1 million?

Built-In Functions

4. a. What is the average weight of a shipment?

b. What is the average weight of a shipment going to Atlanta?

c. How many shipments has customer 433 sent?

d. Which cities in the database have the largest and smallest populations?

e. What is the total weight of packages (shipments) carried in truck 82?

GROUP BY

5. a. For each customer, what is the average weight of a package (shipment) sent by that customer?

b. For each city, what is the maximum weight of a package sent to that city?

c. For each city with population over 1 million, what is the minimum weight of a package sent to that city?

Database Change Operations

6. Write database change operations to accomplish each of the following:

a. Add truck 95 with driver Winston.

b. Delete all cities from the database with population under 5000. Don't forget to update the SHIPMENT relation.

c. Convert the weight of every shipment to kilograms by dividing the weight by 2.2.

■ PROJECTS AND PROFESSIONAL ISSUES

1. Using Zloof's original definition of QBE (Zloof 1975, 1977), perform a comprehensive comparison of SQL and QBE. Examine how the following types of SQL queries could be handled in QBE:

a. noncorrelated subqueries

b. correlated subqueries

c. NOT EXISTS

For each of the above types, use specific queries from Chapter 13, and define how they would be solved in QBE.

2. Obtain a copy of Paradox and investigate the differences, syntactical and otherwise, between its implementation of QBE and the one discussed in this chapter.

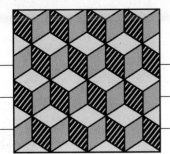

chapter fifteen

MICROCOMPUTER DATABASE MANAGEMENT SYSTEMS

411

Joan Manwaring, CPA and owner of Manwaring Consulting Services, was discussing business strategy with her two project managers. Spud Fields spoke up to say, "Joan, I'm getting an increasing number of inquiries concerning the implementation of database systems for microcomputers. I know that we have programmed a few applications for microcomputer users, but I wonder if we shouldn't be actively pursuing more opportunities for developing micro database systems."

"I'm all for pursuing new business opportunities," Rene Cournot said, "but do we know enough to be competitive in this area?"

"We are already knowledgeable about mainframe DBMSs," Spud said. "I don't see any great problem in transferring that knowledge to microcomputer systems. After all, the most important element of any database system is a sound logical design—and we know how to do that. If anything, implementing a micro DBMS may be simpler than implementing a mainframe system, since micro DBMSs are often cut-down versions of mainframe systems."

Joan agreed. "Undoubtedly, there are some things that we will have to learn, but I think they will be application specific. For example, PARADOX uses a data manipulation language that is very similar to QBE. The details of the syntax differ somewhat, but the concepts are easy to adapt. If this is true for other micro DBMSs, Spud, we may be able to add another useful service for our clients."

As microcomputer database systems become increasingly powerful and popular, they are being used to develop more and more meaningful database systems for large and small businesses. This chapter is devoted to a discussion of the principles of microcomputer DBMSs, especially as they are implemented in some of the better-known and more powerful microcomputer DBMS products.

After reading this chapter, you should be able to:

☐ Explain the potential of microcomputer DBMSs.
☐ Develop an application using PARADOX.
☐ Understand the fundamentals of the RBASE DBMS.
☐ Understand the fundamentals of the ORACLE DBMS.

☐ A ROLE FOR MICROCOMPUTER DBMSs

Given the increasing power available in today's microcomputers, it is no surprise that many DBMSs have been developed for use on microcomputers. Many of these DBMSs are versions of successful mainframe systems and offer sophisticated capabilities for a moderate investment; others have been developed especially for microcomputer use.

This is a potential boon to organizations of all sizes. Large and medium-sized organizations can benefit by the development and use of decentralized database systems, which service the needs of local users. Although some interfacing may be necessary with the corporate database, most local needs can be satisfied readily by a microcomputer database system. This includes the need to use imported data and to function in both standalone and multiuser modes—all of which can be supported by a good microcomputer DBMS.

Small organizations may actually satisfy their management information needs by using one or more microcomputer database installations. This is a particularly attractive option, since microcomputer DBMSs are relatively inexpensive and require less technical expertise than do mainframe systems. Productive applications can be generated very quickly.

Of course, there are some caveats. Uncoordinated use of microcomputer database development can result in redundancy and inconsistency of data. In a growing organization, the limited sizes of microcomputer databases may ultimately require shifting certain applications to a mini- or mainframe environment. Also, the security and integrity mechanisms available in microcomputer DBMSs are not as sophisticated and powerful as those available in mainframe DBMSs. Similarly, backup-and-recovery capabilities are minimal for microcomputer DBMSs, although the situation is improving. In some cases, microcomputer DBMSs support interfacing with a local-area network (LAN). The database to be shared is stored on the file server, where it can be accessed by multiple users. A network environment requires a somewhat more sophisticated DBMS than the single-user environment, but it extends the applicability of microcomputer databases to a new level.

The prospective user needs to be cautious in acquiring a microcomputer DBMS because capabilities range from simple to very complex. Moreover, many products claim to be relational but do not really supply the full range of relational capabilities. In general, a microcomputer DBMS will provide facilities for creating, updating, and deleting records, as well as sorting the database on one or more key fields. Additionally, capabilities should be provided for searching the database according to combinations of required parameters. Typical systems will provide for easy preparation of reports as well. A worthy microcomputer DBMS ought to provide good response time for processes, offer a powerful data manipulation language, and supply a host language to allow the programming of specialized operations on the database.

Because many schools are using microcomputers to give students actual experience in working with a database system, we discuss in this chapter three relational microcomputer DBMSs that are based on languages already discussed in Chapters 8, 13, and 14. Since all of these DBMSs are continually undergoing refinement and revision, we will confine our discussion to general features of each language, without delving too deeply into syntax, which may be changing over time.

PARADOX A microcomputer DBMS whose query language is like QBE.

RBASE A microcomputer DBMS whose query language is based on relational algebra.

ORACLE A microcomputer DBMS whose query language is SQL.

We first discuss **PARADOX,** which is similar to Query-By-Example (QBE). We then look at **RBase,** which is basically an implementation of relational algebra. Finally, we examine **ORACLE,** which incorporates SQL as its query language.

The omission of the dBASE DBMS, which will be familiar to some readers, deserves comment. dBASE, a popular fourth-generation language, was one of the first DBMSs incorporating relational concepts to become available for the microcomputer. However, dBASE is not modeled after any of the established relational languages. It is, nonetheless, quasi-relational and to some extent supports the relational algebra operations of select, project, and join. Other commands included in the language give it considerable power for business processing applications. We have opted, however, to focus on those DBMSs that are most closely aligned with the relational concepts articulated in Chapters 8, 13, and 14.

☐ PARADOX

The first microcomputer DBMS we consider is PARADOX. PARADOX is a DBMS whose query language is similar to the QBE language.

Data Definition and Entry

The PARADOX data definition language is very simple to learn. After entering a name for the database, the user is presented with an empty table and prompted through the process of naming the table and its attributes, as well as specifying the data type and allowable length for each attribute of the table. Example entries to create the PERSNEL relation of Figure 15.1(A) are shown in Figure 15.2. Note that the "*" is used to denote key attributes. The field types, N, A15, and $, indicate numeric, alphanumeric (length 15), and currency fields, respectively. The resulting table before data entries are made is shown in Figure 15.3.

FIGURE 15.1   Relational Schema for Manufacturing Database

(a) PERSNEL (<u>EMPNO</u>, EMPNAME, DEPTNO, PROJNO, SALARY)
(b) DEPTS (<u>DEPTNO</u>, DNAME)
(c) PROJECT (<u>PROJNO</u>, CUSTOMER, LOCATION)
(d) PRPARTS (<u>PROJNO</u>, <u>PARTNO</u>, QUANTITY)
(e) PARTS (<u>PARTNO</u>, VENDOR, COST)

FIGURE 15.2   Specifying the Attributes and Data Types for the PERSNEL Table

STRUCT	FIELD NAME	FIELD TYPE
1	EMPNO	N*
2	EMPNAME	A15
3	DEPTNO	N
4	PROJNO	N
5	SALARY	$

FIGURE 15.3   Table Resulting from Entries in Figure 15.2

PERSNEL	Empno	Empname	Deptno	Projno	Salary

Once the relations (tables) and their attributes are defined, data can be entered using simple menu features. PARADOX allows straightforward implementation of edit checks on data entry—such as limits on ranges of values, validation through lookup tables, and so forth.

Data Manipulation

The PARADOX data manipulation language is implemented through use of the **Ask** command from the main menu. Since the query language is visual, in the manner of QBE, the user does not need to memorize complex query commands. All that is necessary is to use the Ask command to bring up a query form. The tables to be queried and examples of the required data can then be specified.

Selecting Attributes and Rows □ To select attributes on the query form, the user first selects **Ask** from the main menu, enters the table name and presses [Enter]. This causes a blank sample table to appear (see Figure 15.3). The user then moves the cursor to the desired attribute and presses F6 (Checkmark). This places a "✓" in that attribute's column. After F2 **(Do-It!)** is pressed, PARADOX produces an answer table containing all of the values of the checked attributes as they currently exist in the table.

To rename an attribute during a query so that the field name in the answer table is different from the attribute name in the query table, the user simply enters "as" after the selection criterion, followed by the new attribute name. An example is given in Figure 15.4. Here we are seeking the names of all employees in Department 100. Note that we are changing the attribute name "EMPNAME" to "NAME" for the purpose of output only. As you can see, attributes are chosen by use of the "✓," whereas rows are selected based upon supplied criteria—in this case "DEPTNO = 100."

Conjunctive and Disjunctive Queries □ Figure 15.5 extends the query of Figure 15.4 to request the names of all employees in Department 100 who are making more than $30,000 per year. This is a **conjunctive** ("and") **query** in that we are asking for a list of all employees who are in Depart-

conjunctive query A query whose conditions are connected by "and," or an equivalent symbol.

FIGURE 15.4 Renaming an Attribute in a PARADOX Query

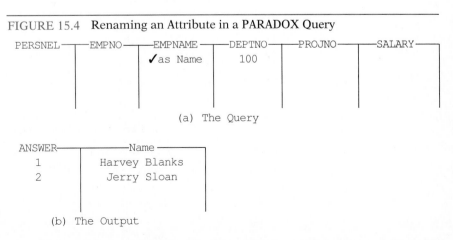

(a) The Query

(b) The Output

PERSNEL	EMPNO	EMPNAME	DEPTNO	PROJNO	SALARY
		✓ as Name	100		>30000

FIGURE 15.5   A Conjunctive Query in PARADOX

ment 100 *and* who are earning over $30,000 per year. Conjunction is readily extended to more than two conditions by simply entering all the "and" conditions on one line of the query. Conjunctions may involve several attributes, as well as several values for a single attribute.

Suppose that we require a conjunction on the values of a single attribute, such as requiring the salary to be greater than $30,000 *and* less than $50,000. This is done as shown in Figure 15.6. The comma between the desired values establishes the required conjunction.

The **disjunctive query** ("or") condition can be indicated in two ways. Two or more rows in a query form serve to indicate an "or" connective between each row, as shown in Figure 15.7. We have requested here a list of all employee names who are in Department 100 *or* who are earning more than $30,000 a year. A second way is illustrated in Figure 15.8 where the word "or" is simply inserted between the conditions. This method can be used only where the "or" condition applies to the contents of a single attribute. In Figure 15.8, we have requested the names of em-

disjunctive query A query whose conditions are connected by "or," or an equivalent symbol.

FIGURE 15.6   A Conjunctive Query with Two Conditions on Salary in PARADOX

PERSNEL	EMPNO	EMPNAME	DEPTNO	PROJNO	SALARY
		✓ as Name	100		>30000, <50000

FIGURE 15.7   One Form of Disjunctive Query in PARADOX

PERSNEL	EMPNO	EMPNAME	DEPTNO	PROJNO	SALARY
		✓ as Name	100		
		✓ as Name			>30000

FIGURE 15.8   A Second Form of Disjunctive Query in PARADOX

PERSNEL	EMPNO	EMPNAME	DEPTNO	PROJNO	SALARY
		✓ as Name	100 or 200		

ployees who are assigned to Department 100 *or* who are assigned to Department 200.

As with any query language, "or" and "and" conditions can be combined within one query. An example is given in Figure 15.9. Here we have requested the names of employees who are assigned to departments 100 or 200 *and* who earn more than $30,000 per year.

Calculations □   Calculations may be performed within the query form. All calculations must be preceded with the CALC operator. An example is seen in Figure 15.10. We have requested a calculation of the average of all salaries. In Figure 15.11, we see a similar example, only here we have requested the average salary by department. Putting a checkmark in the DEPTNO column will perform the indicated calculation for groups of records having the same value in the DEPTNO attribute. In these two examples, we have used the CALC operator in conjunction with the summary operator AVERAGE. Other summary operators include SUM, COUNT, MAX, and MIN. Specialized calculations may also be performed.

Linking Tables □   Queries involving single tables are quite simple since they only require identifying the attributes desired in the output and the conditions that must be satisfied. More complex queries generally involve linking the data in one table with that of another (or several others). This is accomplished in a straightforward way in PARADOX.

An example is shown in Figure 15.12. Here we wish to produce a list of employee names for those individuals assigned to the marketing de-

FIGURE 15.9   A Combined Conjunctive and Disjunctive Query in PARADOX

PERSNEL	EMPNO	EMPNAME	DEPTNO	PROJNO	SALARY
		✓as Name	100 or 200		>30000

FIGURE 15.10   Calculating Average Salary in PARADOX

PERSNEL	EMPNO	EMPNAME	DEPTNO	PROJNO	SALARY
					CALC AVERAGE

FIGURE 15.11   Calculating Average Salary by Department in PARADOX

PERSNEL	EMPNO	EMPNAME	DEPTNO	PROJNO	SALARY
			✓		CALC AVERAGE

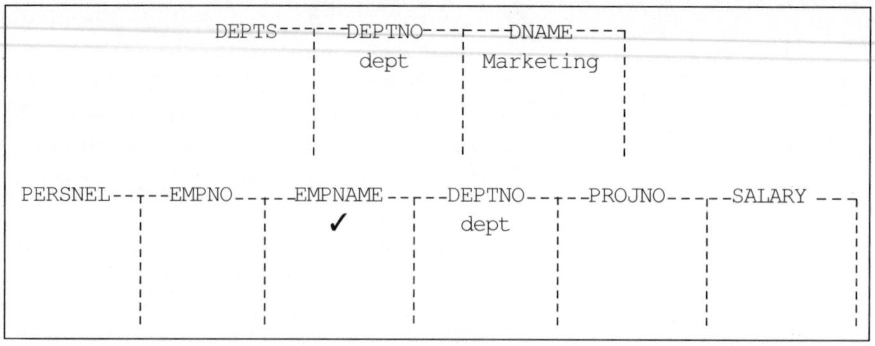

FIGURE 15.12 Linking Tables in PARADOX

partment. The "✓" denotes the attribute whose values we wish to have printed. The "dept" entered into the DEPTNO columns of both the DEPTS and PERSNEL tables acts as a variable by which the tables are linked (we could just as well use "*x*" or "*y*"). However, notice that the "dept" in the DEPTS table is restricted to that value of DEPTNO associated with the name "Marketing." Thus, if we suppose that the marketing department's number is 300, then the only allowable "dept" in DEPTS is 300. When an employee who is associated with DEPTNO 300 is found in the PERSNEL table, the name is retrieved as part of the query solution.

A slightly more complicated example is shown in Figure 15.13. Here we have requested a list of all vendors who supply parts for projects located in Outland. We see that the PRPARTS and PARTS tables are linked by the variable named "part." Whenever a match is found on PARTNO, the two related rows are linked. Looking further at the PRPARTS table, we see that those parts are then linked to those projects in Outland through the variable "proj." This variable connects the rows in the PRPARTS table to the appropriate rows in the PROJECTS table.

FIGURE 15.13 Linking Three Tables in PARADOX

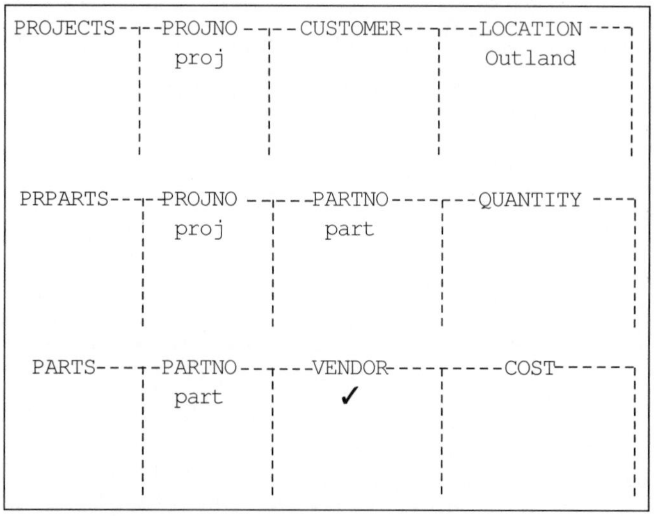

Paradox provides the facility for designing a large variety of reports, which can be constructed from single tables or from multiple tables. Two types of report design are supported: tabular and free form. In a tabular report, information is arranged in rows and columns. A free-form report does not limit the placing of information in columns and rows; it allows positioning information in any two-dimensional format.

Forms are used to enter, edit, and view data in one or several tables. A good example would be creating forms that appear on the screen to facilitate the entry of transaction data into the database. PARADOX includes facilities for standard forms, as well as custom forms. A standard form is automatically created by PARADOX, with each field from a table being presented on a separate line. For users who require more flexibility and more elegant layouts, the custom form is available. Fields that are not contained in the base table can be computed and included on a custom form.

Application Language

PAL PARADOX Application Language, a high-level, structured database programming language.

The PARADOX Application Language **(PAL)** is a high-level, structured database programming language. It provides the user with a method of integrating PARADOX's interactive commands into an application. The writing of programs is usually viewed as a series of statements composed of simple assertions, conditional statements, and iterative statements. We briefly present the general syntax for the latter two structures.

conditional statement A statement that tests for the presence of a condition and directs further processing accordingly.

Conditional Statements □ The general syntax for IF-THEN-ELSE **conditional statements** is as follows:

```
IF <condition>
    THEN <statements>
    ELSE <statements>
ENDIF
```

SWITCH statement A statement that enables testing for a series of conditions.

CASE statement Used with SWITCH statement to direct processing when a condition is found to be true.

SWITCH statements are similar to multiple IF-THEN-ELSE statements. Whereas each IF-THEN-ELSE statement contains just two branches, the SWITCH statement contains one CASE statement for each possible branch. The **CASE statement** contains a condition followed by a colon and a set of commands. Only one of the CASE statements is performed each time the SWITCH statement is executed. Here is one example:

```
SWITCH
    CASE choice = "Customer Data":<list-of-commands-A>
    CASE choice = "Transactions": <list-of-commands-B>
    •
    •
    •
    OTHERWISE: <list-of-commands-K>
ENDSWITCH
```

The first CASE statement having a true condition is performed. If none of the CASE statement conditions is true, then the OTHERWISE statement is performed.

iteration statement A statement that may be repeated a specified number of times.

Iteration Statements □ The general sytax for an **iteration statement** is as follows:

```
WHILE <condition>
     <list of statements to be executed>
ENDWHILE
```

The WHILE condition is checked, and, if it is true, the list of statements is executed. Each time the condition is satisfied the list is executed. The ENDWHILE statement causes execution to be transferred again to the WHILE statement. When the WHILE condition fails program control is passed to the first statement following the ENDWHILE.

□ RBASE

As with PARADOX, the developers of RBASE have made life easier for users by providing a menu-driven architecture. At the operating system prompt, entering "RBASE" brings up the main menu from which one chooses the option to *Define or modify a database.* This brings up a second-level menu from which the user chooses "RBDEFINE." Executing this choice puts the user in the Definition EXPRESS module, whose menu is then displayed. When initially creating a database, the user will select *Define a new database.* At this point, the user is asked for a database name. Upon entry of a database name, an empty table will be displayed as shown in Figure 15.14. The user is then asked to name the table, its attributes, and their corresponding data types as suggested by Figure 15.15. RBASE then allows data to be entered into the table directly from the keyboard or from a file.

FIGURE 15.14 **An Empty RBASE Table**

Enter the name for this table

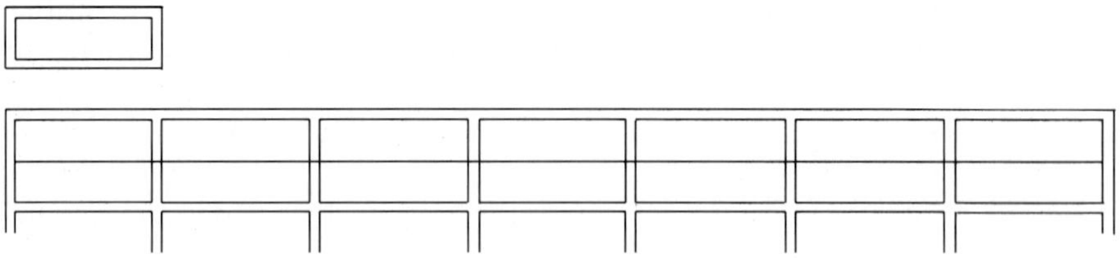

FIGURE 15.15 **An Example of a Completed RBASE Table**

Enter the name for this table

PERSNEL

EMPNO	EMPNAME	DEPTNO	PROJNO	SALARY		
INTEGER	TEXT 15	INTEGER	INTEGER	DOLLAR		

The RBASE data manipulation language is based on relational algebra. However, it is an enhanced version of relational algebra, containing a number of additional, powerful features.

Selecting Attributes and Rows ☐ Limiting the attributes to appear in a solution to a query is accomplished by simply enumerating the names of the attributes required. Suppose that we wish, as before, the names of all employees in Department 100. The query could be written as follows:

```
PROJECT ANSWER FROM PERSNEL USING EMPNAME WHERE DEPTNO = 100.
```

PROJECT creates a table for the solution—in this case called ANSWER. PERSNEL is the table containing the information required. USING specifies the columns to be included in the result. WHERE allows one or more conditions to be applied to the rows that may be selected.

Conjunctive and Disjunctive Queries ☐ We now extend the above query to request the names of all employees in Department 100 who are making more than $30,000 per year. This is a simple conjunctive query in that both conditions must be satisfied. We write the query as follows:

```
PROJECT R FROM PERSNEL USING EMPNAME WHERE DEPTNO = 100 AND
SALARY > 30000.
```

Only a modest imagination is required to see that the conjunctive conditions can easily be extended to many attribute values. As before, we extend the "and" conditions to require that the salary be greater than $30,000 *and* less than $50,000.

```
PROJECT R FROM PERSNEL USING EMPNAME WHERE DEPTNO = 100 AND
SALARY > 30000 AND SALARY < 5000.
```

Turning to the disjunctive form, suppose that we wish a list of employee names who are in Department 100 *or* are earning more than $30,000 per year. Here is the query:

```
PROJECT R FROM PERSNEL USING EMPNAME WHERE DEPTNO = 100 OR
SALARY > 30000.
```

Calculations ☐ Calculations can be completed as the target of a query by using the COMPUTE command. The syntax is illustrated by the following example:

```
COMPUTE AVGSAL AS AVE SALARY FROM PERSNEL WHERE DEPTNO = 300.
```

We have requested the average salary for employees assigned to department number 3. The general form of a COMPUTE statement is

```
                                |AVE      |
        COMPUTE <variable name> AS |COUNT    | <column name>
                                |MAXIMUM  |
                                |MINIMUM  |
                                |SUM      |
        FROM <table> WHERE <condition list>.
```

The AVE, COUNT, MAXIMUM, MINIMUM, and SUM operators are direct counterparts to similarly named operators in PARADOX. RBASE also provides STDDEV (standard deviation) and VARIANCE operators.

Linking Tables ☐ The INTERSECT command creates a new relation from two existing relations. It requires that there be at least one attribute name that is the same in both relations. As with the natural join of relational algebra (see Chapter 8), the new relation contains all the attribute names from the two relations, with no repetitions (meaning attributes in the intersection only appear once). Here's an example. Suppose, as before, we need a list of employee names for those individuals assigned to the marketing department. The query would be as follows:

```
PROJECT NEWTAB FROM DEPTS WHERE DNAME = 'Marketing'
INTERSECT NEWTAB WITH PERSNEL FORMING NEWTAB1 USING EMPNAME
```

In this query, we have first created a new table from DEPTS by choosing only that row that has a DNAME value of Marketing. The INTERSECT command is then used to form a natural join of that relation with PERSNEL. That is, rows from PERSNEL are adjoined to the Marketing row from DEPTS if and only if the value of DEPTNO in the PERSNEL row is equal to the DEPTNO in the Marketing row. The natural join takes place only when employees are found in the PERSNEL relation who are associated with DEPTNO 300. The USING command allows projection of just the EMPNAME from those joined relations, as desired.

Reports and Forms

RBASE provides a report generator called **REPORTS EXPRESS**. It facilitates naming the report; identifying the relations from which the report data will be derived; determining the report layout; and defining which lines on the report layout are to be printed as headers, which as summary lines, and which as detail lines.

RBASE provides an easy procedure for creating forms. RBASE forms come in two varieties: table forms and variable forms. The table form is a single page data entry form. The variable form allows the display of several single-page forms as if they were one multiple-page form.

Application Language

The RBASE application language allows the writing of specialized routines that may be needed by the user. It supplies the capability for expressing the usual programming structures as shown below:

Conditional Statements ☐ The general syntax for *IF-THEN-ELSE* statements in RBASE is as follows:

```
IF <condition-list>
    THEN <statement-block>
    ELSE <statement-block>
ENDIF
```

Iteration Statements □   Iteration in RBASE follows this general syntax:

```
WHILE <condition-list>
    THEN <statement-block>
ENDWHILE
```

The WHILE condition is checked before the execution of the THEN statements. As long as the WHILE condition is true, the statement block will continue to be executed. When the WHILE condition fails, the statement block is skipped, causing the command immediately following the END-WHILE to be executed next.

□ ORACLE

ORACLE uses the SQL data manipulation language, which has become the industry standard. SQL was covered in some detail in Chapter 13.

ORACLE differs from PARADOX and RBASE in that it uses SQL to define, as well as to manipulate, data. The PROJECTS relation of Figure 15.1 would be created as follows:

```
CREATE TABLE PROJECTS (PROJNO NUMBER (2),
                       CUSTOMER CHAR (14),
                       LOCATION CHAR (13))
```

With this command we have created a table named PROJECTS which is made up of attributes PROJNO, CUSTOMER, LOCATION. The first attribute has a numeric data type, with a field length of 2. It is easy to see the meaning of the corresponding specifications for the latter two attributes.

Data is entered as follows:

```
INSERT INTO PROJECTS
VALUES (1, 'BURGER, W.', 'VAUDVILLE');
VALUES (2, 'DOWNING, B.', 'SERIES CITY');
    <etc.>
```

This causes two rows to be added to the PROJECTS relation.

Data Manipulation   ORACLE data manipulation follows SQL data manipulation as described in Chapter 13. It also provides some important enhancements. We give a number of examples for comparison with PARADOX and RBASE.

Selecting Attributes and Rows □   Suppose that we need a list of customers and their locations. We would express the corresponding SQL query as

```
SELECT   CUSTOMER, LOCATION
FROM     PROJECTS;
```

If we wanted only those customers located in Martinsville, we would write

```
SELECT   CUSTOMER
FROM     PROJECTS
WHERE    LOCATION = 'Martinsville';
```

This pattern is easily extended to multiple query conditions. For example,

```
SELECT   PARTNO
FROM     PARTS
WHERE    VENDOR = 'Smith'
         AND COST > 25 AND COST <100;
```

Linking More than One Table ☐ Suppose we again wish a list of all vendors who supply parts for projects located in Outland. The corresponding query would be

```
SELECT    VENDOR
FROM      PARTS,PRPARTS, PROJECTS
WHERE     LOCATION = 'Outland'
          AND PRPARTS.PROJNO = PROJECTS.PROJNO
          AND PRPARTS.PARTNO = PARTS.PARTNO;
```

This query first selects rows from **PROJECTS** where the **LOCATION** is Outland, then joins those rows to rows in **PRPARTS** having the same **PROJNO**. Finally, these rows are joined to rows in **PARTS** having the same **PARTNO**. The **VENDOR** column from these joined rows is then projected for the desired result.

Computing Functions on Groups of Rows ☐ Group functions, a powerful feature of SQL, facilitates the summarization of information from groups of rows. For instance, suppose we want a list of maximum salaries by department. Referring to our Figure 15.1 database, we would write

```
SELECT    DEPTNO, MAX(SALARY)
FROM      PERSNEL
GROUP BY  DEPTNO;
```

The result would be a listing of the department numbers and the maximum salary found for each of those departments.

ORACLE also has a powerful COMPUTE function, which can operate on groups of selected rows. COMPUTE would typically be used in conjunction with the following operators:

```
AVG, COU[NT], MAX, MIN, and SUM.
```

ORACLE provides additional operators such as VAR, STD, and NUM, which are used with COMPUTE to yield variance, standard deviation, and a count of rows. Here is an example of the use of COMPUTE to determine the average salary by department.

```
BREAK ON DEPTNO
COMPUTE AVG OF SALARY ON DEPTNO
SELECT DEPTNO
FROM PERSONNEL
ORDER BY DEPTNO;
```

We use a BREAK statement to indicate the grouping desired. We order the resulting averages by DEPTNO.

Application Language

Pro*C An ORACLE facility that allows applications to be written in the C language.

ORACLE provides a facility called **Pro*C,** which enables applications written in the language C to define and manipulate data in the ORACLE DBMS.

☐ MICROCOMPUTER DBMSs SUMMARIZED

The advent of DBMSs for the microcomputer has made the power of database systems available to the small business. This is not to say that microcomputer DBMSs have all the power of mainframe DBMSs. They do not. They do, however, provide parallel capabilities in the important areas of data sharing, query flexibility, and ease of database creation and maintenance.

Since the development of microcomputer DBMSs is still relatively new, most of them are based on the relational model. Since these products are more marketable if they use less memory—so that they can run on more machines—few systems use sophisticated storage management and indexing methods. The amount of query optimization that takes place is usually limited.

The future for microcomputer systems seems very bright. Indeed, database management capability is even being added to some spreadsheet packages.

☐ APPLICATION ILLUSTRATION (PARADOX)

Since many courses rely on a microcomputer laboratory for "hands-on" database experience, we include an example application in PARADOX. We also return to Manwaring Consulting, a case used earlier in the book.

Case: Manwaring Consulting Services

Joan Manwaring, CPA, has operated Manwaring Consulting Services for the last ten years. Manwaring Consulting employs six consultants who work on projects for Manwaring clients. Each project involves one or more consultants and may last several weeks or several months, depending on the scope of the project.

Estimates. For each engagement taken, Joan must make a proposal for services. The proposal includes a scope, objective, task structure, and fee structure, among other things. The fees Joan charges can vary greatly among the different types of engagements. Fees are based on the benefits provided to the client and the time and effort spent in completing the engagement. All information pertaining to the engagement is kept for future reference. Any adjustments made to the estimate are shown to the client and are recorded.

Cash Receipts. Although many of the smaller engagements are paid for in cash, most of the customers pay on account. Payment is due upon completion of the engagement, unless credit arrangements have been made. The credit accounts are usually paid by the clients on time, but Joan sometimes has to send second notices to the client in order to collect payment.

Cash Disbursements. Although many supplies are charged directly to a specific engagement, some supplies and equipment are associated with multiple engagements or overhead. All supplies are bought on account.

An Object-Oriented Model of Manwaring

An object-oriented model for Manwaring is shown in Figure 15.16. The object-oriented model contains three types of cardinalities, exemplified as follows:

1. The JOB-ESTIMATE relationship is one–one, since each job has only one estimate, and each estimate is associated with just one job.
2. The CUSTOMER-JOB relationship is one–many, since each customer can be associated with several jobs, but any one job can only be related to a single customer.
3. The CASH RECEIPTS-JOB relationship is many–many, since one cash receipt may apply to more than one job (e.g., payments made on three jobs with one check), and one job may be associated with many cash receipts (e.g., a job may be paid for in three installments).

To keep the illustration of Figure 15.16 simple, the attributes of each object and relationship have been omitted. Instead we identify them in the following discussion, which describes the mapping of the model.

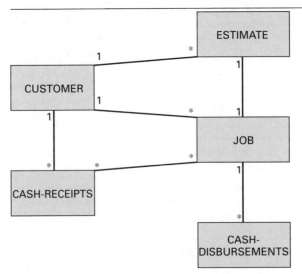

FIGURE 15.16 An Object-Oriented Model of the Manwaring Database

Each of the three types of relationships must be treated differently in the database structure.

One–One Relationships ☐ To establish this relationship, the key of one of the tables must appear as a foreign key in the other table. For example, a one–one relationship exists between ESTIMATE and JOB. Thus, the key of ESTIMATE (ESTNO) may be added to the attributes of JOB as a foreign key. Alternatively, the key of JOB (JOBNO) may be added as a foreign key to the attributes of ESTIMATE.

One–Many Relationships ☐ To establish this relationship, the key of the table derived from the object set on the "one" side of the relationship is added to the attributes of the table derived from the object set on the "many" side of the relationship. For example, a one–many relationship exists between CUSTOMER and JOB. The key of CUSTOMER (CUSTNO) is added to the attributes of JOB.

Many–Many Relationships ☐ To implement many–many relationships, a new table must be created so that the relationship can be represented as two one–many relationships. Figure 15.17 gives an example using the many-many relationship between JOB and CASH-RECEIPTS. The attributes of the CR-JOB relationship must contain at least the two keys from the object sets which it relates (JOB and CASH-RECEIPTS). Other attributes may be added as deemed useful.

Creating Tables

To create a table in PARADOX, select **CREATE** from the main menu. PARADOX then asks for the table name, which can be up to eight characters in length. Enter the table name, and a table structure will appear. You are now ready to enter the attributes (called fields in PARADOX) into the table.

The field names may be up to 25 characters long and should describe a field's contents. Fields may be of four types:

A   *Alphanumeric.* This allows letters, numbers, and special symbols (such as +, %, and so forth). The user must specify the length of the field as well. For example, A15, indicates an alphanumeric field with a maximum allowable length of 15 characters.

FIGURE 15.17   Implementing a Many–Many Relationship

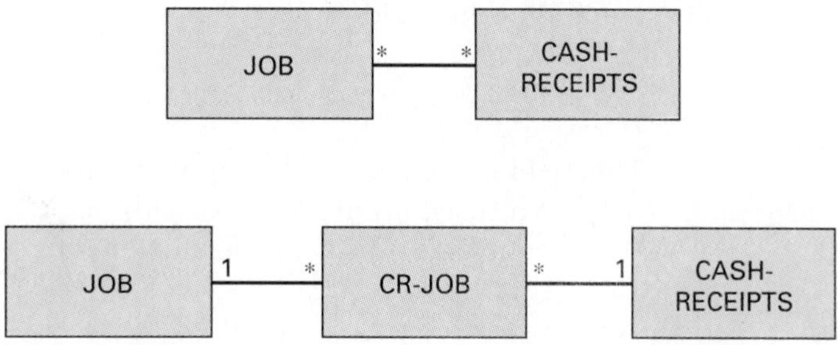

<dl>
<dt>N</dt>
<dd>Numeric. This restricts symbols to numeric digits. No length need be specified.</dd>
<dt>$</dt>
<dd>Currency. This specification allows only numeric digits, which will be automatically rounded to just two decimal places. Commas will also be added to large numbers in the usual way.</dd>
<dt>D</dt>
<dd>Date. This specification provides for calendar dates in several formats, such as: MM/DD/YY, DD-MM-YY, or DD.MM.YY.</dd>
</dl>

To illustrate the creation of a table and its fields, the JOB table of our example will be created. After selecting **CREATE** from the menu, name the table JOB. We are then asked to name the fields comprising JOB. We proceed as follows:

```
JOBNO NAME: JOBNO  DEFINITION: A5*
```

JOBNO is specified as the first field in the table named JOB. The "*" indicates that JOBNO will be a key for the table. It is conventional to place the key attributes as the "leftmost" attributes in a table. (In PARADOX there is another reason, as will be demonstrated later in this section.) Although the job number will be a series of numeric digits, the digits will not be used in calculations; thus, this key can be defined as alphanumeric.

```
CUSTNO NAME: CUSTNO  DEFINITION: A5
```

This attribute is included as a foreign key to link the **CUSTOMER** table to the **JOB** table.

```
DATE NAME: JOBDATE  DEFINITION: D
```

Since the attribute is a date, the proper definition is "D." Thereafter you may choose the form of date that you prefer. If you choose MM/DD/YY, the number 120189 will appear in the table as 12/01/89.

```
AMOUNT NAME: JOBAMOUNT  DEFINITION: $
```

The job amount will be used in calculations such as total customer balance owed. Thus, the field will be defined as currency (numeric would have worked as well).

```
DESCRIPTION NAME: DESCRIPTION  DEFINITION: A20
```

The description will be alphanumeric, since letters and numbers will be entered in this field.

```
ESTNO NAME: ESTNO  DEFINITION: A5
```

This field is defined as alphanumeric for the same reason as JOBNO—it will not be used in calculations. Although ESTNO is a foreign key, PARADOX requires no special indicator for this.

All the necessary attributes have now been defined for JOB. We would now press F2 (**Do-It!**) to save the table structure. The same process may be used to create tables for all other object sets, including CR-JOB. In this table, both RECNO and JOBNO will be defined as A5. The concatenation of these attributes will form the key for the table.

If an error is made in entering the fields, the arrow keys can be used to move data to the proper area to correct the error. If the structure has already been saved, the **Modify/Restructure** option will allow changes. The remainder of the tables are created as shown in Figure 15.18.

Creating Input Forms

Forms are used in PARADOX to simplify the input of data. Although data can be entered directly to the tables, one transaction may affect three or four tables. The use of a form allows the user to enter the data just once, with the data being automatically entered into all the relevant tables.

For example, if Joan has a client come into her office for a simple 1040EZ tax return, she can complete the job and collect payment from the client in a short amount of time. Rather than enter the customer description in the CUSTOMER table, the job description in the JOB table, and the cash receipt in the CASH RECEIPTS table, Joan may enter all this data into a multitable form she has designed in advance.

Step 1: Choosing a Master Table and Related Tables ☐ The first step in creating such a form is the selection of a master table and its related tables. The master table must be created first. Choosing the master table is important in developing useful forms. Three things must be considered when creating a master table:

1. Which table has the most links with other tables?
2. Which table establishes either a one–one or a one–many relationship with other tables?
3. Which table seems a natural master for entering data?

Once the master table is determined, you must create it. You may want to call it MASTER.

FIGURE 15. 18   Table Definitions in PARADOX

CUSTOMER		CASH–REC		CASH–DISB		ESTIMATE	
CUSTNO	A5*	RECNO	A5*	CHECK NO	N*	ESTNO	A5*
LASTNAME	A12	CUSTNO	A5	JOBNO	N	CUSTNO	A5
FIRSTNAME	A8	DATE	D	DATE	D	JOBNO	A5
MIDDLEINIT	A2	AMOUNT	$	AMOUNT	$	DATE	D
ADDRESS	A20					AMOUNT	$
CITY	A15					DESCRIPTION	A20
STATE	A2						
ZIP	A10						
PHONE#	A11						

The related tables will be the remaining tables that relate to the master table. The goal, again, is to input data only once in order to simplify table updating. Thus, the user must consider what data will be entered. In the present case, if a new client comes to Joan for service, she will enter the customer information, such as address and telephone number. She will also enter estimate information, job information, and possibly cash receipts.

Creating the master table follows the same as procedure as creating any other table: Press F10, **Create,** then name the table MASTER. Attributes will be CUSTNO(A5) and CREDITLIMIT($). No key is required for the master. CUSTNO functions as the linking field between the master and its related tables. Those related tables are ESTIMATE, JOB, and CASH-RECEIPTS. Each of these tables links directly to MASTER. The next step is the creation of subforms.

Step 2: Creating of Subforms ☐ Subforms need to be created in each of the related tables and in the master table. To create a subform in the CUSTOMER table, first name the form.

1. Select **Forms** from the main menu.
2. Select **Design** from the next menu, and press return to see a display of table names from which to select. Choose the CUSTOMER table.
3. Select **1.** This allows you to design the form.
4. Name the table something recognizable, such as "C-Input."

Then comes the design.

5. Press **F10** to display the menu.
6. Select **Border, Place, Single (or Double)** to place a border on your subform. Press **RETURN** to locate the starting location for your form (the upper left corner). Size the form to about three or four rows in height and across the screen in length. Then press **RETURN** to finish the sizing and placement.
7. Place the attributes on the form by first moving the cursor to the area in the form where you want the information to appear. Type in text to identify the incoming data, for example, "Customer Name." Then space beyond the text and place the data field by entering **F10, Field, Place, Regular.** PARADOX then prompts for the different attribute names. Select the desired attribute, then press **RETURN** twice to place the data in the form.
8. Enter the desired remaining attributes on the form. Do not place CUSTNO on the form, since CUSTNO is the attribute linking all the related tables to the master table. CUSTNO will be placed on the master, multitable form.
9. The Customer subform should appear approximately as shown in Figure 15.19.
10. Press **F2** to save the subform.

```
Customer Name: _____
Address: _____    City: _____    State: ____    Zip: _____
Phone Number: _____
```

FIGURE 15. 19   The Customer Subform

Following the same steps as above, subforms should be created for the other related tables (ESTIMATE, JOB, and CASH RECEIPTS). Place text and fields in a logical order, remembering not to include CUSTNO on the subforms. Once completed, these subforms should appear approximately as shown in Figure 15.20.

Each of the fields is of the Regular type on the subforms. The other types of fields available are Display-Only and Calculated. Display-Only fields do not allow the user to input any information into that field. Calculated fields in forms are computations of data entered in other fields. A Calculated field is useful, for example, on an invoice form where quantity is multiplied by price in order to compute the amount owed.

Step 3: Creating the Multitable Form ☐ The creation of the multitable form begins with the MASTER table. Its specification proceeds as before:

1. Press **F10** to get the menu.
2. Place a **Border, Single (or Double).** This border should include the whole screen, since each of the subforms will be placed within the border of the master form.
3. Move the cursor to the top of the master form, and type narrative for the attributes of the master table (CUSTNO and CREDITLIMIT). Place these fields with **F10, Field, Place, Regular** choices, as before.
4. Create the customer subform. Place the cursor below the attributes of (3) to begin entering the subforms. The first subform will be the Customer Input form.
5. Press **F10** to display the menu.

FIGURE 15. 20   The Estimate, Job, and Cash Receipts Subforms

```
Estimate Number: _____    Estimate Date: _____
Estimate Amount: _____    Description: _____
```

```
Job Number: _____    Job Date: _____    Estimate Number: _____
Job Amount: _____    Description: _____
```

```
Cash Receipt Number: _____    Cash Receipt Date: _____
Job Number: _____    Amount Received: _____
```

6. Select **Multi, Tables, Place, Linked.** Each subform will be linked in this example because they all have the field CUSTNO in common. Pressing return at this point prompts with the table names. Select CUSTOMER, then select "1," since 1 is the Customer Input form that is to be placed.

7. PARADOX asks for the field on which to link. CUSTNO will be the linking field for all related tables in this example.

8. The screen will now show a highlighted area the size of the Customer Input form. Use the cursor to place this highlighted area within the borders below the attributes already placed. Press **RETURN** to complete the placement. You have now embedded the Customer subform in the multitable form.

9. Create the Estimate, Job, and Cash Receipts subforms. Follow the above directions, which can be summarized as **F10, Multi, Table, Place, Linked,** and **Return.** Then select JOB, ESTIMATE, or CASH RECEIPTS, select "1," link on CUSTNO, and place the highlighted portion within the master form.

10. When completed, the multitable master form should appear approximately as shown in Figure 15.21. Press **F2** to save the complete form.

Step 4: Entering Data in the Multitable Master Form ☐ The benefits of creating these forms are recognized when entering data. This is done in the following way:

1. Press **F10** for the menu.

2. Select **Modify, Edit, Return** to receive prompts for table names. Select MASTER table (or press **F9** for Edit).

FIGURE 15. 21   The Multitable Master Form

3. Press **F10** again for another menu.

4. Select **Image, Pickform, "1"** to get the multitable form on the screen.

PARADOX will place the cursor in the data field areas. The first is customer number followed by credit limit. After entering this data, move the cursor to the next subform. The function key **F4** moves the cursor down to the next subform. **F3** moves the cursor up to the preceding form if needed. Pressing the **RETURN** key moves to a new master or subform record.

As an example, Joan received two checks on February 17, 1990 from customer number 327, Dalyn Casto. This data is entered on the cash receipts subform. After entering information on the first cash received, press **RETURN** to get a new cash receipts subform, and enter information on the second receipt.

■ SUMMARY

As DBMS languages and microcomputers have become more powerful, DBMSs designed for microcomputers have realized widespread acceptance and are used for many interesting applications. A microcomputer DBMS puts significant computational and decision-support capability in the hands of nonprogramming users. This will be an area of continued growth in the near future.

Three representative microcomputer DBMSs have been surveyed in this chapter. All three are descendants of DBMSs that were originally designed for mainframe computing environments. PARADOX is an analog of Query-By-Example (QBE). RBASE is an implementation of relational algebra. ORACLE provides a microcomputer-based version of SQL, which is the industry standard for DBMS query languages. The power of mainframe DBMSs continues to filter down to the microcomputer level, enabling wider use of DBMSs in small businesses.

■ REVIEW QUESTIONS

1. Define each of the following terms in your own words:
   a. PARADOX
   b. ORACLE
   c. conjunctive query
   d. conditional statement
   e. SWITCH statement
   f. CASE statement

2. When would you use a conditional statement, and when would you use a SWITCH statement?

3. How are tables defined in PARADOX? In RBASE? In ORACLE?

4. How are tables linked in PARADOX? In RBASE? In ORACLE?

5. Why do you suppose that the prominent microcomputer DBMSs are relational in structure? Why do DBMSs like dBASE emphasize their relational features?

PROBLEMS AND EXERCISES

1. Match the following terms with their definitions:

__Disjunctive query   a. A microcomputer DBMS whose query language is based on relational algebra

__Pro*C   b. The application language of PARADOX

__Iteration statement   c. An ORACLE feature that allows programs to be written in the C language

__PAL   d. A statement that is repeated a specified number of times

__RBASE   e. A query whose conditions are connected by "or" or an equivalent symbol

2. Write an example *conditional statement*.

3. Write an example *SWITCH statement*.

4. Write an example *iteration statement*.

5. Give an example of a *conjunctive query*.

6. Give an example of a *disjunctive query*.

7. Give an example of a query using both conjunction and disjunction.

8. Using the database structure below, write queries to provide the following information identified in items a through h. (Use the the language specified by your instructor.)

```
POLICY(POLICYNO, INSURED, AGENTNO, COMPANYNO, AMOUNT, PREMIUM)
AGENT(AGENTNO, AGENTNAME, STATE)
COMPANY(COMPANYNO, COMPANYNAME, COMMRATE, REVENUE)
```

a. A list of all companies with revenue exceeding $100 million, who offer a commission rate of less than 15%.

b. A list of policies for an amount exceeding $100,000.

c. A list of insured people who have policies with Travelers.

d. A list of companies having policies with amounts between $50,000 and $100,000, exclusive.

e. A list of commission rates for agents writing policies in Mississippi.

f. All the companies that Sam Stone writes policies for.

9. If you are using PARADOX, create a series of transactions for the Manwaring Company and enter them to update the database. If you are using another language, create the necessary tables for Manwaring and use the report-writing feature to generate a report.

PROJECTS AND PROFESSIONAL ISSUES

1. Compare and contrast the capabilities of three microcomputer DBMSs of your choosing.

2. Write a short report discussing the future of microcomputer DBMSs.

3. Do you think that microcomputer DBMSs are a substitute for mainframe systems? Why or why not? Could they ever operate in a complementary fashion? Discuss these issues.

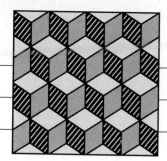

chapter sixteen

KNOWLEDGE-BASE SYSTEMS AND NATURAL LANGUAGES

Sanford Mallon, CIO of International Product Distribution, was having lunch with Billy Clark, who had been a classmate of his at Obelisk University. Billy was now the database administrator at Simpson Technologies, a high-tech manufacturing firm. He had just returned from a visit to the headquarters of his DBMS vendor, Magicware, and was excited about some of the new developments he had seen. "You know, Sandy, we have been very happy with the improvements in management information we have realized from our current database system, and our management has been very receptive to its use. But now management is asking if we can do more."

Sanford replied, "What more could a database system do? We're using the same DBMS as you, and we think that we are a state-of-the-art operation."

"Well," responded Billy, "We have one or two 'new hires' who are asking about knowledge-base systems. I had never heard of them, so I called Magicware to ask what they knew. It turns out that they are developing a product—a knowledge-base system—that will perform the usual database management functions as well as incorporating 'expertise' in the form of rules that operate on the database. I didn't really understand it until I visited Magicware's offices and saw a demonstration. Now I'm pretty excited about presenting its capabilities to our management."

"Wait a minute," said Sanford. "You owe me. How about educating a buddy, so that I can pursue this myself?"

Database technology is currently being extended to include the capabilities of managing not only data, but also rules that operate on that data, to provide more refined information to management. In this chapter, we will briefly survey some of the concepts that are driving this effort and examine some examples of how knowledge-base systems extend the capabilities of database systems. After reading this chapter, you should be able to

☐ Explain how knowledge-base systems can extend the power of database systems to provide information for management.

☐ Identify the ways in which knowledge can be represented in the form of rules.

☐ Discuss languages such as **PROLOG** and **LDL** and explain how they are influencing the development of knowledge-base systems.

☐ Explain the promise and obstacles of developing natural-language systems.

☐ INTRODUCTION TO KNOWLEDGE-BASE SYSTEMS

The development of database systems was initially motivated by a need for efficient storage, management, and retrieval of large amounts and different types of data. As progress has been made in accomplishing these objectives, a parallel interest has arisen in extending the power of the database system to include rules that operate on stored facts (data), allowing other facts to be inferred. This is an exciting prospect, since the incorporation of such expressiveness into a database system advances its capabilities for serving information needs to a higher level.

Incorporating knowledge into a database system was suggested by developments in the field of artificial intelligence (AI), which is devoted to the study of how to program intelligent behavior. AI research includes studies of the representation of logical rules that operate on data. **Expert systems** are a special type of AI development that seek to represent the rules and procedures used by an expert in solving problems in a particular problem domain, such as medicine, diesel engine repair, tax planning, computer design, and so on. Such systems rely upon a knowledge base to reason from input data.

Although expert systems studies have strongly influenced methods of representing knowledge, expert systems are not knowledge-base systems, because they do not provide the full data management capabilities of a DBMS. For example, the PROLOG language, which is a popular expert systems language to be discussed in this chapter, would seem to provide a natural bridge between database systems and knowledge-base systems. PROLOG is based on the predicate calculus, and its predicates may be viewed as relations. Also, it has the capability of expressing the logic that a person might use in converting database facts to information to aid in decision making. Nevertheless, current versions do not provide the necessary range of DBMS capabilities—transaction processing, backup and recovery, and management of secondary storage, for example—required of a knowledge-base system. DATALOG and Logical Data Language (LDL)—extended versions of PROLOG that address this problem—are under development.

Because the study of knowledge-base systems is new, a number of related definitions are not yet refined—a problem that can obscure a discussion of knowledge-base systems. For example, some authors use the term **knowledge-based systems,** whereas we say **knowledge-base systems.** Both terms are widely used to represent the same topic. We have followed the example of Ullman (1990), who has been prominent in the development of knowledge-base system concepts.

To clarify this term, we offer a working definition of a *knowledge-base system (KBS)*, as follows:

A KBS is a computer-based system comprised of the following features:

1. A database of basic facts, as with a database system
2. A database of rules that allows deductions to be made from the database of facts
3. Software, called a **knowledge-base management system (KBMS),** that supports the usual DBMS functions, as well as managing the deductive processes of the rule database.

Although there are a number of slightly different definitions in the literature, we believe that the definition above captures the essential ideas.

Currently, there are a number of active areas of KBS development. Hardware is being designed to enhance the speed with which reasoning with rules is executed. Methods are being developed for the automatic

expert systems Systems that model the decision-making processes of experts in various problem domains, such as medical diagnosis, audit decision making, and so forth; a special type of AI development.

knowledge-based system An alternative term for knowledge-base system.

knowledge-base system A system that provides the full range of database system capabilities for data storage and manipulation, as well as a facility for creating, storing, and executing rules of inference on stored data tables.

knowledge-base management system (KBMS) System software that supports the usual range of DBMS functions, as well as managing the deductive process of the rule database operating on the fact database.

maintenance of the semantic integrity of knowledge bases. The use of logic to express and reason with knowledge involving uncertainty, beliefs, and time is being studied and refined.

In the following sections we will expand on certain of these topics. We first examine the concept of knowledge as it relates to databases.

☐ KNOWLEDGE AND DATABASES

The widespread success of database systems, combined with complex management information needs and developments emanating from the study of artificial intelligence, has resulted in a growing interest in extending database systems to knowledge-base systems. This transition is to a higher level of abstraction of information. For example,

Vendor Smith is located in Los Angeles

is typical of a fact that might be maintained in a database system. One has little difficulty thinking of this information being contained, for example, in the following relational tuple:

vendor(Smith, Los Angeles,...)

On the other hand, information such as

Vendor Smith is a dependable supplier

is not such a precise fact, but represents a higher form of information. Such higher forms of information often depend on logical relationships among database facts. For example, a "dependable vendor" may be identified from relationships among order and delivery dates, as well as complete and partial shipments. Being able to specify such relationships raises the utility of the database to where knowledge can be used to define, control, and interpret the data it maintains. These ideas are formalized in the following taxonomy developed by Wiederhold (1984):

structural knowledge Knowledge about dependencies and constraints among data.

general procedural knowledge Knowledge that can only be described by a procedure.

application-specific knowledge Knowledge that is determined by the rules and conventions that apply to a specific problem domain.

enterprise-directing knowledge Knowledge that helps an enterprise to make decisions.

1. **Structural knowledge** is knowledge about dependencies and constraints among data. For example, "insertion into a CUSTOMER relation is dependent on establishing that the customer has good credit."

2. **General procedural knowledge** is knowledge that can only be described by a procedure. For example, "matching the amount of product ordered with the amount of product received allows payment to be authorized."

3. **Application-specific knowledge** is knowledge that is determined by the rules and conventions that apply to a particular problem domain. For example, "determine the lowest cost plan for a two-week vacation in Hawaii."

4. **Enterprise-directing knowledge** is knowledge that helps an enterprise to make decisions. For example, for a snackfood manufactur-

er, integrating information on costs, revenues, sales, and competitive products by store can help in making market strategy decisions.

The knowledge that exists in the database systems discussed prior to this chapter is made up of facts and instances that are stored in relations. This is termed **extensional knowledge.** Knowledge that is defined beyond the factual content of the database is termed **intensional knowledge.** Most knowledge-base systems under development store the intensional knowledge in the form of logical rules.

Let's clarify these ideas with an example. Examine Figure 16.1. Our database consists of the single table, PARTS, which contains the attributes SUBPART and PART. We can retrieve the names of all parts of which part 250 is a subpart by the relational calculus query:

```
GET(X) :- PARTS(250,X)
```

This syntax is slightly different from the one we saw in Chapter 8 (and we'll have more to say on this), but it is interpreted in a familiar way. In English, this would be read, "From the PARTS relation retrieve all the tuples having the value 250 in the SUBPART column, then assign the corresponding part value to the variable X. Store the value for X as a tuple in the GET relation." In this example, the resulting values for X are 300 and 315.

Taking the information from this query a step farther, we see that part 300, of which part 250 is a subpart, is itself a subpart of part 324. This can be seen by inspecting the PARTS relation. By transitivity 250 is also a subpart of part 324 and so part 324 should probably be in the query solution. Logically, this transitivity of part and subpart could go on and on, but in this example of PARTS, there are only two levels of subparts. We see, however, that it would be convenient if we could write a query to find all the parts for which a given part is a primitive (second level) subpart. (For example, part 250 is a primitive subpart for part 324.) One alternative is the addition of a table that lists parts and their primitive subparts, as illustrated in Figure 16.2. The query to find the parts for which part 250 is a primitive subpart is

```
GET(X) :- PRIMITIVE_PARTS(250,X)
```

The result is 324 and 350.

Unfortunately, the PRIMITIVE_PARTS table contains redundant data, that is, data already available in PARTS. It was derived from the

---

extensional knowledge Facts that are stored in database relations.

intensional knowledge Knowledge that is deduced from extensional knowledge by the applications of rules.

FIGURE 16.1   PARTS Table

PARTS =	SUBPART	PART
	200	315
	250	300
	250	315
	300	324
	315	350

PRIMITIVE_PARTS =	PRIM_PART	PART
	200	350
	250	324
	250	350

FIGURE 16.2   **PRIMITIVE_PARTS Table**

PARTS table using our knowledge that a primitive subpart is a second-level subpart. Constructing special tables to answer every conceivable information need would be very inefficient. It would be better if we could just give the database a rule that establishes the desired relationships and operates directly on the original extensional database. This is roughly the type of capability that is sought by a KBS.

Returning to our example, let **PARTS** be the extensional database. We then define the intensional database as

```
PRIMITIVE_PARTS(X,Z):- PARTS(X,Y) AND PARTS(Y,Z)
```

This may be read as

In the relation PRIMITIVE_PARTS, X is a primitive subpart of Z [PRIMITIVE_PARTS(X,Z)] if (:-), in the relation PARTS, X is a subpart of Y [PARTS(X,Y)] *and* Y is a subpart of Z [PARTS(Y,Z)].

We have simply defined a rule to operate on the **PARTS** table to retrieve primitive subpart information. We may now write a simple query to retrieve the desired information from **PARTS**:

```
GET(Z):- PRIMITIVE_PARTS(250,Z)
```

The result is again 324 and 350, and the problem of maintaining redundant data has been eliminated.

One can imagine the clumsiness of a system where all such queries were satisfied by actually creating separate tables such as PRIMITIVE_PARTS. The intensional form allows specification of the same data in compact form: Redundancy is reduced, and storage space is saved.

To further illustrate fundamental concepts and to give you sufficient knowledge to perform hands-on exercises and projects, we introduce a logic-implementation language. The language concepts we present are simple and provide an easy transition from the examples we have discussed to broader applications in a concrete way. We have chosen PROLOG, an implementation of the same relational calculus ideas we studied in Chapter 8, which also includes the capability for creating rules to operate on extensional databases. Moreover, PROLOG forms the basis for some of the KBS languages that are being developed, such as DATALOG and LDL.

Although most versions of **PROLOG** use more or less standard notation, a few minor differences may occur. Since many readers may have easy access to a microcomputer, we use TURBO PROLOG, one of the more popular versions available for use on the microcomputer.

☐ KNOWLEDGE REPRESENTATION WITH RULES

In this section, we elaborate on mechanisms for expressing logic with rules. We describe basic rule syntax and provide a general example of combining rules into backward-chaining and forward-chaining strategies of evaluation. We then discuss the expression of rules in PROLOG.

Rule Formulation
Rules are a very intuitive method of representing knowledge. We have relied on your intuition in interpreting the rules that were illustrated in the previous discussion, and you could probably write some rules of your own just from studying those examples.

A rule is comprised of a hypothesis and a conclusion. If the hypothesis is satisfied, then a conclusion can be inferred. For instance, "*If* D is a dog (hypothesis), *then* D has four legs (conclusion)." The conclusion may alternatively be an action, as in, "If the fever is accompanied by a cough (hypothesis), one should see the doctor (conclusion-action)."

Simple rules such as these are not often useful until they are combined into richer knowledge representation schemes. There are two general methods for combining rules: One is *forward chaining*, and the other is *backward chaining*. To explain these concepts, we use a simple analogy.

Think of a flight from Salt Lake City to Bangkok as a set of rules where Salt Lake City is the desired starting point and Bangkok is the desired destination. Deduction, which amounts to combining rules, is applied to the task of finding connecting flights between the cities.

There are no direct flights from Salt Lake City to Bangkok. What one must do is to examine the scheduling book that describes all flights and try to find connecting flights that go to, say, Los Angeles, then to Honolulu, then to Tokyo, and then to Bangkok. In this way, a chain of routes is devised.

There are two fundamental ways to solve the problem. One method is to start with Bangkok and then look up the cities from which flights arrive in Bangkok. We find, for example, that there are various flights arriving from Tokyo. Each such segment, from some city to Bangkok, can be viewed as a rule. Thus,

```
GET(X):- SEGMENT(Bangkok,X)
```

generates a list of cities from which flights are scheduled to Bangkok. Tokyo would be in this list. In plain English, this would be expressed as follows:

If a city schedules a flight to Bangkok (hypothesis), then that city is a candidate for our trip (conclusion).

Simplifying a bit, since Tokyo is one of these cities, we can make Tokyo our destination, and look up all the flights that arrive in Tokyo, among which is a flight from Honolulu. We might then make Honolulu the destination and keep working in this manner until we find a connection from

backward chaining A logical
chain of rules proceeding from
a conclusion to a hypothesis.

forward chaining A logical
chain of rules proceeding from
a hypothesis to a conclusion.

Salt Lake City. In this case, we are working backward from Bangkok, a process termed **backward chaining.**

Alternatively, we can begin with Salt Lake City and start going forward. In this instance, we look up all the flights that leave Salt Lake City and see that they go, say, to Los Angeles or Honolulu, or Denver or Chicago; then we try to find a flight from Los Angeles or Honolulu, or Denver or Chicago to go to Tokyo, and then to Bangkok. This is roughly the methodology of **forward chaining.**

Rules in PROLOG

In **PROLOG**, rules are expressed in a familiar way.

```
C:- H₁ & H₂ & . . . & Hₖ.
```

The ":-" symbol can be read as "if," something we have been doing informally. The above PROLOG clause is read as

```
C is true, if H1 and H2 and . . . (so forth) and Hk are true.
```

We could also use "or" instead of "and." The period denotes the end of the rule clause.

Here is a concrete, familiar example.

```
parent(X,Y):- mother(X,Y) or father(X,Y).
```

(By PROLOG convention we have switched to the use of lower case letters to denote relations.) This would be read as

```
X is the parent of Y if X is the mother of Y
    or if X is the father of Y.
```

How do we determine the truth of this question? Is X the parent of Y, or not? To find the answer, X and Y must be bound to actual instances (values) in the database. Then the truth of the statement will depend on the truth of its parts. Suppose that the following facts exist in the extensional database. (Values in PROLOG must begin with a lowercase letter, hence "Jane" is expressed as "jane" and so on.)

```
mother(jane,alex)
mother(tami,anne)
father(john,anne)
```

We now pose the PROLOG query,

```
?parent(john,alex).
```

In the rule for parent, X is now bound to john, and Y is bound to alex. To compute the solution, the rule must be demonstrated to be true or false. In this case, we have

```
mother(john,alex)
```

which is not a database fact, nor is

```
father(john,alex)
```

a database fact. Therefore,

```
parent(john,alex)
```

cannot be deduced from the database, and the answer is FALSE. However, the query

```
?parent(tami,anne)
```

will be interpreted as TRUE, since

```
mother(tami,anne)
```

is a database fact, which is sufficient to establish that

```
parent(tami,anne)
```

is TRUE.

Let's suppose that we want to know who the parents of Anne are. That is,

```
?parent(X,anne).
```

In words we are saying, "Look for any names that qualify as parents of Anne. Then assign them, one by one, to the variable X.' (Variable names in PROLOG must begin with a capital letter.) A search of the database facts finds that

```
mother(tami,anne), and
father(john,anne).
```

Thus the result of the query will be

```
X = tami
X = john.
```

Logic-based languages provide the capability of computing answers to queries that cannot be easily accomplished by conventional database manipulation languages. Although view creation in conventional languages is similar to the use of rules to define intensional databases, the view definition capabilities of relational DBMSs are not as powerful as logical rules. (See Ullman, 1990, for details.) Transitive relationships such as hierarchies of parts, lists of ancestors, and management hierarchies are important examples.

Suppose that we have workers who are managed by department managers, and department managers who are managed by division managers. Both division and department managers may then be involved in evaluating worker performance. We can express this logical relationship recursively, as follows:

```
evaluates(X,Y) :- managerof(X,Y).                    (1)
```

(read "X evaluates Y if X is manager of Y").

```
evaluates(X,Y):- evaluates(Z,Y) & manager of(X,Z). (2)
```

(read "X evaluates Y if Z evaluates Y and X is manager of Z"). Suppose the following facts exist in the extensional database:

```
managerof(john,bob)
managerof(john,ray)
managerof(bob,frank).
```

We pose the following query:

```
?evaluates(john,bob).
```

The result is TRUE by rule (1), since

```
managerof(john,bob)
```

is a fact. We pose another query

```
?evaluates(john,frank).
```

The result is TRUE by rule (2), since

```
evaluates(bob,frank) and managerof(john,bob)
```

are both true.

Suppose we wished a list of all employees who are evaluated by John. This could be expressed as follows:

```
?evaluates(john,X).
```

The result would be

```
X = Bob by rule (1)
X = Ray by rule (1)
X = Frank by rule (2).
```

We have presented an example where the evaluation (hierarchical) path is of length two—there are a maximum of two levels of evaluation. The use of a recursive rule easily extends to paths of any length. We provide a simple demonstration of its extension to a path of length three. Suppose that we add one fact to the above database, as follows:

```
managerof(frank,carl).
```

We pose the following query:

```
?evaluates(john,carl).
```

The result is TRUE by the following train of logic:

1. Rule (2) establishes the truth of "evaluates(bob, carl)," since "evaluates(frank,carl)" is true by rule (1), and "managerof(bob,frank)" is a database fact.
2. One more application of rule (2) yields the result, since "evaluates(bob,carl)" is established, and "managerof (john,bob)" is a database fact.

The basic concepts we have presented are these:

1. Rules can be expressed as clauses that take the form

```
<conclusion> :- <list of hypotheses>.
```

The left-hand side of ":-" is true if the right-hand side of ":-" can be established through database facts or the truth of other rules.
2. Intensional (or deductive) databases can be developed from extensional databases by the addition of such rules.

We now take a closer look at PROLOG as a language for expressing rules.

☐ A SIMPLE PROLOG DATABASE APPLICATION

In this section we outline the fundamental syntax of PROLOG and demonstrate a modest database application.

More PROLOG Fundamentals

first-order logic A logical structure that is characterized by a set of objects, a set of predicates (each of which evaluates to TRUE or FALSE), and a set of functions.

clause In PROLOG, the means by which facts and knowledge are expressed; <conclusion> :- <list of hypotheses>.

PROLOG (*Pro*gramming in *Log*ic) is a language whose statements are formulas of **first-order logic,** the basis for encoding knowledge as rules. PROLOG is the foundation language for the Fifth Generation Computer Systems Project, whose aim is to develop highly intelligent computer systems that can store vast amounts of information. PROLOG is also an important tool in artificial intelligence programming, particularly in the development of expert systems.

The fundamental component of PROLOG is the **clause,** the means by which facts and knowledge are expressed. For instance, Figure 16.3 shows two basic clauses: father(harry,jane) and father(X,jane). The first clause says, "harry is the father of jane." The second clause specifies that "X is the father of jane," where X specifies a variable.

We can also write conditional clauses that express rules in the manner we have seen. For instance, Figure 16.3 shows two rules: The first says that, "X is the parent of Y" is true if "X is the mother of Y" is true (par-

```
CLAUSES
father(harry,jane).
father(X,jane).

CONDITIONAL CLAUSES
parent (X,Y):- mother (X,Y).
parent (X,Y):- father (X,Y).

CONJUNCTIONS AND DISJUNCTIONS
grandfather (X,Y):- father (X,Z), parent (Z,Y).
parent (X,Y):- mother (X,Y); father (X,Y).
```

FIGURE 16.3   Some PROLOG Conventions

ent(X,Y): - mother(X,Y)); the second says, "X is the parent of Y" is true if "X is the father of Y is true" (parent(X,Y): - father(X,Y.)

Conjunctions (ANDs) are denoted by using commas, and disjunctions (ORs) are denoted by semicolons. For example, we may have a basic rule such as X is the grandfather of Y, if X is the father of Z, and Z is a parent of Y.

```
grandfather(X,Y): - father(X,Z),parent(Z,Y).
```

Finally, every clause in PROLOG must end with a period.

The Structure of a PROLOG Application

predicate symbols Names applied to arguments in order to express a predicate.

PROLOG statements are composed of formulas that include **predicate symbols** (such as "parent," "father," or "grandfather") applied to arguments to produce "true" or "false" values. These arguments may include constants (such as "harry" and "jane") and variables (such as X, Y, and Z). (Constants may also be integers.) PROLOG convention specifies that predicate symbols and constants begin with a lower-case letter.

Let's clarify these notions. We first indicate the similarity between a relation name and its attributes and the logical notion of a predicate and its arguments. Refer again to Figure 16.1. We see a relation named PARTS with the associated attributes, SUBPART and PART. In PROLOG, this relation is a predicate, PARTS, having the arguments SUBPART and PART. Thus, if we express the predicate

```
?parts(200,315),
```

the answer TRUE should be returned since the tuple is one of the tuples of the corresponding relation.

A slightly more complex example can be constructed using Figure 16.4. The table names and attribute names have the following interpretation:

Attribute Name	Interpretation
v	vendor
vp	vendor part

```
domains
vname,location,pname,ptype, grade = string
vno,pno,q-rating = integer

predicates
v(vno,vname,location)
vp(vno,pno,q-rating)
p(pno,pname,ptype,grade)

clauses
v(1,james,la).
v(2,cline,london).
v(3,marx,denver).
v(4,myers,sf).
vp(1,25,8).
vp(1,37,9).
vp(1,28,6).
vp(1,29,7).
vp(1,39,9).
vp(2,25,9).
vp(2,37,9).
vp(3,28,7).
vp(3,37,7).
vp(3,29,8).
vp(4,37,8).
vp(3,39,8).
vp(4,28,7).
vp(4,29,7).
p(25,flange,steel,a).
p(28,stirrup,brass,aa).
p(29,bolt,iron,a).
p(37,clip,brass,aa).
```

FIGURE 16.4   Extensional Database in PROLOG

Attribute Name	Interpretation
p	part
vno	vendor number
vname	vendor name
location	location
pno	part number
q-rating	quality rating
pname	part name
ptype	part type
grade	grade

domain The PROLOG term for specification of data type.

predicate An expression that evaluates to TRUE or FALSE.

Notice that **domains** correspond to data types, **predicates** correspond to relational structures, and clauses represent tuples in relations. We define "laview" by the logical rule

```
laview(12,smith):- v(12,smith,la).
```

The rule says that (12,smith) is a fact of laview if (12,smith,la) is a fact of the v (vendor) predicate. A value such as "la" appearing on the right side of ":-", (but not on the left) may be interpreted as an existential condition. That is, for the above rule we may say that

laview(vno,vname) is true if there exists a tuple in v
such that v(vno,vname,la) is true.

We now illustrate the basic structure of a PROLOG implementation by using a simplified version of Figure 16.4.

```
        /* Example */
domains
     vname, location = string
     vno = integer

predicates
     v(vno,vname,location)

clauses
     v(1,james,la).
     v(2,cline,london).
     v(3,marx,denver).
     v(4,myers,sf).
```

The 'domains' section allows the specification of the types of values (data types) that will be provided for the relational schema defined in the "predicates" section. The "clauses" section allows the entry of data, or values, for the respective relational attributes. The clauses section may be viewed as the instances of a relational database. This is the basic structure of all PROLOG implementations.

As it stands, with our simplified version of Figure 16.4, we have created an extensional database. It contains simple facts, and we execute ordinary queries in a straightforward fashion. Suppose we wish to list the names of all vendors in Los Angeles ("la").

Our query is

```
v(_,Vendor_name,la).
```

The result will be

```
Vendor_name = james,
```

How is the query interpreted? Essentially it goes this way:

1. Look in the relation v for tuples having "la" as the value for location. Retrieve the associated value for vname, and assign it to the variable name, Vendor_name.
2. Any word that begins with a capital letter is identified as a variable—in this case, Vendor_name.

3. Any word that begins with a lower-case letter is interpreted as an attribute value.

4. The use of "_" means that the corresponding attribute value has no bearing on the solution to the query and is ignored.

Database Application   We now demonstrate a database application using PROLOG. We represent our database as shown in Figure 16.4. The data that is entered is easily recognizable. Note that character strings are all lowercase letters. We have entered the database instances under the section of the PROLOG program identified as "clauses." As things stand, we have an extensional database. Recall that the "predicates" section requires a definition of the database in terms of relation names and the corresponding attributes, and that the "domains" section defines the types of data that comprise the attribute domains.

So far, so good. To implement an intensional database we need to do a bit more. Suppose we wish to know those vendors whose products are all rated 8 or above. One way of doing this is to find those vendors who supply parts whose rating is greater than or equal to 8; then find those vendors who supply parts that are rated less than 8. The desired information is found by finding those suppliers who are in the first group, but not in the second. We illustrate as follows:

```
First Group: hrating(X):- vp(X,_,Q) and Q>=8.
```

Interpretation: hrating(X) is the result we want for the first group. The relation name "hrating" (for high ratings) has been chosen arbitrarily. Relation names can be any combination of letters, digits, and underscore characters, but they must begin with a lowercase character. X is a variable, and the fact that we have it capitalized means that we want the result printed out. In English, our query could be stated as: If any tuple in the vp relation has a Q value greater than or equal to 8, then its X value (vendor number) is a solution and is a member of the relation hrating.

```
Second Group: lrating(X): -vp(X,_,Q) and Q<8
```

Interpretation: Similar to that described above.

```
Solution: bestquality(X):-hrating(X) and (not(lrating(X))
```

Interpretation: A supplier is in the bestquality relation if it is in the group that supplies parts with quality ratings greater or equal to 8 but is not in the group that supplies parts having quality ratings less than 8.

A combined extensional and intensional database is shown in Figure 16.5. You should convince yourself that typea(X) yields a list of suppliers who provide grade a parts.

```
domains
vname,location,pname,ptype, grade = string
vno,pno,q-rating = integer

predicates
v(vno,vname,location)
vp(vno,pno,q-rating)
p(pno,pname,ptype,grade)

clauses
v(1,james,la).
v(2,cline,london).
v(3,marx,denver).
v(4,myers,sf).
vp(1,25,8).
vp(1,37,9).
vp(1,28,6).
vp(1,29,7).
vp(1,39,9).
vp(2,25,9).
vp(2,37,9).
vp(3,28,7).
vp(3,37,7).
vp(3,29,8).
vp(4,37,8).
vp(3,39,8).
vp(4,28,7).
vp(4,29,7).
p(25,flange,steel,a).
p(28,stirrup,brass,aa).
p(29,bolt,iron,a).
p(37,clip,brass,aa).
p(39,clip,steel,aaa).
hrating(X):- vp(X,_,Q) and Q>=8.
lrating(X):- vp(X,_,Q) and Q<8.
bestquality(X):- hrating(X) and not (lrating(X)).
type1(X):- p(Y,_,_,a) and vp(X,_,_) and not (vp(X,Y)).
type2(X):- vp(X,_,_).
typea(X):- type2(X) and not (type1(X)).
```

FIGURE 16.5   Combined Extensional and Intensional Databases in PROLOG

☐ LOGIC DATA LANGUAGE (LDL)

LDL represents an attempt to provide in one language the expressiveness of **PROLOG** combined with the capability to execute transactions (update, delete, etc.) in the relational database environment. The most important distinction between **PROLOG** and LDL is that LDL provides logical expressiveness as well as the full functionality of a DBMS. The following example is similar to one given by Chimenti et al. (1990):

The record of an employee could have the following form:

```
employee(name(joe,smiley),admin,education(high_school, 1967)).
```

If one wanted to retain more information about the employee, each sub-argument could be refined into a more detailed description. This could lead to a complete educational record for a person, as follows:

```
employee(name(joe,smiley),admin,education({(highschool,1967),(col
lege(harvard,bs,math),1971) (college(har
vard,ms,engr),1973)})).
```

This nesting of sets provides significant flexibility and power. In addition, LDL has adapted PROLOG rule expression conventions into a language that has broader database management capability.

☐ OTHER KNOWLEDGE REPRESENTATION SYSTEMS

Logical expressions of knowledge are the dominant way in which the development of intensional databases is being pursued. There are, however, other representation schemes that are well established in artificial intelligence research and may have future application. These other methods of representation were originally developed because of perceived limitations in the representation of knowledge by logical expression.

Semantic Networks

semantic network A network that shows relationships among facts.

Even though logical expressions are a useful way to express knowledge, they do not provide any mechanism for organizing the knowledge base. **Semantic networks** provide this capability. As with our earlier definition (Chapter 9), we may view a network as a collection of points or nodes connected by lines or edges. In the semantic network, the nodes represent concepts, while the edges denote relationships between concepts. The three examples of Figure 16.6 demonstrate some common interpretations of semantic networks.

1. *Aggregation.* This interpretation shows how parts are related to a whole. That is, as shown in Figure 16.6,
   A *is part of* B.
   Example: Sprocket is part of a bicycle.
2. *Generalization.* This interpretation is identical to the concept of generalization-specialization that was discussed in Chapter 4 in connection with object-oriented modeling. As shown in Figure 16.6, a type of object is related (*is a*) to a more general type of object. Conceptually, we have
   A *is a* B.
   Example: A horse is a mammal and a dog is a mammal.
3. *Script.* The script interpretation shows how concepts are related chronologically. That is, as shown in Figure 16.6,

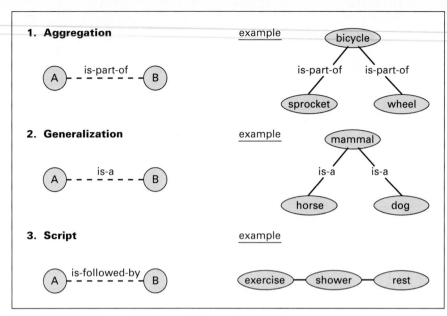

FIGURE 16.6   Semantic Network Examples

A *is followed by* B.
Example: Exercise is followed by taking a shower and by rest.

The major limitation of semantic networks is that there are no rigorous semantic rules to guide reasoning in them.

Frames

frame Data structure for representing a stereotyped situation.

A **frame** is a data structure for representing a stereotyped situation. Frame systems are organized much the same as a semantic network, except that the concept at each node is defined by a collection of attributes (in the same way that a relation is defined by a set of attributes). The frame attempts to represent knowledge in a way that reflects the fact that humans have the ability to interpret new situations on the basis of knowledge gained from experience in similar situations. This circumstance allows knowledge to grow with each experience, rather than beginning from scratch in each case.

For example, based on past experience we expect bicycles to have wheels, tires, sprockets, brakes, and handlebars and to move. These properties can be thought of as defining characteristics that, when taken as a whole, make up our understanding of the concept of a bicycle.

It is convenient to think of a frame as a template into which information is placed. A frame commonly consists of two parts: a name and a list of attribute-value pairs. The attributes are commonly called **slots** and their values are called **fillers.** Links to other frames are created by placing the name of the related frame in a slot whose purpose is to provide a connection to the other frame, thus creating a semantic network. This is illustrated by the SUPPLIERS slot in Figure 16.7.

In addition to the defining characteristics, a frame may also include

slot Frame terminology for attribute names.

filler Frame terminology for values of attribute.

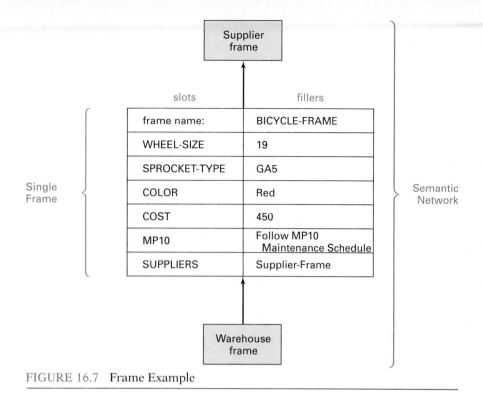

FIGURE 16.7   Frame Example

information about how the frame relates to other frames, default values for the slots, and what procedures are attached to each slot.

Although frames provide a rich representational methodology, no inference mechanisms are available.

☐ NATURAL LANGUAGES

natural language A formal language that uses English-like syntax.

Natural language processing involves the translation of **natural language,** or everyday language, into a formal language that can be processed by a computer. If we were able to translate normal English into COBOL statements, that would be an example of natural language translation. In this way, people could communicate "naturally," and the compiler would be presented with a transformation (COBOL statements) that it can process. However, human language is so complex and fraught with ambiguity that current natural language products often make errors and misinterpretations. Current implementations seem best suited to situations where there is low frequency of use and low task complexity.

The most popular of current natural language implementations are database front ends that understand database queries phrased in unconstrained English, rather than formal query languages. These front ends typically use a mixture of knowledge of syntax (grammar) and semantics (meaning) to interpret human requests for data. The most capable natural language systems can accept a range of queries, each of which may be phrased differently. They can understand sentences with missing parts, and they can handle users who do not speak gramatically correct English.

Even though some implementations are impressive, the ambiguity that is inherent in the English language creates some real obstacles. Suppose a person's weekly pay is $50. Can we unambiguously interpret the following instructions?

Increase the pay to $100 per week

(and later)

Now make the pay $50 per week again.

This seems sufficiently clear and well defined. But suppose the wording of the queries is changed as follows:

Make the pay twice as much

(and later)

Now make the pay half as much again.

"Half as much again" is ambiguous. Does it mean to increase $100 to $150 or to decrease $100 to $50? Since this is ambiguous in human communication, it is difficult to tell the computer how to interpret the instruction.

Here's another example. Suppose we seek a response to the following query:

Which employees have less than the average family size in Indiana?

This is ambiguous. It could mean:

> Of the employees living in Indiana, which have less than the average family size in the U.S. (or the world)?

> Of the employees living in Indiana, which have less than the average Indiana family size?

> Which employees living anywhere have less than the average Indiana family size?

Even though you may receive a response to the query, you may not be able to determine from that response which of the meanings was applied.

Despite these obstacles, work on natural languages is progressing, and one may expect to see viable commercial versions available in the future.

■ SUMMARY

In this chapter we have introduced the fundamental concepts of knowledge-base systems. Knowledge-base systems attempt to extend the power of database systems beyond the data themselves to information that can be derived from the data. With this as a premise, we considered the role of knowledge in database systems and how rules enable the representation of knowledge. We elaborated on this theme by illustrating how a database might be constructed to include knowledge using PROLOG as an explanatory vehicle.

We then summarized LDL, which has extended the capabilities of PROLOG into database management functions as well as knowledge representation. We concluded by a brief look at the potential and problems of natural language developments.

There is a growing interest in extending database systems to incorporate knowledge bases. It is expected that over the next decade interesting and useful developments will occur in this area.

■ REVIEW QUESTIONS

1. Define each of the following terms in your own words:
   a. expert system
   b. knowledge-base system
   c. structural knowledge
   d. general procedural knowledge
   f. application-specific knowledge
   g. enterprise-directing knowledge
   h. extensional knowledge
   i. intensional knowledge
   j. predicate
   k. predicate symbol
   l. semantic network
   m. frame
   n. natural language

2. Contrast predicate and clause in PROLOG. Give an example of each.

3. Discuss how a knowledge-base system is different from a database system.

4. Why might a knowledge-base system be preferred to a database system?

■ PROBLEMS AND EXERCISES

Part A
1. Match each term with its definition.

__Clause	a. A way of combining rules, proceeding from hypothesis to conclusion
__Domain	b. PROLOG term for data type
__Backward chaining	c. A logical structure made up of objects, predicates, and functions
__Forward chaining	d. System software that manages data storage, and data and rule manipulation
__Slot	e. Frame terminology for attribute name
__Filler	f. Frame terminology for attribute values

__First-order logic

g. A way of combining rules, proceeding from conclusion to hypothesis

__Knowledge-base management system

h. An expression of the form
<conclusion> :-<list of hypotheses>

Part B

For each of the queries below, do the following:

a. If the query can be answered using Figure 16.1E, provide the step by step procedures by which the result is found.

b. If the query cannot be answered using Figure 16.1E, indicate the reasons why.

1. Who are the siblings of Alan?
2. Who are the children of Felicia?
3. Who are the parents of Darlene?
4. Who are the sons of Alan?
5. Who are the brothers of Edward?
6. Is Charles the brother of Darlene?
7. Is Grace the sister of Charles?
8. Does Belinda have any sisters?
9. Who is the uncle of Belinda?
10. Who are the uncles of Grace?

FIGURE 16.1E   Intensional Database for End-of-Chapter Exercises

```
mother(X,Y):- parent(X,Y), female(X).
father(X,Y):- parent(X,Y), male(X).
daughter(X,Y):- parent(Y,X), female(X).
son(X,Y):- parent(Y,X), male(X).
sibling(X,Y):- father(Z,X), father(Z,Y),
               mother(W,X), mother(W,Y), (X≠Y).
brother(X,Y):- sibling(X,Y), male(X).
sister(X,Y):- sibling(X,Y), female(X).
uncle(X,Y):- brother(X,Z), parent(Z,Y).
uncle(X,Y):- p arent(Z,Y), sibling(W,Z).
             married(W,X), male(X).


married(alan,belinda).      parent(felicia,john).
male(alan).                 parent(felicia,mary).
female(belinda).            parent(neva,darlene).
male(charles).
female(darlene).
male(edward).
parent(alan,charles).
parent(alan,darlene).
parent(alan,edward).
married(charles,felicia).
married(edward,grace).
female(grace).
female(felicia).
```

Part C

1. For any of the Part B queries that could not be answered from Figure 16.1E, modify the database so that those queries can be satisfied.

2. Modify the rules of the database and add the facts needed to determine grandparent relationships.

Part D

Write queries in **PROLOG** for the following problems. Use Figure 16.4.

1. Which vendors supply parts having quality ratings greater than 8?

2. Which vendors supply bolts?

3. Which vendors supply brass clips?

4. Which parts are made of steel?

5. Where are vendors located who supply iron stirrups?

6. Which vendors supply brass parts?

7. Which vendors supply parts that are grade aa?

8. What parts are supplied by James?

9. For what quality levels does vendor w supply parts?

10. What parts are supplied by vendors located in LA?

PROJECTS AND PROFESSIONAL ISSUES

1. Do some library research on knowledge-base systems. Write an essay on which method of knowledge representation (logic, semantic networks, or frames) is most appropriate for building future KBSs. Explain the reasons for your conclusion.

2. Generate a small database for a hypothetical retail firm. Show how extending it to a knowledge base would enhance decision making in the firm.

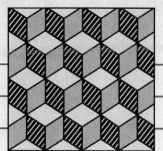

part five

MANAGING THE DATABASE ENVIRONMENT

We gave you an overview of database management issues in Part 1. Now that you know more about the technical issues of database system development and implementation, you are ready to take a more detailed look at the functions and goals of database administration. This is the subject of Chapter 17, which includes an in-depth discussion of the techniques for assuring the integrity, security, and availability of data.

Chapter 18 looks at the development and management of database systems that are distributed among a network of locations and connected by telecommunication links. This is another emerging area of database systems, and it promises to become more important as users in geographically separate locations demand more access to and control over data they create and use in their offices every day. This chapter will give you an overview of the technologies, design issues, typical configurations, and control issues associated with distributed database systems.

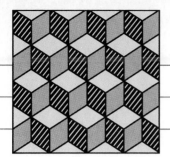

chapter seventeen

DATABASE ADMINISTRATION AND CONTROL

At the weekly staff meeting of Manwaring Consulting Services, the main business was reporting on the status of the various projects under contract. Most of the projects involved database design and development; however, Elmer Nordland was directing a project whose main focus was on administrative and control issues. Joan Manwaring thought it might be instructive for the other project managers to learn about these issues and how Elmer's team was dealing with them.

Joan asked, "Elmer, are the technical problems of database systems separate from administrative and control issues? I've heard people say that good management is good management—that sound management principles do not vary with technology."

Elmer nodded. "There is some justification for that point of view, but as I see things, the two cannot really be considered separately. In fact, we are finding that some problems cannot be easily categorized in one camp or the other. It appears to me that successful database systems implementations are always accompanied by a sound understanding of administrative and control issues."

Information systems are increasingly viewed as resources that require good management, as well as good technical features. Because database systems often form the nucleus of an organization's information system, they are the focus of many administrative issues, which we will address in this chapter. After reading this chapter, you should be able to:

☐ Explain the importance of database administration.

☐ List and describe the functions of the database administrator.

☐ Discuss how data integrity can be maintained.

☐ Describe how data security can be implemented.

☐ List the sources of database failures and compare the various recovery methods.

☐ DATABASE ADMINISTRATION: AN OVERVIEW

data administrator Manager whose responsibilities are focused on establishing policies and procedures for the organization's information system.

database administrator Manager whose responsibilities are focused on managing the technical aspects of the database system.

Database administration (DBA) is basically concerned with ensuring that accurate and consistent information is available to users and applications when needed and in the form required. Thus, database administration interacts with both the system and users (Figure 17.1). Some organizations have split the responsibility for managing information system resources between a **data administrator (DA)** and a **database administrator (DBA).** In such instances, the DA's responsibilities are usually concerned with developing general policies and procedures for the information system, while the DBA's responsibilities tend to be more technical, as suggested by Figure 17.1. The DBA will be concerned with such matters as establishing data definitions; developing programs to generate needed information; adding data to, and deleting data from, the database; implementing security and integrity controls; and managing database operations.

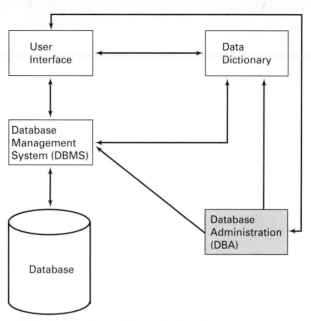

FIGURE 17.1   The DBA in the Database Environment

In addition to these primary responsibilities, the DBA should play a lead role in database planning and development and in educating users. This education includes such areas as

1. How database technology can assist the various levels of management (important to winning and maintaining management support for the database system)
2. The development of realistic expectations for the database system (important for minimizing user complaints)
3. Procedures for solving an information problem (important for maintaining system efficiency and user satisfaction).

We focus our attention on the DBA, since the responsibilities of that function are directly associated with the database system, whereas many of the DA's responsibilities exist in any organization using mechanized data. For example, establishing procedures for data collection and validation may be part of the DA's responsibility, but this responsibility is not dependent on the use of a database system.

Although there are variations in exactly where the DBA is located on the organizational chart, a reasonable location is suggested in Figure 17.2(a). Here the chief information officer (CIO) reports to the chief executive officer, and the DBA reports to the CIO. If the company has a DA, the DBA might be moved downward a notch by reporting to the DA (Figure 17.2(b)).

We now turn to an examination of specific functions that can be the DBA's responsibility.

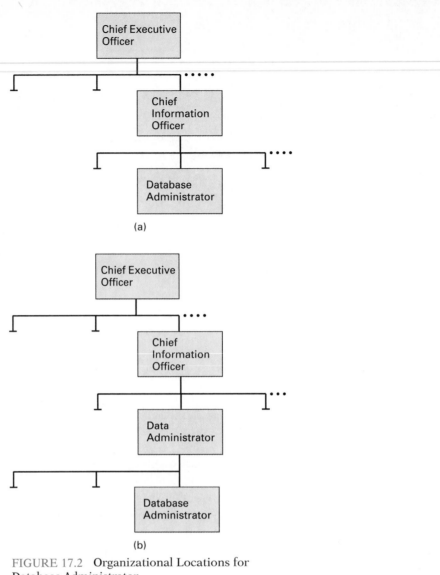

FIGURE 17.2 Organizational Locations for
Database Administrator

□ DBA FUNCTIONS

DBA functions generally fall into the areas of communicating with
database users; planning, designing, and implementing database systems;
and establishing standards and procedures. The planning, designing, and
implementing of database systems has been studied in previous chapters
and is excluded from the following discussion.

Communicating
with Users
Database systems often have three components: a central, widely used
database containing much of the firm's data; several functional databases
(e.g., for accounting) used by a more limited set of programs; and perhaps a few dedicated databases used for a single application (e.g., a bill-

of-materials database). The important organizational issue here is that the general impact of implementing a database system is the centralization of a significant portion of the firm's data.

Centralizing data through a database system tends to eliminate local ownership of data and to reduce redundancy. Ownership and control are transferred to the central data dictionary, which maintains a record of the ownership and use of each data element. Such a shifting of control over data may generate resistance from some users. This resistance can often be mitigated by actively educating users as to the advantages of learning database technology and thereby enhancing their value to the firm. The DBA, in concert with top management, should coordinate this education.

The decision to implement a database system generally signals a commitment to significant changes at the operating levels of the organization. The DBA can foster acceptance of these changes by promoting the database system internally—before implementation is begun. The importance of preparing key staff members for the implementation of a database system is hard to overemphasize. Certain aspects of their current work may be "taken over" by the information system, while standard design frameworks for systems and programs may change significantly. Some ways of doing this preparation include presentations to managers, training sessions for key personnel, and possibly the use of outside consultants. Training can be an especially important part of this preparation.

Training should give personnel a broad view of the function of a database system as an integral part of the firm's information system, as well as giving specific guidance as to how it can be used in the user's daily activities. To be successful, training should be regarded as a continuing process prompted by new hires, new releases of software, and the development of new or improved applications.

Establishing Standards and Procedures

Effective database administration requires the establishment of uniform standards and procedures. Their purpose is to maintain control of data security and data integrity in an efficient way. Standards are particularly applicable to controlling the development and use of database programming and operations.

In the programming area, standards are established to ensure that programs are adequately reviewed and tested before being put into production. These standards may require a review by a competent second party, as well as the use of test data to evaluate how a program handles both correct and erroneous data. The usual procedure includes documenting these test results.

In the area of operations, standards may be established for maintaining transaction logs, and procedures created for error correction, checkpoints, and backup and recovery.

Organizations having few standards and procedures may encounter difficulty in converting to the database environment. The record shows that the integrated data management facilitated by database systems requires good, comprehensive standards and procedures. An organization that is beginning to implement a database system may find it useful to examine the standards in use at other organizations that are already using database systems. For example, the following functions form the nucleus of standards and procedures at the Zeus Corporation.

1. Analysis and Routing of Trouble Reports. At Zeus, a formal trouble-reporting system was established in order to report all errors to the DBA. Trouble reports are analyzed to determine the likely cause of each reported problem. The reports are then routed to the appropriate manager, or user group, for disposition. Each trouble report contains a complete log (time and location of problem) and descriptive information. Each report requires a formal response to the report's initiator specifying how the problem has been resolved.

2. Monitoring of Hardware and Software. The status of all hardware and software is regularly monitored, and reports of failures and consequent action are made to appropriate managers and user groups. Periodic analysis of hardware and software requirements is made, forming the basis for decisions on replacement and upgrading, including needs for additional database storage media.

3. Testing. Performance acceptance testing is conducted to evaluate all new procedures, software, and hardware. Structural and consistency checks of the database are conducted on a regular basis.

4. Security. In consultation with Zeus management, security classifications are implemented that identify which user groups are authorized to access specific data elements in the database and what actions may be performed thereon. Computer operations are frequently monitored to assure that these access controls are functioning in the intended way.

5. Backup and Recovery. Backup and recovery procedures are tested regularly to assure their effectiveness in restoring the database after any disruption of service. A disaster plan (to respond to natural disasters such as flooding or electrical outages) has been drawn up and is tested periodically to make sure it works.

6. Performance Evaluation. Priorities have been assigned to activities that compete for database resources, such as processing transactions, generating reports, and processing queries. System performance is monitored by collecting statistics on transaction volume, response time, error rates, and hardware utilization. Input is elicited from system users to monitor their satisfaction with the system's performance. Database size and growth is also tracked. File expansion programs are run and database reorganizations are performed as necessary. Activity logs and abnormal termination logs are reviewed and summaries prepared for management evaluation.

7. Integrity Checking. Schedules have been developed at Zeus for testing the integrity of the data stored in the database.

☐ DBA GOALS

As you can see, much of the effort involved in database administration is concerned with ensuring the quality and the availability of the database system. This is in keeping with the basic DBA goals: maintaining the integrity, security, and availability of data.

A database must also be protected from accidents, such as input or programming errors, from malicious use of the database, and from hardware or software failures that corrupt data. Protection from accidents that cause data inaccuracies is part of the goal of maintaining **data integrity.** These accidents include failures during transaction processing, logical errors that violate the requirement that transactions preserve database consistency constraints, and anomalies due to concurrent access to the database **(concurrent processing).** Protecting the database from unauthorized or malicious use is termed **data security.** Although the dividing line between data integrity and data security is not precise, a working definition is as follows:

1. *Integrity* is concerned with making certain that operations performed by users are correct and maintain database consistency.
2. *Security* is concerned with limiting users to performing only those operations that are allowed.

The possibility of hardware or software failure requires that **database recovery procedures** be implemented as well. That is, means must be provided so that databases corrupted by system malfunctions can be restored to a consistent state .

These facets of database management are examined in the sections that follow.

data integrity The accuracy and consistency of data values in the database.

concurrent processing (concurrency) Occurs when two or more transactions request access to the same database record at about the same time.

data security Refers to protecting the database system from unauthorized or malicious use.

database recovery procedures The means by which a database that has been corrupted by malfunctions can be restored to a correct and consistent state.

☐ DATABASE INTEGRITY

integrity control (constraint) A restriction applied to a given set of data; used to minimize data entry errors.

A condition or restriction that is applied to a particular set of data is commonly termed an **integrity control** or **constraint.** For example, the values of hours worked in a week might be limited to less than or equal to 60 hours. Integrity controls are designed to minimize data inconsistencies caused when users or application programs make errors while entering or changing data in the database.

By enforcing semantic restrictions on data, it is possible to be reasonably confident that the contents of the database are correct and that no inconsistencies exist among related data. Although integrity constraints apply to all database models (e.g., one may apply set retention constraints in networks), most current developments apply to the relational model. Hence our discussion will focus there.

In relational model terminology, integrity controls may apply to (1) individual attributes, (2) the relationship between two different attributes (perhaps in different relations), or (3) the relationship between tuples of one or more tables. Ideally, the enforcement of integrity constraints would be carried out by the DBMS automatically as each new data item is entered. (Data not satisfying established constraints would be rejected, for example, via an error message.) Unfortunately, few DBMSs currently offer more than limited capabilities for enforcing constraints.

An alternative is to write application programs to control the input of all data to a database. This allows flexibility and comprehensiveness in applying a variety of constraints. The development of such programs, however, can be time-consuming. Sometimes both methods can be used together. The DBMS is used to the extent of its capability for monitoring semantic constraints; then application programs are developed for needs that cannot be handled by the DBMS.

Integrity Constraints in SQL

In the original proposal for SQL, a general-purpose ASSERT statement was to be used to express integrity constraints. A constraint pertaining to a single relation could be expressed as

```
ASSERT <assertion name> ON <relation name> <predicate>
```

As an example, suppose we want to specify an integrity control that the inventory balance can never be negative. We would express this constraint as follows:

```
ASSERT BALANCE_CONSTRAINT ON INVENTORY_ACCT BALANCE >= 0.
```

In this example, BALANCE_CONSTRAINT is the assertion name, IN-VENTORY_ACCT is the relation name, and the predicate is BALANCE > = 0.

Constraint assertions become slightly more complex when more than one relation is involved. Suppose that we do not allow a credit sale unless the customer appears in the APPROVED_CREDIT relation. We write this assertion as follows:

```
ASSERT CREDIT_CONSTRAINT:
(SELECT CUSTOMERNAME
FROM APPROVED_CREDIT)
CONTAINS
(SELECT CUSTOMERNAME
FROM CREDIT SALES)
```

Integrity Constraints in Query-by-Example

Some Query-by-Example (QBE) systems maintain a constraint table for each relation. To create a constraint on a relation R, a table skeleton is created for R. Then one or more rows are entered to specify the constraints. As shown in Figure 17.3,

```
I.CONSTR(I.,U.). I.
```

is entered just below the relation name INVENTORY. The general form of this syntax is

```
I.CONSTR(<condition list>). I. <constraints>
```

"I. CONSTR(<condition list>)" indicates that a constraint is being inserted.

FIGURE 17.3   QBE Constraint on Inventory Balance

INVENTORY	ITEM #	ITEM NAME	BALANCE
I. CONSTR (I., U.). I.			> = 0

The second I. refers to the entries that define the constraint. The condition list may consist of I. (for insert), D. (for delete), and U. (for update or modification), or any combination of these. In Figure 17.3, we show the restriction of inventory balances to positive numbers in the BALANCE column. CONSTR(I.,U.). asserts that the constraint should be tested whenever an insertion (I.) or update (U.) occurs in the relation.

Entries for one or more attributes are placed in the rows of the skeleton. If an entry is a constant, then the tuple being inserted, deleted, or updated must have that constant value for that attribute. In Figure 17.3, we have demonstrated an entry of the form kc, where c is a constant (0) and k is an arithmetic comparison operator (>=). This asserts that the corresponding component of a tuple must stand in relation k to c, whenever the constraint applies to the tuple. In our example, this means that whenever a value is entered into the BALANCE column, that value must not be negative.

An entry may also be blank, or have a variable name beginning with an underscore; both mean that the value can be arbitrary for that attribute. This feature is used in our second QBE example, where we do not wish to allow a credit sale unless the customer appears in the APPROVED_CREDIT relation. We show the QBE integrity constraint in Figure 17.4. We call for CREDIT_SALES and APPROVED_CREDIT skeletons and enter the information shown in Figure 17.4. This constraint asserts that the tuple to be inserted, which defines a value for "_name" in the CUSTNAME attribute in the inserted tuple, must have the same "_name" value occurring in the APPROVED_CREDIT relation.

Transaction Processing

transaction A program unit whose execution preserves the consistency of the database.

atomic transaction A transaction in which all actions associated with the transaction are executed to completion, or none is performed.

Another concept associated with database integrity is termed the database **transaction.** A transaction is a program unit whose execution preserves the consistency of the database. If the database is in a consistent state before a transaction executes, then the database should still be in a consistent state after its execution. To ensure these conditions, transactions must be **atomic,** meaning that either all actions associated with the transaction are executed to completion, or none is performed. For example, a transaction to record a customer payment of $500 might include the following actions:

1. Change the customer record by reducing the balance of the account by $500.
2. Change the cash record by increasing its balance by $500.

FIGURE 17.4   QBE Constraint Involving Two Relations

CREDIT-SALES	CUSTNAME	AMOUNT
I. CONSTR (I.). I.	_name	

APPROVED-CREDIT	CUSTNAME	LIMIT
	_name	

Perhaps the second step fails. Then the accounts will be out of balance. Figure 17.5 shows what happens when these actions are performed as a series of independent steps (a) and when they are performed as a single atomic transaction (b). The key point is that when the actions are performed atomically and one fails, then no changes are applied to the database. Such transactions are said to be **aborted.**

To support transaction processing, a DBMS must maintain a transaction record of *every change* made to the database. One way in which this is done is to use a **log.** When a customer makes a $500 payment on account, the transaction actions include (1) crediting the customer account and (2) debiting the cash account. During the execution of the transaction, all write operations may be deferred until the last action of the transaction has been executed. The resulting updates are recorded on the transaction log. When all actions have been executed, the update information on the log is used to write the updated information to the appropriate database records. If the system fails before the transaction completes its entire execution, the information on the log is never written to those records. We will have more to say about this log when we discuss recovery techniques.

aborted transaction Transaction that is cancelled before changes are applied to the database.

log A record of all transactions and the corresponding changes to the database.

Concurrency Control

Suppose that the League of Women Voters (LWV) in Smithville decides to have a Ham and Turkey Dinner. The Chamber of Commerce (CC) in nearby Johnstown decides that it is also time to reward its members with a Ham and Beans Dinner. Both organizations contact their town's distribution center for Bounty Foods. The LWV wants 25 hams; the CC wants 35 hams. Both orders are transmitted to the database system at the re-

FIGURE 17.5   Independent and Atomic Transactions

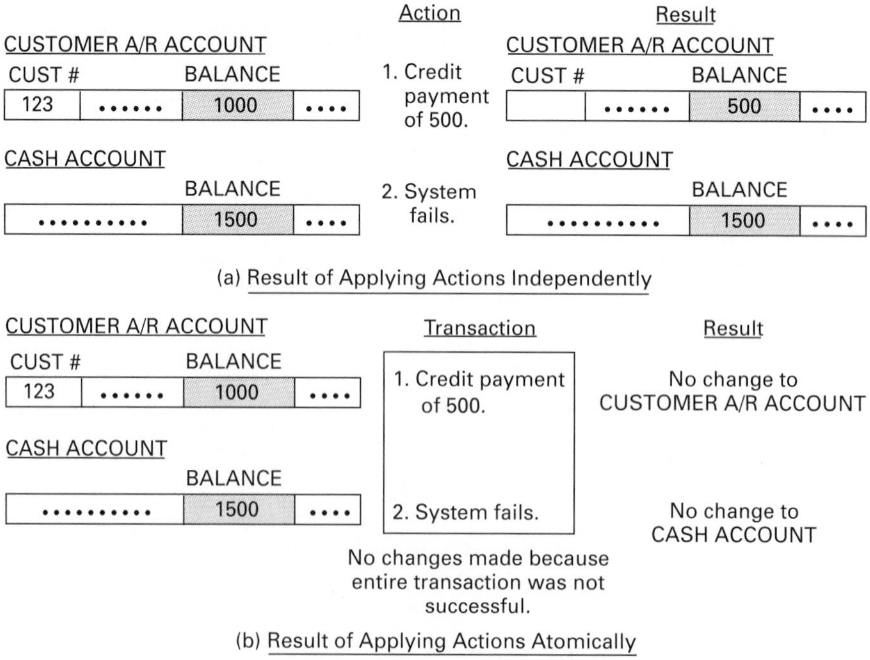

(a) Result of Applying Actions Independently

(b) Result of Applying Actions Atomically

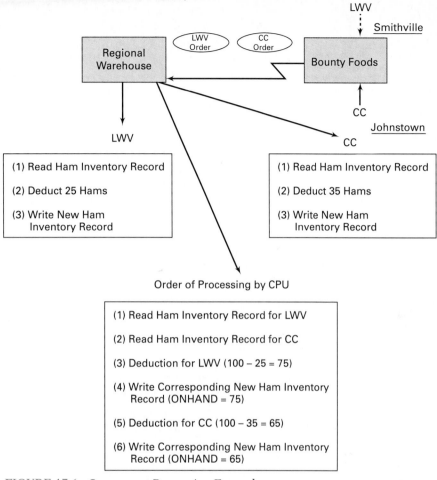

FIGURE 17.6   Concurrent Processing Example

gional warehouse at the same time (Figure 17.6). The LWV order arrives a fraction of a second before the order from the CC. An image of the inventory record for ham is placed into the computer's working area. The inventory record shows that 100 hams are in stock. But before the LWV transaction can be completed and the inventory record updated, the CC transaction also gets a copy of the same inventory record showing 100 hams in stock, which is placed in its working area. Both records show that the order in question can be filled.

Suppose the LWV transaction is completed first. The rewritten inventory record shows 100–25 = 75 hams left in stock. Upon completion of the CC transaction, the inventory record is overwritten with 100–35 = 65 hams in stock. What has really happened is that 60 hams have been sold from a stock of 100, leaving only *40* hams in the warehouse, but the system's inventory balance shows *65* hams on hand. Problems galore! This example illustrates the fundamental nature of concurrent processing: If two or more users are accessing the database at the same time and transactions are interleaved (as in the Bounty Foods example), undesirable results may occur.

A common way of preventing the concurrency problem is through a simple locking policy. In the above example, the first transaction to arrive would **lock** (prevent access by any other transactions) the ham inventory record (Figure 17.7) until the first transaction's processing was complete. When a record is locked by one user, no other user may access it for update. In this case, the CC could not have accessed the record until the LWV's transaction was completed.

Although this approach is simple and useful, it is not foolproof. Suppose both the LWV and the CC wanted to order *ham* and *turkey* (Figure 17.8). Suppose that the LWV requests the turkey inventory record first. Because it is locked, the CC transaction accesses the ham inventory record first. These records are thus locked from use by other users. Within moments both the LWV and the CC have completed their processing on the turkey and ham inventory records, respectively, and are now ready to ac-

lock In transaction processing, prevents access to a database record by a second transaction until the first transaction has completed all of its actions.

FIGURE 17.7 Simple Locking Procedure to Avoid Concurrent Update Problem

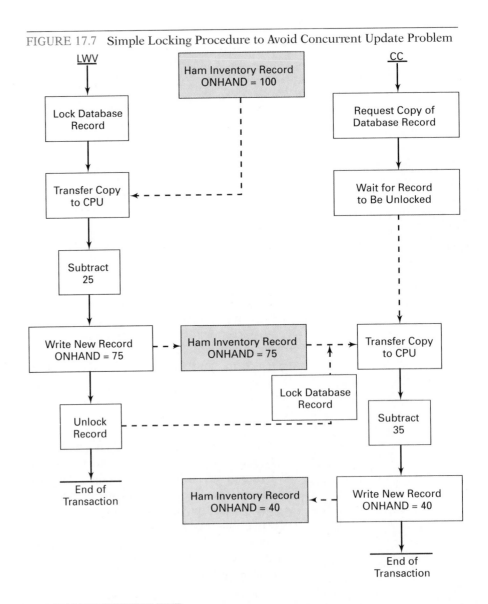

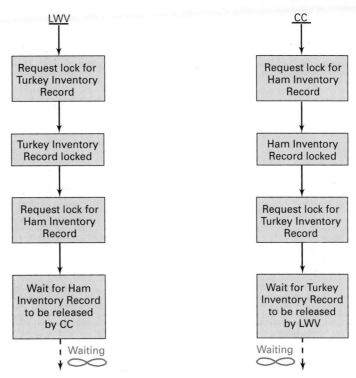

FIGURE 17.8   Locking Scheme Leading to Deadlock Situation

cess the other record. However, neither user has completed its entire transaction, so the records it has accessed remain locked. We are in a **deadlock** situation where neither user can proceed.

There are several methods of dealing with deadlock. One approach is to order the records being locked. That is, if records *A* and *B* are to be accessed, they must always be accessed in that order. In the above instance, requests for the ham and turkey inventory records might be required to access the ham inventory record first and the turkey inventory record second. It is easy to see that the deadlock situation could, thereby, never occur. When the LWV finished processing, all accessed records would be unlocked for use by the CC. This can slow down operations, however, as waiting transactions may become a serious bottleneck. Moreover, if a transaction has to wait too long for a record to unlock, it may be canceled and required to try again later. This tends to give users a low opinion of the database system.

Some DBMSs perform **deadlock detection** by regularly checking to see if the waiting line for any record or resource is too long. Another method of detection is to (in effect) draw an arrow from the transaction to the record being sought and then draw an arrow from that record to the transaction that is currently using it. If the graph has cycles, deadlock is detected. This is illustrated in Figure 17.9. Deadlock-detecting procedures complete their function by canceling one of the transactions and advancing the next transaction in the queue.

Another option for controlling concurrent processing is **two-phase locking.** A transaction is said to follow the two-phase locking protocol if

deadlock Two transactions are mutually excluded from accessing the next record required to complete their transactions; also called a "deadly embrace."

deadlock detection A periodic check by the DBMs to determine if the waiting line for some resource exceeds a predetermined limit.

two-phase locking A method of controlling concurrent processing in which all read and write locks must precede the first unlocking operation.

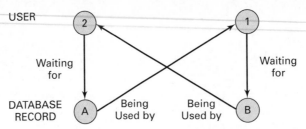

USER

Waiting for

Waiting for

DATABASE RECORD

Being Used by   Being Used by

FIGURE 17.9   Deadlock Detected by Identifying Cycles

read_lock The user has the right to read a given record.

write_lock The user has the right to read and to update the given record.

all locking operations—**read_lock, write_lock**—precede the first unlock operation in the transaction. A read_lock allows reading of a record, while a write_lock, as an upgrade of read_lock, allows both reading and updating of a record.

Two-phase locking has been proven to guarantee serializability, which means that transactions can be executed in such a way that their results are the same as if each transaction's actions were executed in sequence without interruption. Two-phase locking comes with a price, however. It can lead to deadlock unless used in conjunction with a deadlock-prevention protocol.

As an example, in Figure 17.10(a) we see a proper two-phase locking procedure that leads to deadlock. Transaction 1 (T_1) acquires a read_lock on H (for Ham) at the same time that T_2 acquires a read_lock on T (for Turkey). Two steps later, both T_1 and T_2 seek write_locks on

FIGURE 17.10   Example of Incorrect (a) and Correct (b) Two-Phase Locking

T_1	Turkey (T) and Ham (H) Inventory Values	T_2	Turkey (T) and Ham (H) Inventory Values
Read_lock (H)	DISALLOWED	Read_lock (T)	
Read_item (H)	H = 100	Read_item (T)	T = 30
Write_lock (T)	DISALLOWED	Write_lock (H)	
Unlock (H)		Unlock (T)	
Read_item (T)	T = 30	Read_item (H)	
T = T − 25		H = H − 25	
Write_item (T)		Write_item (H)	
Unlock (T)	T = 5	Unlock (H)	

(a)

T_1	Turkey (T) and Ham (H) Inventory Values	T_2	Turkey (T) and Ham (H) Inventory Values
Read_lock (H)			
Read_item (H)	H = 100		
Write_lock (T)			
Unlock (H)		Write_lock (H)	
Read_item (T)	T = 30	Read_item (H)	H = 100
T = T − 25		H = H − 25	
Write_item (T)	T = 5	Write_item (H)	H = 75
Unlock (T)		Unlock (H)	
		Read_lock (T)	
		Read_item (T)	T = 5
		Unlock (T)	

(b)

those database records that are currently held in a read_lock by the other. This action is disallowed because a value might then be changed by a write operation performed by the other transaction. The concurrent holder of the read_lock would then be reading an incorrect value.

The use of two-phase locking with a deadlock-prevention protocol is shown in Figure 17.10(b). We have added the requirement that every transaction lock all of the data items it needs in advance. If any of the data items cannot be obtained, then none of the items is locked, and the transaction is placed on hold until all of the needed items are available. In Figure 17.10(b), we assume that T_1's request has begun momentarily prior to that of T_2. T_2 cannot lock all of its required data items until H is unlocked by T_1. In this way, the deadlock of Figure 17.10(a) is avoided.

□ DATABASE SECURITY

Database integrity problems can be challenging, but they are generally easier to cope with than malicious access to the database, which includes the following:

1. Theft of information
2. Unauthorized modification of data
3. Unauthorized destruction of data.

Thus, database security methods focus on preventing unauthorized users from accessing the database. Because DBMS features that make the database easy to access and manipulate also open doors to intruders, most DBMSs include security features that allow only authorized persons or programs to access data and then restrict the types of processing that can be accomplished once access is made.

Authentication   Database access usually requires user authentication and authorization. For user authentication, the first level of security establishes that the person seeking system entry is an authorized user. His or her identity may be established by (1) something the user knows, such as a log-on number and password, (2) something the user possesses, such as a plastic ID card, or (3) a physical representation of the user, such as a fingerprint or voiceprint.

Passwords, by far the most common and often the least expensive security method, are adequate for many applications. However, once a potential intruder knows the password length and the alphabet from which it is derived, passwords can be repeatedly generated and tried over a period of time until access is eventually gained. For some password schemes, the average time required to do this may be long enough to discourage casual intruders. If the potential payoff is large enough, however, the DBA should devise a password scheme that does not leave this factor to chance.

The ideal password scheme limits unauthorized systems access by creating a password that is difficult to guess, but still easy for the user to remember. For some applications, it may be quite sufficient to specify password parameters such as password length and alphabet to be used, and then let the user devise the password. If this approach is used, it may be advisable to appoint a password supervisor to ensure that password parameters are satisfied and that duplications are avoided.

Whether users select their own passwords or whether passwords are issued from a central authority, it can be useful to designate a supervisor who maintains an encrypted list of all passwords on a disk that is accessible only to that supervisor. (We will discuss encryption in more detail shortly.) Also, when an employee terminates or transfers to a new functional area, all passwords to which that employee had access must be changed. This is very important, since disgruntled ex-employees have been known to sabotage systems.

For extremely sensitive systems, more sophisticated schemes may be considered. One such scheme programs the computer to conduct a question-and-answer session with the user, drawing on questions and answers the user has previously stored in the system. The questions are personal, so only the user is likely to answer them correctly. Question sequences might occur as follows:

- What is your grandfather's middle name?
- When is your daughter's birthday?
- What is special about September 18?

When the user signs on and keys in his or her personal identification number, the computer asks questions randomly selected from the stored data. The selection can also be varied from one time to another to limit the possibility that other persons may observe the answer to all the questions.

Still another method of protecting against unauthorized access is through the use of a prearranged algorithm. That is, the computer gives the prospective user an authentication number chosen at random and asks for a response. The user applies a prearranged transformation on the number and transmits the result. The computer compares the received value with what it has computed. If they match, then access is granted. This is particularly useful if a would-be intruder has tapped into a communication line. All he or she will observe is the result of the algorithm applied to the number. The difficulty of figuring out the algorithm from this information is enormous.

Access control is enhanced if all denied-access attempts produce a log entry and a time delay (the latter increases the time required to gain unauthorized access). The system should automatically log off users who are unable to supply a valid password within a given time or number of tries. It is also desirable that passwords not be displayed on the screen and that users not leave the system unattended after sign-on has been accomplished.

An important aspect of database security is determining when user authentication is sufficient and when it should be combined with specific identification of the terminal. With the increasing incidence of illegal intrusion by so-called "hackers," there have been cases where user authorization was satisfied by someone who was not communicating from any of the legitimate system terminals. In addition, switching mechanisms sometimes misconnect and noise in a communication line can cause a polling mechanism to connect an incorrect device due to address modification. Such errors are often undetected, which degrades reliability and can compromise security. Thus automatic terminal identification is recommended whenever telecommunication switching equipment is used.

Undesirable outside intrusion may alternatively be prevented by implementing dial-up/call-back procedures. With this strategy, anyone attempting to gain system access supplies the necessary authentication information. The system then hangs up and calls back to a legitimate terminal location—assuming one was given. This way, if intrusion does occur, it has to emanate from a legitimate network microcomputer. Dial-up/call-back capabilities can, however, represent a significant additional expense.

Unauthorized system access can be further controlled by allowing only certain types of transactions to be transmitted from a given terminal. Restricting certain terminals to performing a narrow range of tasks can be an effective and easy-to-apply control. For example, terminals in relatively public areas can be limited to read-only functions.

Authorization and Views

view A definition of a restricted portion of a database.

A **view** is a means of providing a user with a personalized model of the database. It is also a useful way of limiting a user's access to various portions of the database: data a user does not need to see is just hidden from view. This simplifies system usage while promoting security. Views can be represented by executing selects, projections, and joins on existing relations. The user might also be restricted from seeing any part of an existing relation, or from executing joins on certain relations.

By creating different views for different classes of users, a high degree of access control is automatically attained. Although a user may be denied direct access to a base relation, the user may be able to access *part* of that relation through a view. A combination of relational-level security and view-level security can be used to limit a user's access to precisely the data that the user needs.

Types of View Access ☐ Different types of access authorization may be allowed for a particular view, such as the following:

1. Read authorization: allows reading, but not modification of data
2. Insert authorization: allows insertion of new data, but no modification of existing data
3. Update authorization: allows modification of data, but not deletion
4. Delete authorization: allows deletion of data.

These types of authorizations are typically made by assigning different passwords to a view. For example, suppose that in a PROJECTS relation (Figure 17.11), we wanted to restrict a particular user, Harry Bean, to having read-authorization access to just the PROJNO and LOCATION attributes. This could be realized by creating a view that includes only the PROJNO and LOCATION attributes, as shown in Figure 17.12. A password with read access may then be defined for PROJNO_LOC, as follows:

```
GRANT READ ACCESS ON PROJNO_LOC TO HARRY BEAN
```

```
PROJECTS
PROJNO    CUSTOMER        LOCATION

   1      BURGER, W.      VAUDEVILLE
   2      DOWNING, B.     SERIES CITY
   3      MCENROE, J.     OUTLAND
   4      DEXTER, M.      MARTINSVILLE
   5      JOINER, W.      ALPENHAGEN
   6      NIXON, R.       SAN CLEMENTE
   7      MARX, K.        OUTLAND
   8      BOND, J.        MARTINSVILLE
   9      ELWAY, J.       ALPENHAGEN
  10      LETTERMAN, D.   OUTLAND
```

FIGURE 17.11   **PROJECTS** Relation

```
PROJNO_LOC
PROJNO    LOCATION

   1      VAUDEVILLE
   2      SERIES CITY
   3      OUTLAND
   4      MARTINSVILLE
   5      ALPENHAGEN
   6      SAN CLEMENTE
   7      OUTLAND
   8      MARTINSVILLE
   9      ALPENHAGEN
  10      OUTLAND
```

FIGURE 17.12   **PROJNO_LOC** Relation

The general form for such SQL authorization is given using the **GRANT** statement:

```
GRANT <privilege list> ON <relation or view name> TO <user
list>
```

The *privilege list* allows several privileges (e.g., read, delete, and/or update) to be granted in a single statement.

Views and Security in SQL

Because SQL has become the de facto standard for relational database languages and provides several facilities for using views for security, we focus on SQL as our model for this section. The general syntax of SQL statements that create views is this:

```
CREATE VIEW viewname (list of attributes desired, if different
from base table)
    AS query
```

Let's consider a concrete example using the **PERSNEL** base relation that has the schema,

```
PERSNEL(ID,NAME,ADDRESS,HWAGE,DEPTNO).
```

Suppose we want to limit access to the PERSNEL table for user U_1 to just those employees in Department 35. We would express this view as

```
CREATE VIEW DEPT_35
    AS SELECT ID, NAME, ADDRESS, HWAGE, DEPTNO
        FROM PERSNEL
        WHERE DEPTNO = 35
```

Read privileges are granted to U_1 in the usual way, and U_1 can now access the DEPT_35 view to see the needed subset of the base table, PERSNEL. Although the values of PERSNEL are actually stored on disk, any views derived from PERSNEL (e.g., DEPT_35) are created at the time they are used. This is unseen by U_1, however, and is generally of no concern to the user.

Suppose that U_1 is to be limited to a view of PERSNEL that excludes salary information (HWAGE). This view would be created in the following way:

```
CREATE VIEW PERS_NO_SAL
    AS SELECT ID, NAME, ADDRESS, DEPTNO
        FROM PERSNEL
```

These two examples demonstrate the creation of views that are, respectively, row and column subsets of the base relation PERSNEL. The next example shows how a view is created that is both a row and column subset of the base relation PERSNEL.

```
CREATE VIEW DEPT_35
AS SELECT ID, NAME, ADDRESS, DEPTNO
    FROM PERSNEL
    WHERE DEPTNO = 35
```

U_1 can now access a view of PERSNEL that includes ID, NAME, and ADDRESS (but not HWAGE) for those employees who are assigned to Department 35.

Some users may be assigned responsibility for maintaining data elements and are thereby permitted to access the SYSTABLES for which they have responsibility. Since the SYSTABLES are themselves relations, views can be created for them, as well. An example follows:

```
CREATE VIEW MY_TABLES
AS SELECT *
    FROM SYSTABLES
    WHERE CREATOR = USER
```

USER is a keyword that requires a value assignment at time of execution. Thus, if user U_1 enters the statement

```
SELECT *
FROM MY_TABLES
```

the system will execute the query as if it were written

```
SELECT *
FROM SYSTABLES
WHERE CREATOR = U₁
```

Views like this are *context-dependent,* since the result that is produced is dependent on the context (U_1) being used.

Views can also be constructed from more than one base relation. Consider the **PERSNEL** and **PLANT** base relations, with the following schemas:

```
PERSNEL(ID,NAME,ADDRESS,HWAGE,DEPTNO,PID)
PLANT(PID,CITY,DEPTNO).
```

We create a view that identifies each employee with the city in which he or she works as follows:

```
CREATE VIEW EMPLOYEE_LOCATION
    AS SELECT ID, NAME, CITY
        FROM PERSNEL, PLANT
        WHERE PERSNEL.PID = PLANT.PID
```

Sometimes a user may be allowed access to summary data maintained in a base relation, but not allowed access to individual values. For example, a user may be allowed access only to the average hourly-wage rate from the **PERSNEL** relation. This constraint could be established by creating the following view:

```
CREATE VIEW AVG_HRATE (ID, NAME, AVRATE, DEPTNO)
    AS SELECT ID, NAME, AVG (HWAGE),DEPTNO
    FROM PERSNEL
    GROUP BY DEPTNO
```

Note what is happening here. An attribute is being created in the view (**AVRATE**) that does not exist in the base table, **PERSNEL**. Its values are created in the **SELECT** statement by specifying that the values in the attribute **HWAGE** be averaged by department number.

Although the use of views can be an effective means of ensuring security, the system must be able to adapt to changing requirements over time. SQL provides this capability through the use of **GRANT** and **REVOKE** privileges. Here are some examples:

```
GRANT SELECT ON TABLE PERSNEL TO JOHN, SYLVIA
```

This means that John and Sylvia are authorized to perform any **SELECT** operations on the **PERSNEL** table.

```
GRANT SELECT, UPDATE (HWAGE) ON TABLE PERSNEL TO HARVEY
```

This means that Harvey has the right to perform **SELECT** operations on the table **PERSNEL**, as well as the right to update the **HWAGE** attribute.

```
REVOKE SELECT ON TABLE PERSNEL FROM JOHN
```

This means that John is no longer authorized to perform SELECT operations on the PERSNEL table.

These examples illustrate a few of the possibilities for granting or revoking authorization privileges. The list of privileges for both base relations and views includes SELECT, UPDATE, DELETE, and INSERT.

The GRANT option may cascade among users. For example, if John has the right to grant authority *A* to another user Sylvia, then Sylvia has the right to grant authority *A* to another user Dale, and so on. Consider the following example.

```
John:
GRANT SELECT ON TABLE PERSNEL TO SYLVIA WITH GRANT OPTION
Sylvia:
GRANT SELECT ON TABLE PERSNEL TO DALE WITH GRANT OPTION
```

As long as a user has received a GRANT OPTION, he or she can confer the same authority to others.

If John later wishes to revoke a GRANT OPTION, he could do so in the following way:

```
REVOKE SELECT ON TABLE PERSNEL FROM SYLVIA
```

This revocation would apply to Sylvia, as well as to anyone to whom she had conferred authority, and so on.

Encryption

encrypt To convert readable text to unreadable text by use of an algorithm; used to protect sensitive data.

The various authentication and authorization measures that are standard for protecting access to databases may not be adequate for highly sensitive data. In such instances, it may be desirable to **encrypt** the data. Encrypted data cannot be read by an intruder unless that party knows the method of encryption. Considerable research has been devoted to developing encryption methods. Some are so simple that they are easy to decipher. Others are very difficult to decipher and provide a high level of protection.

We first demonstrate a simple encryption scheme. We then demonstrate a more complex, but more secure, method.

Simple Substitution Method □ Suppose we wish to encrypt the message **(plaintext)**

plaintext Readable text.

Think snow.

A simple substitution method would be to shift each letter to its immediate successor in the alphabet. (We assume that the "blank" appears immediately before the letter "a," and that it follows the letter "z.") "Think snow" is encrypted **(ciphertext)** to

ciphertext Encrypted plaintext.

uijolatopx.

If an intruder sees only the message "uijolatopx," there is probably insufficient information to break the code. However, if a large number of words are examined, it is possible to statistically examine the frequency with which characters occur, and, thereby, easily break the code. Better encryption schemes use an encryption key, as demonstrated in the next section.

Polyalphabetic Substitution Method □   Suppose that we want to encrypt the same message, but we are now given the encryption key, say, "security." We proceed as follows:

1. Align the key beneath the plaintext, repeating it as many times as necessary to completely cover the plaintext. In this example, we would have

   Thi nk snow

   s e curity s e.

2. Let "blank" occupy the 27th, and last, position in our alphabet. For each character, add the alphabetic position of the plaintext character and that of the key character, divide by 27, and keep the remainder. Replace the plaintext character with the character found in the position computed by the remainder. For our example, T is found in the 20th place in the alphabet, while s is found in the 19th position. Thus,

   (20 + 19) = 39. The remainder on division by 27 is 12. (This process is called "division modulus 27.")

   L is the letter in the 12th position in the alphabet. Thus, the letter T in the plaintext is encrypted as the letter L in the ciphertext.

   This method is still too simple to be of wide use, but it does serve to illustrate the general strategy used in applications.

□ DATABASE RECOVERY

Because information stored on computer media is subject to loss or corruption caused by a wide range of events, it is important to provide means for restoring correct data to the database. Restoring the database to precisely the same state that existed at the time of system failure is not always possible, but database recovery procedures can restore the database to the state that existed shortly before the failure and identify the status of transaction processing at the time of the failure. With this capability, unprocessed transactions can be processed against the restored database to bring it back to a fully current status.

Sources of Failure   The usual classification of failure types includes these:

1. *System errors.* The system has entered an undesirable state, such as deadlock, which prevents the program from continuing with normal processing. This type of failure may or may not result in corruption of data files.

2. *Hardware failures.* Two of the most common types of hardware failures are disk failure and loss of transmission capability over a transmission link. In the former case, the cause usually results from the disk read/write head coming in physical contact with the disk surface (a "head crash").

3. *Logical errors.* Bad data or missing data are common conditions that may preclude a program's continuing with normal execution.

In the next section, we will discuss recovery procedures that are appropriate to common types of failures.

Recovery Procedures

To maintain data integrity, a transaction must be in one of the two following states:

1. *Aborted.* A transaction may not always complete its processing successfully. To be sure that it will not corrupt the consistent state of the database, an uncompleted transaction must be aborted, restoring the database to the state it was in before the transaction began execution.

2. *Committed.* A transaction that successfully completes its processing is said to be **committed.** A committed transaction always leaves the database in a new consistent state.

committed transaction A transaction that successfully completes all its actions.

The log plays a key role in failure recovery. The log is a history of all the changes made to the database, as well as the status of each transaction. A recovery strategy can be pursued by one of two approaches, logging with deferred updates or logging with immediate updates. Checkpointing provides an additional safeguard.

Log with Deferred Updates □   Logging with deferred updates proceeds as follows:

1. When a transaction T begins, a record "<T,BEGIN>" is written to the log.
2. During the execution of transaction T, any writing of a new value, a;, for attribute A, denoted "WRITE(A,a;)," results in the writing of a new record to the log. Often the old value of A is retained in case undo operations are required.
3. Each record of the type described in (2) will consist of the following fields:
   a. The transaction name, T.
   b. The attribute name, A.
   c. The new value of the attribute, a;.
4. If all actions comprising T are successfully executed, we say that T partially commits, and write the record "<T,COMMIT>" to the log. After transaction T partially commits, the records associated with T in the log are used in executing the writes to the affected records in the database.

We illustrate this using our customer payment example once again. Recall that a $500 payment is being made on account.

```
T: READ (A,a₁)          Read the current customer balance
   a₁: = a₁ – 500        Reduce the balance owed by $500
   WRITE (A,a₁)          Write the new balance
   READ (B,b₁)           Read the current cash balance
   b₁: = b₁ + 500        Increase the account balance by $500
   WRITE (B,b₁)          Write the new balance
```

FIGURE 17.13   Transaction Steps for Recording a
Customer Payment of $500

The transaction actions are shown in Figure 17.13. The corresponding log entries are shown in Figure 17.14. Using the log, the DBMS can handle any failure that does not result in the loss of the log information itself.

After a failure has occurred, the DBMS examines the log to determine which transactions need to be redone. A transaction, T, must be redone if the log contains both the record "<T,BEGIN>" and the record "<T,COMMIT>." That is, the database may have been corrupted, but the transaction processing was completed and the new values for the relevant data items are contained in the log. This precludes the need to reprocess the transaction. The log is used to restore the state of the system by using a REDO(T) procedure, which sets the value of all data items updated by transaction T to the new values that are recorded in the log.

To illustrate, suppose that the failure occurred just after the "<T,COMMIT>" record is entered in the log and before the updated records are written to the database. The log appears as shown in Figure 17.15. When the system comes back up, recovery action needs to be taken for T since "<T,COMMIT>" appears in the log. The REDO operation is executed, resulting in the values $500 and $2000 being written to the database as the updated values of A and B.

```
        Log Entries      Database Values
                           A = 1000
                           B = 1500
Time    <T,BEGIN>

        <T,A,500>

        <T,B,2000>

        <T,COMMIT>
                           A = 500
                           B = 2000
```

FIGURE 17.14   Deferred Update Log Entries for Complete Execution of T (Customer Payment of $500)

```
        Log Entries      Database Values
                           A = 1000
                           B = 1500
Time    <T,BEGIN>

        <T,A,500>

        <T,B,2000>

        <T,COMMIT>
```

FIGURE 17.15   Deferred Update Log Entries When Failure Occurs after <T,COMMIT> and Before Updates Are Written to the Database

	Log Entries	Database Values
		A = 1000
		B = 1500
Time	<T,BEGIN>	
	<T,A,500>	
	<T,B,2000>	

FIGURE 17.16 Deferred Update Log Entries When Failure Occurs Before the Action, "WRITE (B,b_1)"

Next, suppose that the failure occurs just before the execution of the action **WRITE**(B,b_1) in Figure 17.13. The log at the time of the failure is shown in Figure 17.16. When the system comes back up, no action is necessary, since no COMMIT record for T appears in the log. The values of A and B in the database remain $1000 and $1500. In this case the transaction must be restarted.

Logging with Immediate Updates ☐ An alternative method using a log for recovery is to make all updates to the database immediately and to keep a record in the log of all changes. As before, if a failure occurs, the log is used to restore the database to a previous consistent state. Similarly, when a transaction begins, a record "<T,BEGIN>" is written to the log. During execution of T, any "WRITE(A,a;)" operation is *preceded* by the writing of a new record to the log. Each log record is written in the following way:

> $<T,A,a_i,a_j)$,
>
> where
>
> A is the attribute name,
>
> a_i is the old value of the attribute, and
>
> a_j is the new value of the attribute.

When T is partially committed, "<T,COMMIT>" is written to the log.

The recovery method for this type of logging requires two procedures:

> REDO(T) (same operation as before)
>
> UNDO(T), which restores the values of all attributes updated by T to their old values.

We illustrate these processes with the same example. First, look at Figure 17.17. This represents what the log would look like after execution of T. After a failure has occurred, the recovery system examines the log to identify those transactions that need to be undone or redone. The logic of this process is as follows:

1. T needs to be undone *if* the log reveals the record "<T,BEGIN>" but does not reveal "<T,COMMIT>." The old values of affected data items need to be restored and the transaction restarted.

	Log Entries	Database Values
		A = 1000
		B = 1500
Time	<T,BEGIN>	
	<T,A,1000,500>	
		A = 500
	<T,B,1500,2000>	
		B = 2000
	<T,COMMIT>	

FIGURE 17.17   Immediate Update Log for Complete Execution of T

2. T can be redone if the log contains both of the above records. The transaction does not have to be restarted.

We will illustrate both of these situations.

Suppose that the system again fails just before the action "WRITE(B,b_1)," as shown in Figure 17.13. Figure 17.18 illustrates what the log would look like at the time of failure. When the system becomes operable, it finds the record "<T,BEGIN>" but no corresponding "<T,COMMIT>". This means that the transaction must be undone, so an "UNDO(T)" is executed. This restores the values of A and B to $1000 and $1500 respectively, and the transaction can be restarted.

Next suppose that the crash occurs just after "<T,COMMIT>" is written to the log, but before the new values are written to the database. The corresponding log entries are shown in Figure 17.19. When the system becomes operable again, a scan of the log shows corresponding "<T,BEGIN>" and "<T,COMMIT>" records. Thus a "REDO(T)" can be performed, after which the values of A and B are $500 and $2000.

Checkpointing □   From the above procedures, one might conclude that recovery only requires scanning the log for entries made by the most re-

	Log Entries	Database Values
		A = 1000
		B = 1500
Time	<T,BEGIN>	
	<T,A,1000,500>	
		A = 500

FIGURE 17.18   Immediate Update Log Entries When Failure Occurs Before the Action, "WRITE (B,b_1)"

	Log Entries	Database Values
		A = 1000
		B = 1500
Time	<T,BEGIN>	
	<T,A,1000,500>	
		A = 500
	<T,B,1500,2000>	
		B = 2000
	<T,COMMIT>	

FIGURE 17.19   Immediate Update Log Entries When Failure Occurs Just after the Action, "<T,COMMIT>" Is Executed

checkpointing Saving copies of the database at predetermined times during processing; database recovery begins or ends at the most recent checkpoint.

cent transaction or by a few of the recent transactions. In principle, there may be no limit on how far back in the log the system must look, since errors may have commenced with the first transaction. This can be very time-consuming and wasteful. A better way is to find a point that is sufficiently far back to ensure that any item written before that point has been done correctly and stored safely. The method by which this is done is called **checkpointing.** During execution, the DBMS maintains the log as we have described but periodically performs checkpoints consisting of the following actions:

1. Temporarily halting the initiation of any new transactions until all active transactions are either committed or aborted.
2. Writing all log records currently residing in primary memory to disk storage.
3. Appending to the end of the log a record indicating that a checkpoint has occurred, and writing it to disk storage.

When the system fails, we initiate the usual recovery procedures, but the log is scanned only as far back as the most recent checkpoint.

■ SUMMARY

A knowledge of administrative and control issues is necessary to the effective management of a database system. Because of multiple-and-concurrent user access of database systems, maintenance of database security and integrity is at once complex and essential.

In this chapter we first addressed the difference between data administration and database administration, focusing on database administration and its goals of maintaining the integrity, security, and availability of the database. Data integrity—the maintenance of accurate, reliable data is ensured by implementing data integrity controls, while security is obtained by implementing data security controls. Data availability is enhanced by implementing backup-and-recovery procedures, which may include a disaster plan.

We then demonstrated some integrity capabilities of commercial query languages such as SQL and QBE. These capabilities do not yet provide all desired features, but this situation is expected to improve in the near future.

Another useful way to maintain database consistency is the atomic transaction, which requires that all transaction processing be completed, or else the transaction is aborted. When used with a log, this ensures that operating failures do not result in the recording of erroneous data.

Concurrent processing can corrupt the database. Simple locking procedures can preclude concurrent processing, but they may greatly restrict the operating efficiency of the database system. Methods such as two-phase locking are available to limit the problems associated with simple locking, while maintaining database integrity.

Database security is primarily concerned with determining who has legitimate access to what data, and then being sure that legitimacy is enforced. Authentication refers to methods of restricting access to the system. Authorization refers to methods of controlling what resources are accessible once system access is gained, and what can be done with those resources.

In relational database systems, the use of views can be an effective way of restricting what the user sees and manipulates, without having to alter stored relations. Using SQL, we demonstrated a number of ways in which views can be applied.

Encryption allows sensitive data to be stored and transmitted in a form which is unintelligible to other than legitimate users.

All database systems must have sound backup-and-recovery procedures to avoid inefficiencies and even catastrophic loss. These methods should be tested periodically to make certain that they are operable, complete, and reliable. Transaction logs (with either deferred or immediate updates), checkpointing, and backup copies of the database are essential elements to backup and recovery.

■ REVIEW QUESTIONS

1. Define each of the following terms in your own words:
   a. data administrator
   b. data integrity
   c. data security
   d. integrity control
   e. atomic transaction
   f. log
   h. deadlock
   i. two-phase locking
   j. write_lock
   k. encrypt
   l. ciphertext
   m. checkpointing
   n. committed transaction

2. What are the DBA's main functions? The DBA's goals?

3. What is the difference between a read_lock and a write_lock?

4. Compare and contrast the meaning of the terms *security* and *integrity*. Give an example of how the database could be affected by a breach of integrity and a breach of security.

5. Describe the role of the database administrator in implementing standards and procedures.

6. What is meant by backup and recovery?

7. Explain how concurrency can lead to an inconsistency in the database.

8. Develop an example, other than the one in the text, showing how a simple locking control could lead to deadlock.

9. Discuss two ways in which deadlock might be detected. What are their advantages and disadvantages?

10. Explain how two-phase locking works.

11. Distinguish between authorization and authentication.

PROBLEMS AND EXERCISES

1. Match the following terms with their definitions:

__Database administrator   a. The means by which a database that has been corrupted by system malfunctions can be restored to a consistent state

__Plaintext   b. Manager whose responsibilities are focused on managing of the technical aspects of the database system

__Concurrent processing   c. Occurs when two or more transactions concurrently request access to the same database record at about the same time

__Database recovery procedures   d. A restricted subset of a stored relation

__Transaction   e. The user has the right to read a given record

__Aborted transaction   f. A program unit whose execution preserves the consistency of the database

__Lock   g. Readable text

__Read_lock   h. Transaction that is cancelled before changes are applied to the database.

__Deadlock detection   i. In transaction processing, prevents access to a database record by a second transaction until the first transaction has completed all of its actions

__View   j. A periodic check by the DBMS to determine if the waiting line for some resource exceeds a predetermined limit

2. Using an example, demonstrate a data integrity problem that could be caused by a concurrent update process.

3. Using an example, illustrate how two-phase locking works.

4. Using the polyalphabetic substitution method and the encryption key, SECURITY, encrypt the plaintext message, "SELL ALL STOCKS."

5. Create the log entries corresponding to the following transactions actions:

T: READ (A, a_1)	Read the current customer balance
a_1: = a_1 + 800	Debit the account by $800
WRITE (A, a_1)	Write the new balance
READ (B, b_1)	Read the current accounts payable balance
b_1: = b_1 + 800	Credit the account balance by $800
WRITE (B, b_1)	Write the new balance

6. Suppose that in (5) a failure occurs just before the execution of the action.

$$WRITE (B, b_1)$$

a. Show the contents of the log at the time of failure.
b. What action is necessary, and why? What are the resulting values of A and B?

6. Suppose that in (5) a failure occurs just after the "<T,COMMIT>" record and before the start of the next transaction.

    a. Show the contents of the log at the time of failure.

    b. What action is necessary, and why? What are the resulting values of A and B?

■ PROJECTS AND PROFESSIONAL ISSUES

1. Do a short research study of what methods the major accounting firms use to audit database systems.

2. Compare and contrast the integrity controls available in SQL and QBE.

3. Compare and contrast the data security controls available in SQL and QBE.

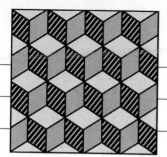

chapter eighteen

DISTRIBUTED DATABASE SYSTEMS

Cordelia Molini and Reggie Townsend were sitting at lunch discussing the progress that had been made in implementing information systems at IPD.

Reggie commented that, "I think we are doing a good job. We have the latest relational technology in-house, we have educated users in every functional area of the business, and there is evidence that our information systems are increasingly being used to support decision making throughout the company."

"Generally, I agree with you," responded Cordelia. "But there is still much to be done. Many of our managers are located at remote sites throughout the world, and I have heard rumors here and there that they would like to have control over that portion of the database system that applies to their operations. In fact, one manager commented to me that she didn't understand why data should be maintained in the corporate database when it was mainly updated and used by her."

"Sounds like we ought to be looking at distributing our database," answered Reggie. "What kinds of changes would we be looking at if we moved in that direction?"

"Well," said Cordelia, "for one thing, we'd have to decide what data could be maintained locally and what data should be maintained centrally. And we'd still want to make certain corporate data available to remote sites. Our system for controlling data access would have to be more sophisticated in order to allow queries to be executed that required data from more than one site. There are other issues, as well, but with our current track record of success, I believe that we are well positioned to begin thinking about a distributed database system."

This chapter provides an introduction to the exciting area of **distributed database systems (DDSs).** It is still a developing area, but by all accounts it will play a major role in business operations over the next decade and beyond. With the impressive advances in communications technology that are occurring, the potential is impressive. After reading this chapter, you should be able to:

☐ Explain why DDSs are of value to organizations.

☐ List and describe the fundamental technologies and the terminology of DDSs.

☐ Discuss the elements of DDS design.

☐ Discuss strategies and objectives that are important for DDSs.

☐ Explain optional configurations that are available for DDSs, along with some of their advantages and disadvantages.

☐ List and discuss the fundamental control problems associated with a DDS and methods for dealing with them.

☐ WHY DISTRIBUTED DATABASES?

distributed database A database that is distributed among a network of geographically separated locations.

So far we have been discussing centralized database systems, with the database located at a central computing facility. In this kind of system, users and application programs access a single database from local sites, as well as from remote locations.

In contrast, a **distributed database** is a database that is not entirely stored in one central location, but is distributed among a network of locations that are geographically separated and connected by communication links. Each location has its own database and is also able to access data maintained at other locations.

distributed database system A collection of locations, each of which operates a local database system, which can participate in the execution of transactions which access data at several locations.

The reasons for the development and use of **distributed database systems** include the following:

1. Organizations often have branches or divisions in different locations. For a given location, L, there may be a set of data that is used frequently, perhaps exclusively, at L. In addition, L may sometimes need data that is used more frequently at another location, L'.

In a retail franchise business, for example, each store may benefit from its own database of inventory, sales, customer accounts, and employees. During business operations, transactions are conveniently processed against the local database. At the end of daily operations, summary results may be transmitted to corporate headquarters, where a franchise-wide database is maintained. Periodically, each store may benefit by being able to access comparative sales and profit information from the corporate database as a way of evaluating its own performance.

In a centralized database system, each site would need to use a communication link to the database for both types of information, and communications could become a significant bottleneck.

2. Allowing each site to store and maintain its own database allows immediate and efficient access to data that is used most frequently. Such data may be used at other sites, as well, but usually with less frequency. Similarly, data stored at other locations is usually needed less often and can be accessed as required.

3. Distributed databases can upgrade reliability. If one site's computer fails, or if a communication link goes down, the rest of the network can probably continue functioning. Moreover, when data is replicated at two or more sites, required data may still be available from a site that is still operable.

4. Allowing local control over the data used most frequently at a site can improve user satisfaction with the database system, since local databases can more nearly reflect an organization's administrative structure and thereby better service its managers' needs.

These are some of the advantages of distributed database systems. There are, however, instances when a distributed database system can be a disadvantage. When a great deal of intersite communication takes place, for example, the overhead incurred by the associated coordination and control tasks can severely degrade performance. This may be especially likely when replicated data is maintained at several sites, which requires extra resources to ensure that concurrent updates are consistent.

The advantages of data replication are the speed gained in processing at sites where the duplicate data is maintained, as well as the availability of backup copies of data in case of a system failure at another location. However, such duplication involves the use of extra storage space, and transaction processing and recovery become more difficult. When a transaction is processed, it may invoke a requirement to read and update data at different sites and to transmit related messages among sites. Before a transaction can be committed, the system must ensure that all the relevant sites have completed their processing. Only if processing has terminated normally at each site should the transaction be committed. Otherwise, the transaction must be undone at each participating site.

Finally, making data available to users throughout a network makes security inherently more complex for a distributed database than with its centralized counterpart.

Although these limitations suggest caution in planning and implementing DDSs, the technology for mitigating such limitations is rapidly improving. In order for firms to be responsive, productive, and competitive, DDSs will increasingly be selected as the central component of an effective information-systems strategy.

□ A GENERAL DDS MODEL

local data Data that is maintained in a network site's own database.

global data Data that is maintained in a database whose location is different from at least one of its users.

link Communications channel between two network sites, which provides for data transfer capability.

distributed database management system (DDBMS) The software which manages the distributed database system.

System for Distributed Databases (SDD) DDBMS marketed by Computer Corporation of America.

R* DDBMS marketed by IBM Corporation.

Distributed INGRES DDBMS marketed by Relational Technology.

A DDS is composed of a collection of sites, each of which operates a local database system for processing activities that require only **local data**. Additionally, each site can process transactions requiring data (called **global data**) that is stored at other sites. This requires that the various database sites be able to communicate data among themselves. The communications connections that provide the necessary data-transfer capabilities are called **links**. The link structure provides the basic architecture of a **distributed database management system (DDBMS)**, which is the systems software that manages the distributed databases.

Several commercial DDBMSs are implemented or are under development. These include **System for Distributed Databases (SDD)** (Computer Corporation of America), **R*** (IBM), and **Distributed INGRES** (Relational Technology). IBM's popular DB2 includes some distributed capabilities, as well. One site using DB2 can execute read operations at another DB2 site. However, updates can only be made at a single site.

A DDBMS is a system composed of several DBMSs running at local sites, which are connected by a message handling facility. The DDBMS data dictionary includes the usual information necessary for data management, in addition to information concerning the location, replication, and fragmentation of data in the various relations of the distributed database. As queries or transactions are processed, the DDBMS data dictionary can provide the required information on location and replication, while assuring that updates are transmitted to the correct locations. The DDBMS data dictionary can be maintained at a central site, or subsets can be distributed among the various sites according to their needs. A full copy of the data dictionary can be obtained by taking the union of all the distributed subsets.

Users interact with the DDBMS by executing programs called **transactions**. Transactions are no longer restricted to single processes controlled by one software module, but they may invoke a set of cooperating processes running at several sites and controlled by independent software modules.

Each of the processes cooperating in the transaction is called an **agent.** A transaction requiring a single, local agent is called a **local transaction**. A transaction requiring several agents is termed a **global transaction**.

Because a given agent can only access the data controlled by its local data management software, accessing data at another site requires cooperation with agents at those sites. Thus, the initiating agent must request the activation of agents at other sites in order to access needed data. Once activated, two or more agents can communicate by message exchange.

Transactions access records by issuing READ and WRITE operations. READ (x) returns the current value of x. WRITE (x, new value) updates the current value of x to the new value. A transaction issues read and write commands to the DDBMS and executes terminal input and output.

Each site participating in the DDBMS typically runs one or more of the following software modules: a transaction manager (TM), a data manager (DM), and a scheduler. Figure 18.1 illustrates their interrelationships. Transactions communicate with TMs; TMs talk to schedulers; schedulers communicate among themselves and also with DMs; and the DMs manage the data. These concepts are further illustrated in Figure 18.2.

transaction The execution of a user program which interacts with the DDBMS.

agent A process that cooperates in completing a transaction.

local transaction A transaction requiring a single agent.

global transaction A transaction requiring several agents.

FIGURE 18.1   DDBMS Architecture

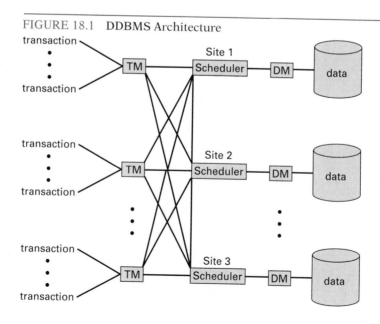

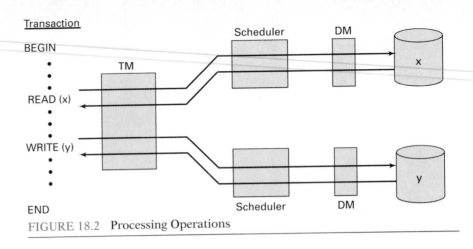

FIGURE 18.2   Processing Operations

Each transaction communicates all of its reads and writes to a single TM. A transaction also issues a BEGIN operation to its TM when it begins executing and an END operation when it is finished. The TM communicates each read and write to a scheduler. Scheduler selection is determined by a concurrency-control algorithm, although the chosen scheduler is most often at the same site as the data being operated on.

The scheduler controls the sequence in which DMs process read and write commands and maintains concurrency control. When a scheduler receives a read or write instruction, the scheduler can process the instruction immediately; delay processing by holding the instruction for later action; or reject the instruction in the case of a transmission error, access violation, or similar problem.

The DM executes each read and write it receives. For a read, the DM scans its local database and returns the requested value. For a write, the DM modifies its local database and returns an acknowledgment to the scheduler, which relays it back to the TM, which relays it back to the transaction.

DDSs often link sites that are widely dispersed geographically. Such systems are called **wide-area networks (WANs)**. Alternatively, distributed database systems can be organized to serve a **local-area network (LAN)**, where the sites are workstations in an office or building that are linked together. In both instances, the sites can be linked in a number of ways.

The linking of sites corresponds to the structure of a graph: The sites correspond to the nodes or vertices of a graph, and the links between sites correspond to the edges of a graph. Usual WAN links are telephone lines, satellite channels, or microwave links. The close proximity (less than a mile) of workstations in a LAN makes it possible to use coaxial cable and fiber optic links, in addition to twisted wire pairs. Typical LAN links are higher speed and subject to lower error rates than WAN links.

Figures 18.3 and 18.4 give possible network configurations. Two generic configurations for WANs are illustrated in Figure 18.3. LAN designs usually follow the architectures shown in Figure 18.4.

The fully connected configuration of Figure 18.3(a) requires [n(n-1)]/2 links, where n is the number of sites. As this term is of order n^2, the

wide-area network (WAN) A computer network with sites that are widely dispersed geographically.

local-area network (LAN) A computer network with the sites located within a short distance (usually less than a mile) of one another.

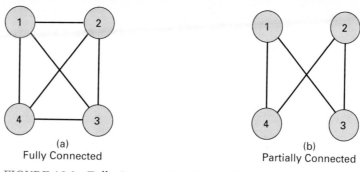

(a)
Fully Connected

(b)
Partially Connected

FIGURE 18.3   Fully Connected and Partially Connected Networks

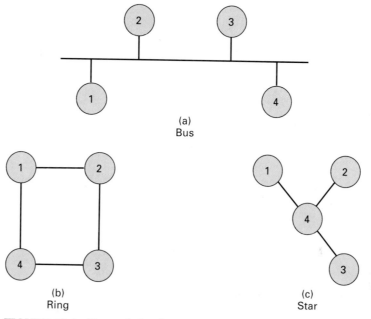

(a)
Bus

(b)
Ring

(c)
Star

FIGURE 18.4   Network Configurations

number of links grows very rapidly with the number of sites, as does the expense of installation and maintenance. Even though the fully connected configuration provides the greatest flexibility and reliability, most installations use a partially connected network architecture as the most cost effective implementation design.

Each site in a distributed database system should be able to process transactions that access data only at that site, as well as transactions that require data from other sites. The choice of one configuration over another is usually a function of

1. The cost of sending a message from station A to station B
2. The frequency with which a link or station fails (reliability)
3. The degree to which data can be accessed despite the failure of some links or stations (availability)

4. The frequency and volume of data that must be accessed
5. The cost of physically linking the stations in the system.

The complexity of optimal network design is such that it is impossible to state generally what configurations these factors favor. It depends on such things as communications volume, communications timing, network transmission media, and other similar factors. Analytical models are being developed to assist in choosing the best configuration in specific situations.

☐ DISTRIBUTED DATABASE SYSTEM DESIGN

The design of a distributed database system can be a complex task. Careful consideration must be given to the objectives and strategies to be served by the design, and parallel decisions must be made as to how the data is to be distributed among the various network sites.

Objectives   Some of the objectives that are common to most distributed database system implementations are discussed in this section.

Location transparency ☐   Location transparency enables a user to access data without knowing, or being concerned with, the site at which the data resides. The location of the data is hidden from the user.

Configuration Independence ☐   Configuration independence enables the organization to add or replace hardware without changing the existing software components of the DDBMS. Configuration independence results in a system that is expandable when its current hardware is saturated.

Integration of Nonhomogeneous DBMSs ☐   It is sometimes desirable to integrate databases maintained by different DBMSs on different computers. Often the DBMSs are supplied by different vendors and may support different data models. One approach to integrating these databases is to provide a single user interface that can be used to access the data maintained by the nonhomogeneous DBMSs. The different data models supported by the nonhomogeneous DBMSs are hidden from the user by this single, system-wide interface.

Strategies   **Data Replication** ☐   As we explained previously, data replication occurs if the system maintains several identical copies of a relation, R, with each copy being stored at a different site. Typically, replication is introduced to increase the availability of the system: When a copy is unavailable due to site failure(s), it should be possible to access another copy.

Replication can also improve performance under routine conditions, since transactions have a greater probability of finding a copy locally. The trade-off is in the extra cost of the added storage and in the maintenance of mutual consistency among copies. The update of a local copy imposes the added overhead of transmitting that update to all sites maintaining a copy of the data.

The advantages of replication then, are that

1. If one of the stations containing relation R fails, the relation can be retrieved from another site, and the system may continue any processing involving R. Thus, database availability is enhanced.

2. If most accesses to R only involve a read of the relation, then several sites can process queries involving R concurrently. The more copies of R there are throughout the network, the better the chance that a query can be executed without requiring data transmission between stations. There is, of course, both a corresponding cost and time savings.

The principal disadvantage is that the system must ensure that all copies of R are identical. Thus, when an update of R occurs, that update must be transmitted to all locations, with the corresponding incurrence of overhead.

For replicated databases, at least two implementation alternatives are available. In one of these, a centralized database is maintained, and copies of portions of the database are extracted for local use. This redundancy may be offset by the reduced communications costs due to the data being stored locally. Reliability is also improved, since loss of data at one location may be restored by the data copy that is maintained at another location.

The second alternative is to omit the centralized database, but to replicate segments of the database at sites that are the most frequent users of those segments. The costs of maintaining the centralized database are thereby avoided, although communications costs may be increased.

Replication transparency ☐ Replication transparency means that the user is unaware of which copy of data is being used. The need for replication transparency occurs when more than one copy of the data exists, since one copy must be chosen when retrieving data, and all copies must be updated when changes are made. This process can be a burden on users. Therefore, a DDBMS should handle all such requirements, freeing the user to concentrate on information needs.

Database Partitioning ☐ Efficiency may result from a strategy that implements a partitioned database. With this approach, the database is distributed so that there is no overlapping, or replication, of data maintained at the various locations. Since there is no duplication of data, the costs associated with storing and maintaining redundant data are avoided. Data availability may be limited, however, if the same segment of data is used at more than one location. Reliability may also be affected since a failure of one computer system means that the data stored at that location is not available to users anywhere in the system. Because the distributed environment of the DDBMS allows the database to be physically partitioned, however, data security may be improved, particularly when the partitioned segments have different security needs.

The most straightforward way of implementing a partitioned database is as a series of independently operated database systems, with the capability of remotely accessing each database. In a somewhat more complex alternative, the database systems are integrated so that a single query by the user may require access to more than one of the database systems. Although the underlying complexities should be transparent to the user, the actual operations may be quite involved. Think, for example, of a relational JOIN operation whose result requires tables maintained in two distinct database locations. We'll look at this problem in more detail shortly.

data fragmentation The partitioning of relations in a DDS.

Data Fragmentation □ **Data fragmentation**, which applies to relational database systems, refers to ways in which relations can be subdivided and distributed among network sites. This is an extension of the data partitioning strategy, which is generally concerned with locating entire relations (or files) from the database at various sites.

If fragmentation is allowed, a given relation is not necessarily stored in its entirety at any single site. Its subsets may be distributed among several sites for performance considerations. Moreover, these subsets may be replicated.

A fragmented relation, R, is divided into subsets (fragments) R_1, R_2, ..., R_n; the union of these fragments reconstructs the original relation R. This fragmentation can be horizontal, which assigns tuples to the various fragments; or it can be vertical, where selected attributes are projected onto the various fragments.

Why is fragmentation a consideration? As Maier (1983) observes, a database of airline reservations might be more effectively used if database subsets are stored at the location of their respective flight origins. Similarly, for a banking database, it may be useful to have database subsets at the branch location where the respective accounts are located.

horizontal fragmentation
Partitioning a relation into subsets of its tuples.

In **horizontal fragmentation,** the division of tuples of a given relation is usually disjoint—that is, no tuple is in more than one fragment, but fragments may also be replicated. In this approach, replication is managed at the fragment level and not at the level of individual tuples.

To illustrate horizontal fragmentation, suppose that the relation R is the FLIGHT relation of Figure 18.5. This relation can be divided into two fragments, each of which consists of tuples identifying a common flight origination location (SF and Den). Such fragmentation is formally defined as a SELECTION on the relation R. That is,

```
R₁ = SELECT (R:<condition>)
```

For our example, we might have

```
FLIGHT_ORIGIND = SELECT (FLIGHT: ORIGIN = 'Den')
FLIGHT_ORIGINSF = SELECT (FLIGHT: ORIGIN = 'SF')
```

The resulting fragments are shown in Figure 18.6. The fragment FLIGHT_ORIGINSF is stored at the San Franscisco airport and fragment FLIGHT_ORIGIND is stored at the Denver airport. The original relation can be restored by performing a UNION operation on FLIGHT_ORIGIND and FLIGHT_ORIGINSF.

FLIGHT			
Origin	Destination	Departure Time	Arrival Time
Den	SF	9A	10A
Den	SLC	7A	8A
Den	SF	1P	2P
Den	SF	6P	7P
SF	Den	8A	11A
SF	Den	12P	3P
SF	Den	5P	8P
SF	SLC	9A	11P

FIGURE 18.5   **FLIGHT** Relation

FLIGHT_ORIGINSF			
Origin	Destination	Departure Time	Arrival Time
SF	Den	8A	11A
SF	Den	12P	3P
SF	Den	5P	8P
SF	SLC	9A	11P

FLIGHT_ORIGIND			
Origin	Destination	Departure Time	Arrival Time
Den	SF	9A	10A
Den	SLC	7A	8A
Den	SF	1P	2P
Den	SF	6P	7P

FIGURE 18.6   Horizontal Fragmentation of **FLIGHT** Relation

The above fragments are horizontally disjoint. That is, no tuple instance occurs in more than one fragment. We could, however, have a particular tuple of R appear in more than one R_i. For example, at San Francisco, we might want to store tuples whose flights originate in San Francisco, as well as those that arrive from Los Angeles.

vertical fragmentation Partitioning a relation by projection of subsets of its attributes.

Vertical fragmentation, the division of the set of attributes of a relation into possibly overlapping subsets, is obtained by projecting the original relation over each set of attributes. To ensure that the projections do not cause the loss of any parts of the relation, each vertical fragment will usually contain a key for the relation. That way, when the fragments are joined again, the resulting relation will be the same as the original relation.

Vertical fragmentation is defined as

```
R₁ = R [<list of attribute names>]
```

R can be reconstructed from the fragments by taking the natural join:

```
R = JOIN (R₁, R₂, . . . , Rₙ)
```

To identify the tuple, vertical fragmentation requires the addition of

```
FLIGHT
Origin        Destination        Departure Time        Arrival Time        TIA
  Den             SF                     9A                   10A             1
  Den             SLC                    7A                    8A             2
  Den             SF                     1P                    2P             3
  Den             SF                     6P                    7P             4
  SF              Den                    8A                   11A             5
  SF              Den                   12P                    3P             6
  SF              Den                    5P                    8P             7
  SF              SLC                    9A                   11P             8
```

FIGURE 18.7   Augmented FLIGHT Relation Showing TIA

```
FLIGHT1
Origin              Departure Time            TIA
  Den                     9A                    1
  Den                     7A                    2
  Den                     1P                    3
  Den                     6P                    4
  SF                      8A                    5
  SF                     12P                    6
  SF                      5P                    7
  SF                      9A                    8


FLIGHT2
Destination          Arrival Time             TIA
  SF                     10A                    1
  SLC                     8A                    2
  SF                      2P                    3
  SF                      7P                    4
  Den                    11A                    5
  Den                     3P                    6
  Den                     8P                    7
  SLC                  11:30P                   8
```

FIGURE 18.8   Vertical Fragmentation of FLIGHT Relation

a surrogate key, the tuple identification attribute (TIA), which is the address for the tuple. Since addresses are unique, the TIA functions as a key for an augmented schema for R. In Figure 18.7, we show the addition of a TIA attribute. In Figure 18.8, we show the FLIGHT relation decomposed vertically into the schemas FLIGHT1 and FLIGHT2. These relations result from computing

```
FLIGHT1 =  FLIGHT [ORIGIN,DEPARTURE_TIME,TIA]
FLIGHT2 =  FLIGHT [DESTINATION,ARRIVAL_TIME,TIA]
```

To reconstruct the original FLIGHT relation from the fragments, we compute

```
FLIGHT = JOIN (FLIGHT1,FLIGHT2)
```

Some database systems support relational databases whose parts are physically separated. Different relations might reside at different sites, multiple copies of a single relation can be distributed among several sites, or one relation might be partitioned into subrelations and these subrelations distributed. In order to evaluate a query posed at a given site, it may be necessary to transfer data between various sites. The key consideration here is that the time required to process such a query will largely be composed of the time spent transmitting data between sites, rather than the time spent on computation or retrieval from secondary storage. These transmission costs can be reduced by using the semijoin operation.

To understand this, let's look at an example. Suppose the relations R and S shown in Figure 18.9 are stored at sites 1 and 2 respectively. If we wish to respond to a query at site 1 that requires the computation

```
JOIN (R,S),
```

we could transmit all of S from site 2 to site 1 and compute the join at site 1. This would involve the transmission of all 24 values (8 tuples × 3 attributes) of S. Notice that in this example most of these value transmissions would be wasted, since only the first three tuples have A2 values that will join with A2 values in R.

Another way would be to compute

```
T = R [A2]
```

at site 1; then send T (6 values) to site 2, and compute

```
U = JOIN (T,S);
```

and finally send U (9 values) to site 1. We can then compute the desired

```
JOIN (R,S),
```

as

```
JOIN (R,U).
```

FIGURE 18.9   R and S Relations to Be Used in Semijoin Example

SITE 1		SITE 2		
R			S	
A1	A2	A2	A3	A4
1	3	3	13	16
1	4	3	14	16
1	6	7	13	17
2	3	10	14	16
2	6	10	15	17
3	7	11	15	16
3	8	11	15	16
3	9	12	15	16

```
1.                    T = PROJECT (R: A2) = A2
                                             3
                                             4
                                             6
                                             7
                                             8
                                             9

2.        U = JOIN (T, S) = A2      A3      A4
                             3       13      16
                             3       14      16
                             7       13      17

3.     JOIN (R, U) = A1      A2      A3      A4
                      1       3       13      16
                      1       3       14      16
                      3       7       13      17
```

FIGURE 18.10   Steps in Using Semijoin to Reduce Transmission Costs

These steps and their results are shown in Figure 18.10. Note, that with this approach we have transmitted only 15 values: 6 for T and 9 for U.

This example provides a basis for defining a semijoin. The **semijoin** of R with S is

```
SEMIJOIN (R,S) = <the portion of R that joins with S>.
```

Therefore,

```
JOIN (R,S) = JOIN (SEMIJOIN (R,S),S).
```

If R and S are at different sites, computing JOIN (R,S) as above saves transmitting data whenever R and S do not join completely, as was demonstrated in Figure 18.10.

DATA INTEGRITY IN DISTRIBUTED DATABASE SYSTEMS

As might be expected, controlling data integrity becomes a harder problem in the network environment. Because data is distributed, the transaction activities may take place at a number of sites, and it can be difficult to maintain a time ordering among actions.

The most common problem is when two (or more) transactions are executing at the same time, and both require access to the same data record in order to complete their processing. (We examined this concurrency problem for centralized database systems in Chapter 17.) The problem is somewhat more complicated in a distributed system, since there may be multiple copies of the same record. All copies must have the same value at all times, or transactions may operate on inaccurate data.

Most concurrency control algorithms for distributed database systems use some form of check to see that the result of a transaction is the same as if its actions were executed serially.

To implement concurrency control, the following must be known:

1. The type of scheduling algorithm used
2. The location of the scheduler
3. How replicated data is controlled.

serializability theory States that a concurrency control algorithm is correct when its results are the same as if processes were executed serially.

These factors provide the basis for constructing rules that determine when a concurrency control algorithm is correct. The rules are based upon **serializability theory.** When transactions are performed sequentially, all the actions of one transaction are performed, and then all the actions of the next transaction are executed. There is no concurrency, and this is called a **serial execution**. When transactions are executed serially, they cannot interfere with one another since only one transaction is active at a time. We saw in an earlier example (Chapter 17) that with concurrent requests to a database by the League of Women Voters and the Chamber of Commerce, transactions are not usually executed serially but are interleaved. An interleaved execution of transactions is said to be serializable if it produces the same result that a serial execution of those same transactions would have produced.

serial execution Actions are executed one after another with no parallel actions.

To enforce serializability, the TMs located at each site must cooperate to provide concurrency control by the use of locking mechanisms or by timestamping. As before, these are methods to prevent data inconsistencies that may arise when transactions are executed in parallel against the database.

We continue our consideration of these issues by examining some of the principal methods of maintaining data integrity in a distributed database system.

Two-Phase Commit Protocol

Earlier, we learned that maintenance of data integrity in database systems requires atomic processing of transactions. In the centralized systems of Chapter 17, this is accomplished by delaying changes to the database until the transaction is committed. In a distributed database system, things are somewhat more involved. Before committing a transaction's updates, each subtransaction (that part of a transaction executed at a given site) must show that it is prepared to commit. Otherwise, the transaction and all of its changes are entirely aborted. The existence of subtransactions at various sites necessitates this rule.

For a subtransaction to be ready to commit, all of its actions must have been completed successfully. If any subtransaction indicates that its actions cannot be completed, then all the subtransactions are aborted, and none of the changes is committed. This idea is illustrated in Figure 18.11.

two-phase commit protocol A protocol consisting of a prepare-to-commit phase and a vote (commit or abort) phase.

Formally, the **two-phase commit protocol** executes as follows:

Phase 1 □ Consider a transaction T, which is initiated at one site and

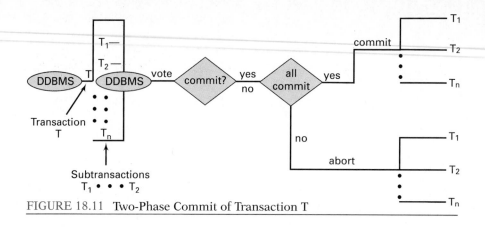

FIGURE 18.11   Two-Phase Commit of Transaction T

invokes subtransactions at other sites, as well as at the home site (where T was initiated). (T consists entirely of subtransactions, each executing at a different site.) The subtransaction at the home site is named as the co-ordinator, C. The other subtransactions are designated as participants. Each subtransaction T_i of T decides whether to commit or abort. C sends a prepare-to-commit message to all sites where a T_i is being executed. T_i responds with a vote-commit or a vote-abort message to C.

Phase 2 ☐   Based on the information received in Phase 1, C determines whether or not T can be committed. C then sends either a commit T or an abort T message to all T_i sites. Since a consensus vote-commit is required for T to be committed, T will not be committed if just one site responds vote-abort.

Distributed Locking   Global transactions may involve a number of local subtransactions, each of which is executed at a different site. The DDBMS must ensure that these transactions are executed in proper sequence.

Example 1 ☐   Suppose that transaction T_1 subtracts 25 turkeys from the inventory at Bounty Foods and transaction T_2 subtracts 35 turkeys from the inventory. Further, suppose that T_1 is initiated at site 1, T_2 is initiated at site 2, and copies of the Turkey Inventory Record (TIR) are maintained at sites 3 and 4. The global transactions T_1 and T_2 consist of local transactions at sites 1, 2, 3 and 4. T_1 must initiate two subtransactions that deduct a number of turkeys from TIR at sites 3 and 4, as must T_2. The effects of these transactions must be coordinated such that the change to one copy of the TIR must not be made unless the same change to the other copies of the TIR is guaranteed.

The DDBMS at each location maintains a local lock manager that administers the lock and unlock requests for data items stored at that site. Locks may be applied in two modes: shared and exclusive. If a transaction locks a record in the shared mode, it can read that record but cannot update it. If a transaction locks a record in the exclusive mode, it can both read and update the record, and no other record can access it while it is exclusively locked. At no time can two transactions hold exclusive locks on the same record. However, any number of transactions should be able to achieve shared locks on the same record at the same time.

If there is only a single copy of a record, then the logical record is identical to its only physical copy. Appropriate locks are maintained by sending lock-request messages to the site at which the copy resides. The TM at that site can grant or deny the lock, returning that result to the user.

When there are several copies of a record, however, the translation from physical locks to logical locks can be executed in a number of ways.

Distributed Two-Phase Locking

As discussed in Chapter 17, two-phase locking (2PL) in a centralized database system synchronizes reads and writes by explicitly detecting and preventing conflicts between concurrent operations. Before reading data item x, a transaction must have a read_lock on x. Before writing into x, it must have a write_lock on x. The ownership of locks is generally governed by two rules:

1. Different transactions cannot simultaneously own conflicting locks.
2. Once a transaction surrenders ownership of a lock, it may not obtain additional locks.

The basis for this method is that a step can always proceed, unless it conflicts with a previous step of an active transaction other than its own. In a distributed database system, the test is exactly the same; the question is how to best carry it out. One way is for the DDBMS to check whether the record accessed by the step in question has been accessed by an active transaction. Using this approach, the TM is required to obtain locks before reading and writing data. That is, the TM must have received a read_lock by the local DBMS from which the data is read. Similarly, before updating a record, a TM must have been provided a write_lock from every database that stores the record in question.

Let's illustrate these ideas with an example.

Example 2 □ Suppose that a transaction T_1 is composed of two actions, as follows:

1. $T_{1.1}$ which runs at site 1 and writes a new value for copy R_1 of record R, and
2. $T_{1.2}$, which runs at site 2 and writes the same new value as in (1) for copy R_2 of R.

Further, consider a second transaction T_2 which has two subtransactions— $T_{2.1}$ running at site 1 and writing a new value to R_1, and $T_{2.2}$ running at site 2 and writing the same value into R_2. Two-phase locking is illustrated in Figure 18.12. Note that pairs of events on each line could occur simultaneously. The events at site 1 suggest that $T_{1.1}$ must precede $T_{2.1}$. At site 2, $T_{1.2}$ must precede $T_{2.2}$.

A two-phase locking technique first goes through a phase of acquiring all the locks for a transaction at a given location, then a phase of releasing them: No lock may be acquired after any lock has been released. Papadimitriou (1988) proved that read and write locks will generate con-

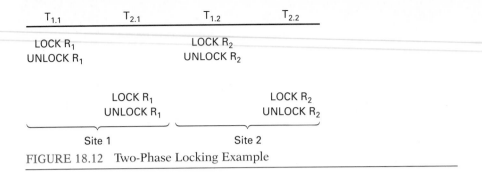

| $T_{1.1}$ | $T_{2.1}$ | $T_{1.2}$ | $T_{2.2}$ |

LOCK R_1 LOCK R_2
UNLOCK R_1 UNLOCK R_2

LOCK R_1 LOCK R_2
UNLOCK R_1 UNLOCK R_2

Site 1   Site 2

FIGURE 18.12   Two-Phase Locking Example

sistent schedules if and only if transactions process in two phases. This requires that the TM evaluate and rearrange, if necessary, the stream of steps arriving at each site. The TM must be a distributed program, with a subprogram, called a module, executing at each site. The computation of a module is a series of actions such as

1. Receiving an action and granting its execution
2. Sending a message to another site
3. Receiving a message.

To show that this strategy always generates consistent schedules, it is necessary to show that the order of locks remains the same as for a serial schedule.

Timestamping

timestamping A method of identifying messages with their time of transmission.

Timestamping involves the use of a global timestamp that indicates when the transaction was initiated. The TM can be called when each transaction begins and a timestamp issued then. Alternatively, a timestamp could be applied to a transaction the first time the TM is asked for access to any record. The issue is how to define the timestamp of each transaction such that it is known to all sites. Consider a request for access to a record, which is taking place at some site. Every record in the database has the timestamp of the transaction that last updated it. If a subsequent transaction seeks to update the same record, and if its timestamp is earlier than that carried in the record, then the transaction is assigned a new timestamp and it is restarted. In this way, a transaction is precluded from processing a record until its timestamp is later than that carried in the record. The obvious result is that it cannot corrupt another transaction.

There are two principal methods of assigning unique timestamps. One is centralized, the other decentralized. In the centralized method, a single site is given responsibility for assigning the timestamps to transactions. With the decentralized scheme, each site is allowed to generate a unique local timestamp. A globally unique timestamp is derived by concatenating the unique local timestamp with (followed by) a unique site identifier. (If the concatenation were reversed, the site with the highest identifier would consistently generate higher timestamps than all other sites.)

Transaction timestamps may be created by having the TM keep a count of the number of transactions it has scheduled, and assigning the next number to each transaction in turn. In this way, no two transactions can receive the same timestamp, and the relative order of the timestamps is consistent with the order in which the transactions are initiated. A second approach is to use the value of the machine's internal clock at the time a process initiates.

How do timestamps enforce the serialization of transaction processing? With each record in the database, two times are identified: read-time, which is the highest timestamp possessed by any transaction to have read the item; and write-time, which is the the highest timestamp possessed by any transaction to have written to the record.

Concurrency is mitigated in the following ways:

1. A transaction having a timestamp t_1 cannot read an item with a write-time of t_2, if $t_2 > t_1$.

2. A transaction with timestamp t_1 cannot write an item with a read-time t_2, if $t_2 > t_1$.

We illustrate these ideas with an example.

Example 3 □ Examine Figure 18.13. T_1 is given a timestamp of 25 and T_2 is given a timestamp of 30. The initial read- and write-times of record R are assumed to be 0. R is given read time 25 when T_1 reads it, and 30 when T_2 reads it. When T_2 writes to R, T_2's timestamp is not less than the read time of R, which is also 30. By the above rule (2), the write is permitted, and the write-time of R is set to 30. Now when T_1 attempts to write at the final step, its timestamp, 25, is less than the read-time of R (30), so by rule (1), T_1 must be aborted.

Suppose T_1 is the LWV turkey order of Chapter 17, and that T_2 is the corresponding CC turkey order. If T_1 were not aborted in the final step of Figure 18.13, then the resulting inventory record balance would read 65, which would be in error. Aborting T_1 and restarting it will result in the proper balance being recorded.

To implement this scheme in the distributed database environment, the following steps need to be followed:

1. Transactions may execute at any site. As they read and write any

---

FIGURE 18.13 Timestamping Example

Timestamp	$\dfrac{T_1}{(25)}$	$\dfrac{T_2}{(30)}$
	1. READ R (25)	READ R (30)
	2. WRITE R (25 < 30 => abort)	WRITE R (30)

copy of the record, their timestamp is captured on the site copy of the record.

2. If a transaction writes a new value for the site copy of the record, the same value must be written to all copies of the record.

☐ DATABASE RECOVERY

In Chapter 17, we outlined recovery strategies based on a transaction log. In a distributed system, a log must be maintained at each site. In addition to the information in a centralized log, the site log must record each message that it sends and receives, as well as which subtransactions were started but did not commit at that site. If the distributed database system fails, the site log is a means of detecting failure and re-establishing the system status at time of failure.

■ SUMMARY

This chapter introduced distributed database systems, their terminology, and the architecture of a general DDBMS model. The underlying structure of a DDBMS is a system of several DBMSs running at separate local sites, which are connected by a message-sending facility. Each site of a DDBMS runs one or more of several software modules, including a transaction manager, a data manager, and a scheduler.

The principal motivating factors for implementing distributed database systems include increased reliability, improved response performance, location and replication independence, configuration independence, integration of nonhomogeneous DBMSs, improved security, and organizational congruence.

Distributed database system design issues were introduced which focused on the following strategies:

1. Replicated database with a centralized database being retained
2. Replicated database with no centralized database being retained
3. Partitioned database implemented as a series of independently operated database systems, but allowing remote access from other sites
4. Partitioned database implemented in an integrated fashion such that a single query requiring access to data at more than one site is handled by the DDBMS, and its functioning is transparent to the user.

Several criteria were suggested to help determine the appropriate configuration.

In processing distributed queries, vertical and horizontal fragmentation of relations can improve response time and user satisfaction. In addition, the use of semijoins can reduce communications costs.

In distributed database systems, integrity can be maintained through a two-phase commit protocol, distributed locking, distributed two-phase locking, and timestamping. Backup and recovery are facilitated by site logs.

Distributed database systems can be complex, but they offer capabilities that extend the advantages of database technology. We can expect to see their widespread use in organizations of many types.

■ REVIEW QUESTIONS

1. Define each of the following terms in your own words:
   a. distributed database system
   b. global data
   c. distributed database management system
   d. R*
   e. transaction
   f. local transaction
   g. WAN
   h. serilizability theory
   i. data fragmentation
   j. vertical fragmentation
   k. two-phase commit protocol
   l. timestamping
   m. distributed database system
   n. horizontal fragmentation

2. Describe how distributed database systems and centralized database systems differ.

3. Describe the software modules of a distributed database management system and how they operate to execute a global transaction (one that requires data from more than one site).

4. Discuss several advantages of a distributed database system.

5. Under what conditions might a distributed database system not function as well as a centralized database system?

6. Describe six objectives/strategies of implementing a distributed database system.

7. Contrast the concepts of partitioned and replicated databases. When might each be preferred to the other?

8. Compare the semijoin to the natural join.

9. What is the purpose of the two-phase commit protocol? How does it work?

10. What is the purpose of timestamping? How does it work?

11. How is database recovery effected in a distributed database system?

■ PROBLEMS AND EXERCISES

1. Match each term with its definition:

   __Local data

   __Link

   __SDD

   __Distributed INGRES

   a. A process that cooperates in completing a transaction

   b. A transaction that requires data from more than one database location

   c. A communications channel between two sites in a computer network

   d. Data that is maintained in the database at one site in a distributed database system

__Agent	e. The actions invoked by a transaction are executed sequentially
__Global transaction	f. A computer network that is limited to a small geographic area
__LAN	g. A DDBMS supplied by Relational Technology
__serial execution	h. A DDBMS supplied by Computer Corporation of America

2. Create a sample relational database for a firm having a database distributed at three locations. Choose a data distribution plan for this database, and justify your plan.

3. Show how vertical fragmentation may be applied to the plan developed in (2).

4. Show how horizontal fragmentation may be applied to the plan developed in (2).

5. Consider a relational schema:

```
EMPLOYEE(ID,NAME,ADDRESS,SKILL,PROJECTNO)
EQUIPMENT(IDNO,TYPE,PROJECTNO)
```

Suppose that the **EMPLOYEE** relation is fragmented horizontally by **PROJECTNO** and each fragment is stored locally at its project site. Assume that the **EQUIPMENT** relation is stored in its entirety at the Seattle location. Describe a good strategy for processing the following queries:

a. Find the join of employee and equipment.
b. Get all employees for projects using R2 Trucks.
c. Get all machines at the Parowan Project.
d. Find all employees for the project using the machine with ID number 12.

6. Compute a semijoin for the following relations

R1 = X Y Z	R2 = Z V W
c b a	a d e
d e f	a f h
c b d	b a b
e a b	c d c
h j k	c b a

■ PROJECTS AND PROFESSIONAL ISSUES

1. Research and then write a short essay on the future of distributed database systems.

2. Do a library research project to gather examples of current implementations of distributed database systems. Can you find any material discussing performance issues?

3. Contact a professional accounting firm, and inquire about the controls that should be present in a distributed processing system. Are there any areas where suitable controls are not in use?

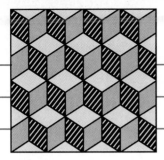

BIBLIOGRAPHY

The following abbreviations are used in this bibliography:

ACM	Association for Computing Machinery
AFIPS	American Federation of Information Processing Societies
CACM	Communications of the ACM
DE	Proceedings of the IEEE Computer Society International Conference on Data Engineering
EDS	Proceedings of the International Conference on Data Engineering
ER	Proceedings of the International Conference on Entity-Relationship Approach
ICIS	Proceedings of the International Conference on Information Systems
IFIP	International Federation for Information Processing
NCC	Proceedings of the National Computer Conference
OOPSLA	Proceedings of the ACM Conference on Object-Oriented Programming Systems, Languages, and Applications
PODS	Proceedings of the ACM Symposium on Principles of Database Systems
SIGMOD	Proceedings of the ACM SIGMOD International Conference on Management of Data
TODS	ACM Transactions on Database Systems
TOOIS	ACM Transactions on Office Information Systems
TSE	IEEE Transactions on Software Engineering
VLDB	Proceedings of the International Conference on Very Large Data Bases

ABRIAL, J. 1974. "Data Semantics." In *Data Base Management,* Klimbie and Koffeman, eds. North-Holland.

AHO, A., BEERI, C., AND ULLMAN, J. 1979. "The Theory of Joins in Relational Databases." TODS 4:3, September 1979.

AHO, A.V., HOPCROFT, E., AND ULLMAN, J.D. 1975. *The Design and Analysis of Computer Programs.* Reading, MA: Addison-Wesley.

ALBANO, A., DE ANTONELLIS, V., AND DE LEVA, A., editors. 1985. *Computer-Aided Database Design: The DATAID Project.* North-Holland.

ALLEN, F., LOOMIS, M., AND MANNINO, M. 1982. "The Integrated Dictionary/Directory System." *Computing Surveys* 14:2.

ANDRIOLE, S. J., ed. 1985. *Applications in Artificial Intelligence.* Princeton, NJ: Petrocelli Books.

ANSI. 1981. Proposed American National Standard for a Data Definition Language for Network Structured Databases. American National Standards Institute, Document ANSI X3H2.

———1986a. American National Standards Institute: The Database Language NDL, Document ANSI X3.133.

———1986b. American National Standards Institute: The Database Language SQL, Document ANSI X3.135.

———1989. American National Standards Institute: Information Resource Dictionary Systems, Document ANSI X3.138.

ASHTON-TATE CORPORATION. 1988. *dBASE IV Language Reference.* Ashton-Tate.

ASTRAHAN, M., et al. 1976. "System R: A Relational Approach to Data Base Management." TODS 1:2.

———1980. "A History and Evaluation of System R." *IBM Research Report RJ2843,* June.

ATRE, S. 1980. *Data Base: Structured Techniques for Design, Performance, and Management.* Wiley.

———1983. *Data Base Management Systems for the Eighties.* QED Information Sciences.

BABAD, Y.M., AND HOFFER, J.A. 1984. "Even No Data Has a Value." CACM 27:8.

BACHMAN, C. 1969. "Data Structure Diagrams." *Data Base* (Bulletin of ACM SIG-FIDET) 1:2.

———1973. "The Programmer as a Navigator." CACM 16:11.

———1974. "The Data Structure Set Model." In *Proceedings of the ACM SIGMOD Debate on Data Models: Data Structure Set Versus Relational,* R. Rustin, ed.

BAROODY, A., AND DEWITT, D. 1981. "An Object-Oriented Approach to Database System Implementation." TODS 6:4.

BATINI, C., LENZERINI, M., AND NAVATHE, S. 1987. "A Comparative Analysis of Methodologies for Database Schema Integration." *Computing Surveys* 18:4.

BATORY, D., et al. 1986. "GENESIS: An Extensible Database Management System." TSE 14:11.

BATRA, D., HOFFER, J. A., AND BOSTROM, R. B. 1988. "A Comparison of User Performance Between the Relational and Extended Entity Relationship Model in the Discovery Phase of Database Design." In ICIS 1988.

———1990. "A Comparison of the Representations Developed Using the Relational and Entity-Relationship Data Models." CACM 33:12.

BAYER, R., AND MCCREIGHT, E. 1972. "Organization and Maintenance of Large Ordered Indexes." *Acta Informatica* 1:3.

BERNSTEIN, P., AND GOODMAN, N. 1981a. "The Power of Natural Semijoins." *SIAM Journal of Computing* 10:4.

———1981b. "Concurrency Control in Distributed Database Systems." *Computing Surveys* 13:2.

BERNSTEIN, P., HADZILACOS, V., AND GOODMAN, N. 1988. *Concurrency Control and Recovery in Database Systems.* Reading, MA: Addison-Wesley.

BERNSTEIN, P. 1976. "Synthesizing Third Normal Form Relations from Functional Dependencies." TODS 1:4.

BHARGAVA, B., ed. 1987. *Concurrency and Reliability in Distributed Systems*. New York: Van Nostrand-Reinhold.

BILLER, H. 1979. "On the Equivalence of Data Base Schemas—A Semantic Approach to Data Translation." *Information Systems* 4:1.

BJORNER, D., AND LOVENGREN, H. 1982. "Formalization of Database Systems and a Formal Definition of IMS." In VLDB 1982.

BLASGEN, M., AND ESWARAN, K. 1976. "On the Evaluation of Queries in a Relational Database System." *IBM Systems Journal* 16:1.

BLASGEN, M., et al. 1981. "System R: An Architectural Overview." *IBM Systems Journal* 20:1.

BLOOMBECKER, J.J. 1989. "Short-Circuiting Computer Crime." *Datamation*. October 1.

BOAR, B.H. 1984. *Application Prototyping*. New York: Wiley.

BOCCA, J. 1986. "Educe—A Marriage of Convenience: Prolog and a Relational DBMS." *Proceedings of the Third International Conference on Logic Programming*. New York: Springer-Verlag, 1986.

BOEHM, B.W. 1981. *Software Engineering Economics*. Englewood Cliffs, NJ: Prentice Hall.

BOHL, M. 1981. *Introduction to IBM Direct Access Storage Devices*. Chicago: Science Research Associates.

BORLAND INTERNATIONAL. 1988. *Paradox 3.0 User's Guide*. Scotts Valley: CA: Borland.

BRACCHI, G., AND PERNICI, B. 1984. "The Design Requirements of Office Systems." TOOIS 2:2.

———1987. "Decision Support in Office Information Systems." In *Decision Support Theory and Application*, Holsapple and Whinston, eds. New York: Springer-Verlag.

BRACHMAN, R., AND LEVESQUE, H. 1984. "What Makes a Knowledge Base Knowledgeable? A View of Databases from the Knowledge Level." In EDS 1984.

BRADLEY, J. 1982. *File and Data Base Techniques*. New York: Holt, Rinehart & Winston.

BRAY, O. 1982. *Distributed Database Management Systems*. Lexington, MA: Lexington Books.

BRODIE, M., MYLOPOULOS, J., AND SCHMIDT, J., eds. 1984. *On Conceptual Modeling*. New York: Springer-Verlag.

BROSEY, M., AND SHNEIDERMAN, B. 1978. "Two Experimental Comparisons of Relational and Hierarchical Database Models." *International Journal of Man-Machine Studies*.

BROWN, R. 1988. "Data Integrity and SQL." *Database Programming and Design*.

BROWNING, D. 1987. "Data Managers and LANs." *PC Tech Journal* 5:5.

BRUCE, T., FULLER, J., AND MORIARTY, T. 1989. "So You Want a Repository." *Database Programming and Design*, May.

BUBENKO, J., BERILD, S., LINDERCRONA-OHLIN, E., AND NACHMENS, S. 1976. "From Information Requirements to DBTG Data Structures." *Proceedings of the ACM SIGMOD/SIGPLAN Conference on Data Abstraction*.

BUNEMAN, P. AND FRANKEL, R. 1979. "FQL: A Functional Query Language." In SIGMOD 1979.

CAMPBELL, D., EMBLEY, D., AND CZEJDO, B. 1985. "A Relationally Complete Query Language for the Entity-Relationship Model." In ER 1985.

———1987. "Graphical Query Formulation For an Entity-Relationship Model." *Data and Knowledge Engineering* 2, 89–121.

CARDENAS, A. 1985. *Data Base Management Systems*, second ed. Newton, MA: Allyn and Bacon.

CAREY, M., DEWITT, D., AND VANDENBERG, S. 1988. "A Data Model and Query Language for Exodus." In SIGMOD 1988.

CAREY, M., DEWITT, D., RICHARDSON, J., AND SHEKITA, E. 1986. "Object and File Management in the EXODUS Extensible Database System." In VLDB 1986.

CAREY, M., et al. 1986. "The Architecture of the EXODUS Extensible DBMS." In *Proceedings of the International Workshop on Object-Oriented Database Systems,* Dittrich and Dayal, eds. IEEECS.

CARLIS, J. AND MARCH, S. 1984. "A Descriptive Model of Physical Database Design Problems and Solutions." In DE 1984.

CASANOVA, M., AND VIDAL, V. 1982. "Toward a Sound View Integration Method." PODS.

CERI, S., ed. 1983. *Methodology and Tools for Database Design.* North-Holland.

CERI, S. AND PELAGATTI, G. 1984. *Distributed Databases: Principles and Systems.* New York: McGraw-Hill.

CERI, S., NAVATHE, S., AND WIEDERHOLD, G. 1983. "Distribution Design of Logical Database Schemas." TSE 9:4.

CHAMBERLIN, D., AND BOYCE, R. 1974. "SEQUEL: A Structured English Query Language." In SIGMOD 1984.

CHAMBERLIN, D., et al. 1976. "SEQUEL 2: A Unified Approach to Data Definition, Manipulation, and Control." *IBM Journal of Research and Development* 20:6.

———1981. "A History and Evaluation of System R." CACM 24:10.

CHAMPINE, G. A. 1977. "Six Approaches to Distributed Data Bases." *Datamation,* May 1977.

CHAN, A., AND WONG, H. K. T. 1990. "Serving Up dBASE." *Data Base Programming & Design,* February.

CHANG, C., AND WALKER, A. 1984. "PROSQL: A Prolog Programming Interface with SQL/DS." In EDS 1984.

CHEN AND ASSOCIATES. 1988. *E-R Designer Reference Manual.* Baton Rouge, LA: Chen and Associates.

CHEN, P. 1976. "The Entity Relationship Model—Toward a Unified View of Data." TODS 1:1.

———1977. *The Entity-Relationship Approach to Logical Data Base Design.* Q.E.D. Information Sciences, Data Base Monograph Series no. 6.

CHIMENTI, D., GAMBOA, R., KRISHNAMURTHY, R., NAQVI, S., TSUR, S., AND ZANIOLO, C. 1990. "The LDL System Prototype." *IEEE Transactions on Knowledge and Data Engineering* 2:1.

CHOUINARD, P. 1989. "Supertypes, Subtypes, and DB2." *Database Programming and Design.* October.

CHRISTODOULAKIS, S., et al. 1984. "Development of a Multimedia Information System for an Office Environment." In VLDB 1984.

CLAYBROOK, B. 1983. *File Management Techniques.* New York: Wiley, 1983.

CODASYL. 1971. Data Base Task Group. April 71 Report, ACM, 1971.

CODASYL. 1978. Data Description Language Journal of Development. Canadian Government Publishing Centre.

CODD, E. 1970 "A Relational Model for Large Shared Data Banks." CACM 13:6.

———1971a. "Relational Completeness of Data Base Sublanguages." *Courant Computer Science Symposium 6, Data Base Systems,* Prentice Hall.

———1971b. "A Data Base Sublanguage Founded on the Relational Calculus," *Proceedings of the ACM SIGFIDET Workshop on Data Description, Access, and Control,* November.

———1972. "Further Normalization of the Data Base Relational Model." In Rustin 1972.

———1974. "Recent Investigations in Relational Database Systems," *Proceedings of the IFIP Congress.*

———1978. "How About Recently? (English Dialog with Relational Data Bases Using Rendezvous Version 1)." In Shneiderman 1978.

———1979. "Extending the Database Relational Model to Capture More Meaning." TODS, 4:4, December.

———1982. "Relational Database: A Practical Foundation for Productivity." CACM, 25:2, December.

————1985. "Is Your DBMS Really Relational?" and "Does Your DBMS Run By the Rules?" *Computerworld,* October 14 and October 21.

————1986. "An Evaluation Scheme for Database Management Systems That Are Claimed to be Relational." in DE.

COMER, D. 1979. "The Ubiquitous B-tree." *Computing Surveys* 11:2.

CONTE, P. 1989. "In Search of Consistency." *Database Programming and Design,* August.

CURTICE, R., AND CASEY, W. 1985. "Database: What's in Store." *Datamation,* December 1.

CURTICE, R. 1981. "Data Dictionaries: An Assessment of Current Practice and Problems." In VLDB.

CZEJDO, B., ELMASRI, R., RUSINKIEWICZ, M., AND EMBLEY, D. 1987. "An Algebraic Language for Graphical Query Formulation Using an Extended Entity-Relationship Model." *Proceedings of the ACM Computer Science Conference.*

DATE, C., AND WHITE, C. 1988a. *A Guide to SQL/DS.* Reading, MA: Addison-Wesley.

————C. 1988b. *A Guide to DB2,* 2nd ed. Reading, MA: Addison-Wesley.

1983a. *An Introduction to Database Systems, Vol. 2.* Reading, MA: Addison-Wesley.

————1983b. "The Outer Join." *Proceedings of the Second International Conference on Databases.*

————1984. "A Critique of the SQL Database Language." *ACM SIGMOD Record* 14:3.

————1986. *An Introduction to Database Systems, Vol. 1,* 4th ed. Reading, MA: Addison-Wesley.

————1987. "Where SQL Falls Short." *Datamation,* May 1.

DAVIES, C. 1973. "Recovery Semantics for a DB/DC System." *Proceedings of the ACM National Conference.*

DBTG. 1971. Report of the CODASYL Data Base Task Group, ACM, April.

DEMARCO, T. 1979. *Structured Analysis and System Specification.* Prentice Hall Yourdan Inc.

DENNING, D., AND DENNING, P. 1979. "Data Security." *Computing Surveys* 11:3.

DIFFIE, W., AND HELLMAN, M. 1979. "Privacy and Authentication." *Proceedings of the IEEE* 67:3.

DITTRICH, K., AND DAYAL, U., eds. 1986. *Proceedings of the International Workshop on Object-Oriented Database Systems.* IEEE CS, September.

DITTRICH, K. 1986. "Object-Oriented Database Systems: The Notion and the Issues." In Proceedings of the International Workshop on Object-Oriented Database Systems, K. Dittrich and U. Dayal, eds.

DODD, G. 1969. "Elements of Data Management Systems." *Computing Surveys* 1:2.

DOS SANTOS, C., NEUHOLD, E., AND FURTADO, A. 1979. "A Data Type Approach to the Entity-Relationship Model." In ER 1979.

DUMPALA, S., AND ARORA, S. 1983. "Schema Translation Using the Entity-Relationship Approach." In ER 1983.

ELLIS, C., AND NUTT, G. 1980. "Office Information Systems and Computer Science." *Computing Surveys* 12:1.

ELLZEY, R.S. 1982. *Data Structures for Computer Information Systems.* Science Research Associates.

ELMASRI, R., AND LARSON, J. 1985. "A Graphical Query Facility for ER Databases." In ER 1985.

ELMASRI, R., AND NAVATHE, S. 1984. "Object Integration in Logical Database Design." In DE 1984.

————1989. *Fundamentals of Database Systems.* Menlo Park, CA: Benjamin/Cummings.

ELMASRI, R., AND WIEDERHOLD, G. 1979. "Data Model Integration Using the Structural Model." In SIGMOD 1979.

———1980. "Structural Properties of Relationships and Their Representation." NCC, AFIPS, 49.

———1981. "GORDAS: A Formal, High-Level Query Language for the Entity-Relationship Model." In ER 1981.

ELMASRI, R., WEELDREYER, J., AND HEVNER, A. 1985. "The Category Concept: An Extension to the Entity-Relationship Model." *International Journal on Data and Knowledge Engineering* 1:1.

FAGIN, R. 1977. "Multivalued Dependencies and a New Normal Form for Relational Databases." TODS 2:3.

———1979. "Normal Forms and Relational Database Operators." In SIGMOD 1979.

———1981. "A Normal Form for Relational Databases That is Based on Domains and Keys." TODS 6:3.

FERNANDEZ, E., SUMMERS, R., AND WOOD, C. 1981. *Database Security and Integrity,* Reading, MA: Addison-Wesley.

FISHMAN, D., et al. 1986. "IRIS: An Object-Oriented DBMS." TOOIS 4:2.

FLAVIN, M. 1981. *Fundamental Concepts of Information Modeling.* Englewood Cliffs, NJ: Yourdon Press.

FLEMING, C., AND VON HALLE, B. 1990. "An Overview of Logical Data Modeling." *Data Resource Management,* Winter.

FRY, J., AND SIBLEY, E. 1976. "Evolution of Data-Base Management Systems." *Computing Surveys* 8:1.

FURTADO, A. 1978. "Formal Aspects of the Relational Model." *Information Systems* 3:2.

GADIA, S. 1988. "A Homogeneous Relational Model and Query Language for Temporal Databases." TODS 13:4.

GALLAIRE, H., AND MINKER, J., eds. 1978. *Logic and Databases.* New York: Plenum Press.

GALLAIRE, H., MINKER, J., AND NICOLAS, J. 1984. "Logic and Databases: A Deductive Approach." *Computing Surveys* 16:2.

GARDARIN, G., AND VALDURIEZ, P. 1989. *Relational Databases and Knowledge Bases.* Reading, MA: Addison-Wesley.

GAREY, M. 1979. *Computers and Intractability: A Guide to the Theory of NP-Completeness.* New York: W. H. Freeman and Company.

GOLDFINE, A., AND KONIG, P. 1988. A Technical Overview of the Information Resource Dictionary System (IRDS), 2nd ed. Washington, DC: National Bureau of Standards, NBS IR 88-3700.

GORMAN, K., AND CHOOBINEH, J. 1990. "An Overview of the Object-Oriented Entity Relationship Model (OOERM)." *Proceedings of the Twenty-Third Annual Hawaii International Conference on Information Systems.*

GOTLIEB, L. 1975. "Computing Joins of Relations." In SIGMOD 1975.

GRAY, J., McJONES, P., AND BLASGEN, M. 1981. "The Recovery Manager of the System R Database Manager." *Computing Surveys* 13:2, June.

GRAY, J. 1981. "The Transaction Concept: Virtues and Limitations." In VLDB 1981.

GREENBLATT, D., AND WAXMAN, J. 1978. "A Study of Three Database Query Languages." In *Databases: Improving Usability and Responsiveness*, B. Shneiderman, ed.

GUIMARAES, T. 1988. "Information Resources Management: Improving the Focus." *Information Resources Management Journal,* Fall.

HAMMER, M., AND McLEOD, D. 1975. "Semantic Integrity in a Relational Data Base System." In VLDB.

———1978. "The Semantic Data Model: A Modelling Mechanism for Data Base Applications." In SIGMOD 1978.

———1981. "Database Descriptions with SDM: A Semantic Data Model." TODS 6:3.

HANSEN, G. 1988. *Database Processing with Fourth Generation Languages.* Cincinnati: South-Western.

HANSEN, G., AND HANSEN, J. 1987. "Procedural and Non-procedural Languages Revisited: A Comparison of Relational Algebra and Relational Calculus." *International Journal of Man-Machine Studies* 26: 683–694.

————1988. "Human Performance in Relational Algebra, Tuple Calculus, and Domain Calculus." *International Journal of Man-Machine Studies* 29:503–16.

HARRINGTON, J. 1987. *Relational Database Management for Microcomputer: Design and Implementation.* New York: Holt, Rinehart, and Winston.

HARRIS, L. 1978. "The ROBOT System: Natural Language Processing Applied to Data Base Query." *Proceedings of the ACM National Conference,* December.

HASKIN, R., AND LORIE, R. 1982. "On Extending the Functions of a Relational Database System." In SIGMOD.

HAWRYSZKIEWYCA, I.T. 1991. Database Analysis and Design, 2nd ed. New York: Macmillan.

HAYES-ROTH, R., WATERMAN, D., AND LENAT, D., eds. 1983. *Building Expert Systems.* Reading, MA: Addison-Wesley.

HELD, G., AND STONEBRAKER, M. 1978. "B-Trees Reexamined." CACM 21:2.

HIMMELSTEIN, M. 1989. "Cooperative Database Processing." *Database Programming and Design,* October.

HOFFER, J., MICHAELE, S., AND CARROLL, J. 1989. "The Pitfalls of Strategic Data and Systems Planning: A Research Agenda." *Proceedings of the Twenty-Second Annual Hawaii International Conference on System Sciences. Vol. IV.*

HOFFER, J. 1982. "An Empirical Investigation with Individual Differences in Database Models." In ICIS.

HOLLAND, R.H. 1980. "Data Base Planning Entails Return to Basics," *Computerworld,* October 27.

HOLSAPPLE, C., AND WHINSTON, A., eds. 1987. *Decision Support Theory and Application.* New York: Springer-Verlag.

HUBBARD, G.U. 1981. *Computer-Assisted Data Base Design.* New York: Van Nostrand Reinhold.

HULL, R., AND KING, R. 1987. "Semantic Database Modeling: Survey, Applications, and Research Issues." *Computing Surveys* 19:3.

IMIELINSKI, T., AND LIPSKI, W. 1981. "On Representing Incomplete Information in a Relational Database." In VLDB 1981.

JACKSON, M.A. 1975. *Principles of Program Design.* Orlando: Academic Press. 1975.

JAQUA, D. 1988. "SQL Database Security." *Database Programming and Design,* July 1988.

JARDINE, D., ed. 1977. *The ANSI/SPARC DBMS Model.* North-Holland.

KAPP, D., AND LEBEN, J. 1978. *IMS Programming Techniques.* New York: Van Nostrand-Reinhold.

KENT, W. 1978. *Data and Reality.* North-Holland.

————1979. "Limitations of Record-Based Information Models." TODS 4:1.

————1983. "A Simple Guide to Five Normal Forms in Relational Database Theory." CACM 26:2.

KIM, W. 1979. "Relational Database Systems." *Computing Surveys* 11:3.

————1982. "On Optimizing an SQL-like Nested Query." TODS 3:3.

KIM, W., REINER, D., AND BATORY, D., eds 1985. *Query Processing in Database Systems.* New York: Springer-Verlag.

KLIMBIE, J., AND KOFFEMAN, K., eds. 1974. *Data Base Management.* North-Holland.

KNUTH, D. 1973. *The Art of Computer Programming, Volume 3: Sorting and Searching.* Reading, MA: Addison-Wesley.

KORTH, H., AND SILBERSCHATZ, A. 1986. *Database System Concepts.* New York: McGraw-Hill.

————1991. Database System Concepts, 2nd ed. New York: McGraw-Hill.

KROENKE, D., AND DOLAN, K. 1988. *Database Processing, 3rd ed.* Chicago: Science Research Associates.

KROENKE, D. 1987. "Developing Object-Oriented Database Applications on Microcomputers." *Proceedings of the Second International Conference on Computers and Applications*, Beijing, June.

KULL, D., 1986. "Anatomy of a 4GL Disaster." *Computer Decisions*, February 11.

LARSON, P. 1978. "Dynamic Hashing." *BIT* 18.

————1981. "Analysis of Index-Sequential Files with Overflow Chaining." TODS 6:4.

LEDERER, A., AND SETHIK, V. 1989. "Pitfalls in Planning." *Datamation*, June 1.

LEFKOVITZ, H. C. 1985. *Proposed American National Standards Information Resource Dictionary System.* QED Information Sciences.

LEISS, E. 1982. *Principles of Data Security.* New York: Plenum Press.

LENZERINI, M., AND SANTUCCI, C. 1983. "Cardinality Constraints in the Entity Relationship Model." In ER 1983.

LIEN, E., AND WEINBERGER, P. 1978. "Consistency, Concurrency, and Crash Recovery." In SIGMOD 1978.

LITWIN, P. 1989. "Faking Multi-Table Forms." *Data Based Advisor.* October.

LITWIN, W. 1978. "Virtual Hashing: A Dynamically Changing Hashing." In VLDB 1978.

————1980. "Linear Hashing: A New Tool for File and Table Addressing." In VLDB 1980.

LIU, K., AND SUNDERRAMAN, R. 1988. "On Representing Indefinite and Maybe Information in Relational Databases." In DE 1988.

LIVADAS, P. 1989. *File Structures: Theory and Practice.* Englewood Cliffs, NJ: Prentice Hall.

LOCKEMANN, P., AND KNUTSEN, W. 1968. "Recovery of Disk Contents after System Failure." CACM 11:8.

LOZINSKI, E. 1986. "A Problem-Oriented Inferential Database System." TODS 11:3.

LYON, L. 1989. "CASE and the Database." *Database Programming and Design.* May.

MAIER, D., STEIN, J., OTIS, A., AND PURDY, A. 1986. "Development of an Object-Oriented DBMS." OOPSLA.

MAIER, D. 1983. *The Theory of Relational Databases.* Rockville, MD: Computer Science Press.

MARKOWITZ, V., AND RAZ, Y. 1983. "Errol: An Entity-Relationship, Role Oriented, Query Language." In ER 1983.

MARTIN, E., DeHAYES, D., HOFFER, J., AND PERKINS, W. 1991. *Managing Information Technology: What Managers Need to Know.* New York: Macmillan.

MARTIN, J. 1977. *Computer Data Base Organization,* 2nd ed. Englewood Cliffs, NJ: Prentice Hall.

————1981. *An End-User's Guide to Data Base.* Englewood Cliffs, NJ: Prentice Hall.

————1982. *Strategic Data Planning Methodologies.* Englewood Cliffs, NJ: Prentice Hall.

————1983. *Managing the Data-Base Environment.* Englewood Cliffs, NJ: Prentice Hall.

McFADDEN, F., AND HOFFER, J. 1991. *Database Management,* 3rd ed. Menlo Park, CA: Benjamin/Cummings.

McGEE, W. 1977. "The Information Management System IMS/VS, Part I: General Structure and Operation." *IBM Systems Journal* 16:2.

MEYER, B. 1988. *Object-Oriented Software Construction.* Englewood Cliffs, NJ: Prentice Hall.

MICRORIM, INC. 1987. *R:BASE for DOS User's Manual.* Redmond, WA: Microrim.

MISSIKOFF, M., AND WIEDERHOLD, G. 1984. "Toward a Unified Approach for Expert and Database Systems." In EDS 1984.

NAFFAH, N., ed. 1982. *Office Information Systems.* North-Holland.

NAVATHE, S., AND GADGIL, S. 1982. "A Methodology for View Integration in Logical Database Design." In VLDB 1982.

NAVATHE, S. AND KERSCHBERG, L. 1986. "Role of Data Dictionaries in Database Design." *Information and Management* 10:1.

NAVATHE, S., AND PILLALAMARRI, M. 1988. "Toward Making the ER Approach Object-Oriented." In ER 1988.

NAVATHE, S., AND SCHKOLNICK, M. 1978. "View Representation in Logical Database Design." In SIGMOD 1978.

NAVATHE, S., ELMASRI, R., AND LARSON, J. 1986. "Integrating User Views in Database Design." *IEEE Computer* 19:1.

NAVATHE, S. 1980. "An Intuitive View to Normalize Network-Structured Data." In VLDB 1980.

NG, P. 1981. "Further Analysis of the Entity-Relationship Approach to Database Design." TSE 7:1.

NIEVERGELT, J. 1974. "Binary Search Trees and File Organization." *Computing Surveys* 6:3.

NIJSSEN, G., ed. 1976. *Modelling in Data Base Management Systems.* North-Holland.

OHSUGA, S. 1982. "Knowledge Based Systems as a New Interactive Computer System of the Next Generation." In *Computer Science and Technologies.* North-Holland.

OLLE, T. W. 1980. *The CODASYL Approach to Data Base Management.* Chichester, England: Wiley.

OZSOYOGLU, G., OZSOYOGLU, Z., AND MATROS, V. 1985. "Extending Relational Algebra and Relational Calculus with Set Valued Attributes and Aggregate Functions." TODS 12:4.

OZSOYOGLU, Z., AND YUAN, L. 1987. "A New Normal Form for Nested Relations." TODS 12:1.

PAPADIMITRIOU, C. 1986. *The Theory of Database Concurrency Control.* Rockville, MD: Computer Science Press.

PARENT, C., AND SPACCAPIETRA, S. 1985. "An Algebra for a General Entity-Relationship Model." TSE 11:7.

PERCY, T. 1986. "My Data, Right or Wrong," *Datamation,* June 1.

REISNER, P. 1977. "Use of Psychological Experimentation as an Aid to Development of a Query Language." TSE 3:3.

———1981. "Human Factors Studies of Database Query Language: A Survey and Assessment." *Computing Surveys* 13:1.

RETTIG, M. 1989. "Gourmet Guide to the DB2 Catalog." *Data Base Programming and Design.* February.

ROTH, M., AND KORTH, H. 1987. "The Design of Non-1NF Relational Databases into Nested Normal Form." In SIGMOD 1987.

ROTHNIE, J., et al. 1980. "Introduction to a System for Distributed Databases (SDD-1)." TODS 5:1.

RUBEL, M. C. 1989a. "Keeping The Garbage Out." *Data Based Advisor,* April.

———1989b. "Entering Data into Screen Forms." *Data Based Advisor,* May.

———1989c. "Creating a Report." *Data Based Advisor,* July.

RUSTIN, R., ed. 1972. *Data Base Systems.* Englewood Cliffs, NJ: Prentice Hall.

———1974. *Proceedings of the ACM SIGMOD Debate on Data Models: Data Structure Set Versus Relational.*

SAYLES, J.S. 1989. "All In a Row." *Data Based Advisor,* December.

SCHAEFFER, H. 1981. *Data Center Operations.* Englewood Cliffs, NJ: Prentice Hall.

SCHEUERMANN, P., ed. 1982. *Improving Database Usability and Responsiveness.* Orlando: Academic Press.

SCHKOLNICK, M. 1978. "A Survey of Physical Database Design Methodology and

Techniques." In VLDB 1978.

SCHMIDT, J., AND SWENSON, J. 1975. "On the Semantics of the Relational Model." In SIGMOD 1975.

SCHUR, S.G. 1989. "Building an Active Distributed Database." *Database Programming and Design,* April 1989.

SHANK, M., BOYNTON, A., AND ZMUD, R. 1985. "Critical Success Factor Analysis as a Methodology for IS Planning." *MIS Quarterly* 9:2.

SHETH, A., LARSON, J., CORNELIO, A., AND NAVATHE, S. 1988. "A Tool for Integrating Conceptual Schemas and User Views." In DE 1988.

SHIPMAN, D. 1981. "The Functional Data Model and the Data Language DAPLEX." TODS 6:1.

SCHNEIDERMAN, B., ed. 1978. *Databases: Improving Usability and Responsiveness.* Orlando: Academic Press.

SIBLEY, E. 1976. "The Development of Database Technology." *Computing Surveys* 8:1.

SMITH, J., AND SMITH, D. 1977. "Database Abstractions: Aggregation and Generalization." TODS 2:2.

SMITH, P., AND BARNES, G. 1987. *Files & Databases: An Introduction.* Reading, MA: Addison-Wesley.

SNODGRASS, R., AND AHN, I. 1985. "A Taxonomy of Time in Databases." In SIGMOD 1985.

SPRAGUE, R., AND MCNURLINK, B. 1986. *Information Systems in Practice.* Englewood Cliffs, NJ: Prentice Hall.

SPRAGUE, R., AND WATSON, H. 1989. Decision Support Systems, 2nd ed. Englewood Cliffs, NJ: Prentice Hall.

STONEBRAKER, M., WONG, E., KREPS, P., AND HELD, G. 1976. "The Design and Implementation of INGRES." TODS 1:3.

STOREY, V.C., AND GOLDSTEIN, R.C. 1988. "A Methodology for Creating User Views in Database Design." TODS 13:3.

TAYLOR, R., AND FRANK, R. 1976. "CODASYL Data Base Management Systems." *Computing Surveys* 8:1.

TEOREY, T., AND FRY, J. 1982. *Design of Database Structures.* Englewood Cliffs, NJ: Prentice Hall.

TEORY, T., YANG, D., AND FRY, J. 1986. "A Logical Design Methodology for Relational Databases Using the Extended Entity-Relationship Model." *Computing Surveys* 18:2.

THOMAS, J., AND GOULD, J. 1975. "A Psychological Study of Query By Example." NCC, AFIPS, 44.

TODD, S. 1976. "The Peterlee Relational Test Vehicle—A System Overview." *IBM Systems Journal* 15:4.

TSICHRITZIS, D., AND KLUG, A., eds. 1978. *The ANSI/X3/SPARC DBMS Framework.* AFIPS Press.

TSICHRITZIS, D., AND LOCHOVSKY, F. 1976. "Hierarchical Data-base Management: A Survey." *Computing Surveys* 8:1.

———1977. *Data Base Management Systems.* New York: Academic Press.

———1982. *Data Models.* Englewood Cliffs, NJ: Prentice Hall.

TSICHRITZIS, D. 1982. "Forms Management." CACM. 25:7.

UHROWCZIK, P. 1973. "Data Dictionary/Directories." *IBM Systems Journal* 12:4.

ULLMAN, J. 1982. *Principles of Database Systems,* 2nd ed. Rockville, MD: Computer Science Press.

ULLMAN, J. 1990. *Principles of Database and Knowledge-Base Systems.* Computer Science Press.

UMBAUGH, R., ed. 1985. *The Handbook of MIS Management.* Auerbach.

VALDURIEZ, P., AND GARDARIN, G. 1989. *Analysis and Comparison of Relational Database Systems.* Reading, MA: Addison-Wesley.

VETTER, M., AND MADDISON, R.N. 1981. *Database Design Methodology.* Englewood Cliffs, NJ: Prentice Hall.

VETTER, M. 1987. *Strategy for Data Modeling.* New York: Wiley.

WELDON, J. 1981. *Data Base Administration.* New York: Plenum Press.

WELTY, C., AND STEMPLE, D. 1981. "Human Factors Comparison of a Procedural and a Nonprocedural Query Language." TODS 6:4.

WERTZ, C. 1986. *The Data Dictionary: Concepts and Uses.* QED Information Sciences.

WHITTEN, J., BENTLEY, L., AND HO, T. 1986. *Systems Analysis and Design Methods.* St. Louis: Times Mirror/Mosby.

WIEDERHOLD, G. 1983. *Database Design,* 2nd ed. New York: McGraw-Hill.

———1984. "Knowledge and Database Management." IEEE *Software* 8:1.

———1986. "Views, Objects, and Databases." *Computer* 19:12.

WYLIE, C. 1957. *101 Puzzles in Thought and Logic.* Mineola, NY: Dover Publications.

WINKLER-PARENTZ, H. B. 1989. "Can You Trust Your DBMS?" *Database Programming and Design,* July.

WIORKOWSKI, G., AND KULL, D. 1989. "Distributed DB2." *Database Programming and Design,* April.

WOOD, D. 1990. "A Primer of Features and Performance Issues of Relational DBMSs." *Data Resource Management* 1:1.

YAO, S. ed. 1985. *Principles of Database Design, Volume 1: Logical Organizations.* Englewood Cliffs, NJ: Prentice Hall.

YOURDON, E., AND CONSTANTINE, L. 1979. *Structured Design.* Englewood Cliffs, NJ: Prentice Hall.

ZANIOLO, C., et al. 1986. "Object-Oriented Database Systems and Knowledge Systems." In EDS 1984.

ZLOOF, M. 1975. "Query By Example." NCC, AFIPS, 44.

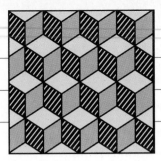

GLOSSARY

A

aborted transaction Transaction that is cancelled before changes are applied to the database.

abstract object set An object set consisting of instances that cannot be printed.

access controls Controls that limit user access to programs and data.

access motion time The time required to position the read/write heads of the disk drive over the desired cylinder.

agent A process that cooperates in completing a transaction.

aggregate object set A relationship viewed as an object set.

alias Alternate name given to a relation.

ancestor In a hierarchy, a segment type that is found on the same path, but at a higher level in the tree.

application-specific knowledge Knowledge that is determined by the rules and conventions that apply to a specific problem domain.

application program A computer program that performs a specific task of practical value in a business situation.

assignment Relational algebra operation that gives a name to a relation.

atomic transaction A transaction in which all actions associated with the transaction are executed to completion, or none is performed.

atomic value Value that is not a set of values or a repeating group.

attribute Functional relationship from an object set to another object set.

attribute domain The set from which an attribute takes its values.

B

backup-and-recovery controls Those controls that provide for restoring the database in case of system failure.

backward chaining A logical chain of rules proceeding from a conclusion to a hypothesis.

base table A table that contains basic or "real" data.

benchmarking A method of comparing DBMS performance by testing its performance on actual applications.

binary relationship A relationship between two object sets.

Boolean connective Any of the logical connectives AND, OR, NOT.

Boyce-Codd Normal Form (BCNF) The property of a relation in which every determinant is a key.

buffer manager Software that controls the movement of data between main memory and disk storage.

built-in function Statistical function that operates on a set of rows—SUM, AVG, COUNT, MAX, MIN.

C

candidate key Any set of attributes that could be chosen as a key of a relation.

cardinality The maximum number of instances of one object set related to a single instance of the other object set.

Cartesian product Result of pairing each row in one table with every row in another table.

CASE statement Used with SWITCH statement to direct processing when a condition is found to be true.

centralized database Data-base physically confined to a single location.

chain A collection of pointers that link a set of physical records—also called a linked list.

character string literals Literals formed from alphanumeric and "special" characters.

checkpointing Saving copies of the database at predetermined times during processing; database recovery begins or ends at the most recent checkpoint.

child The point at the head of the arrow in a hierarchical data structure.

ciphertext Encrypted plaintext.

clause In PROLOG, the means by which facts and knowledge are expressed.

clustering Placing in the same block the records of relations that are likely to be joined frequently.

collision Occurs when the keys of two records hash to the same physical address.

committed transaction A transaction that successfully completes all its actions.

comparison operators =, <>, <, >, <=, >=

complex network A data structure in which one or more binary relationships are many–many.

composite key A key consisting of more than one attribute.

conceptual level Database structural level defining logical schema of database.

conceptual object An object representing a type of thing.

conceptual object set An object set whose instances are conceptual objects.

concurrency controls Controls that maintain database integrity when two or more users simultaneously request a data-base record.

concurrent processing (concurrency) Occurs when two or more transactions access the same database record at the same time.

condition box In QBE, a box in which a complex query condition can be expressed.

conditional statement A statement that tests for the presence of a condition and directs further processing accordingly.

Conference on Data Systems Languages (CODASYL) An organization composed of representatives from hardware vendors, software vendors, and users—known principally for development of the COBOL language.

conjunctive query A query whose conditions are connected by "and," or an equivalent symbol.

constraint A rule that restricts the values in a database.

correlated subquery A subquery whose result depends on the row being examined by an outer query.

count-data format A data format for tracks that uses no external keys.

count-key format A data format for tracks that uses external keys.

currency pointer Contains the address of the segment in the tree that was accessed last.

cursor Embedded SQL facility where the result of an SQL query is stored for subsequent processing.

cylinder The same track extending through all surfaces of the disk storage unit.

D

data Isolated facts.

data administrator Manager whose responsibilities are focused on establishing policies and procedures for the organization's information system.

data-oriented approach Focuses on the analysis of data used by the functions.

Data Definition Language (DDL) The language used to specify a database schema.

data dictionary That part of the DBMS that defines the structure of user data and how it is to be used.

data fragmentation The partitioning of relations in a distributed database system.

data integration Combining data for common use.

data integrity The accuracy and consistency of data values in the database.

data manipulation language (DML) Computer language for querying and updating a database.

data model A conceptual method of structuring data.

data processing system An automated system for processing the data for the records of an organization.

data redundancy Repetition of data in a database.

data security Refers to protecting the database system from unauthorized or malicious use.

data transfer rate The rate at which data can be read from the disk to main memory, or equivalently, the rate at which data is written from main memory to disk.

data view A definition of a restricted portion of the database; also called a view.

database A collection of interrelated, shared, and controlled data that can be processed by one or more application systems.

Database Administration Personnel with responsibility for controlling and protecting the database.

database administrator Manager whose responsibilities are focused on managing the technical aspects of the database system.

database description (DBD) The way in which data is physically stored in IMS (internal database structure).

database development life cycle (DDLC) A process for designing, implementing, and maintaining a database system.

database implementation The steps required to change a logical design to a functioning database.

database management system (DBMS) Systems software that facilitates the management of a database.

database planning Strategic effort to determine information needs for an extended period.

database record An occurrence of a root and all its dependent segment types.

database recovery procedures The means by which a database that has been corrupted by mal-functions can be restored to a correct and consistent state.

database system A database, a database management system, and appropriate hardware and personnel.

Database Task Group (DBTG) A subgroup of CODASYL given responsibility for developing standards for database management systems.

database tree A tree that has a root.

DEA Data envelopment analysis—a quantitative method of evaluating alternative choices.

deadlock Two transactions are mutually excluded from accessing the next record required to complete their transactions; also called a "deadly embrace."

deadlock detection A periodic check by the DBMS to determine if the waiting line for some resource exceeds a predetermined limit.

decision support system Automated system providing strategic information to senior management.

declarative format A qualification expression format that takes the form of a declarative sentence.

decomposition of relations Splitting a relation into multiple relations.

degree of a relation The number of attributes in a relation.

DELETE Operation that removes rows from a relation.

deletion anomaly Unintended loss of data due to deletion of other data.

dependent object set An object set whose instances *must* be related to at least one other instance of another object set.

dependent segment type All record types other than the root segment type.

determinant The attribute(s) on the left side of a functional dependency; determine(s) the value of other attributes in the tuple.

difference Relational algebra operation that creates the set difference of two union compatible relations.

directed graph A mathematical structure in which points or "nodes" are connected by arrows or "edges."

direction of relationship The implied SUBJECT-VERB-OBJECT order for reading the names of a relationship and its object set.

disjoint union A set made up of elements that are in one or the other of two other sets, but not in both.

disjunctive query A query whose conditions are connected by "or," or an equivalent symbol.

disk drive Physical unit that contains the disk storage unit.

DISTINCT Operator that eliminates duplicate rows.

distributed database A database that is distributed among a network of geographically separated locations.

distributed database management system (DDBMS) The software that manages the distributed database system.

distributed database system A collection of locations, each of which operates a local database system, which can participate in the execution of transactions that access data at several locations.

Distributed INGRES DDBMS marketed by Relational Technology.

divide Relational algebra operation that creates a new relation by selecting the rows in one relation that match every row in another relation.

DL/1 Data Language 1, the IMS data manipulation language.

domain The PROLOG term for specification of data type.

dynamically generated set A set whose value varies depending on the particular value of a variable from the target list.

E

economic feasibility Cost-benefit study of proposed database system.

edge Part of a network structure represented by an arrow.

efficient frontier The outer boundary in DEA analysis.

electronic data processing Computer automation of paperwork at the operational level of an organization.

embedded SQL A set of statements that allows SQL to be used with traditional programming languages.

encrypt To convert readable text to unreadable text by use of an algorithm; used to protect sensitive data.

encryption Encoding data to make it unintelligible to unauthorized persons.

enterprise-directing knowledge Knowledge that helps an enterprise to make decisions.

entity integrity rule No key attribute of a row may be null.

equijoin Theta join based on equality of specified columns.

example element In QBE, a variable representing an unspecified value in a column of a table.

example table In QBE, a skeleton table showing the table name and the column names above blank spaces used for entry of query conditions.

existential quantifier Relational calculus expression affirming the existence of at least one row to which a condition applies.

existentially quantified The assertion that, for a given variable, a value exists in the object set.

EXISTS operator Evaluates to true if resulting set is not empty.

expansion path The path from the origin through the reference unit in DEA analysis.

expansion point Any point on the expansion path in DEA analysis.

expert systems Systems that model the decision-making processes of experts in various problem domains, such as medical diagnosis, audit decision making, and so forth; a special type of AI development.

extensional knowledge Facts that are stored in database relations.

external database The user view of the data in IMS.

external key A set of lexical attributes whose values always identify a single object instance.

external level Database structural level defining user views.

F

feasibility study Portion of the DDLC that determines technological, operational, and economic feasibility of database.

FETCH statement A statement that retrieves a single row from an opened cursor.

file manager Software that manages the allocation of storage locations and data structures.

filler Frame terminology for values of an attribute.

First Normal Form (1NF) All attribute values must be atomic.

first-order logic A logical structure that is characterized by a set of objects, a set of predicates (each of which evaluates to TRUE or FALSE), and a set of functions.

flag statements SQL statements embedded in an application program to signal the beginning or end of a set of SQL statements.

foreign key A set of attributes in one relation that constitute a key in some other (or possibly the same) relation; used to indicate logical links between relations.

forward chaining A logical chain of rules proceeding from a hypothesis to a conclusion.

frame Data structure for representing a stereotyped situation.

FROM clause Lists the existing tables referenced by the query.

frontier point Any point on the frontier in DEA analysis.

fully concatenated key Means of identifying the location of a segment in the database.

function-oriented approach Views a system from the perspective of the functions it should perform.

functional relationship A relationship having maximum cardinality 1 in at least one direction.

functional dependency The value of an attribute in a tuple determines the value of another attribute in the tuple.

functionally determine To uniquely determine a value.

G

general procedural knowledge Knowledge that can only be described by a procedure.

generalization An object set that is a superset of (or contains) another object set.

global data Data that is maintained in a database whose location is different from at least one of its users.

global transaction A transaction requiring several agents.

graphical language A computer language that uses pictorial representations to solve problems.

GraphQuery A query language for object-oriented models that uses direct interaction with the model.

GROUP BY clause Indicates that rows should be grouped on a common value of specified column(s).

H

HAVING clause Places conditions on groups.

HDAM IMS access method; provides rapid direct access of segments, but no capability for sequential processing.

head activation time The time required to activate a read/write head.

head list A list of pointers, each of which points to the first record in a file.

HIDAM IMS access method; provides for direct access of root segments, as well as sequential retrieval.

hierarchical data model Data model in which all relationships are structured as trees.

hierarchical occurrence tree Representation of segment occurrences in a tree structure that reflects all PCR types.

higher-level relationship A relationship between three or more object sets.

highlighted attributes Attributes in a GraphQuery solution that indicate the data requested in the user query.

HISAM IMS access method; provides capability for both sequential and direct segment retrieval.

homonym A term that has different meanings in different contexts.

horizontal fragmentation Partitioning a relation into subsets of its tuples.

host language Language of programs in which SQL statements can be embedded.

HSAM IMS access method; very fast for sequential retrieval of segments.

I

important feature A DBMS feature that is not mandatory but makes the DBMS more attractive.

IMS IBM's Information Management System; leading DBMS based on the hierarchical data model.

information Organized or summarized data.

information center An area where users have facilities to do their own computing.

information system An automated system which organizes data to produce information.

inherit The property of a specialization set that causes it to have all the attributes of its generalization set.

INSERT Operation that causes rows to be added to a relation.

insertion anomaly Inability to add data to the database due to absence of other data.

instance Actual record values expressed in a data structure.

Integrated Data Store (IDS) One of the earliest database management systems; its architecture greatly influenced the DBTG recommendations for a network database model.

integrity control (constraint) A restriction applied to a given set of data; used to minimize data entry errors.

intensional knowledge Knowledge that is deduced from extensional knowledge by the applications of rules.

internal level Database structural level defining physical view of database.

interrogative format A qualification expression format that follows the components of the natural language query.

intersection Relational algebra operation that creates the set intersection of two union compatible relations.

intersection record type A dummy record that is created in order to convert a complex network into an equivalent simple network; also called a link record type.

intersection relation A relation representing instances where two other relations meet in a many–many relationship.

inverted list A directory wherein each entry contains pointers to all

physical records containing a specified value.

iteration statement A statement that may be repeated a specified number of times.

J

join Relational algebra operation that connects relations.

K

key A value used for unique identification. In a traditional system it identifies a record in a file. In an object-oriented model, it identifies an instance in an object set. In the relational model it is the value of a minimal set of attributes which identifies a role in a relation.

knowledge-base management system (KBMS) System software that supports the usual range of DBMS functions, as well as managing the deductive process of the rule database operating on the fact database.

knowledge-base system A system that provides the full range of database system capabilities for data storage and manipulation, as well as a facility for creating, storing, and executing rules of inference on stored data tables.

knowledge-based system An alternative term for knowledge-base system.

L

leaf segment In a tree, any segment type that has no child segment types.

lexical object set An object set consisting of instances that can be printed.

link Communications channel between two network sites, which provides for data transfer capability.

linked list A set of physical records that are linked by pointers that are maintained in the records themselves.

load factor The ratio of the number of records to be stored to the number of storage locations.

local data Data that is maintained in a network site's own database.

local-area network (LAN) A computer network with the sites located within a short distance (usually less than a mile) of one another.

local transaction A transaction requiring a single agent.

lock In transaction processing, prevents access to a database record by a second transaction until the first transaction has completed all of its actions.

log A record of all transactions and the corresponding changes to the database.

logical database design Identification of data elements, relationships, and constraints for a database.

logical design Creation of conceptual level schema for database.

logical record A record type as seen from the user's perspective.

M

main memory Storage located in the central processing unit; used for data made available for user operations.

management information Information to support company operations and decision makers.

management information system Automated system focused on information for middle management.

mandatory feature A DBMS feature that must be provided.

many–many Relationship cardinalities of many in both directions.

map To associate elements in one sphere with elements in another sphere.

MARK IV Control Data Corporation's Multi-Access Retrieval System; DBMS based on the hierarchical data model.

member record type The record type on the "many" side of the one–many relationship of a DBTG set.

metadata Data in the data dictionary that describes the database.

model A representation of reality that retains only selected details.

multiple-table query A query involving more than one table.

N

n-ary relationship A relationship between *n* object sets.

natural join Join operation that connects relations when common columns have equal values.

natural language A formal language that uses English-like syntax.

network A data relationship in which a record can be owned by records from more than one file.

network data model Represents data in network structures of record types connected in one–one or one–many relationships.

node Part of a network structure represented by a point.

noise words Words used in a qualification expression that increase readability but do not affect its meaning.

noncorrelated subquery A subquery whose value does not depend on any outer query.

nonprocedural Language that provides a means for stating *what* is desired rather than *how* to get it.

normal forms Rules for structuring relations that eliminate anomalies.

normalization The process of converting a relation to a standard form.

NOT EXISTS operator Evaluates to true if resulting set is empty.

null attribute value An attribute value that does not exist for a specific object instance.

null value The value given an attribute in a tuple if the attribute is inapplicable or its value is unknown.

O

object instance A particular member of an object set.

object-oriented model A model representing real-world entities as objects rather than records.

object set A set of things of the same kind.

occurrence A synonym for instance.

one–many Relationship cardinalities of 1 in one direction and many in the other.

one–one Relationship cardinalities of 1 in both directions.

OPEN cursor statement Embedded SQL statement that causes the DBMS to process a cursor's query and store its result in the cursor.

operational feasibility Determination of availability of expertise and personnel needed for database system.

optional feature A DBMS feature that is of secondary importance; may help to distinguish among otherwise equally rated DBMSs.

ORACLE A microcomputer DBMS whose query language is SQL.

outer query The main query that contains all the subqueries.

outer join Expansion of the natural join that includes all rows from both relations.

owner record type The record type on the "one" side of the one–many relationship of a DBTG set.

P

PAL PARADOX Application Language, a high-level, structured database programming language.

PARADOX A microcomputer DBMS whose query language is like QBE.

parent The point at the tail of the arrow in a hierarchical datastructure.

parent-child relationship type (PCR type) Logical relationship between a parent segment type and a child segment type.

path A set of pointers leading from one index record to another.

physical database design Determination of storage devices, access methods, and indexes for using a database.

physical link A means of connecting records by using the records' disk addresses.

physical object An object representing a specific, physical thing.

physical object set An object set whose instances are physical objects.

physical record A physical block of data.

plaintext Readable text.

pointer A physical address that identifies where a record can be found on disk.

practitioners People responsible for the database system and its associated application software.

predicate An expression that evaluates to TRUE or FALSE.

predicate symbols Names applied to arguments in order to express a predicate.

preliminary planning Planning for a database that occurs during the strategic database planning process.

preorder traversal A method of converting a tree structure to a flat file that retains the necessary information about the hierarchical relationship.

primary key The candidate key designated for principal use in uniquely identifying rows in a relation.

Pro*C An ORACLE facility that allows applications to be written in the C language.

procedural Language that provides a step by step method for solving problems.

procedure Written instructions describing the steps needed to accomplish a given task in a system.

product Relational algebra operation that creates the Cartesian product of two relations.

program communication block (PCB) A component of the PSB.

program specification block (PSB) Specifies the names of each segment an application program will access; corresponds to a user view or subschema.

project Relational algebra operation that creates a relation by deleting columns from an existing relation.

projection Relation resulting from a project operation.

Q

qualification expression A true-false condition that refers to the target list; must hold for the elements in the solution set.

qualifying statement A condition in a relational calculus statement that restricts membership in a solution relation.

query specification Definition of a query used in a view definition, cursor declaration, or other statement.

R

R* DDBMS marketed by IBM Corporation.

random access processing A file access method that provides direct access to a specific record.

RBASE A microcomputer DBMS whose query language is based on relational algebra.

read_lock The user has the right to read a given record.

record section The section of the DBTG schema that defines each record, its data items, and its location.

record type A collection of logically related data items.

recursive foreign key A foreign key that references its own relation.

recursive relationship A relationship that relates an object set to itself.

reference unit The DBMS currently being evaluated in DEA analysis.

referential integrity rule The value of a non-null foreign key must be an actual key value in some relation.

relation A two-dimensional table containing rows and columns of data.

relation attribute A column in a relation.

relational algebra A procedural language for manipulating relations.

relational calculus A nonprocedural language for defining query solutions.

relational data model A data model representing data in the form of tables.

relational database schema A listing showing relation names, attribute names, key attributes, and foreign keys.

relationally complete Having the same logical power as relational algebra or calculus.

relationship A linking between instances of two object sets.

request for proposal (RFP) A formal document that outlines performance requirements and asks vendors to respond with a proposal for meeting those requirements.

requirements definition Determination of management and functional area information requirements.

retrieve only access Database access with no update allowed.

ring structure A linked list whose last record contains a pointer to the first record in the list.

root segment In a tree, the segment type that does not participate as a child segment in any PCR.

rooted tree A hierarchy of index records that has a single index record at the highest level; that record is called the root.

rotational delay The time required for the disk to rotate the sought for record under the read/write head.

S

schema A definition of the logical structure of the entire database.

schema definition Description of a database to the DBMS.

schema owner Person who has authority and responsibility for granting access to tables, columns, and views in a database.

schema section The section of the DBTG schema that names the schema.

Second Normal Form (2NF) No nonkey attribute may be functionally dependent on just a part of the key.

secondary key A data item value that identifies a set of records.

SEGM An IMS statement that defines the fields to be included in a segment to be used by a program.

segment template Program work area format for a segment.

segment type Corresponds to an object in the object-oriented data model; also called a segment.

select Relational algebra operation that uses a condition to select rows from a relation.

SELECT clause Identifies the columns desired in the query.

semantic model A model that captures the meanings of real-world entities and relationships.

semantic network A network that shows relationships among facts.

sensitive segment A segment that is accessible to a program; abbreviated SENSEG.

serial execution Actions are executed one after another with no parallel actions.

serializability theory States that a concurrency control algorithm is correct when its results are the same as if processes were executed serially.

set In the DBTG model, a one–many relationship between two record types.

set-theoretic union A set made up of elements from one or the other or both of two other sets.

set comparison expression A qualification expression that involves comparing two sets to see if one set is contained in the other.

set function A built-in function.

set section The section of the DBTG schema that defines sets and includes owner record types and member record types.

simple network A data structure in which all binary relationships are one–many.

simple query A query involving only one database table.

slot Frame terminology for attribute names.

solution set A set of data values from the database that satisfy the conditions of a query.

specialization An object set that is a subset of another object set.

status flag Field whose value indicates the result of the last database operation (e.g., successful or not successful).

strategy selector Software that translates a user request into an effective form for execution.

structural knowledge Knowledge about dependencies and constraints among data.

subquery A query within a query.

subschema Subsets of the schema which are defined by the user's view of the database.

subtraction The relational algebra difference operation.

superkey A set of attributes that uniquely identifies each row in a relation.

surrogate key A unique, computer system identifier for an abstract object instance; it has no meaning outside the computer system.

SWITCH statement A statement that enables testing for a series of conditions.

synonyms Terms that mean the same thing.

System-2000 SAS Institute's hierarchical DBMS; DBMS based on the hierarchical data model.

system catalog Database containing metadata.

system development life cycle (SDLC) A process for system development.

System for Distributed Databases (SDD) DDBMS marketed by Computer Corporation of America.

T

target list A parenthesized list of variables representing the desired components of a typical member of a query's solution set.

target table In QBE, a table without column headings that is used to define query output.

TDMS System Development Corporation's Time-Shared Data Management System; DBMS based on the hierarchical data model.

technological feasibility Determination of hardware and software availability for database system.

TextQuery A query language for object-oriented models with a text-based syntax.

textual language A computer language whose statements consist of character string symbols.

theta join Join operation that connects relations when values from specified columns have a specified relationship.

Third Normal Form (3NF) The property of a relation in which every determinant is a key.

three-level architecture Standard database structure consisting of conceptual, external, and internal levels.

timestamping A method of identifying messages with their time of transmission.

title division That portion of the DBTG subschema that provides for naming the subschema and its associated schema.

transaction A program unit whose execution preserves the consistency of the database.

tree A hierarchical data structure; that is, a network structure where a child segment type is linked to just one parent segment type.

tuple A row in a relation.

twin segments Segment type occurrences that have the same parent segment type occurrence (more than two segment occur-rences may qualify as twins, so the biological analogy is incomplete).

two-phase locking A method of controlling concurrent processing in which all read and write locks must precede the first unlocking operation.

two-phase commit protocol A protocol consisting of a prepare-to-commit phase and a vote (commit or abort) phase.

U

undesirable feature A DBMS feature that detracts from its value to the firm.

union Relational algebra operation that creates the set union of two union compatible relations.

union compatible Two or more relations that have equivalent columns as to number and domains.

universal quantifier Relational calculus expression stating that some condition applies to every row of some type.

unnecessary feature A DBMS feature that contributes nothing to the value of the DBMS to the firm.

UPDATE Operation that changes column values in rows.

update anomaly Data inconsistency resulting from data redundancy and partial update.

users People who need informa-tion from the database to carry out their primary business responsibility.

V

value constraint A rule defining the permissible values for a specific data item.

variable A symbolic name that represents an unspecified instance in an object set.

vertical fragmentation Partitioning a relation by projection of subsets of its attributes.

view A definition of a restricted portion of the database; also called a data view.

view controls Those controls that restrict access to views (subsets of base relations).

W

WHERE clause Gives the condition for selecting rows from identified tables.

wide-area network (WAN) A computer network with sites that are widely dispersed geographically.

write-lock The user has the right to read and to update the given record.

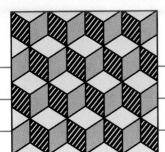

Index

Assignment operation in relational algebra, 232
Atomic transaction, 469–70
Atomic value, 185
Attribute(s), 89–91
  distinguishing between object instances and, 109, 112–13
  foreign key, 182–83
  frames and, 452
  highlighted, 129, 130
  inheritance of, 91
  key, 180–82
  lexical, 90
  relation, 178–79
  selection of
    in ORACLE, 423–24
    in PARADOX, 415
    in RBASE, 421
  specialization/generalization and, 91
  transforming, to relational model, 193
Attribute domain, 179–80
Authentication, 475–77
Authorization, 475, 477–81
Automatic insertion mode, 264
AVG function in SQL, 378

B

Bachman, Charles, 248
Bachman diagram, 248
Backup and recovery, 25–26, 47, 49
  controls, 343
  database maintenance and, 356
  DBA responsibility for, 353–54
  procedures and standards, 466
  See also Database recovery
Backward chaining, 441, 442
Balanced-tree index (B+-Tree), 317–21
Bank data model, 92–96
Base table, 384
Batch processing, 7
Benchmarking, 346–47
Bentley, L., 58, 61
Binary relationships, 139, 140–41
Binary Semantic Data Model, 81
Block, 307
  physical storage, 303–4
  storage formats, 309–10
Boolean connectives, 125–27, 219, 368–69
Boyce-Codd Normal Form (BCNF), 189–90
BREAK statement in ORACLE, 425
B+-Tree, 317–21
Buffer manager, 301
Built-in function
  in Query-by-Example, 402–3
  in SQL, 377–78
    with subqueries, 381–82
Business needs, evolution of database technology and, 5–6

C

Calculations
  in PARADOX, 417
  in RBASE, 421–22
Calculus, relational. *See* Relational calculus
Campbell, D., 108
Candidate key, 181
Cardinality of relationship, 86–88
  example of, 93–94
  one-many, 145, 157
  transformation of relationships and, 194–98
Cartesian product, 369–70
CASE statement in PARADOX, 419
Catalog, system, 386–87
Centralized database, 37–38, 465, 493
Chaining, forward and backward, 441, 442
Chains of pointers, 315
Change, preparing users for, 355–56
Change operations, database
  in Query-by-Example, 406–7
  in SQL, 382–83
Changes to database system, managing, 357
Character string literals, 368
Checkpointing, 484–85
Chen, P., 81
Chief information officer (CIO), 463
Child and twin pointers, 289, 326
Child (hierarchical model), 18, 275
Chimenti, D., 450
Ciphertext, 481
Clause in PROLOG, 445–46, 448, 449
Clustering, 322
COBOL language, 246, 383, 453
CODASYL, 246, 344
  DBTG model, 247
    data definition language, 254–58
    data manipulation language, 258–65
    evaluation, 266–68
Codd, E.F., 20, 21, 176–77, 183, 185, 203, 211, 212, 231, 362, 386
Collision, 312, 314
Column definition, 365–66
Committed transaction, 483
Communication with users, 464–65
Comparison operators, 368
Complex network, 249
Composite key, 181
COMPUTE function in ORACLE, 424
Computer Associates, 247
Computers, 23–24
COMPUTE statement in RBASE, 421–22
Conceptual level, 56
Conceptual object, 143, 145
Conceptual object sets, 154–63
Conceptual schema, 56
Concurrency control, 343, 470–75
  for distributed database systems, 504–5
  timestamping and, 509
Concurrent data access for multiple users, 26
Concurrent processing, 467
Conditional statements

Conditional statements (continued)
    in PARADOX, 419
    in RBASE, 422
Condition box, 399
Conference on Data Systems Languages (CODA-
    SYL), 246, 344
    DBTG model, 247, 266–68
Configuration independence, 498
Conflict resolution between user groups, 45
Conflicts, organizational, 48
Conjunctive query, 415–16, 421
CONNECT command in DBTG DML, 262, 263, 264
Connectives, Boolean, 125–27, 219, 368–69
Consistency, data, 341
Constraints, 183–84. See also Integrity, database
Context-dependent views, 480
Control Data Corporation, 275
Control in file systems, data, 15. See also Database
    integrity; Database security
Correlated subqueries, 374, 375, 381
Costs
    of databases, 47–49, 494
    economic feasibility study of, 65
Count-data format, 307, 308
Count-key format, 307, 308
Criterion-base linear programming model, 351–52
Currency indicators, 259–60
Currency pointers in IMS, 290
Cursor, 383
Cylinder, 302
Czejdo, B., 108

D

Daplex, 108
Data
    consistency, maintaining, 341
    as database system component, 27, 28
    defined, 12
    extensional, 440, 444, 447, 449, 450
    on feature availability and performance, gather-
      ing, 345–47
    global, 494
    local, 494
    localization of, 39. See also Distributed database
      system (DDS)
    logical vs. physical representation of, 55–58
    semantic restrictions on, 467
    shifting of control over, 465
Data administrator (DA), 462
Database
    defined, 13, 33, 39
    extensional, 440, 445, 449, 450, 451
    external, 285
    intensional (deductive), 440, 445, 449, 450, 451
    knowledge and, 438–40
    loading, 356
    management control and, 44–47
    risks and costs of, 47–49
    role in data sharing, 39–40

Database Administration, 40, 41, 44–46, 461–90
    database integrity and, 467–75
    database recovery and, 25–26, 47, 467, 482–87
    database security and, 467, 475–82
    defined, 44
    functions of, 44–46, 47
    as implementation issue, 352–54
    need for sophisticated personnel in, 49
    overview of, 462
Database Administrator (DBA), 16, 44, 462–67
    daily tasks of, 352–54
    defined, 462
    functions, 464–66
    goals, 466–67
    organizational locations for, 463–64
Database architecture, three-level, 55–58, 247
Database description (DBD) in IMS, 285–86
Database design. See Design, database
Database development life cycle (DDLC), 62–71
    defined, 44, 62
    developing skills and, 70–71
    evaluating and enhancing database schema, 70
    feasibility study, 64–65
    implementation, 69–70
    logical design, 68–69
    preliminary planning, 64
    requirements definition, 66–67, 156
    strategic database planning and, 43–44
Database implementation, 69–70
Database integrity, 467–75
    concurrency control, 343, 470–75, 504–5, 509
    integrity constraints, 190, 467
      in Query-by-Example, 468–69
      in relational data model, 183–84, 267, 467
      in SQL, 468
    management control and, 46–47
    transaction processing, 469–70
Database maintenance, 356–57
Database management system (DBMS), 24, 40,
    337–60
    analyzing management information needs, 339–41
    classifying feature requirements, 344–45
    defined, 13
    evaluation models, 347–52
      data envelopment analysis (DEA), 349–52
      scoring model, 347–48
    functions and capabilities, 341–44
    gathering data on feature availability and perfor-
      mance, 345–47
    IDMS/R, 265–66, 341
    implementation issues, 352–57
      database administration, 352–54
      database maintenance, 356–57
      database testing, 354–55
      loading database, 356
      preparing users for change, 355–56
    selection and acquisition of, 69–70
    See also IMS (IBM's Information Management
      System); Microcomputer database manage-
      ment systems
Database partitioning, 499–502
Database planning, 40–44
Database record, 278

Hierarchical data model *(continued)*
    relationship to object-oriented semantics, 276, 277, 281–85
        transforming many-many relationships, 283–85
        transforming object sets and one-many relationships, 281–82
Hierarchical occurrence tree, 279–80
Higher-level relationships, 138–54
Highlighted attributes, 129, 130
HISAM (Hierarchic Indexed Sequential Access Method), 288
Ho, T., 58, 61
Home address, 307
Homonym, 15
Horizontal fragmentation, 500–501
Host language, 383
HSAM (Hierarchic Sequential Access Method), 288
Hull, R., 81

I

IBM, 355, 363, 386, 394
IDMS, 247
IDMS/R, 265–66, 341
IDS system, 246, 247, 248, 275
Implementation, 69–70
    issues of, 352–57
        database administration, 352–54
        database maintenance, 356–57
        database testing, 354–55
        loading database, 356
        preparing users for change, 355–56
    of logical relationships, 314-21
    relational vs. CODASYL DBTG, 267–68
    See also Relational implementation
Important feature, 345
IMS (IBM's Information Management System), 274, 275, 285–94
    access methods, 288–90
    architecture, 285–87
    data manipulation language (DL/1), 285, 290–94
Inconsistency, data, 341
Indexed sequential (ISAM) files, 11, 12, 15
    organization, 311–12
Index records, hierarchy of, 317–21
Information
    defined, 12
    as resource, 12–13
Information center, 46
Information needs
    analyzing management, 339–41
    defining, 66–67
Information processing, progress from data processing to, 1
Information system, 12
INGRES, 363
    distributed, 494
Inheritance of attributes and relationships, 91
Input/output operations, 310

Insert authorization, 477
Insert command
    in DL/1 (INSERT or INSRT), 293–94
    in Query-by-Example, 406–7
Insertion
    automatic insertion mode, 264
    B$^+$-tree resulting from, 320
    manual insertion mode, 264
Insertion anomaly, 185
INSERT operation in SQL, 382
Instances in network data model, 248
Integrated Database Management System/Relational (IDMS/R), 265–66, 341
Integrated Data Store (IDS), 246, 247, 248, 275
Integration
    data, 36, 39, 40. *See also* Data sharing
    of nonhomogeneous DBMSs, 498
    view, 164–66
Integrity, data, 25–26, 343
    DBA and, 353
    defined, 47, 184, 467
    in distributed database, 504–10
Integrity, database, 467–75
    concurrency control, 343, 470–75, 504–5, 509
    integrity constraints, 190, 467
        in Query-by-Example, 468–69
        in relational data model, 183–84, 267, 467
        in SQL, 468
    management control and, 46–47
    transaction processing, 469–70
Integrity checking, 466
Intensional (deductive) database, 440, 445, 449, 450, 451
Intensional knowledge, 439
Internal level, 56–58
Interrogative format, 120
Intersection (link) record type, 249–50
Intersection operation in relational algebra, 215–16, 235
Intersection records, 323
Intersection relation, 196–98
Inverted list, 316–17
    hierarchy mapped to, 326
    in secondary key, 328
Iteration statement
    in PARADOX, 420
    in RBASE, 423

J

Join
    in Query-by-Example, 400–402
    in relational algebra, 222–29, 369
        natural join, 222–26
        outer join, 224, 228–29
        theta join, 226–28
    in SQL, 369–72
Just-in-time (JIT) inventory system, 339

K

Kent, W., 155
Key, 90, 113
  candidate, 181
  composite, 181
  defined, 12
  external, 90, 157, 181, 193–94
  foreign, 182–83
    recursive, 182, 200
  fully concatenated, 287
  primary, 181, 326, 327
  in relational data model, 181–82
  secondary, 326–28
  surrogate, 83, 181, 322
Key attributes, 180–82
King, R., 81
Klug, A., 56
Knowledge
  databases and, 438–40
  taxonomy of, 438–49
Knowledge-base management system (KBMS), 437
Knowledge-base systems (KBS), 435–53
  defined, 437
  introduction to, 436–38
  knowledge and databases, 438–40
  knowledge representation with rules, 441–45
    rule formulation, 441–42
    rules in PROLOG, 442–45
  Logical Data Language (LDL), 437, 450–51
  other knowledge representation systems, 451–53
    frames, 452–53
    semantic networks, 451–52
  simple PROLOG database application, 445–50
    database application, 449–50
    structure of, 446–49
Krishnamurthy, R., 450

L

Language
  graphical, 395
  host, 383
  for manipulating data in tables, 21
  natural, 162, 163, 453–54
  nonprocedural, 212, 239
  object-oriented programming, 81–82
  procedural, 212, 239
  query, 21, 26, 27
  relationally complete, 212
  textual, 395
  visual, 134
  See also Object-oriented data languages; *specific languages*
Latency, 305, 306
Leaf, 317
Leaf segment, 278
Lexical attribute, 90
Lexical object set, 82–83

Linear programming (LP), 351–52
Linked lists, 315–16, 323–24
  hierarchy mapped to, 326
  of secondary keys, 327–28
Linking tables
  in ORACLE, 424
  in PARADOX, 417–18
  in RBASE, 422
Link record type, 249–50
Links
  in distributed database system, 494
  physical, 251
Lists
  inverted, 316–17, 326, 328
  linked, 315–16, 323–24, 326, 327–28
Load factor, 313
Loading database, 356
Local-area network (LAN), 413, 496, 497
Local data, 494
Localization of data, 39
Local transactions, 495
Locations, sharing data between different, 37–39
Location transparency, 498
Locking procedures, 472–73
  distributed, 506–8
  two-phase, 473–75
Log, 510
  with deferred updates, 483–85
  defined, 470
  with immediate updates, 485–86
Logic, first-order, 445
Logical (Boolean) connectives, 125–27, 219, 368–69
Logical database design, 44–45
Logical Data Language (LDL), 437, 450–51
Logical data representation, separating physical and, 55–58
Logical data structures to physical data structures, mapping, 321–26
Logical design, 68–69
Logical errors, 483
Logical records, 251
Logical relationships, implementation of, 314–21
Logical schema, 56
Logic-implementation language, 440. *See also* PROLOG
Logic problems, 98–99
Lotus 1–2–3, 394

M

McLeod, D., 81
Magnetic tape storage, 302, 303
Maier, D., 500
Mainframe, 23
Main memory, 302
Maintenance, database, 356–57
Management
  expectations, evolution of database technology and, 5